100 Most Popular Genre Fiction Authors

**Recent Titles in the
Popular Author Series**

The 100 Most Popular Young Adult Authors: Biographical Sketches and Bibliographies,
Revised First Edition
Bernard A. Drew

Popular Nonfiction Authors for Children: A Biographical and Thematic Guide
Flora R. Wyatt, Margaret Coggins, and Jane Hunter Imber

100 Most Popular Children's Authors: Biographical Sketches and Bibliographies
Sharron McElmeel

100 Most Popular Picture Book Authors and Illustrators: Biographical Sketches and Bibliographies
Sharron McElmeel

100 More Popular Young Adult Authors: Biographical Sketches and Bibliographies
Bernard A. Drew

Winning Authors: Profiles of the Newbery Medalists
Kathleen L. Bostrom

Children's Authors and Illustrators Too Good to Miss: Biographical Sketches and Bibliographies
Sharron McElmeel

100 Most Popular Genre Fiction Authors

Biographical Sketches and Bibliographies

Bernard A. Drew

Popular Authors Series

LIBRARIES
U N L I M I T E D
A Member of the Greenwood Publishing Group

Westport, Connecticut • London

Library of Congress Cataloging-in-Publication Data

Drew, Bernard A. (Bernard Alger), 1950–
    100 most popular genre fiction authors : biographical sketches and bibliographies /
Bernard A. Drew.
        p. cm. — (Popular authors series)
    Includes bibliographical references and index.
    ISBN 1–59158–126–5 (alk. paper)
    1. Novelists, American—20th century—Biography—Dictionaries.   2. Popular
literature—United States—Bio-bibliography—Dictionaries.   3. Popular literature—United
States—Dictionaries.   I. Title: One hundred most popular genre fiction authors.   II. Title.
III. Series.
    PS374.P63D74   2005
    813'.509'03—dc22   2004063836
    [B]

British Library Cataloguing in Publication Data is available.

Library of Congress Catalog Card Number: 2004063836
ISBN: 1–59158–126–5

First published in 2005

Libraries Unlimited, 88 Post Road West, Westport, CT 06881
A Member of the Greenwood Publishing Group, Inc.
www.lu.com

Printed in the United States of America

The paper used in this book complies with the
Permanent Paper Standard issued by the National
Information Standards Organization (Z39.48–1984).

10 9 8 7 6 5 4 3 2 1

Every reasonable effort has been made to trace the owners of copyright materials in this book, but in some
instances this has proven impossible. The author and publisher will be glad to receive information leading to
more complete acknowledgments in subsequent printings of the book and in the meantime extend their
apologies for any omissions.

Contents

Introduction

In autumn 2003, the National Book Foundation announced it would present its annual medal for distinguished contribution to American letters to Stephen King. For some scholars and proponents of literary fiction, that just iced the cake. It seems they couldn't abide the best-selling author rubbing elbows with their treasured John Updike, Arthur Miller, Philip Roth, and Toni Morrison.

Boston Globe columnist Harold Bloom expounded, calling it "extraordinary, another low in the shocking process of dumbing down our cultural life." *Los Angeles Times* book editor Steve Wasserman commented snidely, "I look forward to the day when Danielle Steel, that Balzac of our time, is equally recognized."

Others stepped forward to defend the honor, declaring that King merited the award if for no other reason than he opened the doors to the wonders of pleasurable reading to millions. "Mr. King deserves his due," wrote Janet Maslin in the *New York Times*. "It takes a certain skill to write books (in his case more than 40) so much in demand that no American airport— or library—is complete without one. Writers this popular are such cultural fixtures that they practically create their own weather."

King capably fended for himself at the awards ceremony, challenging literary scribes and critics: "What do you think? You get social academic brownie points for deliberately staying out of touch with your own culture?" (Indeed, Shirley Hazard, who took the year's prize for fiction, sniffed she had not gotten around to a King book, having works by Shakespeare and Joseph Conrad to read instead.)

So is it jealousy, or is it something more?

USA Today's Samuel G. Freedman had this to say: "The carping about King's award reflects an elitism that borders on being a death wish. Strictly as a matter of business, a smart publishing house (and enough of them are not smart) plows some of the windfall from its Stephen Kings or John Grishams into less-commercial writers. In turn, some of them—think of Barbara Kingsolver, Alan Furst or Bruce Feiler—gradually build their own substantial readerships and earning power."

Expect no balanced overview of the literature-vs.-popular-fiction debate in this space; this writer considers literary fiction simply another genre along with mysteries, romances, and fantasy. Literary agent and author Peter Rubie said the same in his book *Telling the Story* and explained that genres came about "as a marketing necessity. . . . Their purpose is basically to help you more easily find what it is you're looking for. They are also guides to let you know, generally, what you can expect to find in a certain type of book."

All genres have their educated and erudite readers. All genres boast shining, well-crafted works. And conversely, literary prose has its duds as well as its novas. Why the bitter rivalry?

"I believe my genre can go anywhere; it just depends how good I am," espionage writer John le Carré told an interviewer in 2004. "In the 1970s, I was some kind of literary star. I couldn't go wrong. But I found myself treated as some tolerated vulgarian. Certainly spy stories, like horror stories—if that's what Stephen [King] writes—can be expanded into love stories, stories of loyalty and divided character."

Likewise, author Jayne Ann Krentz has little patience for those who dismiss romances. She asserts that genre writing comes from the heroic tradition of storytelling. "They feature the ancient heroic virtues: honor, courage, determination and the healing power of love," she told interviewer Claire E. White. "Most modern literary critics are stuck in a time warp that dates back to the middle of the twentieth century when the only fiction that was considered *good* fiction was that which was heavily influenced by existentialism, various social agendas and psychological theory."

Holding nothing against romances, historical-fantasy writer Diana Gabaldon said in a recent e-mail that it irks her not a little that Barnes & Noble insists on placing her novels with romances.

"I wrote my first book—*Outlander*—for practice, never intending to show it to anyone," she said. "That being so, it was quite irrelevant what sort of book it was, and so I used any element of fiction that took my fancy. The result was a book—and now a series of books—that could not be classified by anyone who's ever tried—and believe me, a lot of people have tried!

"The books are essentially Big, Fat, Solid Historical Fiction, of the well-researched and gripping type, à la James Michener and James Clavell," she went on. "However, the main protagonist is a time-traveler. (Cough.) Then we have the Loch Ness monster, a certain amount of witchcraft, religious mysticism, botanical medicine, sex, violence . . . well, what the heck, the books run around 900 pages in hardcover; I have room for a lot of stuff (including a full-fledged murder mystery in each book, though what with all the other stuff going on, this tends not to be the main focus of attention)."

So Barnes & Noble stocks Gabaldon books as romance, including her *Lord John and the Private Matter*, even though "it's a perfectly straightforward historical mystery (and has been so reviewed by everything from *PW* and *Kirkus* to *Booklist* and *Library Journal*). It also has a gay protagonist. No romance. No love story. It doesn't even have 'heterosex,' for goodness sake, and quite a bit of the contrary," Gabaldon sighed.

Gabaldon is not alone. Janet Evanovich was a romance writer who is now shelved with mysteries—though she thinks of her Stephanie Plum novels as "adventures."

Loren D. Estleman is a self-proclaimed genre writer come hell or high water. "I'm pretty popular with myself," he wrote, "but there are times, invariably when the writing isn't going well, when I wonder if anyone cares. But since at this point I couldn't hold down a real job to save myself or the mortgage, I push on."

What publishers and booksellers do not understand, they do not market well. So would it not be simpler without categories? Everything on an equal footing? After all, do not all writers really aspire to be considered literary writers? The hard reality is that genres serve a practical purpose. What readers cannot find, they will not buy or borrow.

"Learn to write a novel that could transcend genre and rise to the top of the bestseller lists!" dares an advertisement for Writer's Digest Book Club, touting Donald Maass's how-to, *Writing the Breakout Novel*.

" 'Transcends the genre' is a phrase that makes me reach for my gun," said mystery writer Ed Gorman, venting about those who disparage popular fiction. "Who says it transcends? And what does 'transcend' mean exactly? And most of all, for me, why should I care if it transcends, even if it does which it probably doesn't?"

If anything, "literary writers" often take a cue from popular writers, suggests literary historian David Pringle. "Just as the Gothic romance influenced the nineteenth-century realistic novel, so sf has infected late twentieth-century 'high literature,' the most serious fiction of the day, with its images, settings and emotional concerns. . . . Very rarely are these high-minded novels described as science fiction, but it's plain that their authors have caught the sf bug."

In his study of popular fiction, *An Aesthetics of Junk Fiction*, critic Thomas J. Roberts feels compelled to distinguish "Plain fiction," or best-seller fiction, "the more respectable of the two kinds of contemporary popular fiction," and "Junk fiction," which he also labels vernacular, category, paperback, or genre fiction in order to justify the popularity of books that have wide readerships. Rubbish.

A rare bright light in looking seriously at popular prose is Diana Tixier Herald's *Genreflecting* reference guide published by Libraries Unlimited, the most recent edition of which continues the first law of reading promulgated by its first editor, Betty Rosenberg: "Never apologize for your reading tastes."

The book in your hands, another in Libraries Unlimited's Popular Authors Series, was a challenge to assemble. There is a surfeit of potential writers to include. We consulted best-seller lists, sales statistics, and fans. Our list was reviewed by a number of librarians and genre experts. Still, it included well over 100 names. Taking comfort that there is always the possibility of a second, companion volume of genre writers, the decision of who to put in went beyond sales figures to look at just who, in the early 2000s, displays creativity, longevity, and influence in each of several categories. We include those black and Hispanic authors who have soared within the genres. As to categories themselves, weight was given to a range of genres even though romances and suspense dominate best-seller lists. All genres contribute to America's rich literary offerings. So all major genres are represented.

It is fascinating to see influences on writers and to learn of their writing styles—some simply jump into a novel and see where the characters take them; others carefully map out every twist and turn.

Dan Brown, for example, whose complex Robert Langdon thriller topped the sales charts in 2003, told interviewer C. M. McDonald that he prepares detailed outlines before he writes. "The outline to *The Da Vinci Code* was over 100 pages. The stories are very intricate and plot-driven. They have a lot of twists, a lot of codes. A lot of surprises. You can't write those freehand—those come from careful planning."

S. J. Rozan, on the other hand, author of the Lydia Chin/Bill Smith detective series (and, along with Ed Gorman, a candidate for future volumes of this reference book series) takes a looser approach. "As soon as the characters start talking and moving around and I see the place, I really don't know what the story will be, although I have a vague idea," she said in a Crime Corner interview.

The authors represented in this collection are surprisingly diverse, yet they do share certain attributes. They all tend to be prolific. They work to fill the voracious reading desires of their fans. Many write in more than one genre, blend genres, or stretch the boundaries of their favored genre. They are usually highly educated, but not likely to be involved in academia. Many of these writers support themselves entirely through their writing. They are fascinating people with fascinating lives.

Because genre fiction "gets no respect," finding information about popular authors can be challenging. Most biographical sources focus on authors with literary credentials—those who are critically acclaimed or award-winners. And if genre writers are included at all, their names are buried among those of the literary elite in vast databases and multivolume sets. Yet genre fans are hungry for information about their favorite authors. And librarians and other professionals who work with readers can only do their jobs successfully if they familiarize themselves with these authors and their works.

The 100 Most Popular Genre Writers gathers in a single volume information about 100 of today's hottest-selling, most successful authors. It is intended as a ready reference for those seeking information about their favorite writers—for research papers, book reports, or simply to satisfy a curiosity. It is equally useful for anyone looking for other titles to read by a beloved author or to find out more about the writing process and what it's like to work as a professional writer.

Teachers will find this book helpful in selecting authors for assignments, as will librarians in choosing titles for their shelves or advising readers. Writers and aspiring writers may well find practical tips, insights, or inspiration.

Librarians and educators reviewed a list of prospective authors and offered suggestions. Selections stress active authors. The focus of this work is on authors who are actively producing new works. A few writers of the past have been enormously influential within their genres—for instance, J.R.R. Tolkien with fantasy, James Michener with doorstopper epics, and Louis L'Amour with westerns—and could not be omitted.

Headers for each entry note the author's year and place of birth. Chapters include biographical information and where possible author insights into the creative process. Complete bibliographies including omnibus editions are offered, as well as authors' works that have been made into motion pictures or television programs. Entries also include selected bibliographies that reflect those works consulted in preparing this book's entries and are not exhaustive.

Readers who wish to comment on this guide or offer suggestions for future volumes in this series are invited to direct their comments to the publisher, Libraries Unlimited, at lubooks@lu.com.

Bernard A. Drew
Great Barrington, Massachusetts

For Further Information

Bloom, Harold. "Dumbing down American readers." *Boston Globe* (September 24, 2003).

"Choose 3 Books Free." Writer's Digest Book Club advertisement. *Write & Publish* (December 2003).

Despain, Robin. "King deserves award for wooing readers" (letter). *USA Today* (December 5, 2003).

Estleman, Loren D. Letter to the author (January 18, 2004).

Freedman, Samuel G. "Stephen King deserves award for creating readers." *USA Today* (October 9, 2003).

Gabaldon, Diana. E-mail to the author (November 2, 2003).

Gorman, Ed. "Transcending?" *Drood Review of Mystery* (March/April 2003).

Herald, Diana Tizier. *Genreflecting: A Guide to Reading Interests in Genre Fiction*, 5th edition. Englewood, CO: Libraries Unlimited, 2000.

"Interview with S. J. Rozan." Crime Corner. *http://www.crime-corner.de/authors-sjrozan.html* (viewed December 29, 2003).

Kirkpatrick, David D. "A Literary Award For Stephen King." *New York Times* (September 15, 2003).

Maslin, Janet. "How's That New Best Seller? Well, the Author's Famous." *New York Times* (November 4, 2003).

McDonald, C. M. "The Dan Brown Interview: The Da Vinci Code." *http://www .modestyarbor./com/dan_brown.html* (viewed January 1, 2004).

Nashawaty, Chris. "The Spy Who Came In From the Cold War." *Entertainment Weekly* (January 16, 2004).

Pringle, David. *The Ultimate Guide to Science Fiction*. New York: Pharos Books, 1990.

Roberts, Thomas J. *An Aesthetics of Junk Fiction*. Athens: University of Georgia Press, 1990.

Rubie, Peter. *Telling the Story: How to Write and Sell Narrative Nonfiction*. New York: HarperCollins Quill, 2003.

"Stephen King blasts 'literary' snobs at book awards." CBC News Online. *http://www .cbc.ca/arts/stories/kingbookaward201103* (viewed December 5, 2003).

White, Claire E. "A Conversation With Jayne Ann Krentz." Writers Write, January–December 2003. *http://www.writerswrite.com/journal/dec02.krentz.htm* (viewed April 29, 2003).

Rochelle Alers

♦ Romance ♦ Romantic suspense

New York, New York
1943

♦ *Hideaway Legacy Series*

Credit: DeVito Studios, Ltd.

About the Author and the Author's Writing

After a decade of reading romance novels for diversion, Rochelle Alers decided to write one of her own. However, she found it was one thing to sit on a sofa and devour a book, but quite another to sit at a desk and try to replicate its subtle rhythms and characterizations. The young writer began her first book in 1984, but it was four years later when one of her manuscripts finally found a publisher. (The first book was eventually published as the first title in her popular Hideaway Legacy series.) Dozens of titles later, the author was still going strong. In a 1995–1996 reader survey, the African American romance writer was voted Arabesque Books' Most Popular Author, and she has garnered other awards since.

Born in New York City in 1943, the author is the daughter of James A. and Minnie L. Ford. She earned a bachelor of arts degree from John Jay College of Criminal Justice of the City University of New York in 1974. She had a double major of psychology and sociology. She worked as an executive assistant for Empire State Medical Equipment Dealers Association for four years beginning in 1987, and then became a community liaison specialist for state-contracted substance abuse programs with the Nassau County Department of Drugs and Alcohol Addiction Services. Now a resident of Freeport, New York, she is divorced with one daughter.

In her novels Alers depicts issues of significance to black women—domestic violence, single motherhood, infertility and missing children. Although many of her books contain elements of suspense and danger, and revolve around edgy themes, they usually have upbeat endings.

The heroines in Alers' books are independent and passionate. Quintin Lord in *Home Sweet Home* thinks nothing of marching into the apartment of her new neighbor and demanding he turn down the sound on his stereo. Summer Montgomery in *Dangerous Masquerade* works undercover for the Drug Enforcement Agency, in the guise of a drama teacher in a

Massachusetts high school. Reporter Dana Nichols returns to Mississippi to ferret out the truth of her parents' years-ago murder/suicide in *Homecoming*.

"Through my novels I show women and men the protocol of courting," the author said on her Web page. "I also want women to say, 'This is how I want a man to treat me.'"

In *Hidden Agenda* Eve Blackwell and Matthew Sterling's marriage is one of convenience—made in order to free her abducted son from his spiteful father—and the two never anticipate they will fall passionately in love. Jolene Walker in *No Compromise* is so dedicated to her work with victimized women, she doubts she has time for a romantic life—until she meets Army Captain Michael Kirkland.

Alers begins each book with a Bible verse in thanks to God for giving her the gift of storytelling. Readers and critics alike seem to appreciate that gift.

"Alers paints such vivid descriptions that when Jolene becomes the target of a murderer, you almost feel as though someone you know is in great danger," commented reviewer Shelley Mosley in *Library Journal*.

This last book reflects the author's own life, in that she writes her novels while maintaining a full-time job. Discipline is the key. Alers generally writes two hours every morning before going to her office. She seldom writes on weekends or at night, unless she needs to meet a deadline. *Private Passions* took longer for the author to write than most of her books—six months—because of the need to wrap up several plot strands. What's the most difficult part of the book to write? The first page, which has to be a grabber, she related to *Shades of Romance Magazine*.

The author has taken her characters to a range of locations. *Hideaway*, for example, is set in Florida as acknowledgment of her southern roots, the author said in an *Arabesque Romance News* interview, and it also afforded the author the opportunity to examine a multicultural locale. Serena Morris-Vega, the heroine of *Heaven Sent*, returns to her childhood home of Costa Rica to help her falsely convicted half-brother secure his release from prison. *Rosie's Curl and Weave* takes place in a Harlem hair salon while *Summer Magic* finds its main character, Caryn Edwards, summering on North Carolina's Marble Island.

The author's ambitious Hideaway Legacy series took a good deal of organization with its floating cast of characters. Matthew Sterling, whom readers met briefly in a scene in *Hideaway*, became a bold hero in *Hidden Agenda*. In that same book, earlier characters Joshua Kirkland and David Cole passed through in one scene for continuity and to give readers a glimpse into a book to come.

Is it all planned? "Sometimes a series or family of characters take on a life of their own," Alers admitted to Romantic Times Book Club. "I was caught off guard to learn my four-book series [Hideaway] wasn't going to end as I had planned. Readers were ready for the second generation to take shape, so I went back to work and further developed family trees."

The author completes detailed character studies before she begins the first chapter. Although in some ways it is easier when characters have already been introduced in other books, that method can create problems. Emily and Chris, the main characters in *Private Passions*, are an example.

"Writing about a couple who are very familiar with each other is not an easy task," the author said in the *Shades of Romance Magazine* interview, "because there are few surprises. Realizing this, I was forced to create situations that would put them at odds with each other. The result is that they actually did not know each other as well as they'd thought they did. Despite their closeness, they still were strangers."

Alers's interests include travel, art, music, and gourmet cooking—activities that appear from time to time in the books she writes. She uses feng shui to create the imaginary furnishings of her characters' homes.

"Music plays a major role in my creative process because I always write to music," she told *Arabesque Romance News*. "I favor soundtracks that at times will convey the mood of the characters or their dilemma." Her broad musical taste runs the gamut from Mozart to Manhattan Transfer to Barry White.

Alers expects eventually to retire from her day job and devote her full energy to her writing. She is nothing if not ambitious; her latest undertaking is a series for Silhouette Books featuring African American families in each of the fifty states, all containing romances and all also looking at traditions and cultural ties to the past.

Works by the Author

Fiction

My Love's Keeper (1991)
Happily Ever After (1994)
Careless Whispers (1995)
Reckless Surrender (1995)
Home Sweet Home (1996)
Gentle Yearning (1998)
Summer Magic (1999)
Secrets Never Told (2003)
Lessons of a Lowcountry Summer (2004)
Let's Get It On (2004)
Long Hot Summer (2004)
Very Private Duty: The Blackstones of Virginia (2004)

Hideaway Legacy Series

Hideaway (1995)
Heaven Sent (1998)
Harvest Moon (1999)
Just Before Dawn (2000)
Hideaway Saga (2004), includes first three books

Hideaway Legacy Series: Sons and Brothers Trilogy

Homecoming (2002)
No Compromise (2002)
Renegade (2003)

Hideaway Legacy Series: Daughters and Sisters Trilogy

Hidden Agenda (1997)
Vows (1997)
Private Passions (2001)

Silhouette Desire Series

1479. *A Younger Man* (2002)

Anthologies

Holiday Cheer (1995)
Love Letters (1997)
Rosie's Curl and Weave (1999)
Della's House of Style (2000)
Island Magic (2000)
Welcome to Leo's (2000)
Going to the Chapel (2001)
Tis the Season (2001)
Island Bliss (2002)
Twilight Moods (2002)
Living Large (2003)
Four Degrees of Hurt (2004)
Love at Leo's II (2004)
A Summer Place (2004)

Written as Susan James

Reckless Surrender (1995)

For Further Information

"Meet the Author: Rochelle Alers." Shades of Romance Magazine. *http://www.sormag.com/alers3.html* (viewed April 22, 2003).

Mosley, Shelley. "No Compromise" review. *Library Journal* (February 15, 2002).

Peacock, Scot, ed. Rochelle Alers entry, *Contemporary Authors*. Vol. 178. Detroit: Gale Research, 2000.

Rochelle Alers interview. Arabesque Romance News (May 1999). *http://authors.aalbc.com/rochelle.html* (viewed March 31, 2003).

Rochelle Alers Web site. *http://www.rochellealers.com/main.htm* (viewed April 22, 2003).

"Spin-Off Characters: Rochelle Alers' Secret Behind Her Hideaway Legacy Series." Romantic Times Book Club. *http://www.romantictimes.com/data/tips/287.html* (viewed March 31, 2003).

Julia Alvarez

◆ Women's Fiction ◆ Historical

New York, New York
1950

◆ *How the Garcia Girls Lost Their Accents*

About the Author and the Author's Writing

"I am a Dominican, hyphen, American," Julia Alvarez remarked in 1994 to Ilan Stavans of *Nation*. She then added, "As a fiction writer, I find that the most exciting things happen in the realm of that hyphen—the place where two worlds collide or blend together."

Much of her writing is about the duality of Hispanic life in America, but Alvarez's writing is also about human travails that override ethnic categories.

Born in New York City in 1950, Alvarez almost immediately moved with her well-to-do family back to their native Dominican Republic. A decade later, the family emigrated to the United States when Alvarez's father was jeopardized by his involvement with attempts to replace the Rafaél Trujillo dictatorship. (Interestingly, her mother's family was on the opposite side of the conflict and fared far better.)

In America Julia attended boarding school and high school. She experienced culture shock, to say the least. As Alvarez told *Contemporary Authors*, "Back home in the Dominican Republic, I had been an active, lively child, a bad student full of fun with plentiful friends. In New York City I was suddenly thrown back on myself. I looked around the schoolyard at unfriendly faces." Life in the Dominican Republic had been without books; the country's culture is largely an oral one. This new environment simultaneously caused anxiety and piqued the interest of the girl. She became an avid reader.

An English class assignment opened Julia's eyes to the possibilities of self-expression, and she began to write stories about her extended family and the way they had lived in the Dominican Republic. Struggling to conquer the English language, the young girl became fascinated with words and began writing poetry. In America, unlike in her traditional homeland, women could pursue careers. Absorbing herself in reading, Julia decided to become a serious writer.

Alvarez attended Connecticut College then transferred to Middlebury College, where she earned a bachelor of arts degree summa cum laude in 1971. She earned her master of fine arts degree from Syracuse University in 1975, and in 1986 attended Bread Loaf School of English on a Robert Frost Poetry fellowship.

From 1975 to 1977 Alvarez served as poet-in-the-schools in Kentucky. She later worked in bilingual and senior-citizen programs in Delaware and North Carolina, respectively. She became a professor of Creative Writing and English at Phillips Andover Academy in Massachusetts, and she instructed students at the University of Vermont and the University of Illinois. In 1984, she was named the Jenny McKean Moore Visiting Writer at George Washington University.

Alvarez is now a professor of English and has taught at Middlebury since 1988. Her writing has earned her numerous awards accolades including a National Endowment for the Arts grant in 1987 and a notable book designation from the American Library Association in 1992. She has published stories, essays, and verses for the *New York Times Magazine*, the *New Yorker*, *Hispanic Magazine*, and other publications.

Whereas her first book was poetry, her second was a novel, *How the Garcia Girls Lost Their Accents*, and it won the PEN Oakland/Josephine Miles Award. The book, which evolves in reverse chronological fashion, is fifteen linked stories about four sisters who, just as Alvarez did, came to New York City from the Dominican Republic and struggled to fit into a hugely different culture in the 1960s and beyond.

Critic Donna Rifkind commented on the book in the *New York Times Book Review*, saying that Alvarez "beautifully captured the threshold experiences of the new immigrant, where the past is not yet a memory and the future remains an anxious dream."

The author returned to the Garcia sisters, and specifically Yolanda (Yo) Garcia, in ¡Yo!. The story of the sister who became a writer is related from the perspectives of those who knew her.

In both books, the author strives to understand her parents' generation—a lost generation in the Dominican Republic. Since the stories come from personal experience, the author told *Atlantic Online*, she sometimes struggled with an impulse to cleanse the situations or alter the characters. But she retained true-to-life descriptions of abortions and illicit trysts and such.

Sisters also feature prominently in the author's *In the Time of the Butterflies*, a historical novel that follows the three Mirabel sisters, "The Butterflies" (Las Mariposas) in their tragic defiance of Trujillo's oppression in the Dominican Republic. (The day the real Mariposas were murdered by secret police, November 25, 1960, became the date for an annual commemoration in Latin America known as the International Day Against Violence Against Women.)

The novel caught the eye of critic Charlotte Rich, who remarked in the journal *Melus* on its structure and on "voices that speak back to and engage in dialogue with the 'official' language of Trujillo's regime, which is voiced by various characters, including Trujillo himself, throughout the novel."

Alvarez wrote the story as prose, rather than biography, as she sought "a way to travel through the human heart," she said on the Women of Hope Web site.

"I believe stories have this power—they enter us, they transport us, they change things inside us, so invisibly, so minutely, that sometimes we're not even aware that we come out of a great book as a different person from the person we were when we began reading it," the author said in a convocation speech at Appalachian State University.

The author's *In the Name of Salom* centers on a late nineteenth-century Dominican Republic poet, Salom Ure, who fought colonial rule and sought to educate women.

Married to physician Bill Eichner since 1989, Alvarez lives in Vermont and has an organic coffee farm called Alta Gracia in the Dominican Republic. She continues to write and to teach at Middlebury, where, according to a profile in *Atlantic Online*, she directs her students to "write about the stuff that isn't quite comfortable inside you, the things that are hard to get at and say."

Works by the Author

Fiction

How the Garcia Girls Lost Their Accents (1990)
In the Time of the Butterflies (1994)
¡Yo! (1997)
En El Tiempo De Las Mariposa (1998)
In the Name of Salom (2000)
The Secret Footprints (2000)
How Tía Lola Came to Stay (2001)
Before We Were Free (2002)
Las Huellas Secretas (2002)
Finding Miracles (2004)

Poetry

The Housekeeping Book (1984)
Homecoming: New and Collected Poems (1996)
The Other Side: El Otro Lado (1996)
The Woman I Kept to Myself (2004)

Editor

Old Age Ain't for Sissies (1979), poetry

Anthologies

The One You Call Sister: New Women's Fiction, edited by Paula Martinac (1989)
The Best American Poetry 1991, edited by David Lehman (1991)
Poems for a Small Planet: Contemporary American Nature Poetry, edited by Robert Pack and Jay Parini (1992)
Growing Up Female: Short Stories by Women Writers from the American Mosaic, edited by Susan Cahill (1993)
Mondo Barbie, edited by Lucinda Ebersole and Richard Peabody (1993)
A Formal Feeling Comes: Poems in Form by Contemporary Women, edited by Annie Finch (1994)
New Writing from the Caribbean (1994)

Nonfiction

Something to Declare: Essays (1998)
A Cafecito Story (2003)

Anthologies

The Writing Life: Writers on How they Think and Work, edited by Marie Arana (2003)

For Further Information

Alvarez, Julia. "A Brief Account of My Writing Life." English @ Middlebury. *http://www.middlebury/edu/~english/alvarez/Alv-autobio.html* (viewed April 15, 2003).

Alvarez, Julisa. "An American Childhood in the Dominican Republic." *American Scholar* (winter 1987).

Athy, Angela. Julia Alvarez entry, *American Ethnic Writers*. Vol. 1, edited by David Peck. Pasadena, CA: Salem Press, 2000.

Bing, Jonathan. "Julia Alvarez: Books That Cross Borders." *Publishers Weekly* (December 16, 1996).

Henao, Edna B. *Colonial Subjects Search for Nation, Culture and Identity in the Works of Julia Alvarez*. Lewiston, NY: Edwin Mellen Press, 2004.

Julia Alvarez biography. "Voices from the Gaps: Women Writers of Color." University of Minnesota. *http://voices.cla.umn.edu/authors/ALVAREZjulia.html* (viewed April 14, 2003).

Julia Alvarez biography. Women of Hope. *http://www.hepm.org/juliaalvarez.htm* (viewed April 15, 2003).

Julia Alvarez biography. *http://www.emory.edu/ENGLISH/Bahri/Alvarez.html* (viewed April 15, 2003).

McClellen, Hilary. "In the Name of the Homeland," Atlantic Online. *http://www.theatlantic.com/unbound/interviews/ba2000-07-19.htm* (viewed April 14, 2003).

Peacock, Scot, ed. Julia Alvarez entry, *Contemporary Authors New Revision Series*. Vol. 101. Detroit: Gale Research, 2002.

Rich, Charlotte. "Talking back to El Jefe: genre, polyphony, and dialogic resistance in Julia Alvarez's In the Time of Butterflies." *Melus* (winter 2002).

Rifkind, Donna. *How the Garcia Girls Lost Their Accents* review. *New York Times Book Review* (October 6, 1991).

Rosario-Sievert, Heather. "The Dominican-American Bildungsroman: Julia Alvarez's *How the Garcia Girls Lost Their Accents.*" *U.S. Latino Literature: A Critical Guide for Students and Teachers*, edited by Harold Augenbraum and Margarite Fernández Olmos. Westport, CT: Greenwood Press, 2000.

Stavans, Ilan. "Las Mariposas." *Nation* (November 1994).

Piers Anthony

♦ Fantasy ♦ Science fiction

Oxford, England
1934

♦ *Xanth Series*

Credit: Carol Jacob.

About the Author and the Author's Writing

Piers Anthony became an instant science fiction fan at age thirteen after he read a Jack Williamson story in *Astounding Science Fiction*. "I credit science fiction with much of the emotional progress I made thereafter, because it provided me with an array of wonderful other worlds, each of which was better than my own. I lived for each new issue of the magazine. Thus I was conversant with the genre of science fiction, and I felt I could be original within it," he related in *Bio of an Ogre*.

The author was born in 1934 in Oxford, England, as Piers Anthony Dillingham Jacob. He has also written essays and reviews under the names Piers A. D. Jacob, Robert Piers, and Piers Xanthony.

The Anthony family moved frequently during Anthony's youth, first to Spain (where his father was briefly and erroneously placed under arrest by the Franco government). Anthony had to repeat first grade twice because of an inability to read. His family came to the United States in 1940, and he became a naturalized citizen eighteen years later. When Piers was fifteen, a cousin died of cancer; his parents divorced when he was eighteen. His psychological discomfort with these events shows in his prose, which often depicts very controled, ordered environments.

Piers majored in creative writing at Goddard College and received his bachelor's degree in 1956. He married Carol Ann (Cam) Marble that year and they have two daughters. He served in the U.S. Army from 1957 to 1959 and worked as a technical writer, teacher, and social worker before he became a full-time writer in 1966.

Anthony's first published short story was "Possible to Rue" published in *Fantastic* in 1962. He received several awards for his first novel, *Chthon*, which came out in 1967. Biographer Michael R. Collings said this novel "weaves a complex tapestry of myth and legend drawn from classical antiquity; from Norseland; from the Christian Eden and *Paradise Lost*; from Dante's *Purgatory*; from the modern mythologies of psychoanalysis and psychology;

from literature; and from folk tales of magicians and dragons." In the book, Aton Five, who is serving a prison sentence inside a rock planet, eventually communicates with and comes to grips with the mineral entity that encompasses him.

Chthon launched Anthony's career writing science fiction and fantasy (there are fewer rules in fantasy, he has said, and it requires less research than science fiction), and he has taken side forays into historical, horror, martial arts, and erotic fiction. Many of Anthony's works are long novels in trilogies or series. This began with his Cluster tales, which eventually extended to five books.

Anthony's Xanth titles start with what he figured would be a stand-alone novel, *A Spell for Chameleon*. The series now numbers twenty-seven, with more promised. Said Don D'Amassa of the series in *Twentieth-Century Science-Fiction Writers*, "Anthony creates an original, magical system, a convincing fantasy world, superimposes an intriguing plot with sympathetic characters, and enlivens the mixture with humor."

"In the land of Xanth, everyone and everything—even a rock or tree—has a magical talent, except Bink," elaborated Deborah A. Stanley in *Authors & Artists for Young Adults*. "*Chameleon* follows Bink on his quest to discover his talent or face exile to the boring, powerless land of Mundania. In the process, Bink gains not only knowledge of his talent but emotional maturity as well."

The Xanth stories are full of puns and other tricks of language because, as the author explained in an ssfworld.com interview, "When I started writing this [Xanth], I found that I simply couldn't take fantasy seriously, so it became humorous, and continued from there. I turned my home state of Florida into the Land of Xanth."

To become a successful fiction writer, Anthony ventured, one needs imagination and desire: one needs to have certain basic skills and to work at the craft. Luck would not hurt, though originality and style are less critical. He partially outlines his books before he begins writing, but never too much so as to deter his muse.

In an interview with Cristopher DeRose, Anthony described his unusual way of overcoming temporary blocks while writing: "I call it the 'bracket' system. When the text stalls, go into brackets [like this] and talk to yourself. State the problem, play with ideas to fix it, and keep doing that—for thousands of words, if need be—until something clicks. Then emerge from the brackets and resume writing text. This does two things: it keeps you writing, which is important for momentum, and it solves your snag." When editing, he simply deletes the bracketed material.

Anthony has been challenged for the sexuality in some of his books, yet he said in an *Ogre's Den* newsletter he has more female readers than male. Many readers commend his ability to create a sense of place. He said in the February 2003 newsletter he literally enters the story when writing; "I am in every scene I write, and I see it through the eyes of every character I write about, male or female."

Piers is prolific, versatile, and seemingly inextinguishable. He went through a well-publicized wrangle with one publisher over compensation issues, was for a time blacklisted, and then did the near-impossible and returned as a best-selling author. He has collaborated with several authors over the years, the general arrangement, he said, being the other writer completes a manuscript that he then revises.

In recent years, Anthony has completed some of his series, has brought some old material back to light through electronic and self-publishing, and has begun a new series, the Chro-Magic books, featuring swords and sorcery on a planet whose volcanoes erupt in different colors of magic.

Will he run out of ideas? It does not seem likely any decade soon.

Works by the Author

Fiction

The Ring, with Robert E. Margroff (1968)
Macroscope (1969)
The E.S.P. Worm, with Robert E. Margroff (1970)
Prostho Plus (1971)
Rings of Ice (1974)
Triple Detente (1974)
But What of Earth?, [heavily revised by Robert Coulson] (1976); restored edition
    (1989)
Steppe (1976)
Hasan (1977)
The Pretender, with Frances Hall (1979)
Mute (1981), complete edition (2002)
Ghost (1986)
Shade of the Tree (1986)
Balook (1989)
Total Recall (1989), novelization of a movie based on the Philip K. Dick story "We
    Can Remember It For You Wholesale"
Dead Morn, with Robert Fuentes (1990)
Firefly (1990)
Hard Sell (1990)
Through the Ice, with Robert Kornwise (1990)
MerCycle (1991)
Tathan Mound (1991)
If I Pay Thee Not in Gold, with Mercedes Lackey (1993)
Killobyte (1993)
The Willing Spirit, with Alfred Tells (1996)
Volk (1996)
Hope of Earth (1997)
Quest for the Fallen Star, with James Richey and Alan Riggs (1998)
Spider Legs, with Clifford Pickover (1998)
Dream a Little Dream, with Julie Brady (1999)
Reality Check (1999)
The Gutbucket Quest, with Ron Leming (2000)
The Secret of Spring, with Jo Anne Taeusch (2000)
Sopaths (forthcoming)

Apprentice Adept Series

Split Infinity (1980)
Blue Adept (1981)
Double Exposure (1982), includes first three books

Juxtaposition (1982)
Out of Phaze (1987)
Robot Adept (1988)
Unicorn Point (1989)
Phaze Doubt (1991)
Caterpillar's Question, with Philip Jose Farmer (1992)

Aton Series

Chthon (1967)
Phthor (1975)
Plasm, by Charles Platt (1987)
Soma, by Charles Platt (1989)

Battle Circle Series

Sos the Rope (1968)
Var the Stick (1972)
Neq the Sword (1975)
Battle Circle (1978), includes first three books

Bio of a Space Tyrant Series

Refugee (1983)
Mercenary (1984)
Executive (1985)
Politician (1985)
Statesman (1986)
Cut by Emerald, by Dana Kramer (1987)
The Iron Maiden (2002)

ChroMagic Books

Key to Chroma (2003)
Key to Havoc (2003)
Key to Destiny (2004)

Cluster Series

Cluster (1977), in England as *Vicinity Cluster* (1979)
Chaining the Lady (1978)
Kirlian Quest (1978)
Thousandstar (1980)
Viscous Circle (1982)

Dragon's Gold Series, with Robert Margroff

Dragon's Gold (1987)
Serpent's Silver (1989)
Adventures of Kelvin of Rud Across the Frames (1990), reprints first, third, and fourth in series
Chimaera's Copper (1990)
Orc's Opal (1990)
Adventures of Kelvin of Rud Final Magic (1992), reprints second and fifth in series
Mouvar's Magic (1993)

Geodyssey Books

Isle of Woman (1993)
Shame of Man (1994)
Hope of Earth (1997)
Muse of Art (1999)
Climate of Change (forthcoming)

Incarnations of Immortality Series

On a Pale Horse (1983)
Bearing an Hourglass (1984)
With a Tangled Skein (1985)
Being a Green Mother (1987)
Wielding a Red Sword (1987)
For Love of Evil (1988)
And Eternity (1990)

Jason Striker Series, with Roberto Fuentes

1. *Kiai!* (1974)
2. *Mistress of Death* (1974)
3. *The Bamboo Bloodbath* (1975)
4. *Ninja's Revenge* (1975)
5. *Amazon Slaughter* (1976)
6. *Curse of the Ninja* (2002)

Mode Series

Virtual Mode (1991)
Fractal Mode (1992)
Chaos Mode (1994)
Doon Mode (2001)

Of Man and Mantra Trilogy

Omnivore (1968)
Orn (1971)
Ox (1976)
Of Man and Mantra (1986), includes all three books

Planet of Tarot Trilogy

God of Tarot (1979)
Faith of Tarot (1980)
Vision of Tarot (1980)
Tarot (1987), includes all three books

Pornucopia Series

Pornucopia (1989), originally *3.97 Erect* as by Tony Pedro
The Magic Fart (2003)

Xanth Series

A Spell for Chameleon (1977)
Castle Roogna (1979)
The Source of Magic (1979)
Centaur Aisle (1981)
The Magic of Xanth (1981), includes first three books
Ogre, Ogre (1982)
Dragon on a Pedestal (1983)
Night Mare (1983)
Crewel Lye: A Caustic Yarn (1985)
Golem in the Gears (1986)
Encyclopedia of Xanth—Crossroads Adventure in the World of Pier Anthony's Xanth, by Jody Lynn Nye (1987)
Vale of the Vole (1987)
Ghost of a Chance—Crossroads Adventure in the World of Pier Anthony's Xanth, by Jody Lynn Nye (1988)
Heaven Cent (1988)
Man from Mundania (1989)
Isle of View (1990)
Question Quest (1991)
The Color of Her Panties (1992)
Demons Don't Dream (1993)
Harpy Thyme (1994)
Geis of the Gargoyle (1995)
Roc and a Hard Place (1995)
Yon Ill Wind (1996)

The Continuing Xanth Saga (1997), reprints *Centour Aisle; Ogre, Ogre;* and *Night Mare*
Faun & Games (1997)
Zombie Lover (1998)
Xone of Contention (1999)
The Dastard (2000)
Swell Foop (2001)
Up in a Heaval (2002)
Cube Route (2003)
Currant Events (2004)

Short Stories

Anthonology (1985)
Uncollected Stars, edited with Barry Malzberg and Martin H. Greenberg (1986)
Alien Plot (1992)
Tales from the Great Turtle, with Richard Gilliam (1994)

Books for Young Adults

Race Against Time (1973)

Anthologies

Nova One: An Anthology of Original Science Fiction, edited by Harry Harrison (1970)
Science Against Man, edited by Anthony Cheetham (1970)
Again, Dangerous Visions, edited by Harlan Ellison (1972)
Generations, edited by David Gerrold (1972)
The Berkley Showcase, edited by Victoria Schochet and John Silbersack (1981)

Nonfiction

Alf Layla Wa Layla (1966)
Bio of an Ogre: The Autobiography of Piers Anthony to Age 50 (1988)
Letters to Jenny (1993)
Piers Anthony's Visual Guide to Xanth, with Judy Lynn Nye (1999)
How Precious Was That While (2001)
Ligeia: The Early Part of Dying (forthcoming)

For Further Information

Clute, John. Piers Anthony entry, *The Encyclopedia of Science Fiction*. Edited by Clute and Peter Nicholls. New York: St. Martin's, 1993.

Collings, Michael R. *Piers Anthony*. San Bernardino, CA: Starmont House, 1983.

"Compleat Piers Anthony Bibliography." Piers Anthony Web site. *http://www .piers-anthony.com/complist.html* (viewed May 15, 2003).

Cowart, David, ed. Piers Anthony entry, *Dictionary of Literary Biography: Twentieth-Century American Science Fiction Writers*, part 1: A–L. Detroit: Gale Research, 1981.

D'Ammassa, Don. Piers Anthony entry, *Twentieth-Century Science-Fiction Writers*. 3rd edition, edited by Noelle Watson and Paul E. Schellinger. Chicago: St. James Press, 1991.

DeRose, Christopher. "Piers Anthony Triumphs Over Writer's Block and the Idiocy of Publishers." SciFi.com. *http://www.scifi.com/sfw/issue218/interview2.html* (viewed March 31, 2003).

Duquette, William H. "Piers Anthony: Oxymandias of Xanth." Ex Libris. *http://www .wjduquette.com/authors/panthony.html* (viewed March 31, 2003).

Jones, Daniel, and John D. Jorgenson, eds. Piers Anthony entry, *Contemporary Authors New Revision Series*. Vol. 73. Detroit: Gale Research, 1999.

"Ogre's Den: From the Desk of Piers Anthony" (February 2003). Piers Anthony Web site. *http://www.hipiers.com/newsletter.html* (viewed March 31, 2003).

Piers Anthony bibliography. Hi Piers Web site. *http://www.hipiers.com/bibliography .html* (viewed March 31, 2003).

Piers Anthony interview. sffworld.com (May 2000). *http://www.ssfworld.com/ authors/a/anthony_piers/interviews/200005.html* (viewed March 31, 2003).

Piers Anthony Web site. *http://www.piers-anthony.com/faq.html* (viewed March 31, 2003).

Stanley, Deborah A. Piers Anthony entry, *Authors & Artists for Young Adults*. Vol. 11, edited by Kevin S. Hile. Detroit: Gale Research, 1993.

Jean M. Auel

◆ Historical ◆ Adventure

Chicago, Illinois
1936

◆ *The Clan of the Cave Bear*

Credit: John Emmerling © 1990.

About the Author and the Author's Writing

Fans had to wait for what seemed like an ice age for the latest of author Jean M. Auel's Earth's Children series, but considering the mammoth amount of research she had to undertake, the result was worth it.

Auel came to popular fiction writing via an unusual route—technical writing, poetry, and MBA research papers. Born Jean Marie Untinen in Chicago in 1936, she was the next-oldest of five children of a painter and decorator and a housewife. As a child she was eager to learn how to read. After high school, she married Ray Bernard Auel. They moved to Portland, Oregon, and eventually had five children. She joined Tektronix in Beaverton, Oregon, in 1965, working her way up from keypunch operator to circuit board designer to technical writer to credit manager.

Reading a magazine article about the high-IQ organization Mensa in 1964, she took a home intelligence test and joined. She felt at home at the group's meetings and was inspired to attend night school to study science, math, and business. When she earned a master's degree in business administration in 1976 from the University of Portland, she quit the electronics firm to look for a suitable new job.

An idea for a short story came to Auel in January 1977, which prompted her to do some research. Her imagination shifted into high gear and she shaped a narrative of a prehistoric girl, an outcast among a new group of more primitive people she came to live with. That story, when she finishes the series, will be the epic adventure of Earth's Children some 25,000 years ago during the Ice Age. Ayla, blond and blue-eyed, a more advanced Cro-Magnon (our close ancestor), falls in love with Jondalar. They live with eastern European Cro-Magnons in Russia before traveling back to his home in France.

Auel's first attempt to put this story together yielded an enormous 450,000-word manuscript, which she produced in a white heat of sixteen-hour days at the typewriter. It became clear the story should be broken into a half-dozen parts. She showed her proposal to Jean Naggar, a New York agent whom Auel had met at a writers' conference. Naggar eventually auctioned the manuscript to publishers. Once the winning bidder had $130,000 committed for North American hardcover rights, there was no way that publisher wasn't going to heavily promote the new writer.

Naggar told *Publishers Weekly* in 2002 she became excited about *Clan* because "at that time, we were seeing a lot of books about ethnic roots—*Roots* had just been published, and *World of Our Fathers*—and my feeling was that Auel's book was powerful because it embraced the roots of our common humanity."

To get a handle on her writing—her previous experience was drafting a technical booklet, *So You Want to Design Circuit Boards*—Auel read such books as Leon Surmelian's *Techniques of Fiction Writing* and Lajos Egri's *The Art of Dramatic Writing*. The author writes at night—she's the "night Auel," she jokes—usually at least eight hours at a shot.

To learn about the Ice Age, she immersed herself in research, devouring books and scientific articles and visiting museums, universities, and archaeological sites.

Among her favorite authors are J.R.R. Tolkien, Robert Heinlein, and Ursula K. Le Guin in fantasy and science fiction and James A. Michener and Mike Waltari in the historical saga realm.

Auel is proud, she said in a *Copperfield Review* interview, "that I'm still writing only to please myself and that the scientific specialists are so positive and enthusiastic about my books."

She rewrote *The Clan of the Cave Bear* four times, she has said, and some sections as many as forty times. It was time well spent, as her Earth's Children books have sold close to 40 million copies around the world. Her stories are popular, the author told Deirdre Donahue of *USA Today*, largely because "it's kind of like everyone's history. We didn't start out building cathedrals."

Digging for information takes a considerable amount of the author's time. She has probed books and papers in libraries and museums in France, Austria, Czechoslovakia, Hungary, Germany, and the Ukraine. She has learned to knapp flint and build a snow cave as well as find and cook wild food and tan an animal hide. She also has taken field courses with anthropologists and survivalists.

Auel has refused publisher advances, as they come with deadlines attached. There was a twelve-year gap between books four and five, not because she wasn't thinking about the new book or working on it, but because she had lots of information to gather, and she had a regular life to live (the Auels have fifteen grandchildren). She visited the restricted caves at Altamira in Spain's Basque country to examine Paleolithic paintings and she traveled to Zimbabwe to view a solar eclipse.

Ice Age people were tall and robust, Auel said. Hunters and gatherers, they were intelligent and displayed psychological reactions that are the same as ours. They had our emotions, they were facile with language, and they were creative.

"These people were the first modern humans," she said in a 1990 Waldenbooks brochure. "It's fairly well accepted by most of the archaeological community that they had the same range of intelligence and the same psychological and emotional reactions as we have, except that theirs were directed in different ways." Neither they nor we would have been comfortable in the other's world, she continued, but that in no way diminishes the intelligence or ability of prehistoric people. The author recognizes a good deal of Ayla's popularity comes from her rather modern strength, tenacity, and intelligence.

At a loss to explain why she writes, Auel said in an Internet interview, "From the beginning, when I first got an idea for a story and wondered if I could write it, it has always been the story that has driven me. The idea led me into the research, which continues to give me more ideas for the story. While I try to make each book a complete novel, the series itself has an overarching story, which I want to finish. Perhaps, in a way, Ayla is sitting on my shoulder telling me to get on with it."

Works by the Author

Fiction

Earth's Children Series

The Clan of the Cave Bear (1980)
The Valley of Horses (1982)
The Mammoth Hunters (1985)
The Plains of Passage (1990)
The Shelters of Stone (2002)

Poetry Anthology

From Oregon With Love, edited by Anne Hinds (1975)

Motion Pictures Based on the Author's Works

The Clan of the Cave Bear (1986)

For Further Information

Allard, Meredith. "An Interview With Jean M. Auel." *Copperfield Review* (winter 2000).

Auel, Jean M. Communication to author. April 26, 2004.

Cochran, Tracy. "The view from mount Auel: Midwife to the Ice Age delivers a long-awaited tale." *Publishers Weekly* (April 22, 2002).

Dirks, Jennifer. "Interview with Jean Auel." Absolute Write. *http://www.absolutewrite.com/novels/jean_auel.htm* (viewed March 30, 2003).

Donahue, Deirdre. "After 12 Years, Auel Revives Ayla." *USA Today* (June 14, 2001).

"Interview with Jean M. Auel." *http://aukon.sf.org/nz/JeanAuel.htm* (viewed March 31, 2003).

Jean M. Auel interview. Waldenbooks book club pamphlet. 1990.

Jean M. Auel Web page. Random House. *http://www.randomhouse.com/features/auel/interviews.html* (viewed March 31, 2003).

Jones, Daniel, and John D. Jorgensen, eds. Jean M. Auel entry, *Contemporary Authors New Revision Series*. Vol. 64. Detroit: Gale Research, 1998.

Linda S. Bergmann. Jean M. Auel entry, *Twentieth-Century Romance and Historical Writers*. 2nd edition, edited by Lesley Henderson. Chicago: St. James Press, 1990.

MacDonald, Jay Lee. "Jean Auel's modern Stone Age family rolls on." BookPage (April 2002). *http://www.bookpage.com/0204bp/jean_auel.html* (viewed March 30, 2003).

"Meet the Writers: Jean M. Auel." Barnes & Noble. *http://www.barnesandnoble. com/writers/writerdetails.asp?userid=0H4KV3ZHMT&cid=967961#bio* (viewed March 31, 2003).

Ross, Deborah. "Queen of Stone Age sex." The Age (June 10, 2002). *http://www.theage. com/au/articles/2002/06/10/1022982811478.html* (viewed March 31, 2003).

"Who is Jean Auel—and how did she come to write this series?" *http://geocities.com/ auelpage/JeanAuel.htm* (viewed March 31, 2003).

Clive Barker

Liverpool, England
1952

◆ *Hellraiser*

Courtesy of Harper-
Collins.

About the Author and the Author's Writing

If Clive Barker didn't have fantastic, frightful nightmares as a child, he certainly did as an adult—transferring them to paper in relentless, gory, and at times uncomfortably humorous prose and bold, horrific motion pictures that have entertained a host of readers and viewers, prompting Stephen King to proclaim him "the future of horror."

Barker was born in Liverpool, England, in 1952, the son of a personnel director and a school welfare officer. He studied English literature and philosophy at Liverpool University. Moving to London at age twenty-one, he scratched out a living as an illustrator. He took to the avant-garde stage scene with Hydra Theatre Company and Theatre of the Imagination, among others. He performed on stage and directed as well as wrote most of the plays. His dramas—with titles such as *Frankenstein in Love*, *Dangerous World*, and *History of the Devil*—early on showed the scary, sexy, comedic, fantastic elements that would soon emerge in his prose writing. (Several of the plays were eventually collected and published in book form.)

Short stories that he wrote during this period were collected in six volumes of the *Books of Blood, 1984–1985*. ("Everybody is a book of blood," Barker has written. "Wherever we're opened, we're red.") With publication of his collections, and of *Damnation Game*, his first novel, and with translation of his works for European markets, he quickly developed a following.

What books and writers have influenced this author? Barker lists the Bible and such writers as Edgar Allan Poe, Ray Bradbury, William Blake, Jean Cocteau, and Herman Melville. But his stories come only from his own head.

His ideas, Barker told Houseofhorrors.com, grow from his subconscious: "I am a Jungian, not a Freudian. I believe that a collective unconscious—a pool of shared images and stories which all humanity is heir to—exists, and the artist dealing in the fantastique is uniquely placed, in that he or she can create stories or paintings which dramatize the eruption of the unconscious into our day to day lives."

In light of the universality Barker sees in his readership—his works are translated in twenty-three languages and are very popular in Russia and Korea—he works to "strip it of particulars," he said in an interview for *January Magazine*. "Like there are no references to what kind of cigarettes people smoke. What kind of booze is going down their throats. There are very few references to movies. I hate it when writers stoop to, as I see it, something which is so particular that it's almost as if they're making a cultural reference to give you shorthand to the feeling."

The author told Bob Graham of the *San Francisco Chronicle* about an experience he had as a five-year-old, watching a parachutist at an air show jump from a plane to his death. He has forever since felt vulnerable.

One thing Barker strives for in his writing is to bring people closer: "The appetite to bridge that gap is based on a kind of despair, actually, about the fact that we're not making a connection. Even those we love, our parents, seem remote," he said.

Displeased with the film results of *Rawhead Rex* and *Transmutations*, which were based on his stories, the author decided to direct one of the scripts himself. *Hellraiser*, based on *The Hellbound Heart*, tells the story of a man's dead monstrous spirit that manipulates a woman into luring and killing people so that he may feed on them. The film raised a cult audience sufficient for the creation of three sequels featuring the pinhead monster, a series of comic books, plastic figurines, and related merchandise. The same phenomena happened when he made a movie called *Nightbreed* from his story "Cabal." Marvel Comics eventually established an entire imprint for Barker storylines.

Meanwhile Barker wrote novels, including the 584-page *Weaveworld*, a fantasy about a magical, Utopian world secreted among the fibers of a carpet. And he expanded his movie credits to include producing (*Candyman*, for example, which is based on his short story "The Forbidden").

Barker moved to Los Angeles in 1991, where he shares a home with his life companion David Armstrong. He devotes considerable energies to his prose writing, all the while involving himself in the whirlwind of moviemaking and television production.

Barker told *Writer's Digest* that his shift from short stories to longer prose forms has enabled him to better delineate his characters and allow them to develop over the course of the action. He has also gone from straight horror into fantasy (*Abarat*) and the supernatural (*Cold Heart Canyon*).

The author begins with plot outlines, particularly on his longest works which may have elaborate backgrounds, though he deviates as necessary. Regarding characters, he told interviewer W. C. Stroby, "Get [the reader] to accept one thing, one weirdness, and then the rest of it must follow realistically. I try not to lie about psychology. I don't think I'm mawkish in my writing, I don't think I'm overly sentimental. I try and be emotionally honest within a framework which has one thing askew."

Barker, in an online interview for *BookEnds*, said he often creates "big, simple, almost mythological characters," their attraction being that myth "takes us out of ourselves, to a place where the world is not muddled. We live in a very muddled world: morally, spiritually, and in terms of the amount of assaultive information being thrown our way. I hope when someone enters any of my books they are going into a place where the battle lines are drawn a little more clearly."

Once the characters are in place, and appreciating that he must persuade his readers to make a leap into the unknown, Barker said he looks for parallel situations. Nearly everyone has felt the lure of the unknown or the dangerous, for example. To make his worlds even more convincing, Barker does considerable research—not necessarily all of it in books. In fact, much of it comes from human experience, putting pains and losses and doubts and angers and loves on paper. Reviewers have frequently made positive note of Barker's commentary on human nature.

An unusual book, in that its story is driven by issues more than character, is *Sacrament*, which looks at the relentless killing of wild animals and the immense threat of AIDS to the gay population. Its main character, Will Rabjohns, is openly, joyously, actively gay, as is Barker himself. Acknowledging to Jane Ganahl of *The Examiner* how personal the book is, Barker stated, "It was a way to wake myself up, to tell myself 'don't just be a witness.' . . . I've had many friends die of AIDS, and it looks like the cure is still years away. Writing this book was a way to reconnect with them, and to make it real for people."

Is there a link between his sexuality and his choice of genres? Yes, Barker said on a Talk Today interactive interview. It comes from the feeling of a gay man or woman of being an outsider in American culture. "What did I find monstrous as a child? Well, not the conventional objects of demonization (I identified with those) but with their oppressors, because even before I fully understood the politics of this I knew in my gut that the oppressors are a universal idea. . . . It's good to be an outsider sometimes."

Works by the Author

Fiction

The Damnation Game (1985)
Weaveworld (1987)
The Hellbound Heart (1988)
Imajica (1991), also published as two volumes: *Imajica I: The Fifth Dominion* and
     Imajica II: The Reconciliation (1995)
London, Volume 1: Bloodline (1993)
The Thief of Always: A Fable (1993)
Lord of Illusion (1995)
Sacrament (1996)
Galilee (1998)
Cold Heart Canyon (2001)
Rare Flesh, with David Armstrong (2004)

Arabat Quartet

Abarat: The First Book of Hours (2002)
Abarat: Days of Magic, Nights of War (2004)

Books of the Art Trilogy

The Great and Secret Show: The First Book of the Art (1989)
Everville: The Second Book of the Art (1994)

Short Stories and Novellas

Clive Barker's Books of Blood, Volume 1 (1984)
Clive Barker's Books of Blood, Volume 2 (1984)
Clive Barker's Books of Blood, Volume 3 (1984)
Books of Blood, Volumes 1–3 (1985), includes first three books
Clive Barker's Books of Blood, Volume 4 (1986), in United States as *The Inhuman Condition: Tales of Terror* (1986)
Clive Barker's Books of Blood, Volume 5 (1986), in United States as *Tales of Terror* (1986)
Clive Barker's Books of Blood, Volume 6 (1986), in United States as *Cabal* (1988)
Books of Blood, Volumes 4–6 (1986), includes previous three books
The Inhuman Condition (1986)
The Essential Clive Barker (1997)
Clive Barker's Tapping the Vein (2002)

Screenplays

Underworld, with James Caplin (1985)
Rawhead Rex (1986)
Hellraiser (1987), also director
Nightbreed (1990), also director
Lord of Illusions (1995), also director and producer
The Thief of Always, with Bernard Rose (1998)

Stage Plays

Incarnations: Three Plays (1995)
Forms of Heaven: Three Plays (1996)

Editor

Night Visions Hardshell (1987)
New Theatre Quarterly 72 (2003)
New Theatre Quarterly 76 (2003)

Introduction

Gods and Monsters: The Shooting Script, by Bill Condon and Ian McKellan (2004)

Anthologies

Silver Scream (1976)
Cutting Edge (1978)
I Shudder at Your Touch: 22 Tales of Sex and Horror (1984)
Millennium (1987)
Gaslight and Ghosts (1988)

Prime Evil (1988)
Between Time and Terror (1990)
The Mammoth Book of Terror (1990)
The Mammoth Book of Vampires (1992)
Best New Horror 4 (1993)
The Year's Best Fantasy and Horror Sixth Annual Collection (1993)
The Giant Book of Terror (1994)
Little Deaths (1994)
Visions of Fear: Foundations of Fear, Volume III (1994)
Night Screams (1995)
Splatterpunks II: Over the Edge (1995)
Dark Terrors 2 (1996)
Dancing with the Dark (1997)
The Reel Stuff (1998)
The Unexplained: Stories of the Paranormal (1998)
Vintage Science Fiction (1999)
Hellraiser: Collected Best II (2003)

Nonfiction

Clive Barker's A-Z of Horror, with Stephen Jones (1984)
Theatre Games (1988)
Clive Barker's Shadows in Eden, edited by Stephen Jones (1991)
Pandemonium: The World of Clive Barker (1991)
Illustrator II: The Art of Clive Barker, edited by Amacker Bullwinkle (1993)

For Further Information

Badley, Linda. *Writing Horror and the Body: The Fiction of Stephen King, Clive Barker, and Anne Rice*. Westport, CT: Greenwood Press, 1996.

Barbieri, Suzanne J. *Clive Barker: Mythmaker for the Millennium*. Stockport, Lancashire: British Fantasy Society, 1994.

Clive Barker biography. Dragoncon. *http://www.dragoncon.org/people/barkerc.html* (viewed April 24, 2003).

Clive Barker interview. Dominion. *http://www.clivebarker.com/html/visions/confess/nonls.scifi/dominion.html* (viewed April 24, 2003).

Clive Barker interview, parts 1 and 2. IGN for Men (December 17 and 20, 1999). *http://formen.ign.com/news/13383.html* and *http://formen.ign.com/news/13415.html* (viewed April 24, 2003).

Clive Barker Web site. *http://www.clivebarker.com/html/visions/confess/cfslist2.html* (viewed March 31 and April 24, 2003).

"Clive Barker's Biography." House of Horrors. *http://www.houseofhorrors.com/barkerbio/htm* (viewed April 24, 2003).

Clive Barker's plays. *http://www.clivebarker.dial.pipex.com/playsindex.html* (viewed April 24, 2003).

"Films of Clive Barker." IGN for Men. *http://www.formen.ign.com/news/13258.html* (viewed April 24, 2003).

Ganahl, Jane. "Hellraiser: Barker on a spiritual quest." *Examiner* (August 11, 1996).

Graham, Bob. "A Demon for Work: Busy horror auteur Clive Barker branches out into erotica." *San Francisco Chronicle* (February 22, 1999).

"Horror in books and movies: Clive Barker." Halloween interview. Talk Today (October 31, 2000). *http://www.usatoday.com/chat/1031barker.htm* (viewed March 31, 2003).

Jensen, Jeff. "Stroke of Genius?" *Entertainment Weekly* (October 4, 2002).

Jones, Daniel, and John D. Jorgensen, eds. Clive Barker entry, *Contemporary Authors New Revision Series*. Vol. 71. Detroit: Gale Research, 1999.

"King of Pain." Salon People Feature. *http://archive.salon.com/people/feature/2000/0204/barker/* (viewed April 24, 2003).

McIntyre, Gina. "Dream Catcher." *Wicked Magazine* (spring 2000). *http://www.clivebarker.com/html/visions/confess/nonls/wicked/wicked2.htm* (viewed April 24, 2003).

"Renaissance man." *Scotsman* (September 18, 1999).

Richards, Linda. "Clive Barker Comes Out." *January Magazine*. *http://www.januarymagazine.com/barker.html* (viewed March 31, 2003).

Stroby, W. C. "Clive Barker: Trust Your Vision." *Writer's Digest* (March 1991).

Wallace, John. Clive Barker interview. BookEnds. *http://62.173.95.217/bookends/chat/barker./asp?TAG=&CID=* (viewed April 5, 2003).

Winter, Douglas E. *Clive Barker: The Dark Fantastic*. New York: HarperCollins, 2002.

Nevada Barr

◆ Mystery ◆ Historical

Yerington, Nevada
1952

◆ *Anna Pigeon Series*

About the Author and the Author's Writing

Many mystery writers root their ongoing series in a specific region of the country: New York, Detroit, California. Nevada Barr's traditional Anna Pigeon mystery novels have a common, but changing setting: Each book takes place in a national park. She's covered nearly a dozen so far, and has 360-plus to go.

The heroine, a National Park Service (NPS) employee, "started out being based on myself," admitted the author in an Amazon.com interview, "because I was working as a park ranger in Guadalupe. But of course she was taller, stronger, smarter—you know, better looking. And over the years she has kind of just evolved into her own person."

Barr was born in 1952 in Yerington, Nevada. Her name, she has said, came from one of her father's favorite fiction characters. She grew up in Susanville, California, where her parents were pilots (her mother was also a mechanic and carpenter) at a small mountain airport eighty miles from Reno. She attended California Polytechnical University, where she earned a bachelor of arts degree in speech and drama. She received a master of fine arts degree in acting from University of California at Irvine.

Her sister Molly became a pilot for USAir, but Nevada pursued a career in theater. She joined the Classic Stage Company in New York City and performed in off-Broadway plays. She also waited tables. After five years and no rise to stardom, she moved to Minneapolis and continued theater work, acted in television commercials and industrial films, and did radio voice-overs.

Beginning in 1978, Barr wrote four historical novels. One of them, *Bittersweet*, was published in 1984. The main character, Imogene Grelznik, falsely accused of having a lesbian affair with a pupil, flees to a small town in Pennsylvania where she ends up, in fact, falling in love with one of her students, Sarah, who has fled an abusive marriage. Traveling together to

Nevada, the pair carve their niche in an otherwise male-dominated world, operating an inn. Although the novel, which was reprinted in 2003, garnered positive reviews, it did not spark a career.

Barr is still drawn to history; her recent *Flashback* includes a lesser-known figure from the time of Abraham Lincoln's assassination, Dr. Samuel Mudd. Historical fiction has its advantages—less modern technology is involved, for instance—but the author told Dorman Shindler of *Publishers Weekly* she wouldn't want to live in any other time "because there's not a tooth in my head that's not filled or crowned—in any other time, I wouldn't have any teeth."

Meanwhile, the author's former husband, a disillusioned actor, became active with the NPS, and Barr did likewise. Long interested in the environmental movement, Barr became first a seasonal park ranger at Mesa Verde National Park in Colorado in 1988. Then, after six years, she was appointed a full-time, uniformed, Sig Sauer-armed ranger at Isle Royale National Park in Michigan. Other postings included Guadalupe Mountain National Park in Texas, Lassen Volcanic National Park and Horsefly Fire Camp in Idaho and a short stint at Cumberland Island National Seashore—all of which would provide background to her mysteries.

While working for the federal government, Barr related campfire stories, taught story-telling, and wrote travel pieces and restaurant reviews, maintaining her skills until she was inspired to wrote her first Pigeon book, *Track of the Cat*, in 1993. It earned her the Agatha Award for Best First Novel and the Anthony Award for Best Novel, both in 1994.

"Urban crime is moving into the parks," Barr told *Outside* writer John Galvin, "and that makes a nice matrix for a murder mystery."

Barr took her character's name from one of her former husband's museum coworkers. Pigeon is a mildly depressed, somewhat alcohol-reliant, tough-talking, feisty widow who has shucked Manhattan in favor of the great wilderness. In the first story, she takes a walk in the backcountry only to stumble upon the body of a fellow ranger who apparently has been clawed to death by a puma.

Pigeon's later assignments also involve murder. Sometimes the settings are cold, as at an island park in the middle of Lake Superior, and sometimes they are arid, as amid the Anasazi ruins at Mesa Verde. In the course of the series, love is not lost; it's just delayed. Pigeon in *Flashback* is looking to avoid a marriage proposal from Paul Davidson.

Barr at times writes bluntly of NPS administrative issues. She's opposed to sportfishing in parks, for example. And in *Ill Wind*, she takes a shot at park concessions: "Anna often wondered how much money the hapless taxpayers had forked out in overtime so fully armed rangers could shoo mice out of the Hostess Twinkies. With the monies concessions pulled in they could easily afford Pinkertons."

However, at heart, Barr is a parks booster. "I want people to love the parks," she said in an interview with Linda M. Rancourt for *National Parks*. "I point out the problems with the Park Service because I write about what I know, and what is true. I want the public still to believe that we're heroes. Because I think everybody needs heroes. Why not let them be us? But I do think [the Park Service] needs to be deglamorized to the point that people realize that there are needs."

After serving with the NPS at the Natchez Trace Parkway in Mississippi, Barr retired as a ranger and in 1997 she became a full-time writer. Her personal life, however, took a bumpy road. She went through an unpleasant divorce and suffered an episode of mental illness. In a nonfiction departure, *Seeking Enlightenment . . . Hat by Hat*, the author relates her family's disdain for organized religion. She one day walked into an Episcopal Church and has since experienced a spiritual awakening. Remarried, she lives in Clinton, Mississippi, with her husband, two dogs, and four cats.

The author has a long list of favorite writers, including Jane Austen and Charles Dickens and mystery-writing contemporaries Anne Perry and Kate Ross.

As the Pigeon series has progressed, Barr has found ways to push herself as a writer. In *Flashback*, she alternates third-person Pigeon scenes with first-person historical chapters. "To do a totally different form and character was marvelously refreshing," she said in *Romantic Times Magazine*. "The difficulty lay in tying the two mysteries [present at Dry Tortugas National Park in Florida, past in a Civil War prison] in a believable way and in capturing the words and language of the 1860s without being stiff or pretentious."

Barr does not consider herself a disciplined writer; she puts in more hours the closer she is to deadline. If she gets hung up on a plot point, she phones her sister for help. Her years acting gave her a basis for understanding character, motivation, and dialogue.

New York Times Book Review's Marilyn Stasio found that *High Country's* "bone-chilling human hunt is a solid piece of adventure writing," despite the transparency of the villains.

How does the author create her compelling stories? She decides on a setting, and if necessary does her research. For *Blood Lure*, Barr told Mystery Guild, "I went to Glacier National Park and spent two weeks looking for bears. I did everything but rub tuna fish oil on my body and wander naked through the meadows. And I never saw a single bear." With a shell of a story in her imagination—who dies and how, and who did the killing—the author explained to Stephanie Swilley for *BookPage*, she jumps in. "I tried once, years ago, to outline it all like a grown-up and write a synopsis for every chapter, and it read like the English assignment from hell. . . . Every bit of spontaneity got sucked right out."

Works by the Author

Fiction

Bittersweet (1984)

Anna Pigeon Series

Track of the Cat (1993)
A Superior Death (1994)
Ill Wind (1995)
Firestorm (1996)
Endangered Species (1997)
Blind Descent (1998)
Liberty Falling (1999)
Deep South (2000)
Blood Lure (2001)
Hunting Season (2002)
Flashback (2003)
High Country (2004)
Hard Truth (2005)

Editor

Nevada Barr Presents Malice Domestic 10: An Anthology of Original Traditional Mystery Stories (2001)

Anthologies

Women on the Case, edited by Sara Paretsky (1996)
AZ Murder Goes . . . Artful, edited by Susan Mailing and Barbara Peters (2001)
Naked Came the Phoenix: A Serial Novel, edited by Marcia Talley (2001)

Nonfiction

Seeking Enlightenment . . . Hat by Hat: A Skeptic's Look at Religion (2003)

For Further Information

Davies, Jon M. "Nevada Barr." Mississippi Writers Page. *http://www.olemiss.edu/depts/english/ms-writers/dir/barr_nevada/* (viewed March 30, 2003).

Gavin, John. "Mystery writer Nevada Barr's stiff-brimmed recipe for murder." *Outside* (April 1996).

Jackson, Gordon. "Cumberland researcher settles with author." *Savannah Morning News* (August 9, 1999).

Nevada Barr interview. Mystery Guild. *http://www.mysteryguild.com/doc/browse/author/author_interview.jhtml?authorId=1000193* (viewed March 30, 2003).

Nevada Barr Resource Page. *http://members.tripod.com~MindHarp/nbarr.html#pub* (viewed March 20, 2003).

Nevada Barr Web site. *http://www.nevadabarr.com/books/booksmain.htm* (viewed March 30, 2003).

"Nevada Barr: You're Not Going to Get Rich Saving the World." iVillagers interview. *http://www.ivillage.com/books/intervu/myst/articles/0,11872,2407-95_85057,00.html* (viewed March 30, 2003).

Peacock, Scot, ed. Nevada Barr entry, *Contemporary Authors*. Vol. 161. Detroit: Gale Research, 1998.

"Pigeon Sweeps Manhattan: An Interview with Nevada Barr." Amazon.com. *http://www.amazon.com/exec.obidos/ts/feature/4840/1022562698-9751302* (viewed March 30, 2003).

Prokop, Mary. *Seeking Enlightenment* review. *Library Journal* (June 1, 2003).

"Raising the Barr." *Romantic Times Magazine* (February 2003).

Rancourt, Linda M. "Murder She Writes." *National Parks* (September/October 1995).

Shindler, Dorman. "Taking on History's Mysteries." *Publishers Weekly* (January 27, 2003).

Silet, Charles L. P. "Nevada Barr." *Mystery Scene* no. 53 (May/June 1996).

Stasio, Marilyn. *High Country* review. *New York Times Book Review* (February 22, 2004).

Swanson, Jean, and Dean James, eds. Nevada Barr entry, *By a Woman's Hand: A Guide to Mystery Fiction by Women*. 2nd edition. New York: Berkley, 1996.

Swilley, Stephanie. "On the trail with Nevada Barr." BookPage. *http://www.bookpage .com/0103bp/nevada_barr.html* (viewed March 31, 2003).

Peter Benchley

◆ Adventure

New York, New York
1940

◆ *Jaws*

About the Author and the Author's Writing

Peter Benchley's *Jaws*, the ideal beach-blanket read, spent some forty weeks on the *New York Times* bestseller list and its motion picture version—with a screenplay by the author—filled movie theaters in 1975.

Although it was the author's first novel, Benchley enjoyed a certain familiarity with readers, as both his father, Nathaniel Benchley, and his grandfather, humorist Robert Benchley of Algonquin Round Table fame, were authors as well.

Still, *Jaws* stood on its own merits. It was a fright story, a thriller about a flesh-hungry shark roaming the South Shore of Long Island and the unlikely team of police chief, oceanographer, and fishing captain that pursues the creature.

The author's inspirations, he told *People* in 1974, were his own experiences on family swordfish angling jaunts off Nantucket, where the family summered, and a news account of a 4,500-pound great white shark caught off Long Island's Montauk Point. "My God, if that kind of thing can happen around the beaches of Long Island, and I know Southampton, why not put the two together?"

Benchley was born in New York City in 1940. He attended school there before pursuing his secondary school education at Phillips Exeter Academy in New Hampshire. He majored in English at Harvard College, graduating in 1961. After traveling the globe for a year, he wrote a nonfiction book about his adventures, and later he served six months in the Marine Corps Reserves. In 1964 he married Winifred B. Wesson, with whom he has three children.

Benchley joined the *Washington Post* and later worked for *Newsweek*. In 1967, he became a speechwriter for President Lyndon B. Johnson, leaving two years later to freelance write movie reviews, travel pieces, television scripts, and for newspapers. He wrote a couple of pieces about sharks, and in 1971 the idea for a novel began to gel. He worked on it three or four days a week, and spent the rest of the time writing television or newspaper stories. It took about a year to finish his manuscript.

As he explained on his Web page, this book *Jaws* and later adventure tales were well-grounded in research. "Everything I've written is based on something that has happened to me or something that I know a great deal about. In *Jaws* I knew a great deal about sharks. In *The Deep*, I had been lucky enough to learn about Bermuda and to meet Teddy Tucker, a great Bermudan treasure diver. . . . With *Beast*, I had been fishing for giant squid for years with no luck. . . ." In each case, he took a real experience and stretched it by "what if " speculation.

Years later, Benchley admitted that new research has changed a lot of what we know about sharks—and he would not be able to write the same twenty-million-copy best-seller *Jaws* today. The author has sustained a strong interest in the ocean, and as a *National Geographic* special about sharks was set to air in 2002, he told an Associated Press news reporter that he could no longer use the premise of a shark hanging around a specific beach because it had developed a taste for human meat.

"I attributed to them a kind of marauding monsterism that became what *Jaws* was," he told David Bauder. "Now we know that sharks do not attack boats. The way they decide what to eat is by biting it." Immediately after the shark bites into flesh, it makes a snap determination as to whether it carries sufficient nutrition to be worth killing and eating, Benchley explained. Sharks prefer fatty seals to bony men or women, so they often spit out humans after taking a first nip.

"It was OK to demonize a shark in 1974," Benchley told U.S. travel writers in 2001, "but in the last 25 years we've learned a lot about the oceans. About the delicacy and fragility of the ocean and having respect for the creatures of the ocean."

A frequent scuba diver, Benchley was diving off the coast of Bermuda in the early 1980s when he and a shark, converging from opposite sides of a mound of sea wreckage, came face to face, surprised each other, and immediately fled. He has had other encounters, including another time when, bleeding from a cut on his leg after having been caught in a fisherman's line, he had to evade a white-tip shark that came close, attracted by the scent.

As a champion of the ocean, Benchley has expressed dismay at how little the public knows about ocean safety, how few recognize the ocean for the vast frontier wilderness that it remains. "The sea is right there, in our backyard, and it doesn't occur to us that there could be any peril in plunging into it," he said in a *Meet the Writers* interview. "One of the most astonishing facts I came across while doing research for *Shark Trouble* is that more than 80 percent of all living things on earth live in the sea. And they all, naturally, have to eat."

Benchley points to no single author has having influenced his writing, though he enjoys Ernest Hemingway, F. Scott Fitzgerald, and John Steinbeck, and lists T. H. White's *The Once and Future King* and James Boswell's *Life of Johnson* as among his favorite books.

Even before publication of *Jaws*, Benchley worked on a screenplay. He also wrote scripts for his own *The Deep* and *The Island* (for a cool $4 million salary) and was executive producer for a television miniseries, *The Beast*, and a series, *The Amazon*. The last is about an airplane crash in the jungle whose survivors must learn how to survive before they can escape. (One novel has appeared based on the series, written by Rob MacGregor.) Benchley appeared briefly in two of the films based on his books and in *Mrs. Parker and the Vicious Circle*. *Jaws* inspired three sequel films written by others.

In recent years, Benchley has written less fiction and more nonfiction, including *Shark Trouble*. What's the lure of the shark? "To me, they were (and are) like dinosaurs—mysterious, fascinating, dangerous and, best of all, still alive," he told *BookPage*. The most common shark myth is "that sharks target humans, that they are man-eaters," he explained Brian Handwerk for *National Geographic* News. "Nothing could be further from the truth."

Benchley said in a *Time* Internet chat event that he hopes his writing helps readers better understand and appreciate the ocean. Hooper, the scientist in *Jaws*, was the author himself, he said, "urging the populace not to embark on some mad vendetta against an animal that was just doing what nature programmed it to do. If there's an underlying theme in the books I've written about marine creatures, it's that man has a responsibility to co-exist with his environment, not to try to dominate it."

Works by the Author

Fiction

Jaws (1974)
The Deep (1976)
The Island (1979)
The Girl of the Sea of Cortez (1982)
Tiburon (1983), retitled *Tiburon Blanco* (1995)
Q Clearance (1986)
Lush (1989)
Rummies (1989)
Beast (1991)
Three Complete Novels (1994), includes first three books
White Shark (1994)
Peter Benchley's Creature (1997)

Screenplays

Jaws, with Carl Gottlieb (1975)
Jeremiah of Jacob's Neck (1975)
The Great Houdini (1976), television movie
The Deep, with Tracy Keenan Wynn (1977)
The Island (1980)
Jaws 3-D (1983)
Cruel Jaws (1995)
Amazon (1999), television series (executive producer)

Motion Picture or Television Adaptations

Jaws (1975)
The Deep (1977)
The Island (1980)
Dolphin Cove (1989), television series
The Beast (1996), television miniseries
Peter Benchley's Creature (1998), television miniseries

Nonfiction

Jonathan Visits the White House (1964), young adult
Time and a Ticket (1964)
Shark Trouble: True Stories About Sharks and the Sea (2002)
Shark!: True Stories and Lessons from the Deep (2002)
Healing the Ocean: Solutions for Saving Our Seas, with Rod Fujita (2003)

Editor and Contributor

Ocean Planet: Writings and Images of the Sea, with Judith Gradwohl (1994)

For Further Information

Bauder, David. "Benchley Wouldn't Write Same Jaws Today." *The Trentonian* (April 5, 2000).

Handwerk, Brian. "Jaws Author Peter Benchley Talks Sharks." *National Geographic News* (June 7, 2002). *http://news.nationalgeographic.com/news/2002/06/0606_shark5.html* (viewed May 4, 2003).

"Jaws 25 Years Later." *People Weekly* (June 19, 2000).

Jones, Daniel, and John D. Jorgensen, eds. Peter Benchley entry, *Contemporary Authors New Revision Series*. Vol. 66. Detroit: Gale Research, 1998.

Kanner, Ellen. "Reality Bites: Peter Benchley marks the 30th anniversary of Jaws." *Pages* (January/February 2004).

McEvoy, Chris. "Shark Summer II?" *National Review* online. *http://www.natinoalreview.com/script/printpage/asp?ref=/mcevoy/mcevoy.asp* (viewed May 4, 2003).

"Meet Peter Benchley." BookPage. *http://www.bookpage.com/0207bp.meet_peter_benchley.html* (viewed May 4, 2003).

"Meet the Writers: Peter Benchley." Barnes & Noble. *http://www.barnesandnoble.com/writers/writerdetails.asp?userid=0H4KV3ZHMT&cid=57569#bio* (viewed May 4, 2003).

Oliver, Joan. "A Third Benchley Has a Whale of a Novel." *People* (April 15, 1974).

Peter Benchley filmography. IMDB. *http://www.imdb.com/Name?Benchley,+Peter* (viewed May 4, 2003).

Peter Benchley Web site interview. *http://www.peterbenchley.com/interview.htm* (viewed April 15, 2003).

"Sharks Getting Bad Rap, 'Jaws' Author Tells U.S. Travel Writers in Bermuda." PR Newswire (September 5, 2001).

"Visions of the 21st Century: Novelist Peter Benchley." Time Chat Event, transcript (November 4, 1999). *http://www.tim.com/time/community/transcripts/1999/110499benchley.html* (viewed April 15, 2003).

Elizabeth Berg

♦   Women's Fiction

St. Paul, Minnesota
1948

♦   *Durable Goods*

About the Author and the Author's Writing

The key to success as a writer, according to Elizabeth Berg in her how-I-did-it-and-you-can-too book *Escaping Into the Open*, "is a fierce desire to put things down on paper."

Berg thrives on writing, though it took her a while to discover her passion. She was a law firm receptionist, a hotel clerk, an actress, a waitress, a lead singer in a rock-and-roll band—and she was a forty-five-year-old woman before she wrote and sold her first novel, *Durable Goods*. That book and a sequel, *Joy School*, earned her American Library Association Best Book of the Year designations. Her 2000 novel *Open House* was selected as an Oprah Book Club featured selection and Berg appeared on Oprah Winfrey's television program three times—greatly expanding her already large audience of readers.

The author was born Elizabeth Hoff in St. Paul, Minnesota, in 1948. Her very first writing effort was a story she sent to *American Girl Magazine*. It was rejected, but that did not deter her from majoring in English her first year at the University of Minnesota. She switched to humanities for a year before dropping out. After going through a variety of jobs, she went back to school at St. Mary's Junior College in Minneapolis and trained as a nurse. She was a registered nurse in medical/surgical units, and then intensive-care units, for ten years. She married marketing director Howard Berg in 1974 and they had two daughters. A longtime resident of eastern Massachusetts, the author now lives in Chicago.

At the urging of friends, she began writing in 1985, winning $500 in a *Parents* magazine essay contest. She sold articles and stories to national publications such as *Good House-keeping* and *Woman's Day*. Random House accepted her first novel, which was based on experiences from her own youth. Her family had moved frequently, depending on her soldier-father's assignments. Katie Nash, the twelve-year-old heroine of *Durable Goods*, similarly leads a disjoined life. Her mother died of cancer, and she now lives at an Army base in rural Texas with an abusive father. She is infatuated with her sister Diane's boyfriend. Her periods are starting, and her breasts are swelling.

"The novel came about because I was thinking one day about how it felt as an Army brat to leave a place. How it felt when we left a place to be sitting in the back seat and not being able to cry when you wanted to cry. It was just really a haunting experience," Berg related to interviewer Craig McDonald. She wrote a section of the book, liked what she had, and developed it into a full-length story. She had some qualms about what she had written, particularly the closeness of the depiction of her heroine's father with her own father, but finally went ahead because "I wanted to find a way to bring compassion to my real father through a fictional character finding it within herself for her father."

Berg brought Katie Nash back for two more books. In *Joy School*, the character's father has been transferred to Missouri, she misses her mom, and now she misses her old friends. By *True to Form*, the now-thirteen-year-old's new stepmother turns out to be her ally.

That time in her life was still fresh in the author's mind, and creating a youthful heroine came comfortably, she said. The father in the book is a little larger-than-life than Berg's own father. Although many true-life people and experiences show up in her books, Berg said they are transformed and not necessarily recognizable. Just two of her own experiences gave her plenty to write about: her own divorce after twenty-three years of marriage and the misdiagnosis in 1985 of life-threatening cancer and only five years to live. (It turned out to be mycosis fungoides, a chronic T-cell lymphoma affecting the skin.)

Berg's favorite authors include Anne Tyler and Alice Munro. Although she is decidedly a women's writer—in the view of reader Elisabeth Sherwin, "Berg is the ultimate writer of what are sometimes called 'chick books.' Women love her, they identify with her and her characters, and they appreciate her optimism"—she also has a readership of men, some of whom were urged to read her *The Pull of the Moon* and afterward told her they then understood more about their wives. The book is about a woman, just turned fifty, who impulsively leaves her husband for new horizons.

Noted for her sincere, unpretentious yet emotionally charged stories, Berg has said she does not outline her books before she writes, though she may jot down scatterings of dialogue or brief scenes. She may have an idea of how it will end, but not how the characters will get there. She writes first thing in the morning for three or four hours—more than that is difficult as her stories, she said, can be emotionally draining. A self-confessed computerphobe—she does not yet have a Web site—she nevertheless composes her novels on one, or she writes longhand on a pad if she is traveling.

Berg has explored a variety of themes in her books. *Until the Real Thing Comes Along* is about a real estate agent whose biological clock is ticking and turns to a gay man to help her bear a child; *Say When*'s hero is living single again after his wife of ten years abandons him for an affair; the main character in *Never Change* is a fifty-one-year-old nurse, who never married, and who unexpectedly is hired to care for a man who was once the golden boy in high school.

Is there an underlying message in her books? "Forgiveness, acceptance?" she told Writerspace. "I write from consciousness not trying to put out a message but looking back over my body of work, I think that all of my books contain a unified message—affirming our lives as we live them."

In a *Bookreporter* interview Berg stated, "I think writers are born, not made later. It's some fire in you. A need. In my case, I would write whether I were published or not."

Works by the Author

Fiction

Talk Before Sleep (1994)
Range of Motion (1995)
The Pull of the Moon (1996)
What We Keep (1998)
Open House (2000)
Until the Real Thing Comes Along (2000)
Never Change (2001)
Say When (2003)
The Art of Mending (2004)

Katie Nash Series

Durable Goods (1993)
Joy School (1998)
True to Form (2002)

Short Stories

Ordinary Life (2002)

Nonfiction

Family Traditions: Celebrations for Holidays and Everyday (1992)
Escaping Into the Open: The Art of Writing True (2000)

Television Movies Based on the Author's Works

Range of Motion (Lifetime Television)

For Further Information

"Author Profile: Elizabeth Berg." Bookreporter. *http://www.bookreporter.com/authors/au-berg-elizabeth.asp* (viewed March 31, 2003).

Bankoff, Lisa. *Say When* review. *Publishers Weekly* (May 12, 2003).

Durable Goods review. Neeter Skeeter's Place. *http://www.neeterskeeper.com/durablegoods.html* (viewed May 4, 2003).

Elizabeth Berg biography. Barnes & Noble. *http://www.barnsandnoble.com/writers/writerdetails.asp?userid=0H4KV3ZHMT&cid=883100#bio* (viewed March 31, 2003).

Elizabeth Berg biography. The Best Reviews. *http://www.thebestreviews.com/author101* (viewed May 4, 2003).

Elizabeth Berg. The Feminine Critique. *http://www.lewispublishing.com/auth35.htm* (viewed March 31, 2003).

"Elizabeth Berg: The Purpose of Writing." iVillage. *http://www.ivillage.com/books/intervu/fict/articles/0,192468_85069,00.html* (viewed March 31, 2003).

Handschuh, Judith. *Joy School* review. Bookreporter. *http://www.bookreporter.com/reviews/0345423097.asp* (viewed May 4, 2003).

Hill, Nancy Milone. *Ordinary Life: Stories* review. Fiction Readers' Advisory. *http://www.noblenet.org/wakefield/.zraberg.htm* (viewed May 4, 2003).

"Interview with Elizabeth Berg." Writerspace (May 14, 2002). *http://www.writerspace.com/interviews/berg0602.html* (viewed May 4, 2003).

Jepsen, Cara, and Mimi O'Connor. "Elizabeth Berg's Writing Life—How Sweet It Is." *Book Magazine* (September/October 1999).

Klausner, Harriet. *True to Form* review. The Best Reviews. *http://thebestreviews.com/review5198* (viewed May 4, 2003).

McDonald, Craig. "Elizabeth Berg Interview: True to Form" (June 2002). *http://www.modestyarbor.com/elizabethberg.html* (viewed March 31, 2003).

"Meet the Author; Elizabeth Berg." BookPage (July 2000). *http?www.bookpage.com/0007bp/elizabeth_berg.html* (viewed March 31, 2003).

Peacock, Scot, and Pamela Willworth Ave, eds. Elizabeth Berg entry, *Contemporary Authors*. Vol. 147. Detroit: Gale Research, 1995.

Pull of the Moon review. *Library Journal* (August 1995).

Range of Motion review. Neeter Skeeter's Place. *http://www.neeterskeeter.com/rangeofmotion.html* (viewed May 4, 2003).

Scribner, Susan. *Open House* review. The Romance Reader. *http://www.theromancereader.com/berg-open.html* (viewed May 4, 2003).

Sherwin, Elisabeth. "Elizabeth Berg combines wit, domesticity, joy, tears." Printed Matter. *http://www.dcn.davis.ca.us/~gizmo/2001/berg1.html* (viewed May 4, 2003).

Talk Before Sleep review. Bookreporter. *http://www.bookreporter.com/reviews/038531782.asp* (viewed May 4, 2003).

Urquhart, Anita. *Until the Real Ting Comes Along* review. Amazon.com. *http://www.amazon.com/exec/obidos/tg/detail/-/034543739X/104-3961905-2055953?vi=glance* (viewed May 4, 2003).

Wachsmith, Maudeen. *Never Change* review. The Best Reviews. *http://www.thebestreviews.com/review180* (viewed May 4, 2003).

What We Keep review. *Publishers Weekly*. *http://www.amazon.com/exec/obidos/tg/detail/-/0345435028/qid=1052054269/sr=1-9/ref=sr 1 9/104-3961905-2055953? v=glance&s=books* (viewed May 4, 2003).

Wilkinson, Joanne. *Say When* review. *Booklist* (March 1, 2002).

You Gotta Have Heart review. Amazon.com. *http://www.amazon.com/exec/obidos/tg/detail/-/0060929294/qid=1052054604/sr=1-13/ref=sr 1 13/104-3961905-2055953? v=glance&s=books* (viewed May 4, 2003).

Maeve Binchy

◆ Women's Fiction ◆ Romance

Dublin, Ireland
1940

◆ *Tara Road*

Credit: Liam White.

About the Author and the Author's Writing

A journalist's ear and close observation of ordinary people give Maeve Binchy's prose its depth, sparkle, and charm. The author is constantly taking notes: "I watch people," she told interviewer Ellen Kanner for BookPage. "I'll wonder about this woman—I bet she's out for her first date. And that man knows his son is on drugs. I'm never bored by anything. I'm very interested in the small details of people's lives, I almost have to be dragged away from them."

Born in Dalkey, a hamlet outside Dublin, Ireland, in 1940, Maeve was one of four children in the household. The author retained a love for country life, which shows up in her recreations of village life in her novels and short stories. Taking note of the recent and often dark nonfiction works of Frank McCourt and Nuala O'Faolain, Binchy told *People Weekly* her childhood was far from dire. "I had two overprotective parents who thought their daughter was so dazzling that if I were out after midnight, it would be a temptation for all the men in Ireland to have their way with me. It was flattering but bore very little relationship to reality."

After attending Holy Child Convent, a progressive school in Killiney County, Dublin, Binchy went on to secure a bachelor of arts degree in education from University College in Dublin in 1960. She settled into life as a teacher of history and French at Zion Schools and Pembroke School, both in Dublin, for seven years beginning in 1961.

But while vacationing during the summers, she dabbled in travel writing. While in Israel, she decided to join a kibbutz. She wrote of her experiences during tense conditions in the country in weekly letters to her father. When he sold one for publication to *The Irish Times* for £18—more than she had made teaching—a new career dawned.

Commenting on her popularity in an interview carried on the Maeve Binchy Web page, the author said, "I want my books to draw the readers into the tale that is being unfolded. I do not write poetry. I do not have a particular literary style. I am not experimental, nor have I explored a new form of literature. I tell a story and I want to share it with my readers. In today's world, where audiences want to lose themselves for a while, there does seem to be a place for the stories I write, I am delighted to say."

In 1968, Binchy moved to London and worked as a twice-weekly columnist for *The Irish Times*, becoming known for her wit. She married Gordon Thomas Snell in 1977. Snell, a BBC broadcaster, later wrote humor books and books for children. Binchy's short stories were published in books in 1978 and 1980, but it was her first novel, *Light a Penny Candle*, that caught the full attention of the reading public. The author drew on her own experiences—though she has cautioned she was not writing memoir—in her stories of the travails and successes of young Irish women growing up during wartime. The novel relates the story of Aisling and Elizabeth, friends over two decades, the former an Irish girl marrying an alcoholic and becoming locked in her marriage, the latter an English girl finding a life of more opportunity and less oppression abut no fewer personal problems.

In *Circle of Friends*, the main character, Benny, is stifled by her small-town, small-minded parents and struggles to break away. She befriends Eve, whose Protestant mother has died. Rejected by her family, Eve is raised by nuns. "Two worlds are again juxtaposed: professional upper-middle-class Dublin and a small country town," observed a Binchy profile on the Read Ireland Web site. "Benny herself loves and loses but learns that she can be a person in her own right."

Binchy credits her Irish storytelling heritage as helping in her success. "The Irish don't really think about writing, it is just a natural extension of what we do all the time, which is talking," she wrote in a "Writers on Writing" column for the *New York Times*. "I grew up in a time when children were told to be seen and not heard, or were advised, 'Don't speak until you have something to say,' or 'it is better a listener than a talker be.' No self-respecting Irish child ever heard anything as negative and upsetting. In Ireland talk was always great, any old kind of talk."

When her novel *Tara Road* became an Oprah Winfrey Book Club selection, Binchy's novels enjoyed an enormous boost among readers in the United States. That book, set in recent times, finds the closed Irish society of Binchy's earlier works opening up to change. "The very firm hold of an organized religion is losing its grip, young Irish people are now more educated and travel the world," she explained on her Web site.

Ria and her friend Marilyn Vine have little in common, one living in a family-bustling home on Tara Road, the other attending university in Connecticut. Chance—and good plotting—bring them together, and they exchange homes for the summer, neither anticipating the changes the swap will bring not only to their own troubled lives, but to each other.

Binchy has said that her attorney-father soundly advised her to never use real people as the basis for her characters, at the risk of being sued. However, she told interviewer Joan Higgins for Bookreporter, "I am constantly borrowing traits from people I know well, and from slight acquaintances. I am always interested in the self-destructive characteristics of those who have no idea that their manner and behavior alienates everyone else."

She said in an interview with Jana Siciliano for *Bookreporter* that she was the least-educated of her siblings, but she always appreciated her father's definition of the word "education": "My father had this theory that the word education was derived from the Latin word 'educere,' which means to lead out. Education led you out into things, into the light and information." To her mother, Binchy credited the confidence to step out and be herself.

What the author writes about has evolved over the years, but the way she writes—quickly and with little conscious style—remains unchanged. She allows no influences among other writers, saying her favorites such as Alice Munro or Fay Weldon or Kurt Vonnegut have styles far different from her own. She writes every day, usually from 7 in the morning until 1 in the afternoon, sharing a large desk with her husband.

She announced in 2000 that *The Scarlet Feather* would be her last novel, and that she wished to retire from writing—or at least, slow down. But in 2002, *Quentins* appeared. The story follows Ella Brady as she compiles a documentary film about a famous Dublin restaurant and its requisite group of eccentrics, dallies with a financial backer, and has a bad experience with an investment advisor. (Fans will recognize Cathy from *Scarlet Feather*, Nora from *Evening Class* and Ria from *Tara Road* making return visits.) Let us hope the stories keep coming.

Works by the Author

Fiction

Light a Penny Candle (1982)
Echoes (1985)
Firefly Summer (1987)
Silver Wedding (1988)
Circle of Friends (1991)
Maeve Binchy: Three Complete Books (1995), reprints *The Lilac Bus*, *Firefly Summer*, and *Silver Wedding*
The Glass Lake (1996)
Evening Class (1997)
Tara Road (1999)
Scarlet Feather (2001)
Quentins (2002)
Maeve Binchy: Two Complete Novels (2003), reprints *Circle of Friends* and *Copper Beech*
Maeve Binchy Value Collection (2003), includes *Copper Beech*, *Circle of Friends*, and *The Glass Lake* (abridged)

Short Stories

Central Line: Stories of Big City Life (1978)
Victoria Line (1980)
Maeve Binchy's Dublin Four (1982), retitled *Dublin Four* (1984)
London Transports (1983), includes *Central Line* and *Victoria Line*
The Lilac Bus: Stories (1984)
The Copper Beech (1993)
This Year Will Be Different and Other Stories: A Christmas Treasury (1997)
The Return Journey and Other Stories (1999)
Nights of Rain and Stars (2004)

Anthologies

Portrait of the Artist as a Young Girl, edited by John Quinn (1976)
Territories of the Voice: Contemporary Stories by Irish Women Writers, edited by Louise DeSalvo, Kathleen Walsh D'Arcy, and Katherine Hogan (1989)

Murder on the Railways (1996)
Irish Girls About Town, edited by Kathy Kelly (2003)
Ladies Night in Finbar's Hotel (2003)

Stage Plays

End of Term (1976), produced in Dublin
Half Promised Land (1979), produced in Dublin

Radio Play

Deeply Regretted By (1976)

Teleplay

Ireland of the Welcomes (1980)
Echoes (1988)

Nonfiction

My First Book (1976)
Maeve's Diary (1979)
Aches and Pains (2000)

Motion Pictures or Telefilms Based on the Author's Works

The Lilac Bus (1992)
Circle of Friends (1995), starring Minnie Driver

For Further Information

Binchy, Maeve. "For the Irish, Long-Windedness Serves as a Literary Virtue." *New York Times* (November 4, 2002).

Cheakalos, Christina, and Eileen Finan. "A Novel Retirement: After 11 bestsellers, Ireland's Maeve Binchy looks forward to smelling the roses." *People Weekly* (August 28, 2000).

Higgins, Joan. Maeve Binchy Interview. Bookreporter. *http://www.bookreporter.com/authors/au-binchy-maeve.asp* (viewed April 3, 2003).

Kanner, Ellen. "Maeve Binchy: finding the heroes among ordinary people." Book-Page. *http://www.bookpage.com/0103bp/maeve_binchy.html* (viewed March 31, 2003).

Maeve Binchy Web page. *http://www.randomhouse.com/features/binchy/author.html* (viewed April 3, 2003).

Maeve Binchy. Read Ireland. *http//www.readireland.ie/aotm/Binchy.html* (viewed April 3, 2003).

O'Hara, Roberta. *Irish Girls About Town* review. Bookreporter.com. *http://www.bookreporter.com/reviews/0743457463.asp* (viewed April 11, 2003).

Robertson, Karen. Maeve Binchy entry, *Twentieth-Century Romance and Historical Writers*. 2nd edition, edited by Lesley Henderson. Chicago: St. James Press, 1990.

Siciliano, Jana. Maeve Binchy interview. Bookreporter. *http://www.bookreporter.com/authors/au-binchy-maeve.asp* (viewed April 3, 2003).

Smith, Joan. "Real Life Writ Large." *Guardian* (May 4, 2000).

Lawrence Block

◆ Mystery

Buffalo, New York
1938

◆ *Burglar Series*

Credit: Athena Gassoumis.

About the Author and the Author's Writing

Lawrence Block's favorite advice to aspiring writers is to please themselves, and after more than sixty books, that's how he keeps his prose fresh. "I write only what I want to write," he said in a *Mystery Ink* interview, "and I try to avoid paying attention to the expectations of others."

Keeping his muse forever on the alert, the Mystery Writers of America Grand Master and Crime Writers Association Cartier Diamond Dagger Award recipient for lifetime achievement doesn't think more than one book ahead. Fans may demand a new Bernie Rhodenbarr caper or Keller commission—and those works may appear—but just don't rush him. "I rarely know what I'm going to write next, and, on those rare occasions when I think I know, I'm generally wrong. Which is fine with me—if I'd wanted a world of schedules and certainties I'd have gone into some other line of work."

Block was born in Buffalo, New York, in 1938. (When traveling, he and his second wife go out of their way to visit other Buffaloes—they have logged about eighty so far.) He took English, history, and other classes at Antioch College from 1955 to 1959, but dropped out to pursue his writing. Divorced and with three daughters (and now two granddaughters), he married Lynne Wood in 1983.

Block worked only two day jobs his entire life. One was as an editor for the Scott Meredith literary agency in 1957–1958 and the other was as an editor for a Whitman Publishing coin collecting periodical in 1964–1966. He worked freelance before and since. He taught at Hofstra University in 1981 and conducted his Write for Your Life seminars on the East Coast from 1983 to 1988.

Block's first published work was a story for the *Salvation Army* magazine. His first crime story was "You Can't Lose" for *Manhunt* in 1958. Perfecting his craft, he wrote pulpish stories for digests and men's magazines and publishers of lurid paperbacks (these publishers accepted anything he wanted to write, as long as there were enough sex scenes), the latter works ones he generally disclaims today. The author also wrote a monthly how-to column for *Writer's Digest* for fourteen years, collecting the material in later nonfiction books.

Early on in his career, the author developed a fondness for short stories, and he continues to turn them out (*Enough Rope* collects the first eighty-four), even though his novels have a large following. Although it wasn't his intention, he also developed a fondness for crime stories.

Block juggles several series, featuring a variety of protagonists. Evan Tanner, who since he was wounded in Korea has lost his ability to sleep, supports himself writing term papers for college students and traveling the world in support of political causes. Matthew Scudder is a recovering alcoholic, a retired police officer who wasn't where he should have been when his partner was shot. Now he solves crimes on his own hook. Bernie Rhodenbarr is a bibliophile and gentleman thief; Keller is a lonely hitman; Chip Harrison is girl-hungry assistant to the large detective Leo Haig; and Martin Ehrengraf, a lawyer, never loses a case.

"I tend to find anti-heroes more interesting than white knights," Block told Katy Kelly of *USA Today*. In fact, he makes it his mission to lure his readers into liking his characters. "It seems to me there's nothing terribly challenging about making a reader like Alan Alda. Everybody likes Alan Alda."

Block travels extensively between books; thus when he does write, he writes intensely. After an idea has kicked around in his head for a year or so, he goes into seclusion at a hotel or writer's colony.

The author has honed his craft over the years, to the point where it seems totally effortless and natural. The writer told Tom Callahan in a *Writer* interview, "My feeling about writing is that most of the hard work gets done on an unconscious level anyway. It's hard to tell when you are working or not. Sometimes, from my own perspective, it comes easy. Sometimes it's very, very hard, and I'm not able to determine any qualitative difference between the two. It comes out about as well either way."

Block claims he doesn't do a lot of research. For the Tanner series, which hops around a variety of locations, from Canada to Latvia to Afghanistan to Africa, "I would get hold of a certain amount of real data but beyond that I would just fake my way through it with an atlas and an encyclopedia," he told a BookEnds interviewer. He added that he writes without an outline—making the Burglar books with their intricate plots the hardest to do.

Current events can trigger a book plot. The first Burglar book, he explained in *Mystery Scene*, no. 64, grew from a period when he couldn't find suitable work. The idea for the latest one came from news stories of a woman who had a love affair with reclusive writer J. D. Salinger.

"Except in the light books—Bernie, Chip—I never set out to be funny," Block told Ali Karim for *Shots* magazine. "It's my experience that, if I create clever characters, they're going to say some amusing things now and then." His Scudder books are particularly dark, and although Block admits some readers find they have lightened in tone, to his thinking, except that the hero is going to AA and is now married, his tales are, if anything, more violent and troubling.

"Most characters in similar kinds of fiction don't age or change," Block observed to Claire E. White. "But because of the level of realism operating in the series, it became clear to me around the fourth book that I couldn't really have him unaffected by his own history as it developed. I couldn't have him *not* altered by the experiences he would undergo in one book. So things just happened to him, and he's changed and aged, even as you and I."

The Greenwich Village resident said he has never run into what many would call writer's block. But he's had his problems with books, for example the Scudder mystery *Like a Lamb to*

Slaughter. "I wrote ten pages a day, five days a week, and when I hit a hundred pages it was like hitting a wall. I took a day off. I took another day off. But I went back the third day, and I hung in there, and even when it didn't go well," he said in *Writer's Digest* in June 1984. By page 130, after sending his character on useless errands, he gave up. He will not force a story that is just not working. He went on to something else. Some of Block's work has been adapted for films. However, so far Hollywood has not done well by him, in its wisdom transferring the location of *Eight Million Ways to Die* to Los Angeles and changing the gender of Bernie Rhodenbarr in *Burglar* to a woman.

The author has no issue with being cast as a mystery writer. "I think the mystery is getting more respect than it used to," he said in an *Armchair Detective* interview, "both commercially and critically, so one is less apt to feel, you know, a stepchild."

Still, he long wanted to tackle a "big book." He finally did with *Small Town*, which is about New York City. "I was ten and a half when I fell in love with New York," he said in a January 2003 newsletter on his Web site. "That was in December of 1948 when my father and I took the train down from Buffalo to spend a long weekend in the city of his birth. We rode the subways and the Third Avenue El, saw Ray Bolger in *Where's Charley?*, went to Bedloe's island to gape at the Statue of Liberty and caught a light telecast of Toast of the Town."

Inevitably Block moved to the city and embraced its whir and jangle. He uses the city for the setting of most of his books (Tanners being exceptions). In 1993, he came up with the idea of a city book; in 2000 he proposed it to his publisher. He completed 100 pages of manuscript in summer 2001, and then the September 11 attacks happened. The city he was writing about was no longer the same. He set the story aside, but returned to it in summer 2002, recasting some of the story but otherwise continuing with what he had begun.

"I saw the skeleton of a different book there from the one I'd been writing, a bigger, darker novel with more scope, one that took place in the spring and summer of 2002, in the aftermath of the attack," he told interviewer Ed Gorman in *Mystery Scene*, no. 78. "The Red Sox had a left-hander a generation ago of whom it was said that he pitched like his hair was on fire, and that's how I wrote *Small Town*."

The result, as he explained on his Web page, was definitely what he needed to write to exorcise the feelings that came after the Twin Towers attacks. And readers proved him right.

Works by the Author

Fiction

Babe in the Woods (1960)

$20 Lust (1961), published pseudonymously, retitled *Cinderella Sims* as by Lawrence Block (2003)

Death Pulls a Doublecross (1961), retitled *Coward's Kiss* (1987)

Markham: The Case of the Pornographic Photos (1961), retitled *You Could Call It Murder* (1987)

Mona (1961), retitled *Sweet Slow Death* (1986), retitled *Grifter's Game* (2004),

The Girl With the Long Green Heart (1963)

After the First Death (1969)

The Specialist (1969)

Ronald Rabbit Is a Dirty Old Man (1971)

Ariel (1980)
Code of Arms, with Harold King (1981)
Deadly Honeymoon (1981)
Into the Night, with Cornwell Woolrich (1987)
Random Walk (1988)
Dead Honeymoon (2003)
Small Town (2003)
Such Men Are Dangerous (2003)

Burglar (Bernie Rhodenbarr) Series

Burglars Can't Be Choosers (1977)
The Burglar in the Closet (1978)
The Burglar Who Likes to Quote Kipling (1979)
The Burglar Who Studied Spinoza (1980)
The Burglar Who Painted Like Mondrian (1983)
The Burglar Who Traded Ted Williams (1994)
The Burglar Who Thought He Was Bogart (1995)
The Burglar in the Library (1997)
The Burglar in the Rye (1999)
The Burglar on the Prowl (2004)

Evan Tanner Series

The Canceled Czech (1966)
The Thief Who Couldn't Sleep (1966)
Tanner's Twelve Swingers (1967)
Two for Tanner (1967), retitled *The Scoreless Thai* (2001)
Here Comes a Hero (1968), retitled *Tanner's Virgin* (2003)
Tanner's Tiger (1968)
Me Tanner, You Jane (1970)
Tanner on Ice (1998)

John Keller Series

Hit Man (1999)
Hit List (2000)

Matthew Scudder Series

In the Midst of Death (1976)
The Sins of the Fathers (1976)
Time to Murder and Create (1976)
A Stab in the Dark (1981)
Eight Million Ways to Die (1982)

When the Sacred Ginmill Closes (1986)
Out on the Cutting Edge (1989)
A Ticket to the Boneyard (1990)
A Dance at the Slaughterhouse (1991)
A Walk Among the Tombstones (1992)
The Devil Knows You're Dead (1993)
A Long Line of Dead Men (1994)
Even the Wicked (1997)
Everybody Dies (1998)
Hope to Die (2001)
All the Flowers Are Dying (2005)

Collections

Sometimes They Bite (1983)
Like a Lamb to Slaughter (1984)
Some Days You Get the Bear (1993)
By the Dawn's Early Light: And Other Stories (1994)
Ehrengraf for the Defense (1994)
Collected Mystery Stories (1999)
One-Night Stands (1999)
The Lost Cases of Ed London (2001)
Enough Rope: Collected Stories (2002)

Anthologies

Alfred Hitchcock Presents: Once Upon a Dreadful Time, edited by Alfred Hitchcock (1964)
The Late Unlamented and Other Tales of Evil, edited by Alfred Hitchcock (1967)
Alfred Hitchcock Presents: A Month of Mystery, edited by Alfred Hitchcock (1969)
Murders on the Half-Skull, edited by Alfred Hitchcock (1970)
Alfred Hitchcock Presents: Terror Time, edited by Alfred Hitchcock (1972)
Best Detective Stories of the Year—1975, edited by Allen J. Hubin (1975)
The Year's Best Mystery and Suspense Stories—1977, edited by Edward D. Hoch (1977)
The Year's Best Mystery and Suspense Stories—1978, edited by Edward D. Hoch (1978)
Alfred Hitchcock Presents: The Master's Choice, edited by Alfred Hitchcock (1979)
Alfred Hitchcock's The Best of Mystery (1980)
The Best of Ellery Queen 2 (1982)
Alfred Hitchcock's A Choice of Evils, edited by Elana Lore (1983)
Alfred Hitchcock's Borrowers of the Night, edited by Cathleen Jordan (1983)
Ellery Queen's Crimes and Punishments, edited by Eleanor Sullivan (1984)
The Eyes Have It, edited by Robert J. Randisi (1984)

The Year's Best Mystery and Suspense Stories—1984, edited by Edward D. Hoch (1984)

Chapter and Hearse, edited by Marcia Muller (1985)

The Year's Best Mystery and Suspense Stories—1985, edited by Edward D. Hoch (1985)

101 Mystery Stories, edited by Bill Pronzini (1986)

Alfred Hitchcock's Tales of Terror, edited by Eleanor Sullivan (1986)

The Year's Best Mystery and Suspense Stories—1986, edited by Edward D. Hoch (1986)

Ellery Queen Masters of Mystery (1987)

Mystery Scene Reader 1, edited by Ed Gorman (1987)

Prime Suspects, edited by Bill Pronzini (1987)

The Year's Best Mystery and Suspense Stories—1987, edited by Edward D. Hoch (1987)

Alfred Hitchcock: Portraits of Murder (1988)

Ellery Queen's Media Favorites, edited by Eleanor Sullivan (1988)

The Mammoth Book of Private Eye Stories, edited by Bill Pronzini (1988)

The Second Black Lizard Anthology of Crime Fiction, edited by Ed Gorman (1988)

American Detectives, edited by Martin H. Greenberg (1989)

Ellery Queen's 11 Deadly Sins, edited by Eleanor Sullivan (1989)

Felonious Assaults, edited by Bill Pronzini (1989)

Justice for Hire, edited by Robert J. Randisi (1990)

The New Edgar Winners (1990)

Dark Crimes (1991)

Scarlet Letters (1991)

Hardboiled (1992)

High Adventure (1992)

Murder Takes a Holiday (1992)

Crimes of Passion (1993)

Dark Crimes 2 (1993)

Monsters in Our Midst (1993)

Murder on Main Street (1993)

The King Is Dead: Tales of Elvis Post-Mortem (1994)

Murder on Trial (1994)

Bad Behavior (1995)

Blowout in Little Mans Flats (1995)

Murder by the Book (1995)

Murder Is My Business (1995)

Murder Most Medical (1995)

Night Screams (1995)

No Alibi (1995)

The Eyes Still Have It (1996)

First Cases (1996)

Win, Lose or Die (1996)

American Pulp (1997)

Best American Mystery Stories 1997, edited by Robert B. Parker (1997)
First Cases 2 (1997)
Funny Bones (1997)
Hot Blood: Crimes of Passion (1997)
Law and Order (1997)
Love Kills (1997)
Mystery's Most Wanted (1997)
The Plot Thickens (1997)
Whydunit (1997)
Best American Mystery Stories 1998, edited by Sue Grafton (1998)
The Best of the Best (1998)
Cutting Edge (1998)
Murder for Revenge (1998)
Murder on the Run (1998)
Best American Mystery Stories 1999, edited by Ed McBain (1999)
Death Cruise: Crime Stories on the Open Sea (1999)
First Cases 3 (1999)
Master's Choice (1999)
Best American Mystery Stories of the Century, edited by Otto Penzler and Tony Hillerman (2000)
Creme de la Crime (2000)
Master's Choice 2 (2000)
Murder Among Friends (2000)
Opening Shots (2000)
Over the Edge (2000)
World's Finest Mystery and Crime Stories, edited by Edward Gorman (2000)
The Best American Mystery Stories 2001 (2001)
Blood, Threat & Fears (2001)
Century of Great Suspense Stories, edited by Jeffrey Deaver (2001)
Death by Horoscope (2001)
Flesh & Blood (2001)
Murder on the Ropes (2001)
Murder Most Postal (2001)
Murderer's Row (2001)
Opening Shots 2 (2001)
Speaking of Greed (2001)
Speaking of Lust (2001)
A Century of Noir (2002)
Most Wanted, edited by Robert J. Randisi (2002)
Mothers and Sons (2002)
Murder in the Family (2002)
Murder is My Racquet (2002)
Murder on the Ropes: Original Boxing Mysteries, edited by Otto Penzler (2002)
Speaking of Wrath (2002)

World's Finest Mystery and Crime Stories: Third Annual Collection, edited by Ed
    Gorman (2002)
Death by Horoscope, edited by Anne Perry (2003)
World's Finest Mystery and Crime Stories: Fourth Annual Collection, edited by Ed
    Gorman and Martin H. Greenberg (2003)

Editor

Best American Mystery Stories 2001 (2001)
Blood on Their Hands (2003)

Introduction

Gotham Central (2003)

Written as Chip Harrison

Chip Harrison Series

No Score (1970)
Chip Harrison Scores Again (1971)
Make Out With Murder (1974), in the United Kingdom as *The Five Little Rich Girls*
The Topless Tulip Caper (1975)
A/K/A/ Chip Harrison (1984), as by Lawrence Block, reprints second two books
Introducing Chip Harrison (1984), as by Lawrence Block, reprints first two books

Written as Paul Kavanagh

Such Men Are Dangerous (1969), later editions as by Lawrence Block
The Triumph of Evil (1971), later editions as by Lawrence Block
Not Comin' Home to You (1974), later editions as by Lawrence Block

Written as William Ard

Lou Largo Series

Babe in the Woods (1960)

Nonfiction

Swiss Shooting Talers and Medals, with Delbert Ray Krause (1965)
Writing the Novel: From Plot to Print (1979)
Real Food Places, with Cheryl Morrison (1981)
Telling Lies for Fun and Profit (1981)
Spider, Spin Me a Web: A Handbook for Fiction Writers (1988)
After Hours: Conversations with Lawrence Block, with Ernie Bulow (1995)
Gangsters, Swindlers, Killers, and Thieves (2004)

Motion Pictures Based on the Author's Works

Nightmare Honeymoon (1973), based on *Deadly Honeymoon*
Eight Million Ways to Die (1985)
Burglar (1987)
Keller (announced)
Burglars Can't Be Choosers (announced)
A Walk Among the Tombstones (announced)

For Further Information

Ayers, Jeff. Enough Rope review. *Library Journal* (June 1, 2002).

Block, Lawrence. "A Burglar's-Eye View of Greed." Lawrence Block Web site. *http://www.lawrenceblock.com/articlepage-1.htm* (viewed May 16, 2003).

Block, Lawrence. "Burning the Raft at Both Ends." *Mystery Scene*, no. 60 (1998).

Block, Lawrence. "Creative Plagiarism." *Mystery Scene*, no. 59 (1997).

Block, Lawrence. "Gone Shopping." *Writer's Digest* (June 1984).

Block, Lawrence. "Let's Hear It for Sex and Violence." *Writer's Digest* (November 1983).

Block, Lawrence. "Novel Approaches." *Mystery Scene*, no. 55 (1996).

Block, Lawrence. "The Burglar in the Rye." *Mystery Scene*, no. 64 (1999).

Block, Lawrence. "The Carrot and the Stick." *Mystery Scene*, no. 56 (1997).

Block, Lawrence. "The Plot's the Thing." *Mystery Scene*, no. 54 (1996).

Callahan, Tom. "Lawrence Block: master of mystery." *The Writer* (July 2003).

Gorman, Ed. "Small Town Boy: A Conversation with Lawrence Block." *Mystery Scene*, no. 78 (winter 2003).

Hughes, Martin. "Lawrence Block: The Author in the Library." *Crime Time*, no. 10 (1997).

Jones, Daniel, and John D. Jorgenson, eds. Lawrence Block entry, *Contemporary Authors New Revision Series*. Vol. 63. Detroit: Gale Research, 1998.

Karim, Ali. "Lawrence Block talks to Shots about his latest novel, *Small Town*." *SHOTS*: The Crime & Mystery Magazine. *http://www.shotsmag.co.uk/SHOTS%2018/Lawrence%Block%20Interview.htm* (viewed May 16, 2003).

Kelley, George. Lawrence Block entry, *Twentieth-Century Crime and Mystery Writers*. 3rd edition, edited by Lesley Henderson. Chicago: St. James Press, 1991.

Kelly, Katy. "Lawrence Block, Mystery Man." *USA Today* (October 13, 1998).

Lawrence Block interview. BookEnds. *http:62.173.217.bookends/chat/block.asp?TAG= &CID=* (viewed April 5, 2003).

Lawrence Block interview. Mystery Ink (October 10, 2001). *http://www .mysteryinkonline.com/interview1block.htm* (viewed May 16, 2003).

Lawrence Block interview. Mystery One Bookstore. *http://www.mysterone.com/ LawrenceBlockInterview.htm* (viewed May 16, 2003).

"Lawrence Block Interviews Matthew Scudder." Lawrence Block Web site. *http://www .lawrenceblock.com/content_1b-interviews-ms.htm* (viewed May 16, 2003).

Lawrence Block Newsletter. *http://www.lawrenceblock.com/content_newsletter-2003 .htm* (viewed February 27, 2003).

Lawrence Block Web site. *http://www.lawrenceblock.com* (viewed December 20, 2002).

"Legendary Lawrence Block on Ariel." *Mystery Scene*, no. 62 (1999).

Meyer, Adam. "Telling Lies for Fun and Profit: An Interview with Lawrence Block." *The Armchair Detective* (spring 1994).

Tribute to Lawrence Block special issue. *Mystery Scene*, no. 74 (2002).

White, Claire E. "A Conversation with Lawrence Block." Writers Write (October– November 2001). *http://www.writerswrite.com/journal/nov01.block2.htm* (viewed May 16, 2003).

Ray Bradbury

◆ Fantasy ◆ Science Fiction ◆ Poetry

Waukegan, Illinois
1920

◆ *Fahrenheit 451*

About the Author and the Author's Writing

Ray Bradbury is the dean of writers of imaginative fiction, described as "the most widely recognized spokesman for the genre, and particularly for the romantic attitudes toward space flight and technology that it sometimes embodies," by Gary K. Wolf in *Twentieth-Century Science Fiction Writers*. Wolf adds that ironically much of Bradbury's writing indicts unreined technological and scientific advancement.

Two of Bradbury's best-known works from the early 1950s remain pillars of the genre: *The Martian Chronicles*, in which humans colonize and dominate Mars after Earth is destroyed in a nuclear war, and *Fahrenheit 451*, in which the written word is outlawed and rebels, out of necessity, memorize important books. The themes, obviously, have overtones of a postwar generation on the brink of space exploration, grappling with the Cold War and myriad social issues.

Ray Douglas Bradbury was born in Waukegan, Illinois, in 1920. Whereas his parents chose the middle name from the swashbuckling actor Douglas Fairbanks, Bradbury's great adventures would be at the typewriter, turning out hundreds of short stories and poems and dozens of plays, screenplays, essays, and novels. Bradbury had a happy childhood (he depicted his home community as "Greentown," a comfortable, safe place in his works). He grew up with a large extended family that moved back and forth between Illinois and Tucson, Arizona. He began writing at age eleven, purportedly on butcher paper.

In 1934 the Bradburys relocated to Los Angeles, and young Ray came to know movie special effects master Ray Harryhausen and comedian George Burns, who was responsible for his first professional sale (a joke that Burns used on his radio program). Bradbury was active in the drama club at Los Angeles High School, but at the urging of his teachers, decided to pursue writing rather than acting. He joined the poetry club at school, and the Los Angeles Science Fiction League out of school.

Earning money as a newsboy, Ray continued his postsecondary studies at night at the local library; and he wrote. He published his own science fiction fan publication and produced articles for others, until he sold his first short story, "Pendulum," to *Super Science Stories* in 1941. Among his favorite writers in those years were Henry Kuttner, Robert Heinlein, Leigh Brackett, and Henry Hass. Bradbury became a full-time writer of short stories in 1945.

"It's amazing," the author told interviewer Joshua Klein. "I never thought it would happen. I wrote stories to please myself, and it's very gratifying to see that *Fahrenheit*, or *The Martian Chronicles*, or *Something Wicked* [*This Way Comes*] are in schools all over the country."

In 1946, Bradbury married Marguerite "Maggie" McClure, a clerk in a bookstore that he frequented. (They would eventually have four daughters.) That same year, his first book, a collection of stories titled *Dark Carnival*, came into print. The stories are "wonderfully evocative and succinct," in the view of Baird Searles in *A Reader's Guide to Fantasy*.

Bradbury's work began to gain critical momentum with awards such as the O. Henry Memorial. Eventually, he would be named Science Fiction Writers of America Grand Master and receive the World Fantasy Award for Lifetime Achievement. He has been president of Science-Fantasy Writers of America (1951–1953) and a member of Screen Writers Guild of America (1957–1961). An Apollo astronaut named the Dandelion Crater after Bradbury's novel *Dandelion Wine*.

"Science fiction is the most important literature in the history of the world," Bradbury is quoted on his Web page, "because it's the history of ideas, the history of our civilization birthing itself."

Although he is known as a science fiction writer, Bradbury once asserted that he's actually written only one science fiction work, *Fahrenheit 451*. The rest are fantasy stories— stories that never really could happen. *Fahrenheit*, interestingly, considering its theme, has gone through some transmutations in the publishing world. Bradbury's publisher once excised and censored about seventy-five pages. More recently, screenwriters transforming it into a new movie felt compelled to rewrite his original dialogue.

In 1991, Bradbury told interviewer Robert Couteau that he rises in the morning and listens to his internal voices: "I call it my morning theater; it's inside my head. And my characters talk to one another, and when it reaches a certain pitch of excitement I jump out of bed and run and trap them before they are gone. So I never have to worry about a routine; they're always in there talking." He added that too much planning can ruin the creative impulse; the writer has to live the story and let it emerge of its own power.

He continued his routine through his eightieth birthday and beyond, writing three or four thousand words a day. "The feeling I have every day is very much the same as it was when I was twelve," he said in August 2000.

Ever since seeing *The Hunchback of Notre Dame* and *The Lost World*, Bradbury has adored movies. He wrote his own screenplays for Hollywood feature films (he was nominated for an Academy Award for the animated picture *Icarus Mongtolfier Wright*), and teleplays for such television programs as *Alfred Hitchcock Presents* and *The Twilight Zone*. He later developed his own series, *Ray Bradbury Theater*, which ran on cable from 1986 to 1992, many of the episodes based on his own stories. All the while he continued to write short stories, essays, and poems. He was creative consultant for the United States Pavilion at the 1964 World's Fair and a contributor to Walt Disney's Spaceship Earth at the EPCOT Center in Florida.

As future-reaching as the author has been, he was wary of the merits of the Internet. "Who wants to be in touch with all those people?" he asked in the *Brown Daily Herald* in 1995. He still writes on an IBM Selectric, with his daughter later entering the material into a computer and making corrections.

To those interested in becoming writers, Bradbury has urged the reading of not only literature's best, but also its commonplace and terrible. "The snob who refuses knowledge in mediocrities remains always second-rate himself," he said in *Twentieth-Century Science Fiction Writers*.

As for his own creative genius, Bradbury brushed it off with a statement on his Web page: "God, here and there, makes madness a calling."

In a recent volume of 100 of Bradbury's short works, the author made the selections; but that shouldn't be taken as sign he is giving up writing. The same year there appeared a new Bradbury poetry volume, published in Ireland, which shows what *Publishers Weekly* called "his evergreen touch-accessible, humorous, quietly emotional" touch.

In an eighty-second birthday message to fans, Ray Bradbury said, "The act of writing is, for me, like a fever—something I must do. And it seems I always have some new fever developing, some new love to follow and bring to life."

Works by the Author

Fiction

Fahrenheit 451 (1953)
Dandelion Wine (1957)
Something Wicked This Way Comes (1962)
Autumn People (1965)
The Ghosts of Forever (1980)
Death Is a Lonely Business (1985)
Fever Dream (Night Lights) (1987)
A Graveyard for Lunatics: Another Tale of Two Cities (1990)
Green Shadows, White Whale (1992)
Ahmed and the Oblivion Machines: A Fable (1998)
From the Dust Returned: A Family Remembrance (1999)
Let's All Kill Constance (2002)

Short Story Collections

Dark Carnival (1947), in the United Kingdom as *The Small Assassin* (1962)
The Martian Chronicles (1950), also published as *The Silver Locusts* (1951)
The Illustrated Man (1951)
The Golden Apples of the Sun: And Other Stories (1953)
The October Country (1956)
A Medicine for Melancholy (1959), in the United Kingdom as *The Day It Rained Forever* (1959)
Twice 22 (1959), omnibus
The Machineries of Joy (1964)
The Pedestrian (1964)
The Vintage Bradbury (1965)
Tomorrow Midnight (1966)

I Sing the Body Electric!: And Other Stories (1969)

Block and Bradbury (1969), in the United Kingdom as *Fever Dream And Other Fantasies* (1970)

Selected Stories, edited by Anthony Adams (1975)

The Best of Bradbury (1976)

Long After Midnight (1976)

The Small Assassin (1976)

Colonies in Space (1978)

Beyond 1984: A Remembrance of Things Future (1979)

To Sing Strange Songs (1979)

The Last Circus, and The Electrocution (1980)

The Stories of Ray Bradbury (1980)

Dinosaur Tales (1983)

A Memory of Murder (1984)

The Smile (1984)

The Million Year Picnic: And Other Stories (1986)

Cuts (1987)

A Sound of Thunder (1987)

The Dragon (1988)

Lord John Ten (1988)

The Toynbee Convector (1988)

Classic Stories 1 (1990)

Classic Stories 2 (1990)

Folon's Folons (1990)

The Smile (1991)

Quicker Than the Eye (1992)

The Ravine and Here There Be Tigers (1994)

Dogs Think That Every Day is Christmas (1997)

Driving Blind (1997)

A Chapbook for Burnt Out Priests, Rabbis And Ministers (1998)

Kaleidoscope (1998)

Ray Bradbury Collected Short Stories (2001)

I Live by the Invisible (2002)

One More for the Road (2002)

The Best of the Ray Bradbury Chronicles (2003)

Bradbury Stories: 100 of His Most Celebrated Tales (2003)

The Cat's Pajamas: New Stories (2004)

Books for Children

Switch on the Night (1955)

R Is for Rocket (1960)

S Is for Space (1966)

The Halloween Tree (1972)

Books for Young Adults

Ray Bradbury Presents Series, by Stephen Leigh

Ray Bradbury Presents Dinosaur Planet (2004)
Ray Bradbury Presents Dinosaur Samurai (2004)
Ray Bradbury Presents Dinosaur Warriors (2004)
Ray Bradbury Presents Dinosaur World (2004)

Poetry

Old Ahab's Friend, and Friend to Noah, Speaks His Piece: A Celebration (1971)
When Elephants Last in the Dooryard Bloomed: Celebrations for Almost Any Day in the Year (1973)
That Son of Richard III: A Birth Announcement (1974)
Where Robot Mice and Robot Men Run Round in Robot Towns: New Poems, Both Light and Dark (1977)
The Bike Repairman (1978)
Twin Hieroglyphs That Swim the River Dust (1978)
The Aqueduct (1979)
This Attic Where the Meadow Greens (1979)
The Author Considers His Resources (1979)
The Haunted Computer and the Android Pope (1981)
Imagine (1981)
The Complete Poems of Ray Bradbury (1982)
The Love Affair (1982)
Two Poems (1982)
With Cat for Comforter (1997)
They Have Not Seen the Stars: The Collected Poems of Ray Bradbury (2001)
I Live by the Invisible: New and Selected Poems (2003)

Stage Plays

The Meadow in Best One-Act Plays of 1947–48, edited by Margaret Mayorga (1949)
The Anthem Sprinters And Other Antics (1963)
The World of Ray Bradbury (1964)
The Pedestrian (1966)
Christus Apollo (1969)
The Leviathan 99 (1972)
Pillar of Fire And Other Plays (1973)
The Wonderful Ice Cream Suit: And Other Plays for Today, Tomorrow, and Beyond Tomorrow (1975), includes *Kaleidoscope* and *The Foghorn*
A Device Out of Time (1976)
That Ghost, That Bride of Time: Excerpts from a Play-in-Progress (1976)
The Foghorn (1977)
The Martian Chronicles (1977)

Twin Hieroglyphs That Swim the River Dust (1978)
Fahrenheit 451 (1979)
Dandelion Wine (1980)
The Veldt (1980)
Forever and the Earth (1984), radio drama
The Day It Rained Forever (1988)
On Stage: A Chrestomathy of His Plays (1991)

Screenplays and Teleplays

It Came From Outer Space (1953)
Moby Dick (1956)
King of Kings (1961)
Icarus Montgolfier Wright (1962), with George C. Johnston
American Journey (1964)
Picasso Summer (1972), written as Douglas Spaulding, with Edwin Booth
All Summer in a Day (1982), PBS
Something Wicked This Way Comes (1983)
Quest (1983)
The Ray Bradbury Theater (1985–1987), HBO and USA Network television series
The Coffin (1988)
The Halloween Tree (1993), animated program
It Came from Outer Space, four screenplay treatments edited by Donn Albright (2004)

Bradbury has written television scripts, based on his own short stories or as original plots, for *Alfred Hitchcock, Jane Wyman's Fireside Theater, Rendezvous, Trouble Shooters, Alcoa Premiere Television, The Twilight Zone, Curiosity Shop, NBC Peacock Theater, CBS Library,* and *Ray Bradbury Theater.*

Editor

Timeless Stories for Today and Tomorrow (1952)
Circus of Dr. Lao and Other Improbable Stories (1956)
Irish Tales of Terror (1995)

Anthologies

Who Knocks? (1946)
The Night Side (1947)
Timeless Stories for Today and Tomorrow (1952)
The Best from Fantasy and Science Fiction 4th Series (1955)
Alfred Hitchcock Presents (1957)
The Best from Fantasy and Science Fiction 6th Series (1957)
Best Fantasy Stories (1962)

Best Tales of Terror (1962)
Time Machines: The Best Time Travel Stories Ever Written (1964)
Everyman's Book of Classic Horror Stories (1965)
The Pseudo-People (1965)
Beyond the Curtain of Dark (1966)
Science Fiction for People Who Hate Science Fiction (1966)
Summoned from the Tomb (1966)
Tomorrow's Children (1966)
The Evil People (1968)
The Future Makers (1968)
Great Science Fiction of the 20th Century (1968)
The Midnight People (1968)
The Stars and Under (1968)
Three to the Highest Power (1968)
The Unspeakable People (1969)
The Witchcraft Reader (1969)
The Freak Show (1970)
The Hollywood Nightmare (1970)
Nova 1 (1970)
A Sea of Space (1970)
A Wilderness of Stars (1970)
The Ghouls Book 2 (1971)
Again Dangerous Visions Book 1 (1972)
Into the Unknown (1973)
The Hounds of Hell (1974)
More of Christopher Lee's New Chamber of Horrors (1974)
Space 2 (1974)
Space Opera (1974)
Tales of Terror From Outer Space (1975)
Black Water (1976)
Christopher Lee's Archives of Evil (1977)
The Rivals of Dracula (1977)
Tales of Unknown Horror (1978)
More Tales of Unknown Horror (1979)
Dark Forces (1980)
A Century of Science Fiction 1950–1959 (1981)
A Treasury of Modern Fantasy (1981)
Magic for Sale (1983)
The Mammoth Book of Fantasy All-Time Greats (1983), also retitled *The Fantasy Hall of Fame*
The Second Omni Book of Science Fiction (1983)
Vampires, Wine and Roses (1983)
Masques: All New Works of Horror and the Supernatural (1984)
The Penguin Book of Ghost Stories (1984)

The Penguin Book of Horror Stories (1984)
Random Access Messages of the Computer Age (1984)
Top Fantasy (1984)
Top Science Fiction (1984)
Urban Horrors (1984)
Dangerous Vegetables (1985)
The Great SF Stories 13: 1951 (1985)
A Magic-Lover's Treasury of the Fantastic (1986)
Masters of Darkness (1986)
Science-fiction Classics: The Stories That Morphed Into Movies (1986)
A Century of Horror 1970–1979: The Greatest Stories of the Decade (1987)
The Dark Descent: The Colour of Evil (1987)
The Mammoth Book of Haunted House Stories (1987)
Scaremongers (1987)
Simulations: 15 Tales of Virtual Reality (1987)
The Book of Fantasy (1988)
Supernatural Stories (1988)
Dinosaurs (1989)
Into the Mummy's Tomb (1989)
Masques 3 (1989)
Tales of the Occult (1989)
Between Time and Terror (1990)
Dark Voices: The Best from the Pan Book of Horror Stories (1990)
Nebula Awards 24 (1990)
Masterpieces of Terror and the Unknown (1993)
Monsters in Our Midst (1993)
The Ultimate Witch (1993)
The Best from Fantasy And Science Fiction: The 50th Anniversary Anthology (1994)
Bruce Coville's Book of Aliens: Tales to Warp Your Mind (1994)
Reel Future (1994)
Tomorrow Sucks (1994)
David Copperfield's Tales of the Impossible (1995)
Night Screams (1995)
Tales in Space (1995)
The Vampire Omnibus (1995)
The Year's Best Fantasy and Horror Eighth Annual Collection (1995)
American Gothic Tales (1996)
The SFWA Grand Masters, Volume 2 (1996)
Virtuous Vampires (1996)
The Wizards of Odd: Comic Tales of Fantasy (1996)
Ackermanthology (1997)
Dark Terrors 3 (1997)
Dragons: The Greatest Stories (1997)
Free Space (1997)

The Fantasy Hall of Fame (1998)
Knights of Madness: Further Comic Tales of Fantasy (1998)
The Playboy Book of Science Fiction (1998)
The Year's Best Fantasy and Horror Eleventh Annual Collection (1998)
Year's Best SF 3 (1998)
California Sorcery (1999)
Technohorror: Tales of Terror, Suspense, and Intrigue (1999)
Vintage Science Fiction (1999)
October Dreams: A Celebration of Halloween (2000)

Nonfiction

Teacher's Guide: Science Fiction, with Lewy Olfson (1968)
Mars and the Mind of Man (1973)
Zen and the Art of Writing and the Joy of Writing (1973)
The Mummies of Guanajuato (1978), photographs by Archie Lieberman
About Norman Corwin (1979)
Beyond 1984: Remembrance of Things Future (1979)
The Ghosts of Forever (1981)
Los Angeles (1984), photographs by West Light
The Art of Playboy (1985), text
Orange County (1985), photographs by Bill Ross and others
Zen in the Art of Writing (1990)
Yestermorrow: Obvious Answers to Impossible Futures (1991)
Back There Where the Past Was: A Small-Town Boyhood, with Charles Champlin
      (1999)
Rod Steiger: Memoirs of a Friendship (2000)
60 Greatest Science Fiction Shows Selected By Ray Bradbury (2001)
Imagining Space: Achievements, Predictions, Possibilities: 1950–2050, with Roger
      D. Launius (2001)

Anthologies

The Writing Life: Writers on How they Think and Work, edited by Marie Arana (2003)

Motion Pictures and Television Movies Based on the Author's Works

Beast From 20,000 Fathoms (1952)
Fahrenheit 451 (1967)
The Illustrated Man (1969)
The Picasso Summer (1969)
The Screaming Woman (1972)
The Martian Chronicles (1979), miniseries
Any Friend of Nicholas Nickleby Is a Friend of Mine (1981)

Bradbury stories have been adapted for *Tales of Tomorrow, Lights Out, Out There, Suspense, CBS Television Workshop, Alfred Hitchcock,* and *G.E. Theater. The Black Ferris* (1954) aired as a series pilot.

Comic Book Adaptations

The Autumn People (1965)
Tomorrow Midnight (1966)

For Further Information

Aggelis, Steven L., ed. *Conversations with Ray Bradbury.* Jackson: University Press of Mississippi, 2004.

Berger, Roger A. *Bradbury Stories* review. *Library Journal* (August 2003).

Couteau, Robert. "The Romance of Places: An Interview with Ray Bradbury." *http://members.tripod.com/more_couteau/bradbury.htm* (viewed April 3, 2003).

Eller, Jonathan R., ed. *Ray Bradbury: The Life of Fiction.* Kent, OH: Kent State University Press, 2004.

Elliot, J. M. *Science Fiction Voices No. 2: Interviews with Ray Bradbury, A. E. Van Vogt, Robert Silverberg and Others.* 1990.

I Live by the Invisible review. *Publishers Weekly* (September 23, 2002).

Indick, Benjamin P. *The Drama of Ray Bradbury.* Baltimore, MD: T-K Graphics, 1977.

Indick, Ben P. "Ray Bradbury: Still Talking and Still Listening." *Publishers Weekly* (October 22, 2001).

Jepsen, Chris, and Richard Johnston. Ray Bradbury biography. Ray Bradbury Online. *http://www.spaceagecity.com/bradbury/* (viewed April 3, 2003).

Johnson, Wayne L. *Ray Bradbury.* New York: Ungar, 1980.

Klein, Joshua. Ray Bradbury interview. Onion A.V. Club. *http://www.theavclub.com/avclub/3523/avfeature3523.html* (viewed May 19, 2003).

Mass, Wendy. *Ray Bradbury: Master of Science Fiction and Fantasy.* Berkeley Heights, NJ: Enslow Publishers, 2004.

Mogen, David. *Ray Bradbury.* Boston: Twayne, 1986.

Nolan, William F. *The Ray Bradbury Companion.* Detroit: Gale Research, 1975.

Olander, Joseph D., and Martin H. Greenberg, eds. *Ray Bradbury.* New York: Taplinger, 1980.

Peacock, Scot, ed. Ray Bradbury entry, *Contemporary Authors New Revision Series.* Vol. 75. Detroit: Gale Research, 1999.

Ray Bradbury entry, *St. James Guide to Horror, Ghost & Gothic Writers*. Detroit: St. James Press, 1988.

Ray Bradbury Web site. *http://www.raybradbury.com* (viewed April 3, 2003).

Searles, Baird, Beth Meacham, and Michael Franklin. *A Reader's Guide to Fantasy*. New York: Avon, 1982.

Slusser, George Edgar. *The Bradbury Chronicles*. San Bernardino, CA: Borgo Press, 1977.

Toupence, William F. *Ray Bradbury and the Poetics of Reverie: Fantasy, Science Fiction, and the Reader*. Ann Arbor, MI: UMI Research Press, 1984.

Toupence, William F. *Ray Bradbury*. Mercer Island, WA: Starmont House, 1989.

Wolfe, Gary K. Ray Bradbury entry, *Twentieth-Century Science Fiction Writers*. 3rd edition, edited by Noelle Watson and Paula E. Schellinger. Chicago: St. James Press, 1991.

Marion Zimmer Bradley

◆ Fantasy ◆ Science fiction

Albany, New York
1930–1999

◆ *The Mists of Avalon*

About the Author and the Author's Writing

Never mind mail-order writing courses or college workshops if you want to become a writer, Marion Zimmer Bradley suggested in 1980. To become a writer you have to write—and write some more. "Apply the seat of the pants firmly to the seat of the chair and just get down to it," she stated in an essay available on the Marion Zimmer Bradley Literary Works Web page.

That's how she got started; and by perseverance and solid honing of her ideas and language, Bradley has become one of today's most highly respected fantasy authors.

Born in Albany, New York, in 1930, Marion Zimmer was the daughter of a carpenter and a historian. She grew up on an upstate farm during the Great Depression. She attended New York State College for Teachers (now called State University of New York at Albany) from 1946 to 1948. She gave up on hopes for a music career when she married Robert Alden Bradley in 1949, but fourteen years later they divorced.

Bradley completed her bachelor of arts degree at Hardin-Simmons College in Abilene, Texas, in 1964 and took graduate courses at the University of California at Berkeley the next three years. She married Walter Henry Breen in 1964, but divorced him sixteen years later. She had three natural and several foster children.

Bradley's writing career began with her short stories—thus it was appropriate that in 1988 she became editor of *Marion Zimmer Bradley Fantasy Magazine*, which nurtured other practitioners of the short form. She wrote for fan publications until 1953, when she sold a story to a newsstand publication, *Vortex Science Fiction*. She dabbled in gothics, historicals, and occult novels, but her major output during this time was the Darkover Series of science fiction novels. These books, which share a setting at the edge of the Galactic Empire, are only loosely chronological and may be comfortably read out of sequence.

Offspring of colonists on the chill planet, the inhabitants of Darkover refuse to be absorbed into the Empire's politics or society. Many among them are telepathic. As the series progressed, Bradley delved into issues of sexual politics, for example, she included homosexuals among her characters. (Bradley's second husband was gay and she for several years was a counselor at the Gay Pacific Center near where she lived in Berkeley, California.) Darkover was so well-received that it inspired a sequence of shared universe anthologies with other authors reworking the Bradley themes and filling gaps in Darkovan history.

Some of Bradley's early science fiction books were of the space opera and barbarian sort; in 1984 she edited a continuing series of annual anthologies, Sword and Sorceress, giving a feminist twist to an existing genre. Midcareer, Bradley swung more to fantasy, and wrote her most popular book, *The Mists of Avalon*, which inspired several sequels. It is a retelling of the Arthurian legend with the focus on the women, Arthur's sister Morgaine and his wife, Gwynhefar, among them.

"Her ability to create strong believable female characters is astounding, as is her ability to work with the intricacies of female-centered religions and goddess worship," suggested a writer on the Raven's Reviews Web page. "Her female-female interactions are portrayed with a unique insightfulness. Ms. Bradley writes very well in a historically based setting, changing the familiar male perspectives to the female point of view."

Although some have called Bradley the "mother of feminist science fiction," Laura Murphy in *Dictionary of Literary Biography* notes, "Though her interest in women's rights is strong, her works do not reduce to mere polemic."

Rosemarie Arbur in *Leigh Bracket, Marion Zimmer Bradley, Anne McCaffrey: A Primary and Secondary Biography* said Bradley does not enter politics unless there is good reason in the story. "Her emphasis is on character, not political themes."

Bradley wrote of the collapse of Atlantis in two novels (collected as *The Fall of Atlantis*) and of Kassandra and the Trojan War in *Firebrand*. A trio of witch novels, set in modern times, includes *Witch Hill*, originally issued under a penname. In later years, the author refused to recognize many of her pseudonymous early books, as they were somewhat lurid works written under duress, to bring in money to support an ill husband and two children.

Bradley was a frequent collaborator (and her work continues to be used even after her death from a heart attack in 1999). Her brother Paul Edwin Zimmer helped with battle scenes in *Hunters of the Red Moon*, and Bradley was so pleased with the result, she asked him to work with her on a sequel. Mercedes Lackey, Holly Lisle, Deborah J. Ross, and Diana L. Paxon have all shared a byline with Bradley.

In the view of Laurie A. Rivers-Fakhroo, Bradley had "the marvelous ability to bring into her stories (in other periods, on other planets, including other planes of existence) issues that affect us in this world. From colonial power struggles to the issue of the empowerment of women. . . . [Bradley] addresses the issue . . . in a realistic manner via her multi-dimensional characters, without the soapboxes and lectures that so many authors are unable to avoid. She is a reader's writer."

Works by the Author

Fiction

The Door Through Space (1961)
Seven from the Stars (1962)
Falcons of Narabedla (1964)
Castle Terror (1965)

Souvenir of Monique (1967)
Bluebeard's Daughter (1968)
The Brass Dragon (1970)
In the Steps of the Master (1973), novelization of teleplay
Can Ellen Be Saved (1975), novelization of teleplay
The Endless Voyage (1975)
Drums of Darkness (1976)
The Catch Trap (1979)
The Endless Universe (1979)
The Ruins of Isis (1980)
Survivor Ship (1980)
House Between the Worlds (1981)
Colors of Space (1983)
Web of Darkness (1983)
Web of Light (1983)
Night's Daughter (1985)
Warrior Woman (1985)
Fall of Atlantis (1987), joins *Web of Light* and *Web of Darkness*
The Firebrand (1987)
Tiger Burning Bright, with Andre Norton, Mercedes Lackey, and Elisabeth Waters (1995)

Avalon Series

The Mists of Avalon (1983)
The Forest House, with Diana L. Paxon (1994), retitled *Forests of Avalon* (1998)
The Lady of Avalon, with Diana L. Paxon (1997)
Priestess of Avalon, with Diana L. Paxon (2000)
The Ancestors of Avalon, with Diana L. Paxon (2004)

Claire Moffatt Series

Dark Satanic (1972)
Witch Hill (1972), as Valerie Graves; revised (1990) as by Marion Zimmer Bradley
The Inheritor (1984)

Darkover Series

Planet Savers (1962)
Sword of Aldones (1962)
The Bloody Sun (1964), rewritten as sequel to *Forbidden Tower* (1979)
Star of Danger (1965)
Winds of Darkover (1970)
World Wreckers (1971)

Darkover Landfall (1972)
The Spell Sword (1974)
Heritage of Hastur (1975)
Shattered Chain (1976)
Forbidden Tower (1977), sequel to *The Spell Sword*
Stormqueen (1978)
Two to Conquer (1980)
Sharra's Exile (1981), retells events of *Sword of Aldones*; sequel to *Heritage of Hastur*
Hawkmistress (1982)
Thendara House (1983), sequel to *Shattered Chain*
City of Sorcery (1984), sequel to *Thendara House*
Rediscovery, with Mercedes Lackey (1993)
Exile's Song, with Adrienne Martine-Barnes (1996), also retitled *Return to Darkover*; sequel to *Sharra's Exile*
Shadow Matrix by Adrienne Martine-Barnes (1998); sequel to *Exile's Song*
Reluctant King (in progress at author's death)
Thunderlord (in progress at author's death)
A World Divided (2003), collects *Star of Danger, The Bloody Sun*, and *Darkover*

Darkover Clingfire Trilogy, with Deborah J. Ross

Fall of Neskaya (2001)
Zandru's Forge (2003)
Flame in Hali (forthcoming)

Darkover Shared Universe Anthologies

The Keeper's Price (1980)
Sword of Chaos (1982)
Free Amazons of Darkover (1985)
Other Side of the Mirror (1987)
Red Sun of Darkover (1987)
Four Moons of Darkover (1988)
Domains of Darkover (1990)
Leroni of Darkover (1991)
Renunciates of Darkover (1991)
Marion Zimmer Bradley's Darkover (1993)
Towers of Darkover (1993)
Snows of Darkover (1994)

Glenraven Books, with Holly Lisle

Glenraven (1996)
Glenraven 2: In the Rift (1998)

Hunters Books, with Paul Edwin Zimmer

Hunters of the Red Moon (1973)
The Survivors (1979)

Trillium Series

Black Trillium, with Andre Norton and Julian May (1990)
Golden Trillium, with Andre Norton and Julian May (1993)
Lady of the Trillium, with Elisabeth Waters (1995)

Witchlight Series, with Rosemary Edghill

Ghostlight (1995)
Witchlight (1996)
Gravelight (1997)
Heartlight (1998)

Collections

The Dark Intruder and Other Stories (1964)
The Jewel of Arwen (1974)
The Parting of Arwen (1974)
Lythande (1986)
The Best of Marion Zimmer Bradley, edited by Martin H. Greenberg (1988)
Jarnie: And Other Stories (1988)
Marion Zimmer Bradley's Fantasy Worlds (1998)
The Forbidden Circle (2002)

Anthologies

Women of Wonder (1974)
The Year's Best Fantasy Stories (1975)
A Century of Science Fiction 1950–1959 (1981)
Sword of Chaos (1982)
100 Great Fantasy Short Short Stories (1984)
A Magic-Lover's Treasury of the Fantastic (1986)
Ghor, Kin-Slayer: The Saga of Genseric's Fifth-Born Son (1987)
Spells of Wonder (1989)
The Merlin Chronicles (1991)
The Norton Book of Science Fiction (1993)
New Eyes; Science Fiction About the Extraordinary Women of Today and Tomorrow (1994)
Excaliber (1995)
Space Opera (1996)
Out of Avalon: Tales of Old Magic and New Myths, edited by Jennifer Roberson (2001)

Editor

Greyhaven (1983)
Sword and Sorceress 1 (1984)
Sword and Sorceress 2 (1985)
Sword and Sorceress 3 (1986)
Sword and Sorceress 4 (1987)
Sword and Sorceress 5 (1989)
Sword and Sorceress 6 (1990)
Sword and Sorceress 7 (1990)
Sword and Sorceress 8 (1991)
Sword and Sorceress 9 (1992)
Sword and Sorceress 10 (1993)
Best of Marion Zimmer Bradley's Fantasy Magazine 1 (1994)
Sword and Sorceress 11 (1994)
Best of Marion Zimmer Bradley's Fantasy Magazine 2 (1995)
Sword and Sorceress 12 (1995)
Sword and Sorceress 13 (1996)
Sword and Sorceress 14 (1997)
Sword and Sorceress 15 (1998)
Sword and Sorceress 16 (1999)
Sword and Sorceress 17 (2000)

Written as Lee Chapman

I Am a Lesbian (1962)

Written as John Dexter

No Adam for Eve (1966)

Written as Miriam Gardner

The Strange Woman (1962)
My Sister, My Love (1963)
Twilight Lovers (1964)

Written as Morgan Ives

Spare Her Heaven (1963)
Knives of Desire (1966)

Translator

El Villano en su Rincon, by Lope de Vega (1971)

Nonfiction

A Complete, Cumulative Checklist of Lesbian, Variant, and Homosexual Fiction (1960)
Men, Halflings, and Hero Worship, with Barbara Grier (1973)
The Necessity for Beauty: Robert W. Chamber and the Romantic Tradition (1974)
A Gay Bibliography (1975)
Essays Lovecraftian (1976), contributor
Experiment Perilous: Three Essays in Science Fiction, with Alfred Bester and Norman Spinrad (1976)

Motion Pictures Based on the Author's Works

Mists of Avalon (2001), television movie

For Further Information

Alpers, J. J., ed. *Marion Zimmer Bradley's Darkover*. New York: Corian, 1983.

Arbur, Rosemarie. *Leigh Bracket, Marion Zimmer Bradley, Anne McCaffrey: A Primary and Secondary Biography*. Boston: G. K. Hall, 1982.

Arbur, Rosemarie. *Marion Zimmer Bradley*. West Linn, OR: Starmont House, 1985.

Clute, John. Marion Zimmer Bradley entry, *The Encyclopedia of Science Fiction*. Edited by Clute and Peter Nicholls. New York: St. Martin's Press, 1983.

Marion Zimmer Bradley biography. Electronic Edition (November 1, 1999). *http://www.inconjunction.org/coj/newsletters/1999/11.shtml* (viewed May 19, 2003).

Marion Zimmer Bradley biography. Raven's Reviews. *http://tatooine.fortunecity.com/leguin/405/ko/marionb.html* (viewed April 5, 2003).

Marion Zimmer Bradley biography. The Knitting Circle: Literature. *http://www.sbu.ac.uk/stafflag/marionbradley./html* (viewed May 19, 2003).

Marion Zimmer Bradley books. Twomoons.com. *http://www.twomoons.com/books/bradley.htm* (viewed April 5, 2003).

Marion Zimmer Bradley LiteraryWorks Trust Web page. *http://mzbworks.home.att/net/* (viewed April 5, 2003).

Murphy, Laura. Marion Zimmer Bradley entry, *Dictionary of Literary Biography*. Vol. 8. Detroit: Gale Research, 1981.

"Paul Edwin Zimmer: Swordsman and Poet." *Mythprint* (December 1997).

Peacock, Scot, ed. Marion Zimmer Bradley entry, *Contemporary Authors New Revision Series*. Vol. 75. Detroit: Gale Research, 1999.

Rivers-Fakhroo, Laurie A. "The Worlds of Marion Zimmer Bradley." Empirezine. *http://www.empirezine.com/spotlight/zimmer/zimmer-bio.htm* (viewed April 5, 2003).

Roberson, Jennifer, ed. *Return to Avalon: A Celebration of Marion Zimmer Bradley*. New York: Daw, 1996.

Schwartz, Susan. Marion Zimmer Bradley entry, *Twentieth-Century Science-Fiction Writers*. 3rd edition, edited by Noelle Watson and Paul E. Schellinger. Chicago: St. James Press, 1991.

Spivack, Charlotte. *Merlin's Daughters: Contemporary Women of Fantasy*. Westport, CT: Greenwood Press, 1987.

Terry Brooks

Sterling, Illinois
1944

◆ *Shannara*

About the Author and the Author's Writing

In a time long ago, in a place shaded and peaceful, half-elf Shea Ohmsford has no inkling of the forces of evil, none, that is, until the giant and powerful Allanon begins his reign of terror. Shea is the last of his people who may rightfully wield the Sword of Shannara.

Epic fantasy: sure, J.R.R. Tolkien invented it; but Terry Brooks soared with it. His *The Sword of Shannara* was the first fantasy novel to leap onto the *New York Times* trade paperback best-seller list in 1977.

Born in Sterling, Illinois, in 1944, Brooks was the son of a printer and a housewife. He majored in English literature at Hamilton College in 1966, but changed direction and earned an LL.B. degree from Washington and Lee University three years later. In 1987, divorced and with one child, Brooks wed Judine Elaine Alba. A member of the Illinois bar from 1969 to 1986, he now lives in Seattle, Washington, and is a full-time writer.

As a lawyer, one might expect Brooks to write legal thrillers. But as he told a BookEnds interviewer, "This may be because a great deal of my writing stems from the way I grew up, always writing and reading long before I began practicing law. Of course, now I tell people that if I'd known how well John Grisham was going to do, then I would have written that kind of thing!"

His early favorite reads were action stories by Zane Grey, Edgar Rice Burroughs, and James Fennimore Cooper and the adventures of Walter Scott, Robert Louis Stevenson, and Alexander Dumas. Once he had discovered science fiction, he read Isaac Asimov, Andre Norton, and Robert Heinlein. It was not much of a stretch, the author has said, to write adventure stories with an exotic, fanciful setting. After a few stabs at writing westerns, science fiction, and war stories, he took a cue from Tolkien, whose works he read only after he began college. He sent his manuscript to DAW and received a nice rejection letter with the suggestion he try a new imprint at Ballantine Books. He did, and publisher Lester Del Ray, anticipating a largely untapped market for fantasy, gave the novel a big push.

It was not easy being a lawyer and a writer at the same time. It took Brooks several years to complete *The Sword of Shannara*. As to sequels, "[e]ach took a number of years to write. *Sword* took six or seven all together, *Elfstones* took almost three," he recalled in a SciFi.com interview. "That was after a misstep on what was going to be the second book, so there was a five-year gap between book one and book two. The next one, *Wishsong*, took another two or three years to write—there were big gaps of time in there, when I wasn't a full-time writer." After *Magic Kingdom*, he retired from law practice.

After several series with traditional fantasy settings, his *Running with the Demon* took a contemporary backdrop. The action is in a small Illinois town where, again, evil and good are at loggerheads. Brooks said he began the book with the idea that we as a civilization are ruining ourselves.

"The real impetus came from my wish to do a story on the transition from being a child to being an adult, where our belief in what's real and our perceptions of the world undergo a momentous change," the author said in an ssfworld.com interview. "We hang onto something of the magic of children, but we cross over into realities that deny the truths of that magic as well."

After finishing his novel, for a real change of pace, Brooks adapted the film script of the Star Wars movie *The Phantom Menace*. He accepted the assignment on condition he be given a degree of artistic license, which he was.

Brooks stresses the importance of imagination in fiction writing, to draw people away from true crime stories and tattletale biographies. He has led writing workshops at the Maui Writers Retreat in Hawaii and the Odyssey Writer's School in New Hampshire; and he has compiled a book's worth of thoughts on the writing craft, *Sometimes the Magic Works*. He urges novice writers to spend a lot of time shaping and outlining their stories before they write (though he notes there needs to be some elasticity to allow for creative writing). In answer to a question from a fan on his Web site, Brooks explained that he spends considerable time planning so he doesn't have to rely on some easy trick, such as magic, to relieve a plot gnarl.

Brooks averages five to eight pages of manuscript a day when he's writing; trying to push a book by writing more, he said, could lead to unwanted burnout. He claims he does not write for a particular gender or age group, though he acknowledges his first fans were teenaged males. By his second book, he included strong female characters. He has continued to look for the broadest appeal he can. "I always thought that was true about European adventure story writers. I thought *Treasure Island* was a book where it didn't matter—that anybody could enjoy it," he told interviewer Robert Neilson.

Although he has read mythology and other fantasy, everything that goes into his prose is his own. "I hate research," he remarked to Bookreporter. "That's too much hard work! I like to make it up."

Works by the Author

Fiction

Hook: A Novel (1992)
Star Wars: Episode I, The Phantom Menace (1999)

Heritage of Shannara Series

The Scions of Shannara (1990)
The Druid of Shannara (1991)
The Elf Queen of Shannara (1992)
The Talismans of Shannara (1993)

High Druid of Shannara Series

Jarka Ruus (2003)
Tanequil (2004)

Magic Kingdom of Landover Series

Magic Kingdom for Sale—Sold! (1986)
The Black Unicorn (1987)
Wizard at Large (1988)
The Tangle Box (1994)
Witches' Brew (1995)

Shannara Series

The Sword of Shannara (1977)
The Elfstones of Shannara (1982)
The Wishsong of Shannara (1985)
First King of Shannara (1996), prequel to *The Sword of Shannara*

Voyage of the Jerle Shannara Series

Ise Witch (2000)
Antrax (2001)
Morgawr (2002)

The Word and the Void Series

Running with the Demon (1997)
A Knight of the Word (1998)
Angel Fire East (1999)

Editor

Trolltown I (1998)
Trolltown II (1998)
Trolltown III (1998)
World of Shannara, by Teresa Patterson (2001)

Anthologies

Once Upon a Time (1991)
Legends II, edited by Robert Silverberg (2003)

Nonfiction

Sometimes the Magic Works: *Lessons from a Writing Life* (2003)

For Further Information

"About Terry Brooks." BookEnds. *http://62.173.95.217/bookends/chat/brooks.asp? TAG=&CID=* (viewed April 5, 2003).

"An Interview with Terry Brooks." Random House. *http://www.randomhouse.com/ features/brooks/author/interview.html* (viewed May 16, 2003).

Chapman, Jeff, and Pamela S. Dean, eds. Terry Brooks entry, *Contemporary Authors New Revision Series*. Vol. 51. Detroit: Gale Research, 1996.

Doorly, Sean. "Terry Brooks Interview." Bookreporter. *http://www.doorly.com/ writing/TerryBrooks.htm* (viewed May 16, 2003).

Hennessey-DeRose, Christopher, and Michael McCarty. "Terry Brooks' many magic kingdoms are still for sale." SciFi.com. *http://www.scifi.com/sfw/issue286/ interview.html* (viewed May 16, 2003).

Neilson, Robert. "An Interview with Terry Brooks." Albedo One (winter 1997–1998).

Terry Brooks entry, *Contemporary Popular Writers*. Chicago: St. James Press, 1997.

Terry Brooks entry, *St. James Guide to Fantasy Writers*. Chicago: St. James Press, 1996.

Terry Brooks interview. sffworld.com. *http://www.sffworld.com/authors/b/brooks_ terry/interviews/199909.html* (viewed May 16, 2003).

Terry Brooks Web site. *http://www.terrybrooks.net/bio.html* (viewed April 5, 2003).

Dan Brown

◆ Suspense

Exeter, New Hampshire
1964

◆ *The Da Vinci Code*

About the Author and the Author's Writing

If you've read any of his books, you just know little Danny Brown must have had one of those solve-codes-and-ciphers books as a boy. After all, he grew up to write some of the most intense and complex thriller novels today, including the cryptic blockbuster *The Da Vinci Code*, which went back to press fifty-six times in its first thirteen months in print, selling 7.35 million copies.

Brown was born in Exeter, New Hampshire, in 1964. His father taught mathematics and his mother sang sacred music professionally. He attended Phillips Exeter Academy and returned there to teach English after graduating from Amherst College in 1986. This was after a year in California writing songs. His wife, Blythe, is an art historian and painter.

Brown's reading interests were largely classical. William Shakespeare was appreciated for the superior wordplay, John Steinbeck for the masterful descriptions. But when Brown was vacationing in Tahiti in 1994, he found a copy of Sydney Sheldon's *Doomsday Conspiracy*. He became hooked from the first page—and immediately vowed to write a book of his own. Robert Ludlum's *The Bourne Identity* gave Brown a further blueprint for a high-concept, international suspense novel. Once he had a manuscript, Brown found a publisher within three weeks.

Digital Fortress, published in 1998, takes place within the (real) National Security Agency where an ultrasophisticated code-breaking computer meets a message it cannot crack. Head cryptographer Susan Fletcher becomes caught up in an accelerating maze of secrecy and lies. The code is so ingenious, so complex, so devious, it threatens to bring down the entire American intelligence network.

Technology's double-edged promise of dangers and blessings is a recurring theme in Brown's books. Although he admires science's gains in preventing and curing disease, broadening food sources, and engendering new fuel options, the author said he, at the same time, is fearful of spacecrafts' ability to deliver precision warheads and distrustful of how genetic engineering might be misused.

Brown followed his first novel with *Angels & Demons*, the first adventure of Harvard symbologist Robert Langdon. Traveling to Switzerland to examine a mysterious design branded on a murdered physicist, Langdon is shocked by what he sees. It is the sign of an ancient brotherhood, the Illuminati, the most powerful and secret organization ever, a rabid enemy of the Catholic Church. With the assistance of Vittoria Vetra, an Italian scientist, Langdon races against time to prevent a disaster at the Vatican.

A visit to a concealed tunnel beneath Vatican City sparked Brown to write the book. "Secret societies like the Illuminati go to enormous lengths to remain covert," the author said on his Web site. "Although many classified intelligence reports have been written on the brotherhood, few have been published." Illuminati, Brown amplified, are suspected of infiltrating everything from the British Parliament, the United States Treasury, and the international Freemasonry.

Brown asserts that technical background in his novels is accurrate; he uses the Freedom of Information Act and other resources to uncover obscure reference materials. While writing *Angels & Demons*, he even had a group audience with Pope John Paul II.

As for his leisure activities, the author admits to enjoying the Indiana Jones action movies and Pink Panther comic capers, as well as *Fantasia, Life Is Beautiful, Annie Hall*, and Zeffirelli's *Romeo and Juliet*. Musically, he sways to Spanish singer Franco de Vita, Sarah Mclachlan, Enya, and the Gypsy Kings. It's a rare day he is not at his desk writing by 4 a.m. He takes hourly breaks to do a few quick stretches and exercises.

After another techno-thriller, *Deception Point*, in which a bold scientific deception could influence a presidential election, Brown returned to the Langdon series with the phenomenally popular *The Da Vinci Code*.

The book's labyrinthian plot forced Brown to write an outline of more than 100 pages. It took him about nine months to research, another nine to write. "For me the most astonishing aspect of researching *The Da Vinci Code*," Brown told BookBrowse, "was the realization that one of history's greatest 'secrets' is not nearly as secret as we think. Clues to its true nature are all around us . . . in art, music, architecture, legend, and history. In the words of Robert Langdon, 'The signs are everywhere.' "

Beyond a solid reader hook, Brown told journalist Claire E. White that setting is important in crafting a bestselling novel. "If you're writing a love story, don't set the story in the middle of a parking lot. Set the scene in a location that has an interest factor so that the setting itself is interesting. . . . If you wrote a story in a private school and didn't reveal any inside information about what it's like to work or study at a private school then you've got a boring setting."

Not surprisingly, Brown's list of ten favorite books includes Fred Wrixon's *Codes, Ciphers & Other Cryptic & Clandestine Communications* and James Bamford's *The Puzzle Palace*—nonfiction looks at two realms of deception, codes, and the Central Intelligence Agency. *The Da Vinci Code* also owes something to *Holy Blood, Holy Grail* by Michael Baigent and others.

The Da Vinci Code finds hero Langdon being summoned to the Louvre where a curator has been murdered. Near the body is a puzzling riddle—which leads to hidden symbols in the art of Leonardo da Vinci. With an assist from French cryptologist Sophie Neveu, Langdon uncovers another secret society, the Priory of Sion, which has for centuries kept hidden a certain religious relic. A second clandestine organization, the fundamentalist Catholic sect Opus Dei, is out to gain the same information as Langdon, and it is a race to see who gets there first.

Brown said he first learned of secret messages in da Vinci's paintings while studying art at the University of Seville in Spain. Later in the Vatican library, he tripped over more information about da Vinci. He visited the Louvre, and spent a year, with assistance from his wife, researching the background for *The Da Vinci Code.*

"Leonardo da Vinci was a man centuries ahead of his time," Brown told *CNN Sunday Morning.* "He was fascinated with secrets. He was one of the first cryptologists, and he devised many ways to keep information secret, and portray it in ways that most people, when you look at a painting, don't really see. That's really what the book is about. When you look at paintings like the *Mona Lisa*, the *Last Supper*, there is really more there than meets the eye."

The book's publication triggered a reaction within the religious community. Whereas some supported Brown's research and conclusions and believe they draw logically from the information he uncovered, others called him heretical.

"A great deal of the novel's appeal is its feminist sensibility, particularly its translation of feminist critiques of Christianity and Catholicism into popular fiction," Patrick McCormick wrote in *U.S. Catholic.* "The book suggests—as some feminist scholars have been arguing for a while—that the original Jesus movement was much more welcoming to women, marriage, and sexuality than the church Constantine and Augustine handed on to us."

In terms of the novel, is the red-haired figure to Jesus's left in da Vinci's painting of the Last Supper really Saint John?

Collin Hansen, writing for *Christianity Today*, is a skeptic. "Though unoriginal in its allegations, *The Da Vinci Code* proves that some misguided theories never entirely fade away. They just reappear periodically in a different disguise. Brown's claims resemble those of Arius and his numerous heirs throughout history, who have contradicted the united testimony of the apostles and the early church they built. Those witnesses have always attested that Jesus Christ was and remains God himself. It didn't take an ancient council to make this true. And the pseudohistorical claims of a modern novel can't make it false."

Gerald O'Collins, a Jesuit writing in *America*, faulted Brown's facts and conclusions, and suggested the author "belittles the Jewish roots of Christianity."

There were secular critics as well. Laura Miller was so troubled by the appearance of several new books keying off the wild popularity of *The Da Vinci Code* that she wrote an exposé for *The New York Times Book Review*, decrying the novel's entire background as a mammoth hoax. "The only thing more powerful than a worldwide conspiracy, it seems, is our desire to believe in one," she concluded.

Brown didn't set out to create controversy—though it hasn't hurt sales—he just wanted to craft an entertaining novel. "When the book came out, I was a little bit nervous about the response," he told interviewer C. M. McDonald. "The response from priests, nuns—all sorts of people in the church—for the most part has been overwhelmingly positive. There have been a few people for whom the book was shocking and was upsetting, but less than 1 percent."

Theology aside, "The book moves at a breakneck pace," said *New York Times* reviewer Janet Maslin, "with the author seeming thoroughly to enjoy his contrivances. Virtually every chapter ends with a cliffhanger, not easy, considering the amount of plain old talking that gets done. And Sophie and Langdon are sent on the run, the better to churcn up a thriller atmosphere. To their credit, they evade their pursuers as ingeniously as they do most everything else."

At this writing, the author is hard at work on a third Langdon thriller.

Works by the Author

Fiction
Digital Fortress (1998)
Deception Point (2001)

Robert Langdon Series
Angels & Demons (2000)
The Da Vinci Code (2003), special illustrated edition (2004)
Solomon's Key (forthcoming)

Motion Pictures Based on the Author's Works
The Da Vinci Code (announced)

For Further Information

Adler, Jerry. "Deciphering Code." *Newsweek* (May 26, 2003).

Angels and Demons review. *Publishers Weekly* (May 1, 2000).

Ayers, Jeff. *Deception Point* review. *Library Journal* (October 1, 2001).

Baigent, Michael, Richard Leigh, and Henry Lincoln. *Holy Blood, Holy Grail*. New York: Delacorte, 1980.

Bock, Darrell L. *Breaking The Da Vinci Code*. Nashville, TN: Thomas Nelson, 2004.

Burstein, Daniel. *Secrets of the Code: The Unauthorized Guide to the Mysteries Behind The Da Vinci Code*. New York: CDS Books, 2004.

"Conversation with Dan Brown, author of The Da Vinci Code." BookBrowse. *http://www.bookbrowse.com/indez.cfm?page=author&authorID=226&view=interview* (viewed January 1, 2004).

Court, Ayesha. " 'Da Vinci Code' inspires fervent deciphering." *USA Today* (May 8, 2003).

Dan Brown entry, *Contemporary Authors Online*. Reproduced in Biography Resource Center: Gale Group, 2003. *http://galenet.galegroup.com/servlet/BioRC* (viewed December 30, 2003).

Dan Brown interview. Meet the Writers, Barnes & Noble. *http://btob.barnesandnoble.com/writers/writerdetails.asp?cid=1040938&userid=0H4KV3ZHMT#Interview* (viewed January 1, 2004).

Dan Brown Web site. *http://www.danbrown.com/* (viewed December 30, 2003).

Digital Fortress review. *Publishers Weekly* (December 22, 1997).

"Fact or Fiction? Cracking The Da Vinci Code." *Pages* (September/October 2003).

Garlington, Lela. "Anticipation high for talk on 'heretic' best-seller." *Journal-Constitution* (October 30, 2003).

Hansen, Collin. "Breaking The Da Vinci Code." *Christianity Today* (November 7, 2003). *http://www.christianitytoday.com/history/newsletter/2003/nov7.html* (viewed January 1, 2004).

"Interview With Dan Brown." CNN Sunday Morning (May 25, 2003). *http://www.cnn.com/TRANSCRIPTS/0305/25/sm.12.html* (viewed January 1, 2004).

Lampman, Jane. "Who was Mary Magdalene? The buzz goes mainstram." *Christian Science Monitor* (November 14, 2003).

Mariampolski, Ruth. Dan Brown interview. Borders. *http://www.bordersstores.com/features/feature.jsp?file=browndan* (viewed January 1, 2004).

Maryles, Daisy. "Brown Rocks." *Publishers Weekly* (August 18, 2003).

Maryles, Daisy. "From Angels to Demons." *Publishers Weekly* (January 12, 2004).

Maryles, Daisy. "The greening of Brown." *Publishers Weekly* (December 15, 2003).

Maryles, Daisy. "Veni, Vidi, Da Vinci." *Publishers Weekly* (March 31, 2003).

Maslin, Janet. "Spinning a Thriller From the Louvre." *New York Times* (March 17, 2003).

McCormick, Patrick. "Painted out of the picture: Part of the best-selling appeal of The Da Vinci Code is a conspiracy that has kept women from taking their rightful place in the church." *U.S. Catholic* (November 2003).

McDonald, C. M. Dan Brown Interview: The Da Vinci Code. *http://www.modestyarbor.com/dan_brown.html* (viewed January 1, 2004).

Miller, Laura. "The Da Vinci Con." *New York Times Book Review* (February 22, 2004).

Minzesheimer, Bob. " 'Code' Deciphers Interest in Religious History." *USA Today* (December 11, 2003).

Mnookin, Seth. "Page-Turner: A Stolen 'Da Vinci'—Or Just Weirdness? It's a Real-Life Mystery." *Newsweek* (June 9, 2003).

Morris, Edward. "Explosive new thriller explores secrets of the church." *BookPage* (April 2003).

O'Collins, Gerald. "Sensational Secrets." *America* (December 15, 2003).

Today show transcript. June 9, 2003. Dan Brown Web site. *http://www.danbrown.com/media/todayshow.htm* (viewed December 30, 2003).

White, Claire E. "Interview with Dan Brown." Writers Write. *http://www.writerswrite.com/journal/may98/brown.htm* (viewed January 1, 2004).

Sandra Brown

◆ Romance ◆ Women's fiction ◆ Romantic suspense

Waco, Texas
1948

◆ *Slow Heat in Heaven*

Credit: Gregory Hessler.

About the Author and the Author's Writing

When her novel *The Alibi* appeared at number one on the *New York Times* best-seller list, author Sandra Brown felt she had realized a major career achievement. Even though she already had thirty-seven novels appear on the tally, making the very top "represented the achievement of a career goal," she noted in a Bookreporter.com interview. At the same time, it upped the pressure on the writer, who started out crafting category romances, to attain similar achievements with subsequent novels.

Born in Waco, Texas, the author grew up in Fort Worth and early on developed a love for reading and storytelling. She majored in English at Texas Christian University. After her sophomore year, she married Michael Brown and continued her studies at Oklahoma State University and the University of Texas at Arlington. She performed in local theater, managed a cosmetics store, modeled clothing, and appeared in television commercials before joining the syndicated *PM Magazine* as a feature reporter. After being let go from the TV program, she responded to a dare from her husband: You've always wanted to write, so do it. She attended a writer's conference and took a stab at writing a romance novel. She sold her first two books within two weeks of each other. Soon Brown was so busy with book contracts (with more than one publisher), that she began writing under four pseudonyms.

Raising two children (Rachel and Ryan, who loaned their names for one of her pen-names), she was mom morning and night, but writer in the middle of the day. On her Web page, she describes having once worked out the plot for a story during a school field excursion to the circus. Ideas can come from anywhere, she said, including an idea for a character, a particular subject of interest, a scene, or a snatch of dialogue. She makes up her characters from scratch.

Which writers does Brown admire? She lists Tennessee Williams, Taylor Caldwell, and Evelyn Anthony as among those who have influenced her writing.

In 1987, at age thirty-nine, the author shifted genres, from romance to women's (or mainstream) fiction. In 1990, her book *Mirror Image* became the first of a string of her novels to appear on the best-seller list. Brown received the Romance Writers of America Lifetime Achievement Award in 1998.

An avid traveler, Brown has a new home in Texas (built on the site of an old house that was burned down as part of an episode of the television series *Walker, Texas Ranger*) and a vacation place on Hilton Head Island, South Carolina. She has three pet longhorn steers, a wedding anniversary gift from her husband. One is named Boudreaux, after the hero of *Slow Heat in Heaven*, her breakout novel from 1988.

"By the time I had written about forty romance books, I was eager to try something new," the author told Phillip Tomasso III. "I made a gradual venture into the mainstream market. Mainstream has enabled me to plot without being constrained by the boundaries of a genre. As a writer, I welcome a challenge with each book that I write. This helps my characters become interesting."

Although she now produces only one book a year, she finds she puts in just as much work as when she was writing several, as she spends more time researching topics, shaping characters, and developing plots. Brown writes at an office away from her home, five days a week (more if under deadline), generally from noon to six. Mornings are for answering mail and dealing with business. Although she writes a synopsis for each book for her editor, she seldom refers to it when actually writing. She knows the beginning and the ending, but not the route the characters will take to get there.

Writing the types of books she does these days often entails considerable research, the author said in an interview with Writers Review. *The Switch*, for example, required knowledge of ranching and artificial insemination. "I try and make my settings another character in the story," she said, "so that my reader gets a real sense of place. I want the reader to vicariously experience the climate, taste the regional food, smell the scents, all of which requires me to experience it myself."

For *Fat Tuesday*, which is set in New Orleans, she interviewed a former police officer, a man who had left the department under disgrace, to get a true picture of the facets of corruption. She and her husband toured the bayou with a Cajun guide and went to Mardi Gras. For *The Alibi*, she spoke with a county prosecutor in Charleston, South Carolina.

Research is the least favorite part of her work, the author confessed. Storytelling is her favorite part. Being a native Texan, she acknowledges the Lone Star State's storytelling tradition and its heroic heritage since the days of Davy Crockett and the Alamo.

With some sixty books under her belt, the author claims she is fairly confident that she has a distinct voice and knows what appeals to her readers. At the same time, she writes to satisfy herself; if she gets nervous reading a scene, then her fans are likely to as well.

Brown has described herself as a girl who grew up with four younger sisters, was anxious to please, made the honor roll, served on the student council, and essentially made a role model of herself. Her writing has afforded her an opportunity to release some of her pent-up feelings, to craft vile characters, write steamy sex scenes, and depict violent crimes. Writing about villain lawyers and extremist hate groups brings a level of excitement to what otherwise might be considered a pretty routine life.

Works by the Author

Fiction

Slow Heat in Heaven (1988)
Best Kept Secrets (1989)
Mirror Image (1990)
Breath of Scandal (1991)
French Silk (1992)
Where There's Smoke (1993)
Charade (1994)
The Witness (1995)
Exclusive (1996)
Fat Tuesday (1997)
Unspeakable (1998)
The Alibi (1999)
Standoff (2000)
The Switch (2000)
Envy (2001)
The Crush (2002)
Hello, Darkness (2003)
Sunny Chandler's Return (2004)
White Hot (2004)

Coleman Series

Another Dawn (1985)
Sunset Embrace (1985)

Harlequin American Series

1. *Tomorrow's Promise* (1983)

Loveswept Series

1. *Heaven's Price* (1983)
66. *In a Class by Itself* (1984)
79. *Thursday's Child* (1985)
115. *Riley in the Morning* (1985)
136. *The Rana Look* (1986)
154. *22 Indigo Place* (1986)
185. *Sunny Chandler's Return* (1987)
197. *Demon Rumm* (1987)
229. *Tidings of Great Joy* (1988)
263. *Hawk O'Toole's Hostage* (1988)
300. *Long Time Coming* (1989)

336. *Temperatures Rising* (1989)
366. *A Whole New Light* (1989)

Loveswept Series, "Mason Sisters Books"

217. *Fanta C* (1987)
252. *Adam's Fall* (1988)

Loveswept Series, "Breakfast in Bed Books"

22. *Breakfast in Bed* (1983)
51. *Send No Flowers* (1984)

Loveswept Series, "Second Chance at Love Books"

106. *Relentless Desire* (1983)
137. *Temptation's Kiss* (1983)
164. *Tempest in Eden* (1983)

Tyler Family Series

Texas! Lucky (1990)
Texas! Chase (1991)
Texas! Sage (1991)
Texas! Trilogy (1992), includes all three books

Written as Rachel Ryan (later editions as by Sandra Brown)

Candlelight Ecstasy Series

7. *Love's Encore* (1981)
29. *Love Beyond Reason* (1981)
49. *A Treasure Worth Seeking* (1982)
59. *Eloquent Silence* (1981)
151. *Prime Time* (1983)·

Written as Erin St. Claire

Silhouette Desire Series

7. *Not Even for Love* (1982)
41. *Seduction by Design* (1983)
73. *A Kiss Remembered* (1983)
139. *Words of Silk* (1984)
488. *The Thrill of Victory* (1989), later editions as by Sandra Brown

Silhouette Intimate Moments Series

29. *A Secret Splendor* (1983), later editions as by Sandra Brown
76. *Bittersweet Rain* (1984)
93. *Sweet Anger* (1985)
112. *Tiger Prince* (1984), later editions as by Sandra Brown
120. *Led Astray* (1985), sequel to *The Devil's Own*; later editions as by Sandra Brown
133. *Above and Beyond* (1986), later editions as by Sandra Brown
144. *Honor Bound* (1986), later editions as by Sandra Brown
180. *The Devil's Own* (1987), later editions as by Sandra Brown
213. *Two Alone* (1987), later editions as by Sandra Brown

Written as Laura Jordan

Hidden Fires (1982), later editions as by Sandra Brown
The Silken Web (1982), later editions as by Sandra Brown

Television Movies Based on the Author's Works

French Silk (1994)

For Further Information

Hello, Darkness review. *Publishers Weekly* (July 7, 2003).

Jones, Daniel, and John D. Jorgenson, eds. Sandra Brown entry, *Contemporary Authors New Revision Series*. Vol. 63. Detroit: Gale Research, 1998.

Kemp, Barbara E. Sandra Brown entry, *Twentieth-Century Romance and Historical Writers*. 2nd edition, edited by Lesley Henderson. Chicago: St. James Press, 1990.

Sandra Brown interview. Bookreporter.com. *http://www.bookreporter.com/authors/au-brown-sandra.asp* (viewed April 5, 2003).

Sandra Brown interview. Writers Review. *http://jez.cc/writersreview/authors/sandra_brown.htm* (viewed May 19, 2003).

Sandra Brown Web site. *http://www.sandrabrown.net* (viewed April 5, 2003).

Tomasso, Phillip III. "An Interview with Bestselling Author Sandra Brown." *Charlotte Austin Review* (January 28, 2001).

von Pier, Sandi. Sandra Brown interview. RebeccasReads.com. *http://rebeccasreads.com/interview/authors/092301_brown_interview_svp.html* (viewed May 19, 2003).

Lois McMaster Bujold

◆ Science fiction

Columbus, Ohio
1949

◆ *Miles Vorkosigan Series*

About the Author and the Author's Writing

Lois McMaster Bujold's science fiction hero Miles Vorkosigan is rooted in a curious mix of history and personal experience in Lawrence of Arabia (a fierce fighter of short stature); in young Winston Churchill; in a disabled hospital pharmacist the author knew; and in the author's relationship with her father, a prominent welding engineering professor at Ohio State University.

Born to a class of warriors, Vorkosigan, who suffers from very fragile bones, a large head, and a limp, at first attempts to follow in his father's footsteps by applying to military school. Rejected, he strikes out on his own.

Born to a class of educators, "I've been a voracious reader all my life," the author explained on her Web page, "beginning with a passion for horse stories in grade school. I began reading adult science fiction when I was nine, a taste picked up from my father."

Robert Charles McMaster, who held two Ph.Ds from Cal Tech, magna cum laude, devoured science fiction magazines and paperbacks while flying around the country as a consultant. When he was through with them, he passed them on to his daughter. Among her favorite science fiction writers were Poul Anderson, James H. Schmitz, Andre Norton, Zenna Henderson, and Anne McCaffrey.

Lois McMaster was born in 1949 in Columbus, Ohio. She majored in English at Ohio State University from 1968 to 1972 and took a six-week biology study tour of East Africa as a photographer. (She later incorporated details of the countryside in her science fiction landscape.) She married fellow science fiction fan John Frederic Bujold in 1971 and settled in Marion, Ohio, but they divorced twenty-one years later. Since 1995, the author has lived in Minneapolis, Minnesota.

Bujold worked as a pharmacy technician from 1972 to 1978, then was a homemaker. Encouraged by the literary energies of an old high school friend, Bujold began writing in 1982, jotting her stories longhand and carrying the pages around with her in a three-ring binder so she could work on them in spare moments, such as when she went to the Marion Public Library. She completed three novels and a handful of short stories, which she circulated to potential publishers. One of the stories sold to *Twilight Zone Magazine* in 1985.

She still has the postcard acceptance. "I was ecstatic," she said in a sf-f.org online chat. "The meager money was soon spent, but the morale boost was critical to power me through the following year and third novel until my final vindication, when I sold the three completed manuscripts to Baen books."

Baen Books discovered her novels in the "slush pile" of unagented submissions. (Bujold did not have an agent until seven of her books were in print.) Her message to would-be writers in this experience is: Don't stop with just one manuscript, keep writing. Her fourth novel, *Falling Free*, gained the author a Nebula award. Her story "The Mountains of Mourning," which appeared in *Analog*, her father's favorite magazine, earned both Hugo and Nebula Awards for best novella in 1989. And *The Vor Game* and *Barrayar* won Hugos for best novel in 1991 and 1992, respectively. Her three Hugo awards tie Bujold with science fiction giant Robert A. Heinlein.

Bujold envisions the Vorkosigan stories much like the C. S. Forester Horatio Hornblower historical sea sagas—with each novel freestanding, but fitting into an umbrella biography of one character.

The author has told interviewers she believes that character is vital to a good novel, whereas short stories tend to be idea driven. Characters can't stand by themselves, she said, because they must react to situations and interact with other people. She has said she sometimes places her characters in a little what's-the-worst-thing-I-can-do-to-them scenario.

"I tend to assemble my settings around the characters," she told a Girl's World Internet interviewer. "And setting offers [openings] for me. Once I've got a setting going, I'll get ideas about it and that will trigger more ideas for plot incidents which will then in turn feed into characterization. In science fiction you're always making up a culture and a history and there should be things about the characters that are special and unique to their culture that is different from ours. Otherwise, why write science fiction?"

Bujold has given her character Miles Vorkosigan more than the usual depth, calling on her experiences raising two children to craft an appropriate background for him, to provide sensible motivation and complexity. When asked about any problems with being a female writing about a male character, Bujold shrugs off any concerns. There are, after all, only two genders, and she has had plenty of experience with a father, a grandfather, a husband, brothers, a son, male colleagues, and male bosses.

As to the universe of Barrayar, she told *Science Fiction Chronicle*: "One of my earlier parameters that I chose back when I was writing *Shards of Honor* was that in Miles' universe, which in some ways is a very ornery universe, I'd take what everybody does and do the opposite. Everybody has aliens, so I'm not going to have any aliens in Miles' universe. We'll just have genetically-engineered humans. If I want aliens, I'll do another universe."

Bujold hasn't shied from atypical themes; *Ethan of Athos*, for example, explores gender role reversal. She decided to take off on some of the Amazon-planet tales of the 1950s— written by men, of course. "What would happen on a world where the men had to do all the housework? Stir in my medical background, make my hero an obstetrician who takes on the quintessential female role of 'technological' childbearing for his woman-free planet, and the thing grew from there," she said in a SciFi.com interview.

The author wrote a historical fantasy, *The Spirit Ring*, set in an alternate history Renaissance Italy where there really is magic, before returning to the story of Miles Vorkosigan in

Mirror Dance, also a Hugo and Locus Award winner in 1995. In 2001, she set off in a new fantasy direction with *The Curse of Chalion*.

Bujold, who has taught writing workshops at Thurber House and Ohio State University, does not enjoy revising her manuscripts, so she works hard for as clean a first draft as she can manage. She shows her manuscript to trusted readers to spot any obvious problems.

"I do a lot of pre-planning and outlining," she said in an interview with Mike Houlahan, "down to the scene and even paragraph level, before I take my penciled notes to the computer to commit first draft. There is no way I could *remember* it all, else. I do not, however, outline the whole book in advance, bur rather take it in small bites, clearing my mental buffers of one section before turning to the next."

Works by the Author

Fiction

The Spirit Ring (1992)

Curse of Chalion Series

The Curse of Chalion (2001)
Paladin of Souls (2003)

Vorkosigan Series

Ethan of Athos (1986)
Shards of Honor (1986)
The Warrior's Apprentice (1986)
Test of Honor (1987), includes first two books
Falling Free (1988)
Borders of Infinity (1989)
Brothers in Arms (1989)
The Vor Game (1990)
Vorkosigan's Game (1990), includes *Borders of Infinity* and *The Vor Game*
Barrayar (1991)
Mirror Dance (1994)
Cetanganda: A Vorkosigan Adventure (1996)
Cordelia's Honor (1996), includes *Barrayar* and *Shards of Honor*
Memory (1996)
Young Miles (1997), includes "The Mountains of Mourning," *The Warrior's Apprentice*, and *The Vor Game*
Komarr: A Miles Vorkosigan Adventure (1998)
A Civil Campaign: A Comedy of Biology and Manners (1999)
Miles, Mystery and Mayhem (2001), includes "Labyrinth," *Cetaganda*, and *Ethan of Athos*
Miles Errant (2002), includes *Borders of Infinity, Brothers in Arms*, and *Mirror Dance*
Diplomatic Immunity (2002)

Collections

Dreamweaver's Dilemma: Short Stories and Essays, edited by Suford Lewis (1995)

Anthologies

Far Frontiers 5 (1986)
Alien Stars 4: Freelancers (1987)
Free Lancers, edited by Elizabeth Mitchell (1987)
Nebula Awards 25, edited by Michael Bishop (1991)
Commando Brigade 3000, edited by Martin H. Greenberg and Charles Waugh (1994)
Nebula Award-Winning Novellas, edited by Martin H. Greenberg (1994)
The New Hugo Winners 3, edited by Connie Willis and Martin H. Greenberg (1994)
Intergalactic Mercenaries, edited by Sheila Williams and Cynthia Manson (1996)
Wondrous Beginnings, edited by Steven H. Silver and Martin H. Greenberg (2003)
Irresistible Forces, edited by Catherine Asaro (2004)
Irresistible Forces 2, edited by Catherine Asaro (2004)

Editor

Women at War, with Roland J. Green (1995)

Author's Works Adapted for Television

Tales from the Darkside (1986), episode based on short story "Barter"

For Further Information

Allen, Corrina. "The Curse of Chalion." *Barnes & Noble Explorations* (August/September 2001).

Bartter, Martha A. Lois McMaster Bujold entry, *Twentieth-Century Science Fiction Writers*. 3rd edition, edited by Noelle Watson and Paul E. Schellinger. Chicago: St. James Press, 1991.

Bujold, Lois McMaster. "Beyond Genre Barriers." *Ohio Writer Magazine* (May/June 1992).

Bujold, Lois McMaster. "My First Novel." *Bulletin of the Science Fiction Writers of America* (winter 1990).

Hennessey-DeRose, Christopher, and Ryan Timothy Grable. "Award-winning author Lois McMaster Bujold is a slush-pile survivor." SciFi.com. *http://www.scifi.com/sfw/issue291/interview.html* (viewed April 6, 2003).

Houlahan, Mike. Lois McMaster Bujold interview (April 1, 2003). *http://www.dendarii.com/int=nz.html* (viewed April 6, 2003).

Lois McMaster Bujold interview. SciFi.com. *http://www.scifi.com/transcripts/2001/loisbujold.html* (viewed May 26, 2003).

Lois McMaster Bujold interview. "Women Who Rock the World." A Girl's World. *http://www.agirlsworld.com/amy/pajama/wmhistory/careers/lois/mylife.html* (viewed April 6, 2003).

"Lois McMaster Bujold Responds to Your Questions." sf-f.org. *http://sf-f.org/index/php?p=forView&id=1333&cnt=1* (viewed April 6, 2003).

Lois McMaster Bujold Web site. The Bujold Nexus. *http://www.dendarii.com/biolog.html* (viewed April 6, 2003).

Morgan, Tina. "Interview with Lois McMaster Bujold." Fiction Factor. *http://www.fictionfactor.com/interviews/LoisBujold.html* (viewed May 26, 2003).

Peacock, Scot, ed. Lois McMaster Bujold entry, *Contemporary Authors New Revision Series.* Vol. 87. Detroit: Gale Research, 2000.

Rand, Ken. "SFC Interview: Talking with the *Real* Lois McMaster Bujold." *Science Fiction Chronicle* (October–November 1995).

Rico, Lail. "Lois McMaster Bujold, inhabitant of Barrayar." Cyberdark.net. *http://www.cyberdark.net/portada.php?edi=3&cod=2* (viewed May 26, 2003).

James Lee Burke

◆ Mystery

Houston, Texas
1936

◆ *Dave Robicheaux Series*

About the Author and the Author's Writing

James Lee Burke's writing career hasn't always been easy. After three books with three publishers, he experienced a thirteen-year drought before he found an imprint for his fourth. It was 111 rejection slips and nine years before he placed a fifth book, a crime novel, in 1986. But that one was nominated for a Pulitzer Prize.

The next year, the first of Burke's Dave Robicheaux books appeared and the author had the satisfaction of seeing the series steadily rise in popularity. As dark as the Louisiana bayous that provide their setting, these are dense, meaty, and thoroughly engaging novels.

"The writing is beautiful, as always," observed *Publishers Weekly* of *Last Car to Elysian Fields*, laced with the author's signature descriptions: "The sepia-tinted light in the trees and on the bayou seemed to emanate from the earth rather than the sky."

Robicheaux is a fourteen-year member of the New Orleans Police Department in *The Neon Rain*, a story of violence, corruption, drugs, and illegal arms. He and his half brother Jimmie were raised by their father, a commercial fisherman and offshore derrick man. A recovering alcoholic, Robicheaux periodically faces new demons.

A two-time Edgar Award recipient (for *Black Cherry Blues* and *Cimarron Rose*), Burke has been called by some "the Faulkner of crime fiction." The writer in fact nods to Faulkner and George Orwell, both of whom suggested "the artist has an obligation to give voice to those people who have none, and ultimately the artist must tell the truth about the period in which he lives and expose those who would exploit their fellow men and make the earth an intolerable place," he said in *Twentieth-Century Crime and Mystery Writers*.

"He writes about man's depravity and his grace," explained journalist R. Reese Fuller in *The Times of Acadiana*, "his beauty and his vulgarity. His novels have engaged millions of readers all over the world, propelling him to the top of the *New York Times*' bestseller list. But life hasn't always been a gravy train for the author. The ride to the top has been riddled with detours and unexpected delays."

Born in Houston, Texas, on December 5, 1936, Burke grew up on the Texas-Louisiana Gulf Coast. The only detective fiction he read as he grew up was an occasional Mickey Spillane novel. He attended the University of Southeastern Louisiana Institute–Lafayette, then earned bachelor's (1959) and master's (1960) degrees from the University of Missouri–Columbia. Burke found higher education challenging; he related to journalist Fuller the story of his freshman English instructor who gave him D minuses on his papers. The professor explained the grades: "Your penmanship, Mr. Burke, is like an assault upon the eyeballs. Your spelling makes me wish the Phoenicians had not invented the alphabet, but you write with such heart, I couldn't give you an F." With diligence and hard work, Burke raised his grade to a B, published his first short story in the university's literary journal, and thus launched an otherwise hopeless literary career.

The author has taught English at the University of Southwestern Louisiana–Lafayette, University of Montana–Missoula, Miami-Dade Community College in Florida, and Wichita State University in Kansas. He has also worked as a reporter, an oil company landman and pipeliner, a land surveyor, a social worker on Los Angeles's Skid Row, as U.S. Forest Service truck driver in the Dan'l Boone National Forest, and a U.S. Job Corps instructor.

In 1960, he married Pearl Pai Chu. They have four children, and homes in Missoula, Montana, and New Iberia, Louisiana. A practicing Roman Catholic, Burke describes himself politically as a Jeffersonian liberal and his avocational interests include fishing, weightlifting and sports, and bluegrass music.

Burke's fictional Cajun hero has gone through severely stressful episodes in the course of the series—an alcoholic, frequently haunted by memories of the Vietnam War, he quits the police force in the very first book. In the course of the series, he encounters right-wing retired generals, drug-smuggling Nicaraguans, a Mafia boss, and assorted psychopaths and thugs. He also meets and falls in love with social worker Anne Ballard.

It is Burke's intention that the individual books be self-contained, each with its own theme and plotting. "The challenge is to encapsulate events and characters out of the past in such a way that the reader is familiar with the larger story, without being repetitive," he told interviewer Dave Weich for Powells.com. "That's what art is."

Relationships are important in the Robicheaux books, particularly the main character's ties with his mother, his wife, and his adopted daughter Alafair, an El Salvadoran whom he pulled from the wreck of an airplane that had crashed when her mother attempted to smuggle the girl into the United States. His former partner, Cletus Purcel, is a coarse if generally amusing second banana in the books.

Burke considers *Black Cherry Blues* his breakthrough novel—the one, as he told Steven Womack for *The Armchair Detective*, that allowed him to become a full-time writer. It is a rough book, but "[T]he violence that we see in Dave's life is inherent to the situation of a police officer. But in all the novels, Dave indicates one conclusion about violence: that it's reprehensible, that he's repelled by it. And even though on occasion he has acted violently, he always indicates to the reader that violence is a failure, that it represents the failure of everything that is decent and good in human beings."

Burke asserts that one need never have actually been a police officer to write convincingly about them—it is enough to know their psychology, the occupation is secondary. To budding writers he has advised, stick to your vision, come what may.

The Robicheaux books are going strong, and Burke has begun a second series, which evolved from two earlier books, *Two for Texas* and *Lay Down My Sword and Shield*, based on the Hollands, his mother's family. He even retained actual names in his retelling of true events from the Civil War era. *Cimarron Rose*, for instance, relates exploits of his great-grandfather as a cattle drover and gunfighter during Reconstruction. Although it may appear risky to depart from a successful series, Burke embraces the challenge. "Safe and predictable isn't art," he told Alden Mudge for BookPage.

Cimarron Rose, the first Billy Bob Holland book, "is about redemption," Burke told Mudge. "All of us have mistakes in our past we need to address. In Billy Bob's case, it's the fact that he killed his best friend, L. Q. Navarro. It was an accident, but it is the reason Billy Bob is where he is when he book begins."

The author has been Guggenheim, Breadloaf and National Endowment for the Arts fellows. His short stories have appeared in several periodicals. His success, he told interviewer Fuller, has come from slowly building a readership. "It's like the oil business," he said. "It's gushers or dusters."

Burke writes nearly every day. "I have never thought of my vocation as work," he wrote in the *New York Times* in 2002. "I never had what is called writer's block, nor have I ever measured the value of what I do in terms of its commercial success. I also believe that whatever degree of creative talent I possess was not earned but was given to me by a power outside myself, for a specific purpose, one that has little to do with my own life."

Works by the Author

Novels

Half of Paradise (1965)
To the Bright and Shining Sun (1970)
Lay Down My Sword and Shield (1971)
Two for Texas (1983)
The Lost Get-Back Boogie (1986)
White Doves at Morning (2002)

Dave Robicheaux Series

The Neon Rain (1987)
Heaven's Prisoners (1988)
Black Cherry Blues (1989)
A Morning for Flamingoes (1990)
A Stained White Radiance (1992)
In the Electric Mist with Confederate Dead (1993)
Dixie City Jam (1994)
Burning Angel (1995)
Cadillac Jukebox (1996)
Sunset Limited (1998)
Purple Cane Road (2000)
Jolie Blon's Bounce (2002)
Last Car to Elysian Fields (2003)

Billy Bob Holland Series

Cimarron Rose (1997)
Heartwood (1999)
Bitterroot (2001)
In the Moon of Red Ponies (2004)

Short Stories

The Convict and Other Stories (1985)

Nonfiction

Ohio's Heritage, with Kenneth E. Davison (1989)
Texas City, Nineteen Forty-Seven (1992)

Motion Pictures or Telefilms Based on the Author's Works

Heaven's Prisoners (1996), with Alec Baldwin

For Further Information

Ashley, Mike. James Lee Burke entry, *Mammoth Encyclopedia of Modern Crime Fiction.* New York: Carroll & Graf, 2002.

Burke, James Lee. "Seeking a Vision of Truth, Guided by a Higher Power." *New York Times* (December 2, 2002).

Carter, Dale. "Trouble in The Big Easy." *Armchair Detective* (winter 1992).

Fuller, R. Reese. "The Man Behind Dave Robicheaux." *Times of Acadiana* (June 5, 2002).

James Lee Burke interview. Bookreporter. *http://www.bookreporter.com/authors/au-burke-james-lee.asp* (viewed April 5, 2003).

James Lee Burke Web site. *http://www.jamesleeburke.com/about_the_author.html* (viewed April 5, 2003).

Jeffrey, David K. James Lee Burke entry, *Twentieth-Century Crime and Mystery Writers.* 3rd edition, edited by Lesley Henderson. Chicago: St. James Press, 1991.

Last Car to Elysian Fields review. *Publishers Weekly* (August 11, 2003).

Mudge, Alden. James Lee Burke interview. BookPage. *http://www.bookpage.com/9708bp/firstperson2.html* (viewed April 5, 2003).

Weich, Dave. James Lee Burke interview. Powells.com. *http://www.powells.com/authors/burke.html* (viewed April 5, 2003).

Womack, Steve. "A Talk with James Lee Burke." *Armchair Detective* (spring 1996).

Octavia E. Butler

Pasadena, California
1947

◆ *Kindred*

About the Author and the Author's Writing

Ever since publication of her first story, "Crossover," in the 1971 *Clarion* anthology, Octavia Estelle Butler has proven herself to be a powerful, if not prolific, writer of science fiction. As with many of her later works, "Crossover" quilts African American history and futuristic social themes.

Hugo and Nebula award-winning Butler was born in Pasadena, California, in 1947. Her father died while she was a baby, and her mother went to work as a domestic to support her. While growing up, the young girl heard many family stories from her mother and grandmother. Octavia began writing science fiction at the age of twelve, after seeing the motion picture *Devil Girl from Mars* and declaring she could write something better.

In 1968 she received an associate's degree from Pasadena City College, and she subsequently attended California State University and the University of California in Los Angeles as part of the Screen Writers' Guild Open Door Program. As good fortune would have it, one of her instructors was Harlan Ellison. She also attended the Clarion Science Fiction Writers Workshop. The author was drawn to science fiction, she said in *Twentieth-Century Science Fiction Writers*, because it allowed her as a writer the most creative freedom.

Butler's first novel, *Patternmaster*, began a five-book series about elite telepaths ruled by a 4,000-year-old immortal African named Doro, who has the ability to jump into the minds of others and destroy them. Doro and his group seek to establish a super race. Anyanwu, a shapeshifter forced to bear children by Doro and his son, enters into a struggle with Doro to control the global network of "talents."

"The series' strength," in the view of critic John Clute, "is in the author's capacity to inhabit her venues with characters whose often anguished lives strike the reader as anything but frivolous."

While working at a variety of blue-collar jobs, Butler completed *Kindred*, a novel she had begun while in college. The story was based on a comment made by a friend that there were too many old black people around, holding the younger generation back. The friend obviously felt no ties to his roots. He didn't understand or appreciate what people such as Butler's mother went through, suffering verbal abuse and racism in order to make a living, buy a home, and educate a child.

"I realized that he didn't understand what heroism was," Butler told *Locus Magazine*. "That's what I want to write about: when you are aware of what it means to be an adult and what choices you have to make, the fact that maybe you're afraid, but you still have to act."

Kindred is about a black woman who time-travels to a Southern slave plantation where she ends up rescuing her white, slave-owning ancestor. She must grapple with torn emotions as she owes her being to a man who was an oppressor of her race.

This story creates "a dialectic between two specific historical moments in American history: the period of chattel slavery and the richly symbolic bicentennial year of 1976," explains Angelyn Mitchell in a critical piece in the periodical *Melus*. "When Mona [the main character, a writer], Gerima's protagonist [in a story she is writing], travels to the past in order to learn about the history she has forgotten or never knew, the audience does so as well. Likewise, when Butler's twentieth-century protagonist travels to antebellum Maryland, she learns how the past shaped and continues to shape the present. Butler's readers also learn the same lesson."

Butler is known for her richly depicted strong women characters and her tight but swift prose style. According to critic Rosemary Stevenson, her "work is both fascinating and highly unusual; character development, human relationships, and social concerns predominate over intergalactic hardware."

"Her stories do not insist upon particular solutions," observed John Pfeiffer in *Twentieth-Century Science Fiction Writers*. "They do encourage hope that some kind of enlightened species, related to humanity, can survive."

Butler's Xenogenesis stories are about the Oankali, a genetically impoverished alien race that wants to interbreed with humans in order to survive in the postnuclear era. Selected humans, who have pretty much destroyed Earth, are held in suspended animation. The Oankali abhor human class divisions and conflict and hope to breed those qualities out of their future offspring. The heroine Lilith is chosen the first human to start this new race.

The Parable books are a psychological exploration of people in a world now gone mad. Butler looks at the use of power and the appropriateness of religion in political power.

"As one of the few African-American writers in the science-fiction field, and the only black woman, Butler's racial and sexual perspective is unique," *Contemporary Authors* noted.

Butler has written short stories for *Isaac Asimov's Science Fiction Magazine, Omni*, and *Future Life*. Her "Bloodchild" novella won both the Hugo and Nebula Awards. It is about men who bear children of an alien race—putting a twist on issues of power and gender.

In 1995, Butler received a MacArthur Foundation five-year, $295,000 "genius grant" fellowship for her unusual synthesis of science fiction with mysticism, mythology, and African-American spiritualism. But Butler remains modest in the wake of her achievements.

"I'm not writing for some noble purpose, I just like telling a good story," she told Robert McTyre. "If what I write about helps others understand this world we live in, so much the better for all of us."

Works by the Author

Fiction

Kindred (1979)

Parable Books

Parable of the Sower (1994)
Parable of the Talents (1998)

Patternist Series

Patternmaster (1976)
Mind of My Mind (1977)
Survivor (1978)
Wild Seed (1980)
Clay's Ark (1984)

Xenogenesis Trilogy

Dawn (1987)
Adulthood Rites (1988)
Imago (1989)

Short Stories or Novellas

Bloodchild and Other Stories (1995) [collection]
Lilith's Brood (2000) [3 novellas]

For Further Information

Clute, John. Octavia E(stelle) Butler entry, *The Encyclopedia of Science Fiction.* Edited by Clute and Peter Nicholls. New York: St. Martin's Press, 1993.

"Four Blacks among 24 MacArthur Foundation Fellowship Winners." *Jet* (July 3, 1995).

Jones, Daniel, and John D. Jorgenson, eds. Octavia E(stelle) Butler entry, *Contemporary Authors New Revision Series.* Vol. 73. Detroit: Gale Research, 1999.

McTyre, Robert E. "Octavia Butler: Black America's first lady of science fiction." *Michigan Chronicle* (April 26, 1994).

Mitchell, Angelyn. "Not enough of the past: feminist revisions of slavery in Octavia E. Butler's *Kindred.*" *Melus* (fall 2001).

Octavia Butler biography. Voices from the Gaps: Women Writers of Color, University of Minnesota. *http://voices.cla.umn.edu/authors/BUTLERoctavia.html* (viewed April 7, 2003).

Octavia Butler biography. *http://www.math.buffalo.edu/~sww/butler/butler_octavia_bio.html* (viewed April 7, 2003).

Octavia Butler interview. National Public Radio (September 1, 2001). *http://www.npr.org/programs/specials/racism/010830.octaviabutler.html* (viewed April 7, 2003).

Octavia E. Butler biography. *http://www.geocities.com;shaithis.rm/ octavia_e_butler.html* (viewed April 7, 2003).

"Octavia E. Butler: Persistence." *Locus Magazine* (June 2000).

Pfeiffer, John. Octavia Butler entry, *Twentieth-Century Science-Fiction Writers.* 3rd edition, edited by Noelle Watson and Paul E. Schellinger. Chicago: St. James Press, 1991.

Stevenson, Rosemary. *Black Women in America: An Historical Encyclopedia.* Brooklyn, NY: Carlson Publications, 1993.

Xenogenesis and other reviews. Raven's Reviews. *http://tatooine.fortunecity.com/leguin/405/ko/octaviab.html* (viewed April 7, 2003).

Yaszek, Lisa. " 'A grim fantasy': remaking American history in Octavia Butler's *Kindred." Signs* (summer 2003).

Bebe Moore Campbell

◆ Women's fiction

Philadelphia, Pennsylvania
1950

◆ *Brothers and Sisters*

About the Author and the Author's Writing

A leading African American voice in the blossoming genre of women's fiction, Bebe Moore Campbell wrote a well-received memoir, *Sweet Summer, Growing Up With and Without My Dad*, before penning four *New York Times* best-seller list novels. Among the best-sellers was *Your Blues Ain't Like Mine*, which garnered the author a National Association for the Advancement of Colored People Image Award for outstanding literary work (fiction).

In a *Jet* magazine interview in 1998, Campbell said that until the 1990s, mainstream publishers believed blacks didn't read or buy books and whites wouldn't buy books written by ethnic writers. But as authors such as Terry McMillan, Toni Morrison, Alice Walker, and Campbell herself broke onto the bestseller lists, there came a change. "I really think the publishing world has really learned better," she said. "They are beginning to know that black people read a variety of books. You don't have to write the same book for us over and over again."

Bebe Moore was born in Philadelphia in 1950. By the time she reached school age, she was spending nine months of the year in a multiethnic neighborhood in Philadelphia with her mother and maternal grandmother and summers in North Carolina with her father and paternal grandmother—the split home she wrote of in *Sweet Summer*. She credits both parents with helping shape her writing career. Her mother set aside Sundays for church and for going to the library. George Moore, left a paraplegic following a car accident, listened attentively to the stories his daughter wrote to entertain him and draw his reaction. (The experience of living in two places also provided the author with differing views of subtle inequities and racism in the two sections of the country.)

Moore earned a bachelor of science degree summa cum laude in elementary education from the University of Pittsburgh. She taught for five years but decided to give up the career to become a writer. After taking a class with author Toni Cade Bambara, she began freelance writing for the *New York Times*, the *Washington Post, Ebony, Essence*, and other publications. She eventually became a commentator on National Public Radio's *Morning Edition*.

The author's marriage to Tiko F. Campbell ended in divorce. She and her second husband, Ellis Gordon Jr., live in Los Angeles. She has two children.

Her first book, *Successful Women, Angry Men*, examines marital relationships as women rise higher on the success ladder than their husbands. She followed that with *Sweet Summer, Growing Up With and Without My Dad*, a remembrance of coming to grips with being a child of divorce.

Dipping her toe into fictional waters, Campbell came up with the winning *Your Blues Ain't Like Mine*, a look at the impact on families, black and white, of a racially motivated killing in the 1950s.

On her Web site, the author said ideas usually gestate in her mind; and in the case of *Your Blues Ain't Like Mine*, the gestation lasted for three years. It drew inspiration from the 1955 murder of Chicago teen Emmett Till, slain because he spoke with a white woman.

"When an idea for a book hits me I sit on it for a while to see if it will go away," she said. "If it doesn't, I begin to play with it in my mind. I shuffle beginnings, endings and the so-elusive middle. Characters begin to emerge, usually the main ones. That's all I need to begin. After some time it will take on a life of its own."

It's not a regular habit, but the author also said she occasionally journals her feelings, particularly in time of personal crisis.

Brothers and Sisters uses the backdrop of unrest and rioting in Los Angeles in 1992 after the Rodney King verdict to explore the friendship between two women—one black, the other white—as they each face sexual discrimination, failed relationships, and "glass ceilings."

"As in *Blues*, Campbell demonstrates [in *Brothers and Sisters*] an uncanny ability to write from many different perspectives, black and white, male and female," observed the Voices from the Gaps Web site.

In a *Washington Post*-sponsored Internet chat Campbell said she hoped the book would stir dialogue about race, class, and other issues. "I certainly hoped people would think about the issue of race and I wanted people to realize that subtle discrimination—a la the waitress who pays no attention to the diner of color—is as emotionally and psychologically damaging as being restricted to the back of the bus."

The book features a range of characters; and Campbell has commented that her years as a journalist writing for *Essence* particularly exposed her to the many facets of human personalities.

Singing in the Comeback Choir is about a television producer seeking to boost the spirits of her now-past-prime jazz-singer grandmother, the grandmother who raised her but has now suffered a stroke. It is a book about second chances. Singing is a natural background for the novel, and particularly the loss of voice, as Campbell grew up in a household of women who sang a lot, and she belonged to a youth choir in the Baptist church.

It further examines the importance of roots, particularly to that segment of the population that has had to take a back seat to the rest, including African Americans, Asians, Native Americans, and Hispanics. To go beyond the success level of the community in which they live, in other words, people often must move up to another community.

"I think that a lot of people who have achieved success have to struggle with the duality and don't give up the good part of the community that has molded us," she said in a Bookreporter interview. "But I do think that it is a struggle to remember where you came from and see where you are going."

Three other books withered in the trying before the author completed *What You Owe Me*, which looks at the unraveling of a business partnership between Hosanna Clark, now a maid after working in the Texas farm fields, and Gilda Rosenstein, a Holocaust survivor who is working at the same hotel. The book is an examination of betrayal and of healing.

As a child, the author read the works of the Bronte sisters, Mark Twain, and Charles Dickens. Toni Morrison influenced her as a young adult. Then and now, she reads classics and fairy tales, the last for their liveliness and moral instruction.

Campbell obviously delights in black culture. On her Web site, she answered her own question, What is your idea of the ultimate dinner party? with the response that it would be one with guests Harriet Tubman, emancipator of slaves; Mary McLeod Bethune, founder of a black college; C. J. Walker, beauty industry entrepreneur; Billie Holiday, jazz singer; and Katherine Dunham, a dancer who espoused African and Caribbean movement.

Works by the Author

Fiction

Your Blues Ain't Like Mine (1992)
Brothers and Sisters (1994)
Singing in the Comeback Choir (1998)
What You Owe Me (2001)
72-Hour Hold (2005)

Radio Plays

Old Lady Shoes
Sugar on the Floor

Children's Books

Sometimes My Mommy Gets Angry (2003)

Nonfiction

Successful Women, Angry Men: Backlash in the Two-Career Marriage (1986)
Sweet Summer: Growing Up With and Without My Dad (1989)

For Further Information

"Author Bebe Moore Campbell says publishers now recognize the importance of Black authors, readers." *Jet* (March 30, 1998).

Bebe Moore Campbell biography. Voices from the Gaps: Women Writers of Color, University of Minnesota. *http://voices.cla.umn.edu/authors/CAMPBELLbebemoore.html* (viewed April 7, 2003).

Bebe Moore Campbell interview. Bookreporter (April 14, 1998). *http://www .bookreporter.com/authors/au-campbell-bebe-mmore.asp* (viewed April 7, 2003).

Bebe Moore Campbell Web site. *http://www.bebemoorecampbell.com/* (viewed April 7, 2003).

Benton, Jacquelyn. Bebe Moore Campbell entry, *American Ethnic Writers.* Vol. 1, edited by David Peck. Pasadena, CA: Salem Press, 2000.

Brown, DeNeen L. "Transcript of Bebe Moore Campbell's Live Chat." *Washington Post* (November 25, 1997). *http://www.washingtonpost.com/wp-srv/zforum/97/ campbell.htm* (viewed April 7, 2003).

Peacock, Scot, ed. Bebe Moore Campbell entry, *Contemporary Authors, New Revision Series.* Vol. 81. Detroit: Gale Research, 1999.

See, Lisa. "Bebe Moore Campbell: Her Memoir of 'A Special Childhood' Celebrates the Different Styles of Her Upbringing in a Divided Black Family." *Publishers Weekly* (June 30, 1989).

What You Owe Me review. *Publishers Weekly* (July 9, 2001).

Orson Scott Card

◆ Science fiction ◆ Historical

Richland, Washington
1951

◆ *Ender's Game*

Credit: Bob Henderson, Henderson Photography, Inc.

About the Author and the Author's Writing

Orson Scott Card's vibrant and dramatic fiction writing grows from his years of crafting plays. Although his reputation is in writing science fiction, he also has penned books of Mormon fiction and novels with historical and biblical settings.

Born in Richland, Washington, in 1951, Card is the son of a teacher and a secretary and administrator. He grew up in California, Arizona, and Utah, and was in missionary service for the Mormon Church in Brazil, 1970–1971. In 1975 he earned a bachelor of arts degree in theater, with distinction, from Brigham Young University and he received a master's from the University of Utah in 1981. He married Kristine Allen in 1977; they have three children.

Card operated a repertory theater, proofread and edited manuscripts for a university press, served as a senior editor for a book publisher, freelance wrote and edited, and taught writing at various workshops before becoming a full-time writer in 1978. He still offers writing advice on his Web site Hatrack River. Among other tips, he suggests beginning writers not write in the first person, as it is too limiting; avoid too much structure in their stories; strive for clarity and let style come naturally; and allow drama and comedy emerge naturally from the characters.

Card also advises that those interested in writing fantasy or science fiction must be familiar with Hugo Award winners' works and those in the Science Fiction Hall of Fame, as well as stories in Harlan Ellison's *Dangerous Visions* and *Again Dangerous Visions*. "These stories are the root of the field. If you don't know them," he said on the Web site, "you will try to reinvent the wheel; and since the readers do know them, it will kill your work."

Besides novels, he has written short fiction (under his own name and as Brian Green and Byron Walley), edited anthologies, and written and directed plays. The author has garnered numerous science fiction awards including Nebula and Hugo Awards in 1986 for *Ender's Game*.

The hero of this story, Andrew "Ender" Wiggin, was nurtured in his youth for his ability with electronic games only to become a powerful weapon. After Card's short story was nominated for a Hugo, he expanded it into a novel. Throughout his works, Card shows an interest in how his young heroes confront issues of morality. His own feelings of the role of the individual in the world are grounded in his Mormon faith.

In 2000, the author told *Publishers Weekly* that he has no trouble writing in the voice of a child genius: "To children, life is real. They don't think of themselves as cute or sweet. I translate their thoughts from the language available to children into the language available to adults. Every fear or terror that a child feels is more important, more real than it is to an adult, and children are every bit as complex."

Science fiction worlds also allow the author to omit all contemporary philosophies and explore new ideas.

"What I want to write about is people who are committed members of the community and therefore have a network of relationships that define who they are," he told *Publishers Weekly* in 1990. "I think if you're going to write about people, you have to write about storytelling."

The Seventh Son series is set in a fantasy version of pioneer America and follows the seventh son of a seventh son who has mystical powers. The Homecoming books are set on the planet Harmony, where the global computer Oversoul controls everything and everyone.

With *A Woman of Destiny*, Card has ventured into pure historical fiction. The story takes place in the 1800s and is about Dinah Kirkham, an English woman who converts to Mormonism through the persuasion of Joseph Smith, the religion's founder. She becomes Smith's second wife, and after he is murdered, goes to Utah to become a leader and a wife of Brigham Young, Smith's successor as church leader.

The author's latest trilogy begins with *Sarah* and is about the women of the Old Testament Book of Genesis.

"I have always loved their story and I remember as a little kid even when I was reading about Abraham and Isaac and Jacob thinking that a lot of the really cool stuff and sometimes the most dangerous and difficult stuff was done by the woman. . . . Women are very important in the Bible," he told Internet interviewer Doug Wright.

Although Card does not see his writing as being in conflict with his religion, not all Mormons see it that way. "I find that my Mormon faith coincides with reality far more accurately than any other belief system I have found, and the Mormon community is the one to which I have the most allegiance and whose purposes I am most committed to advancing," he said on his Web site in a conversation with Claire E. White. "The more deeply I explore Mormon thought and Mormon life, the more truth and virtue I find within both."

Ultimately, it is an openness to the environment that gives a writer strength, Card asserted in an interview with *Locus* in 2002: "I tell my writing students, 'Everybody walks past a thousand story ideas every day. The good writers are the ones who see five or six of them. Most people don't see any.' "

Works by the Author

Fiction

Hot Sleep: The Worthing Chronicle (1978)
A Planet Called Treason (1979), revised as *Treason* (1988)
Songmaster (1980)

Hart's Hope (1982)
A Woman of Destiny (1983), as *Saints* (1988)
The Worthing Chronicle (1983)
Wyrms (1987)
Eye for Eye—The Tunesmith, with Lloyd Biggle (1990)
Worthing Saga (1990)
The Abyss (1991)
The Changed Man (1992)
Cruel Miracles (1992)
Flux (1992)
Lost Boys (1992)
Monkey Sonatas (1992)
The Ships of Earth (1992)
Children of the Mind (1996)
Pastwatch: The Redemption of Christopher Columbus (1996)
Treasure Box (1996)
Homebody (1997)
Stone Tables: The Story of Moses (1998)
Folk of the Fringe (2001)
Saints (2001)

Ender Series

Ender's Game (1985)
Speaker for the Dead (1986)
Xenocide (1991)
First Meetings (2002)

Homecoming Series

The Call of Earth (1992)
The Memory of Earth (1992)
The Ships of Earth (1993)
Earthfall (1994)
Earthborn (1995)

Mayflower Series with Kathryn H. Kidd

Lovelock (1994)
Rasputin (forthcoming)

Shadow Series

Ender's Shadow (1999)
Shadow of the Hegemon (2001)

Shadow Puppets (2002)
Shadow of the Giant (forthcoming)

Tales of Alvin Maker

Seventh Son (1987)
Red Prophet (1988)
Prentice Alvin (1989)
Alvin Journeyman (1995)
Heartfire (1998)
The Crystal City (2003)

Women of Genesis Trilogy

Sarah (2000)
Rebekah (2001)
Rachel and Leah (2004)

Short Stories

Capitol: The Worthing Chronicle (1978)
Unaccompanied Sonata and Other Stories (1980)
The Folk of the Fringe (1990)
Maps in a Mirror: The Short Fiction of Orson Scott Card (1990)

Editor

Dragons of Light (1980)
Dragons of Darkness (1981)
Future on Fire, with Martin H. Greenberg (1991)
Hitting the Skids in Pixeltown, volume 2 with Larry Niven (2003)
Masterpieces: The Best Science Fiction of the Twentieth Century (2004)

Anthologies

Legends: Short Novels by the Masters of Modern Fantasy, volume 1, edited by Robert
    Silverberg (1999)
Legends II, edited by Robert Silverberg (2003)

Introduction

War of the Worlds, by H. G. Wells (2004)

Stage Plays

Tell Me You Love Me, Junie Moon (produced 1969), adaptation of work by Marjorie
    Kellogg
The Apostate (produced 1970)
In Flight (produced 1970)
Across Five Summers (1971)
Of Gideon (produced 1971)
Stone Tables (produced 1973)
A Christmas Carol (produced 1974), adaptation of work by Charles Dickens
Father, Mother, Mother, and Mom (produced 1974)
Liberty Jail (produced 1975)
Rag Mission (written as Brian Green) in *Ensign* (1977)
Fresh Courage Take (produced 1978)
Elders and Sisters (produced 1979)
Wings (produced 1982)

Nonfiction

Listen, Mom and Dad (1978)
Saintspeak (1981)
Ainge (1982)
Compute's Guide to IBM, PCjr Sound and Graphics (1984)
Cardography (1987)
Characters and Viewpoint (1988)
How to Write Science Fiction and Fantasy (1990)

For Further Information

Card, Orson Scott. "Does a Writing Career Always Mean Novels?" Uncle Orson's
    Writing Class on Hatrack River: The Official Web Site of Orson Scott
    Card. *http://www.hatrack.com/writingclass/lesson02.shtml* (viewed January 19,
    2003).

Ciporen, Laura. "PW Talks with Orson Scott Card." *Publishers Weekly* (November
    20, 2000).

Clute, John. Orson Scott Card entry, *Encyclopedia of Science Fiction*. Edited by
    Clute and Peter Nicholls. New York: St. Martin's Press, 1993.

Collings, Michael R. *Storyteller—The Official Bibliography and Guide to the Works
    of Orson Scott Card*. Westport, CT: Greenwood Press, 1990.

Decandido, Graceanne A., and Keith R. A. Decandido. "PW Interview: Orson Scott
    Card." *Publishers Weekly* (November 30, 1990).

Lupoff, Richard A. Orson Scott Card entry, *Twentieth-Century Science-Fiction Writers*. 3rd edition, edited by Noelle Watson and Paul E. Schellinger. Chicago: St. James Press, 1991.

"Orson Scott Card: Casting Shadows." *Locus* (December 2002).

Tyson, Edith S. *Orson Scott Card: Writer of the Terrible Choice*. Chicago: Rowman & Littlefield, 2003.

White, Claire E. "A Conversation With Orson Scott Card." Writers Write (September 1999) as reproduced on Hatrack River: The Official Web site of Orson Scott Card. *http://www.hatrack.com/research/interviews/1999-09-writerswrite.shtml* (viewed January 19, 2003).

Wright, Doug. "An Interview with Orson Scott Card." Everyday Lives, Everyday Values Web site. *http://deseretbook.com/products/3957659/interview.html#content* (viewed November 13, 2000).

C. J. Cherryh

♦   Science fiction   ♦   Fantasy

St. Louis, Missouri
1942

♦   *Chanur Series*

About the Author and the Author's Writing

C. J. Cherryh—born Carolyn Janice Cherry in St. Louis, Missouri, in 1942—is equally comfortable writing science fiction and fantasy. Early on in her writing career, she caught the attention of her peers, collaring the John W. Campbell Best New Author Award in 1977. Her more than forty novels published since 1976 have garnered her the genres' top honors including Nebula, Hugo, World Fantasy and British Fantasy Society Awards.

But she paid her dues before enjoying that success. The daughter of a Social Security representative, she studied Latin in high school and chose that as her college major. A Woodrow Wilson fellowship enabled her to obtain her master's degree at Johns Hopkins University. She taught Latin and ancient history in the Oklahoma City Public Schools from 1965 to 1977. She later worked as an artist and residence and teacher for Central State University, 1980–1981. In her spare time, she wrote, abided rejection slips for several years, and then finally found a receptive editor.

"I've written since I was ten," the author told Amazon.com, [and] "went full time back in 1977. I write both sf and fantasy, usually in alternation, because they stretch different muscles. I trained as a Classicist, archaeology of the Bronze Age Med, but I have interests in wide-ranging things such as physics and biology. Everything is related to everything—especially in my writing."

Themes that recur in Cherryh's works are absolute power and character as shaped by culture. The author explores the fate of the outcast and the woman as a military leader. Her heroes and heroines are often capable but threatened, caught in complex political situations. Critics have variously labeled her a speculative anthropologist and a writer of "soft science fiction." Her characters include the human, the alien, and the manufactured.

Cherryh's significance, in the view of Thomas P. Dunn in *Twentieth-Century Science Fiction Writers*, is "her broad and systematic exploration of the concept of 'humanity' itself seeking to discover what of this basic idea can survive the great range of adverse conditions made possible by today's and tomorrow's knowledge of human and animal behavior."

In *Encyclopedia of Science Fiction* John Clute notes that Cherryh's bookshelf is a large one, and the author's vision, which is becoming increasingly clear, may take some sorting out.

Many of the author's science fiction tales are set in a future time, in which Earth has established colonies on orbiters around distant stars. There emerge three general peoples: Terrans on Earth; merchanters, who travel space; and stationers, who live in the space ports. The latter are rebellious against renewed attempts at political control by Terrans. The Company Wars, Merchanter, and Cyteen stories fit immediately in this universe; the Faded Sun, Brothers of the Earth, and other books are loosely connected.

"The reach for space and its resources is the make-or-break point for our species," Cherryh asserts in *Twentieth-Century Science-Fiction Writers*, "and the appropriate use of technology and the adjustment of human viewpoint to a universe not limited to a blue sky overhead and the curvature of the horizon are absolutely critical to our survival. Therefore I write fiction about space and human adjustment to the unfamiliar."

Cherryh's "total immersion into character viewpoint is the underlying secret to her incredibly believable aliens as well as her lovable but nuttier-than-a-fruitcake protagonists . . . ," suggests Jane Francher in program notes for Bucconeer Con. "Combined with CJ's incredible control of language (fluency in several languages doesn't hurt), her vast imagination, her warped and subtle sense of humor, her sheer talent, and her incredible productivity (*Cuckoo's Egg*, nominated for a Hugo, took two weeks to write. . . .) [Y]ou have all the raw materials for a Phenomenon."

"[S]he continues to produce some of the most thoughtful and thought-provoking 'soft science' fiction, enriched with speculative ethnology, invented linguistics and thoroughly imagined civilizations," according to the Internet critic known as dancingbadger.

Cherryh wrote her first stories as a youth with fat-lead pencils on an inexpensive tablet. She eventually began to use a typewriter, and she has said the loss by three different editors of the manuscript to *Hunter of Worlds*, forcing her each time to retype the manuscript, solidified her writing talents "because I kept having to improve it, and I learned on every pass." These days she works on a laptop computer, but she told ssfworld.com, "The current generation of writers that never retypes, because there's always a computer file, might try re-entering an unsold novel or two and seeing if they can't be bettered with a thorough re-write."

The author's manuscripts and working notes are held at Eastern New Mexico University at Portales. Outside interests include weaving, boating, maintaining a marine tank, and exploring the Internet. She frequently attends science fiction fan conventions.

How does the author conceive her complex settings? "I just go where that same daydream-spot inside my head that I'm pretty sure all of us have," she said in an interview with sfworld.com. "Thinking up new ideas and characters isn't hard. Writing day and night for months—that's hard."

Works by the Author

Fiction

Hestia (1979)
Serpent's Reach (1980)

Wave Without a Shore (1981)
Forty Thousand in Gehenna (1983)
Alien Stars, with Joe W. Haldeman and Timothy Zahn (1985)
Glass and Amber (1987)
The Paladin (1988)
Smuggler's Gold (1988)
The Goblin Mirror (1992)
Faery in Shadow (1993)
Rider at the Gate (1995)
Cloud's Rider (1996)
Lois and Clark: Superman (1996)
Devil to the Belt (2000)

Age of Exploration Series

Port Eternity (1982)
Voyager in Night (1984)
Cuckoo's Egg (1985)
Alternate Realities (2000), includes *Port Eternity*, *Voyager in Night*, and *Wave Without a Shore*

Arafel Series

Ealdwood (1979)
The Dreamstone (1983)
The Tree of Swords and Jewels (1983)
The Dreaming Tree (1997), includes the three books

Chanur or Compact Space Series

The Pride of Chanur (1981)
Chanur's Venture (1984)
The Kif Strike Back (1985)
Chanur's Homecoming (1986)
Chanur's Legacy (1992)
The Chanur Saga (2000), includes earlier novels

Company Wars Series

Downbelow Station (1981)
Rimrunners (1989)
Heavy Time (1991)
Hellburner (1992)

Cyteen Series

The Betrayal (1988)
The Rebirth (1988)
The Vindication (1989)

Faded Sun Series

Kesrith (1978)
Shon'Jir (1979)
Kutath (1980)
The Faded Sun Trilogy (2000), includes the three books

Foreigner Series

Foreigner (1994)
Invader (1995)
Inheritor (1996)
Precursor (1999)
Defender (2001)
Explorer (2002)

Gene Wars Series

Hammerfall (2001)
Forge of Heaven (2004)

Hanan Rebellion Series

Brothers of Earth (1976)
Hunter of Worlds (1976)
The Hanan Rebellion (2000), includes the two books; rereleased as *At the Edge of
    Space* (2003)

Heroes in Hell Series

1. *The Gates of Hell*, with Janet Morris (1986)
9. *Kings in Hell*, with Janet Morris (1987)
10. *Legions of Hell* (1987)

Merchanter Series

Merchanter's Luck (1982)
Tripoint (1994)
Finity's End (1997)

Merovian Nights Series

Angel with the Sword (1985)
Festival Moon (1987)
Fever Season (1987)
Merovian Nights (1987)
Trouble Waters (1988)
Divine Right (1989)
Flood Tide (1990)
Endgame (1991)

Morgaine Series

Claiming Rites (1976)
Gate of Ivrel (1976)
Well of Shiuan (1978)
Fires of Azeroth (1979)
Chronicles of Morgaine (1985)
Witchfires of Leth—Crossroads Adventure in the World of C. J. Cherryh's Morgaine,
    by Dan Greenberg (1987)
Exile's Gate (1988)
The Morgaine Saga (2000), includes all books except *Exile's Gate*.

Rusalka Series

Rusalka (1989)
Chernevog (1990)
Yvgenic (1991)

Swords of Knowledge Series

A Dirge for Sabis, with Leslie Fish (1989)
Reap the Whirlwind, with Nancy Asire, Leslie Fish, and Mercedes R. Lackey (1989)
Wizard Spawn, with Nancy Asire (1989)

Tristan Series

Fortress in the Eye of Time (1995)
Fortress of Eagles (1998)
Fortress of Owls (1998)
Fortress of Dragons (2000)

Collections

Sunfall (1981)
Festival Moon (1987)

Visible Light (1986)
Troubled Waters (1988)
Collected Short Fiction (2004)

Anthologies

Women of Wonder (1974)
The Year's Best Fantasy 3 (1977)
The 1979 Annual World's Best SF (1979)
The Best Science Fiction of the Year (1980)
Nebula Winners 14 (1980)
Elsewhere (1981)
Flashing Swords 5 (1981)
Hecate's Children (1981)
Fantasy Annual V (1982)
Shadows of Sanctuary (1982)
The Year's Best Fantasy (1982)
The John W. Campbell Awards Volume 5 (1984)
A Magic-Lover's Treasury of the Fantastic (1986)
Thieves' World 12: Stealer's Sky (1989)
The Year's Best Fantasy and Horror Fifth Annual Collection (1992)
Strange Dreams (1993)
Future on Ice (1998)
The Unexplained: Stories of the Paranormal (1998)

Translator

The Green Gods, by Charles and Nathalie Henneberg (1980)
Star Crusade, by Pierre Barbet (1980)
The Book of Shai, by Daniel Walther (1984)

For Further Information

"Amazon.com Talks to C. J. Cherryh." Amazon.com. *http://www.amazon.com/exec/ obidos/show-interview/c-c-herryhj/ref%3Dpm%Fdp%5Fln%5Fb%5F8/ 102-5492614-9851310* (viewed April 10, 2003).

Bacon-Smith, Camille. "Military Command in Women's Science Fiction: C. J. Cherryh's Signy Mallory." *The Swan*, vol. 1, 2000. *http://www.dm.net/~theswan/ baconsmith.html* (viewed April 19, 2003).

C. J. Cherryh Interview. ssfworld.com. *http://www.ssfworld.com/authors/c/cherryh_ cj/interviews/200001.html* (viewed April 6, 2003).

"C. J. Cherryh, Science Fiction, and the Soft Sciences." *http://www.dancingbadger .com/cherryh.htm* (viewed April 19, 2003).

Clute, John. C. J. Cherryh entry, *Encyclopedia of Science Fiction*. Edited by John Clute and Peter Nicholls. New York: St. Martin's Press, 1993.

Dunn, Thomas P. C. J. Cherryh entry, *Twentieth-Century Science-Fiction Writers*. 3rd edition, edited by Noelle Watson and Paul E. Schellinger. Chicago: St. James Press, 1991.

Eagen, Tim. "C. J. Cherryh: The Outcast and the Uncertain Mind." September 1997. *http://www.stmoroky/com/reviews/authors/cherryh/htm* (viewed April 19, 2003).

Ex Libris Archives: C. J. Cherryh. *http://www.wjduquette.com/authors/cjcherryh.html* (viewed April 6, 2003).

Fancher, Jane. "So, Who is This CJC and Why is She GoH of Bucconeer?" Bucconeer Progress Report Four, June 1998. *http://www.bucconeer.worldcon.org/PR4/jfancher.htm* (viewed April 21, 2003).

Stephenson-Payne, Phil. *C. J. Cherryh: A Working Bibliography* (chapbook, 1992).

Universes of C. J. Cherryh. *http://www.cherryh.com/www/univer.htm* (viewed April 5, 2003).

Wiloch, Thomas. C. J. Cherryh entry, *Contemporary Authors New Revision Series*. Vol. 10, edited by Ann Ivory and Linda Metzger. Detroit: Gale Research, 1983.

Tom Clancy

◆ Adventure ◆ Thriller

Baltimore, Maryland
1947

◆ *Jack Ryan Series*

About the Author and the Author's Writing

An insurance broker, a fascination with naval history, a first novel published by a small publisher—these elements would not seem to be the tinder for a sure-fire best-selling author, one whose books President Ronald Reagan would declare "non-put-downable." But in Tom Clancy's case, the blaze surged sky high.

Clancy was born in 1947 in Baltimore, Maryland, the son of a mail carrier and a credit company employee. In 1969, he graduated from Loyola College with a degree in English. He was never in the service, rejected for health reasons. He married Wanda Thomas, manager of an insurance agency, in 1969 and they have four children. He was working as an insurance agent when he wrote his first novel, *The Hunt for Red October*—the gripping story of efforts by naval leaders in America and the USSR to find a Soviet submarine whose captain wants to defect.

Clancy's novels are packed with details of armaments and operations—it is not surprising Naval Institute Press was his first publisher—to the extent that some reviewers have called his books "techno-thrillers." But the author disdains the label: "I've never written the same book twice. All [at that time] nine of my novels are different," he said in a Quill Academy interview.

A major inspiration to his writing, Clancy told Verbosity, was Frederick Forsyth's *Day of the Jackal*. "The book is perhaps the best thriller ever done—and more than that, it redefined the thriller novel, converting it into a highly respectable genre. Then I asked myself, 'Why are all the good thriller writers Brits? Why can't an American do it?' So I did, and I guess it worked."

The series character Jack Ryan, the author concedes, is largely a fictional version of himself. He wants his characters to be humans, not super-heroes, he said, with human issues to deal with, human virtues, and human flaws.

Reviewers don't always find humanity in Clancy's characters, however. "There is something very creepy about Clancy's protagonists," Bill Bell carped in a review of *The Teeth of the Tiger*. "All are developmentally arrested, all are obsessed with manliness and machinery, and all are posturing frat boy conversationalists."

Clancy is continually conducting research for his books and has been welcomed by military personnel to, among other facilities, the National Training Center in Fort Irwin, California, to witness Army war games. He has not, however, ever been privy to classified documents.

However, contrary to what some readers may believe, the author has no security clearance; what he writes about is based on material openly available. He interviewed Edward L. Beach, a World War II submarine captain, and Arkady Shevchenko, a Soviet defector, for firsthand details (never having been aboard a submarine before drafting *The Hunt for Red October* or inside a Politburo meeting before writing *Red Storm*).

Clancy is so popular among "techno-fetishists" that there have grown a number of Internet sites such as *www.clancy.faq.com* and *www.tcic.org*, which provide the latest advance notice of new books or films, define obscure terms, provide plot summaries, and profile characters in the books.

Clancy has been uncannily prescient in his writing; in his novel *Debt of Honor*, a character named Sato flies an airplane into the U.S. Capitol, killing most of the government leaders. Touring ground zero in New York after September 11, 2001, Clancy is quoted in *The Writer* as saying, "You can't keep up with reality right now. Nobody has a big enough imagination."

Besides his own two series featuring CIA operatives Ryan and John Clark (a darker but more humorous variation on Ryan) and his nonfiction works, Clancy with Martin H. Greenberg has created the concept and universe for the Power Plays series. With Steve Pieczenik he has created the Net Force and Net Force Explorers series for young adults and the Op Center series, all written by authors other than Clancy.

The author's enormous popularity has given him a soapbox to air his views:

On the superiority of the American military in the Persian Gulf War, he told interviewer Jesse Kornbluth, "This was simply the best trained, best led army I'm aware of—and I've been reading military history since I was a kid. This army was as good an army since Caesar's army invaded Gaul."

On the 2001 terrorist attacks, in an essay in the *Wall Street Journal*, he bemoaned the country's lack of confidence in the Central Intelligence Agency, which with better resources and support might have prevented the hijackings: "The loss of so many lives in New York and Washington is now called an 'intelligence failure,' mostly by those who crippled the CIA in the first place, and by those who celebrated the loss of its invaluable capabilities."

On the United States' future, he's upbeat, as he stated in an Intellectual Capital interview: "As long as we can keep the Constitution in place, which has served us well, it will continue to serve us well. Which is why other countries throughout the world are emulating it."

Not all critics have welcomed the Clancy hawkish Republican stance. Jason Cowley, who labels Clancy "the John Wayne of fiction," writing in *New Statesman* in 1996, wondered aloud about what Clancy calls the "Ryan doctrine" of warfare, striking first and fast to take out a major enemy. " 'To me, the Ryan doctrine is the logical extension of military technology,' Clancy told me. 'Killing people doesn't worry me so long as you have a good enough reason. The Ryan doctrine gives you a reason.' As do irrational messianic fervor (Bin Laden) and wounded indignation (George Bush)."

But in spite of the criticisms, no one can dispute the success of this writer. The bottom line is that readers love his work. Clancy told *Publishers Weekly's* Jeff Zaleski his readers are "people who want to know how the world really works. My covenant with my readers is that I tell them the way things really are. If I say it, it's real."

Is the writing life all pleasure? Not by a long shot, Clancy told Lev Grossman for *Time*: "I don't recommend writing as a form of employment, because it's such miserable work. That's how you tell a rookie: if they actually think the writing's fun. I guess it is for the first one or two, but after that it just becomes miserable work, like digging in the dirt with a shovel. But it's something you have to do. You can't not do it."

Works by the Author

Fiction

Red Storm Rising, with Larry Bond (1986)
The Teeth of the Tiger (2003)

Jack Ryan Series

The Hunt for Red October (1984)
Patriot Games (1987)
Cardinal of the Kremlin (1988)
Clear and Present Danger (1989)
The Sum of All Fears (1991)
Debt of Honor (1994)
Executive Orders (1996)
The Bear and the Dragon (2000)
Red Rabbit (2002)

Jack Ryan Jr. Series

The Teeth of the Tiger (2003)

John Clark Series

Without Remorse (1993)
Rainbow Six (1998)

Net Force Series, created by Tom Clancy and Steve Pieczenik

Net Force, by Steve Perry and Steve Pieczenik (1998)
Hidden Agendas, by Steve Pieczenik (1999)
Night Moves, by Steve Pieczenik (1999)
Breaking Point, by Steve Perry and Steve Pieczenik (2000)
Cybernation, by Steve Perry and Steve Pieczenik (2001)
Point of Impact, by Steve Perry and Steve Pieczenik (2001)
State of War, by Steve Perry (2002)
Changing of the Guard, by Steve Perry and Larry Segriff (2003)

Cloak and Dagger, by Steve Pieczenik, John Helfers, and Russell Davis (2003)
State of War, by Steve Perry and Larry Segriff (2003)

Net Force Explorers Series (Books for Young Adults), created by Tom Clancy and Steve Pieczenik

The Deadliest Game, by Bill McCay (1998)
End Game, by Diane Duane (1998)
Virtual Vandals, by Diane Duane (1998)
Cyberspy, by Bill McCay (1999)
One Is the Loneliest Number, by Diane Duane, Steve Perry, and Steve Pieczenik (1999)
The Ultimate Escape (1999)
Deathworld, by Diane Duane (2000)
Duel Identity, by Bill McCay (2000)
Gameprey, by Mel Odom (2000)
Private Live, by Bill McCay (2000)
Safe House, by Diane Duane (2000)
Shadow of Honor, by Mel Odom (2000)
Cold Case, by Bill McCay (2001)
High Wire, by Mel Odom (2001)
Runaways, by Diane Duane (2001)
Death Match, by Diane Duane (2003)

Power Plays Series, created by Tom Clancy and Martin H. Greenberg

Politika (1997)
Ruthless.com (1998)
Shadow Watch (1999)
Bio-Strike (2000)
Cold War, by Jerome Preisler (2001)
Cutting Edge, by Jerome Preisler (2002)
Wild Card, by Jerome Preisler (2004)

Splinter Cell Series, created by Tom Clancy, based on video game

Splinter Cell, by David Michaels (2004)

Tom Clancy's Op-Center Series, created by Tom Clancy and Steve Pieczenik

Mirror Image, by Steve Pieczenik (1995)
Op-Center, by Steve Pieczenik (1995)
Acts of War, by Steve Pieczenik (1996)
Games of State, by Steve Pieczenik (1996)
Balance of Power, by Steve Pieczenik (1998)

State of Siege, by Steve Pieczenik and Jeff Rovin (1999)
Divide and Conquer, by Jeff Rovin (2000)
Line of Control, by Jeff Rovin (2001)
Mission of Honor, by Jeff Rovin (2002)
Sea of Fire, by Jeff Rovin (2003)
Call to Treason, by Jeff Rovin (2004)
War of Eagles, by Jeff Rovin (2004)

Nonfiction

Submarine: A Guided Tour Inside a Nuclear Warship (1993)
Armored Cav: A Guided Tour of an Armored Cavalry Regiment (1994)
Fighter Wing: A Guided Tour of an Air Force Combat Wing (1995)
Marine: A Guided Tour of a Marine Expeditionary Unit (1996)
SSN: Strategies of Submarine Warfare (1996)
Airborne: A Guided Tour of an Airborne Task Force (1997)
Carrier: A Guided Tour of an Aircraft Carrier (1999)
Special Ops (2000)

Commander Series

Into the Storm: A Study in Command, with Gen. Fred Franks (1997)
Every Man a Tiger, with Gen. Charles Horner (1999)
Shadow Warriors, with Gen. Carl Stiner (2002)
Battle Ready, with Gen. Tony Zinni (2004)

Motion Pictures and Television Series Based on the Author's Works

The Hunt for Red October (1990)
Patriot Games (1992)
Clear and Present Danger (1994)
Net Force (1998)
Op Center (1999)
The Sum of All Fears (2002)

For Further Information

Bell, Bill. "It's Clancy Fun in the Son." *New York Daily News* (August 13, 2003).

Clancy, Tom. "First We crippled the CIA. Then we blamed it." *Wall Street Journal* (September 18, 2001).

Cowley, Jason. "He is the most popular novelist on earth, whose images of catastrophe animate the modern American psyche." *New Statesman* (September 24, 2001).

Donnelly, John. Tom Clancy interview. Salon.com. *http://www.salon.com/june97 .clancy970604.html* (viewed April 7, 2003).

Garson, Helen S. *Tom Clancy: A Critical Companion*. Westport, CT: Greenwood Press, 1996.

Goldstein, Bill. "Some Best-Seller Old Reliables Have String of Unreliable Sales." *New York Times* (January 20, 2003).

Grossman, Lev. "10 Questions For Tom Clancy." *Time* (July 29, 2002).

Hormann, Richard. "Secret Agent Men: Web spooks dig deep for intelligence on thriller writer Tom Clancy." *Entertainment Weekly* (June 7, 2002).

"Is There a Clear and Future Danger? An Interview with Tom Clancy." Intellectual Capital (June 26, 1997). *http://hem.passagen.se/clancy/interv9.htm* (viewed June 5, 2003).

Jones, David, and John D. Jorgenson, eds. Tom Clancy entry, *Contemporary Authors New Revision Series*. Vol. 62. Detroit: Gale Research, 1998.

Kornbluth, Jesse. Tom Clancy interview. Book Report (1997). *http://hem/passagen.se/ clancy.interv3.htm* (viewed June 5, 2003).

Maryles, Daisy. "Clancy's lucky 13th." *Publishers Weekly* (August 25, 2003).

Moire, Allen. "Tom Clancy's timing remarkable." *The Writer* (May 2002).

Stern, Carol Simpson. Tom Clancy entry, *St. James Guide to Crime & Mystery Writers*. 4th edition, edited by Jay P. Pederson. Detroit: St. James Press, 1996.

Tom Clancy interview. Quill Academy. *http://hem/.passagen.se/clancy.interv10.htm* (viewed June 5, 2003).

Tom Clancy interview. Verbosity. *http://hem.passagen.se/clancy./interv6.htm* (viewed June 5, 2003).

Tom Clancy Web page. Penguin Putnam. *http://www.penguinputnam.com* (viewed April 7, 2003).

Tom Clancy Web site. *http://www.clancyfaq.com/books/htm#books* (viewed April 7, 2003).

Vinciguerra, Thomas. "Word for Word: The Clancy Effect; Quick! Man the F56 Kryton Hydro Thermal-Sensitive Torpedoes!" *New York Times* (August 18, 2002).

Zaleski, Jeff. "The Hunt for Tom Clancy." *Publishers Weekly* (July 13, 1996).

Mary Higgins Clark

♦ Mystery ♦ Suspense

New York, New York
1929

♦ *Where Are the Children?*

About the Author and the Author's Writing

Called by some the "Queen of Suspense," author Mary Higgins Clark in 2003 became only the seventh recipient of the Christopher Life Achievement Award for her contributions to publishing and national literacy campaigns. "Clark's resilience and determination," according to a PR Newswire report, "enabled her to succeed as an author, despite overwhelming challenges, without compromising her faith, values or convictions. Her inspiring life and career as the author of 27 best sellers in as many years reflects the essence of the Christopher Awards."

Mary Higgins was born in 1929 in New York City, the daughter of a restaurant owner and a professional buyer. As a girl, she wrote poetry and skits for her friends to perform. She attended Villa Maria Academy but left before graduation, because of the death of her father and the need to support her mother and two brothers, to attend Ward Secretarial School. She attended New York University and received a bachelor of arts degree in philosophy summa cum laude in 1979 from Fordham University. Higgins worked as an advertising assistant for Remington Rand in 1946. As a flight attendant with Pan American Airlines from 1949 to 1950, she traveled to Europe, Africa, and Asia. In 1949, she married airline executive Warren F. Clark (they had known each other as neighbors since she was sixteen) and they had five children.

The author, who now lives in Saddle River, New Jersey, and Manhattan, was a radio scriptwriter and producer with Robert G. Jennings from 1965 to 1970; then vice president, partner, creative director, and producer of radio programming with Aerial Communications in New York for a decade beginning in 1980. She credits her radio work with honing her writing and her ability to pen suspense. In 1980, she became chairman of the board and creative director of David J. Clark Enterprises.

A widow since 1964, Clark rose at 5 in the morning to write for a couple of hours before sending the children to school and leaving for work. It took six years and forty rejections before her first story, "Last Flight from Danubia," about a flight attendant and a revolutionary, appeared in *Extension* magazine in 1956. "She received that first acceptance slip when she was seven months pregnant with me," daughter Carol Higgins Clark said in *Mystery Scene*. "The heroine's name was Carol, hence my name. I always thank God it wasn't Hepsibah."

Clark was regularly selling short stories when her first book, *Aspire to the Heavens*, about George Washington, came out in 1969. It was based on a radio series she scripted, Portrait of a Patriot.

The Washington book was not a best-seller. Looking around for ideas, Clark said, she considered what she liked to read: As a girl she'd devoured Nancy Drew and graduated to Agatha Christie and Arthur Conan Doyle. She was also fascinated by a 1957 New Jersey crime, Edgar Smith's stalking and killing of teenager Vickie Zielinski. So she wrote a suspense novel. Two publishers were disinterested—children in jeopardy didn't seem to have a strong chance for success—but Simon and Schuster offered the author a $3,000 advance. Paperback rights sold to Dell for $100,000. Clark wrote another book, "and then I was offered $500,000 for the hardback rights and $1 million for the paperback," she said in a BookEnds interview. "The publisher told me to think it over. I said: 'Honey, I don't need to think it over!' Something inside told me I was going to make it."

Clark credits her success to good storytelling. She praised her teacher and mentor William Byron Mowery for urging her to provide minimal description and let the reader's imagination kick in and to create and exploit a style or setting so it would make the author instantly recognizable.

"I write about very nice people whose lives are invaded by evil," Clark said in an interview with Lucy Freeman for *The Armchair Detective*. "I grew up among very nice people whose lives were invaded by the human condition with its peaks and valleys. From them I learned that it is not always how we *act* but how we *react* that is the measure of our worth."

Clark shuns blood and gore, believing what is not seen is scarier than what's blatant. She paces the action quickly. "We're all used to bites of news," she told Betta Ferrendelli of *Mystery Scene*. "You can't take forty pages to get from the car to the house, and see the daffodils and the shadows on the house—forget it. Not today. You've got to get something happening."

Clark often incorporates current topics, from health maintenance organizations to capital punishment. "I like to use something that's in the news," she said in an interview with David Weich. "When I wrote *Where Are the Children*, for the first time children were starting to be picked up."

Clark has also written several stories featuring the detective team of Henry Parker Britland IV, retired president of the United States, and his wife, Sandra (nicknamed Sunday), who is newly elected to Congress.

If any further proof of Clark's popularity were needed, it surely came with the 1996 launch by *Family Circle* of *Mary Higgins Clark Mystery Magazine*, a quarterly that published works by the eponymous author as well as P. D. James, Elmore Leonard, and Walter Mosely. Nearly a dozen of the author's works have been sold for motion picture or television adaptation, including *A Cry in the Night*, which starred the author's daughter (and mystery novelist), Carol Higgins Clark.

Critical of some of the works based on her novels, Mary Higgins Clark has observed Hollywood looks at a book with a female protagonist as a telefilm, not a feature movie.

In 1996, Clark married John Conheeney, a retiree to whom she was introduced by one of her daughters. She has collected her memoirs in the book *Kitchen Privileges*. In it she reveals her steadfast confidence she would become a successful writer. "My mother was always supportive," Clark told *Publishers Weekly*. "So many parents discourage children. I say praise the creativity. Don't talk about the child's penmanship or spelling. It's so easy to snuff [creativity] out when the child is sensitive."

The writing process is a slow one for Clark, who in a *USA Today* chat in 2002 said, "Would to God I could write straight through. I edit and edit and edit, and change and change and change, particularly the first couple of chapters. Then that wonderful happening occurs: the characters are so grounded that they take over the story and tell it themselves. That's when writing is a joy."

Works by the Author

Fiction

Where Are the Children? (1975)
A Stranger is Watching (1978)
The Cradle Will Fall (1980)
A Cry in the Night (1982)
Stillwatch (1984)
Murder in Manhattan, with Thomas Chastain and others (1986)
Weep No More, My Lady (1987)
While My Pretty One Sleeps (1989)
Loves Music, Loves to Dance (1991)
All Around the Town (1992)
Missing in Manhattan: The Adams Round Table (1992)
I'll Be Seeing You (1993)
Remember Me (1994)
Let Me Call You Sweetheart (1995)
Mary Higgins Clark; Three Complete Novels (1995), includes first three books
Silent Night (1995)
Mary Higgins Clark, Three New York Times Bestsellers (1996), includes *While My Pretty One Sleeps, Loves Music, Loves to Dance*, and *All Around the Town*
Moonlight Becomes You (1996)
Pretend You Don't See Her (1997)
All Through the Night (1998)
We'll Meet Again (1999)
Before I Say Goodbye (2000)
Mount Vernon Love Story: A Novel of George and Martha Washington (2000)
The Plot Thickens (2000)
He Sees You While You're Sleeping (2001)
On the Street Where You Live (2001)
Daddy's Little Girl (2002)
The Second Time Around (2003)
Night Time Is My Time (2004)

Regan Riley Series, conceived by Carol Higgins Clark

Deck the Halls, with Carol Higgins Clark (2000)
The Christmas Thief, with Carol Higgins Clark (2004)

Editor

Murder on the Aisle: The 1987 Mystery Writers of America Anthology (1987)
Women of Mystery, with Faye Kellerman and Cynthia Manson (1992)
The Plot Thickens (1997)

Collections

The Anastasia Syndrome and Other Stories (1989)
Death on the Cape and Other Stories (1993)
Mists from Beyond: Twenty-Two Ghost Stories and Tales from the Other Side (1993)
Stowaway and Milk Run (1993)
The Lottery Winner: Alvirah and Willy Stories (1994)
My Gal Sunday (1996)

Anthologies

The Best Saturday Evening Post Stories (1962)
I, Witness (1978)
Alfred Hitchcock's Grave Suspicions, edited by Cathleen Jordan (1984)
Murder in Manhattan (1986)
Mistletoe Mysteries, edited by Charlotte MacLeod (1989)
A Body Is Found (1990)
Justice in Manhattan (1994)
The International Association of Crime Writers Presents Bad Behavior (1995)
Murder on the Run (1996)
The Best of Sisters in Crime (1997)
The Plot Thickens (1997)
Best American Mystery Stories 1998, edited by Sue Grafton (1998)
The Night Awakens (2000)
Murder in the Family (2002)

Nonfiction

Aspire to the Heavens: A Biography of George Washington (1969)
Kitchen Privileges: A Memoir (2002)

Anthologies

The Writing Life: Writers on How they Think and Work, edited by Marie Arana (2003)

Motion Pictures or Television Movies Based on the Author's Works

A Stranger Is Watching (1982)
The Cradle Will Fall (1984)
A Cry in the Night (1985)
Where Are the Children? (1986)
A Cry in the Night (1992)
Weep No More My Lady (1992)
Pretend You Don't See Her (2002)
Loves Music, Loves to Dance (2003)

For Further Information

About Mary Higgins Clark. BookEnds. *http://62.173.95.217/bookends/chat/clark.asp?TAG=&CID=* (viewed April 5, 2003).

Baker, John F. "Clarks to Combine on Xmas Novel." *Publishers Weekly* (June 26, 2000).

"Best-Selling Author and Literacy Advocate Mary Higgins Clark to Receive the 2003 Christopher Life Achievement Award." PR Newswire (February 25, 2003).

Block, Lawrence. "There's Something About Mary." *Mystery Scene*, no. 73 (2001).

Clark, Carol Higgins. "Mary Higgins Clark." *Mystery Scene*, no. 73 (2001).

Clark, Mary Higgins. "Edgar Smith: The Human Copperhead." *Mystery Scene*, no. 63 (1999).

Davis, Dorothy S. "Mary Higgins Clark." *Mystery Scene*, no. 73 (2001).

Ferrendelli, Betta. "Mary Higgins Clark and the Adams Round Table." *Mystery Scene*, no. 51 (January/February 1996).

Fisher, Rachel. "French toast pulp fiction queen." *Variety* (August 31, 1998).

Freeman, Lucy. "Interview with Mary Higgins Clark." *The Armchair Detective* (summer 1985).

Grape, Jan. "Mary Higgins Clark is a Wicked Lady." *Mystery Scene*, no. 73 (2001).

Hall, Parnell. "Did you hear the one about Mary Higgins Clark?" *Mystery Scene*, no. 73 (2001).

Hart, Carolyn. "Mary Higgins Clark." *Mystery Scene*, no. 73 (2001).

Healy, Jeremiah. "A Tribute to Mary Higgins Clark." *Mystery Scene*, no. 73 (2001).

Hirschhorn, Joel. "Novelist's advice: write what you know." *Publishers Weekly* (November 4, 2002).

Hoch, Edward D. Mary Higgins Clark entry, *St. James Guide to Crime & Mystery Writers*. 4th edition, edited by Jay P. Pederson. Detroit: St. James Press, 1996.

Isaacs, Susan. "Mary Higgins Clark." *Mystery Scene*, no. 73 (2001).

Kelman, Judith. "Mary's Golden Wing." *Mystery Scene*, no. 73 (2001).

Marylea, Daisy. "The fiction leader is anonymous no longer." *Publishers Weekly* (April 15, 1995).

Peacock, Scot, ed. Mary Higgins Clark entry, *Contemporary Authors New Revision Series*. Vol. 76. Detroit: Gale Research, 1999.

Pelzer, Linda Claycomb. *Mary Higgins Clark: A Critical Companion*. Westport, CT: Greenwood Press, 1995.

Pinkus, Sam. *Kitchen Privileges* review. *Publishers Weekly* (November 4, 2002).

Quinn, Judy. "Mary Higgins Clark mystery mag launched." *Publishers Weekly* (July 15, 1996).

Scott, Justin. "Tribute to Mary." *Mystery Scene*, no. 73 (2001).

USA Today Book Club: Mary Higgins Clark. *http:cgil.usatoday.com/mchat/20021204005/tscript.htm* (viewed December 20, 2002).

Weich, David. Mary Higgins Clark interview (May 1999). Powells. *http://www.powells.com/authors/hjigginsclark.html* (viewed April 5, 2003).

Arthur C. Clarke

◆   Science fiction

Minehead, Somerset, England
1917

◆   *2001: A Space Odyssey*

About the Author and the Author's Writing

For a generation, the music of "Thus Spake Zarathustra" has brought to immediate mind the monolith, Hal the computer, and the motion picture *2001: A Space Odyssey*, based on a script science fiction giant Arthur C. Clarke wrote with director Stanley Kubrick in 1968.

Clarke has kept the science in science fiction. He "has displayed an uncanny ability to see the future," according to critic Frank Houston. "In 1945, a year before the death of [H. G.] Wells and twelve years before Sputnik, Clarke predicted a global relay system of radio and television signals using geocynchronous satellites—a communications revolution that began taking shape twenty years later. The first draft of the article 'Can Rocket Stations Give World-wide Radio Coverage?' is now in the Smithsonian."

Arthur Charles Clarke was born in 1917 in Minehead, Somerset, England, one of four children of a farming family. When the author was thirteen, his father died. Clarke attended Huish's Grammar School in Somerset, and in his youth, experimented with telescopes and made his own map of the moon. He also experimented with rockets, foretelling an aspect of his future career. He earned a bachelor of science degree in mathematics and physics with honors at King's College, University of London, in 1948. During his years of study, he wrote and in 1946 he sold his first science fiction story, "Loophole," to *Astounding*. He married an American, Marilyn Mayfield, in 1953; they divorced eleven years later.

Clarke has had a long and varied career, not only as a writer. He was an auditor with the British Exchequer and Audit Department in London from 1936 to 1941. For the next five years, he worked as a radar instructor (he wrote the novel *Glide Path* based on this time), then as flight lieutenant for the Royal Air Force. Returning from the service, he joined the British Interplanetary Society and used some of its equipment for experiments. From 1949 to 1950, Clarke was assistant editor for *Science Abstracts* in London, a publication of the Institution of

Electrical Engineers. He began writing imaginative fiction in 1951, when his first novel *The Sands of Mars* came out.

His novels *Childhood's End, 2001: A Space Odyssey*, and *Rendezvous with Rama* are all considered classics. Biographer Eric S. Rabkin asserts it is Clarke's vision that sets him apart from other science fiction writers, his "humane and open and fundamentally optimistic view of humankind and its potential in a universe which dwarfs us in physical size but which we may hope some day to match in spirit."

Still, Clarke has to wonder about the future of humankind, and particularly the effects of some religious zealots. "One of the great tragedies of mankind is that morality has been hijacked by religion," he told Council for Secular Humanism's Matt Cherry. "So now people assume that religion and morality have a necessary connection. But the basis of morality is really very simple and doesn't require religion at all. It's this: 'Don't do unto anybody else what you wouldn't like to be done to you.' It seems to me that that's all there is to it." Clarke considers himself a Buddhist of sorts, though generally he is against organized religion.

During his long career as a writer, Clarke has written both fiction and nonfiction, including technical reports. As the result of his "Extra-Terrestrial Relays" paper about satellites in 1945, he was made a Fellow of King's College and given its Marconi International Fellowship in 1982. The report did not end Clarke's interest in satellites; in 1954 he put forth the value of satellites in meteorological research and forecasting. He also suggested the viability of reusable spacecraft and the mobile telephone.

In 1956, Clarke moved permanently to Sri Lanka. He explored and photographed the Great Barrier Reef off Australia and also the coast of Ceylon (now Sri Lanka) from 1954 to 1964 with his partner Mike Wilson. They discovered a 250-year-old shipwreck off the Great Basses Reef. In 1964, Clarke began working with film director Stanley Kubrick to adapt Clarke's short story "The Sentinel" (from *Expedition to Earth*) into what became the major motion picture, *2001: A Space Odyssey*, for which the two shared an Academy Award nomination.

At the time of the Apollo missions, 1968–1970, Arthur Clarke worked as a television commentator with Walter Cronkite. He hosted two of his own television programs, *Arthur C. Clarke's Mysterious World* and *Arthur C. Clarke's World of Strange Powers*, in 1980 and 1984, respectively. He also has been a director of Rocket Publishing; an owner of Underwater Safaris, a founder and patron of Arthur C. Clarke Centre for Modern Technologies; and chancellor of University of Morutuwa, all in Sri Lanka, among other positions. He has received a long list of awards, beginning with the International Fantasy Award in 1952 and including the Science Fiction Writers of America Grand Master Award in 1986 and the Jupiter Award from Instructors of Science Fiction in Higher Education in 1974 for *Rendezvous with Rama*. He is in the Aerospace Hall of Fame (1988) and received the special achievement award from the Space Explorers Association in 1989.

Clarke was named a Commander, Order of the British Empire, in 1989; and he was knighted by Queen Elizabeth in 1999 for services to literature.

Age and post-polio syndrome have barely slowed the writer's pace, though he has had to give up scuba diving. He maintains a state-of-the-art communications center at his compound in Colombo where he lives with an adopted family, Hector and Valerie Ekanayake, their children, and Pepsi the Chihuahua.

Examining images returned to Earth by the Mars Global Surveyor in 2001, Clarke expressed his continued belief that the red planet could sustain life. "Something is actually moving and changing with the seasons that suggests, at least, vegetation," he told writer Leonard David.

Thrilled with the progress the world has made in space exploration, the author told interviewer John L. Coker III in 1999 of an entrepreneur who was "going to take some of my hair and it's going to be shot out into outer space. Then, in maybe a hundred million years someone can clone me. It's called 'Project Encounter.' It's an interesting idea, isn't it?"

What does the future bode? Clarke, calling them extrapolations rather than predictions, suggested to interviewer Gyles Brandwreth that the microchip had created a revolution; new sources of energy would be perfected, genetic modification would be expanded. "And there'll be a change in our personal fuel, too. We'll be able to synthesize all our food quite soon. All it will take is water, air, and a few basic chemicals. Unquestionably, we are going to see the end of agriculture and the end of animal husbandry, so-called. That could happen within my lifetime."

Works by the Author

Fiction

Prelude to Space (1951), retitled *Master of Space* (1961) and *The Space Dreamers* (1969)
The Sands of Mars (1951)
Islands in the Sky (1952)
Against the Fall of Night (1953)
Childhood's End (1953)
The City and the Stars (1955)
Earthlight (1955)
The Deep Range (1957)
Across the Sea of Stars (1959), includes *Childhood's End* and *Earthlight*
A Fall of Moondust (1961)
From the Oceans, from the Stars (1962), includes *The Deep Range* and *The City and the Stars*
Dolphin Island: A Story of the People of the Sea (1963)
Glide Path (1963)
An Arthur C. Clarke Omnibus (1965), includes *Childhood's End, Prelude to Space,* and *Expedition to Earth*
Prelude to Mars (1965), includes *Prelude to Space* and *The Sands of Mars*
2001: A Space Odyssey (1968), screenplay with Stanley Kubrick
A Second Arthur C. Clarke Omnibus (1968), includes *A Fall of Moondust, Earthlight,* and *The Sands of Mars*
The Lost Worlds of 2001 (1972)
Imperial Earth: A Fantasy of Love and Discord (1975)
Four Great Science Fiction Novels (1978), includes *The City and the Stars, The Deep Range, A Fall of Moondust,* and *Rendezvous with Rama*
The Fountains of Paradise (1979)
Selected Works (1985)
The Songs of Distant Earth (1986)
Cradle, with Gentry Lee (1988)
A Meeting with Medusa (1988)

Beyond the Fall of Night, with Gregory Benford (1990)
The Ghost from the Grand Banks (1990)
The Hammer of God (1993)
Breaking Strain: The Adventures of Yellow Dog (1995)
Richter 10, with Mike McQuay (1996)
The Trigger, with Michael P. Kube-McDowell (1999)

Odyssey Series

2001: A Space Odyssey (1968)
2010: Odyssey Two (1982)
2061: Odyssey Three (1988)
3001: The Final Odyssey (1997)

Rama Series

Rendezvous with Rama (1973)
Rama II, with Gentry Lee (1989)
The Garden of Rama, with Gentry Lee (1991)
Rama Revealed, with Gentry Lee (1993)

Time Odyssey Series

The Light of Other Days, with Stephen M. Baxter (2000)
Time's Eye, with Stephen M. Baxter (2003)

Short Story Collections

Expedition to Earth (1953)
Reach for Tomorrow (1956)
Tales from the White Hart (1957)
The Other Side of the Sky (1958)
Tales of Ten Worlds (1962)
Sunjammer (1965)
The Nine Billion Names of God (1967)
Earthlight and Other Stories (1968)
The Lion of Comarre and Other Stories (1968)
Of Time and Stars: The Worlds of Arthur C. Clarke (1972)
The Wind from the Sun (1972)
The Best of Arthur C. Clarke (1973), edited by Angus Wells, published in two volumes as *The Best of Arthur C. Clarke 1937–1955* (1977)
The Best of Arthur C. Clarke; 1956–1972 (1977)
Possessed and Other Stories (1978)
The Lion of Comarre and *Against the Fall of Night* (1983)
The Sentinel: Masterworks of Science Fiction and Fantasy (1983)

Tales from Planet Earth (1989)
A Meeting With Medusa and Other Stories (1990)
The Collected Stories of Arthur C. Clarke (2001)
The Shining Ones and Other Stories (2001)

Editor

Time Probe: The Science in Science Fiction (1966)
Three for Tomorrow (1972)
The Science Fiction Hall of Fame, Volume 3: The Nebula Winners, with George Proctor
    (1982)
Project Solar Sail (1986)
Hal's Legacy, with David G. Stork (1996)

Nonfiction

Interplanetary Flight: An Introduction to Astronautics (1950)
The Exploration of Space (1951)
The Young Traveler in Space (1953), retitled *Going into Space* (1954); revised as *Into
    Space: A Young Person's Guide to Space*, with Robert Silverberg (1971)
The Cost of Coral (1956)
The Making of a Moon: The Story of the Earth Satellite Program (1957)
The Scottie Book of Space Travel (1957)
Boy Beneath the Sea, with Mike Wilson (1958)
Voice Across the Sea (1958)
The Challenge of the Spaceship: Previews of Tomorrow's World (1959)
The First Five Fathoms: A Guide to Underwater Adventure, with Mike Wilson
    (1960)
Indian Ocean Adventure (1961) with Mike Wilson
Profiles of the Future: An Inquiry into the Limits of the Possible (1962)
Indian Ocean Treasure, with Mike Wilson (1964)
Man and Space, with the editors of *Life* (1964)
Voices from the Sky: Previews of the Coming Space Age (1965)
The Promise of Space (1968)
First on the Moon, with Neil Armstrong, Michael Collins, Edwin E. Aldrin Jr., Gene
    Farmer, and Dora Jane Hamblin (1970)
Beyond Jupiter, with Chesley Bonestell (1972)
Report on Planet Three and Other Speculations (1972)
The View from Serendip (1977)
Arthur C. Clarke's Mysterious World, with Simon Welfare and John Fairley (1980)
1984: Spring—A Choice of Futures (1984)
Arthur C. Clarke's World of Strange Powers, with Simon Welfare and John Fairley
    (1984)
*Ascent to Orbit, a Scientific Autobiography: The Technical Writings of Arthur C.
    Clarke* (1984)

The Odyssey File, with Peter Hyams (1985)

Arthur C. Clarke's July 20, 2019: Life in the 21st Century (1986)

Arthur C. Clarke's Chronicles of the Strange and Mysterious, edited by Simon Welfare and John Fairley (1987)

Astounding Days: A Science Fiction Autobiography (1989)

Opus 700 (1990)

How the World Was One; Beyond the Global Village (1992)

By Space Possessed (1993)

The Apollo 11 Moon Landing (1994)

Arthur C. Clarke's A–Z of Mysteries (1994)

The Colors of Infinity (1994)

The Snows of Olympus: A Garden on Mars (1995)

The Supernatural A–Z, with James Randi (1995)

Rama: The Official Strategy Guide (1996)

Macroshift: Navigating the Transformation to a Sustainable World (1997)

Arthur C. Clarke and Lord Dunsany: A Correspondence, with Lord Dunsany (1998)

Arthur C. Clarke's Mysteries, with John Fairley (1998)

Greetings, Carbon-Based Bipeds! (1999)

Welcome to the Wired World; The New Networked Economy (1999)

Sri Lanka: The Emerald Island (2000)

Arthur C. Clarke and C. S. Lewis: A Correspondence, with C. S. Lewis (2001)

Moonwatcher's Memoir: A Diary of 2001, a Space Odyssey, with Dan Richter (2002)

From Narnia to a Space Odyssey: The War Letters Between Arthur C. Clarke and C. S. Lewis (2003)

Editor

The Coming of the Space Age: Famous Accounts of Man's Probing of the Universe (1967)

Motion Pictures and Television Series Based on the Author's Works

2001: A Space Odyssey (1968)

Arthur C. Clarke's Mysterious World (1980)

Arthur C. Clarke's World of Strange Powers (1984)

For Further Information

Allen, Jamie. CNN Interactive. *http://www.cnn.com/2000/books/news/02/02/clakr .baxter/* (viewed April 20, 2003).

Arthur C. Clarke biography. ACC Biography. *http://library/thinkquest.org/27864 .data/clarke/acebio/html* (viewed April 20, 2003).

Arthur C. Clarke biography. The Vision of Arthur C. Clarke Web page. *http://www .sciencemuseum.org/uk/on-line/clarke/biog.asp* (viewed April 20, 2003).

Brandreth, Tyles. "Space Odyssey's visionary has new predictions for the future." *London Sunday Telegraph. http://pub23.exboard.com/fmonsffafrm7.show Message?topicalID=2.topic* (viewed April 20, 2003).

Cherry, Matt. "A Chat With Arthur C. Clarke." Council for Secular Humanism. *http://www.secularhumanism.org/library/fi/clarke_19_2.html* (viewed April 20, 2003).

Coker, John L. III. "A Visit With Arthur C. Clarke." *Locus Magazine* (September 1999).

David, Leonard. "Arthur C. Clarke Stands By His Belief in Life on Mars." *http:// www.space/com/peopleinterviews/clarke_mars_010601.html* (viewed April 20, 2003).

Hollow, John. *Against the Night, the Stars: The Science Fiction of Arthur C. Clarke.* New York: Harcourt, 1983; Athens, OH: Ohio University Press, 1987, expanded.

Houston, Frank. Arthur C. Clarke biography. Salon.com. *http://dir.salon.com/people/ bc/2000/03/07/clarke/index.html* (viewed April 20, 2003).

Jonas, Gerald. *Time's Eye* review. *New York Times Book Review* (January 4, 2004).

McAleer, Neil. *Arthur C. Clarke: The Authorized Biography.* Chicago: Contemporary Books, 1992.

Moskowitz, Sam. *Seekers of Tomorrow: Masters of Science Fiction.* New York: World Publishing, 1966.

Olander, Joseph D., and Martin H. Greenberg, eds. *Arthur C. Clarke.* New York: Taplinger, 1977.

Peacock, Scot, ed. Arthur C. Clarke entry, *Contemporary Authors New Revision* Series. Vol. 74. Detroit: Gale Research, 1999.

Rabkin, Eric S. *Arthur C. Clarke.* San Bernardino, CA: Starmont House, 1979.

Rabkin, Eric S. Arthur C. Clarke entry, *Twentieth-Century Science-Fiction Writers.* 3rd edition, edited by Noelle Watson and Paul E. Schellinger. Chicago: St. James Press, 1991.

Jackie Collins

◆ Romance ◆ Women's fiction

London, England
1941

◆ *Chances*

About the Author and the Author's Writing

Joseph Collins, a theatrical booking agent in London, was determined that his two daughters would find homes on the stage. Joan Collins, indeed, would go on to become a Hollywood star. But her sister, Jackie Collins, found more appeal in the written word and became a best-selling novelist.

Jackie Collins was born in London in 1941. By age eight she was writing stories. Suffering a rebellious adolescence, she was expelled from school when she was fifteen. She left home and married Wallace Austin in 1959, and they had two children. They divorced after four years.

In 1966, she married nightclub owner Oscar Lerman, but he died in 1992. Later in the 1990s, her fiancé of five years, shopping mall developer Frank Calcagnini, died of cancer. Her recent companion has been producer Arnold Kopelson.

Collins had followed her sister to Los Angeles, hoping for a career in films. (Joan, it should be noted, has also written some fiction, beginning with *Prime Time* in 1988.) Jackie wrote her first novel of power, lust, and violence in Hollywood, drawing on her own and her sister's experiences, in 1968, and *The World Is Full of Married Men* became a huge hit, the first of several.

"The important thing is I get people into the bookstores who probably wouldn't be there otherwise," she told Books and Writers.

Her novels are about the American dream, the author told another interviewer. *Hollywood Husbands*, typically is about talk show host Jack Python, Orpheus Studios maven Howard Soloman, and movie star Mannon Cable, all multiply divorced and multiply jaded, but all taken with copper-haired Jade Johnson. The author followed this with the aptly titled *Hollywood Kids* and *Hollywood Wives*.

The multitalented author has not restricted her career to the printed word. Several of Collins's works have been adapted for the screen, and she has also served as executive producer for the *Lucky* and *Chances* miniseries. In 1998, she had her own talk show, "Jackie Collins Hollywood," but ended it after eight weeks and seventy-five celebrity guests because it allowed her no time to write. She has even released her own CD, *Lethal Seductions; A Compilation of Jackie's Favorite Singers.*

The Hollywood character Lucky Santangelo has proved an enduring Collins creation. After first appearing in *Chances* in 1981, she has returned for further adventures, including in *Lady Boss* (1989), in which she takes charge of Panther Studios. Lucky is in a longtime struggle with the Bonnatti family, which, in *Vendetta*, kidnaps her husband, Lennie Golden.

"The Lucky series bring[s] together all the required ingredients of a Collins cocktail: the rich and famous, the shifty Hollywood shenanigans, scheming opportunists and a bug-on-the-wall vantage point of every—or every other—bedroom in the 90210 zip code," claims a Meet the Writers column on the Barnes & Noble Web site.

A second Collins series features Madison Castelli, a journalist introduced in *L.A. Connections*, who is less wild than Lucky but is struggling in her relationship with her father Michael Castelli.

Calling herself an instinctive, self-taught writer, Collins said in an iVillage interview, "I don't believe in writing anything that I don't know about or haven't researched about personally. I like to transport the reader to places, and in order to do that I have to do the research." She often bases characters on famous people—but mixes their traits and won't tell who is who. She said she often falls in love with her characters, even the villains.

She has an idea of what a book will be about before she begins putting words to paper—she had to research the early 1900s before she started *Chances*, for example—but doesn't necessarily know where the writing will take her. Working from a study in her home, the author usually starts at 6:30 in the morning and writes all day, with soul music playing in the background. It can take nine months to a year to complete a book. She writes the first draft, an assistant types it, and Collins does further editing, sometimes several times before she is satisfied.

Collins said her own favorite authors these days are Elmore Leonard, Robert B. Parker, and Laurence Shames—fast-paced, male-oriented fiction writers, but ones remindful of her own work, with honest and direct relationships.

Collins is often identified with a racy prose. During the Bill Clinton impeachment hearings, "Everybody said that the Monica Lewinsky stuff in the Starr report was like a Jackie Collins book," the author told the *Chicago Tribune* in 2001. "But if I'd written it, the sex would have been better."

The Arts & Entertainment television network in 2002 declared Collins one of the "15 Sexiest People in the 20th Century." Collins views such designations with a bit of amusement, recalling how she was raising three small children when she traveled to promote her first book: "There I am, supposedly this big sex writer from London, and I'm in Chicago with three little kids in the room behind me," she mused to *Entertainment Weekly's* Rebecca Ascher-Walsh.

Are her books too sexy? "It's extremely amusing because there is so much sex on TV now," the author said in a Simon & Schuster Web page interview. "My novels should not shock people, yet they do. Is it because I'm a woman writing about sex? Or is it because people feel sex is much more personal when it's captured in a book? I don't know. I only know that I prefer writing erotic sex to rude sex, and also, I write great married sex—contrary to popular belief, that does take place."

Works by the Author

Fiction

The World Is Full of Married Men (1968)
The Stud (1970)
Sinners (1971)
Sunday Simmons and Charlie Brick (1971), retitled *The Hollywood Zoo* (1975)
Lovehead (1974), retitled *The Love Killers* (1975)
The World Is Full of Divorced Women (1975)
Lovers and Gamblers (1977)
The Bitch (1979)
Hollywood Husbands (1986)
Rock Star (1988)
American Star: A Love Story (1993)
Hollywood Kids (1994)
Thrill! (1998)
Hollywood Wives: The New Generation (2001), sequel to *Hollywood Wives*
Hollywood Divorces (2003)

L.A. Connection Series

Obsession (1998)
Murder (1998)
Power (1998)
Revenge (1998)
L.A. Connection (1999)

Madison Castelli Series

Lethal Seduction (2000)
Deadly Embrace (2002)

Lucky Santangelo Series

Chances (1981)
Lucky (1985)
Lady Boss (1990)
Vendetta: Lucky's Revenge (1996)
Dangerous Kiss (1999)

Screenplay

Yesterday's Hero (1979)

Motion Pictures and Television Movies Based on the Author's Works

Hollywood Wives (1985)
Hollywood Kids
The Stud (1978)
The Bitch (1979)
The World Is Full of Married Men (1979)
Lucky/Chances (1990)
Lady Boss (1992)
Jackie Collins' Hollywood Wives: The New Generation (2003)

For Further Information

Ascher-Walsh, Rebecca. "L.A. Confidential: Once Again, Novelist Jackie Collins Dives Into the Steamy Love Lives of Hollywood's Beautiful People." *Entertainment Weekly* (August 3, 2001).

Collins, Joan. *Past Imperfect: An Autobiography*. New York: Simon & Schuster, 1984.

Crimp, Susan. *Hollywood Sisters; Jackie and Joan Collins*. New York: St. Martin's, 1989.

Hughes, Cassidy. *Sex, Death, Glitter and Lots of Money: Jackie Collins and the Blockbuster Novel*. New York: Hyperion, 1992.

Jackie Collins biography. Barnes & Noble Meet the Writers. *http://www.barnesandnoble.com/writers/writerdetails.asp?userid=0H4KV3ZHMT&cid=115590#bio* (viewed April 20, 2003).

Jackie Collins biography. Books and Writers. *http://www.kirjasto.sci.fi/jcollins.htm* (viewed April 20, 2003).

Jackie Collins biography. SimonSays.com. *http://www.simonsays./com/subs/txtobj.cfm?areaid=13&pagename=bio* (viewed April 20, 2003).

Jackie Collins interview. SimonSays.com. *http://www.simonsays.com/subs/txtobj.cfm?areaid=13&pagename=qa* (viewed April 20, 2003).

Jackie Collins Web site. *http://www.jackiecollins.com/* (viewed April 20, 2003).

"Jackie Collins: The Importance of Sex." ivillage.com. *http://www.ivillage.com/books/intervu/romance/articles/0,,192503_87890,00.html* (viewed April 20, 2003).

Jones, Daniel, and John D. Jorgenson, eds. Jackie Collins entry, *Contemporary Authors New Revision Series*. Vol. 64. Detroit: Gale Research, 1998.

Maryles, Daisy. "Embraced by her fans." *Publishers Weekly* (June 24, 2002).

Bernard Cornwell

◆ Historical ◆ Adventure

London, England
1944

◆ *Richard Sharpe Series*

About the Author and the Author's Writing

Richard Sharpe, the maverick officer in Lord Wellington's British army, through his courageousness and daring (it didn't hurt that he once saved Wellington's life) has risen rapidly in rank during the nineteenth-century colonial confrontations in India and the Napoleonic Peninsular Wars and goes on to best enemies on battlefields in Chile. An orphan who honed his survival skills as a youth, he is at times an amoral character.

"In the character of Richard Sharpe, the grim, scarred rifle officer commissioned from the ranks, [author Bernard] Cornwell has created a fitting hero for his canon," praised Geoffrey Sadler in *Twentieth-Century Romance and Historical Authors*. "Low-born and illegitimate, a ruthless professional soldier, Sharpe is convincingly presented as a man of strong and complex desires, his unremitting hatred for the enemy counter-balanced by his fierce attachment to the men under his command, his physical lusts matched by an austere code of honour from which he never deviates."

Richard Sharpe was born in a basement flat on Cortnell Street in London one winter's night in 1980. His creator, Bernard Cornwell, was planning to marry an American and settle in that country, but he was ineligible for a green card. He decided his best recourse was to become a writer. He had a firm idea of who he wanted to write about: an adventurer in the C. S. Forester mold, only his character would be a soldier rather than a sailor. He had years before formed this hero in his mind, as an escape from his oppressive childhood.

"I wasted hours trying to find my hero's name," he said on the Sharpe Appreciation Society Web site. "I wanted a name as dramatic as Horatio Hornblower, but I couldn't think of one (Trumpetwhistler? Cornetpuffer?)." Figuring it would be temporary, Cornwell began writing using the name of a well-known rugby player, Richard Sharp, adding an "e" on the end. It stuck. The first tale garnered Cornwell a seven-book contract.

The author initially figured he would follow his hero through the Waterloo campaign, not reckoning with reader demand—particularly with the television portrayal of the character by actor Sean Bean. The author has since expanded the series and has many more adventures in mind.

Cornwell was born in London in 1944, a "war baby" of a Canadian airman father and a British Women's Auxiliary Air Force mother, who was married, had children, and was waiting for her husband to return from the front. Left at an orphanage, Cornwell was adopted and raised by a family in Essex. His adoptive family belonged to the strict fundamentalist Peculiar People religious sect.

"With hindsight, I do have things to be grateful to my parents for," he said in an interview with Charles Laurence. "I learnt from them that childhood is a trap and that growing up is learning how to get out of it. And a seventeenth-century mentality has proved useful to a historical novelist."

His adoptive father was a thriving contractor who sent the rebellious Cornwell to Monkton Combe boarding school. After attending London University (where he received a bachelor of arts degree in 1967), Cornwell broke ties with his family and taught for a time. He joined BBC Television and worked for a decade as a researcher and producer. He married and divorced his first wife, with whom he had one child.

Cornwell became head of Current Affairs Television in Northern Ireland, 1976–1979. He then became a television news editor for Thames Television's "Thames at Six" in London, 1979–1980. It was in Belfast that he met the woman who became his wife, Judy Acker, a travel agent with three children from a previous marriage. They wed in 1980 and moved to Cape Cod in Massachusetts. Cornwell continued to pursue his writing—for which he did not need a work permit—and he later became an American citizen.

The author has long held a fascination with history. Besides the Sharpe books, he has written about Nathaniel Starbuck in stories set during the American Civil War and about King Arthur. His Thomas of Hookton books are about a fourteenth-century archer in the English army who quests for the religious relic stolen from his village church. All show meticulous research, sometimes taking the author to such locations as northern France.

There's quite a bit of establish-your-characters-and-let-them-go in Cornwell's series, he acknowledged in a HarperCollins Internet interview. Describing his book *Harlequin*, he said, "I had no idea what was going to happen until I wrote it down. Well, I knew it was going to Crecy . . . I always think for readers the joy of reading is finding out what happens. Basically it's the same with writing—you sit down every morning and find out what is going to happen."

Cornwell's characters joke, drink, carouse, and fall in love. "I have a firm belief that human nature doesn't change," he told the interviewer at Bookselling This Week's Web site, "though the people might just have different circumstances."

His research sometimes surprises him, Cornwell said in the same interview. When working on *Stonehenge*, for example, he learned archers in 2000 B.C. had longbows made of the same yew used centuries later. The technology changed little; it was simple and deadly.

Each morning that he is writing, the author said he reviews the previous day's work. When the manuscript is completed, he evaluates it again. Cornwell works nine-and-a-half-hour days much of the year, if not researching or writing, then promoting. For two months every summer, he hoists sail on his twenty-four-foot Cornish crabber, *Royalist*, and takes to sea.

Cornwell has also written a trio of books with his wife (issued under the name Susannah Kells), some of which have been reissued under his name. Some early books were issued under the Michael Joseph name. The few other historical writers he reads are Patrick O'Brian and George MacDonald Fraser.

Dismissing his writing as not being hard work, he told *January Magazine* reporter Linda Richards that he is a storyteller, not a literary stylist. "From the time I was 14, 15 [it was] all I wanted to do. I thought it would be great; better than working. it's true, it is. It's *much* better than working. You sit down and you tell stories. It's *fun* . . . My great fear is that I'll be caught out."

Works by the Author

Fiction

Redcoat (1988)
Wildtrack (1988)
Sea Lord (1989), in the United Kingdom as *Killer's Wake* (1989)
Crackdown (1990), in the United Kingdom as *Murder Cay* (1990)
Stormchild (1991)
Scoundrel (1993)
Stonehenge (2000)
Gallows Thief (2002)

Grail Quest Series

Harlequin (2001), in the United States as *The Archer's Tale*
Vagabond (2002)
Heretic (2003)

Nathaniel Starbuck Series

Rebel (1983)
Copperhead: Ball's Bluff 1862 (1994)
Battle Flag (1995)
The Bloody Ground: Battle of Antietam, 1862 (1996)

Richard Sharpe Series

Sharpe's Eagle: Richard Sharpe and the Talavera Campaign, July 1809 (1981)
Sharpe's Gold: Richard Sharpe and the Destruction of Almeida, August 1810 (1981)
Sharpe's Company: Richard Sharpe and the Siege of Badajoz, January to April 1812 (1982)
Sharpe's Enemy: Richard Sharpe and the Defense of Portugal, Christmas, 1812 (1983)
Sharpe's Sword: Richard Sharpe and the Salamanca Campaign, June and July, 1812 (1983)
Sharpe's Honor: Richard Sharpe and the Victoria Campaign, February to June, 1813 (1985)
Sharpe's Regiment: Richard Sharpe and the Invasion of France, June to November 1913 (1986)

Sharpe's Siege: Richard Sharpe and the Winter Campaign, 1814 (1987)
Sharpe's Rifles: Richard Sharpe and the French Invasion of Galicia, January 1809 (1988)
Sharpe's Revenge: Richard Sharpe and the Peace of 1814 (1989)
Sharpe's Waterloo: Richard Sharpe and the Waterloo Campaign, 15 June to 18 June 1815 (1990)
Sharpe's Devil: Richard Sharpe and the Emperor, 1820–1821 (1992)
Sharpe's Battle: Richard Sharpe and the Battle of Fuentes de Onoro, May, 1811 (1995)
Sharpe's Tiger: Richard Sharpe and the Siege of Seringapatam, 1799 (1997)
Sharpe's Triumph: Richard Sharpe and the Battle of Assaye, September 1803 (1998)
Sharpe's Fortress: Richard Sharpe and the Siege of Gawlighur, December 1803, 1803 (1999)
Sharpe's Trafalgar: Richard Sharpe and the Battle of Trafalgar, October 1805 (2001)
Sharpe's Prey: Richard Sharpe and the Siege of Copenhagen, 1807 (2002)
Sharpe's Skirmish (2002)
Sharpe's Christmas (2003), short stories
Sharpe's Havoc Richard Sharpe and the Campaign in Northern Portugal, Spring 1809 (2003)
Sharpe's Escape: *Richard Sharpe and the Bussaco Campaign, 1810* (2004)

Warlord Trilogy

The Winter King: A Novel of Arthur (1996)
Enemy of God: A Novel of Arthur (1997)
Excalibur: A Novel of Arthur (1997)

Written as Susannah Kells, with Judy Cornwell

A Crowning Mercy (1983), later editions as by Bernard Cornwell and Susannah Kells
The Fallen Angels (1984), later editions as by Bernard Cornwell and Susannah Kells
Coat of Arms (1986), in the United States as *Aristocrats*

BBC Television Movies Based on Cornwell Books

Sharpe's Battle
Sharpe's Company
Sharpe's Eagle
Sharpe's Enemy
Sharpe's Gold
Sharpe's Honour
Sharpe's Justice
Sharpe's Mission
Sharpe's Regiment
Sharpe's Revenge

Sharpe's Rifles
Sharpe's Siege
Sharpe's Sword
Sharpe's Waterloo

For Further Information

"Bernard Cornwell Brings History to Life." Bestselling This Week. *http://news.bookweb.org/features/989.html* (viewed May 8, 2003).

Bernard Cornwell interview. HarperCollins. *http://www.fireandwater.com/Authors/interview.asp?interviewid=147* (viewed May 8, 2003).

Bernard Cornwell Web site. *http://www.bernardcornwell.net/* (viewed May 8, 2003).

Heretic review. *Publishers Weekly* (August 11, 2003).

Kenney, Michael. "From Cape Cod, he plots Napoleonic Wars; Bernard Cornwell has become military fiction's Sharpe-shooter." *Boston Globe* (July 30, 1996).

Lawrence, Charles. "Bernard Cornwell Interview." *Daily Telegraph* (April 14, 2000). *http://www.comleatseanbean.com/cornwell2.html* (viewed May 8, 2003).

Peacock, Scot, ed. Bernard Cornwell entry, *Contemporary Authors New Revision Series*. Vol. 92. Detroit: Gale Research, 2000.

Richards, Linda. "January Interview Bernard Richards." *January Magazine.* *http://www.januarymagazine.com/profiles./bcornwell.html* (viewed May 8, 2003).

Sadler, Geoffrey. Bernard Cornwell entry, *Twentieth-Century Romance and Historical Writers*. 2nd edition, edited by Lesley Henderson. Chicago: St. James Press, 1990.

Sharpe Appreciation Society Web page. *http://www.bernardcornwellbooks.com/bio/html* (viewed May 8, 2003).

Sharpe's Havoc review. *Library Journal* (April 15, 2003).

Sharpe television movies. Napoleonic Guide. *http://www.napoleonguide.com/sharpe/htm* (viewed May 8, 2003).

Patricia Cornwell

◆ Mystery

Miami, Florida
1956

◆ *Dr. Kay Scarpetta Series*

About the Author and the Author's Writing

In 1991, Patricia Cornwell's first novel, *Postmortem*, took the crime writing world by storm, pocketing her Edgar, John Creasey, Anthony and Macavity Awards—as well as the Prix du Roman d'Adventure. Over the next decade she became firmly entrenched as one of the most fascinating new talents of the mystery genre.

Patricia Daniels was born in 1956 in Miami, Florida, the daughter of an attorney and a secretary. Her parents divorced when she was seven, and Patricia and two siblings moved with their mother to North Carolina. In 1979, she received a bachelor of arts degree in literature from Davidson College. She married Charles Cornwell in 1980, but they divorced a decade later. The author now lives in Greenwich, Connecticut.

Patricia was a crime reporter for the *Charlotte Observer* in North Carolina from 1979 to 1981, and she also squeezed in time to write a nonfiction book. Her biography of Ruth Bell Graham, the wife of evangelist Rev. Billy Graham, came out in 1983. Cornwell grew up living just down the road from the Grahams, got to know Ruth Graham as a teenager, and heeded Graham's urging to start writing short stories and poetry. The friendship is reminiscent of Cornwell's featured character Dr. Kay Scarpetta's mentoring relationship with her gay niece, Lucy, in later books.

From 1985 to 1991, Cornwell worked as a computer analyst in the office of the chief medical examiner in Richmond, Virginia. This experience, as well as her earlier service as a volunteer police officer for the city of Richmond, provided plenty of background for a crime novel. The author witnessed autopsies, attended medical school lectures, sat in on trials, and conducted research in medical libraries.

In the meantime, Cornwell wrote three fiction manuscripts that never sold. Then *Postmortem*, the first book in her Scarpetta series, found a publisher. *Postmortem* follows the chief medical examiner, her right-hand Detective Sergeant Pete Marino, and the Richmond police as they pursue a serial killer who has brutalized and strangled three women in their own bedrooms.

For *Postmortem*, Cornwell received a $7,500 advance in a two-book contract. Soon afterward, she inked a deal for *Body of Evidence* paperback rights for $385,000. And by the late 1990s, she received $24 million for three Scarpetta books in a package with Putnam's.

Cornwell's work has a strong ring of authenticity. "One of the reasons I've been fortunate enough to have access to a lot of places [including the FBI's Quantico headquarters] is because I have a platform of legitimacy from my profession and background," the author told Paul Duncan for *Mystery Scene*.

Although Cornwell has modeled some of her characters on real people (including Utah Senator Orrin Hatch, Virginia's chief medical examiner Marcella F. Fierro, and forensic anthropologist William Bass), Scarpetta herself is all fabrication—or perhaps she is Cornwell herself. Discussing *The Last Precinct* in an iVillage interview, the author asserted that the story "is a crime scene because she was almost killed, and she is now a victim of a murder investigation. The important thing is, because of all the scrutiny Kay is undergoing, she is forced to reveal much of herself. . . . I've done so much research on Kay that, by revealing so much of her, you'll find out more about me."

In 1995, Cornwell herself was thrown into the spotlight when an FBI agent attempted to kill his wife after he suspected she had had a brief affair with Cornwell. "That episode, says Cornwell, gave her the 'thick skin' she needs to stand up to her critics," according to Galina Espinoza's profile of the author in *People Weekly*.

Cornwell is very close to Scarpetta and her other regular characters, but has no interest in becoming so intimate with her villains. "These people are not an abstraction," she told Rosemary Herbert in *The Armchair Detective*. "They are evil to me, and I do not want them to connect with me at all. And I think that, when you've seen enough of the signatures of that, when you've seen enough of the signatures of what they do, if you've been to the crime scenes, you've seen the bodies, and you have talked with the profilers, *believe you me*, if you've got any intuition at all, you can piece together what you're dealing with, and that's about as close as I want to get."

The supremely villainous Temple Brooks Gault plays a role in three Scarpetta novels beginning with *Cruel & Unusual*. In 1997, the author began a second series featuring the Charlotte Police Chief Judy Hammer.

Cornwell returned to nonfiction in 2002 with *Portrait of a Killer*, her take on the Jack the Ripper crime spree of 1880s London. The book generated some controversy. It concludes the perpetrator was a respected artist of his day, Walter Sickert, in large part based on tests made on some 250 letters (some of them certainly fakes) in Scotland Yard files, sent by Jack the Ripper to police. Some letters were written on the same paper as stationery the painter Sickert used.

Though she obviously relished the detective work—and purportedly spent an estimated $6 million of her own money in the investigation—Cornwell with some relief reentered the imaginary world and the writing of another Scarpetta case in 2003.

Works by the Author

Fiction

Judy Hammer and Andy Brazil Series

Hornet's Nest (1997)
Southern Cross (1999)
Isle of Dogs (2001)

Dr. Kay Scarpetta Series

Body of Evidence (1991)
Postmortem (1991)
All That Remains (1992)
Cruel & Unusual (1993), first of Gault trilogy
The Body Farm (1994), second of Gault trilogy
From Potter's Field (1995), third of Gault trilogy
Cause of Death (1996)
Three Complete Novels (1997), includes *Postmortem*, *Body of Evidence*, and *All That Remains*
Unnatural Exposure (1997)
Point of Origin (1998)
Black Notice (1999)
The Last Precinct (2000)
Blow Fly (2003)
Trace (2004)

Nonfiction

A Time for Remembering: The Story of Ruth Bell Graham (1983), retitled *Ruth, a Portrait: The Ruth Bell Graham Story* (1997)
Food to Die For: Secrets from Kay Scarpetta's Kitchen, with Marlene Brown (2001)
Portrait of a Killer: Jack the Ripper—Case Closed (2002)

Anthologies

The Writing Life: Writers on How they Think and Work, edited by Marie Arana (2003)

For Further Information

Beahm, George. *The Unofficial Patricia Cornwell Companion: A Guide to the Best-selling Author's Life and Work*. New York: St. Martin's Minotaur, 2002.

Chapman, Jeff, Pamela S. Dear, and John D. Jorgenson, eds. Patricia Cornwell entry, *Contemporary Authors New Revision Series*. Vol. 53. Detroit, Gale Research, 1997.

Cornwell, Patricia. "Black Notice." *http://www.familyhaven.com/books/blacknotice .html* (viewed May 13, 2003).

Duncan, Paul. "Patricia Cornwell: Verbal Evidence." *Mystery Scene*, no. 57 (1997).

Espinoza, Galina, with Diane Herbst. "Killer Instinct: Author Patricia Cornwell thinks she has unmasked a notorious serial killer. Critics say she doesn't know Jack." *People Weekly* (December 9, 2002).

Herbert, Rosemary. "All That Remains." *The Armchair Detective* (fall 1992).

"Meet the Author: Patricia Cornwell." BookPage. *http://www.bookpage.com/9908bp/ patricia_cornwell.html* (viewed May 13, 2003).

Muller, Adrian. Patricia Cornwell entry, *St. James Guide to Crime & Mystery Writers.* 4th edition, edited by Jay P. Pederson. Detroit: St. James Press, 1996.

Patricia Cornwell: A Reader's Checklist and Reference Guide. CheckerBee, 1999.

Patricia Cornwell Web site. *http://www.patriciacornwell.com/about_main.html* (viewed May 13, 2003).

Patricia Cornwell Web page, Bastulli Mystery Library. *http://www.bastulli.com/ Cornwell/CORNWELL.htm* (viewed May 13, 2003).

"Patricia Cornwell: Kay and I Went Through the Same Pain." iVillage. *http://www .ivillage.com/books/intervu/myst/articles/0,11872,240795_192641,00.html* (viewed May 13, 2003).

"Q&A With Patricia Cornwell." ABCNews.com. *http://abcnews.go.com/sections/ primetime/2020/PrimetimeQA_010111_patriciacornwell_feature.html* (viewed May 13, 2003).

Catherine Coulter

◆ Historical ◆ Romance ◆ Romantic suspense ◆ Mystery

London, England
1934

◆ *Devil's Embrace*

About the Author and the Author's Writing

Author Catherine Coulter does her homework, especially when writing one of her popular crime thrillers. "You try your best to get this stuff right," she said in an interview with Brianna Yamashita, "but sometimes it's impossible. Sometimes, when I can't grind something out, I'll think, 'If I were the FBI, what would I do in this case?' And then I think, 'Well, we're dealing with a huge bureaucracy.' So I always do the opposite of what common sense would dictate. I have some readers in the FBI, but they're forgiving."

Known as a genre-jumper, Coulter began writing mysteries after exhausting her romantic suspense energies, though she still alternates mysteries with her historicals. The Texas-born author's first novel, *The Autumn Countess*, was published in 1978. She chose to write a Regency romance because "as any publisher will tell you, it's best to limit the unknowns in a first book, and not only had I grown up reading Georgette Heyer, but I earned my M.A. degree in nineteenth-century European history," she said on the Authors on the Web site. She wrote a half dozen more Regencies before completing her first long historical, *Devil's Embrace*. She continued in that genre until she moved into the present century with *False Pretenses* in 1988.

"My major period is the Napoleonic Era," the author told *Contemporary Authors*, "or that period between 1800 and 1820. To combine history with the relationship between two people is always enjoyable, and sitting down at my computer every morning isn't a chore, believe me. Also, learning about a new time period and a new place is not only hours of research but also fun, pure and simple fun."

The daughter of a painter/singer and a concert pianist/organist, the author grew up on a horse ranch. She graduated from the University of Texas and received her master's degree from Boston College. She traveled in Europe, and then, as she always found writing easy, she took a job writing speeches for the president of a company on Wall Street before becoming a full-time fiction writer. (Or, as she has said in one interview, those speeches were actually fiction as well.)

She began writing novels while her husband Anton attended medical school at Columbia Presbyterian. Reading romance after romance, she threw one aside in disgust and swore she would write one better. She and her husband worked out the plot for *The Autumn Countess* and she wrote it in six months. The first editor she sent it to accepted it and offered a three-book contract.

Now living in Marin County, California, the author said each of the genres she works in requires different writing approaches. In addition to settings and characters, she has to be particularly careful of plot consistencies with the mysteries. She feels more comfortable placing eccentric characters in the historicals than in the procedurals.

She didn't set out to create a series around Lacey Sherlock and Dillon Savich. Rather, Savich was a secondary character in her first crime book, *The Cove*, and Sherlock appeared in the second, *The Maze*. They made an obvious team. In the recent *Eleventh Hour*, for example, the married couple joins FBI Agent Dane Carver to solve the killing of Father Michael Joseph. The only witness is "Nick" Jones, a homeless woman with a past. In *Blindside*, the pair momentarily abandon their pursuit of a serial killer to intercede in a kidnapping case involving the son of a friend.

Whether set in the past or present, there is a bit of Coulter in each of her books. "Particularly in the heroine," she told Gabrielle Saveri for *People Weekly*. "There's always some of you in your main character." The author added that she believes in happy endings. "I like reaffirming that to love somebody is a good thing." She also revisits old characters, even in the historicals, because she likes to see what they've been up to, she said in one interview. Coulter shuns graphic sex scenes, but that doesn't mean she doesn't include plenty of sensuality.

How are her romances different? "I aim for humor," she said in a *Charlotte Austin Review* interview, "and for people who are very, very real and not just so utterly 'perfect' in both mind and body. I try to always write cleanly, clearly, and crisply. I like to laugh; falling in love should be filled with fun. . . . Keep the reader guessing, I guess that's something I always try to do. If you can go in two directions, always chose the road less traveled."

Works by the Author

Fiction

The Autumn Countess (1979), rewritten as *The Countess* (1999)
The Rebel Bride (1979)
Lord Deverill's Heir (1980), retitled *The Heir* (1996)
Lord Harry's Folly (1980), rewritten as *Lord Harry* (1995)
The Generous Earl (1981), also titled *The Duke* (1995)
The Devil's Embrace (1982)
Devil's Daughter (1985), sequel to *Devil's Daughter*
False Pretenses (1989)
Impulse (1990)
Beyond Eden (1992)
Warrior's Song (2001)

FBI Agent Series

The Cove (1996)
The Maze (1997)
The Target (1998)
The Edge (1999)
Riptide (2000)
Hemlock Bay (2001)
Eleventh Hour (2002)
Blindside (2003)
Blowout (2004)

Haraldsson Viking Series

Season in the Sun (1991)
Lord of Hawkfall Island (1993)
Lord of Raven's Peak (1994)
Lord of Falcon Ridge (1995)

Legacy Series

The Nightingale Legacy (1994)
The Wyndam Legacy (1994)
The Valentine Legacy (1995)

Magic Series

Midsummer Magic (1987)
Calypso Magic (1988)
Moonspun Magic (1988)

Night Series

Night Fire (1989)
Night Shadow (1989)
Night Storm (1990)

Sherbrooke Bride Series

The Hellion Bride (1992)
The Sherbrooke Bride (1992)
The Heiress Bride (1993)
Mad Jack (1999)
The Courtship (2000)
The Scottish Bride (2001)
Pendragon (2002)
Sherbrooke Twins (2004)

Silhouette Intimate Moments Series

Aftershocks (1986)
Afterglow (1987), sequel to *Aftershocks*

Silhouette Special Edition

The Aristocrat (1986)

Song Series

Chandra (1984), retitled *Warrior's Song* (2001)
Fire Song (1985)
Earth Song (1990)
Secret Song (1991)
Rosehaven (1996)
The Penwyth Curse (2003)

Star Series

Sweet Surrender (1984), revised as *Evening Star* (1996)
Midnight Star (1986)
Jade Star (1987)
Wild Star (1987)

Trilogy

An Honorable Offer (1981), retitled *The Offer* (2003)
An Intimate Deception (1983), retitled *The Deception* (2003)
The Wild Baron (1997)

Anthologies

Forever Yours (2000)

For Further Information

Austin, Charlotte. Catherine Coulter interview, *Charlotte Austin Review*. *http://collection.nlc-bnc/100/202/300/charlotte/2000/07-31/pages/interviews/authors/catherinecoulter.htm* (viewed June 13, 2003).

Blindside review. *Publishers Weekly* (June 30, 2003).

Catherine Coulter entry, Contemporary Authors Online (2003). Biography Resource Center. *http://www.galenet.com/servlet/BioRC* (viewed June 27, 2003).

Catherine Coulter interview. A Romance Review. *http://www.aromancereview.com/interviews/catherinecoulter.phtml* (viewed June 13, 2003).

Catherine Coulter Web site. *http://www.catherinecoulter.com* (viewed June 12, 2003).

Catherine R. Coulter biography. Authors on the Web. *http://www.authorsontheweb.com/features/authormonth/0207coulter/coulter-catherine.asp* (viewed June 13, 2003).

Maryles, Daisy. "Coulter Rides the Tide." *Publishers Weekly* (July 24, 2000).

Saveri, Gabrielle. "Loving the love stuff." *People Weekly* (September 23, 1996).

Yamashita, Brianna. "From history to mystery: A genre-jumper explains." *Publishers Weekly* (June 30, 2003).

Robert Crais

◆ Mystery

Baton Rouge, Louisiana
1954

◆ *Elvis Cole Series*

Credit: Patrik Giardino.

About the Author and the Author's Writing

Robert Crais honed his mystery-writing skills producing scripts for a variety of crime action television programs in the 1970s and 1980s—*Baretta, Vega$, Quincy, M.E., Joe Dancer, Hill Street Blues* (for which he received an Emmy nomination), *Cagney & Lacy, L.A. Law, Miami Vice*, and *The Equalizer* among them—and he continues to write for shows such as *Earth II* and *JAG*.

Robert Crais was born in 1954, in Baton Rouge, Louisiana, where many of his family members were police officers or worked for an oil refinery. Thus, the darker side of his adopted Los Angeles comes from experiences moving there in 1976. "My Los Angeles is different from [Raymond] Chandler's," Crais stated in an interview with Nick Hasted in 2001. "It's more ethnically diverse now, there are places which are purely Chinese, Vietnamese, Lithuanian. But it always has been a feeding ground where people from all over the world come, hungry to reach their dreams. And any time you have so many people risking so much, there's a potential for crisis, and crime."

Indeed, Los Angles has changed, and Crais's hip hero Elvis Cole is a far cry from Chandler's dour Philip Marlowe. According to Ariel Swartley of *Los Angeles Magazine*, the Cole mysteries' "subversive pleasure is seeing an every-Angeleno—a man who plots his routes around favorite takeout and waits for a whiff of eucalyptus after rain—pit his cockiness against a series of Goliaths. In the course of his career he has triumphed over the yakuza, the Mafia, corrupt cops, and the Russian mob."

Crais began his writing career haphazardly. He studied a few scripts to see how they were put together. He had no television in his apartment, so he watched shows when he could in department store displays. "Then I started writing scripts," he explained in a *BookPage* interview. "I found an agent through a friend, and eventually one of them sold."

The author found scriptwriting a competitive and wrenching field in which his final work was often changed by others. Long aspiring to produce books, it took the death of Crais's father and his need to work out some of his fears and frustrations to force him to write one. Although he could not control things happening in his own life, he could manipulate his characters in a book.

Crais's first private-eye novel was 1987's *The Monkey's Raincoat*, which followed the wisecracking, Vietnam veteran Elvis Cole, who is fond of Hawaiian shirts. The protagonist's darker half is the seldom talking, grim, hard as nails Joe Pike, also a Vietnam vet and loyal to Cole.

"Elvis and Joe believe something that most people want to believe, namely, that everyone matters," Crais said in a Mystery Ink interview. "Not just the rich or the famous; each of us has depth, and that depth deserves respect. Elvis sees that depth in people, and he cares. Maybe my readers are responding to the subliminal message that we can affect the course of our own lives—we can make a difference. We can rise above ourselves."

"Novels are more personal than television. . . . Books are much more intimate. You work with your editor and publisher, but the final product is yours. Books are freedom," the author told Amazon.com. "That's what it's about. Having that freedom."

Crais studied mechanical engineering in college. Once he decided on a different career route, he attended the Clarion Writers' Workshop in Michigan in 1975 and studied with such science fiction writers as Gene Wolfe and Samuel R. Delany. Guiding his writing, in whatever media, was his exposure as a youth to Stan Lee's Marvel comics, which often featured troubled, flawed teen heroes, and the science fiction of Robert Heinlein, in which young male characters often overcame their dismal pasts.

Where do his characters come from? "To write honestly and well, you have to invest yourself—even in the bad guys. So yeah, I'm the heroes, Elvis and Joe Pike, but I'm also the bad guys, the self-serving detective, the homeless guy, even the serial killer. It's all me in some way or another," Crais ventured in a *Cincinnati Enquirer* interview.

Crais featured Pike in *L.A. Requiem*, then took a break from the Cole series to write two books, *Demolition Angel* (Carol Starkey works for the LAPD bomb squad) and *The Hostage* (actor Bruce Willis bought rights to make a movie and play the hero, suburban police chief Jeff Talley). "The stand-alones give me the freedom to write with new characters and settings," Crais said on the Random House Web page, "but Elvis and Joe are old and trusted friends."

Crais returned to his series with *The Last Detective* to give Cole the same treatment he gave Pike in *L.A. Requiem*. The author often has to make tough choices, including one about Cole's ongoing relationship with Louisiana lawyer Lucy Chenier. *The Last Detective* only opened the door on Cole's character; Crais wanted to know more. "*The Forgotten Man* grows out of my realization that Elvis Cole's driving reason for being a detective is that, first and foremost, the detective must find himself. To that end, *The Forgotten Man* continues the journey that began in *The Last Detective* as Elvis continues the search up-river for his own 'heart of darkness,' " Crais said in his e-mail newsletter.

Some of Cole's clients have been unusual characters. In *Indigo Slam*, he helps three children find their father, and in *Free Fall* he helps Jennifer Sheridan's boyfriend. Families and relationships are important to Cole, a theme the author explores further in *The Last Detective*. In that book, Crais has taken a few risks with point of view, at times using Pike and Ben Chenier, his girlfriend's son, as well as Cole. Crais also tinkers with the genre itself—merging suspense novel with police procedural and mystery.

Crais has also begun to probe his female character more. "It's liberating in that it allows me to explore an area of life that, normally, I haven't in my books. I'm serious about my writing. I don't want to write the same story over and over and over again. I want my work to grow, to be a better writer," he said in a *January Magazine* interview with Kevin Burton Smith.

Crais does not intend to ever stop writing about Cole and Pike. "If you write series," he said in *Publishers Weekly* in 2000, "you always have two totally different audiences: the old people, who have read everything that has come before, and the new people, those for whom this particular title is their first exposure to the series. The story has to be framed in such a way that both audiences get it without insulting the intelligence of the old people or confusing the new people."

Although Crais did not mind selling movie rights to his two independent novels, he has refused to sell rights for the Cole-Pike series, despite receiving eighteen or nineteen offers. "He is my life's work; my collaboration with my readers. I want to preserve that collaboration; I'm concerned that committing him to film will change the collaboration."

Works by the Author

Fiction

Demolition Angel (2000)
Hostage (2001)

Elvis Cole Series

The Monkey's Raincoat (1987)
Stalking the Angel (1989)
Lullaby Town (1992)
Free Fall (1993)
Voodoo River (1995)
Sunset Express (1996)
Indigo Slam (1997)
L.A. Requiem (1998)
The Last Detective (2003)
The Forgotten Man (2005)

Anthologies

The American Tricentennial, edited by Edward Bryant (1977)
Clarion SF, edited by Kate Wilhelm (1977)
Raymond Chandler's Philip Marlowe: A Centennial Celebration, edited by Byron Preiss (1988)

Introduction

The Private Eye Writers of America Presents Mystery Street, edited by Loren D. Estleman (2001)

Screenplays

In Self Defense (1987)
Cross of Fire (1989)

For Further Information

Ashley, Mike ed. Robert Crais entry, *The Mammoth Encyclopedia of Modern Crime Fiction*. New York: Carroll & Graf, 2002.

Batten, Jack. "Deadly sleuths good to go." *Toronto Star* (April 20, 2003).

Buckley, James Jr. "Elvis has left the city." BookPage. *http://www.bookpage.com/9906bp/robert_crais.html* (viewed July 26, 2003).

"Forgotten Man." RobertCrais.com e-mail newsletter, September/October 2003.

Hasted, Nick. "Crime pays in the city of angels." *Guardian* (March 24, 2001).

Indigo Slam review. *Publishers Weekly* (April 14, 1997).

Knippenberg, Jim. "Robert Crais talks about his life of crime." *Cincinnati Enquirer* (June 22, 1999).

Memmott, Carol. "*Last Detective* is first-rate read." *USA Today* (March 5, 2003).

Niebuhr, Gary Warren. Robert Crais entry, *St. James Guide to Crime & Mystery Writers*. 4th edition. Detroit: St. James Press, 1996.

Peacock, Scot, ed. Robert Crais entry, *Contemporary Authors*. Vol. 187. Detroit: Gale Research, 2000.

Perkins, Christine. *L.A. Requiem* review. *Library Journal* (June 1, 1999).

"Q&A With Robert Crais." Random House. *http://www.randomhouse.com/features/lastdetective/interview.html* (viewed July 26, 2003).

Robert Crais biography. Mostly Fiction. *http://mostlyfiction.com/sleuths/crais.htm* (viewed July 26, 2003).

Robert Crais interview. Amazon.com. *http://www.amazon.com/exec/obidos/tg/features/-/34392/102-4898291-5917764* (viewed July 26, 2003).

Robert Crais interview. Mystery Ink. *http://www.mysterinkonline.com/interviewrcrais.htm* (viewed July 26, 2003).

Robert Crais Web site. *http://www.robertcrais.com/* (viewed July 25, 2003).

Smith, Kevin Burton. "The Explosive Talents of Robert Crais." *January Magazine*. *http://www.januarymagazine.com/profiles/rcrais.html* (viewed July 26, 2003).

Swartley, Ariel. "Elvis is back." *Los Angeles Magazine* (March 2003).

"What's Your MOTIVE?" *Publishers Weekly* (October 23, 2001).

Michael Crichton

◆ Adventure ◆ Thriller

Chicago, Illinois
1942

◆ *Jurassic Park*

About the Author and the Author's Writing

Michael Crichton's books, including *The Andromeda Strain* and *Airframe*, have been megasellers. His movies, such as *Jurassic Park*, have dominated the box office. And his television show *ER* has been a ratings winner. Crichton is undoubtedly a prince of all media.

John Michael Crichton was born in 1942 in Chicago, Illinois, and grew up in Roslyn, New York. He received his A.B. from Harvard University in 1964, summa cum laude, Phi Beta Kappa. He was a Henry Russell Shaw Traveling Fellow 1964–1965 and visiting lecturer in anthropology at Cambridge University in England in 1965. He wanted to be a writer, as his father was, but doubted he could make a good living at it. So he decided to become a doctor.

A graduate of Harvard Medical School in 1969, he served a year as a postdoctoral fellow at California's Salk Institute for Biological Sciences. By that time, he had already written a handful of novels under pennames (including *A Case of Need*, about a Chinese American obstetrician accused of performing an illegal abortion) and *The Andromeda Strain* under his own name, to help pay his way through school. So a career change was inevitable.

Crichton has been hailed as one of the originators of the "techno-thriller" for his science-based suspense novels starting with *The Andromeda Strain*, in which a satellite crashlands on Earth bearing a life-threatening bacteria.

He watched others turn his best-selling novels into popular films and began to script and direct films himself, beginning with the television movie *Binary*, released in 1972, and the theatrical film *Westworld*, released the following year. Long interested in computers, Crichton's software firm FastTrack pioneered special effects that won him an Academy of Motion Pictures Arts and Sciences Technical Achievement Award in 1992.

Other awards range from an Emmy and a Peabody (for *ER*) and Mystery Writers of America Edgar Allan Poe Awards (for *A Case of Need* and *The Great Train Robbery*). In fact, a recently discovered species of dinosaur was named for him in 2000, the *Bienosaurus crichtoni*.

Four times married and three times divorced, with one daughter, he lives in Los Angeles and has homes in New York and Hawaii.

Crichton has said his novels are generally driven by concepts that interest him, such as nanotechnology (in *Prey*), the science of extreme miniaturization of machines, which could lead to vastly smaller computers or medical breakthroughs such as treatment for cancer. Many of Crichton's books were long in gestation, from concept to print: *The Great Train Robbery*, three years; *Jurassic Park*, eight years; *Sphere*, twenty. *Prey*, however, took only nine months. He usually plans his novels closely, as they are plot driven rather than character driven. Crichton believes his story lines are far more interesting and significant than personality issues.

The author does his research largely through reading. "I start with journals and reviews—symposiums on artificial life and things like that," he told interviewer Benjamin Svetkey. "The goal is to find the state of knowledge in a particular field. For example, with *Prey* I had to figure out what a nanotechnological assembly line would look like. I struggled with it and was never satisfied. Then I read in a journal that somebody had figured it out."

Although he often raises troubling issues about scientific advances, Crichton points out it is not a new issue, as the industrialized world has already come to accept such things as hip replacements, medicinal implants, cellular telephones, and global positioning systems. How far-fetched was *Jurassic Park*—in which DNA extracted from amberized mosquitoes was used to clone dinosaurs—given the great interest in cloning in recent years?

Yes, he is at times prescient. But Crichton explained in a *Playboy* interview how he decides his plots: "In the past, certain stories were fueled by my outrage, but then I would lose the outrage and wouldn't have the motor to do that project anymore. I'd outgrow it. Sometimes events bypass it. And sometimes somebody else does a project that makes the issues go away."

Crichton deviates from the adventure-thriller genre slightly in *The Rising Sun* to write of crime and political intrigue and in *Disclosure* of corporate sexual politics. The author said he anticipated that the latter, in which a male was the victim, would stir a reaction among feminists, but he was caught by surprise to be accused of racism in his depiction of ruthless Japanese businessmen in the former. For *Jurassic Park*, Crichton was accused of being anti-science, to which he countered the book and film helped trigger a renewed interest in the dinosaur age at natural history museums. He hit on a hot current topic—global warming—in his latest, *State of Fear*.

Crichton claims he finds good points and bad in his duo-faceted career. Book writing provides greater control of the end product, but it is a solitary endeavor. Filmmaking and television are collaborative efforts in which the end product seldom reflects a single artistic vision. Yet each can be enormously satisfying.

Some have suggested he writes his novels with movie sales in mind, but the author has countered that other writers, such as Robert Louis Stevenson, are also very cinematic writers—and there were no movies in Stevenson's day.

Works by the Author

Fiction

The Andromeda Strain (1969)
The Terminal Man (1972)
The Great Train Robbery (1973)

Westworld (1974)
Eaters of the Dead (1976), also titled *The 13th Warrior* (1999)
Congo (1980)
Sphere (1987)
Rising Sun (1991)
Disclosure (1993)
Michael Crichton: A New Collection of Three Complete Novels (1994), includes
    Cargo, *Sphere*, and *Eaters of the Dead*
Airframe (1996)
Twister, with Ann-Marie Martin (1996)
Timeline (1998)
The Michael Crichton Collection (2000), includes *Jurassic Park*, *The Lost World*, and
    The Andromeda Strain
Prey (2002)
State of Fear (2004)
Three Complete Novels (2004), includes *Andromeda Strain*, *Terminal Man* and *The
    Great Train Robbery*

Jurassic Park Books

Jurassic Park (1980)
The Lost World (1995)

Written as Jeffrey Hudson

A Case of Need (1968)

Written as John Lange

Odds On (1966)
Scratch One (1967)
Easy Go (1968), retitled *The Last Tomb* (1974)
The Venom Business (1969)
Zero Cool (1969)
Drug of Choice (1970)
Grave Descent (1970)
Binary (1972)

Screenplays

Extreme Close-up (1973)
Westworld (1973), based on his novel
Coma (1977), based on the Robin Cook novel
The Great American Train Robbery (1978), based on his novel
Looker (1981)

Runaway (1984)
Twister (1996)

Motion Pictures Based on the Author's Works

The Andromeda Strain (1971)
A Case of Need (1972)
Pursuit (1972), based on *Binary*
The Terminal Man (1974)
Jurassic Park (1994)
Congo (1995)
The Lost World (1997)
The 13th Warrior (1999), based on *Eaters of the Dead*
Jurassic Park III (2001)
Timeline (2003)

Nonfiction

Five Patients: The Hospital Explained (1970)
Jasper Johns (1977), revised (1994)
Electronic Life: How to Think About Computers (1983)
Travels (1988)

For Further Information

Kirschling, Gregory. " 'Fear' Factory." *Entertainment Weekly* (December 19, 2004).

Michael Crichton interview. ReadersRead. *http://www.readersread.com/features/michaelcrichton.htm* (viewed June 3, 2003).

Michael Crichton Web site. *http://www.crichton-official.com/* (viewed June 3, 2003).

Peacock, Scot, ed. Michael Crichton entry, *Contemporary Authors New Revision Series*. Vol. 76. Detroit: Gale Research, 1999.

Rezek, John, and David Sheff. Michael Crichton interview. *Playboy* (January 1999).

Svetkey, Benjamin. "Michael Crichton Gets Small." *Entertainment Weekly* (November 29, 2002).

Zibart, Eve. "Is Michael Crichton a Jap-basher? Xenophobic? Worried? No. No. Sort of." BookPage (March 1992). *http://www.bookpage.com/BPinterview/crichton392.html* (viewed June 3, 2003).

Clive Cussler

◆ Adventure

Aurora, Illinois
1931

◆ *Dirk Pitt Series*

Credit: Paul Peregrin.

About the Author and the Author's Writing

When has a book been so good that a college considered it the equivalent of a Ph.D. thesis—and awarded a degree accordingly? When the book is Clive Cussler's *The Sea Hunters* and the school is the Maritime College, State University of New York, which awarded the author a doctor of letters degree in May 1997.

Cussler has since published a second book of stories of deep-sea diving and exploration, but he is perhaps best known to the reading public for his ongoing series of adventures featuring Derek Pitt.

Clive Eric Cussler was born in 1931 in Aurora, Illinois, and grew up in Alhambra, California. He attended Pasadena City College from 1949 to 1950, and then during the Korean War, served in as an aircraft mechanic and flight engineer in the Military Air Transport Service, rising to the rank of sergeant. He later went to Orange Coast College in California. In 1955, he married Barbara Knight; they have three children.

Cussler started Bestgen & Cussler Advertising in Newport Beach, California, in 1961, but left it in 1965 to become creative director for three years for Darcy Advertising in Hollywood. He was vice president and creative director of broadcast for Mefford, Wolff, and Weir Advertising in Denver, Colorado, from 1970 to 1975, winning numerous international awards for radio and television commercials. Later, he joined the sales staff of Aquatic Marine Dive Equipment in Newport Beach, California.

Cussler began writing in 1965, taking a cue from adventure and intrigue author Alistair MacLean. It was eight years before Cussler's first novel was published. "I sent *Pacific Vortex* out and kept getting rejections," Cussler told interviewer J. A. Hitchcock. "In the meantime, I began writing the second book, and finished it in 1969, then found an agent. . . . He tried to get me published, but couldn't and after a couple of years even his bosses said to dump me because it wasn't going anywhere." The agent hung in, and finally *The Mediterranean Caper* came into print in paperback in 1973. Two years later *Iceberg* came out in hardcover, but in an edition of only 5,000. However, *Raise the Titanic* in 1976 was a turning point, and it even inspired a motion picture. (The film did not inspire the author, however, who withdrew his novels from consideration by Hollywood film interests until just recently, when he sold fourteen of them as a package to a production company—retaining script and casting approval rights.)

The hero Dirk Pitt's first name, Derek, the author borrowed from his son. (He also borrowed his son's bedroom to use as an office to write that book.) To make his character and story different, the author, a longtime scuba diver, decided to use a maritime setting. That first book was actually *Pacific Vortex*, which didn't come into print until 1983 when it became sixth in the series.

Not just anyone could play Dirk Pitt. "I cast around for a hero who cut a different mold," the author said in *St. James Guide to Crime & Mystery Writers*. "One who wasn't a secret agent, police detective, or a private investigator. Someone with rough edges, yet a degree of style, who felt equally at ease entertaining a gorgeous woman . . . or downing a beer with the boys . . . A congenial kind of guy with a tinge of mystery about him."

When writing, Cussler knows how each adventure will start and how it will end, but the middle comes only in the writing. "It's all in my head," he told Bookreporter in a 1999 interview. "The only thing I put down in notes is who's got green eyes and red hair, things like that."

Cussler's books are based on thorough historical research and sometimes futuristic anticipation. *Valhalla Rising* describes an attempt to ram the World Trade Center foundation with a propane gas-loaded tanker ship.

Cussler created the fictional National Underwater & Marine Agency (NUMA)—which with the help of writer Paul Kemprecos is the focus of its own series of books featuring Kurt Austin and Joe Zavala—as the organization that employs Pitt and other running characters. But when Cussler was doing underwater exploration at his own expense, it was suggested he establish a nonprofit foundation. He did, and took the NUMA name. One of NUMA's recent finds was the *Carpathia*, the ship that sailed to the rescue of *Titanic* survivors.

A recognized authority on shipwrecks, the author serves as founder and chairman of NUMA, which has gone on to discover more than sixty sunken ruin sites, including that of the *CSS Hunley*, the first submarine to ever fire upon and sink an enemy ship (the USS *Housatonic*) in battle. Avocationally, Cussler is a fellow of the Explorers Club of New York and the Royal Geographic Society of London. He maintains a collection of some eighty-five vintage automobiles including a Stutz, a Pierce-Arrow, and an Allard. (Some of his collector cars turn up in the Pitt novels.) He maintains homes in Colorado and Arizona.

It took Cussler about nine months to write the early Pitt books; these days, it is more apt to be fourteen or fifteen months. More and more he relies on the help of a coauthor, such as Craig Dirgo on the new Oregon Files books.

Reversing the fiction-into-reality paradigm, Cussler wrote himself into one of his novels, *Atlantis Found*. Pitt is at a classic car meet and introduces himself to an older, greybearded gentleman. "[B]efore I knew it I had typed in 'Hello, my name is Clive Cussler,'" the author explained in a Time2watch interview. "I stopped and looked around and said, 'Gee, why did I do that?' Then I got to joking around and had them look at each other. Then Pitt says, 'You know, the name sounds familiar, but I just can't place the face.' So I left it in as a joke, figured the readers would get a laugh out of it."

Works by the Author

Fiction

White Death (2003)

Dirk Pitt Series

The Mediterranean Caper (1973), retitled *Mayday!* (2002)
Iceberg (1975)
Raise the Titanic (1976)
Vixen 03 (1978)
Night Probe! (1981)
Pacific Vortex! (1983)
Deep Six (1984)
Cyclops (1986)
Clive Cussler; Iceberg, Dragon, Deep Six (1988), omnibus
Treasure (1988)
Dragon (1990)
Sahara (1992)
Inca Gold (1994)
The Mediterranean Caper and Iceberg (1995), omnibus
Clive Cussler Gift Set: Treasure, Dragon and Sahara (1996), omnibus
Shock Wave (1996)
Flood Tide (1997)
Atlantis Found (1999)
Clive Cussler: Two Novels (2001), includes *Flood Tide* and *Cyclops*
Flood Tide and Cyclops (2001), omnibus
Valhalla Rising (2001)
Trojan Odyssey (2003)
Black Wind, with Dirk Cussler (2004)

NUMA Files Series, with Paul Kemprecos

Serpent (1999)
Blue Gold (2000)
Fire Ice (2002)
The NUMA Files Collection (2002), omnibus
Lost City (2003)
Lost City (2004)
White Death (2004)

Oregon Files, with Craig Dirgo

Golden Buddha (2003)
Sacred Stone (2004)

Nonfiction, with Craig Dirgo

The Sea Hunters (1996)
Clive Cussler and Dirk Pitt Revealed (1998)
The Sea Hunters II: Diving the World's Seas for Famous Shipwrecks (2002)

Motion Pictures Based on the Author's Works

Raise the Titanic! (1980)

For Further Information

Clive Cussler interviews. Bookreporter, September 11, 2001, and November 6, 1999. *http://www.bookreporter.com/authors/au-cussler-clive.asp* (viewed May 30, 2003).

Clive Cussler Web page. *http://www.bradland.com/cussler/clive/index.html* (viewed May 30, 2003).

Clive Cussler Web page. Penguin Putnam. *http://www.penguinputnam.com/static/ packages/us/clivecussler/* (viewed May 30, 2003).

Golden Buddha review. *Publishers Weekly* (August 25, 2003).

Hinckley, Karen. Clive Cussler entry, *St. James Guide to Crime & Mystery Writers.* 4th edition, edited by Jay P. Pederson. Detroit: St. James Press, 1996.

Hitchcock, J. A. "Clive Cussler may very well be the best author you're probably not reading." *Mothership* (April 17, 2000).

Levesque, Marc. "An Interview with Dr. Clive Cussler." Time2watch.net. *http://www .time2watch.net/cusslerinterview.htm* (viewed May 30, 2003).

National Underwater & Marine Agency Web site. *http://www.numa/net/* (viewed May 30, 2003).

Peacock, Scot, ed. Clive Cussler entry, *Contemporary Authors New Revision Series.* Vol. 91. Detroit: Gale Research, 2000.

Valero, Wayne. *The Collector's Guide to Clive Cussler.* 2000.

Janet Dailey

◆ Romance ◆ Historical

Storm Lake, Iowa
1944

◆ *This Calder Range*

About the Author and the Author's Writing

The bank wants to foreclose on his ranch. His sister has died and left him responsible for her four rowdy children. Eben MacCalister is at a loss for what to do, until his neighbor Maddie Williams offers a hand. Will their romance rekindle in *Scrooge Wore Spurs*? Is this a Janet Dailey novel? Of course love will blossom.

Janet Ann Haradon was born in 1944 in Storm Lake, Iowa, the daughter of farmers. She attended public schools in Independence, Iowa, then secretarial school. Working in the office of William Dailey's construction company in Omaha, Nebraska, she fell in love with and married the boss in 1963 and helped raise his children. Janet boasted once too often she could write a better novel than the one she was currently reading, and her husband dared her to actually do it. She did write a book, and Harlequin published *No Quarter Asked* in 1976, launching her writing career, which was sufficiently successful to support a twenty-acre plantation in Branson, Missouri.

William Dailey continues to assist his wife with research for her novels, including visiting all fifty states in preparation for the fifty-volume Americana series. Janet has contributed more than a dozen titles to the Silhouette romance line.

"She is known for her strong, decisive characters, her extraordinary ability to re-create a time and place, and her unerring courage to confront important, controversial issues, like alcoholism and sexual abuse, in her stories," according to a HarperCollins Web page. Readers can count on "Dailey's flair for creating vivid characters that tickle the heart and funny bone," attests a reviewer in *Publishers Weekly*.

Dailey seldom parted from a standard romance pattern—reluctant heroine, rich hero, heroine resists hero, heroine succumbs to hero's sexual charms, heroine falls in love with hero—until she shifted to the mass market field in 1979 with *Touch the Wind*, her first book on the *New York Times* best-seller list. In her longer works she broadened as a writer, sometimes exploring historical settings. *The Proud and the Free*, for example, is set during the Trail of Tears, the Cherokee trek to Oklahoma, while *Legacies* takes place on the eve of the Civil War.

"It is as if in writing about outlaws and Indians, ranching and riding she comes much closer to her own emotional center of gravity, either because these are activities she knows or because they spring from her personal fantasy life," observed critic Nancy Regan.

Dailey defended romance novels in an interview with *Redbook*: "Romance novels, don't forget, allow women to see other women moving into jobs and careers, competing with men, having identity crises. But they retain their femininity. They find love—and that's what readers want, so the books are reassuring."

Perhaps best known are the author's Calder books, which follow members of a ranching family in Montana. In *Green Calder Grass* (2002), set on the Triple C ranch, Ty Calder and his bride Jessy are expecting twins and at the same time are ensnarled in a political wrangle over a large parcel of government land surrounded by Calder land. A group of environmentalists wants to get its hands on the acreage and is fighting the ranchers all the way.

Dailey, in 1997, was accused in her novel *Notorious* of copying situations and whole paragraphs from the novel *Sweet Revenge* by another popular author, Nora Roberts. The revelation came within months of Dailey's induction into the Writers Hall of Fame in Springfield, Missouri. Dailey apologized to Roberts and her readers, claiming she had recently suffered family losses and had an unspecified affliction. Roberts was at first inclined to accept the apology, then discovered that more than one of Dailey's books had borrowed from her work. She sued, and the authors reached an agreement out of court. Dailey purportedly paid an unspecified amount to Literacy Volunteers of America. The incident appears to have had an effect on Dailey's publishing arrangement with HarperCollins—in 2001 she changed publishers, to Kensington, in a seven-figure deal for four novels—but not on her popularity with readers. *Scrooge Wore Spurs* spent five weeks on the *USA Today* best-seller list; *Shifting Calder Wind* appeared for four weeks on the *New York Times* tally.

Works by the Author

Fiction

Touch the Wind (1979)
Ride the Thunder (1980)
The Rogue (1980)
Night Way (1981)
Silver Wings, Santiago Blue (1984)
The Glory Game (1985)
The Pride of Hannah Wade (1985)
The Great Alone (1986)
Heiress (1988)
Rivals (1989)
Masquerade (1991)
Tangled Vines (1992)
The Proud and the Free (1994)
Legacies (1995)
Notorious (1996)

A Capital Holiday (2001)

Scrooge Wore Spurs (2002)

Maybe This Christmas (2003), includes revised *Darling Jenny* and *Strange Bedfel-
lows*

Western Man and *Leftover Love* (2004), repackages two earlier novels

Janet Dailey Americana Series

1. *Dangerous Masquerade* (1986)
2. *Northern Magic* (1986)
3. *Sonora Sundown* (1986)
4. *Valley of the Vapours* (1986)
5. *Fire and Ice* (1986)
6. *After The Storm* (1986)
7. *Difficult Decision* (1986)
8. *The Matchmakers* (1986)
9. *Southern Nights* (1986)
10. *Night of The Cotillion* (1986)
11. *Kona Winds* (1986)
12. *The Traveling Kind* (1986)
13. *The Lyon's Share* (1986)
14. *The Indy Man* (1986)
15. *The Homeplace* (1986)
16. *The Mating Season* (1987)
17. *Bluegrass King* (1987)
18. *The Bride of The Delta Queen* (1987)
19. *Summer Mahogany* (1987)
20. *Bed of Grass* (1987)
21. *That Boston Man* (1987)
22. *Enemy in Camp* (1987)
23. *Giant of Mesabi* (1987)
24. *A Tradition of Pride* (1987)
25. *Show Me* (1987)
26. *Big Sky Country* (1987)
27. *Boss Man From Ogallala* (1987)
28. *Reilly's Woman* (1987)
29. *Heart of Stone* (1987)
30. *One of the Boys* (1987)
31. *Land of Enchantment* (1987)
32. *Beware of the Stranger* (1987)
33. *That Carolina Summer* (1987)
34. *Lord of the High Lonesome* (1987)
35. *The Widow and the Wastrel* (1987)
36. *Six White Horses* (1987)

37. *To Tell the Truth* (1987)
38. *The Thawing of Mara* (1987)
39. *Strange Bedfellow* (1987)
40. *Low Country Liar* (1987)
41. *Dakota Dreamin'* (1987)
42. *Sentimental Journey* (1987)
43. *Savage Land* (1988)
44. *A Land Called Deseret* (1988)
45. *Green Mountain Man* (1988)
46. *Tidewater Lover* (1988)
47. *For Mike's Sake* (1988)
48. *Wild and Wonderful* (1988)
49. *With A Little Luck* (1988)
50. *Darling Jenny* (1988)

Aspen Series

Aspen Gold (1991)
Illusions (1997)

Calder Saga

This Calder Range (1982)
Calder Born, Calder Bred (1983)
Stands A Calder Man (1983)
This Calder Sky (1983)
Calder Pride (1998)
Green Calder Grass (2002)
Shifting Calder Wind (2003)
Calder Promise (2004)

Harlequin Presents Series

124. *No Quarter Asked* (1976)
131. *Boss Man From Ogalla* (1976)
139. *Savage Land* (1976)
147. *Fire and Ice* (1976)
151. *Land of Enchantment* (1976)
159. *The Homeplace* (1976)
167. *After The Storm* (1976)
171. *Dangerous Masquerade* (1977)
180. *Night of The Cotillion* (1977)
183. *Valley of The Vapours* (1977)
192. *Fiesta San Antonio* (1977)
200. *Show Me* (1977)

203. *Bluegrass King* (1977)
208. *A Lyon's Share* (1977)
211. *The Widow and The Wastrel* (1977)
219. *The Ivory Cane* (1978)
223. *The Indy Man* (1978)
227. *Darling Jenny* (1978)
231. *Reilly's Woman* (1978)
236. *To Tell The Truth* (1978)
239. *Sonora Sundown* (1978)
244. *Big Sky Country* (1978)
248. *Something Extra* (1978)
252. *The Master Fiddler* (1978)
256. *Beware The Stranger* (1978)
259. *Giant of Mesabi* (1978)
264. *The Matchmakers* (1978)
267. *For Bitter Or Worse* (1979)
272. *Green Mountain Man* (1979)
275. *Six White Horses* (1979)
279. *Summer Mahogany* (1979)
284. *The Bride of The Delta Queen* (1979)
292. *Tidewater Lover* (1979)
296. *Strange Bedfellow* (1979)
308. *Sweet Promise* (1979)
313. *For Mike's Sake* (1979)
319. *Sentimental Journey* (1979)
326. *A Land Called Deseret* (1980)
332. *Kona Winds* (1980)
338. *That Boston Man* (1980)
343. *Bed of Grass* (1980)
349. *The Thawing of Mara* (1980)
356. *The Mating Season* (1980)
363. *Lord of The High Lonesome* (1980)
369. *Southern Nights* (1980)
373. *Enemy in Camp* (1980)
386. *Difficult Decision* (1980)
391. *Heart of Stone* (1980)
399. *One of The Boys* (1980)
416. *Wild and Wonderful* (1981)
421. *A Tradition of Pride* (1981)
445. *Dakota Dreamin'* (1981)
475. *Northern Magic* (1982)
482. *With A Little Luck* (1982)
488. *That Carolina Summer* (1982)

Silhouette Romance Series

82. *The Hostage Bride* (1981)
106. *The Lancaster Man* (1981)
118. *For The Love of God* (1981)
153. *Wildcatter's Woman* (1982)
177. *The Second Time* (1982)
195. *Mistletoe and Holly* (1982)
213. *Separate Cabins* (1983)
231. *Western Man* (1983)

Silhouette Special Edition Series

1. *Terms of Surrender* (1982)
36. *Foxfire Light* (1982)
132. *The Best Way to Lose* (1983)
150. *Leftover Love* (1984)

Anthologies

Marry Me, Cowboy (1995)
Flower Girls (1996)
A Spring Bouquet (1996)
Homecoming (1997)
Unmasked (1997)
The Only Thing Better (2002)

Nonfiction

The Janet Dailey Companion: A Comprehensive Guide to Her Life and Novels, with Martin H. Greenberg (1996)

For Further Information

Baker, John F. "Kensington's Big Buy: Janet Dailey." *Publishers Weekly* (April 23, 2001).

Falk, Kathryn. *Love's Leading Ladies*. New York: Pinnacle, 1982.

Green Calder Grass review. *Publishers Weekly* (June 17, 2002).

Janet Dailey entry, *Contemporary Popular Writers*. Detroit: St. James Press, 1997.

Janet Dailey interview. *Redbook* (June 1983).

Janet Dailey Web page. HarperCollins. *http://www.harpercollins.com/catalog/author_xml.asp?authorID=2227* (viewed June 20, 2003).

Janet Dailey Web site. *http://www.janetdailey.com/* (viewed June 20, 2003).

Jones, Daniel, and John D. Jorgenson, eds. Janet Dailey entry, *Contemporary Authors New Revision Series*. Vol. 63. Detroit: Gale Research, 1998.

Maybe This Christmas review. *Publishers Weekly* (September 8, 2003).

Patrick, Diane. "Daily, Roberts settle." *Publishers Weekly* (May 4, 1998).

Regan, Nancy. Janet Dailey entry, *Twentieth-Century Romance and Historical Writers*. 2nd edition, edited by Lesley Henderson. Chicago: St. James Press, 1990.

"Resolved." *People Weekly* (May 4, 1998).

Rist, Curtis. "Bodice Rip-Off." *People Weekly* (August 18, 1997).

"Roberts will sue Dailey after all." *Publishers Weekly* (September 8, 1997).

Scrooge Wore Spurs review. *Library Journal* (November 15, 2002).

Shifting Calder Wind review. *Publishers Weekly* (June 30, 2003).

Samuel R. Delany

◆ Science fiction ◆ Fantasy

New York, New York
1942

◆ *Nevèryon Series*

About the Author and the Author's Writing

By age twenty-six, Samuel R. Delany had already pocketed four Nebula Awards for his science fiction writing—the first for his debut novel *The Jewels of Aptor* in 1962—and over the next decades he would further make his mark on the genre. He did this even while, as a gay man and an African American, he remained something of an outsider. He used his unique perspective to explore touchy topics. For example, his apocalyptic 1975 novel *Dhalgren* explores bisexual themes and his Nevèryon series touches on the AIDS crisis.

"Samuel R. Delany is one of today's most innovative and imaginative writers of science-fiction," commented biographer Jane Branham Weedman.

Samuel Ray "Chip" Delany was born in 1942 in Harlem. His father ran a funeral home and his mother was a library clerk. As a child, he was drawn to both math and the sciences and to literature, music, and drama. He undertook psychotherapy at age ten after his mother discovered his homosexual preference. At age thirteen, he began writing imaginative fiction and composing music. He attended Dalton School, Bronx High School of Science, and City College (later City University of New York) in the early 1960s and was editor of its poetry publication *Promethean*. He married poet Marilyn Hacker in 1961, but they divorced nineteen years later. They had one child.

In *The Motion of Light in Water: Sex and Science Fiction Writing in the East Village, 1957–1965*, the author's 1988 memoir, Delany writes of his life cruising the nighttime sexual underground of New York. "His curiosity about his experience as a gay black man is utterly scrupulous in its quest for honest expression and true explanation," observes Brian Stableford, "and his attempts to understand and explain the different experiences of others are marked by great generosity of spirit and critical insight."

In 1967, Delany performed music with the group Heavenly Breakfast. He lived in a commune in 1967–1968. All the while, he wrote. "The core fiction of the 1960's, from *The*

Jewels of Aptor up to *Nova*, is astonishing both for its inventiveness and its story-telling verve," asserts critic Paul Brazier. "Quasi-medieval societies, beggars, mutants, spaceships, and quests mingle in pyrotechnic story-telling. Along with the wonder and adventure, however, there are more serious themes." These themes include the power of linguistics and pornography (*The Tides of Lust*).

Delany has been Butler Professor of English at State University of New York at Buffalo (1975); a senior fellow at the Center for Twentieth Century Studies at the University of Wisconsin in Milwaukee (1977) and at the Society for the Humanities at Cornell University (1987); and a professor of comparative literature at the University of Massachusetts in Amherst (1988).

The author's well-delineated futuristic novels of the 1970s gave way in the next decade to the Nevèryon stories, sword-and-sorcery fantasy in the Robert E. Howard and Fritz Leiber vein, following the adventures of Gorgik from slavery to power in a raw world.

These complex stories, suggests critic Sandra Y. Govan, "unveil sophisticated examinations of the movement of a barbarian, preindustrial society as it slowly evolves to a market economy and moves from barter to a cash system. Along with this development Delany investigates slavery, political intrigues, the power of signs, and an emphasis which could be called 'womanist mythologies.'"

"Delany is as much concerned with showing how fact turns into legend as with narrative; one of the many threads that weave the series together is the gradual revelation of the true story of particularly bloody political intrigue among the ruling family of Nevèryon—on which is based a rhyme chanted by children as they bounce rubber balls," explains *St. James Guide to Fantasy Fiction*.

Delany disdains face-to-face interviews, preferring, as a writer, to compose written responses to questions. "My thoughts are formed by writing. When I want to think with any seriousness about a topic, I write about it. Writing slows the thought processes down to where one can follow them—and elaborate on them—more efficiently," he told interviewer K. Leslie Steiner. "Writing is how I do my thinking. Thus, if you want to understand what I think, ask me to write—not to speak."

Delany thus wrote of his place in the American literary scene in *Silent Interviews*: "The constant and insistent experience I have as a black man, as a gay man, as a science fiction writer in racist, sexist, homophobic America, with its carefully maintained tradition of high art and low, colors and contours every sentence I write. But it does not delimit and demarcate those sentences, either in their compass, meaning, or style. It does not reduce them in any way."

Works by the Author

Fiction

The Jewels of Aptor (1962)
The Ballad of Beta-2 (1965)
Babel-17 (1966)
Empire Star (1966)
The Einstein Intersection (1967)
Nova (1968)
The Tides of Lust (1973), revised as *Equinox* (1994)
Dhalgren (1975)

Triton (1976)
Trouble on Triton: An Ambiguous Heterotopia, with Kathy Acker (1976)
Empire: A Visual Novel (1978)
Stars in My Pocket Like Grains of Sand (1984)
The Star Pit (1989)
We, in Some Strange Power's Employ, Move on a Rigorous Line (1990)
Hogg (1994)
The Mad Man (1994)
Bread and Wine: An Erotic Tale of New York (1998)
1984 (2000)

Fall of the Towers Series

Captives of the Flame (1963), revised as *Out of the Dead City* (1968)
The Towers of Toron (1964)
City of a Thousand Suns (1965)
Out of the Dead City (1968)
The Fall of the Towers (1971), includes revised *Out of the Dead City, The Towers of Toron*, and *City of a Thousand Suns*

Nevèryon Series

Tales of Nevèryon (1975), short stories
Flight from Nevèryon (1978), short stories
Nevèryona: Or The Tale of Signs and Cities (1983), short stories
The Bridge of Lost Desire (1987), retitled *Return to Nevèryon* (1989), short stories
They Fly at Ciron (1992)

Collections

Driftglass: Ten Tales of Speculative Fiction (1971)
Distant Stars (1981)
The Complete Nebula Award-Winning Fiction (1986)
Atlantis: Model 1924 (1995)
Aye and Gomorrah: And Other Stories (2003)

Anthologies

Nebula Award Stories 3 (1967)
Nebula Award Stories 5 (1969)
Partners in Wonder (1971)
Modern Science Fiction (1974)
Modern Classic Short Novels of Science Fiction (1993)
The Norton Book of Science Fiction (1993)
Off Limits: Tales of Alien Sex (1996)

Editor

Quark 1, with Marilyn Hacker (1970)
Quark 2, with Marilyn Hacker (1971)
Quark 3, with Marilyn Hacker (1971)
Quark 4, with Marilyn Hacker (1971)
Nebula Award Stories 13 (1979)

Stage Plays

Wagner/Artaud (1988)

Nonfiction

The Jewel-Hinged Jaw: Notes on the Language of Science Fiction (1977)
The American Shore: Meditations on a Tale of Science-Fiction by Thomas M. Disch—Angoulene (1978)
Heavenly Breakfast: An Essay on the Winter of Love (1979)
Times Square Red, Times Square Blue (1983)
Starboard Wine (1984)
The Straits of Messina (1986)
The Motion of Light in Water: Sex and Science Fiction Writing in the East Village, 1957–1965 (1988)
Silent Interviews: On Language, Race, Sex, Science Fiction, and Some Comics: A Collection of Written Interviews (1994)
Longer Views (1996)
Shorter Views (1999)
Black Gay Man, with Robert Reid-Pharr (2001)

For Further Information

Aye and Gomorrah review. *Library Journal* (March 15, 2003).

Barbour, Douglas. *Worlds Out of Words: The SF Novels of Samuel R. Delany*. Frome, Somerset: Bran's Head, 1979.

Brazier, Paul. Samuel R. Delany entry, *Twentieth-Century Science-Fiction Writers*. 3rd edition, edited by Noelle Watson and Paul E. Schellinger. Chicago: St. James Press, 1991.

Govan, Sandra Y. "Silent Interviews: On Language, Race, Sex, Science Fiction, and Some Comics." *African American Review* (spring 1997).

McAuley, Paul J. Samuel R. Delany entry, *St. James Guide to Fantasy Writers*. Edited by David Pringle. Detroit: St. James Press, 1996.

McEvoy, Seth. *Samuel R. Delany*. New York: Ungar, 1984.

Peplow, Michael W., and Robert S. Bravard. *Samuel R. Delany: A Primary and Secondary Bibliography, 1962–1979*. Boston: G.K. Hall, 1980.

Samuel R. Delany biography. *http://www.uic.edu/depts/quic/history/samuel_delaney.html* (viewed June 20, 2003).

Samuel R. Delany entry, *Gay & Lesbian Biography*. Edited by Michael J. Tyrkus. Detroit: St. James Press, 1997.

Slusser, George Edgar. *The Delany Intersection: Samuel R. Delany Considered as a Writer of Semi-Precious Words*. San Bernardino, CA: Borgo, 1977.

Slusser, George. Samuel R. Delany entry, *St. James Guide to Science Fiction Writers*. Edited by Jay P. Pederson. Detroit: St. James Press.

Stableford, Brian. Samuel R. Delany entry, *American Ethnic Writers*. Vol. 1, edited by David Peck. Pasadena, CA: Salem Press, 2000.

Steiner, K. Leslie. "An Interview with Samuel R. Delany." *Review of Contemporary Fiction* (fall 1996).

Trosky, Susan M., ed. Samuel R. Delany entry, *Contemporary Authors New Revision Series*. Vol. 43. Detroit: Gale Research, 1994.

Weedman, Jane Branham. *Samuel R. Delany*. Mercer Island, WA: Starmont House, 1982.

Barbara Delinsky

◆ Women's fiction ◆ Romance

Boston, Massachusetts
1945

◆ *Lake News*

About the Author and the Author's Writing

There are no details too small when it comes to crafting a novel, author Barbara Delinsky explains on her Web site. Consider the matter of naming characters such as ones for her novel-in-progress, *The Summer I Dared*. "How to decide on a name? It's a gut thing, really. I go through names and names from baby books, phone books, news reports, even obituary pages, until something just clicks. I can't tell you why one name clicks over another; but at the same time that I'm running through names, my character is taking on a personality."

The author of *The Vineyard, Coast Road*, and *Lake News* shifted to mainstream novels after several years of writing more formulaic romances for Silhouette and Harlequin. Fiction writing wasn't an early career goal for the Boston native. Born Barbara Ruth Greenberg in 1945, she lost her mother eight years later, but otherwise experienced a normal childhood of piano and flute lessons, ballet dance classes, and summer camp. She earned a bachelor of arts degree in psychology at Tufts University and a master's in sociology at Boston College, the last in order to better position herself in the job market so she could support her husband, Stephen R. Delinsky (they married in 1967) as he attended law school, she explained on her Web site.

Delinsky worked as a researcher for Massachusetts Society for the Prevention of Cruelty to Children in Boston from 1967 to 1969, and then taught photography in the Dover-Sherborn school system from 1978 to 1982. She began writing while working as a photographer and reporter for the *Belmont Herald*. She later did volunteer work for various hospital groups and served as a director of Friends of the Massachusetts General Hospital Cancer Center and the Massachusetts General Hospital Cancer Advisory Board.

It was the chance reading of a newspaper article about three women writers that inspired her—with three children at home—to research and write a romance novel. She read a stack of Harlequin novels. She analyzed their plots, studied their content, and wrote her own book in about three weeks. It sold. That was 1980.

After producing a steady flow of books for more than a decade, she decided to make a change. (Most of her early books written under the bylines Bonnie Drake and Billie Douglass were later rereleased under her own name.) Although her books still contain elements of romance, other elements have come to the fore. "Plotting is intricate and in depth with subplots and different narrative threads woven throughout," commented Arlene Moore in *Twentieth-Century Romance and Historical Writers*. "Character development is multi-faceted, with strong individualizing detail."

The shift in genres was natural and comfortable for the author, considering her growing interest in psychology and sociology, Delinsky explained on her Web page. "People fascinate me; social dynamics fascinate me. Year by year, book by book, my stories became more complex until they had simply outgrown that initial format."

However, the change forced Delinsky to alter the way she worked. A new agent "believed that the more time I spent in preparation, the better the finished product would be," the author said in an article for *The Writer*. "I wasn't sure I agreed. I wanted to be writing, not just thinking or jotting down notes. I had been weaned on genre fiction, which rewarded productivity over passive pondering. I didn't wait for inspiration to strike, but made it happen. Writer's block was a luxury in which I never indulged."

But the extended effort paid off. By *More Than Friends* in 1993, she was on the *New York Times* best-seller list.

Delinsky writes novels of emotional intensity. They have complex but familiar, everyday characters and well-drawn secondary characters. They have involved but inspiring plots and offer fresh voices.

She wrote her first novels with pencil and pad while supervising her children, typing the material at night. These days she writes on a computer. Time spent on research varies from book to book. "The only research required for *For My Daughters*, for instance, was about flowers that grow on the Maine coast," she said on her Web page. "*The Vineyard*, on the other hand, called for research on the subjects of grape-growing, photo restoration, dyslexia, the trees and flowers of Rhode Island, the Great Depression, and World War II, to name a few."

A lifelong New Englander, Delinsky feels most comfortable writing about that region. Some books emerge around characters (in *The Vineyard*, the author said she knew she wanted to depict a young woman, grappling with modern-day problems, who finds comfort in the past) and others from plot (such as *Lake News*, in which she wanted to look at what happens when a rampant media ruins an innocent woman).

Lake News takes a strong stand on the subject of today's journalists. "The news media scares me," Delinsky told interviewer Claire E. White for Writers Write. "The day and age of reporting news is gone. Reporters now take it upon themselves to interpret the news, and in the process, often make the news. How do they get away with that? Beats me. Yes, I think the media goes too far. As I said in *Lake News*, they splash lurid accusations across the front page, then let a story die in an obscure spot when the accusations prove unfounded. That's wrong. It's unethical."

Her ideas come from everywhere, Delinsky said, but mostly from reading newspapers and magazines, going to movies and keeping up with current events. One of her husband's cases provided impetus for *Finger Prints*, she said; and she took inspiration from a country music song for *Heart of the Night*. Her own family experiences show up in the books; *Together Alone* is about the empty-nest syndrome, for example.

Delinsky generally works from a dozen-page outline, and a new novel may take as long as nine months to produce, including extensive shaping and rewriting. She has a home office, which is often visited by her cat. She has both an agent and an assistant, who manages her Web site, answers mail, and does marketing and promotional work.

When a book is in full progress, she sometimes will work eleven-hour days, minus interruptions. When she is concentrating on a book, "I can't seem to turn off the characters and their plot," she said on her Web page. "They're with me round the clock, seven days a week. There are days when I wish I worked nine-to-five and could just come home, put it all out of my mind, and relax."

The author has written two books with a shared setting and some intermingled characters, *Lake News* and *An Accidental Woman*. The background of the first is a newspaper, the second a New Hampshire maple sugar plantation. She initially thought it would save time. "Wrong," she told interviewer Roberta O'Hara for Bookreporter. "I discovered that when you go back to a setting from another book, you have to make sure that everything is the same as it was in the previous book, and that's hard! You also have to work within certain preset guidelines, though your new plot may cry out for things to be different."

One departure for the author has been a nonfiction book about cancer survivors, *Uplift*. "I put *Uplift* together because, as a survivor, I saw the need for a book that treated breast cancer as a do-able experience—and, indeed, the response to it has been remarkable," the author told readers on her Web page. In addition to providing solid information, Delinsky admitted to Barnes & Noble in a Web page interview, she knew it was important to those with cancer to "see me as a healthy, active, vibrant woman—learn that I'd had breast cancer and had not only survived but emerged better than ever. I felt that if I could be a role model for women now grappling with breast cancer—if I could be a source of hope for them—my career success would be turned into something even more positive than it is."

Is writing hard work? Yes, but the author told interviewer Mary Prince for the *Boston Herald*, "Basically, I have a great time. . . . I get as much enjoyment from writing escapist literature as the reader gets from reading it."

Works by the Author

Fiction

Finger Prints (1984)
Within Reach (1986)
Twilight Whispers (1987)
Commitments (1988)
Heart of the Night (1989)
Facets (1990)
A Woman Betrayed (1991)
The Passions of Chelsea Kane (1992)
More Than Friends (1993)
For My Daughters (1994)
Suddenly (1994)
Variation on a Theme (1994)
Together Alone (1995)
Shades of Grace (1996)
A Woman's Place (1996)

Three Wishes (1997)
Coast Road (1998)
Moment to Moment (1998)
Rekindled (1998)
Lake News (1999)
The Vineyard (2000)
The Woman Next Door (2001)
An Accidental Woman (2002), sequel to *Lake News*
Flirting With Pete (2003)
The Summer I Dared (2004)

Crosslyn Rise Trilogy, Harlequin Temptation Series

317. *The Dream* (1990)
321. *The Dream Unfolds* (1990)
325. *The Dream Comes True* (1990)
Dreams (1999), includes first three books

Harlequin Intrigue Series

34. *Threats and Promises* (1986)

Harlequin Temptation Series

17. *Bronze Mystique* (1984)
65. *Secret of the Stone* (1985)
79. *Chances Are* (1985)
87. *First Things First* (1985)
Jasmine Sorcery (promotion 1986, retail 1992)
98. *Straight From the Heart* (1986), also issued as Men Made in America Series no. 7
    (1993)
116. *First, Best and Only* (1986)
130. *The Real Thing* (1986)
144. *Twelve Across* (1987)
150. *A Single Rose* (1987)
164. *Cardinal Rules* (1987)
173. *Heat Wave* (1987)
199. *TLC* (1988)
218. *Fulfillment* (1988)
249. *Through My Eyes* (1989)
280. *Montana Man* (1989)
297. *Having Faith* (1990)
357. *The Stud* (1991)
385. *The Outsider* (1992)

Jordana/Pat Sequence, Harlequin Temptation Series
4. *A Special Something* (1984)
41. *The Forever Instinct* (1985)

Phyllida Moon Mystery Series
Naked Witness (2004)

Anthologies
With This Ring (1991)
Expecting (1996)
Summer Lovers (1998)
Dangerous Desire (1999)
Forever Yours (2000)
Impulse (2000)
Heatwave (2000)
Family Passions (2002)
In Too Deep (2003)
Take 5, volume 6 (2002)

Written as Bonnie Drake
Candlelight Ecstasy Romances

3. *The Passionate Touch* (1981)
9. *Surrender by Moonlight* (1981)
18. *Sweet Ember* (1981)
32. *Sensuous Burgandy* (1981)
42. *The Ardent Protector* (1982)
70. *Whispered Promise* (1982)
85. *Lilac Awakening* (1982)
101. *Amber Enchantment* (1982)
114. *Lover from the Sea* (1983)
132. *The Silver Fox* (1983)
146. *Passion and Illusion* (1983)
186. *Gemstone* (1983)
219. *Moment to Moment* (1984)

Written as Billie Douglass
Silhouette Desire Romances

38. *Sweet Serenity* (1983)
56. *Flip Side of Yesterday* (1983)
74. *Beyond Fantasy* (1983)

Silhouette Intimate Moments Romances

80. *Variation on a Theme* (1985)

Silhouette Special Edition

6. *Search for a New Dawn* (1982)
32. *A Time to Love* (1982)
58. *Knightly Love* (1982)
80. *Fast Courting* (1983)
123. *An Irresistible Impulse* (1983)
133. *The Carpenter's Lady* (1983)

Nonfiction

Uplift: Secrets From the Sisterhood of Breast Cancer Survivors (2001)

Contributor

How to Write a Romance and Get It Published: With Intimate Advice from the World's Most Popular Romance Writers, edited by Kathryn Falk (1983)
Writing and Selling the Romance Novel, edited by Sylvia K. Burack (1983)

Television Movies Based on the Author's Works

Three Wishes
For My Daughters
A Woman's Place
Coast Road

For Further Information

Delinsky, Barbara. "Blueprint for a Novel." *The Writer* (May 1993).

Delinsky, Barbara. "The Birth of a Novel." *Book Club Reader* (spring/summer 2003).

Barbara Delinsky Web site. *http://www.barbaradelinsky.com* (viewed March 29, 2003).

"Meet the Author: Barbara Delinsky." BookPage. *http://www.bookpage.com/9907bp/barbara_delinsky.html* (viewed March 30, 2003).

"Meet the Writers: Barbara Delinsky." Barnes & Noble. *http://www.barnesandnoble.com/writers/writerdetails.asp?userid=0H4KV3ZHMT&cid=883221#bio* (viewed March 30, 2003).

Moore, Arlene. Barbara Delinsky entry, *Twentieth-Century Romance and Historical Writers*. 2nd edition, ed. Lesley Henderson. Chicago: St. James Press, 1990.

O'Hara, Roberta. Barbara Delinsky interview, July 26, 2002. Bookreporter. *http://www.bookreporter/com/authors/au-delinsky-barbara.asp* (viewed March 30, 2003).

Peacock, Scot, ed. Barbara Delinsky entry, *Contemporary Authors New Revision Series*. Vol. 89. Detroit: Gale Research, 2000.

Prince, Mary. "A Day in the Life; Romancing the Novel." *Boston Herald* (March 21, 1993).

White, Claire E. "A Conversation with Barbara Delinsky." Writers Write. *http://www.writerswrite.com/journal/jun00/delinsky.htm* (viewed March 30, 2003).

Charles de Lint

♦ Fantasy   ♦ Horror

Bussum, Netherlands
1951

♦ *Moonheart*

Credit: MaryAnn Harris.

About the Author and the Author's Writing

Charles de Lint, a master of the modern fantasy in an urban setting, often weaves into his stories elements of horror, romance, and suspense. Explaining his mythic fiction, the author told Clinton Cyril Somerton, "The main thrust of my work is contemporary—taking place in a contemporary setting—involving ordinary people and how their lives are changed or not changed by some kind of extraordinary occurrence. It's very much mainstream writing with a fantasy or mythic element."

"Unlike most fantasy writers who deal with battles between ultimate good and evil," observed Tanya Huff in *Quill and Quire*, "de Lint concentrates on smaller, very personal conflicts."

Charles Henri Diederick Hoefsmit de Lint was born in Bussum, Netherlands, in 1951 and emigrated with his parents to Canada the next year. His father was a survey project manager, his mother a high school teacher. The family lived in western Canada, Turkey, and Lebanon before settling near Aylmer, Quebec. In 1961, de Lint became a Canadian citizen, and he places most of his fiction writing in and around Ottawa, Ontario, where he now lives. He attended Aylmer and Philemen Wright high schools, but left before graduation. (He later noted the irony of his gravitating to a career of writing reviews and doing research into history and geography, which he disliked while in school.) He has long loved Celtic music and has played it with a band called Wickentree. He married MaryAnn Harris in 1980.

Until 1983, when he became a writer, de Lint held clerical, music store retail, and construction jobs. From 1977 to 1984 he was owner-editor of Triskell Press, which published literary and fine art works. He has been a regular contributor to various periodicals including a review column for *Fantasy & Science Fiction*. He admits to a range of authors as influences at varying times, from William Morris to Robert E. Howard to Robert Vachss.

The world has become an ever more harsh place, and de Lint said through his prose he tries "to remind my readers of the wonders that are still present and the need to preserve those wonders and mysteries, doing so through the exaggerated technique of fantasies set in the contemporary world," he told *Contemporary Authors.*

The author stresses character and plot in his short stories and novels. "I write books I'd like to read but no one else has written yet," he told James Schellenberg and David M. Switzer. "I do it for the enjoyment—I entertain myself. It's not that I don't care about my readers—I like them a lot and I'm really appreciative of them. But if I'm going to spend 12 or 16 months with this book I want to make sure that I'm at least having some fun."

With *Moonheart,* which is about Tamson House, a link between our world and a mystical place, "de Lint began also his peculiar blending of Canadian mythologies, using traditions found in Native Indian shamanism and in Welsh Druidism," according *Authors & Artists for Young Adults.* He populated the book with an apprentice mage, a Mountie, and magical little manitous.

De Lint has also written mystery and science fiction, but finds himself in some ways confined to the fantasy genre. His publishers, he has said, have even promoted his contemporary works as Tolkienesque "high fantasy," which they are not. When readers were surprised to find the de Lint novel *Mulengro* was actually a horror work, he used the penname Samuel M. Key for three other books, doing little to hide his identity.

After experimenting in traditional fantasy, de Lint began writing stories set in the city of Newford, beginning with "Uncle Dobbin's Parrot Fair." The novel *Someplace to Be Flying,* part of the series, is about a photojournalist named Lily and a cabbie named Hank who are thrown together in the aftermath of a shattering experience and find themselves in a different world of shape-shifters called the First People.

"It's my corvid book—corvids are crows, ravens, magpies, etc.," the author said in an interview with Chuck Lipsig. "The novel is built upon the idea that the first people here were animal people, a distinct race of beings who could be animals or people. They're still with us now and the novel is about people discovering these animal people living among us."

De Lint has said there's a great comfortable level with the Newford setting—which is really Ottawa—and its repertory of continuing characters. He plays something of the role of a journalist chronicling news events there.

Gypsies and other characters are of a kind, de Lint said in an interview with Lawrence Schimel. "[T]he characters I like to write about the most are the outsiders who don't fit into regular society, even in my secondary world books. Now some choose to be outsiders, some have no choice, but they're all fascinating."

Often praised for his depictions of female characters, de Lint said he thinks it comes from his open-mindedness and his great curiosity about things he cannot experience himself.

Does he believe in magic? De Lint stated on his Web page that he accepts "an everyday sort of magic—the inexplicable connectedness we sometimes experience with places, people, works of art and the like, the eerie appropriateness of moments of syncronicity; the whispered voice, the hidden presence, when we think we're alone. These are magics that many of us experience, parts of a Mystery that can't—and perhaps shouldn't—be explained."

As an organic, as opposed to methodical, writer, de Lint disdains outlines in favor of charging into a piece with only theme and character in mind. This at times has its risks; he's had to discard dozens, even a hundred pages, such as was the case when he took a wrong turn with *Trader.* His wife, who is his musical partner as well as first reader of his manuscripts, suggested the cut, and he agreed.

As his career has advanced, writing has become more difficult, de Lint told Mike Timonin: "It's strange, when I started writing, I thought it would get easier as I went on, but it doesn't. It actually gets harder, each novel I write. I have to find something new to say, and because I don't want to repeat what I've said before, I have to go deeper, further."

Works by the Author

Fiction

Moonheart: A Romance (1984)
The Riddle of the Wren (1984)
The Harp of the Grey Rose (1985)
Mulengro: A Romany Tale (1985)
Yarrow: An Autumn Tale (1986)
Ascian in Rose (1987)
Jack, the Giant Killer (1987)
Greenmantle (1988)
Wolf Moon (1988)
Berlin (1989)
Svaha (1989)
Westlin Wind (1989)
The Dreaming Place (1990)
The Fair in Emain Macha (1990)
Ghostwood (1990)
Death Leaves an Echo (1991)
Ghosts of Wind and Shadow (1991)
The Little Country (1991)
Our Lady of the Harbour (1991)
Paperjack (1991)
Uncle Dobbin's Parrot Fair (1991)
From a Whisper to a Scream (1992)
Merlin Dreams in the Mondream Wood (1992)
Into the Green (1993)
The Wishing Well (1993)
The Wild Wood (1994)
Jack of Kinrowan (1995), omnibus
The Buffalo Man (1999)
The Road to Lindoonvarna (2001)
Spirits in the Wires (2003)

Newford Series

From a Whisper to a Scream (1992), as by Samuel M. Key
Dreams Underfoot (1993), collection
I'll Be Watching You (1994), as by Samuel M. Key
Memory and Dream (1994)

The Ivory and the Horn (1995), collection
Trader (1997)
Someplace to be Flying (1998)
Moonlight and Vines (1999), collection
Forests of the Heart (2000)
The Onion Girl (2001)
Seven Wild Sisters (2002)
Tapping the Dream Tree (2002), collection

Philip José Farmer's The Dungeon Series

3. *The Valley of Thunder* (1989)
5. *The Hidden City* (1990)

Collections

De Grijze Roos (The Grey Rose) (1984)
Hedgework and Guessery (1991)
Spiritwalk (1992)
The Newford Stories (1999), omnibus
Triskell Tales (2000)
Waifs and Strays (2002)
A Handful of Coppers; Collected Early Stories, Vol. 1: Heroic Fantasy (2003)

Anthologies

Swords Against Darkness 4, edited by Andrew J. Offutt (1979)
Year's Best Fantasy Stories 8, edited by Arthur W. Saha (1982)
Sword and Sorceress, edited by Marino Zimmer Bradley (1984)
Sword and Sorceress 2, edited by Marion Zimmer Bradley (1985)
Dragons and Dreams, edited by Jane Yolen, Martin H. Greenberg, and Charles G. Waugh (1986)
Liavek: The Players of Luck, edited by Will Shetterly and Emma Bull (1986)
Spaceships and Spells, edited by Jane Yolen, Martin H. Greenberg, and Charles G. Waugh (1987)
Sword and Sorceress 4, edited by Marion Zimmer Bradley (1987)
Tales of the Witch World, edited by Andre Norton (1987)
Annual Review of Fantasy and Science Fiction (1988)

Books for Children

A Circle of Cats (2003)

Written as Samuel M. Key

Angel of Darkness (1990)

For Further Information

Charles de Lint entry, *Authors and Artists for Young Adults*. Vol. 33. Detroit: Gale Research, 2000.

Charles de Lint Web page. *http://www.cyberus.ca/~cdl* (viewed June 22, 2003).

Charles de Lint Web page. *http://www.sfsite/com/charlesdelint/* (viewed June 22, 2003).

Charles de Lint Web page. *http://www.sfsite/com/charlesdelint/spirts1.htm* (viewed June 22, 2003).

Hall, M. M. "PW Talks with Charles de Lint." *Publishers Weekly* (October 22, 2001).

Handful of Coppers review. *Publishers Weekly* (January 27, 2003).

Huff, Tanya. "Rising Stars in Fantasy Worlds." *Quill and Quire* (May 1993).

Lipsig, Chuck. "Interview with Charles de Lint." *http://www.sfsite/com/charlesdelint/interview4.htm* (viewed June 22, 2003).

Mathew, David. "Flying Solo: Charles de Lint Interviewed." *Odyssey*, no. 7 (1998).

Schellenberg, James, and David M. Switzer. "Interview with Charles de Lint." Challenging Destiny. *http:home.golden.net/~csp/interviews/delint/htm* (viewed June 22, 2003).

Schimel, Lawrence. "An Interview with Charles de Lint." *Marion Zimmer Bradley's Fantasy Magazine* (summer 1996).

Spirits in the Wires review. *Library Journal* (August 2003).

Sumerton, Clinton Cyril. "Charles de Lint Takes Readers Someplace to Be Flying." *http://www.sfsite/com/charlesdelint/interview4.htm* (viewed June 22, 2003).

Timonin, Mike. "Interview with Speculative Fiction Author Charles de Lint." *Wordsworth* (January 1998).

Trotsky, Susan M., ed. Charles de Lint entry, *Contemporary Authors*. Vol. 126. Detroit: Gale Research, 1989.

Jude Deveraux

Louisville, Kentucky
1947

◆ *The Mulberry Tree*

About the Author and the Author's Writing

Jude Deveraux, a writer of historicals, has gradually emerged into the present to dance on the edge of the fantastical.

Jude Gilliam White was born in 1947 in Louisville, Kentucky, the daughter of an electrician and his wife. The Whites moved when Jude was seven and, missing her large extended family, the young girl began making up her own fanciful stories with historic settings, featuring herself as the heroine.

She received a bachelor of science degree from Murray State University in 1970 and a teaching certificate from the College of Santa Fe three years later. In 1976, she added a remedial reading certificate, earned at the University of New Mexico.

From 1973 to 1977, she taught elementary school in Santa Fe, New Mexico, then began writing full-time. Twice married and twice divorced, she has one son. She has had homes in Connecticut, North Carolina, and Badolato, Italy.

Deveraux quickly gained a following with her historical romances featuring members of the Montgomery family (and she since has featured family members in contemporary romantic suspense novels). The early entries in the Montgomery Annals are set in fifteenth- and sixteenth-century England, with feisty heroines a hallmark.

"I was tired of women who hid behind some granite-sheeked, taciturn man, who fought off villains and later threw her on a bed," the author told *Contemporary Authors*.

In *The Raider*, a Montgomery son in Maine before the American Revolution adopts a masked disguise to fight the king of England's forces. In *The Temptress*, set in the American West, Christiana Montgomery, determined to become a journalist, becomes intrigued by the rugged scout Tynan. *High Tide*, set in modern day, is about doll maker Fiona Burkenhalter, Ace Montgomery, a murder, flight, and pursuit. *Publishers Weekly* called it a "corny but sassy love story."

Motherhood brought a change in Deveraux's writing. "I find that now I'm not so interested in the events that happen between a man and woman," she told Barnes & Noble. "Now I want to know more about the character of a man, because now whether or not he would be a good father is of utmost importance."

Twin of Fire and *Twin of Ice* center on another clan of masculine heroes, the Taggarts, and takes place in nineteenth-century Colorado. The James River Trilogy follows yet another family in another time, the French Revolution. Nicole Courtalain seeks refuge in England, is mistaken for her benefactor, and is abducted out of the country to Virginia.

Knight in Shining Armor is something of a departure—it features a time-traveling protagonist. *The Summerhouse* is a story of female friendship. *Wild Orchids* is about a morose widower mystery writer, Ford Newcombe, who is sparked to begin a new book and a new relationship when he meets university research assistant Jackie Maxwell. "The key to this taut eerie thriller is the lead protagonists who are complete people still feeling respective tragedies from their pasts," observed reviewer Harriet Klausner. Who is the villain in the book? It is the devil himself.

In *Forever* and *Forever and Always*, Deveraux introduces Darci Montgomery in a paranormal mystery with touches of romance (though not enough to please some readers, judging by the responses of buyers on Amazon.com).

Deveraux, in an interview on a German Web site, said of her heroes, "I want him to be honest, loyal, and have a great sense of humor. If a man makes you laugh, you can put up with a lot from him."

Works by the Author

Fiction

The Enchanted Land (1978)
Casa Grande (1982)
Twin of Fire (1985)
Twin of Ice (1985), sequel to *Twin of Fire*
The Temptress (1986)
The Princess (1987)
The Raider (1987)
The Awakening (1988)
The Maiden (1988), sequel to *The Princess*
A Knight in Shining Armor (1989)
The Taming (1989)
Wishes (1989)
Mountain Laurel (1990)
The Conquest (1991), sequel to *The Taming*
The Duchess (1991)
Eternity (1992)
Sweet Liar (1992), sequel to *The Raider*
The Invitation (1994), three novellas
Remembrance (1994)
The Heiress (1996)

Legend (1996)
Twin of Fire/Twin of Ice (1997), omnibus
An Angel for Emily (1998)
The Blessing (1998)
High Tide (1999)
Temptation (2000)
The Summerhouse (2001)
The Mulberry Tree (2002)
Wild Orchids (2003)

Darci Montgomery Series

Forever: A Novel of Good and Evil, Love and Hope (2002)
Holly (2003)

Forever Trilogy

Forever and Always (2003)
Always (2004)

James River Trilogy

Counterfeit Lady (1984)
Lost Lady (1985)
River Lady (1985)

Tapestry Romances Series

15. *Sweetbriar* (1983)

Velvet Series

The Black Lyon (1980)
The Velvet Promise (1981)
Highland Velvet (1982)
Velvet Angel (1983)
Velvet Song (1983)

Anthologies

A Holiday of Love (1994)
A Gift of Love (1995)
Simple Gifts (1997)
Upon a Midnight Clear (1997)
A Season in the Highlands (2000)

For Further Information

Forever and Always review. *Publishers Weekly* (August 11, 2003).

High Tide review. *Publishers Weekly* (October 15, 1999).

"Interview with Jude Deveraux." *http://www.die-buecherecke.de/deverz/.HTM* (viewed June 22, 2003).

Jude Deveraux biography. Barnes & Noble. *http://www.barnesandnoble.com/writers/ writerdetails.asp?userid-0H4KV2ZHMT&cid-883224#bio* (viewed June 22, 2003).

Jude Deveraux biography. Romantic Times. *http://www.romantictimes.com/data/ authors/102.html* (viewed June 22, 2003).

Jude Deveraux Web page. SimonSays.com. *http://www.simonsays.com/subs/txtobj .cfm?areaid-186&pagename=bio* (viewed June 22, 2003).

Klausner, Harriet. *Wild Orchids* review. The Best Reviews. *http://www.thebestreviews .com/review11469* (viewed June 22, 2003).

Mayles, Daisy. "Wild About Orchids." *Publishers Weekly* (May 5, 2003).

Peacock, Scot, ed. Jude Gilliam White entry, *Contemporary Authors New Revision Series.* Vol. 89. Detroit: Gale Research, 2000.

Wild Orchids review. *Publishers Weekly* (March 31, 2003).

Tananarive Due

♦ Romantic suspense ♦ Historical ♦ Horror ♦ Fantasy

Tallahassee, Florida
1966

♦ *The Between*

About the Author and the Author's Writing

After initially establishing a niche writing supernatural suspense tales with a distinct African American flavor, author Tananarive Due has since written a historical novel and a family memoir of the civil rights era. Still at the beginning stages of her writing career, she has already shown enormous talent.

Born in Tallahasse, Florida, in 1966, Tananarive was one of three daughters of civil rights activists. (Her first name was taken from the capitol city of Madagascar.) Born too late to experience much of the racial turmoil of the 1960s firsthand, she does recall at age three covering herself with baby powder to become white, as her mother had been unable to find a school in Florida that would enroll a black child. Tananarive grew up in an integrated neighborhood, but she never felt accepted in that or in the black community. When she was six, she watched the television miniseries *Roots* and immediately wrote her own family's history.

After earning a bachelor of science degree in journalism from Northwestern University, Due secured a master's in English literature from University of Leeds in England, where she was a Rotary Foundation Scholar and specialized in Nigerian literature.

Due has worked as a journalism intern for the *New York Times* and *Wall Street Journal* and as a feature writer and columnist for the *Miami Herald* for a decade. She has taught at the Clarion Science Fiction and Fantasy Writers' Workshop at Michigan State University and the University of Miami. The author has also taught creative writing at the Imagination conference at Cleveland State University.

Avocationally, she has been a keyboard player and vocalist with fellow writers Stephen King, Dave Barry, and Amy Tan in the music group Rockbottom Remainders. She and her husband, novelist and television writer Steven Barnes (they met at a conference for writers), and a daughter live in Longview, Washington.

When working as a reporter and hoping to some day become a science fiction writer, she once interviewed author Anne Rice and was heartened when the famous author scoffed at those who were critical of her "wasting her talents" writing about vampires. Due began her own first novel, *The Between*, writing chapters in the morning before going to work. *Essence* called the book "a major breakthrough in supernatural suspense writing."

The Between was nominated for the Bram Stoker Award for Superior Achievement in a First Novel by the Horror Writers Association.

In Due's second novel, *My Soul to Keep*, a woman reporter discovers her husband is really 500 years old and belongs to a secret group of immortal Ethiopians. The author wrote in the horror realm, she has said, because until then it had not seen an African American voice. Beyond that, Due, because of her own rich family experience, crafts characters in her books with dimension and feeling. As one small example, Jessica, the heroine in *My Soul to Keep*, is a practicing Christian—as is a large segment of the black community.

In 2001, Due told *Publishers Weekly's* Stefan Dziemianowicz that she gravitated to the supernatural field to do something different from those who have become so well-established as African American writers of fiction, such as Toni Morrison, Gloria Naylor, or Alice Walker. "By looking at the world through a supernatural prism I can step back from my own real-life fears of loss and death, and make them feel a little bit safer when I write stories with characters who are facing things that I'll never have to face."

"Fear has actually propelled most of my writing," she elaborated for *Essence* that same year. "I wrote *My Soul to Keep* and *The Living Blood* to conquer my own fears of the unknown. . . . There is a misconception that I write about gore. For the most part, I don't have buckets of blood in my novels. My novels really are about ordinary people in the midst of extraordinary circumstances and how they deal with these situations." *The Living Blood* garnered a 2002 American Book Award.

Although she feels pretty much limited to an ethnic readership, Due, in a Dark Echo Horror interview, noted it has been in her favor that "the black community draws on so many belief systems that they take the supernatural for granted. I also find that a lot of black readers are willing to share their stories of prophetic dreams or ghost sightings, and to them, that isn't horror or dark fantasy, it's true life." She credits writers Terry McMillan, Samuel R. Delany, and Octavia Butler for opening the market for black genre writers.

The Alex Haley estate approached Due to use the late author's notes to complete the biographical novel *The Black Rose*, about millionaire makeup queen C. J. Walker. "I was incredibly flattered," she said in an interview found on her Web site, "just to be asked—and then Madam Walker's life is such a testament to vision and endurance. I found that it inspired me. I couldn't say no." Due's maternal grandmother had graduated from the Madam C. J. Walker School of Beauty Culture in Indianapolis, giving her a further personal connection. That book was nominated for an NAACP Image Award.

The author felt it her life's mission to, with her mother, write a family memoir of the 1960s struggle for civil rights, *Freedom in the Family*. She had long heard the stories of sit-ins, arrests, marches, speeches. "In the Due house, Freedom songs were every bit as much of the family sing-a-long repertoire as nursery songs," she said in a HorrorWorld interview. "We were raised attending NAACP national conventions, protests and speeches. Our exposure was very deep from the beginning. . . . I consider this book a tribute to my parents as well as all those other 'foot-soldiers' my mother taught us about." Though she had worked as a reporter and feature writer, she said, she found it difficult to write the nonfiction work containing such emotion and memories.

"I hope one of the prime effects of *Freedom in the Family* will be to give people a sense of context," she said in an Africana interview. "For example, when you look at what happened in Florida during the 2000 elections, hearing complaints about discrimination and how the machines weren't working and there were people being turned away, observers and outsiders tend to think that it was exaggeration. When you understand the history of Florida, it suddenly becomes a lot less farfetched."

Reviewer Evelyn C. White praised Due's *The Good House* as "a thriller that features upscale black folk grappling with issues of family, community and career while fighting off demons and other supernatural threats," and she goes on to say that the book "will remain on my bookshelf as an unforgettable read. What with characters fashioning hex-breaking crosses out of discarded Kentucky Fried Chicken drumstick bones, the imagery in the novel lingers."

Works by the Author

Fiction

The Between (1995)
My Soul to Keep (1997)
The Black Rose (2000)
The Living Blood (2001), sequel to *My Soul to Keep*
The Good House (2003)

Contributor

Naked Came the Manatee (1997)

Anthologies

The Year's Best Science Fiction: 17th Annual Collection, edited by Gardner R. Dozois (2000)
Year's Best SF 6, edited by David G. Hartwell (2000)
Dark Matter: Reading the Bones, edited by Sheree R. Thomas (2004)

Nonfiction

Freedom in the Family: Mother-Daughter Memoir of the Fight for Civil Rights, with Patricia Stephens Due (2002)
The Ghost of Scott Joplin (forthcoming)

For Further Information

Baker, John F. "First Black Millionaire." *Publishers Weekly* (November 8, 1999).

Bass, Patrick Henry. "The Living Blood." *Essence* (May 2001).

Dziemianowicz, Stefan. "PW Talks to Tananarive Due." *Publishers Weekly* (March 19, 2001).

Freedom in the Family review. *Publishers Weekly* (December 23, 2002).

Good House review. *Entertainment Weekly* (September 19, 2003).

Grant, Gavin J. Steven Barnes interview. BookSense.com. *http://www.booksense.com/people/archive/barnesteven.jsp* (viewed June 21, 2003).

Guran, Paula. "Tananarive Due: Unique Name for a New Dark Star." Dark Echo Horror. *http://www.darkecho.com/darkecho/archives/due.html* (viewed June 21, 2003).

Henderson, Ashyia, ed. Tananarive Due entry, *Contemporary Black Biography*. Vol. 20, Detroit: Gape Research, 2001.

Patricia Stephens Due interview. Tananarive Due Web site. *http://www.tananarivedue.com/* (viewed June 21, 2003).

Peacock, Scot, ed. Tananarive Due entry, *Contemporary Authors*. Vol. 170. Detroit: Gale Research, 1999.

Sherwin, Elisabeth. " 'Black Rose' describes life of Madam C. J. Walker." *http://www.dcn.davis.ca/us/go/gizmo/2000/due.html* (viewed June 21, 2003).

Tananarive Due interview. Africana.com. *http://www.africana.com/articles/qa/bk20030218due.asp* (viewed June 21, 2003).

Tananarive Due interview. *horrorworld.cjb.net* (viewed June 21, 2003).

Tananarive Due interview (March 17, 2002). Tananarive Due Web site. *http://www.tananarivedue.com/* (viewed June 21, 2003).

Tananarive Due Web site. *http://www.tananarivedue.com/* (viewed June 21, 2003).

White, Evelyn C. *The Good House* review. *Washington Post Book World* (October 19, 2003).

Loren D. Estleman

◆ Mystery ◆ Western ◆ Historical

Ann Arbor, Michigan
1952

◆ *Amos Walker, Page Murdock*

Credit: Deborah Morgan.

About the Author and the Author's Writing

"I'm exactly like Walker: handsome, strong, courageous, and honest. Criminals blanch at the mention of my name and I shake women off my lapels like snow," Loren D. Estleman described himself, tongue in cheek, to interviewer Jon Jordan, referring to his long-running private detective series character, Amos Walker. He might as comfortably have given a thumbnail portrait of Page Murdock, his western lawman, for the author is equally comfortable in both genres and both heroes are equally appealing. Switching back and forth, he told interviewer Steven Law, is "a kind of literary crop rotation. The variety preserves the challenge."

Estleman is a genre writer come hell or high water. "I'm pretty popular with myself," he wrote, "but there are times, invariably when the writing isn't going well, when I wonder if anyone cares. But since at this point I couldn't hold down a real job to save myself or the mortgage, I push on."

As author Linda Fairstein has expressed it, Estleman is "one of the best American writers working today. Forget genre and categories. His characterizations are brilliant, his dialogue is dead-on, and his settings are backdrops for universal themes, whether a Detroit back alley or a Southwest corral."

Born in Whitmore Lake, near Ann Arbor, Michigan, in 1952, the son of a truck driver and a postal clerk, Estleman as a child watched *Gunsmoke* and *The Untouchables* on a black-and-white television. His grandmother knew and told the author stories about Al Capone; his mother knew a member of the Purple Gang; and his father, legally blind at age fifty after a freak accident, was often watching old movies when young Loren came home from school. Is it any wonder his first novel was based on the 1930s exploits of Wilbur Underhill, Public Enemy No. One? Or that in *Never Street*, Amos Walker studies old movies in order to find clues to the whereabouts of a missing husband? Or that novels *This Old Bill* and *Aces and Eights* are about historical figures Buffalo Bill Cody and Wild Bill Hickok, respectively?

Estleman knew he wanted to be a writer from an early age. He wrote and sent out his first short story hoping to find a publisher when he was fifteen. In 1974, he received a bachelor of arts degree in literature and journalism from Eastern Michigan University. (Years later, in 2002, EMU presented Estleman with an honorary doctorate in letters.) Through 1980, he worked as a reporter or editor for the *Ypsilanti Press*, *Community Foto-News*, the *Ann Arbor News*, or the *Dexter Leader*.

Estleman's first novel came out in 1976, with its title, *The Oklahoma Punk*, chosen by the publisher. It was more appropriately called *Red Highway* when reissued several years later. From this has sprung a bookshelf of more than fifty works in both mystery and western series, book and movie reviews, and short stories—all still being produced on a manual typewriter.

In 1980, after a handful of freestanding historical novels (*The Hider* is about a man and boy hunting the last surviving bison in 1898) and Sherlock Holmes pastiches (produced in the afterglow of Nicholas Meyer's *The Seven-Per-Cent Solution*), Estleman wrote the first of his long-running Walker books. The city of Detroit is as much a character as the hero in these gritty books. "Amos goes with the flow," the author told Mary Ann Tennenhouse for *Publishers Weekly*. "Anything that happens in Detroit he's willing to embrace because it might bring him work. Like me, he has a love-hate relationship with the city so, as much fun as he has kicking apart what's wrong, he celebrates what's right."

Poison Blonde, typically, finds Walker working for Gilia Christobal, trying to find out what happened to the blackmailer who is holding potential scandal over the famous Latina diva's head. Walker is a loner, trading barbs with one of his few friends, Inspector John Alderdyce, and exchanging blows with a villain you almost like, Hector Matador. Walker is a throwback; he has no cell phone, no Internet computer. He lives alone, with his television set, in the largely Polish community of Hamtramck. He solves crimes the old-fashioned way, by phone, on foot, and by direct contact. All of the conventions of the Raymond Chandler-style noir private detective novel are there, but very much with Estleman's own twists.

"Amos Walker is a compendium of every police officer I have ever known and part of myself, or what I would like to be," he told *Armchair Detective* interviewer Keith Kroll, admitting his fictional character is actually a little taller, slimmer, and better looking than he is. "He says on the spot what I think of on the elevator on the way down. For what it's worth, there's some of me in Amos Walker. I wish there were more of Amos Walker in me."

As far as Estleman is concerned, a crime novel doesn't have to fit all whodunit conventions to work. It can as easily be about why a crime was committed or what snaking route the detective must follow in order to sort things out.

Estleman sees parallels between cowboy and private eye fiction: both involve a hero trying to tame a frontier someone else wants to keep unfettered. His Murdock is a deputy United States marshal called on in *Stamping Ground* to quell a blood reprisal in Cheyenne country and in *The High Rocks* to bring in for trial mountain man Bear Anderson, who is hiding in the Montana Bitterroot Mountains.

Estleman's *Billy Gashade* follows one frontier character through seventy years and, the author has said, allowed himself to stretch himself professionally and use western lore he had accumulated over the years. Estleman firmly believes in the western genre even as, following a period of formulaic, poorly written books glutting the market, the genre struggles today. He advocates pushing boundaries. "Propagating the myth is what cost the western its broad popularity," he told interviewer Law. "Why lie when the truth is so much more fascinating?" As president of Western Writers of America, the author urged fiction writing members to shun the depictions of white, male, quick-draw artists and explore everything as

Cormac McCarthy or Larry McMurtry or Annie E. Proulx and Jane Kingsolver do. "Theirs is the direction our form must go in, in order to survive and prosper."

Estleman snorts at most prose and movie depictions of quick-on-the-draw gunfights: "There was no such thing as the fast draw between two cowboys," he told Lev Raphael of the *Detroit Free Press*. "You'd try to sneak up on someone, your gun drawn, and shoot him in the back." What else can westerns be about, then? "Hispanics, women and Native Americans weren't just minor figures in the landscape, they played central roles," he said.

The flawed, gritty characters of *Lonesome Dove* or *Dances With Wolves* or *Unforgiven* are the wave of the future, Estleman asserted in *The Writer* in 1997: "They presented raw, unflinching portraits of imperfect humanity that audiences the world over recognized as genuine."

Peter Macklin, featured in another series, is a hitman (the latest book is told from the point of view of his young wife, who is ignorant of his vocation), whereas Valentino, who has appeared so far only in short stories, is a film archivist and amateur crime solver. The Detroit books cover a rich period of crime and history in Michigan's major city.

Estleman averages two books a year. He is a methodical writer, generally spending six hours a day (or as long as it takes to finish five good pages) working at his craft, rewriting and polishing as he goes, "writing for the wastebasket" as he calls it, consuming many a cola as he works. He starts with the title—and begins writing when he's come up with a story to go with it. Among the writers who came to inspire him are Jack London, Edgar Allan Poe, W. Somerset Maugham, Ernest Hemingway, Raymond Chandler, and Edith Wharton.

Estleman lives in Michigan with his wife, mystery novelist Deborah Morgan. He is an avid collector of books, modern firsts and reference books (about 15,000 titles), and of recorded movies (at least 1,300 titles).

He has received national writing awards from the Private Eye Writers of America, the Western Writers of America, and the Cowboy Hall of Fame and has been nominated for others including the Pulitzer Prize and the National Book Award. He's gotten fan mail from an unlikely range of readers, from singer Mel Tormé to The Amazing Kreskin to pulp novelist John D. MacDonald.

Works by the Author

Fiction

The Oklahoma Punk (1976), retitled *Red Highway* (1987)
The Hider (1978)
Aces and Eights (1981)
Mr. St. John (1983)
The Wolfer (1983)
This Old Bill (1984)
Gun Man (1985)
Bloody Season (1988)
Peeper (1989)
Sudden Country (1991)
Billy Gashade (1997)

The Rocky Mountain Moving Picture Association (1999)
The Master Executioner (2001)
Black Powder, White Smoke (2002)

Amos Walker Series

Motor City Blue (1980)
Angel Eyes (1981)
The Midnight Man (1982)
The Glass Highway (1983)
Sugartown (1984)
Every Brilliant Eye (1985)
Lady Yesterday (1987)
Downriver (1988)
General Murders: Ten Amos Walker Mysteries (1988), short stories
Silent Thunder (1989)
Sweet Women Lie (1990)
Never Street (1996)
The Witchfinder (1998)
The Hours of the Virgin (1999)
A Smile on the Face of the Tiger (2000)
Sinister Heights (2002)
Poison Blonde (2003)
Retro (2004)

Detroit Novels

Whiskey River (1990)
Motown (1991)
King of the Corner (1992)
Edsel (1995)
Stress (1996)
Jitterbug (1998)
Thunder City (1999)

Page Murdock Series

The High Rocks (1979)
Stamping Ground (1980)
Murdock's Law (1982)
The Stranglers (1984)
City of Widows (1994)
White Desert (2000)
Port Hazard (2003)

Peter Macklin Series

Kill Zone (1984)
Roses Are Dead (1985)
Any Man's Death (1986)
Something Borrowed, Something Black (2002)

Sherlock Holmes Series

Sherlock Holmes vs. Dracula: *The Adventures of the Sanguinary Count* (1978)
Dr. Jekyll and Mr. Holmes (1979)

Collections

The Best Western Stories of Loren D. Estleman, edited by Bill Pronzini and Martin H.
    Greenberg (1989)
People Who Kill (1993)

Anthologies

The Eyes Have It: The First Private Eye Writers of America Anthology, edited by
    Robert J. Randisi (1984)
Best of the West, edited by Joe R. Lansdale (1986)
The Mean Streets (1986)
The Year's Best Mystery and Suspense Stories, 1986, edited by Edward D. Hoch
    (1986)
A Matter of Crime, edited by Matthew J. Bruccoli and Richard Layman (1987)
An Eye for Justice, edited by Robert J. Randisi (1988)
A Matter of Crime 3 (1988)
Raymond Chandler's Philip Marlowe, edited by Byron Preiss (1988)
Westeryear, edited by Edward Gorman (1988)
The Arizonans, edited by Bill Pronzini and Martin H. Greenberg (1989)
The Fatal Frontier (1989)
The New Frontier, edited by Joe R. Lansdale (1989)
Christmas Out West, edited by Bill Pronzini and Martin H. Greenberg (1990)
The Northwesterners, edited by Bill Pronzini and Martin H. Greenberg (1990)
Invitation to Murder (1991)
Deals with the Devil (1994)
For Crime Out Loud (1995)
Holmes for the Holidays, edited by Martin H. Greenberg, Jon L. Lellenberg, and
    Carol-Lynn Waugh (1996)
Homicide Hosts Presents (1996)
Western Hall of Fame Anthology, edited by Dale L. Walker (1997)
Best American Mystery Stories 1997, edited by Robert B. Parker (1997)
Best of the American West, edited by Ed Gorman and Martin H. Greenberg (1998)

The Fatal Frontier (1998)
Best of the American West II, edited by Ed Gorman and Martin H. Greenberg (1998)
Best American Mystery Stories 1999, edited by Ed McBain (1999)
Legend (1999)
More Holmes for the Holidays, edited by Martin H. Greenberg, Jon L. Lellenberg, and Carol-Lynn Waugh (1999)
The Night Awakens (2000)
The Shamus Game (2000)
Tin Star, edited by Robert J. Randisi (2000)
Murder on Baker Street, edited by Martin H. Greenberg, Jon L. Lellenberg, and Daniel Stashower (2001)
Mysterious Press Anniversary Anthology: Celebrating 25 Years (2001)
Murder, My Dear Mr. Watson, edited by Martin H. Greenberg (2002)
Murder on the Ropes: Original Boxing Mysteries, edited by Otto Penzler (2002)
Wild Crimes, edited by Dana Stabenow (2004)

Editor

P.I. Files, with Martin H. Greenberg (1990)
Deals with the Devil, with Martin H. Greenberg and Mike Resnick (1994)
American West: Twenty New Stories from the Western Writers of America (2001)

Introduction

Fer-de-lance, by Rex Stout (1983)
Complete Sherlock Holmes, by Sir Arthur Conan Doyle (1986)

Stage Plays

Dr. and Mrs. Watson at Home, in *The New Adventures of Sherlock Holmes*, edited by Martin H. Greenberg and Carol-Lynn Rössel-Waugh (1987)

Nonfiction

The Wister Trace: Classic Novels of the American Frontier (1987)
Writing the Popular Novel (working title, 2004)

For Further Information

Crider, Bill. Loren D. Estleman entry, *Twentieth-Century Western Writers*. 2nd edition, edited by Geoff Sadler. Chicago: St. James Press, 1991.

Dundee, Wayne. "Estleman—Meeting the Challenges." *Hardboiled*, no. 2 (1985).

Estleman, Loren D. Letters to the author, January 18 and 29, 2004.

Estleman, Loren D. "No Trap So Deadly: Recurring Devices in the Private Eye Story." *Alfred Hitchcock's Mystery Magazine* (December 1983)

Estleman, Loren D. "Plus Expenses: The Private Eye as Great American Hero." *Alfred Hitchcock's Mystery Magazine* (September 1983).

Estleman, Loren D. "The Road to *Never Street.*" *Mystery Scene*, no. 56 (1997).

Estleman, Loren D. "Twilight for High Noon: Today's Western." *The Writer* (July 1997).

Estleman, Loren D. "Westerns: Fiction's Last Frontier." *The Writer* (July 1981).

Jordon, Jon. "Interview with Loren Estleman." October 12, 2001. *http://www.booksnbytes.com/auth_interviews.loren_estleman.html* or *http://www.mysteryone.com/LorenEstlemanInterview.htm* (viewed April 20, 2003).

Kroll, Keith. "The Man from Motor City." *The Armchair Detective* (winter 1991).

Loren D. Estleman bibliography. Fantastic Fiction. *http://www.fantasticfiction.co.uk/authors/Loren_D_Estleman.html* (viewed April 20, 2003).

Loren D. Estleman biography. *http://www.twbookmark.com/authors.68/266/* (viewed April 20, 2003).

Loren D. Estleman interview. ReadWest. *http://www.readwest.com/lorend.htm* (viewed April 20, 2003).

Loren D. Estleman Web site. *http://www.lorenestleman.com/* (viewed April 20, 2003).

Morgan, Deborah. Loren D. Estleman profile. Lore D. Estleman Web site. *http://www.lorenestleman.com/author.htm* (viewed April 20, 2003).

Peacock, Scot, ed. Loren D. Estleman entry, *Contemporary Authors New Revision Series.* Vol. 74. Detroit: Gale Research, 1999.

Raphael, Lev. "50 years, 50 books: Loren Estleman reaches a milestone with 'Poison Blonde,' his latest mystery with a Detroit bent." *Detroit Free Press* (April 7, 2003).

Tennenhouse, Mary Ann. "PW Talks with Loren D. Estleman." *Publishers Weekly* (April 21, 2003).

Yates, Donald A. Loren D. Estleman entry, *Twentieth-Century Crime and Mystery Writers.* 3rd edition, edited by Lesley Henderson. Chicago: St. James Press, 1991.

Janet Evanovich

◆ Mystery ◆ Romance

South River, New Jersey
1943

◆ *Stephanie Plum Series*

About the Author and the Author's Writing

Janet Evanovich has put the "ha-ha" in hard-boiled crime fiction with her humorous bounty hunter series featuring onetime discount lingerie buyer Stephanie Plum.

"The appeal of Janet Evanovich's popular creation is that she's not much better than the average Jersey girl would be at nabbing criminals," observed reviewer Laura Miller, noting Stephanie Plum doesn't know kung fu, refuses to exercise, and eats recklessly.

The author was born in South River, New Jersey, in 1943, the daughter of a machinist and a housewife. Walter Farley's Black Stallion books were a favorite when she was growing up. When she completed high school, she entered Douglass College planning to become a fine artist. She married high school friend Peter Evanovich, who was a doctoral candidate studying mathematics at Rutgers University. For a time they moved frequently because of his Navy postings. During that time, Janet worked as an office temp, waitress, insurance claims adjuster, and hospital supplies and used car saleswoman. Juggling parental and household responsibilities, she began writing.

She sold none of her manuscripts for ten years. Then her first romance novel, *Hero at Large*, found a home with the Second Chance at Love imprint. She used the pseudonym Steffie Hall on that and a dozen subsequent romances, mostly for Bantam Loveswept. But Evanovich gave up on romances, as she told Robert Allen for *The Writer*, because "she ran out of sexual positions."

However, writing romances provided great opportunity, she said in a conversation with Art Taylor for *Mystery Scene*. "I was writing a lot of books very quickly, and it gave me the opportunity to decide what I liked and what I didn't like. I realized that I like the positive characters. I loved writing with humor. . . . I didn't like writing the very specific sex scene. What I liked was the adventure of the sexual tension—the chase, the hunt. About two-thirds of the way through that career, I realized that I probably was in the wrong genre, because I wanted more action."

The author elaborated for *Charlotte Austin Review*, "I actually was forced out of romance. I wanted to write bigger books with more action, sort of like the movie *Romancing the Stone*, and I couldn't get any of the romance editors to give me a contract. . . . Truth is, the Plum series is probably neither romance or mystery. I think the Plum series is adventure."

It took two years before the first Stephanie Plum novel appeared. "I spent two years retooling—drinking beer with law enforcement types, learning to shoot, practicing cussing. At the end of those years I created Stephanie Plum. I wouldn't go so far as to say Stephanie is an autobiographical character," she said on her Web site, "but I will admit to knowing where she lives."

Plum's profession was influenced by Robert De Niro's role as a character working for a bail bondsman in the motion picture *Midnight Run*. "It had such a cachet, the Wild West thing," she told interviewer Andrea Sachs. "It was something with a lot of personal freedom to it. Then I had to find out what bounty hunters do."

What do they do? They improvise a lot. "I got to be friends with a couple of bounty hunters and tried to figure out what kind of people they were," she told Adrian Muller for *Mystery Scene*. "It turned out that they flew by the seat of their pants, responding to all sorts of situations. They look at a bond agreement, see who's put up the bond, or trace people who are important to the felon. Then they start from there. They stake that person and wait for this guy to come visit his girlfriend."

Evanovich soon had a contract assuring at least ten titles. Plum and her ensemble of Southern New Jerseyites, humor-wise, are the female, Hungarian Italian equivalent of Jerry Seinfeld, the author told Allen. Among the cast of characters are Lula, the former prostitute; Grandma Mazur, who hangs out at Stiva's Funeral Home; vice cop Joe Morelli and fellow bondsman and mentor Ranger; and Rex the hamster.

The author's literary influences are perhaps atypical, according to Allen, from Little Lulu to Betty and Veronica.

"There were two early influences on my work," Evanovich told interviewer Eve Tan Gee. "The first would have to be Carl Barks. When I was a kid I read Donald Duck and Uncle Scrooge comics and I developed a love for the adventure story. The second would have to be Robert B. Parker. When I made the decision to move from romance to crime I read all the Parker books and decided I wanted to be just like him when I grew up. He's such an incredible technician. He makes reading easy."

Her favorite writers today include Amanda Quick, Lisa Scottoline, Michael Connelly, Robert Crais, and Nora Roberts. Favorite stories include Barks's "Back to the Klondike" and Mary Jo Putney's *The Rake*.

Evanovich's Plum novels sparkle with sassy wit and brisk verbal exchanges. To improve her ability in this area, she took improvisational acting classes.

The author says she is in no hurry to return to romances. She said in an interview for BookBrowse.com, "I write with alot of humor and I think humor can get tedious so I prefer a short book. . . . I prefer writing action to relationship, because I suck at internal narrative. I have more freedom of language with mystery. Okay, so I have a trash mouth. I'm from Jersey, what can I say?"

Evanovich likes to experiment. She ended *High Five* with a cliffhanger; readers had to wait until *Hot Six* to find out who Plum's new lover was. (One group of fans was so eager to find out, it bid more than $460 on the eBay Internet auction service for an advance reading copy.) Sometimes the author brings a rock band to her book signings and professional wrestlers to read the parts of Plum's lovers. She also encourages customers to dress up as Grandma Mazur.

Now living in Hanover, New Hampshire, Evanovich spends long hours in her office overlooking the Connecticut River, seated at her computer, devouring Cheez Doodles and drinking Coke. She has a second series that grew from one of her earlier romances. She and friend and author Charlotte Hughes took *Full House*, expanded it and followed it with further stories.

Is she comfortable in the writing life? The author answered this question in a BookPage interview: "Basically, I'm just a boring workaholic. I motivate myself to write by spending the money I make before it comes in."

Works by the Author

Fiction

Metro Girl (2004)

Loveswept Romance Series

254. *The Grand Finale* (1988)
289. *Thanksgiving* (1988)
303. *Manhunt* (1988)
343. *Ivan Takes a Wife* (1989)
537. *Naughty Neighbor* (1992)

Loveswept/Elsie Hawkins Series

362. *Back to the Bedroom* (1989)
392. *Smitten* (1990)
422. *Wife for Hire* (1990)
460. *The Rocky Road to Romance* (1991)

Stephanie Plum Series

One for the Money (1994)
Two for the Dough (1995)
Four to Score (1998)
Three to Get Deadly (1998)
High Five (1999)
Hot Six (2000)
Seven Up (2001)
Hard Eight (2002)
Visions of Sugar Plums (2002)
To the Nines (2003)
3 Plums in One (2004), includes first three books
Ten Big Ones (2004)

Full Series

Full House, with Charlotte Hughes (2002), revision of Steffie Hall title
Full Tilt, with Charlotte Hughes (2002)
Full Speed, with Charlotte Hughes (2003)
Full Blast, with Charlotte Hughes (2004)

Anthologies

The Plot Thickens (1997)

Written as Steffie Hall

Second Chance at Love Series

409. *Hero at Large* (1987)
456. *Foul Play* (1989)
466. *Full House* (1989), revised (2002)

For Further Information

Court, Ayesha. "Evanovich's fans are 'Plum crazy.'" *USA Today* (July 24, 2003).

Evanovich, Janet. *Have You Met Stephanie Plum?* New York: St. Martin's Press, 2003.

James, Pamela Cornwell. Janet Evanovich interview. *Mystery Scene*, no. 64 (1999).

James, Pamela. "Three To Get Deadly: An Interview with Janet Evanovich." *The Armchair Detective* (winter 1997).

Janet Evanovich entry. Biography Resource Center Online, Gale Group, 2002. *http://www.galenet.com/servlet/BioRC* (viewed July 1, 2003).

Janet Evanovich interview. Bestsellersworld.com. *http://www.bestsellersworld.com/interviews-evanovich.htm* (viewed June 30, 2003).

Janet Evanovich interview. Bookbrowse. *http://www.bookbrowse.com/index.cfm?page-author&authorID=232&view=interview* (viewed June 30, 2003).

Janet Evanovich Web site. *http://www.evanovich.com* (viewed July 1, 2003).

Maryles, Daisy. "Janet's plum spot." *Publishers Weekly* (July 1, 2002).

Maryles, Daisy. "This plum gets juicier." *Publishers Weekly* (July 28, 2003).

"Meet the Author: Janet Evanovich." BookPage. *http://www.bookpage.com/980/by/janet_evanovich.html* (viewed June 30, 2003).

Miller, Laura. "A Plum Assignment." *Entertainment Weekly* (July 18, 2003).

Muller, Adrian. "Janet Evanovich." *Mystery Scene*, no. 54 (1996).

Nunn, P. J. Janet Evanovich interview. *Charlotte Austin Review*. *http://www.collection.nk-bnc.ca/100/202/300/charlotte/2000/07-31/pages/interviews/authors/janetevanovich.htm* (viewed June 30, 2003).

Papinchak, Robert Allen. "Janet Evanovich: It's all in the family." *The Writer* (August 2002).

Peacock, Scot, ed. Janet Evanovich entry, *Contemporary Authors*. Vol. 167. Detroit: Gale Research, 1999.

"Quickie with Janet Evanovich On Her Stephanie Plum Series." All About Romance. *http://www.likesbooks.com/quick20.html* (viewed July 1, 2003).

Sachs, Andrea. "Late Bloomer." Time (2002), Biography Resource Center Online, Gale Group, 2002. *http://www.galenet.com/servlet/BioRC* (viewed July 1, 2003).

Smith, Janet. Janet Evanovich interview. Writer's E-Zine. *http://www.thewritersezine.com/t-zero/archives/2003-texts/2003-06-ahtor.shmtl* (viewed July 1, 2003).

Smith, Jill M. *Full Tilt* review. *RT Book Club* (February 2003).

Tan Gee, Eve. Janet Evanovich interview. Crime Time. *http://www.crimetime.co.uk/interviews/janetevanovich.html* (viewed June 30, 2003).

Taylor, Art. "Visions of Sugar Plums: An Interview with Janet Evanovich." *Mystery Scene*, no. 77 (2002).

Tierney, Bruce. Janet Evanovich interview. ProMotion (June 2000). *http://www.bookpage.com/0007bp/janet_evanovich.html* (viewed June 30, 2003).

Tierney, Bruce. "Janet Evanovich: Mystery maven keeps readers coming back for more." BookPage (July 2000). *http://www.bookpage.com/0007bp/janet_evanovich.html* (viewed March 31, 2003).

White, Claire E. "A Conversation with Janet Evanovich." Writers Write (January 1999). *http://www.writerswrite.com/journal/jan99/evanovich.htm* (viewed July 1, 2003).

Ken Follett

◆ Suspense ◆ Adventure ◆ Historical

Cardiff, Wales
1949

◆ *Eye of the Needle*

About the Author and the Author's Writing

When researching *Hammer of Eden*—in which terrorists hold San Francisco at bay and threaten to trigger a man-made earthquake—writer Ken Follett questioned California Government Pete Wilson about how he would respond. "He gave the answer I anticipated," Follett said in an interview with Salon.com. "He said, No matter what the threat, you couldn't give in because if you did, then next week there would be another threat."

Ken Follett was born in Cardiff, Wales, in 1949, the son of a tax inspector and a housewife. He became an avid reader at a young age, in part because his born-again Christian parents would not allow him to watch television or go to movies. The family moved to London when he was ten and he attended public schools; then received a bachelor of arts degree in philosophy (with honors) from University College in London in 1970.

Follett credits the discipline of his studies with helping him develop as a writer. "When you study philosophy you deal with questions like: 'Here we are sitting at a table, but is the table real?' Now that's a daft question because of course the table is real," he said on his Web page. "When you study philosophy, however, you need to take that sort of thing seriously and you have to have an off-the-wall imagination. It's the same with fiction which is all about imagining situations that are different from the real world." The politically volatile Vietnam War gave Follett and other students plenty of food for thought. He later became active in the Labour Party.

While in college, Follett played guitar and was drawn to Bob Dylan's songs. He is still an active amateur musician with a blues band called Damn Right I Got the Blues and with another called ClogIron. He has two children by his first wife, Mary Emma Ruth Elson. His second wife is Barbara Broer Follett, a member of Parliament from Stevenage, Hertfordshire, where they have a home. They also have places in London—where Follett, an enthusiast of the Bard, frequently attends performances of the Royal Shakespeare Company—and Antigua.

Follett worked for several years as a newspaper reporter for the *South Wales Echo* (1970 to 1973) then the *London Evening News* (1973 to 1974). While a journalist, he generally covered breaking news events, although he once interviewed members of Led Zeppelin and singer Stevie Wonder. He began to write novels in part to pay for a car repair and because he heard through a friend it was easy to get a book advance. He wrote three books under the pen-name Symon Myles. They featured Apples Carstairs, a sexy and violent hero whom the author now considers far short of his standard.

Follett continued to write as he went to work for a publisher, Everest Books (1974–1977), first as a deputy managing director, then as editorial director. *The Shakeout* and *The Bear Raid* feature Piers Roper, an industrial spy. As with the Apples books, Follett has allowed these titles to go out of print. Deviating from that theme, he wrote *Amok: King of Legend*, a King Kong-ish adventure written hastily on commission, and *Capricorn One*, the novelization of a screenplay about a faked space flight to the moon. He wrote mystery and science fiction for younger readers, under his own name and as Martin Martinsen.

Follett credits his American agent, Al Zuckerman, with helping him improve his prose writing. One tip was to better flesh out his characters to give them a past and motivations. Responding to a question about criticism of some of his villains as being too empathetic, Follett said in an Amazon.com interview, "Well, the problem is that when the villain is a point-of-view character, you as the reader are going to spend a lot of time in his company. So he has to be interesting, and he has to be kind of likable, otherwise you're going to put the book down."

Follett, who became a full-time writer in 1977, finally caught the public's attention in 1978 with his eleventh book, the suspenseful *Eye of the Needle*, a work with a strong female protagonist. *Needle* spent thirty weeks on the *New York Times* best-seller list, eventually earned its author a Mystery Writers of America Edgar Award, and was made into a popular motion picture.

The author has continued to write thrillers—*The Key to Rebecca* and *Lie Down With Lions* among them—but has also given readers a few surprises such as *Pillars of the Earth*, which is set against the construction of a Middle Ages cathedral, and *On Wings of Eagles*, a true account of the rescue of two employees of Ross Perot from Iran during the 1979 revolution.

Follett comes up with plots at the edge of the news, whether terrorist blackmail or, as in *The Third Twin*, secret experiments in genetic engineering. He has delved into history with *Code to Zero*, which is about the Cold War space race, and *Jackdaws*, which is set during World War II.

"Follett's forte—in fiction and nonfiction—is the variation upon history," observed Anne Janette Johnson. "Every human relationship is somehow blighted or molded by the complexities of world politics, and all the emotional and sexual entanglements are played out against a backdrop of historical events."

Believing accurate details give the reader a strong feeling of authenticity in a story, Follett uses a professional researcher in New York, Dan Starr, to locate books and articles and track down professionals, but he does his own interviews. For *Hornet Flight*, he talked to an engineer who was particularly knowledgeable about a small biplane aircraft called the Hornet Moth and accompanied him on a flight. He visited locations in Denmark and Sweden to capture the feel of places there in his depiction of a flight from German control during World War II.

What is the continued fascination with that time period? "It is the greatest drama in human history," Follett told Bookreporter.com in December 2002, "the biggest war ever and a true battle of good and evil. I imagine that writers will continue to get stories from it, and readers will continue to love them, for many more years."

It generally takes a year or so for Follett to prepare for a new novel. He carefully outlines before he begins writing, then gives flesh to that skeleton in his first draft. This, to him, is the most difficult part of the writing process. He then revises his manuscript before submitting it to his publisher. He describes the writer's mission on his Web page: to craft an imaginary yet very real-to-the-reader world and then pull the reader into that world. He lists among his favorite writers Ian Fleming, Thomas Harris, Charles Dickens, Jane Austen, and Stephen King.

"Versatility does not seem to diminish Follett's popularity," suggested critic Jane S. Bakerman. "Indeed it may help to increase it with an even wider audience since Follett is a successful writer who takes pride in his craft and is constantly trying to improve."

Works by the Author

Fiction

The Shakeout (1975)
The Bear Raid (1976), sequel to *The Shakeout*
Eye of the Needle (1978)
Triple (1979)
The Key to Rebecca (1980)
The Man from St. Petersburg (1982)
Lie Down with Lions (1986)
The Pillars of the Earth (1989), retitled *Pillars of the Almighty* (1994)
Night Over Water (1991)
Under the Streets of Nice (1991)
A Dangerous Fortune (1993)
A Place Called Freedom (1995)
The Third Twin (1996)
The Hammer of Eden (1998)
Code to Zero (2000)
Jackdaws (2001)
Hornet Flight (2002)
Whiteort (2004)

Books for Juvenile Readers

The Secret of Kellerman's Studio (1976), retitled *Mystery Hideout* (1990)

Screenplays

Fringe Banking (1978)
A Football Star, with John Sealey (1979)
Lie Down with Lions (1988)

Written as Bernard L. Ross

Amok: King of Legend (1976)
Capricorn One (1978)

Written as Martin Martinsen

The Power Twins and the Worm Puzzle: A Science Fantasy for Young People (1991), published as *The Power Twins* (1991), by Ken Follett

Written as Symon Myles

Apples Carstairs Series

The Big Black (1974)
The Big Needle (1994), retitled *The Big Apple* (1975), by Ken Follett (1986)
The Big Hit (1975)

Written as Zachary Stone

The Modigliani Scandal (1976), by Ken Follett (1985)
Paper Money (1977), by Ken Follett (1987)

Motion Pictures or Television Movies Based on the Author's Works

Eye of the Needle (1981)
The Key to Rebecca (1985)
On Wings of Eagles (1985)
Lie Down with Lions (1994)
The Third Twin (1997)

Nonfiction

The Heist of the Century, with Rene Louis Maurice (1978); retitled as *The Gentlemen of 16 July* (1980); revised as *Under the Streets of Nice: The Bank Heist of the Century* (1986)
On Wings of Eagles (1983)

For Further Information

Bakerman, Jane S., updated by Peter Kenney. Ken Follett entry, *St. James Guide to Crime & Mystery Writers*. 4th edition, edited by Jay P. Pederson. Detroit: St. James Press, 1996.

Bowman, David. "The Salon Interview; Ken Follett." Salon.com. *http://dir.salon.com/books/int/1998/12/cov_02intc.html* (viewed July 5, 2003).

Johnson, Anne Janette. Ken Follett entry, *Contemporary Authors New Revision Series*. Vol. 54, edited by Jeff Chapman and John D. Jorgenson. Detroit: Gale Research, 1997.

Ken Follett entry, *Authors and Artists for Young Adults.* Vol. 50. Detroit: Gale Group, 2003.

Ken Follett interview. Amazon.com. *http://www.amazon.com/exec/obidos/tg/feature/-/115584/ref=ed_cp_2_3_b/102-8920117-1500149* (viewed July 5, 2003).

Ken Follett interviews. Bookreporter.com. *http://www.bookreporter.com/authors/au-follett-ken.asp* (viewed July 5, 2003).

Ken Follett Web site. *http://www.ken-follett.com* (viewed July 5, 2003).

"Top Author Talks About Reading." *http://www.huyton-today.merseyside.org/issue6/kenfollettinterview.html* (viewed July 5, 2003).

Frederick Forsyth

Ashford, Kent, England
1938

◆ *Day of the Jackal*

About the Author and the Author's Writing

French President Charles de Gaulle was one of literature's famous figures by simply being himself—the target of a meticulous, tenacious professional killer in Frederick Forsyth's 1971 gripping fiction debut, *The Day of the Jackal*. It was the book "that practically invented the political assassination subgenre," said a writer in MysteryGuide.com. Its close attention to Cold War governmental dynamics and to the technical detail of how a sniper would prepare for his victim make it a classic.

Forsyth, of course, is far from a single-book writer. His *The Odessa File*, *The Dogs of War*, and *The Avenger* (in which Osama bin Laden is a real-life character) have established him as a keen political observer and purveyor of top-notch thrillers. Regarding bin Laden and international terrorists, Forsyth in a British Broadcasting Corporation interview with Gavin Esler suggested that "resentment and envy" were at the root of the attacks on the Twin Towers in 2001. He faults the Clinton administration for depriving American intelligence of necessary resources to predict and fight terrorists by barring the use of unsavory individuals as sources. "Well, try telling that to the CID (Criminal Investigation Department) at Scotland Yard that they're not allowed to talk to grasses because they're disreputable."

Forsyth was born in 1938 in Ashford, in rural East Kent, England. He attended Tonbridge School and then Granada University in Spain then joined the Royal Air Force and became one of its youngest pilots at age nineteen. He served from 1956 to 1958, and then became a reporter for the *Eastern Daily Press* in Norfolk. It was as a Reuters correspondent in 1961 in Paris, then in Germany and Czechoslovakia, that he garnered a deep knowledge of national and international politics. He shifted to radio and television when he worked for the BBC in the mid-1960s. He left after a disagreement over coverage of the Biafra-Nigeria war in 1967. His notebooks were full of details, however, and he used them to write the nonfiction work *Biafra*. But afterward, fiction became his realm.

Forsyth abandoned journalism (by now he had also worked for the *Daily Express* and *Time* magazine) to write *Day of the Jackal*. "It was my first attempt at fiction," he said in a Books at Transworld interview. "I had little idea I could even tell a story, but I had to give it a try because I was flat broke!" The gist of his plot had long simmered in his head; it grew from an actual incident in Paris in the early 1960s when Organization of American States agents really tried six times to kill de Gaulle because of his support for an independent Algeria. The manuscript was not immediately grabbed up by a publisher; in fact, it circulated among several editors' desks before it found a home. The book won the Mystery Writers of America Edgar Allan Poe Award for best novel.

Forsyth brings a journalist's digging instinct and fondness for detail to his fiction; in fact, his descriptions of forged passports and incendiary devices raised questions from some as to whether real-life terrorists were not adopting and using his techniques. The man charged with assassinating Yitzhak Rabin in 1995, according to *St. James Encyclopedia of Popular Culture*, had a copy of *The Day of the Jackal* in his apartment.

Forsyth employed a journalist as the hero in *The Odessa File*. Crime reporter Peter Miller tracks down the former commander of a concentration camp, against the wishes of an organization of former Nazi security officers.

Forsyth eventually found writing just thrillers limiting. Some critics complained that he paid too much attention to details, too little attention to characterization. The author apparently felt so, too. Following a dinner conversation with old friend and theater impresario Andrew Lloyd Webber, he decided to pick up the story of the Phantom of the Opera. Forsyth allowed that it was in large part vanity that prompted him to write a sequel delving into the main character's, well, character. Exiled to America, the Phantom, naturally, is reunited with his fond Christine de Chagny.

The author told Larry King on CNN he felt shackled to the spy genre. "I had done mercenaries, assassins, Nazis, murderers, terrorists, special forces soldiers, fighter pilots, you name it, and I got to thinking, could I actually write about the human heart, and I'm vain enough to think, maybe I could."

Twice married, and with two sons, Forsyth in leisure time is an avid fisherman. He has a country estate in Hertfordshire.

Forsyth is getting older, and so are his heroes. He returned to his thriller hallmark with, *Avenger*, in which the hero, a former Vietnam War tunnel rat, has dedicated himself to making things right ever since his daughter was kidnapped and murdered, and his wife committed suicide. Believing himself retired, Colin Dexter reluctantly hires out to find and bring back a young man who is being held captive by a Serbian warlord. The old spark shone bright. "Forsyth's extraordinary care with detail, his solid voice, and his exquisite pacing make this a totally engrossing thriller," write Connie Fletcher for *Booklist*.

Summed up critic Andrew F. Macdonald, the author's " 'docudrama' genre, interweaving truth and fiction, was not Forsyth's invention—numerous writers have practiced it as well—but he is certainly its most prolific exponent."

Works by the Author

Fiction

The Day of the Jackal (1971)
No Comebacks: Collected Short Stories (1972)

The Odessa File (1972)
The Dogs of War (1974)
The Shepherd (1976)
The Devil's Alternative (1979)
The Fourth Protocol (1984)
The Negotiator (1989)
The Deceiver (1991)
The Fist of God (1994)
Icon (1996)
The Phantom of Manhattan (1999), sequel to Gaston Leroux's *The Phantom of the Opera*
Quintet (2000), electronic book
The Veteran and Other Stories (2001)
Avenger (2003)

Screenplay

The Fourth Protocol (1987)

Editor

Great Flying Stories (1991)

Nonfiction

The Biafra Story (1969)
Emeka (1982)
I Remember: Reflections on Fishing in Childhood (1995)

Motion Pictures or Television Movies Based on the Author's Works

The Day of the Jackal (1973)
The Odessa File (1974)
The Dogs of War (1981)
The Fourth Protocol (1987)
Jackal (1997)

For Further Information

Avenger review. Bookfinder. *http://www.bookfinder.us/review1/031319517.html* (viewed June 17, 2004).

Bedell, Geraldine. "Ready, Freddie, Go." *Observer* (May 12, 2002).

Brown, Derek. "Frederick Forsyth." *Guardian* (September 18, 2000). *http://www .guardian.co.uk/netnotes/article/0,6729,370388,00.html* (viewed June 17, 2004).

Cabell, Craig. *Frederick Forsyth: A Matter of Protocol: The Authorized Biography.* London: Robson Books, 2003.

Clark, Judy. *Avenger* review. Mostly Fiction. *http://mostlyfiction.com/spy-thriller/ forsyth.htm* (viewed June 14, 2004).

Day of the Jackal review. Mystery Guide. *http://www.mysteryguide.com/bkForsyth Jackal.html* (viewed June 17, 2004).

Esler, Gavin. "Bin Laden in Forsyth Thriller." BCC News. *http://news.bbc.co/uk/hi/ programmes/hardtalk/3101598.stm* (viewed June 14, 2004).

Farndale, Nigel. "Looking for Other Icons." *Sunday Times* (August 31, 1997).

Frederick Forsyth entry, *Contemporary Novelists*. 7th edition. Detroit: St. James Press, 2001.

Frederick Forsyth entry, *Contemporary Popular Writers*. Detroit: St. James Press, 1996.

Frederick Forsyth entry, *St. James Encyclopedia of Popular Culture*. Detroit: St. James Press, 2000.

Frederick Forsyth interview. Books at Transworld. *http://www.booksattransworld .co.uk/catalog/interview.htm?command=search&db-twmain.txt&eqisbndata= 0593050932* (viewed June 14, 2004).

Jerome, Helen M. "Return to Formula: Frederick Forsyth is back in business." *Book* (November/December 2001).

Larry King Live Weekend transcript, April 15, 2000. CNN.com. *http://www.cnn .com/TRANSCRIPTS/0004/15/lklw.00.html* (viewed June 17, 2004).

Macdonald, Andrew F. Frederick Forsyth entry, *St. James Guide to Crime & Mystery Writers*. 4th edition, edited by Jay P. Pederson. Detroit: St. James Press, 1996.

McCormick, Donald. *Who's Who in Spy Fiction*. New York: Taplinger, 1977.

Panek, LeRoy L. *The Special Branch: The British Spy Novel*. Bowling Green, OH: Bowling Green University Popular Press, 1981.

Veteran review. *Publishers Weekly* (November 20, 2000).

Dick Francis

Tenby, Pembrokeshire, Wales
1920

◆ *Dead Cert*

About the Author and the Author's Writing

Dick Francis proved as adept at whipping a mystery novel into the winner's circle as he was a spirited race horse.

"Dick Francis and his highly popular horse-racing thrillers . . . [are] rich in detail, seemingly modern but at heart exponents of Golden Age storytelling," asserts critic Maxim Jakubowski.

Born Richard Stanley Francis in Tenby, Pembrokeshire, Wales, in 1920, the author was the son of a horse trainer/stable manager and a housewife. He attended Maidenhead County School but dropped out at age fifteen to become a jockey. He served in the Royal Air Force from 1940 to 1946, becoming a flying officer and piloting bombing runs to Europe during WWII.

Older and slightly heavier, he became an amateur steeplechase rider from 1946 to 1948, then turned professional jockey from 1948 to 1957. Francis rode the Queen Mother's entry, Devon Loch, in the 1956 Grand National, and was ten strides from the Ainslee track's finish line when the gelding inexplicably fell. No reason was ever determined for the mishap; it was a true mystery. And, the author liked to say, once he retired from the track, it spurred him to write mysteries.

The author married Mary Benchley, a teacher and assistant stage manager, in 1947 and they had two sons. Mary Francis suffered polio and was for years tragically confined to an iron lung—but this provided raw material for the mystery *Rat Race* that was to come years later. After his jockey career ended, Francis exercised horses and judged at shows. His first writing was as a racing correspondent for London's *Sunday Express*, from 1957 to 1973.

His first fictional work, *Dead Cert*, about bet fixing at a steeplechase track, found an immediate audience in the early 1960s, and he produced virtually a book a year through the end of the 1990s. Francis has said that he prefers the research to the writing of his mysteries.

As solid as his mysteries were, some critics, such as mystery writer Julian Symons in the *New York Times Book Review*, found him lacking when it came to depictions of female characters. "Mr. Francis might reply that a writer of his kind of thriller cannot afford psychological intricacies, and very likely he would be right. In the end, action is the name of the Dick Francis game."

Although there is little gore in the Francis books, there is violence. The hero invariably goes through some episode of intense physical pain—whether due to a fall from a horse or a beating from a foe. Francis told interviewer Axthelm for *Newsweek* that such pain was one detail of his mysteries he never had to make up; he had broken both collarbones, an arm, a wrist, vertebra, his nose, and even his skull in the course of his career.

Francis, speaking with interviewer Robert J. Guttman, likened writing to horse racing: "When you're going into a fence, you try and get your horse going so well that you jump the fence better than the opposition, and maybe gain a length at every fence. . . . When I get to the end of a chapter, I like to have it such that the people can't stop, they've got to go on to the next one. That's a good comparison between riding and writing."

Although jockey-turned-investigator Sid Halley appeared in four books (in part because he had become popular on television) and Kit Fielding in two (because Francis had just wrapped up his biography of jockey Lester Piggott and didn't want to have to find new characters right away), Francis has preferred to develop new protagonists and new situations for his novels. His general pattern has been to begin writing a novel in January and complete it in May, spending the rest of the time developing new ideas and gathering information. He has had homes in England, Florida, and the Cayman Islands.

"I know before I start writing what the main crime is going to be and who the culprit and victims are," the Mystery Writers of America Grand Master said in an interview with Alvin P. Sanoff in 1988, "but the subplots develop as I write. My crooks are an amalgam of a number of people. As for my heroes, I won't say they're autobiographical, but I wouldn't ask them to do anything I wouldn't do myself."

After a while, the horse racing element receded in the Francis novels, despite the expectations of many readers. One theme remained, however. "Almost universally in Francis's world," observed Michael N. Stanton in *The Armchair Detective*, "the motive for ill-doing is greed . . . the basic line of Francis's books is the uncovering of a wrongful scheme which is in-place or being put in place, and the identification of the agents and principals involved. Except in *Nerve, Enquiry*, and *Bonecrack*, the object of every scheme is to make money wrongly, and one could argue about *Enquiry*."

Following the death of Mary Francis in 1999, journalists and unofficial biographer Graham Lord voiced their belief that she did much of the writing of the Francis mysteries. The author in fact long credited her with checking his spelling, editing his stories, and doing research. "Mary never allowed her name to be on the books, but it was a double act, really," Francis told journalist Gretchen Allen.

On another occasion, the author told an iVillager interviewer in 1995, "We [Francis and his wife] talk about the books a lot while I'm writing. It's a joint affair. There are passages about the females in them and how females think, and Mary's always a great help with that."

Francis biographer Melvyn Barnes found it difficult to place Dick Francis within the context of crime fiction, as he felt the horse racing thrillers are of a higher literary standard and explore more positive themes than some of his predecessors such as Edgar Wallace. Francis himself told Barnes, "I consider my books to be adventure stories rather than thrillers."

And that is a satisfactory legacy, is it not?

Works by the Author

Fiction

Dead Cert (1962)
Nerve (1964)
For Kicks (1965)
Flying Finish (1966)
Blood Sport (1967)
Forfeit (1968)
Enquiry (1969)
Rat Race (1970)
Bonecrack (1971)
Smokescreen (1972)
Slay-Ride (1973)
Knock Down (1974)
High Stakes (1975)
In the Frame (1976)
Risk (1977)
Trial Run (1978)
Reflex (1981)
Twice Shy (1981)
Banker (1983)
The Danger (1984)
Proof (1985)
Bolt (1986), sequel to *Break In*
Hot Money (1987)
The Edge (1988)
Straight (1989)
Longshot (1990)
Comeback (1991)
Driving Force (1992)
Decider (1993)
Wild Horses (1994)
Break In (1995)
To the Hilt (1996)
10 Lb. Penalty (1997)
Second Wind (1999)
Shattered (2000)
Win, Place or Show (2004), includes *Odds Against*, *Whip Hand* and *Come to Grief*

Sid Halley Series

Odds Against (1965)
Whip Hand (1979)
Come to Grief (1995)

Collections

Field of 13 (1998)

Editor

Best Racing and Chasing Stories, with John Welcome (1966)
Best Racing and Chasing Stories II, with John Welcome (1969)
Racing Man's Bedside Book (1969)
The Dick Francis Treasury of Great Racing Stories, with John Welcome (1991)
The New Treasury of Great Racing Stories, with John Welcome (1991)

Anthologies

Winter's Crimes 5, edited by Virginia Whitaker (1973)
Great Stories of Suspense, edited by Ross Macdonald (1974)
Stories of Crime and Detection, edited by Joan D. Berbrich (1974)
Ellery Queen's Crime Wave (1976)
Ellery Queen's Searches and Seizures, edited by Ellery Queen (1977)
John Creasey's Crime Collection 1977, edited by Herbert Harris (1977)
Verdict of Thirteen, edited by Julian Symons (1978)
Masterpieces of Mystery: The Seventies, edited by Ellery Queen (1979)
Best Detective Stories of the Year—1980, edited by Edward D. Hoch (1980)
The Best of Winter's Crimes 1, edited by George Hardinge (1986)
The Mammoth Book of Modern Crime Stories, edited by George Hardinge (1986)

Nonfiction

The Sport of Queens (1957)
A Jockey's Life: The Biography of Lester Piggott (1986), in England as *Lester: The Official Biography* (1986)

Motion Pictures and Television Movies Based on the Author's Works

Dead Cert (1973)
The Racing Game (1970), for Yorkshire Television and PBS's *Mystery* based on *Odds Against*
Dick Francis: Blood Sport (1989)
Dick Francis Mysteries (1989)

For Further Information

Allen, Gretchen. "Mystery Writer Says Wife Helped." Associated Press. *http://members/ optushome.com/au/dibingham/DF0910.htm* (viewed July 5, 2003).

Ashley Mike, ed. Dick Francis entry, *The Mammoth Encyclopedia of Modern Crime Fiction.* New York: Carroll & Graf, 2002.

Axthelm, Pete. "Writer With a Whip Hand." *Newsweek* (April 6, 1981).

Bargainnier, Earl. F., ed. *Twelve Englishmen of Mystery.* Bowling Green, OH: Bowling Green University Popular Press, 1984.

Barnes, Melvyn. *Dick Francis.* New York: Ungar, 1986.

Barnes, Melvyn. Dick Francis entry, *St. James Guide to Crime & Mystery Writers.* 4th edition, edited by Jay P. Pederson. Detroit: St. James Press, 1996.

Davis, J. Madison. *Dick Francis.* Boston: Twayne, 1989.

"Dick Francis: The Queen Mother's Horse." iVillage.com. *http://www.ivillage.com/ books/intervu/myst/articles/(1,240795_97134,00.html?arrivalSA=1&arrival_ freqCap=1&pba=adid=5804264* (viewed July 5, 2003).

Fuller, Bryony. *Dick Francis: Steeplechase Jockey.* London: Joseph, 1994.

Guttman, Robert J. Dick Francis interview. *Europe* (November 1996).

Jakubowski, Maxim. "Two or Three Things You Should Know About British Crime Fiction." *The Fine Art of Murder*, edited by Ed Gorman, Martin H. Greenberg, Larry Segriff, with Jon L. Breen. New York: Carroll & Graf, 1993.

Jones, Daniel, and John D. Jorgenson, eds. Dick Francis entry, *Contemporary Authors New Revision Series.* Vol. 68. Detroit: Gale Research, 1998.

Lord, Graham. *Dick Francis: A Racing Life.* New York: Time Warner, 2000.

Nolan, Tom. "Dick Francis on a Winning Streak." *Mary Higgins Clark Mystery* (spring 1997).

Sanoff, Alvin P. "Finding intrigue wherever he goes." *U.S. News & World Report* (March 28, 1988).

Stanton, Michael N. "Dick Francis: The Worth of Human Love." *The Armchair Detective.* Vol. 15, no. 2 (1982).

Symons, Julian. Reflex review. *New York Times Book Review* (March 29, 1981).

"Who Done It? Millions of books later, a mystery gallops up on Dick Francis: Did his wife cowrite his bestsellers?" *People Weekly* (November 22, 1999).

Diana Gabaldon

♦ Historical

Williams, Arizona
1952

♦ *Outlander*

Credit: Barbara Schnell.

About the Author and the Author's Writing

Diana Gabaldon's introduction to professional writing was, rather surprisingly, creating comic book scripts for Walt Disney! Well, is it such a stretch to think about a connection between Duckburg multibillionaire Scrooge McDuck and the Scots heroes of the author's popular Outlander series?

"I wrote my first book—*Outlander*—for practice, never intending to show it to anyone," the author said in an e-mail. "That being so, it was quite irrelevant what sort of book it was, and so I used any element of fiction that took my fancy. The result was a book—and now a series of books—that could not be classified by anyone who's ever tried—and believe me, a lot of people have tried!

"The books are essentially Big, Fat, Solid Historical Fiction, of the well-researched and gripping type, a la James Michener and James Clavell," she went on. "However, the main protagonist is a time-traveler. (Cough.) Then we have the Loch Ness monster, a certain amount of witchcraft, religious mysticism, botanical medicine, sex, violence . . . well, what the heck, the books run around 900 pages in hardcover; I have room for a lot of stuff (including a full-fledged murder mystery in each book, though what with all the other stuff going on, this tends not to be the main focus of attention)."

Diana Gabaldon was born in Williams, Arizona, in 1952, of Hispanic American ancestry. She now lives in Scottsdale, Arizona, but does some of her writing at the family home she grew up in and inherited in Flagstaff. She says she was born with a knack for telling stories, "to myself, or to my sister (we shared a room until I was fourteen or so, and told long, interactive stories far into the night)—for as long as I can recall. Still, there's a major difference between having a story in your head and being able to get it to come out convincingly on paper," she told interviewer Chris Chamberline. "Writing well takes a lot of work, no matter who you are."

At Arizona State University, she earned a bachelor's degree in zoology in 1973 and a master's in marine biology two years later. At Northern Arizona University she earned a Ph.D. in behavioral ecology in 1978. (Her dissertation topic was "Nest Site Selection in Pinyon Jays.") She married Doug Watkins, whom she met while each played French horn in the university's marching band, and they have three children.

Gabaldon received two National Science Foundation postdoctoral appointments, at the University of Pennsylvania and University of California at Los Angeles. During the latter assignment, from 1979 to 1980, she sought out Walt Disney Productions' comic book producers and landed freelance work for the foreign comics program: "stories about Mickey Mouse, Donald Duck, the Beagle Boys and Uncle Scrooge, etc. My first foray into fiction—and where I learned most of what I know about the mechanics of storytelling," she said on her Web page.

From there, she spent a dozen years, from 1980 to 1992, as a field ecologist and then assistant research professor at Arizona State University, writing articles and reviews for scientific journals and computer programs designed to store data on bird gizzards. All the while, she continued to write nonfiction freelance. She left the academic world with the sale of her novel *Dragonfly in Amber*.

That book was her second novel, a sequel to *Outlander*, and it tells the story of an English nurse, Claire Beauchamp Randall, who is visiting Scotland during the time of World War II and time travels to 1743 and the Second Jacobite Rising. Claire ultimately has husbands in both worlds, marrying Scots warrior Jamie Fraser in the past. Admirers of the Claire and Jamie novels have their own Web site: Ladies of Lallybroch. In fact, the Internet helped propel the author onto best-seller lists. Gabaldon, on her Web site, posted selections from her newest novels, along with maps and information on Scottish clans.

"I think the Internet has played quite a bit of a role in the success of my books," the author told the *Wall Street Journal's* David D. Kirkpatrick when *Drums of Autumn* was released. Gabaldon was quite comfortable using the Internet—she engaged an agent after posting portions of her first novel on a writer's forum on CompuServe.

She had decided to write a novel with a strong historical setting so she would have something to fall back on, lest she run out of plot. The time travel idea arose after she watched an episode of the British science fiction series *Doctor Who* that featured a kilted young Scot. She wrote the book without any expectation of selling it for publication. This, she said, accounts for its brashness. (And it also handily allows the heroine to speak in tart twentieth-century language.)

Booksellers struggle with figuring out what kind of books Gabaldon is writing. Historical? Romance? Adventure? Fantasy? Her publisher, Delacorte, treats them as general fiction; Barnes & Noble, to the author's dismay, shelves them as romances.

"I like romance novels," the author told interviewer Anne Stephenson. "But I think most romance writers are redoing either Cinderella or Beauty and the Beast, and my books don't fit that standard. There's a good love story in them, and a certain amount of sex, but there the resemblance ceases." In a reversal of the usual approach, it is experienced Claire in *Outlander* who introduces virginal Jamie to the world of sensual pleasure.

Gabaldon found she had to defend her hybrid novel. "I used to hear a certain amount of muttering about how 'everyone' knew that you couldn't do that—'that' ranging from writing a book in the first person (I guess nobody told Herman Melville, Charles Dickens or Robert Louis Stevenson, poor saps) to having a female protagonist be older than her lover, to allowing characters to go to the bathroom, to having a book be longer than 100,000 words to . . . well, all the books are still in print in hardcover—and people quit muttering a long time ago," she said in an iVillage interview.

Because of the great fan interest, and the volume of inquiries that swamped her Internet site, the author wrote *The Outlandish Companion* to answer historical and other questions.

Gabaldon does not write detailed outlines of her novels; she has a story concept in mind when she begins writing and lets it pour out. She explained her approach to writing in *The Outlandish Companion*: "I not only don't write with an outline, I don't write in a straight line. I write in bits and pieces, and glue them together, like a jigsaw puzzle."

Hellfire is a nonseries book—or was meant to be, at first—still set in the eighteenth century, as the author had insufficient time to research another country or time period. She liked the hero, Lord John Grey, and featured him in a short story for editor Maxim Jukabowski's *Past Poisons*. She had an idea of writing another story with the same character, but it turned into the next novel, *Lord John and the Private Matter*, in which the main character is troubled to come upon a case of syphilis in an aristocrat who is about to wed his cousin.

The author has contracted to write two contemporary mystery novels, the first tentatively titled *Red Ant's Head*. With fans demanding more to the Claire and Jamie story, a sixth book in progress will wrap up the second trilogy. After that . . .

Works by the Author

Fiction

Hellfire (1998), electronic book
Red Ant's Head (forthcoming)

Lord John Grey Series

Past Poisons: An Ellis Peters Memorial Anthology of Historical Crime, edited by Maxim Jakubowski (1998), short story
Lord John and the Private Matter (2003)
Legends II, edited by Robert Silverberg (2004), short story

Outlander Series

Dragonfly in Amber (1991)
Outlander (1991), also titled *Cross Stitch*
Voyager (1993)
The Drums of Autumn (1996)
The Fiery Cross (2001)
A Breath of Snow and Ashes (forthcoming)

Anthologies

Excalibur, edited by Richard Gilliam (1995)
Mothers & Daughters: Celebrating the Gift of Love, edited by Jill M. Morgan (1998)
Fathers & Daughters: A Celebration in Memoirs, Stories and Photographs, edited by Jill M. Morgan (2000)
Naked Came the Phoenix, edited by Maria Talley (2001)

Out of Avalon: Tales of Old Magic and New Myths, edited by Jennifer Roberson (2001)
Mothers & Sons, edited by Jill Morgan (2001)
Legends II, edited by Robert Silverberg (2003)

Introductions

Ivanhoe: A Romance, by Sir Walter Scott (2001)
Common Sense, by Thomas Paine (2004)

Nonfiction

The Outlandish Companion: In Which Much Is Revealed Regarding Claire and Jamie Fraser, their Lives and Times, Antecedents, Adventures, Companions, and Progeny, with Learned Commentary (and Many Footnotes) by their Humble Creator (1999), also titled *Through the Stones: The Diana Gabaldon Companion*

For Further Information

Baker, John F. "Millions for New Gabaldon Series." *Publishers Weekly* (October 28, 2002).

Bliss, Laurel *Lord John and the Private Matter* review. *Library Journal* (September 1, 2003).

"Books by Diana Gabaldon." January *Magazine. http://www.januarymagazine/com/profiles/gabaldon2002.html* (viewed July 5, 2003).

Chamberline, Chris. "An Interview with Diana Gabaldon." *RestStop Writers' Newsletter* (June 1999).

Clute, John. Diana Gabaldon entry, *Encyclopedia of Fantasy*. New York: St. Martin's Press, 1999.

"Diana Gabaldon: The Truth About Men in Kilts." iVillage. *http://www.ivillage.com/books/intervu/romance/articles/0,,192468_51837,00.html* (viewed July 5, 2003).

Diana Gabaldon Web page. *http://www.cco.caltech.edu/~gatti/gabaldon/gabaldon/html* (viewed July 5, 2003).

Gabaldon, Diana. E-mail to the author, November 2, 2003.

"Gaga for Gabaldon." *Maclean's* (January 14, 2002).

Intini, John. "John Intini starts a sentence . . . Diana Gabaldon finishes it." *Maclean's* (December 8, 2003).

Jones, Daniel, and John D. Jorgenson, eds. Diana Gabaldon entry, *Contemporary Authors New Revision Series*. Vol. 72. Detroit: Gale Research, 1999.

Kirkpatrick, David D. "Little Known Writer Makes Big Splash with the Help of the Net." *Wall Street Journal* (January 9, 1997).

Lacitis, Erik. "Author Diana Gabaldon owes some of her success to her fans in cyber-space." *Seattle Times* (January 17, 1997).

"Modern Romance—in 1745." *Maclean's* (February 17, 1997).

"Ovations for Outlander." *Publishers Weekly* (November 19, 2001).

"Plaid to the bone." *People Weekly* (April 14, 1997).

"Romantic Web." *Time* (January 20, 1997).

Stephenson, Anne. "Diana Gabaldon: Her novels flout convention." *Publishers Weekly* (January 6, 1997).

Sturgeon, Julie. "Private Firest Class." *Pages* (November/December, 2003).

"Tying up loose ends." *Maclean's* (August 9, 1999).

Julie Garwood

Historical   ◆   Romance   ◆   Suspense

Kansas City, Missouri
1946

◆   *Clayburne Roses Series*

About the Author and the Author's Writing

Strong, appealing characters and delightful prose sprinkled with wit and unexpected plotlines make Julie Garwood's romance fiction distinctive and draw a loyal readership. Noting the author bases her heroines' quirks on her own, an All About Romance interviewer commented, "That includes having a poor sense of direction, being 'kind of a klutz,' and . . . having a charming ability to obfuscate and change the direction of conversation to the consternation, frustration, but eventual acceptance of the other party."

Julie Murphy was born in Kansas City, Missouri, in 1946, the daughter an Irish American boxer and a homemaker. She missed a lot of school because of tonsillitis and only fully learned to read when she was in sixth grade, when a nun tutor introduced her to Nancy Drew mysteries. Sister Mary Elizabeth made reading fun and encouraged Julie to keep a journal.

At first it was a diary, the author said in a Bookreporter interview, "but I soon tired of what I thought was a very boring life. Going to school during the day and doing homework at night wasn't exciting to me. Making up stories was much more fun. . . . I made sure that they had wonderful adventures."

The author attended Avila College to study nursing. Required to take a humanities course, she studied Russian history and found she enjoyed it. In 1967, she married Gerald Garwood, a physician, with whom she has three children. They have since divorced.

Garwood began her writing career when the youngest of her children started school. She found an agent who placed her young adult romance novel with Scholastic. She soon moved on to adult historicals with few preconceptions about the genre. The result was books with vibrant heroines such as *The Lion's Lady*, in which a young princess raised in the American West in the early nineteenth century returns to her native England on a secret mission; or *The Bride*, in which a young woman in medieval times weds a Highlander and becomes his equal as an adventurer. Among the distinctions of her writing: there's an element of humor.

She began writing contemporary romantic suspense with *Heartbreaker*. She came up with the unusual plot of a man, in the sanctity of the confessional, asking a priest for forgiveness in advance for killing a woman—the priest's sister. "My mentor Sister Mary Elizabeth would have had a fit," Garwood said in a BookPage interview. "I was sitting in a 400-year-old church in London, plotting a crime. The novel follows FBI Agent Nicholas Buchanan, who responds to a frantic plea from his childhood friend, Father Tommy Madden, and—this is a romance after all—is immediately drawn to the priest's younger sister, Laurant."

Garwood's *For the Roses*, about four brothers who raise a foundling, prompted several sequels and was made into a television movie in 1997. All the brothers in the books were based on the author's only brother, Thomas Murphy, who died of a brain tumor in 1994, at age fifty-seven. To Garwood, writing this book was a way of saying good-bye. Family, it is obvious in the books, is important to the author.

Garwood, who now lives in Leawood, Kansas, was accustomed to family noise and says she still works best with it. "Each morning she's up for work at 5 a.m., turning on CNN full blast," revealed *People Weekly* in 1997. "She likes it even more if her three children . . . are home to add decibels."

Garwood has found her old fans want more historicals; her new ones are excited about the romantic suspense books. Writing in either genre takes time for research. She writes with a general outline, but at times, as with *Killjoy*, a novel about a sociopath, "there were a couple of twists that surprised even me as I was writing," she told Rose Chastain. "The name came to me as I was writing a scene. The antagonist says to the heroine, 'Don't be a killjoy,' and I knew I had the title."

"The Irish are great storytellers who relish getting all the details and nuances of every situation," Garwood said on Wabaweb.com. "Add in the fact that I was the sixth of seven children. Early in life I learned that self-expression had to be forceful, imaginative and quick."

Works by the Author

Fiction

Honor's Splendor (1987)
The Bride (1989)
The Prize (1991)
The Secret (1992)
Saving Grace (1993)
Prince Charming (1994)
The Wedding (1996), sequel to *The Bride*
Ransom (1999), sequel to *The Secret*
The Murder List (2004)

Buchanan Brothers Series

Heartbreaker (2000)
Mercy (2001)
Killjoy (2002)

Clayborne Roses Series

For the Roses (1995)
Come the Spring (1997)
One Pink Rose (1997)
One Red Rose (1997)
One White Rose (1997)

Lyon Series

The Lion's Lady (1988)
Guardian Angel (1990)
The Gift (1991)
Castles (1993)

Tapestry Romances Series

Gentle Warrior (1985)
Rebellious Desire (1986)

Books for Young Adults

What's a Girl to Do, with Emily Chase (1985)
A Girl Named Summer (1986)

Television Movies Based on Author's Works

Rose Hill (1997), based on *For the Roses*

For Further Information

Chastain, Rose. Julie Garwood interview. A Romance Review. *http://www.aromance review.com/interviews/juliegarwood.phtml* (viewed July 5, 2003).

Julie Garwood biography. Bookreporter. *http://www.bookreporter.com/authors/talk-garwood-julie.asp* (viewed July 5, 2003).

Julie Garwood's Readers and Fans Web site. *http://www.wabaweb.com/JulieGarwood .about/.htm* (viewed July 5, 2003).

"Lunch With Julie Garwood." All About Romance (January 1, 1998). *http://www .likesbooks.com/garwood.html* (viewed July 5, 2003).

Maryles, Daisy. "Garwood Scores a Double." *Publishers Weekly* (September 24, 2001).

Maryles, Daisy. "Julie's All Heart." *Publishers Weekly* (July 17, 2000).

Olendorf, Donna, ed. Julie Garwood entry, *Contemporary Authors*. Vol. 138. Detroit: Gale Research, 1993.

Smith, Kyle. "Talking with . . . Julie Garwood: coming up roses." *People Weekly* (April 28, 1997).

Trotter, Karen. "Julie Garwood breaks rank, ventures into the realm of thrillers." Book-Page. *http://www.bookpage.com/0007bp/julie_garwood.html* (viewed March 31, 2003).

Sue Grafton

◆ Mystery

Louisville, Kentucky
1940

◆ *Kinsey Milhone Series*

Credit: Steven Humphrey.

About the Author and the Author's Writing

Along with Sara Paretsky and Marcia Muller, Sue Grafton is one of the mothers of the modern female private detective, one of the "Lady Gumshoes: Boiled Less Hard," as a *New York Times Book Review* headline writer put it.

Sue Taylor Grafton was born in 1940 in Louisville, Kentucky, the daughter of bond attorney Chip Warren Grafton and his wife, Vivian Bousseau Harnsberger Grafton, a high school chemistry teacher. The author's grandparents on both sides were Presbyterian missionaries, and her parents grew up in China. "Both of them were alcoholics," she said in a *Mystery Scene* interview, "so I grew up in a very dysfunctional situation. Sometimes I think it was a very perfect upbringing, because I was raised with a great deal of freedom. It was a very unstructured household, and I lived in my imagination. There was no television back then; and what kids did was, we *played*. We *played*; we played intense games. There were about 12 kids in our neighborhood, and there was always just some drama being acted out. And I think that was very good for me."

Grafton earned a bachelor of arts degree in English literature with minors in humanities and fine arts from University of Louisville in 1961. (Two of her college years were spent at Western Kentucky State Teachers College.)

She married Steven F. Humphrey, a philosophy professor, in 1978. She has three children by two earlier marriages. She has homes in Montecito, California, and Louisville.

Grafton worked as a hospital admissions clerk, cashier, and medical secretary before starting her writing career with two novels, *Kezia Dane* and *The Lolly-Madonna War*. She spent a decade in Hollywood writing television and motion picture scripts. Going through a lengthy and bitter divorce and custody battle, she dreamt of ways to commit murder. She decided to put her dreams on paper and, at the same time, provide herself with an escape from screenwriting, which she'd come to dislike. By the time *G Is for Gumshoe* came out, she was able to leave Tinseltown without regrets.

"There's nothing like a film script to teach you structure, which is what the mystery is about," Grafton said in a *Publishers Weekly* interview in 1998. "What I hated about Hollywood was doing business. I hated the democratic process where everybody got a vote. I am not a team player. I was not a good sport. I spent a lot of that time trying to suppress a natural rage that came billowing out when people tried to tell me how to do my work." Consequently, she has refused to sell movie rights to her popular Kinsey Milhone books.

Grafton knew she wanted to write mysteries, but she didn't know a whole lot about private investigators. "In the course of writing that first book, I began the long (and continuing) task of educating myself," she is quoted in *G Is for Grafton: The World of Kinsey Milhone.* "I read books on forensics, toxicology, burglary and theft, homicide, arson, anatomy, and poisonous plants, among many others."

When she began the mystery series, she considered linking the titles by use of color. But John D. MacDonald had done that. Days of the week? Harry Kellerman took that. How about the alphabet—as artist Edward Gorey did?

The author gained helpful insights about her craft from her father, who wrote three mystery novels in the 1940s. "He talked a lot about how to survive as a writer," she said in an interview with Bruce Taylor, "how to deal with rejection, how to roll with the punches. He taught me how to write with clarity and simplicity. He said it was never my job to revise the English language or to play games with punctuation, spelling, or capitalization. . . . He talked often about the fact that you can always write the big scenes. But you have to pay attention to the transitions, because if you don't handle the small things well, you won't have a reader by the time you get to the big scenes."

Kinsey Milhone remains blessedly single, if for no other reason than that it's a major challenge for the author to figure out what to do with a love interest while dealing with the crime story. "The problem any mystery writer runs into, when it comes to the question of romance, is what the heck to do with the guy before, during, and after," she explained in an iVillage interview. "Often, your choices are send him off to the foreign legion, kill him, or have him marry your heroine. None of these alternatives suit me." Grafton does make the promise her heroine, sometime before Z, will have a relationship.

The mysteries are on a slower time track than the real world; *O Is for Outlaw*, for example, still has the heroine in 1986, before cellular telephones or the Internet. This may derive from the author's religious background and her missionary grandparents. "The Presbyterians believe that in the mind of God there is no time, which makes sense," she said, with a bit of humor, on the Writers Write Web site. "In God's mind, it can't be Monday, August 23rd. In God's mind, it's all over, beginning, middle and end, all through the end of time." Consequently, if all history already exists, her task is simplified: Just sit at the keyboard and type the story again.

Grafton says she does not outline before she writes. However, she does maintain a journal where she tries out some what-ifs. She often discards more ideas than she keeps as she gets into the rhythm of a particular novel. Does she get into trouble? Yes.

But for the adventuresome writer, that's the reward. In an article in *Writer's Yearbook 1996*, she described how *E Is for Evidence* came together. Her plot came to a dead end and she "didn't have the faintest idea how the book was going to end. I thought, I sure hope this book ends with a bang and not a whimper. And a little voice said, 'Put a bomb in it, Grafton.' So the book ends with a bombing. People who outline don't have nearly the fun we do," referring to fellow mystery writer, and non-outliner, Tony Hillerman.

For background, the author interviewed a host of cops, investigators, lawyers, coroners, and others, and she read widely. Although her character is a great part of her own personality, Grafton said she works hard to maintain Milhone's perspective and not let hers take over. She doesn't know everything about her heroine's life; when she decided to write about Milhone's ex-husband, Mickey Magruder, the author said she knew little more than that he was a police officer, a little older than Milhone, and that Milhone had walked out on their marriage. She learned the details only as they emerged in her writing.

Grafton admits that sometimes she fails. Readers are quick to point out errors. "[T]here's the famous error in *B Is for Burglar* where Kinsey leaves her car keys in the ignition of the VW before she creeps down into some dark and spidery basement," Grafton said on her Web page. "When she's caught, she uses the very same set of keys to loosen a screw on the door she's hoping to open. Oops. Loyal readers always swear she carries a second set of keys for just such occasions."

What gives Milhone her great appeal, Grafton expects, is her real dimension. She has no college degree. She's a hard worker; she makes her own way; she pays her bills promptly. "Readers are convinced she's real," the author said in a 1996 interview that appears on her Web site. "I don't idolize her; she isn't larger than life; she's human-sized. She makes mistakes."

What does she like about writing mysteries? "I love a well-structured story," she said in *The Writer* in 2002. "I'm interested in what motivates an individual to do good or ill and I'm fascinated by the dark side of human nature. Basically, any mystery writer is both magician and moralist . . . two species of artist in short supply. Sometimes I claim I write because I put in an application at Sears and they've never called back."

Works by the Author

Fiction

Keziah Dane (1967)
The Lolly-Madonna War (1969)

Kinsey Milhone Series

A Is for Alibi (1982)
B Is for Burglar (1985)
C Is for Corpse (1986)
D Is for Deadbeat (1987)
E Is for Evidence (1988)
F Is for Fugitive (1989)
G Is for Gumshoe (1990)
H Is for Homicide (1991)
I Is for Innocent (1992)
J Is for Judgment (1993)
K Is for Killer (1994)
L Is for Lawless (1995)
M Is for Malice (1996)

N Is for Noose (1998)
Sue Grafton: Three Complete Novels A, B & C (1999), omnibus
O Is for Outlaw (2001)
P Is for Peril (2001)
Q Is for Quarry (2002)
R Is for Ricochet (2004)

Anthologies

Mean Streets, edited by Robert J. Randisi (1986)
The Year's Best Mystery and Suspense Stories, edited by Edward D. Hoch (1987)
Criminal Elements, edited by Bill Pronzini (1988)
An Eye for Justice, edited by Robert J. Randisi (1988)
Lady on the Case, edited by Marcia Muller (1988)
City Sleuths and Tough Guys, edited by David Willis McCullough (1989)
Deadly Doings, edited by Martin H. Greenberg (1989)
Match Me Sidney! (1989)
Sisters in Crime, edited by Marilyn Wallace (1989)
Sisters in Crime 2, edited by Marilyn Wallace (1990)
Under the Gun, edited by Ed Gorman (1990)
Best American Mystery Stories 2000, edited by Donald E. Westlake (2000)
Best American Mystery Stories of the Century, edited by Otto Penzler and Tony Hillerman (2001)
Most Wanted, edited by Robert J. Randisi (2002)

Teleplays

Lolly-Madonna War (1973)
Sex and the Single Parent (1979)
Walking Through the Fire (1979)
Mark, I Love You (1980)
Nurse (1980)

Written with Steven F. Humphrey

Seven Brides for Seven Brothers (1982)
A Caribbean Mystery (1983)
Killer in the Family (1983)
Sparkling Cyanide (1983)
Love On the Run (1985)
Tonight's the Night (1987)

Nonfiction
Editor

Writing Mysteries

For Further Information

Ashley, Mike ed. Sue Grafton entry, *The Mammoth Encyclopedia of Modern Crime Fiction*. New York: Carroll & Graf, 2002.

Bing, Jonathan. "Sue Grafton: death and the maiden." *Publishers Weekly* (April 20, 1998).

Chapman, Jeff, and John D. Jorgenson, eds. Sue Grafton entry, *Contemporary Authors New Revision Series*. Vol. 55. Detroit: Gale Research, 1997.

Fish, Peter. "Gumshoe in paradise." *Sunset* (September 1999).

Geherin, David. Sue Grafton entry, *St. James Guide to Crime & Mystery Writers*, 4th edition. Detroit: St. James Press, 1996.

Goodman, Susan. " '2' Is for Bestsellers." *Writer's Yearbook 1996* (1996).

Grafton, Sue. "How I Write." *The Writer* (May 2002).

Kaufman, Natalie Hevener, and Carol McGinnis Kay. *G Is for Grafton: The World of Kinsey Milhone*. New York: Holt, 1997.

Nolan, Tom. "Seven Down and Nineteen to Go." *Mystery Scene*, no. 72 (2001).

Stasio, Marilyn. "Lady Gumshoes: Boiled Less Hard." *New York Times Book Review* (April 28, 1985).

Sue Grafton entry, *Authors and Artists for Young Adults*. Vol. 49. Detroit: Gale Group, 2003.

"Sue Grafton: M Is for Mysteries." iVillager. *http://www.ivillage.com/books/intervu/myst/articles/0,,240795_39443.html* (viewed July 27, 2003).

Sue Grafton Web site. *http://www.suegrafton.com* (viewed July 27, 2003).

Taylor, Bruce. "G Is for (Sue) Grafton." *The Armchair Detective* (winter 1989).

White, Claire, E. "A Conversation with Sue Grafton." Writers Write. *http://www.writerswire/com/journal/oct99/grafton.htm* (viewed July 27, 2003).

W.E.B. Griffin

◆ Adventure ◆ Science fiction ◆ Mystery

Newark, New Jersey
1929

◆ *Brotherhood of War Series*

About the Author and the Author's Writing

Is there a genre W.E.B. Griffin hasn't written in, under one of his dozen pseudonyms? Auto racing, romance, military, humor, epics, sports, historical, suspense, mystery, aviation—Griffin has done them all.

William Edmund Butterworth III, to use the author's given name, was born in 1929 in Newark, New Jersey, and grew up in New York City and Wallingford, a suburb of Philadelphia. He has been married twice and has three children.

In 1946, he enlisted in the U.S. Army, where he trained in counter-intelligence and was assigned to the Army of Occupation in Germany. He was later a member of the staff of Major General I. D. White, who had command of the U.S. Constabulary. He attended Phillips University at Marburg an der Lahn in Germany, but he was recalled to active duty, again under White, serving at Fort Knox and in Korea. He was a combat correspondent and information officer and received the Expert Combat Infantryman's Badge. Upon his discharge in 1953, he became chief of the U.S. Army Signal Aviation Test & Support Activity's Publications Division at Fort Rucker, Alabama.

The author began a long career of genre writing in the 1960s, under his own and other names. He wrote car racing and athletics stories for young adults; he wrote nonfiction books about astronomy and automobiles; and he coauthored a series of M*A*S*H novels with Richard Hooker, who wrote the original novel that inspired a motion picture and long-running television series.

Butterworth began using the W.E.B. Griffin penname in 1982 to write novels for adult readers, beginning with the Brotherhood of War series about the military. Spanning the years from World War II to Vietnam, the books have been praised for their historical and technical accuracy. As that series was underway, he began others: *The Corps*, depicting the valor of members of the U.S. Marine Corps from World War II to Korea; *Honor Bound*, about Office for Strategic Services operatives working against pro-Nazi Peron in Argentina during World War II; and *Badge of Honor*, about members of the Philadelphia Police Department. Men at War novels, about members of Colonel William "Wild Bill" Donovan's Office of Strategic Services during the Second World War, were originally published in paperback under the by-line Alex Baldwin by Pocketbooks, but are now being rereleased by Putnam in hardcover, with some revisions, under the Griffin byline.

Called "the poet laureate of the American military" by the Los Angeles *Daily News*, Griffin alternates his five series, taking upwards of nine months to research and write a new book. Badge of Honor books, he said on his Web site, are based on real cases investigated by Philadelphia police. His main characters are fictional ones placed against historical backgrounds and often interacting with historical figures.

"You have to really think about how an actual person would behave in a given circumstance," Griffin said of his writing in an interview with Barnes & Noble. "I've been very lucky all along in either (rarely) knowing the character myself, or being with people who knew them intimately, and have been willing to tell me about them, and their behavior in private."

Griffin, who has homes in Alabama and in Buenos Aires, has won numerous awards, including the Brigadier General Robert L. Dening Memorial Distinguished Service Award of the U.S. Marine Corps Combat Correspondents Association. He has received an honorary doctor of philosophy in military fiction degree from Norwich University and holds honorary memberships in the Special forces Association, the Marine Corps Combat Correspondents Association, and the U.S. Army Otter & Caribou Association. In 2003, he became a life member of the Police Chiefs Association of Southeastern Pennsylvania, Southern New Jersey, and Delaware.

Griffin puts in long hours at his craft, but there's a big payoff. "Nothing honors me more than a serviceman, veteran, or cop telling me he enjoys reading my books," the author said on his Web site.

Works by the Author

Fiction

By Order of the President (2004)

Badge of Honor Series

Men in Blue (1988)
Special Operations (1989), originally written as by John Kevin Dugan
The Victim (1990)
The Witness (1991)
The Assassin (1992)
The Murderers (1995)
The Investigators (1998)
Final Justice (2003)

Brotherhood of War Series

The Captains (1982)
The Lieutenants (1982)
The Colonels (1983)
The Majors (1983)
The Berets (1985)
The Generals (1986)
The New Breed (1987)
The Aviators (1988)
Special Ops (2001)

Corps Series

Semper Fi (1986)
Call to Arms (1987)
Counterattack (1990)
Battleground (1991)
Line of Fire (1992)
Behind the Lines (1995)
Close Combat (1995)
In Danger's Path (1999)
Under Fire (2002)
Retreat, Hell! (2004)

Honor Bound Series

Honor Bound (1993)
Blood and Honor (1997)
Secret Honor (2000)

Written as Alex Baldwin, Reissued as by W.E.B. Griffin

Men at War Series

The Last Heroes (1985)
The Secret Warriors (1985)
The Soldier Spies (1986)
The Fighting Agents (1987)

Written as Allison Mitchell

Wild Harvest (1984)
Wild Heritage (1985)

Written as Eden Hughes

The Wiltons (1981)
The Selkirks (1983)

Written as Edmund O. Scholefield

Tiger Rookie (1966)
Bryan's Dog (1967)
L'il Wildcat (1967)
Maverick on the Mound (1968)
Yankee Boy (1971)

Written as Jack Dugan

The Deep Kill (1984)

Written as James McM. Douglas

Hunger for Racing (1967)
Racing to Glory (1969)
The Twelve-Cylinder Screamer (1970)
Drag Race Driver (1971)
A Long Ride on a Cycle (1972)

Written as Patrick J. Williams

Fastest Funny Car (1967)
Grand Prix Racing (1968)
The Green Ghost (1969)
Racing Mechanic (1969)
Up to the Quarterdeck (1969)

Written as Walker E. Blake

Heartbreak Ridge (1962)
The Level and the Lost (1962)
Once More With Passion (1964)
Doing What Comes Naturally (1965)

Written as W. E. Butterworth

Comfort Me With Love (1961)
Hot Seat (1961)
The Court-Martial (1962)
The Girl in the Black Bikini (1962)

Hell on Wheels (1962)
The Love-Go-Round (1962)
Where We Go From Here (1962)
Le Falot (1963)
Fast Green Car (1963)
Stock Car Racer (1966)
Air Evac (1967)
Helicopter Pilot (1967)
Road Racer (1967)
Orders to Vietnam (1968)
Redline 7100 (1968)
Grand Prix Driver (1969)
Stop and Search (1969)
Wheel of a Fast Car (1969)
Fast and Smart (1970)
Marty and the Micro Midgets (1970)
Moving West on 122 (1970)
Steve Bellamy (1970)
Susan and Her Classic Convertible (1970)
Crazy to Race (1971)
My Father's Quite a Guy (1971)
The Race Driver (1971)
Return to Racing (1971)
Team Racer (1971)
Dateline: Talladega (1972)
The Narc (1972)
Flying Army (1973)
Race Car Team (1973)
Yankee Driver (1973)
Dave White and the Electric Wonder Car (1974)
Return to Daytona (1974)
Stop Thief! (1974)
The Roper Brothers and Their Magnificent Steam Automobile (1976)
Christina's Passion (1977)
The Air Freight Mystery (1978)
Net Stop Earth (1978)
Tank Driver (1978)
Under the Influence (1979)
LeRoy and the Old Man (1980)
Skyjacked! (1982)

M*A*S*H Series, written with Richard Hooker

M*A*S*H Goes to Maine (1972)
M*A*S*H Goes to Paris (1974)

M*A*S*H Goes to Morocco (1975)
M*A*S*H Goes to New Orleans (1975)
M*A*S*H Goes to Hollywood (1976)
M*A*S*H Goes to Las Vegas (1976)
M*A*S*H Goes to London (1976)
M*A*S*H Goes to Miami (1976)
M*A*S*H Goes to San Francisco (1976)
M*A*S*H Goes to Vienna (1976)
M*A*S*H Goes to Montreal (1977)
M*A*S*H Goes to Texas (1977)
M*A*S*H Goes to Moscow (1978)

Written as Webb Beech

No French Leave (1960)
Article 92: Murder-Rape (1965)
Warrior's Way (1965)
Make War in Madness (1966)

Nonfiction as W. E. Butterworth

The Wonders of Astronomy (1964)
The Wonders of Rockets and Missiles (1964)
Soldiers on Horseback: The Story of the United States Cavalry (1966)
The Image Makers (1967)
Flying Army: The Modern Air Arm of the U.S. Army (1971)
Wheels and Pistons: The Story of the Automobile (1971)
The High Wind: The Story of NASCAR Racing (1972)
Tires and Other Things: Some Heroes of Automotive Evolution (1974)
Black Gold: The Story of Oil (1975)
Careers in the Service (1976)
Mighty Minicycles (1976)
An Album of Automobile Racing (1977)
Hi-Fi: From Edison's Phonograph to Quadraphonic Sound (1977)

For Further Information

Hall, Elizabeth. "Tell It of the Marines." *Pages* (March/April 2004).

Jones, Daniel, and John D. Jorgenson, eds. W. E. Butterworth entry, *Contemporary Authors New Revision Series*. Vol. 64. Detroit: Gale Research, 1998.

Official W.E.B. Griffin Web page. *http://www.nmark.com/webgriffin/author.html* (viewed June 30, 2003).

W.E.B. Griffin biography. Barnes & Noble. *http://www.barnesandnoble.com/writers/writerdetails/.asp?userid-0H4KV3ZHTM&cid=883328#bio* (viewed June 30, 2003).

W.E.B. Griffin Web site. *http://www.webgriffin.com/* (viewed June 30, 2003).

John Grisham

◆ Mystery ◆ Suspense

Jonesboro, Arkansas
1955

◆ *The Firm*

About the Author and the Author's Writing

Each decade has a favorite author of courtroom stories: Arthur Train, Erle Stanley Gardner, and John Grisham have provided their respective generations with hours of fascinating reading. Grisham, whose novels include *The Firm* and *Runaway Jury*, was the best-selling author of the 1990s, according to a *Publishers Weekly* top-100 list, just edging out Stephen King and Danielle Steel.

"The best-selling single book from the list was Grisham's 'The Pelican Brief,' which registered 11,232,480 copies sold. Number two was also a Grisham title, 'The Client,' which sold 8.1 million copies," CNN.com reported.

John Grisham was born in 1955 in Jonesboro, Arkansas, the son of a construction worker and his homemaker wife. As a boy, John hoped to become a professional baseball player. Growing up he read the usual Dr. Seuss, Hardy Boys, Chip Hilton, Mark Twain, and Charles Dickens, but one of his earliest recollections of a book that made a strong impression on him was John Steinbeck's *Tortilla Flat*.

Grisham received a bachelor of science degree in accounting from Mississippi State University and a J.D. from the University of Mississippi. He married Renee Jones; they have two children and own a farm in Mississippi and a plantation in Virginia.

Admitted to the bar in Mississippi in 1981, Grisham was in private practice in Southaven, Mississippi, for a decade, putting in sixty to seventy hours a week in criminal defense and personal injury litigation cases. His Christian faith prompted him to turn down some cases—he wouldn't do divorces, believing the laws too lax. "I turned down certain criminal defendants because I couldn't bring myself to believe them or fight for them," he told *Saturday Evening Post*, adding, "I did a lot of pro bono work for churches [that had] an assortment of legal problems."

Grisham served in the Mississippi House of Representatives from 1984 to 1990. Despite this heavy workload, he found time to write, inspired by an account he heard from a twelve-year-old rape victim. It took him three years to complete *A Time to Kill*, which Wynwood Press brought out in a 5,000-copy print run in 1988. It quietly went out of print.

"The day after Grisham completed *A Time to Kill*, he began work on another novel," according to the author's Web site, "the story of a hotshot young attorney lured to an apparently perfect law firm that was not what it appeared. When he sold the film rights to *The Firm* to Paramount Pictures for $600,000, Grisham suddenly became a hot property among publishers, and book rights were bought by Doubleday. Spending 47 weeks on *The New York Times* bestseller list, *The Firm* became the best-selling novel of 1991."

Grisham followed that book with *The Pelican Brief* and *The Client*, by which time Doubleday reissued *A Time to Kill*. He was on a roll.

Although he had left the law profession, Grisham returned to the courtroom in 1996 to fulfill an old promise to represent the family of a brakeman who was killed when pinned between two rail cars. Counsel secured a jury award of $683,500.

That case is emblematic of Grisham's fiction. As he has said of his view of humanity—something he recognizes from his love of Steinbeck's fiction—he favors the underdog against the bully.

Grisham also has "a fascination with life on the run," as he told interviewer Ellen Kanner. "I really get into it. I did a lot of criminal work as an attorney, and learned a lot about it from that. It's not as difficult as it may seem, to disappear. I always wonder why people would voluntarily show up in court and go to jail for ten years. Some people have absolutely nothing to lose if they disappear."

Renee Grisham, John's wife, is an important part of the family writing machine. "I constantly inundate Renee with all sorts of story ideas, and it's her job to tell me to shut up and keep searching," the author told Jesse Kornbluth of Bookreporter. "She has an uncanny ability to spot a good story; I tend to think that almost anything will work. Once I start writing, she is merciless as the chapters pour forth. She enjoys picking a good brawl over a subplot, a weak character, an unnecessary scene. I accuse her of looking for trouble—and, inevitably, I return to the typewriter and fix whatever troubles her."

Grisham has no intention of staying forever in the courtroom, even in his writing; in later books he has ventured elsewhere. "I always try to tell a good story," he said in an Amazon.com.uk interview, "one with a compelling plot that will keep the pages turning. That is my first and primary goal. Sometimes I can tackle an issue—homelessness, tobacco litigation, insurance fraud, the death penalty—and wrap a good story around it. These are the best books, the ones with a story and a message. Other times, I simply want to entertain."

Grisham lightened up considerably for *The Brethren*. "After my last two books [*The Street Lawyer* and *The Testament*], which were a little heavy, my wife told me to stop preaching and write something fun," the author said in an interview with *Entertainment Weekly's* Benjamin Svetkey. "So I tried to write the funniest thing I could think of without going into all-out comedy. But, you know, all the books I've ever written have had a lot of jokes in them, a lot of one-liners. I just always end up cutting them out."

Further outside chambers is Grisham's 2001 release, *Painted House*, a family story related by seven-year-old Luke Chandler about growing up on a cotton farm in rural Arkansas Delta country in 1952. It is a very personal book. "The stories have been around forever, ever since I was a little kid," the author told Jennifer Harden of *USA Today*. "A lot of the stories were just old family tales, handed down from a father and grandfather, both with a great sense of exaggeration. So I don't know what's true and what's not."

Grisham has maintained his writing routine from his schedule when he was still a lawyer and legislator, rising early to sit at the keyboard. The difference is that now he races to meet a November deadline every year. Considering the intricacies of his plots, it's not surprising his stories are thoroughly thought out in advance.

Grisham outlines extensively, he said in an interview published in *Mystery Scene*, noting the process can sometimes take as long as a year. "But it makes you see the whole story. And when you write suspense it's sort of like writing mystery: you have to drop off clues along the way, you have to make sure you've got your main plot that works, and your core subplot that works. And you've got to be able to see that when you start. You can't predict everything that's going to happen; you can't predict every character you're going to come up with."

Bleachers, the author's story of a former high school quarterback who goes to see his old dying coach, prompted different critical reactions. "To call these characters cardboard is a slander against paper dolls," complained Jennifer Reese in *Entertainment Weekly*, whereas Bill Sykes in *Sports Illustrated* found "Grisham tells a lean and well-paced tale." *Entertainment Weekly's* Gregory Kirschling put the issue in perspective when reviewing the author's recent *The King of Torts*. "Sustaining momentum, not building character, is Grisham's specialty," he opined.

Does being a best-selling author inhibit his writing? "The only pressure I put on myself is to write the best book I can write," Grisham explained to Jeff Zaleski of *Publishers Weekly*. "I guess one of these days I'm going to publish a book, and it's going to be a real dud that will sell half of what the last one sold. At that point, I'll probably worry about sales."

Works by the Author

Fiction

A Time to Kill (1989)
The Firm (1991)
The Pelican Brief (1992)
The Client (1993)
The Chamber (1994)
The Rainmaker (1995)
The Runaway Jury (1996)
The Partner (1997)
The Street Lawyer (1998)
The Testament (1999)
The Brethren (2000)
A Painted House (2001)
Skipping Christmas (2001)
The Summons (2002)
Bleachers (2003)
The King of Torts (2003)
The Last Juror (2004)

Collection
John Grisham (1993)

Anthologies
Legal Briefs (1998)

Screenplays
The Gingerbread Man, written as Al Hayes
Mickey

Motion Pictures and Television Series Based on the Author's Works
The Firm (1993)
The Client (1994)
The Pelican Brief (1994)
John Grisham's 'The Client' (1995–1996), CBS television series
The Chamber (1996)
A Time to Kill (1996)
The Rainmaker (1997)
The Runaway Jury (2003)

For Further Information

"Author Profile: John Grisham." Collect Books. *http://collectbooks.about.com/library/weekly/aa011903a.htm* (viewed July 4, 2003).

Best, Nancy, and Leonard David Baer, eds. *Readings on John Grisham*. San Diego, CA: Greenhaven, 2004.

Donahue, Dick. "Tasty top 'torts.'" *Publishers Weekly* (February 17, 2003).

Ferranti, Jennifer. "Grisham's law." *Saturday Evening Post* (March–April 1997).

"Grisham plagiarism suit dismissed." *Publishers Weekly* (October 20, 1997).

"Grisham ranks as top-selling author of decade." CNN.com. *http://www.cnn.com/1999/books/nbews/12/31/1990.sellers/* (viewed December 20, 2002).

Harden, Jennifer. "'Painted House' freshens the past." *USA Today* (April 17, 2003).

John Grisham entry, *Authors and Artists for Young Adults*. Vol. 47. Detroit: Gale Group, 2003.

John Grisham interview. Academy of Achievement (June 2, 1995). *http://www.achievement.org/autodoc/page/gri0int-1* (viewed July 4, 2003).

John Grisham interview. Amazon.com.uk. *http://www.amazon.co.uk/exec/obidos.tg/feature/-/137103/ref%3Ded%Fcp%5F%5Fi%5F2%5F2%5F2/026-4610415-2502819* (viewed July 5, 2003).

John Grisham Room. Mitchell Memorial Library, Mississippi State University. *http://library/msstate.edu/grisham_room/grisham.htm* (viewed July 5, 2003).

John Grisham Web site. *http://www.randomhouse.com/features/grisham/author.html* (viewed July 4, 2003).

Johnson, Ted. "Home Again." *TV Guide* (April 26, 2003).

Jones, Daniel, and John D. Jorgenson, eds. John Grisham entry, *Contemporary Authors New Revision Series*. Vol. 69. Detroit: Gale Research, 1999.

Jordan, Tina. "Grisham v Grisham." *Entertainment Weekly* (February 13, 2004).

Kanner, Ellen. John Grisham interview. Bookpage. *http://www.bookpage.com/BPinterviews/grisham392.html* (viewed July 4, 2003).

Kennedy, Dean. "The Jury is in." *Entertainment Weekly* (June 7, 1996).

Kirshling, Gregory. "Laws of Motion." *Entertainment Weekly* (February 14, 2003).

Kornbluth, Jesse. John Grisham interview. Bookreporter (May 1997). *http://www.bookreporter.com/authors/att-grisham-john.asp* (viewed July 4, 2003).

Last Juror review. BookPage (February 2004).

Murphy, Stephen M. *Their Word Is Law: Best-selling Lawyer-Novelists Talk About Their Craft*. New York: Berkley, 2002.

Nolan, Tom. "John Grisham Testifies." *Mystery Scene* (spring 2003).

Reese, Jennifer. "Incomplete Pass: John Grisham Tackles a Gridiron Novel with *Bleachers* but Fumbles the Ball." *Entertainment Weekly* (September 12, 2003).

Summer, Bob. " 'Oxford American' relaunched." *Publishers Weekly* (February 10, 2003).

Svetkey, Benjamin. "Making His Case." *Entertainment Weekly* (February 11, 2000).

Syken, Bill. "Gridiron Grisham: The best-selling author winningly draws on his quarterback days." *Sports Illustrated* (September 1, 2003).

Zaleski, Jeff. "The Grisham business." *Publishers Weekly* (January 19, 1998).

Zeitchik, Steven M. "Court Rejects Grisham Suit." *Publishers Weekly* (March 9, 1998).

Carl Hiaasen

◆ Mystery ◆ Humor

Fort Lauderdale, Florida
1953

◆ *Strip Tease*

Credit: Elena Seibert.

About the Author and the Author's Writing

Carl Hiaasen quickly credits his home state, which teems with curious characters, with spawning his particularly twisted, comedic take on the crime novel.

Born in 1953 in Fort Lauderdale, Florida, Hiaasen was the son of a lawyer and his wife. Growing up, he was an eager reader of everything from Ian Fleming's spy fiction and J. D. Salinger's coming-of-age novel to biographies of sports legends Lou Gehrig and Vince Lombardi. Early on he knew he wanted to become a writer. "I think it's some sort of extension of being a class clown—that if you could write something and make somebody laugh, it was a good gig to have," he said in *The Writer*. "I think there was an element of psychotherapy—it was a legal outlet for some of the ideas I was wanting to express as a kid."

Hiaasen attended Emory University from 1970 to 1973 and received a bachelor of science degree in journalism from the University of Florida in 1974. He has twice been married and has one son by each marriage, as well as one stepson and two grandchildren. He lives in the Florida Keys.

For two years beginning in 1974, the author was a reporter for *Cocoa Today*. He joined the *Miami Herald* in 1976, first as a general-assignment reporter, then as part of an investigative team, which won awards for articles on physicians, land speculators, and drug corruption. He taught at Barry College in 1978 and 1979. In 1985, Hiaasen became a *Herald* columnist. (His publisher Putnam has brought out two collections of these columns.)

Hiaasen's first fiction effort was during his college years, assisting Dr. Neil Schulman with a pair of books (he received no byline). Then, as a *Herald* reporter, he worked with a fellow journalist, Bill Montalbano, on three thrillers set against Miami's late 1970s cocaine war. With *Tourist Season*, Hiaasen finally went out on his own.

Besides his adult fiction, Hiaasen has written one book for younger readers, *Hoot*, in which heroes Roy and Mullet Fingers work to stave off the destruction of an owl's burrow. He has also written a nonfiction expose of the Walt Disney empire, *Team Rodent*.

Hiaasen has his characters in mind, and a plot premise, when he sets about writing a novel, but no firm outline. He came to despise outlines while writing assignments in college. "I want the freedom to change directions if needed," he said on his Web site, "and I want to be surprised by my characters. Those are the great joys of writing novels. If I wanted to know in advance how my books were to end, I'd write nonfiction instead."

Hiaasen lists as author influences Joseph Heller, Kurt Vonnegut, John Irving, and John D. MacDonald. He often takes stories from the headlines—convenient, since he is often writing stories to go with those headlines—to shape his novel premises, usually with oddball characters. Chemo in *Skin Tight*, for example, is a hit man with a Weed Whacker affixed to the stump of his arm; Skink in *Double Whammy* is a former-governor-turned-hermit who takes vengeance on any who would desecrate nature; and Jack Tagger in *Basket Case* is a newspaper obituary writer who has memorized the death dates of famous people.

For that last novel, which involves the premature death of a rock-and-roll musician, Hiaasen's publisher requested a complete song by Jimmy and the Slut Puppies to go with lyrics he made up for the storyline. He enlisted his musician friend, the late Warren Zevon, to help him come up with a real song, which ended up on a Zevon CD. (Hiaasen makes few claims to musicianship, but he did fill in for an absent Stephen King to play with columnist Dave Barry and others in the all-author Rock Bottom Remainders at the Miami Book Fair one year.)

Hiaasen has brought Skink back for brief visits in other novels, and he's reintroduced homicide detective Al Garcia. But he shuns series books. "With the main characters I like to start fresh with each book," he told *The Armchair Detective*, "because I feel it makes me actually think them through and write them out. If I have the same lead guy every time, I know myself and I know I'd get lazy."

Are his sometimes demented Florida yarns too far-fetched? Hiaasen points to the Elian Gonzalez story or the "dangling chads" and miscast butterfly votes in the 2000 U.S. national election and rests his case. Land use—or misuse—in Florida is a natural topic for one of the author's novels. "Now you have land use attorneys whose job it is to get around master plans and zoning restrictions, and they make good livings off finding loopholes or making loopholes so people can build something where they weren't intended to build it," said Hiaasen—himself the son and grandson of attorneys—in a BookPage interview. "A good example is Key West. . . . They live off the Hemingway mystique, they trade on the Hemingway mystique, constantly. If Hemingway were alive, he'd take a flame-thrower to Duval Street, and that's the truth. Fifty T-shirt shops? Give me a break."

O. J. Simpson? "The minute I heard he was leaving California," Hiaasen said in a *Book* interview, "I turned to someone and said, 'That sonuvabitch is moving to Florida!' Why did he come here? One, he loves to golf and he can golf all year round here, and two, the bankruptcy laws in Florida protect scoundrels like him."

Hiaasen summed up his writing philosophy in a *January* magazine interview: "The idea of using suspense or a suspense novel as a framework for satire is just useful to me and it's natural to me from doing newspaper work. . . . Especially in South Florida whether it's violent crime or good old-fashioned corruption, a lot of what we write about is right or wrongdoing."

Works by the Author

Fiction

Tourist Season (1986)
Double Whammy (1987)
Skin Tight (1989)
Native Tongue (1991)
Stormy Weather (1993)
Strip Tease (1993)
Lucky You (1997)
Sick Puppy (2000)
Basket Case (2002)
Skinny Dip (2004)

Written with Bill Montalbano

Powder Burn (1981)
Trap Line (1982)
A Death in China (1984)

Contributor

Naked Came the Manatee (1996)

Books for Children

Hoot (2002)

Nonfiction

Paradise Screwed: Selected Columns of Carl Hiaasen (2001)
Kick Ass: Selected Columns of Carl Hiaasen (1999)
Team Rodent: How Disney Devours the World (1998)

Motion Pictures Based on the Author's Works

Strip Tease (1996)

For Further Information

Brookman, Rob. Carl Hiaasen interview. *Book* magazine (January/February 2002).

Carl Hiaasen biography. Amazon.com. *http://www.authorsontheweb.com/features/authormonth/0202hiaasen-carl.asp* (viewed July 15, 2003).

Carl Hiaasen biography. Barnes & Noble. *http://www.barnesandnoble.com/writers/ writerdetails/asp?userid=2UHJZHFY29&cid=88302#bio* (viewed July 15, 2003).

Carl Hiaasen Web site. *http://www.carlhiaasen.com/* (viewed July 15, 2003).

Hiaasen, Carl. "How I Write." *The Writer* (June 2003).

Hiaasen, Carl. "Writers on Writing: Real Life, That Bizarre and Brazen Plagiarist." *New York Times* (April 24, 2000).

Huang, Jim. Carl Hiaasen entry, *St. James Guide to Crime & Mystery Writers*. 4th edition, edited by Jay P. Pederson. Detroit: St. James Press, 1996.

Jones, Daniel, and John D. Jorgenson, eds. Carl Hiaasen entry, *Contemporary Authors New Revision Series*. Vol. 65. Detroit: Gale Research, 1998.

MacDonald, Jay Lee. "Carl Hiaasen takes a bite out of crimes against the environment." BookPage. *http://www.bookpage.com/0001bp.carl_hiaasen.html* (viewed July 15, 2003).

Richards, Linda. "January Interview with Carl Hiaasen." *January Magazine*. *http://www.janmag.com/profiles.hiaasen.html* (viewed July 15, 2003).

Silet, Charles L. P. "Sun, Sand and Tirades; An Interview with Carl Hiaasen." *The Armchair Detective* (winter 1996).

Eleanor Hibbert

◆ Romance ◆ Romantic suspense ◆ Historical

London, England
1906–1993

◆ *Mistress of Mellyn*

About the Author and the Author's Writing

Most readers never knew her real name. The prolific Eleanor Alice Burford Hibbert, the "Queen of Romantic Suspense," wrote under seven aliases. Whatever name she used, she always did her research, carefully crafted her plots and rounded out her female characters to the delight of hundreds of thousands of readers.

Burford was born in London's East End in 1906, the daughter of a dock worker and his wife. She was a typist, and later worked for a gemologist. She was working as a shop clerk when she met George Percival Hibbert, a leather goods manufacturer. They moved in together, though he had two children by his first marriage. In 1935 they wed. They had no children of their own.

Eleanor began her writing career drafting nine long novels, which forever remained in the drawer. In the meantime, she wrote and sold short stories to British newspapers. An editor for the *Daily Mail* urged her to write a romantic novel, which would likely find a publisher. She did, and it did, appearing in print in 1941 under her name. She began writing historicals under the Jean Plaidy penname (she lived near Plaidy Beach at the time) in 1945. These novels generally featured English royals and other real figures from the past.

She took command of the gothic romance tradition with *Mistress of Mellyn* under the Victoria Holt pseudonym (the name borrowed from Holt's Bank in London) in 1960, most of them set during the time of Queen Victoria. "Holt's touch is so assured, her presentation of late nineteenth-century Cornwall so loving, her heroine so (almost anachronistically) spirited that even a jaded curmudgeon like this reviewer has no objection to reading the old story once more," opined Anthony Boucher in the *New York Times Book Review*.

A *Kirkus* reviewer likewise enjoyed the telling of Victorian governess Martha Leigh's arrival at a great country manor house, assuming charge of young Alvean and coming to love the master of the estate. "This gaslit, gothic novel with its labyrinthine mansion, its intimations of ghosts, its whispers of scandal and treachery, is a legitimate descendant of Jane Eyre."

Allowing each of her author names its own style, Hibbert used Phillipa Carr for family sagas. She wrote these romantic suspense novels from different times, fictional journals from the English Reformation to World War II. The *Daily Telegraph* called them "thumping good yarns which offered plentiful opportunity for retailing colourful episodes from the past." And as Eleanor Burford, Elbur Ford, Kathleen Kellow, and Ellalice Tate she filled in whatever gaps there remained in the genre.

"Keep on giving them books, so they don't forget your name," the author once told the *Daily Telegraph.*

Hibbert wrote at least five hours a day, every day, to produce a steady stream of books. She built a loyal following through library sales. She was well compensated for her books, and purchased King's Lodge in Sandwich, which she decorated in gothic style only to realize it was a mistake and move back to a flat in London.

Critic Kay Mussell acknowledged the brilliance of the author's earliest publications. "Her best work is probably her first five or six Victoria Holt novels when she was setting standards for a host of authors who imitated her formula. . . . *Mistress of Mellyn*, however, deserves a place among the most important gothic romances of the century, placing Hibbert (as Holt) near the top of her field as an heiress of Daphne du Maurier, whose *Rebecca* remains the premier gothic romance of our time."

"I write with great feeling and excitement and I think this comes over to the reader," the author once told *Contemporary Authors.* She continued to write up until her death in 1993 while on a ship cruise from Athens to Port Said.

The Hibbert legacy is huge: some 200 novels in sixteen series and under her own and six pennames in five decades.

Works by the Author

Fiction
Written as Elbur Ford

The Flesh and the Devil (1950)
Poison in Pimlico (1950)
Bed Disturbed (1952)
Such Bitter Business (1953), in the United States as *Evil in the House* (1953)

Written as Eleanor Burford

Daughter of Anna (1941)
Passionate Witness (1941)
The Married Lover (1942)
When All the World Is Young (1943)
So the Dreams Depart (1944)
Not in Our Stars (1945)
Dear Chance (1947)
Alexa (1948)

The House at Cupid's Cross (1949)
Believe the Heart (1950)
The Love Child (1950)
Bright Tomorrow (1952)
Dear Delusion (1952)
Saint or Sinner? (1952)
Leave Me My Love (1953)
When We Are Married (1953)
Castles in Spain (1954)
Heart's Afire (1954)
Two Loves in Her Life (1955)
When Other Hearts (1955)
Begin to Live (1956)
Married in Haste (1956)
To Meet a Stranger (1957)
Blaze of Noon (1958)
The Dawn Chorus (1959)
Pride of the Morning (1959)
Red Sky at Night (1959)
Night of Stars (1960)
Now That April's Gone (1961)
Who's Calling (1962)

Written as Ellalice Tate

Defenders of the Faith (1956)
The Scarlet Cloak (1957)
The Queen of Diamonds (1958)
Madame du Barry (1959)
This Was a Man (1961)

Written as Jean Plaidy

Together They Ride (1945)
Beyond the Blue Mountains (1948)
The Goldsmith's Wife (1950)
Daughter of Satan (1952)
Lilith (1954)
Melisande (1955)
The Scarlet Cloak (1957)
Milady Charlotte (1959)
Evergreen Gallant (1965)

Ferdinand and Isabella Trilogy

Spain for the Sovereigns (1960)
Daughters of Spain (1961)
Katharine of Aragon (1968)
Isabella and Ferdinand (1970)

French Revolution Series

Louis the Well-Beloved (1956)
The Road to Compiegne (1959)
Flaunting, Extravagant Queen (1957)
Milady Charlotte (1958)

Georgian Series

The Princes of Celle (1967)
Queen in Waiting (1967)
Caroline, The Queen (1968)
The Prince and the Quakeress (1968)
Perdita's Prince (1969)
The Third George (1969)
Indiscretions of the Queen (1970)
Sweet Lass of Richmond Hill (1970)
Goddess of the Green Room (1971)
The Regent's Daughter (1971)
Victoria in the Wings (1972)

Harlequin Romance Series

203. *Daughter of Satan* (1952)
268. *The Unholy Woman* (1954)

Lucrezia Borgia Series

Light on Lucrezia (1958)
Madonna of the Seven Hills (1958)
Lucrezia Borgia (1976)

Mary Queen of Scots Series

Royal Road to Fotheringay (1955)
The Captive Queen of Scots (1963)
Mary Queen of Scotland: The Triumphant Years (1968)
Mary Queen of Scots; The Fair Devil of Scotland (1975)

Medici Trilogy

Madame Serpent (1951)
The Italian Woman (1952)
Queen Jezebel (1953)

Norman Trilogy

The Bastard King (1974)
The Lion of Justice (1975)
The Passionate Enemies (1976)

Plantagenet Series

The Plantagenet Prelude (1976)
The Heart of the Lion (1977)
The Revolt of Eaglets (1977)
The Battle of the Queens (1978)
The Prince of Darkness (1978)
Hammer of the Scots (1979)
The Queen from Provence (1979)
The Follies of the King (1980)
The Vow on the Heron (1980)
Epitaph for Three Women (1981)
Passage to Pontefract (1981)
The Star of Lancaster (1981)
Red Rose of Anjou (1982)
The Sun in Splendor (1982)

Queen Victoria Series

The Captive of Kensington Palace (1972)
The Queen and Lord M (1973)
The Queen's Husband (1973)
The Widow of Windsor (1974)

Queens of England Series

Myself the Enemy (1983)
Queen of This Realm (1984)
Victoria Victorious (1985)
The Lady in the Tower (1986)
The Courts of Love (1987)
In the Shadow of the Crown (1988)
The Queen's Secret (1989)

The Reluctant Queen (1990)
The Pleasures of Love (1991)
The Rose Without a Thorn (1993)
William's Wife (1993)

Stuart Series

A Health Unto His Majesty (1956)
The Wandering Prince (1956)
Here Lies Our Sovereign Lord (1957)
The Murder in the Tower (1964)
The Three Crowns (1965)
The Haunted Sisters (1966)
The Queen's Favorites (1966)

Tudor Series

Murder Most Royal (1949)
The Sixth Wife (1953)
Mary, Queen of France (1954)
The Spanish Bridegroom (1954)
St. Thomas' Eve (1954)
Gay Lord Robert (1955)
Katharine, the Virgin Widow (1961)
The King's Secret Matter (1962)
The Shadow of the Pomegranate (1962)
The Thistle and the Rose (1963)
Uneasy Lies the Head (1982)

Nonfiction

A Triptych of Poisoners (1958)
The Rise of the Spanish Inquisition (1959)
The Growth of the Spanish Inquisition (1960)
The End of the Spanish Inquisition (1961)
Mary Queen of Scots: The Fair Devil of Scotland (1975)
The Spanish Inquisition (1994)

Written as Kathleen Kellow

Danse Macabre (1952)
Rooms at Mrs. Oliver's (1953)
Lilith (1954)
It Began in Vauxhall Gardens (1955)
Call of the Blood (1956)

Rochester, the Mad Earl (1957)
Milady Charlotte (1959)
The World's a Stage (1960)

Written as Phillipa Carr

The Witch from the Sea (1975)
Saraband for Two Sisters (1976)
Lament for a Lost Lover (1977)
The Song of the Siren (1979), sequel to *Saraband for Two Sisters*
The Return on the Gypsy (1985)
A Time for Silence (1991)
The Gossamer Cord (1992)
We'll Meet Again (1993), sequel to *Gossamer Cord*
Daughters of England (1995)

Cador Series

Midsummer's Eve (1986)
The Pool of St. Branock (1987)
The Changeling (1989)
The Black Swan (1990)

Ransome Series

Will You Love Me in September? (1981)
The Adulteress (1982)
Knave of Hearts (1983)
Voices in a Haunted Room (1984)

Reformation Series

The Miracle at St. Bruno's (1972)
The Lion Triumphant (1974)
The Love Child (1978)

Written as Victoria Holt

Mistress of Mellyn (1960)
Kirkland Revels (1962)
Bride of Pendorric (1963)
The Legend of the Seventh Virgin (1964)
Menfeya in the Morning (1966)
The King of the Castle (1967)

The Queen's Confession (1968)
The Shivering Sands (1969)
The Secret Woman (1970)
The Shadow of the Lynx (1971)
On the Night of the Seventh Moon (1972)
The Curse of the Kings (1973)
The House of a Thousand Lanterns (1974)
Lord of the Far Island (1975)
The Pride of the Peacock (1976)
The Devil on Horseback (1977)
My Enemy the Queen (1978)
The Spring of the Tiger (1979)
The Mask of the Enchantress (1980)
The Judas Kiss (1981)
The Demon Lover (1982)
The Time of the Hunter's Moon (1983)
The Landower Legacy (1984)
The Road to Paradise Island (1985)
Secret for a Nightingale (1986)
The Silk Vendetta (1987)
The India Fan (1988)
The Captive (1989)
Snare of the Serpents (1990)
Daughter of Deceit (1991)
Seven for a Secret (1992)
The Black Opal (1993)

Books for Children, written as Jean Plaidy

The Young Elizabeth (1961)
The Young Mary Queen of Scots (1963)

Stage Plays Based on the Author's Works

Mistress of Mellwyn (1981)

For Further Information

"Biography of Jean Plaidy." *http://www.cybcity.com/angryducklet/biography.html* (viewed May 24, 2003).

Boucher, Anthony. *Mistress of Mellyn* review. *New York Times Book Review* (September 11, 1960).

Eleanor Hibbert obituary. *London Daily Telegraph* (January 21, 1993).

Jones, David, and John D. Jorgenson, eds. Eleanor Alice Burford Hibbert entry, *Contemporary Authors New Revision Series*, vol. 59. Detroit: Gale Research, 1998.

Mistress of Mellyn review. *Kirkus Reviews* (July 1, 1960).

Mussell, Kay. Victoria Holt entry, *Twentieth-Century Romance and Historical Writers.* 2nd edition, edited by Lesley Henderson. Chicago: St. James Press, 1990.

"Victoria Holt (1906–1993)." *http://www.geocities.com/Athens/Forum/8078/holt.html* (viewed May 24, 2003).

Victoria Holt Web site. *http://holt.org/victoriaholt.html* (viewed May 24, 2003).

Tony Hillerman

◆   Mystery

Sacred Heart, Oklahoma
1925

◆ *Joe Leaphorn/Jim Chee Series*

Credit: Kelly Campbell.

About the Author and the Author's Writing

There are police procedural novels. And then there are Tony Hillerman's police procedurals: Navajo mysteries that are about as far removed as you can get from the genre's usual urban settings.

Hillerman grew up in Sacred Heart, Potawatomie County, Oklahoma, where he was born in 1925, alongside Potawatomie, Cree, Cherokee, Choctaw, Comanche, and Seminole playmates and neighbors.

"I grew up knowing that the only difference between me and them was very marginal and totally cultural. Race wasn't a factor," he said on the PBS Web site on the Internet.

From 1943 to 1945 Hillerman, the son of a farmer/storekeeper and his wife, served in the U.S. Army, was severely wounded at Alsace, spent six months in the hospital in recovery, and was presented the Silver Star, Bronze Star, and Purple Heart.

Around that time, a newspaper reporter wrote a feature story on Hillerman, relating his war experiences. She read some of the letters he had sent home to his mother and commented he should be a writer. He talked it over with a cousin, and they decided to attend journalism school together. He attended the University of Oklahoma in 1943, where he earned a bachelor of arts degree in 1946. In 1948, he married Mary Unzner; they have six children.

Hillerman worked as a reporter for the *Borger* (Texas) *New Herald* in 1948, then became city editor for the *Morning Press-Constitution* in Lawton, Oklahoma, for two years. He joined United Press International in Oklahoma City as a political reporter for two years, then from 1952 to 1954 was the Santa Fe, New Mexico, bureau chief. From 1954 to 1963 he worked as a political reporter and executive editor for the *New Mexican* in Santa Fe. He earned a master's degree at the University of New Mexico in 1966. After starting out as an associate professor at University of New Mexico in Albuquerque in 1965 and 1966, he rose to full professorship, and in 1985, he became professor emeritus of journalism.

Hillerman long nursed the idea for a story. He had been exposed to Navajo culture in 1945, after he returned from World War II. Working a job driving a truck to the reservation, he witnessed part of an Enemy Way ceremony, a gathering of an entire community in Crownpoint, New Mexico, to comfort Navajo Marines just back from the South Pacific. It gave him the spark of an idea for his first series book, *The Blessing Way*.

The novel introduced Lt. Joe Leaphorn, at first a walk-on character whose role was expanded after the book was accepted by editor Joan Kahn of Harper and Row.

"Leaphorn emerged from a young Hutchinson County, Texas, sheriff who I met and came to admire in 1948 when I was a very green crime and violence reporter for a paper in the high plains of the Panhandle," Hillerman said on the HarperCollins Web site. "He was smart, he was honest, he was wise and humane in his use of police powers—my idealistic young idea of what every cop should be but sometimes isn't."

When the plot of *People of Darkness* required a more brash police officer, Hillerman came up with Sgt. Jim Chee, "a mixture of a couple of hundred of those idealistic, romantic, reckless youngsters I had been lecturing to at the University of New Mexico."

The author put his two series cops together after a comment made by a reader at a book signing. When she asked why he had changed the name of his hero, he explained that they were two different characters. But she said she couldn't distinguish them. Recovering from the shock—he thought them completely different—he put them in the same story. "I wanted to look at them side by side," he told Jan Grape of *Mystery Scene*. "So Chee was the main character in *Skinwalkers* but I dumped Leaphorn in there too. So that lady whoever she was gets the credit and it turned out to be a good idea."

Hillerman has admitted he likes Leaphorn best, and he has allowed him to grow older (by *The First Eagle*, Leaphorn has lost his wife to cancer and has retired from the force) and confront some of the issues Hillerman himself faces (the writer suffers from his war wounds, plus rheumatic arthritis, cancer now in remission, and a minor heart attack).

Raised a Catholic, Hillerman gives great importance to one's relationship with God; Native American spiritualism also plays an important role in his novels.

And so does the setting, which he described in *Louis L'Amour Western Magazine* as "an arid landscape, inhospitable, almost empty, with none of the lush green that spells prosperity. It is built far out of human scale, too large for habitation, making man feel tiny, threatened, aware of his fragility and mortality. Perhaps that is why it is good for me—why I seem to need it, and return at every excuse."

After years devoted to his Leaphorn/Chee novels, Hillerman made a departure in *Finding Moon*, resurrecting a story he had developed not long after World War II, when Belgians pulled out of the Belgian Congo and factions battled for control. The author struggled with the idea, then in 1980 tried again, moving the setting to Southeast Asia. Unable to gain entry to Vietnam or Cambodia, he did research in the Philippines.

Hillerman returned to his familiar series with *The Sinister Pig*, in which Navajo policewoman Bernie Manuelito joins the Border Patrol. That idea, he told *Publishers Weekly*, came from a woman reader who works for the Customs Service who told me of the federal government recruiting Shadow Wolves, or trackers. "So I thought, well, why not? I'll look into it. And then a friend of this same lady, who'd been with the Treasury Department, told me about a committee she was on about abandoned pipelines. That got me thinking. My brother had been a well logger, a petroleum geologist. I knew a little bit about the oil business—we grew up at the edge of the oil patch in Oklahoma. I decided to get Bernie Manuelito involved."

It generally takes Hillerman a year to write a novel, he said on the PBS Web site. He does not outline. Instead he starts with a general idea and knows the place and the time of year. If he gets stuck, he drives out to the reservation. He rewrites each chapter as he goes, then turns in the resulting draft. Although he tries to remain faithful to physical details, he once relocated a place called Burnt Water—which he loved—200 miles from its actual spot so he could use the name without having it discovered. And he placed limestone caves in a setting where they don't exist. Those were intentional; unintentional, however, were his putting time meters in taxi cabs in Washington, D.C., and giving the city Walgreen drug stores in *Talking God*—details his New York-based editor also missed.

"I am always worried about getting it wrong," Hillerman confided in an interview with Bob Hoover. "I read everything I can find and I try to run my writing past my Navajo friends, but I still make mistakes."

Hillerman is a Mystery Writers of America Grand Master and has been awarded the organization's Edgar Award for his work. He has also earned the Western Writers of America Silver Spur Award and the Navajo Tribe's Special Friend Award.

Right at home with his southwest characters and settings, Hillerman has worked hard to make them comfortable to his readers. He stresses, for example, differences among tribal people such as the Hopi, settled agrarians, and Navajo, traditionally nomadic herders, both thrown together by arbitrary federal fiat. In both cases, he sees the yearning of the people to maintain their traditions.

"I know what I write about seems exotic to a lot of people, but not for me," he said in a BookPage interview. "The first time I pulled up to an old trading post and saw a few elderly Navajos sitting on a bench in the shade, I felt right at home. It was like a time warp taking me back to Sacred Heart."

Works by the Author

Fiction

A Fly on the Wall (1970)
Finding Moon (1995)

Jim Chee Mysteries

People of Darkness (1980)
The Darkwind (1982)
The Ghostway (1984)
The Jim Chee Mysteries (1992)

Joe Leaphorn Mysteries

The Blessing Way (1970)
Dance Hall of the Dead (1973)
Listening Woman (1978)
The Joe Leaphorn Mysteries (1989)

Joe Leaphorn and Jim Chee Mysteries

Skinwalkers (1986)
A Thief of Time (1988)
Talking God (1989)
Coyote Waits (1990)
Leaphorn and Chee: Three Classic Mysteries Featuring Lt. Joe Leaphorn and Officer Jim Chee (1992), omnibus
Sacred Clowns (1993)
Fallen Man (1996)
The First Eagle (1998)
Hunting Badger (1999)
The Wailing Wind (2002)
The Sinister Pig (2003)
Skeleton Man (2004)

Books for Young Adults

Diablo the Devil Steer, with William J. Buchanan (2004)

Books for Children

The Boy Who Made Dragonfly: A Zuni Myth (1972)
Buster Mesquite's Cowboy Band (2001)

Editor

The Spell of New Mexico (1992)
The Mysterious West (1994)
The Oxford Book of American Detective Stories, with Rosemary Herbert (1996)
Best American Mystery Stories of the Century (2000)

Tony Hillerman's Frontier Series

People of the Plains by Ken Englade (1996)
The Soldiers by Ken Englade (1996)
The Tribe by Ken Englade (1996)
Battle Cry by Ken Englade (1997)
Brother's Blood by Ken Englade (1998)
Cold Justice by Will Camp (1998)
Comanche Trail by Will Camp (1999)

Anthologies

Crime Wave (1981)
The Ethnic Detectives, edited by Bill Pronzini (1985)

The New Black Mask 7, edited by Matthew J. Bruccoli and Richard Layman (1986)
Mystery Scene Reader 1, edited by Ed Gorman (1987)
Criminal Elements, edited by Bill Pronzini (1988)
2nd Culprit (1993)
New Mystery (1993)
Best American Mystery Stories 2000, edited by Donald E. Westlake (2000)
Century of Great Suspense Stories, edited by Jeffrey Deaver (2001)

Nonfiction

Great Taos Bank Robbery and Other Indian Country Affairs (1973)
Indian Country (1987)
Hillerman Country: A Journey through the Southwest with Tony Hillerman (1991)
The Best of the West: An Anthology of Classic Writing from the American West (1992)
New Mexico, Rio Grand and Other Stories (1993)
Seldom Disappointed: A Memoir (2002)

Television Movies Based on the Author's Works

Skinwalkers (2002)
Coyote Waits (2003)
A Thief of Time (2003)

For Further Information

Anderson, Marc Duane. "Seldom Disappointed: A Memoir." *The Writer* (February 2002).

"Anthropological thrillers." *The Economist* (August 14, 1993).

Bates, Judy. "Politics and the reservation." *Publishers Weekly* (April 14, 2003).

"Biography of Tony Hillerman." *http://www.umsl.edu/~smueller/bio./htm* (viewed July 25, 2003).

Brisman, Fred. *Tony Hillerman*. Boise, ID: Boise State University, 1989.

Bulow, Ernie, and Tony Hillerman. *Talking Mysteries: A Conversation with Tony Hillerman*. Albuquerque: University of New Mexico Press, 1991.

Cox, Ana Marie. "New Frontiers." *Washington Post Book World* (June 29, 2003).

Foote, Timothy. "Inside the Beltway With Chee and Leaphorn." *New York Times Book Review* (June 18, 1984).

Fredriksson, Karl G. and Lillian. Tony Hillerman entry, *St. James Guide to Crime & Mystery Writers*. 4th edition. Detroit: St. James Press, 1996.

Goodman, Susan. " '2' Is for Bestsellers." *Writer's Digest Yearbook '96* (1996).

Grape, Jan. Tony Hillerman interview. *Mystery Scene*, no. 58 (1997).

Hillerman, Tony. "Our Own Holy Land." *Louis L'Amour Western Magazine*, no. 1 (1993).

Hoover, Bob. "No mystery to Tony Hillerman's success as a best-selling author." *Post-Gazette* (October 31, 1998). *http://www.post-gazette.com/magazine/19981031hmiller3.asp* (viewed July 25, 2003).

Jones, Daniel, and John D. Jorgenson, eds. Tony Hillerman entry, *Contemporary Authors New Revision Series*. Vol. 65. Detroit: Gale Research 1996.

Mariampolski, Ruth. "Native Speaker: An Interview with Tony Hillerman." Borders. *http://www.bordersstores.com/features/feature.jsp?file=hillerman* (viewed July 25, 2003).

"Online Q&A with Tony Hillerman." PBS. *http://www.pbs.org/als/feature/hillerman/#questions* (viewed July 25, 2003).

Reilly, John M. *Tony Hillerman: A Critical Companion*. Westport, CT: Greenwood Press, 1996.

Scanlan, Tom. "An Interview with Tony Hillerman." *http://www.geocities.com/SoHo/Museum/2852/aniinterviewwithtonyhillerma2.html* (viewed July 25, 2003).

Sobol, John. *Tony Hillerman: A Public Life*. Toronto, Ontario: BCW Press, 1994.

Stead, Deborah. "Tony Hillerman's Cross-Cultural Mystery Novels." *New York Times* (August 16, 1988).

Tony Hillerman entry, *Authors and Artists for Young Adults*. Vol. 40. Detroit: Gale Group, 2001.

Tony Hillerman Web site. *http://www.tonyhilermanbooks.com/* (viewed July 25, 2003).

"Two New Hillerman Adaptations for PBS's Mystery." PR Newswire (April 30, 2003).

Zibart, Rosemary. "Sitting down and setting out with Tony Hillerman." Book Page. *http://www.bookpage.com/9809bp/tony_hillerman.html* (viewed July 25, 2003).

John Jakes

◆ Historical ◆ Western ◆ Mystery ◆ Fantasy

Chicago, Illinois
1932

◆ *Kent Family Chronicles*

Credit: Rob Kaufman.

About the Author and the Author's Writing

John Jakes' first book, published in 1956, is a western, *Wear a Fast Gun. Charleston*, released in 2002, is a historical saga. In the nearly half century and six dozen books in between, Jakes has written in just about every genre, turning out stories of brawny barbarians, suave private detectives, valiant Civil War soldiers, and California gold seekers.

Labeled variously "the people's author," "America's history teacher," and the "godfather of the historical novel," he was the first author to bullet three books on the *New York Times* best-seller list simultaneously. Jakes showed his mastery of huge casts and sweeping thematic panoramas in the Kent Family Chronicles and the North and South Trilogy, following American history from the time of the Revolution through slavery plantations and westward expansion and into the early twentieth century.

Jakes was born in Chicago in 1932. His father was a general manager for Railway Express, his mother a homemaker. When he sold a story for $25 in 1950, while a freshman majoring in acting at Northwestern in Chicago, Jakes steered in a new career direction (though years later he would return to theater with his hometown playhouse on Hilton Head Island). He enrolled in DePauw University's creative writing program, earning an A.B. degree in 1953. A year later, he accepted his master's in arts degree from Ohio State University.

Jakes worked as a copywriter for Abbott Laboratories in North Chicago for six years beginning in 1954, then joined the advertising agency Rumrill in Rochester, New York, 1960–1961. After a four-year stint at freelance writing, he became senior copywriter for another ad group, Kirchner Helton & Collett, until 1968, when he became copy chief, and eventually vice president, of Oppenheim, Herminghausen, Clarke, both in Dayton, Ohio. Jakes became creative director for Dancer Fitzgerald Samle, also in Dayton, 1970–1971. Then he again took up creative writing full-time.

While with the pharmaceuticals company and various advertising agencies, Jakes had started writing short stories in his evening hours, eventually selling some 200 of them. He also had begun writing the first of what is now a shelf of some sixty books, two of which (*North and South* and *Homeland*) were nominated for Pulitzer Prizes.

The author made several attempts at fiction series, featuring such characters as Johnny Havoc, a private eye; Brak, a sword-swinging barbarian; and Gavin Black, a space adventurer. He also wrote nonfiction, and books for children. He worked under two pseudonyms and completed three mysteries in the Lou Largo series begun by the late William Ard. But major success eluded him.

Then in the early 1970s, book packager Lyle Kenyon Engel approached Jakes to write five books in the proposed American Bicentennial Series. Jakes takes no credit for the general concept—which, once it became successful, reached to eight novels—but he does claim the story and the characters.

Jakes had already written a half dozen paperback original historicals, so he felt comfortable accepting the new project. "I accepted the commission to do the novels because I thought it a tremendous opportunity to enjoy relearning some American history, and presenting my feelings about the country," he amplified for interviewer Meredith Allard for *Copperfield Review*. "I hadn't the slightest idea that the series would become the monumental bestseller that it has. When last I looked, *The Bastard* [the first volume] was in something like its 68th printing."

The author has said he enjoys crafting sagas, as their large families automatically afford opportunity for conflict and have a natural excuse to flow through a whole period of time. To prepare for each book or series, he delves into the best secondary sources to come up with ideas for characters and story threads. Once he has identified subjects that interest him—perhaps the rise of aviation—he delves into biographies, diaries, letters, and other primary materials. How he blends the real past with fiction is a matter of his years of experience as a writer.

When he completed the Kent saga, he reached agreement with his publisher to explore the Civil War and was particularly taken during his research to learn all the graduates of the military academy at West Point who knew each other as students, then went on to fight on opposite sides during the conflict. He later moved to later time periods, but he returned to the Civil War era for *On Secret Service*, triggered by material found during his research for *North and South*.

Although Jakes didn't have great success with his early series—after three or four books, he found them repetitious, he said in an article for *The Armchair Detective*—he had no problem sustaining his historical series. "I avoided the problem with The Kent Family Chronicles and The North and South Trilogy by shifting each succeeding novel into a new, intrinsically different historical period, each with its own interesting research challenge."

John Clute praised one of the author's science fiction books, noting *Black in Time* "presents vignettes from Black history dramatized through a timetravel device." An interest in race history reemerged in the author's sagas, where slavery and greed, as critical biographer Mary Ellen Jones has pointed out, are treated accurately and head-on.

Jakes has a long list of admired writers, among them Balzac, Dumas, Tolstoy, Kenneth Roberts, F. Scott Fitzgerald, and John D. MacDonald. But Charles Dickens is his favorite. As he told Bookreporter, "What I find so inspiring about Dickens is his genius. Some commercial novelists are skillful with plot—i.e., with keeping you turning pages. So-called literary writers are often skilled with the language. There are just a few writers, truly deserving of the term genius, who are skilled with both, and Dickens stands at the top of that class in my estimation."

Jakes is a master of history and period detail, though some critics find his prose pedestrian. "Look not for subtlety in these pages. Elegant turns of phrase; rich, evocative descriptions of people and places; and finely drawn, complex characters are not to be found," pronounced reviewer Tom Linthicum in the *Baltimore Sun*. "Contrasts are stark; labels are clear."

In *Twentieth-Century Romance and Historical Writers*, critic Marion Hanscom relished Jakes' afterwords in his saga books: "It is as if he were having a personal conversation with the reader—revealing the happenings in his life that occurred while writing, the family deaths, his own illness, giving up cigarettes, even what he thinks about his own work."

Jakes was a University of South Carolina Department of History research fellow in 1989 and has served as a trustee for Depauw University. He and his wife, Rachel Ann Payne, a teacher whom he married in 1951, have four children. They have homes in South Carolina and Connecticut. The author's hobbies include golf, swimming, acting, and directing community theater.

The John Jakes Papers, 1973–2001, including notes and correspondence, are on deposit with the Rare Books and Special Collections Department, University of South Carolina.

Works by the Author

Fiction

A Night for Treason (1956)
Wear a Fast Gun (1956)
The Devil Has Four Faces (1959)
G.I. Girls (1963)
The Asylum World (1969)
The Hybrid (1969)
The Last Magicians (1969)
Secrets of Stardeep (1969)
Tonight We Steal the Stars (1969)
Black in Time (1970)
Mask of Chaos (1970)
Monte Cristo 99 (1970)
Six-Gun Planet (1970)
Conquest of the Planet of the Apes (1972)
Mention My Name in Atlantis (1972)
On Wheels (1973)
California Gold (1989)
John Jakes' Mullkon Empire (1995)
The Bold Frontier (2000)
On Secret Service (2001)
Charleston (2002)
Savannah: Or, A Gift for Mr. Lincoln (2004)

Kent Family Chronicles or American Bicentennial Series

The Bastard (1974), in Great Britain as two volumes, *Fortune's Whirlwind* (1975)
    and *To an Unknown Shore* (1975)
The Rebels (1975)
The Seekers (1975)
The Furies (1976)
The Patriots (1976), includes first two books
The Pioneers (1976), includes second two books
The Titans (1976)
The Warriors (1977)
The Lawless (1978)
The Americans (1980)

Brak the Barbarian Series

Brak the Barbarian (1968)
Brak the Barbarian vs. the Sorceress (1969)
Brak vs. the Mark of the Demons (1969)
Brak When the Idols Walked (1978)
Fortunes of Brak (1980), collection

Crown Family Saga

Homeland (1993)
American Dreams (1998)

Dragonard Series

When the Star Kings Die (1967)
The Planet Wizard (1969)
Time Gate (1972)

Gavin Black Series

Master of the Dark Gate (1970)
Witch of the Dark Gate (1972)

Johnny Havoc Series

Johnny Havoc (1960)
Johnny Havoc Meets Zelda (1962), retitled *Havoc for Sale* (1990)
Johnny Havoc and the Doll Who Had "It" (1963), retitled *Holiday for Havoc*
    (1991)
Making It Big (1968), retitled *Johnny Havoc and the Siren in Red* (1991)

North and South Trilogy

North and South (1982)
Love and War (1984)
Heaven and Hell (1988)

Written as Alan Payne

Murder, He Says (1958)
This Will Slay You (1958)

Written as Jay Scotland

The Seventh Man (1958), reissued under John Jakes byline (1981)
I, Barbarian (1959), reissued under John Jakes byline (1979)
Strike the Black Flag (1961)
Sir Scoundrel (1962)
Veils of Salome (1962), reissued under John Jakes byline as *King's Crusader* (1976)
Arena (1963)
Traitor's Legion (1963), reissued under John Jakes byline as *The Man from Cannae* (1977)

Written as William Ard

Lou Largo Series

Make Mine Mavis (1961)
And So to Bed (1962)
Give Me This Woman (1963)

Collections

The Best of John Jakes, edited by Martin H. Greenberg and Joseph D. Olander (1977)
The Best Western Stories of John Jakes, edited by Bill Pronzini and Martin H. Greenberg (1991)
In the Big Country: The Best Western Stories of John Jakes (1993)

Stage Plays

Dracula, Baby (1970), lyrics
A Spell of Evil (1972)
Stranger with Roses (1972)
Violence (1972)
Wind in the Willows (1972), book and lyrics
Gaslight Girl (1973), book and lyrics
Doctor, Doctor! (1973), book and lyrics
Shepherd Song (1974), book and lyrics
Great Expectations (1999), book and lyrics

Editor

Civil War Ghosts, with Charles G. Waugh (1991)
New Trails: Twenty-Three Original Stories of the West from Western Writers of America, with Martin H. Greenberg (1994)
Great Stories of the American West, with Martin H. Greenberg (1995)
Great Stories of the American West II, with Martin H. Greenberg (1996)
A Century of Great Western Stories (2000)

Anthologies

Dark Mind Dark Heart (1962)
Frights (1976)
100 Twisted Little Tales of Torment (1984)
Masterpieces of Terror and the Unknown (1993)
Great Writers and Kids Write Spooky Stories (1995)
The Bold Frontier (2001)
Crime Time (2001)
Westward: A Fictional History of the American West, edited by Dale L. Walker (2003)

Nonfiction

The Texans Ride North: The Story of the Cattle Trails (1952)
Tiros: Weather Eye in Space (1966)
Famous Firsts in Sports (1967)
Great War Correspondents (1967)
Great Women Reporters (1968)
Mohawk: The Life of Joseph Brant (1969)
The Bastard Photostory (1980)
Susanna of the Alamo: A True Story (1986)

Television Miniseries Based on the Author's Work

Kent Family Chronicles (1982)
North and South (1985), ABC TV
North and South: Book II (1986), ABC TV
John Jakes' Heaven and Hell: North and South Part III (1994), ABC TV

For Further Information

Allard, Meredith. "An Interview with John Jakes." *Copperfield Review* (winter 2003).

Bowler, Joe. "Portrait of John Jakes." John Jakes Web site. *http://www.johnjakes.com/johnjakes.htm* (viewed March 31, 2003).

Carter, Lin. *Imaginary Worlds*. New York: Ballantine, 1973.

Clute, John. John Jakes entry, *The Encyclopedia of Science Fiction*. Edited by Clute and Peter Nicholls. New York: St. Martin's Press, 1993.

Hawkins, R. *The Kent Family Chronicles Encyclopedia*. New York: Bantam, 1979.

Interview with John Jakes (November 12, 2000). *http://home.wandadoo.nl/~swayze/johnjakes.htm* (viewed March 31, 2003).

Jakes, John. "Havoc Returns." *The Armchair Detective* (fall 1991).

John Jakes biography. Amazon.com. *http://www.authorsontheweb./com/features/authormonth/0208jakes/jakes-john.asp* (viewed April 25, 2003).

John Jakes biography. Authors on the Web. *http://www.authorsontheweb/com/features/lists/li-jakes-john.asp* (viewed March 31, 2003).

John Jakes biography and interview. Bookreporter (August 9, 2002). *http://www.bookreporter.com/authors/au-jakes-john.asp* (viewed March 31, 2003).

John Jakes Papers, 1973–2001. University of South Carolina. *http://www.sc.edu/library/spcoll/amlit/jakes.html* (viewed March 31, 2003).

John Jakes Web site. *http://www.johnjakes.com/* (viewed March 31, 2003).

Jones, Daniel, and John D. Jorgensen, eds. *Contemporary Authors new Revision Series*, vol. 66. Detroit: Gale Research, 1998.

Jones, Mary Ellen. *John Jakes: A Critical Companion*. Westport, CT: Greenwood Press, 1996.

Kelley, George. John Jakes entry, *Twentieth-Century Western Writers*. Edited by Geoff Sadler. Chicago: St. James Press, 1991.

Linthicum, Tom. "Historical Novel: It's a bodice ripper! A history lesson! A potboiler! A John Jakes extravaganza!" *Baltimore Sun* (August 28, 2002).

Shuey, Andrea Lee. John Jakes entry, *Twentieth-Century Romance and Historical Writers*. Edited by Lesley Henderson. Chicago: St. James Press, 1990.

P. D. James

Oxford, England
1920

◆ *Death of an Expert Witness*

Credit: Alixe Buckerfield de la Roche.

About the Author and the Author's Writing

P. D. James has taken the British mystery tradition of Dorothy L. Sayers, Margery Allingham, and Ngaio Marsh soaring to new heights with her Inspector Adam Dalgliesh procedural and Cordelia Gray private detective novels.

The "Queen of Crime" was named an Officer of the Order of the British Empire in 1983, a life Peer of the United Kingdom in 1991 (as Baroness James of Holland Park), and a Mystery Writers of America Grand Master in 1999.

"Brilliant to say the least, P. D. James is one of the few crime writers to be placed in the higher literature category," proclaimed the Bastilli Mystery Library Web site.

Phyllis Dorothy James was born in Oxford, England, in 1920, the oldest of three children of an Inland Revenue officer and his wife. She has described her family as only moderately well off and not very close. Family vacations were to the East Anglia countryside (later the setting for *Death in Holy Orders*). She attended Cambridge High School for Girls from 1931 to 1937, but left before receiving a diploma. She married a doctor, Ernest Connor Bantry White, in 1941. White's experiences in the Royal Army Medical Corps during World War II left him emotionally traumatized, and he was in and out of psychiatric institutions until he died in 1964. His wife became the sole parent to two daughters.

This stressful period in her life brought great awareness to the author. "I am infinitely grateful to life and health, and aware of how brief and uncertain life is," she told Nan Robertson of the *New York Times*. "We must live each day to the fullest."

James worked as a tax office assistant and an assistant stage manager at Festival Theatre in Cambridge, England, until the war, when she became a Red Cross nurse and worked at the Ministry of Food. Burdened by her husband's probable schizophrenia, the author got by with some help from her in-laws and gradually worked her way up through the British Home Office bureaucracy. During a thirty-year civil-service career, from 1949 to 1968, she was a principal administrative assistant for the North West Regional Hospital board. She was responsible for making appointments to the country's forensics laboratories and advised ministers on issues dealing with juvenile crime. She later worked for four years with the Department of Home Affairs' Police Department, then for seven years was with the Criminal Policy Department. (She has also chaired the British Society of Authors and served as a local magistrate.)

Realizing in the late 1950s there might never come a comfortable time to write a book, she began her first Dalgliesh novel, *Cover Her Face*, while riding to work on the commuter train. It took her three years to write, but the book immediately found a publisher. She used the gender-neutral name P. D. James, shortened from her own, as a pseudonym. She wrote mostly in early mornings, before going to the office, or on weekends.

Although she intended her first mystery as a trial run for a more ambitious literary novel, she soon found her niche as a mystery and crime writer. She "discovered that within the detective form I could write a novel that has a moral ambiguity and psychological subtlety like a serious novel," she explained to *Armchair Detective's* Rosemary Herbert. "Writing within the constraints isn't in fact inhibiting; it's positively liberating!"

Following the success of the novel *Death of an Expert Witness*, she decided to retire in 1979 to become a full-time writer.

One of her favorite writers is Jane Austen, whom she has called "an absolute mistress of construction." From Allingham the author gleaned a strong sense of setting, from Sayres English wit and style.

It is important to the reader, James wrote in an essay for the *New York Times* in 1983, to be immediately comfortable upon beginning a mystery. "With what mixture of excitement, anticipation and reassurance we enter that old brownstone in Manhattan, that gentle spinster's cottage in St. Mary Mead (never fully described by Agatha Christie but so well imagined), that bachelor flat in London's Piccadilly where Bunter deferentially pours the vintage port, that cozy Victorian setting room on Baker Street."

A sense of place is integral to James novels. Observed reviewer Nicola Upson, "Fascinated by institutions—churches, hospitals, publishing houses and now museums [*The Murder Room*]—she evokes the tensions and alliances that underpin tight-knit communities." And though she hasn't yet found a way to do it, James has said she would love to set a crime story in the British House of Lords.

One departure for James was *The Children of Men*, a futuristic work; another was a memoir, *Time to Be in Earnest*. Of the latter, critic Adam Smyth expressed disappointment that the "the real and fascinating question the book provokes—why, particularly amid these concerns over moral degeneracy, is P. D. James so inexorably attracted to murder—is left unanswered."

Seen by many critics as a more literary Agatha Christie, James broke away from the strict formulas of her early books to develop strong characterization and probe social issues. "The detective story has moved much closer to mainstream fiction," the author told Robert McCrum for the *Guardian*. "It no longer affirms with such confidence the probity of the state system, including the police. Detectives are far less creatures of fantasy or romantic wish-fulfillment. They tend to be professionals doing a difficult job in a modern world."

In her novels James has dealt with serious issues—incest, child abuse, school violence, and dysfunctional families. A non-series mystery, *Innocent Blood*, is about a woman, Philippa Palfrey, who was adopted as a child and who harbors vivid fantasies about her birth parents. She looks into records and learns a shocking secret—her birth mother was a victim of rape, her father a murderer.

Most of the mysteries feature the complex and fascinating Dalgliesh, initially chief inspector and later commander of London's Metropolitan Police Force. Dedicated, extremely efficient and a poet by avocation, Dalgliesh was widowed when his wife died in childbirth. However, two books are about the head of the Pryde Detective Agency, young and resourceful Cordelia Grey.

James told Kate Kellaway for the *Guardian* that the violence in the books is necessary, "There's a sort of catharsis of horror." Her characters emerge on their own. "The process is mysterious, it feels as if the characters exist in limbo and I am getting in touch with them. It's revelation rather than creation. My writing is visual, I write as if I were shooting film."

James is content to maintain only two series characters, whose lives fleetingly touch in *Unsuitable Job for a Woman.* In an essay for *Murder Ink*, she ventured to answer the question, What if Adam were to marry Cordelia? claiming that she supported the view of Sayers that detectives should solve crimes and "not spend their time chasing young women." (In *The Murder Room*, Dalgliesh begins a romantic entanglement with a Cambridge University lecturer.)

In a three-way dialogue with *New York Times* crime reviewer Marilyn Stasio and American hard-boiled novelist Lawrence Block in 1988, James summed up reasons for the mystery's stronger-than-ever popularity in an age of international disruption and violence: These and other problems such as racial tension and drug abuse are "literally beyond our ability to solve, [and] it seems to me very reassuring to read a popular form of fiction which itself has a problem at the heart of it. One which the reader knows will be solved by the end of the book; and not by supernatural means or good luck, but by human intelligence, human courage and human perseverance. That seems to me one of the reasons why the crime novel, in all its forms and varieties, does hold its place in the affections of its readers."

Works by the Author

Fiction

Innocent Blood (1980)
The Children of Men (1999)

Cordelia Gray Series

An Unsuitable Job for a Woman (1972)
The Skull Beneath the Skin (1982)

Inspector Adam Dalgliesh Series

Cover Her Face (1962)
A Mind to Murder (1963)
Unnatural Causes (1967)
A Shroud for a Nightingale (1971)
The Black Tower (1975)
Death of an Expert Witness (1977)
Crime Times Three (1979), omnibus

Murder in Triplicate (1982), omnibus
Trilogy of Death (1984), omnibus
A Taste for Death (1986)
P. D. James: Three Complete Novels (1987)
Devices and Desires (1989)
An Omnibus P. D. James (1990)
A Dalgliesh Trilogy (1991), omnibus
Original Sin (1994)
A Certain Justice (1997)
Death in Holy Orders (2001)
The Murder Room (2003)

Stage Plays

A Private Treason (1985)

Anthologies

Ellery Queen's Murder Menu (1969)
Winter's Crimes 5, edited by Virginia Whitaker (1973)
Ellery Queen's Masters of Mystery (1975)
Winter's Crimes 8, edited by Hilary Watson (1976)
Crime Writers (1978)
Masterpieces of Mystery: Stories Not To Be Missed, edited by Ellery Queen (1978)
Fourth Bedside Book of Great Detective Stories, edited by Herbert van Thal (1979)
Mysterious Visions, edited by Charles G. Waugh (1979)
Verdict of Thirteen, edited by Julian Symons (1979)
Best Detective Stories of the Year—1980, edited by Edward D. Hoch (1980)
John Creasey's Crime Collection 1981, edited by Herbert Harris (1981)
John Creasey's Crime Collection 1982, edited by Herbert Harris (1982)
85 Great Murder Mysteries, edited by Mary Danby (1983)
An International Treasury of Mystery and Suspense, edited by Marie R. Reno (1983)
The Web She Weaves, edited by Marcia Muller (1983)
Winter's Crimes 15, edited by George Hardinge (1983)
Great Detectives, edited by David Willis McCullough (1984)
Murder Most Foul (1984)
The Penguin Classic Crime Omnibus, edited by Julian Symons (1984)
John Creasey's Crime Collection 1985, edited by Herbert Harris (1985)
The Mammoth Book of Great Detective Stories, edited by Herbert van Thal (1985)
Best of Winter's Crimes 1, edited by George Hardinge (1986)
Mammoth Book of Modern Crime Stories, edited by George Hardinge (1986)
Ellery Queen's Masters of Mystery (1987)
Ladykillers (1987)
Prime Suspects, edited by Bill Pronzini (1987)
Suspicious Characters, edited by Bill Pronzini (1987)

Criminal Elements, edited by Bill Pronzini (1988)
English Country House Murders, edited by Thomas F. Godfrey (1988)
Great Murder Mysteries (1988)
Deadly Doings, edited by Martin H. Greenberg (1989)
Felonious Assaults, edited by Bill Pronzini (1989)
The Best Crime Stories (1990)

Nonfiction

The Maul and the Pear Tree: The Ratcliffe Highway Murders, 1811, with Thomas A.
    Critchley (1971)
Time To Be In Earnest: A Fragment of an Autobiography (2000)

PBS Television Adaptations of Author's Works

Cover Her Face
Unnatural Causes
The Black Tower
A Taste for Death
Devices and Desires
Death of an Expert Witness
Shroud for a Nightingale

For Further Information

Arndt, Frances. "A Suitable Job for a Woman." *Armchair Detective* (winter 1991).

Gidez, Richard B. *P. D. James*. Boston: Hall, 1986.

Gussow, Mel. "Savoring Old Murders, Spinning Tales of New One." *New York Times*
    (January 10, 2004).

Herbert, Rosemary. "A Mind to Write: An Interview with P. D. James." *The Armchair
    Detective* (fall 1986).

James, P. D. "A Fictional Prognosis." *Murder Ink: The Mystery Reader's Companion*,
    edited by Dilys Winn. New York: Workman, 1977.

James, P. D. "In Mystery Fiction, Rooms Furnished One Clue at a Time." *New York
    Times* (August 25, 1983).

James, P. D. "One Clue at a Time." *The Writer* (February 1984).

James, P. D. "Ought Adam to Marry Cordelia?" *Murder Ink: The Mystery Reader's
    Companion*, edited by Dilys Winn. New York: Workman, 1977.

Jones, Daniel, and John D. Jorgenson, eds. P. D. James entry, *Contemporary Authors
    New Revision Series*. Vol. 65. Detroit: Gale Research, 1998.

Keating, H.R.F. "P. D. James: A Taste for Death." *The Fine Art of Murder*, edited by Ed Gorman, Martin H. Greenberg, Larry Segriff, with Jon L. Breen. New York: Carroll & Graf, 1993.

Kellaway, Kate. "On the case of the Baroness." *Observer* (October 16, 1994).

McCrum, Robert. P. D. James talks to Robert McCrum about God, realism and Agatha Christie." *Guardian* (March 4, 2001).

Stasio, Marilyn. "No Gore Please—They're British." *New York Times* (October 9, 1988).

Patrick, Bethanne Kelly. "Roomful of Clues." *Pages* (November/December 2003).

P. D. James biography. Guardian. *http://books.guardian.co.uk/authors/author/0,5917.93,00.html* (viewed May 5, 2003).

P. D. James biography. *http://www.bol.ucla.edu/!ryoder/mystery/james-bio.html* (viewed April 11, 2003).

P. D. James interview. Bastulli Mystery Library. *http://www.bastulli.com/James/PDJAMES.htm* (viewed April 11, 2003).

P. D. James resources. Wyoming Council for the Humanities. *http://www.uwyo.edu/wch/bdpcrimedd.htm* (viewed May 5, 2003).

Robertson, Nan. "Phyllis Dorothy White Uncovers The Secret Face of P. D. James." *New York Times* (December 11, 1977).

Siebenheller, Norman. *P. D. James*. New York: Ungar, 1981.

Smyth, Adam. "P. D. James's Uncomfortable Autobiography. *Contemporary Review* (October 2000).

Stedman, Jane W.P.D. James entry, *Twentieth-Century Crime and Mystery Writers*. 3rd edition, edited by Lesley Henderson. Chicago: St. James Press, 1991.

Swanson, Jean, and Dean James. P. D. James entry, *By A Woman's Hand: A Guide to Mystery Fiction by Women*. 2nd edition. New York: Berkley Prime Crime, 1996.

Upson, Nicola. "Behind the scenes at the museum." *New Statesman* (July 28, 2003).

J. A. Jance

Watertown, South Dakota
1944

◆ *Joanna Brady Mysteries*

Courtesy of J. A. Jance.

About the Author and the Author's Writing

Mystery writer J. A. Jance is gender neutral when it comes to writing; she's equally comfortable with a male leading character (J. P. Beaumont) or a female (Joanna Brady).

Jance—born Judith Ann Busk in 1944 in Watertown, South Dakota—credits the introduction to L. Frank Baum's Wizard of Oz series of fantasy books in second grade as having instantly sparked her interest in becoming a fiction writer. Growing up she read Nancy Drew, Dana Girls, and Hardy Boys series mysteries, later John D. MacDonald and Lawrence Block. One of her more recent favorite books is Fannie Flagg's *Fried Green Tomatoes at the Whistle Stop Café*.

Judith pursued her interest to the University of Arizona, where she received her bachelor of arts degree in English and secondary education in 1966. An M.Ed degree in library science followed four years later. She taught high school English in Tucson for two years then was kindergarten-to-grade-twelve librarian for the Oasis School District near Tucson for five years. In 1980, she received a C.L.U. degree from American College.

An experience in college disgusted her; the professor who taught creative writing at the University of Arizona refused to accept female students. He believed girls should become teachers or nurses. One man who was allowed in, however, became Judith's husband. But he never pursued a writing career of his own, she has said in interviews, and he discouraged her from writing. So she wrote poetry late at night, out of his sight.

More than a decade later, in 1982, resettled from Arizona to Seattle, divorced and raising two children, selling life insurance full-time, Judith decided to write a book. It was based on a string of murders in the Tucson area in 1970 to which she had had a peripheral involvement. The book ran 1,200 pages. Her agent suggested she might do better to try fiction writing, which she did, and the result was the first Beaumont case, *Until Proven Guilty*, which appeared in paperback edition in 1985.

At a retreat, she met a widower, William Alan Schilb, an engineer. They became friends, and eventually they married and merged their families.

All of these personal experiences have had a telling effect on her series characters. "The eighteen years I spent while married to an alcoholic have helped shape the experience and character of Detective J. P. Beaumont. My experiences as a single parent have gone into the background for Joanna Brady—including her first tentative steps toward a new life after the devastation of losing her husband in *Desert Heat*," she explained on her Web site. And the nasty writing professor? He shows up in the stand-alone book *Kiss of the Bees*.

Jance based her Seattle detective Beaumont partly on a Pima County homicide cop she met when he was investigating the Arizona serial killings. He had a drinking problem and was struggling to overcome it. Jance on her Web site said her characters are like old friends to her, and as they age, things change in their lives. When she's been away from Beaumont for a time, to write a Brady or other book, coming back is like visiting again with an old friend. As the Beaumont series proceeded, Jance said her agent was the one who suggested starting a second series, to alternate with the first. She opted for a change in setting at the same time, to arid Arizona, where she had been living for many years. (She has homes in both Arizona and Washington.) Unlike many crime fiction protagonists, Jance's heroine comes with a family—a daughter, helpful in-laws, a pushy mother, a new husband—and a lot of complications.

It was Jance's agent's idea she use the intentionally gender-vague initials "J. A.," because at the time there were very few police procedural mysteries on the market by women writers.

At the urging of readers, Beaumont and Brady shared a case involving a dead Arizona artist—someone who had been in the Washington state witness protection program—in *Partner in Crime*.

The writer's other fiction consists of two novels, *Hour of the Hunter*—written when she began to tire of Beaumont—and *Kiss of the Bees*, separated by two decades but using the same setting and some of the same characters.

Because doing research is easier than writing a book, Jance said in a Bestsellers World interview, she tries to limit the time she spends digging up background material. She added that she mostly writes on deadline.

Jance told iVillager she does not outline her books: "First, I usually come up with a name; then I figure out who's dead. I spend the rest of the book trying to find out who did it, and why."

The first twenty percent of the book is the most critical, she said in a piece for *The Writer*. It is when the characters are introduced, the setting established, the tone set. "Like the foundation of a house," she wrote, "those first few chapters have to be strong enough to support the rest of the book. They also have to be interesting and engaging."

The spark for *Dead to Rights*, she explained, was a friend's loss of his wife to a drunk driver. Jance opens her novel with a man handing out Mothers Against Drunk Driving leaflets outside the office of a veterinarian. The man's wife was killed by the vet in a DWI accident. When the vet soon turns up dead, the man is the first, but of course wrong, suspect. The dead dentist in *Improbable Cause*? "I finally managed to wreak personal revenge on a sadistic dentist who had haunted a whole generation of kids in my hometown by practicing Novocain-free dentistry," she wrote in *Mystery Scene*.

Without knowing the resolution, does she ever get stuck? If she does, she told *January Magazine* interviewer Linda Richards, there's something wrong in the motivation of her characters. "So what I've learned to do is go back and tweak the motivation instead of throwing everything away. And because in the mysteries the murder hardly ever happens onscreen, all I have to do is the hardest thing authors ever do which is change my mind and decide somebody else is the killer." This not knowing the outcome, she ventured, added to the tension of the story; the teller is as eager to learn the resolution as the reader.

Jance said in a Barnes & Noble interview that the storyteller's mission "is to beguile the time. And that's how I see my book—as storytelling. There's no higher praise than to be told that reading my books helped someone through the long waiting-room hours of a loved one's serious illness."

Works by the Author

Fiction

Hour of the Hunter (1992)
Kiss of the Bees (2000)
Day of the Dead (2004)

Joanna Brady Mysteries

Desert Heat (1993)
Tombstone Courage (1994)
Shoot, Don't Shoot (1995)
Dead to Rights (1996)
Skeleton Canyon (1997)
Rattlesnake Crossing (1998)
Outlaw Mountain (1999)
Devil's Claw (2000)
Paradise Lost (2001)
Exit Wounds (2003)

Joanna Brady and J. P. Beaumont Mystery

Partner in Crime (2002)

J. P. Beaumont Mysteries

Until Proven Guilty (1985)
Injustice for All (1986)
Trial by Fury (1986)
Taking the Fifth (1987)
Improbable Cause (1988)
More Perfect Union (1988)
Dismissed with Prejudice (1989)
Minor in Possession (1990)
Payment in Kind (1991)

Without Due Process (1992)
Failure to Appear (1993)
Lying in Wait (1994)
Name Withheld (1995)
Breach of Duty (1999)
Birds of Prey (2001)

Anthologies

Cat Crimes, edited by Martin H. Greenberg and Ed Gorman (1991)
The Mysterious West (1994)
Partners in Crime (1994)
No Alibi (1995)
Vengeance Is Hers (1997)
Midnight Louie's Pet Detective (1998)
More Murder, They Wrote (1999)
Fathers & Daughters, edited by Jill Morgan (2000)
First Cases IV (2002)
Dangerous Women, edited by Otto Penzler (2004)

Poetry

After the Fire (1984)

Nonfiction

Books for Children

Dial Zero for Help: A Story of Parental Kidnapping (1985)
It's Not Your Fault (1985)
Welcome Home, Stranger: A Child's View of Family Alcoholism (1986)

For Further Information

Exit Wounds review. *Publishers Weekly* (June 9, 2003).

Goldberg, Rylla. "J. A. Jance." *Mystery Scene* (January/February 1996).

J. A. Jance biography. Meet the Writers, Barnes & Noble. *http://www.barnesandnoble.com/writers/writer.asp?cid=881721* (viewed May 6, 2003).

J. A. Jance books. Mystery Women Authors. *http://members.fortunecity.com/le10/authors/authorsH-P/jajance.htm* (viewed May 6, 2003).

J. A. Jance interview. BestsellersWorld (June 2, 2002). *http://www.bestsellersworld.com/interview-jajance.com* (viewed April 11, 2003).

J. A. Jance interview. iVillagers. *http://www.ivilage.com/books/intervu/myst/articles/0,11872,240795_91812,00.html* (viewed April 11, 2003).

J. A. Jance profile. *January Magazine. http://www.januarymagazine.com/profiles/jajance.html* (viewed April 11, 2003).

J. A. Jance Web site. *http://jajance.com/* (viewed April 11, 2003).

Jance, J. A. "Dead to Rights." *Mystery Scene* (July/August 1996).

Jance, J. A. "The long slide home: the author of 30 mysteries shares her secrets for getting from start to finish." *The Writer* (January 2004).

Jones, Daniel, and John D. Jorgenson, eds. J. A. Jance entry, *Contemporary Authors New Revision Series*. Vol. 61. Detroit: Gale Research, 1998.

Richards, Linda. J. A. Jance interview. *January Magazine* (February 2001). *http://www.januarymagazine.com/profiles/jajance.html* (viewed May 6, 2003).

Sturgeon, Julie. "Stranger than Fiction: With J. A. Jance, the line between the two blurs beautifully." *Pages*, September/October 2003.

Swanson, Jean, and Dean James. *By a Woman's Hand: A Guide to Mystery Fiction by Women*, 2nd edition. New York: Berkley Prime Crime, 1996.

Jerry B. Jenkins

Kalamazoo, Michigan
1949

Credit: © 2003 Tyndale House Publishers.

Tim LaHaye

◆ Christian ◆ Science fiction

Detroit, Michigan
1926

◆ *Left Behind Series*

About the Authors and the Authors' Writing

The twelve-volume Left Behind series by Tim LaHaye (who guides the biblical philosophy) and Jerry B. Jenkins (who writes the books) is about Christians who, following the vanishing of millions of people during the Rapture, the subsequent reign of chaos, and the emergence of a harsh dictator Nicolae the antichrist, struggle to survive until the arrival of the King of Kings.

These works by Jenkins and LaHaye charged Christian fiction into the mainstream. *Armageddon*, the eleventh in the series, debuted at the number one spot on four leading national best-seller lists, and the books have been stocked in Wal-Mart and other chain stores.

"We continue to be amazed at the crossover success of these books . . . ," Jenkins said on the Left Behind Series Web site. "It's a thrill to be involved in fiction that not only entertains, but also changes lives."

For indeed, the writers have a second agenda beyond entertaining readers; they want to leave them with a strong Christian message. It is a message LaHaye has frequently preached:

What will be the fate of Christians with the arrival of "end times" as predicted in the Book of Revelation? And LaHaye also dealt with the subject of the return of Christ and the final battle against Satan in nonfiction books such as *The Rapture: Who Will Face the Tribulation?* and *Revelation Unveiled.*

Minister and national speaker on Bible prophecy, LaHaye is founder and president of Tim LaHaye Ministries and cofounder of the Pre-Trib Research Center. Born in Detroit, Michigan, in 1926, he served in the military during World War II. He attended Bob Jones University, receiving a bachelor of arts degree in 1950, and he earned a doctorate in ministry in 1977 from Western Conservative Baptist Seminary. He also holds a doctor of literature degree from Liberty University. He has served as pastor of Baptist churches in Pickens, South Carolina; Minneapolis, Minnesota; and El Cajon, California. In addition, he founded two accredited Christian high schools. Between 1970 and 1976, he established and served as president of Christian Heritage College. Since 1982, he and his wife, Beverly (Ratcliffe), have cohosted a weekly television program, "LaHayes on Family Life." (She is chairman and founder of Concerned Women for America.) In 2001, Wheaton College's Institute for the Study of American Evangelicals named LaHaye the most influential evangelical leader of the last quarter century.

LaHaye's reputation and his prophecy expertise brought the Left Behind books to notice among both Christian and secular readers. It is Jenkins, however, who actually writes the books.

Born in Kalamazoo, Michigan, in 1949, Jenkins attended Moody Bible Institute, Loop College, and William Rainey Harper College. He married Dianna Louise Whiteford in 1971. Suffering a sports-related injury in high school, Jenkins began covering games for the school paper—and found writing was his calling. He worked in radio and print news for several years before becoming executive editor for *Moody Monthly* in 1973. He went on to become editor then director of Moody Press. In 1985, he became vice president of Moody Bible Institute's Publishing Branch. He wrote articles for *Reader's Digest*, *Parade*, and dozens of Christian periodicals over the years. He also wrote or cowrote a number of sports and other biographies and nonfiction books, including Dr. Billy Graham's memoirs. In addition, he wrote three popular Christian fiction series including the Jennifer Grey mysteries and the Baker Street Sports Club books. Today he is writer-at-large for the Moody Institute. And he scripts the syndicated Gil Thorp daily newspaper comic strip.

Jenkins told one interviewer that he believes the Christian market has yet to attract many strong writers and is open and accepting of new writers in any of the genres. He explained in an Amazon.com interview some of what he believes has helped make the Left Behind series so popular: "I do believe there is a hunger for God among the general population and a curiosity over what the Bible says and what some people believe is going to happen at the end of the world." Highly respectful of LaHaye's beliefs—which Jenkins fully accepts—he said he feels a stewardship to the coming cosmic event.

The series' success, Jenkins said, allowed him to ease his writing burden; he now only writes two books a year. On the other hand, he now feels as if thousands of readers are looking over his shoulder as he works. Although the series has a biblical direction, Jenkins has not had a detailed outline as he has written the individual books. Rather he immerses himself in LaHaye's directions. "I write as a process of discovery," he said in *Insight on the News*, "so I write to see what happens. Sometimes I'm surprised and shocked when somebody ends up dead."

The series was originally envisioned as a single book, but as Jenkins began writing, it became obvious there was more to be said. The single book expanded to three, then six, and finally twelve. (The creators are already hinting there may be a prequel series to relate the stories of the main characters up to the Rapture.)

LaHaye told the interviewer at FamilyChristian.com he believes they have become more sophisticated as the series has progressed. "Slowing it down has been a real help, because there's a world of material that's going to happen during these seven years and what makes it so exciting is that there's more space in the Bible, more material on the seven year Tribulation period than anything but the life of Jesus."

LaHaye notes several reasons for the books' appeal. "Timing is one thing," he told Dee Ann Grand for BookPage. "All people, even secular people, are seeing books on the market like *The End of History*. It makes them start thinking, where is this world going? People recognize something's going to happen, and they'd better get ready."

A number of critics have condemned the series for its intolerance: Gershom Gorenberg in *American Prospect*, stated that the books "promote conspiracy theories; they demonize proponents of arms control, ecumenicalism, abortion rights and everyone else disliked by the Christian right; and they justify assassination as a political tool. Their anti-Jewishness is exceeded by their anti-Catholicism. Most basically, they reject the very idea of open, democratic debate."

The books are futuristic—or are they absolutely current? Perhaps the latter, considering the ascendancy of a born-again Christian president of the United States and a battle against international terrorism and an assault on a scourge in Iraq.

Time writer John Cloud theorizes "in this volatile moment [after the September 11 terrorist attacks in the United States], many people are starting to read the Left Behind books not as novels but as tomorrow's newspapers. LaHaye believes that the Scriptures lay out a precise timetable for the end of the world, and the Left Behind books let us in on the chronology."

Joan Didion, writing in the *New York Review of Books*, explores the relationship of the books' philosophy and the course pursued by the Bush administration in Washington, which has taken international affairs into its own hands to fight terrorism. "In many ways it is from this assumption of competences," she wrote, "of the ability to manage a hostile environment, that the series derives both its potency and its interest: This is a story that feeds on wish fulfillment, a dream of the unempowered, the kind of dream that can be put to political use, and can also entrap those who would use it."

The LaHaye-Jenkins team also has recast the Left Behind series toward teens, following the trials of four youths who face Earth's last days together. A motion picture based on the adult series failed to live up to expectations; a federal court in 2003 dismissed LaHaye's lawsuit against the producer, Cloud Ten Pictures, for making a movie of lower quality than it had promised.

LaHaye is the idea man behind the Left Behind series, but he also writes—he has more than forty nonfiction books to his credit on topics ranging from prophesy, family life, sexuality, and temperament. With another coauthor, Bob DeMoss, LaHaye is producing books for teen readers in the Soul Survivor series. The books deal with topical issues such as abortion, drug abuse, and the dangers of computer chat rooms. Jenkins, too, has found time for a sports novel, *American Leather*, set in a football factory in a small town in Alabama.

Fiction

Written by Jerry Jenkins and Tim LaHaye

Left Behind Series

Left Behind: A Novel of the Earth's Last Days (1995)
Tribulation Forces: The Continuing Drama of Those Left Behind (1996)
Nicolae: The Rise of Antichrist (1997)

Soul Harvest: The World Takes Sides (1998)
Apollyon: The Destroyer Is Unleashed (1999)
Assassins: Assignment Jerusalem, Target-Antichrist (1999)
The Indwelling: The Best Takes Possession (2000)
The Mark: The Beast Rules the World (2000)
The Desecration: Antichrist Takes the Throne (2001)
The Remnant: On the Brink of Armageddon (2002)
Armageddon: The Coming Battle of the Ages (2003)
Glorious Appearing: The End of Days (2004)

Left Behind: The Kids Series

Facing the Future (1998)
Second Chance (1998)
Through the Flames (1998)
The Vanishings (1998)
Busted (1999)
Nicolae High (1999)
The Underground (1999)
Death Strike (2000)
Earthquake! (2000)
Into the Storm (2000)
On the Run (2000)
The Search (2000)
Battling the Commander (2001)
Fire from Heaven (2001)
Judgment Day (2001)
The Showdown (2001)
Terror in the Stadium (2001)
The Attack of Appolyon (2002)
A Dangerous Plan (2002)
Darkening Skies (2002)
Escape from New Babylon (2002)
Horsemen of Terror (2002)
Secrets of New Babylon (2002)
Breakout (2003)
Death at the Gala (2003)
Escape to Masada (2003)
The Mark of the Beast (2003)
Murder in the Holy Place (2003)
Uplink from the Underground (2003)
War of the Dragon (2003)
Wildfire (2003)
Attack on Petra (2004)
Bounty Hunters (2004)

Heat Wave (2004)
Ominous Choices (2004)
Perils of Love (2004)
The Rise of False Messiahs (2004)
The Road to War (2004)
Triumphant Return (2004)

Left Behind Political Series

End of State, by Neesa Hart (2003)
Impeachable offense, by Neesa Hart (2004)
Necessary Evils, by Neesa Hart (2004)

Left Behind Military Series

Apocalypse Dawn: The Earth's Last Days: The Battle Begins, by Mel Odam (2003)
Apocalypse Burning, by Mel Odam (2004)
Apocalypse Crucible, by Mel Odam (2004)
   Note: There have also been five Left Behind graphic novels and five Tribulation Force graphic novels.

Written by Tim LaHaye

A Novel of the Earth's Last Days (1996)

Written by Tim LaHaye and Bob Demoss

Soul Survivor Series

The Mind Siege Project (2001)
All the Rage (2002)
The Last Dance (2002)
Black Friday (2003)

Written by Tim LaHaye and Greg Dinallo or Bob Phillips

Babylon Rising, with Greg Dinallo (2003)
The Secret of Ararat, with Bob Phillips (2004)

Written by Jerry B. Jenkins

American Leather (2001)
Underground Zealot (2004)

Bradford Family Adventure Series

Daniel's Big Surprise (1984)
The Clubhouse Mystery (1984)
The Kidnapping (1984)
Two Runaways (1984)

Blizzard! (1985)
Fourteen Days to Midnight (1985)
Good Sport/Bad Sport (1985)
Marty's Secret (1985)
Before the Judge (1986)
Daniel's Big Decision (1986)
In Deep Water (1986)
Mystery at Raider Stadium (1986)

Dallas O'Neil and the Baker Street Sports Club Series

The Angry Gymnast (1986)
The Bizarre Hockey Tournament (1986)
The Mysterious Football Team (1986)
The Scary Basketball Player (1986)
The Secret Baseball Challenge (1986)
The Silent Track Star (1986)
The Strange Swimming Coach (1986)

Jennifer Grey Mystery Series

Gateway (1983)
Heartbeat (1983)
Three Days in Winter (1983)
Too Late to Tell (1983)
The Calling (1984)
Veiled Threat (1984)

Margo Mystery Series

Margo (1979)
Hilary (1980)
Karlyn (1980)
Allyson (1981)
Paige (1981)
Erin (1982)
Shannon (1982)
Courtney (1983)
Janell (1983)
Lindsey (1983)
Meaghan (1983)
Lyssa (1984)
Margo's Reunion (1984)

Nonfiction
Written by Tim LaHaye and Jerry B. Jenkins

Have You Been Left Behind? (1999)
Fire From Heaven (2001)
Perhaps Today (2001)
A Visual Guide to the Left Behind Series (2001)
God Always Keeps His Promises (2003)

Written by Tim LaHaye and Thomas Ice

Charting the End Times: Prophecy Study Guide (2002)
The End Time Controversy (2003)
The Second Coming Under Attack (2003)

Written by Tim LaHaye and Beverly LaHaye

Family (1998)
Gathering Lilies from Among the Thorns: Finding the Mate God Has for You (1998)

Written by Tim LaHaye

Spirit-Controlled Temperament (1966)
How to Be Happy Though Married (1968)
Transformed Temperaments (1971)
The Beginning of the End (1972)
How to Win Over Depression (1973)
Revelation Illustrated and Made Plain (1973), revised *Revelation Unveiled* (1999)
The Act of Marriage (1974)
Ten Steps to Victory Over Depression (1974)
The Act of Marriage After 40 (1976)
The Bible's Influence on American History (1976)
How to Study the Bible for Yourself (1976)
The Battle for the Mind (1980)
The Battle for the Family (1981)
Anger Is a Choice (1982)
The Battle for Public Schools (1982)
How to Manage Pressure Before Pressure Manages You (1983)
How to Manage Your Pressures Before They Manage You (1983)
Your Temperament: Discover Its Potential (1984)
Sex Education Is for the Family (1985)
Faith of Our Founding Fathers (1987)
Why You Act the Way You Do (1988)
If Ministers Fall, Can They Be Restored? (1990)
Transforming Your Temperament (1991)

Against the Tide: How to Raise Sexually Pure Kids, with Beverly LaHaye (1993)
Transformed Temperaments (1993)
Nation Without a Conscience (1994)
The Spirit-Controlled Woman (1996)
Alike in Love: When Opposites Attract (1998)
The Power of the Cross (1998)
Jesus: Who Is He? (1997)
Are We Living in the End Times? (1999)
Bible Prophecy: What You Need to Know (1999)
Revelation: Unveiled (1999)
Tim LaHaye Prophecy Study Bible (2000)
Prophecy Bible Study (2000)
Finding the Will of God in a Crazy, Mixed-Up World (2001)
I Love You, But Why Are We so Different? (2001)
The Mind Siege, with David Noebel (2001)
Understanding Bible Prophecy for Yourself (2001)
Understanding the Male Temperament (2001)
The Merciful God of Prophecy and His Loving Pain for You in the End Times (2002)
The Rapture (2002)
The Rapture: Who Will Face the Tribulation? (2002), previously titled *Rapture Under Attack*
Seduction of the Heart (2002)
Soul Harvest (2002)
Understanding Bible Philosophy for Yourself (2002)
World (2002)
The Promise of Heaven (2003)

Written by Jerry B. Jenkins

Sammi Tippit: God's Love in Action (1973)
You CAN Get thru to Teens (1973)
Bad Henry, with Hank Aaron and Stan Baldwin (1974)
The Story of the Christian Booksellers Association (1974)
VBS Unlimited (1974)
Stuff It: The Story of Dick Motta, Toughest Little Coach in the NBA (1975)
Three Behind the Curtain, with Sammy Tippit (1975)
The World's Strongest Man, with Paul Anderson (1975)
Running for Jesus, with Madeline Manning Jackson (1977)
Light on the Heavy: A Simple Guide to Understanding Bible Doctrines (1978)
Sweetness, with Walter Payton (1978)
You, Me, He, with B. J. Thomas (1978)
The Luis Palau Story (1980)

The Night the Giant Rolled Over (1981)
Teaching the Word, Reaching the World, with Robert Flood (1985)

Written by Jerry B. Jenkins and Pat Williams

The Gingerbread Man: Pat Williams Then and Now (1974)
The Power Within You (1983)
Rekindled: How to Keep the Warmth in Marriage (1985)

Motion Pictures Based on LaHaye and/or Jenkins Books

Left Behind: The Movie (2001)
American Leather (2002)

For Further Information

"Author Profile: Tim LaHaye." Page-Turner's Journal. *http://www.tyndale.com/journal/fiction/lahaye_bio.html* (viewed April 2, 2003).

Cherry, Sheila. "Tour Guides to the Tribulation." *Insight on the News* (August 26, 2002).

Cloud, John. "Meet the Prophet: How an Evangelist and Conservative Activist Turned Prophecy into a Fiction Juggernaut." *Time* (July 1, 2002).

"Conversation with Jerry Jenkins & Tim LaHaye." FamilyChristian.com. *http://www.familychristian.com/books/jenkins.lahaye.asp* (viewed April 2, 2003).

Didion, Joan. "Mr. Bush & the Divine." *New York Review of Books* (November 6, 2003).

"Federal judge in March dismissed Left Behind co-author Tim Lahaye's Lawsuit against Cloud Ten Pictures." *Christianity Today* (July 2003).

Foster, Julie. "Tim LaHaye 'most influential leader': Institute says 'Left Behind' creator No. 1 evangelical." WorldNetDaily. *http://www.worldnetdaily.com/news/article.asp?ARTICLE_ID=23070* (viewed April 2, 2003).

Gates, David. "The Pop Prophets." *Newsweek* (May 24, 2004).

"God in the End times: An interview with Jerry B. Jenkins." Amazon.com. *http://www.amazon.com/exec/obidos/tg/feature/-/39251/104-3961905-2055953* (viewed April 2, 2003).

Gorenberg, Gershom. "Intolerance: the bestseller." *American Prospect* (September 23, 2002).

Grand, Dee Ann. "Left Behind series co-author tackles familiar turf." BookPage. *http://www.bookpage.com/0104bp/jerry_jenkins.html* (viewed April 2, 2003).

Grand, Dee Ann. "Tim LaHaye keeps readers enraptured with tales of those Left Behind." BookPage. *http://www.bookpage.com/0104bp/tim_lahaye.html* (viewed April 2, 2003).

Ivory, Ann, and Linda Metzger, eds. Tim LaHaye entry, *Contemporary Authors New Revision Series*. Vol. 9. Detroit: Gale Research, 1983.

Jerry B. Jenkins Web site. *http://www.jerryjenkins.com/* (viewed April 2, 2003).

Left Behind Web site. *http://www.leftbehind.com/* (viewed April 2, 2003).

Meet the Writers; Jerry B. Jenkins & Tim LaHaye. Barnes & Noble. *http://www.barnesandnoble.com/writers/writerdetails.asp?userid=0H4KV3ZHMT&cid=968101#bio* (viewed April 2, 2003).

Metzger, Linda, and Deborah A. Straub, eds. Jerry B. Jenkins entry, *Contemporary Authors, New Revision Series*. Vol. 20. Detroit: Gale Research, 1987.

Minzesheimer, Bob. "Search for meaning motivates mainstream readers." *USA Today* (March 29, 2004).

Murphree, Randall. "New Novel For Teens Tackles Abortion Issue." AFA Online. *http://headlines.agapepress.org/archive/3/afa/102003f.asp* (viewed May 2, 2003).

Potter, Megan. "An interview with Jerry B. Jenkins, co-author of the Left Behind series of books." Writing Corner. *http://writingcorner.com/tips/writerslife/ jerry_b_jenkins.htm* (viewed April 20, 2003).

Rosenthal, Shane. "An Interview With . . . Tim LaHaye." ModernReformation.Org. *http://www.modernreformatin.org/mr95/marapr/mr9502interview.html* (viewed April 2, 2003).

Tim LaHaye Web site. *http://www.timlahaye.com/* (viewed April 2, 2003).

Robert Jordan

◆ Fantasy

Charleston, South Carolina
1948

◆ *Wheel of Time Series*

Credit: Jack Alterman.

About the Author and the Author's Writing

A nuclear physicist crafting the sword-swinging adventures of Conan the Barbarian? Hey, anything goes in the world of fiction writing.

James Oliver Rigney Jr. was born in 1948 in Charleston, South Carolina, where he still lives, in a 1797 Colonial home. His older brother helped him learn to read, and by the age of five he was devouring the works of Mark Twain and Jules Verne. He also read *Gulliver's Travels* and Freddy the Pig books. These days he can list a host of favorite writers, from Jane Austen and Charles Dickens to Patrick O'Brian and James Patterson, Robert Heinlein, Louis L'Amour, and John D. MacDonald.

From 1968 to 1970 Jordan served two tours in Vietnam with the U.S. Army, receiving the Distinguished Flying Cross, the Bronze Star with "V," and two Vietnamese Crosses of Gallantry. In 1974, he graduated from The Citadel, the Military College of South Carolina. The author married Harriet Stoney Popham McDougal in 1981. She is an executive editor for Jordan's publisher, Tor. His avocations include hunting, fishing and sailing, poker, chess, and pool.

Jordan worked as a U.S. Civil Service nuclear engineer from 1974 to 1978, then became a freelance writer. He long toyed with writing a serious Vietnam novel under his own name, so he used the pennames Jackson O'Reilly (for a western) and Reagan O'Neal (for family historicals) for his early books. His Robert Jordan alias stuck through his popular continuations of Robert. E. Howard's barbarian tales and his even more popular original Wheel of Time sequence.

Jordan stated his strong commitment to fantasy in an Orbit interview: "Some stories need to be told in certain genres, and fantasy allows the writer to explore good and evil, right and wrong, honour and duty without having to bow to the mainstream belief that all of these things are merely two sides of a coin."

After sharpening his blade on Conan, Jordan moved on to create the Wheel of Time series, beginning with *The Eye of the World*. In these books, Rand, a questing sheepherder who grew up in a small village, is often saved from dire situations by a mysterious crack of lightning. Unlike Conan, who is essentially a loner (or loses his companions in combat), Rand has friends, the wolfer Perrin and the lucky Mat. Also unlike Conan, the Wheel books have strong women characters such as girlfriend Egwene, wisewoman Nynaeve, and Moraine, a female mage.

Because Jordan wants readers to follow the series from the first book, he doesn't make it easy to jump in with later entries. His slow pace annoys some, such as critic Douglas C. Lord, who panned *Crossroads of Twilight* as an "annoyingly intricate and sprawling soap opera." Others disagree. Wendy Bradley, in *St. James Guide to Fantasy Writers*, found Jordan's Conan novels "vigorous, lusty and full of excellent scene setting."

The author thinks big. He has quoted his grandfather as saying: "Boy, would you rather hunt rabbits or leopards?" Obviously, Jordan wants leopards.

Jordan doesn't closely outline his books; he may have some scenes or themes in mind, and once he's figured out how they will fit together, and how things will probably end, he starts writing. His Wheel universe has become so large, he keeps a file for every individual, city, and culture he creates.

A typical writing day finds him lifting weights or swimming before he goes to his carriage house office to deal with correspondence and calls. He usually spends at least eight hours at writing, though he will put in as many as fourteen when in the heat of finishing a book. Although his publisher's intent has been to bring out one book a year, Jordan has fallen behind on the schedule—for the simple reason it takes him more than a year to write one of the 700-plus page epics. Some of his books have come out within two months of the delivery of a manuscript; this speedy turnaround has necessitated Jordan and his wife going to New York to revise pages as quickly as a copy editor turned them in.

Jordan said he tries hard to get inside the players he is writing about at a particular moment, and sometimes succeeds too well, as when his wife will comment, once he leaves work, that he's being a Padan Fain that day.

Complex women (as well as men) characters, Jordan has said, are a given if you want to write involved, satisfying novels. Of Tuon, for example, he told *Publishers Weekly*, "She's an intelligent, capable woman who has grown up in a competitive and highly deadly atmosphere. She and her siblings must compete to prove their worth. The winner will be the heir to the throne. She is short, slender, and wishes she had more bosom and height, so she thinks she has no presence and must make up for it by her skill."

Jordan plans to end the Wheel series, but he's not saying if it will take two more books or ten. Jordan said in a *Locus* interview, "In a normal historical novel, you can simply let some things go by because the reader of historical fiction knows these, or has the concept of them. But this is not the medieval period, not a fantasy with knights in shining armor. If you want to imagine what the period is, imagine it as the late seventeenth century without gunpowder. I had to do more explaining about cultural details, and that meant things got bigger than I had intended."

Jordan's fantasy contains lots of fighting, something he has known firsthand from his military experience. He learned "that being in a battle is confusion," he said in an Amazon.com interview. "You know what you can see; you don't know what is happening beyond your sight. That's what comes from the military. To tell you the truth, the battles aren't nearly as interesting as the people. I like the interactions of the people—the character development, the way people play off one another."

Which character's point of view he uses for a particular scene, Jordan said in a Dragonmount discussion with fans, "is a matter of choosing whose eyes are the best to see a scene. What do I want the reader to know in that scene? What do I want to leave them uncertain about? . . . Faile and Perrin, for example, will not see the same event in exactly the same way or react to it in the same way, nor will Min and Rand, or Nynaeve and Elayne and Egwene, or Rand and Perrin and Mat."

In *Lord of Chaos* there's a jarring scene in which Rand memorizes the face of a maiden who has died to protect him from assailants. It came from the author's heart. "[T]hat particular thing came from the only time I was really shaken in combat in shooting at somebody . . . ," he recalled for a Fast Forward television interview. "[A] woman came out and pulled up an AK-47, and I didn't hesitate about shooting her. That stuck with me. I was raised in a very old-fashioned sort of way. You don't hurt women—you don't *do* that. That's the one thing that stuck with me for a long time."

Works by the Author

Fiction

Conan the Barbarian Series

Conan the Defender (1982)
Conan the Invincible (1982)
Conan the Triumphant (1983)
Conan the Unconquered (1983)
Conan the Destroyer (1984)
Conan the Magnificent (1984)
Conan the Victorious (1984)
King of Thieves (1984)
The New Adventures of Conan (1985)
The Conan Chronicles (1995), omnibus
The Conan Chronicles II (1997), omnibus
The Further Chronicles of Conan (1998), omnibus

Eye of The World Series

From the Two Rivers (2002)
To the Blight (2002)

Wheel of Time Series

The Eye of the World (1990)
The Great Hunt (1990)
The Dragon Reborn (1991)
The Shadow Rising (1992)
The Fires of Heaven (1993)
Robert Jordan Wheel of Time (1993), includes first three books

Lord of Chaos (1994)
A Crown of Swords (1996)
The Path of Daggers (1998)
The Best of Robert Jordan (1999), includes second four books
Winter's Heart (2000)
Crossroads of Twilight (2003)
New Spring: The Novel (2004)

Written as Jackson O'Reilly, reissued as by Robert Jordan

Cheyenne Raiders (1982)

Written as Reagan O'Neal, reissued as by Robert Jordan

Fallon Series

The Fallon Pride (1981)
The Fallon Legacy (1982)
The Fallon Blood (1995)

Anthologies

Visions of Wonder (1985)
Legends (1986)
Legends: Short Novels by the Masters of Modern Fantasy, volume 1, edited by Robert
 Silverberg (1999)

Nonfiction

The World of Robert Jordan's The Wheel of Time (1997) with Teresa Patterson

For Further Information

"About Robert Jordan." *http://www.geocities.com/iliana._sedai.index.html* (viewed
 May 20, 2003).

Bradley, Wendy. Robert Jordan entry, *St. James Guide to Fantasy Writers*. Detroit: St.
 James Press, 1996.

Indick, Ben P. "The Wheel Turns Another Notch." *Publishers Weekly* (December 23,
 2002).

Jones, Daniel, and John D. Jorgenson, eds. James Oliver Rigney Jr. entry, *Contemporary Authors New Revision Series*. Vol. 62. Detroit: Gale Research, 1998.

Lord, Douglas C. *Crossroads of Twilight* review. *Library Journal* (June 15, 2003).

"Meet Robert Jordan." BookPage. *http://www.bookpage.com/0301bp/meet_robert _jordan.html* (viewed May 20, 2003).

Norén, Karl-Johan. Robert Jordan interview. Sun Fantasy Convention (June 17, 1995). *http://hem.passagen.se/kjnoren/jordan/rj-talk1-html* (viewed May 20, 2003).

Robert Jordan interview. Amazon.com. *http://www.amazon.com/exec/obidos/ts/ feature/11690.002-4508949-0718447* (viewed May 20, 2003).

Robert Jordan interview. Barnes & Noble. *http://www.barnesandnoble.com/writers/ writer.asp?cid=883023* (viewed May 20, 2003).

Robert Jordan interview. Dragonmount (December 9, 2002). *http://www.dragonmount .com/Interviews/2002-12-09_rj.aspx* (viewed May 20, 2003).

Robert Jordan interview. Fast Forward: Contemporary Science Fiction (November 1, 1994). *http://www.gocities.com/Area51/2593/frjfastf.htm* (viewed May 20, 2003).

Robert Jordan interview. Orbit (November 2001). *http://www.sffworld.com/authors/ j/.jordan_robert/interviews/200111.html* (viewed May 20, 2003).

"Robert Jordan: The Name Behind the Wheel." *Locus* (March 2000).

Jan Karon

◆ Romance ◆ Christian

Lenoir, North Carolina
1937

◆ *Mitford Years*

About the Author and the Author's Writing

"In my books I try to depict not a glorious faith with celestial fireworks but a daily faith, a routine faith, a seven-days-a-week faith," Jan Karon said in a Penguin readers guide to her Mitford Years series. ". . . I try to depict how our faith may be woven into our daily life, like brandy poured into coffee. I believe that spirituality needs to be basic, common, everyday."

The author was born Janice Meredith Wilson in Lenoir, North Carolina, in 1937. She and her sister grew up on their grandparents' farm and, although she disliked it at the time, she said she is now appreciative of her rural upbringing.

"I went with my grandfather to swap mules and horses, to buy bird dogs, to buy nails for roofing and seed corn for planting," she told interviewer Betty Smartt Carter. "I got to be around a lot of different people. The world opened up to me. I developed, without even knowing it, an ear for dialect."

From her grandmother, an herbalist and storyteller, she felt the compulsion to write. "I grew up hearing words like snakeroot, sassafras, mullein," the author told *People Weekly*, "things that had wondrous, mysterious sounds in their names."

Karon knew she wanted to be a writer by the time she was ten. She wrote her first story on Blue Horse binder pages. Despite her best efforts, her sister found the manuscript and pointed out the single swear word in it to their grandmother. Never forgetting the scolding she received, Karon has never included another curse word in her prose. She left school after eighth grade.

At her first job, as a receptionist for an advertising agency, she constantly left samples of her writing and finally her boss noticed. She went on to spend thirty years in the advertising field, handling accounts such as Honda and British Airways, and received numerous awards and held an executive position with a national agency. Divorced, she has a daughter, Candace Freeland, a photojournalist and musician.

After a good deal of praying, the author left her profession. She settled in North Carolina to be near her brother. "I immediately responded to the culture of village life," Karon said on the Mitford Books Web site. A town of some 1,800 people in the Blue Ridge mountains, Blowing Rock serves as the model for Mitford. Although the community is populated with individuals normal and eccentric—as are her books—none is specifically a character in her prose.

Karon so absorbed her small-townness, that Zachary Karabel in the *Los Angeles Times Book Review* called her "a writer who reflects contemporary culture more fully than almost any other living novelist. Karon spins a fantasy of a town full of lovable yet decent people who struggle with love and marriage, with domestic disputes and unpredictable weather, with ghosts of their past and, most of all, with faith and God."

She wrote her first book tentatively, based on a simple mental image that came to her of the characters. She took her manuscript to the local newspaper editor for his comments. He began to run chapters in the paper for the next two years, providing her with invaluable feedback. She found readers particularly felt close to the characters.

At Home in Mitford, the opening book in her series, finds Episcopal priest Tim Kavanath, drained after a dozen years with his parish, with his secretary, who still treats him as child; a huge black dog, Barnabas; a belligerent mountain boy, Dooley, in his care; and a growing friendship with a neighbor, Cynthia Coppersmith, a children's book author and illustrator. (She is not this character, the author has insisted; Cynthia has betterlooking legs.) Readers loved Mitford, its characters, and the gentle tale Karon spun.

Those characters who simply pop out of the page work best, the author said in a DKOnline interview. The Rev. Absalom Greer, as an example, is preaching at a revival meeting in These High Green Hills. "Nothing was happening. He saw this young girl sitting in the tree. She was about 13–14 years old, dirty, hair mangled, and clothes torn. All of a sudden, she jumped from the tree and landed right in front of Absalom. Here's a character I had never planned on."

Karon's characters are not all perfection; Cynthia the fun-loving neighbor has a messy divorce in her past, and once went through a suicidal depression, for example.

"These people are flawed just like you and me," Karon explained to journalist Phyllis ten Eishof of *Christian Reader*. "They're people in whom we find ourselves." (Though as *Christianity Today* writer Lauren F. Winner pointed out, there are no major controversies, such as women priests or homosexuals, in the books.)

Mitford appears to be the ideal, comfortable town, but the author stresses in the stories that it takes all the inhabitants to make that town so wonderful; they don't come ready-made.

Although most of her writing is about Mitford, Karon has written two children's books, including *Miss Fannie's Hat*, about her grandmother; she also is working on a Mitford cookbook.

Karon writes in her properly decorated home office, working at a word-processing computer sometimes two hours a day, sometimes twelve. She said in the readers guide she learned her craft from radio, where listeners have to fill in a lot of the blanks, have to imagine a lot for themselves.

In the face of her books' huge popularity, and a constant flow of fans to her home, the author out of desperation for creative privacy purchased a home in Virginia where she now writes. She still visits Blowing Rock, where she has family and friends. Her characters likewise had to step outside Mitford for awhile. Father Tim felt compelled to retire from Lord's Chapel in *A New Song*, though it is not long before he and his now-wife Cynthia relocate to Whitecap Island off the North Carolina coast where the pastor will serve on an interim basis at Saint John's in the Grove. If Father Tim expected any great change, he was in for a surprise. The new town's people have as many issues as the old one's.

Works by the Author

Fiction

The Trellis and the Seed (2003)

Mitford Years Series

At Home in Mitford (1994)
A Light in the Window (1996)
These High, Green Hills (1996)
Out to Canaan (1997)
A New Song (1999)
A Common Life: The Wedding Story (2001)
The Mitford Years (2001), includes first five books
The Mitford Snowmen: A Christmas Story (2001)
Patches of Godlight: Father Tim's Favorite Quotes (2001)
Esther's Gift: A Mitford Christmas Story (2002)
In This Mountain (2002)
Shepherd's Abiding (2003)

Short Stories

A Southern Style Christmas: Holiday Treasures by Jan Karon (2000)

Books for Children

Miss Fannie's Hat (1998)
Jeremy: The Tale of an Honest Bunny (2000)

Nonfiction

Mitford Cookbook and Kitchen Reader (2004)
Mitford Beside Companion (forthcoming)

For Further Information

Carter, Betty Smartt. "Postmarked Mitford: Readers Are Finding a Home in Jan Karon's Novels." *Christianity Today* (September 1, 1997).

Cheakalos, Christina, with Fran Brennan. "Comfort Zone: Writer Jan Karon Created Imaginary Mitford, N.C., and Millions of Readers Call It Home." *People Weekly* (September 10, 2001).

Jan Karon interview. DKOnline. *http://www.daviskidd.com/html/karonarchive.html* (viewed March 31, 2003).

Karabel, Zachary. "Look Homeward Angel: Why the Literati Snub the Christian Fiction of Jan Karon." *Los Angeles Times Book Review* (August 22, 1999).

"Karon's Agenda: The frustrated Episcopalian is not a frustrated evangelist." *Christianity Today* (July 12, 1999).

Maryles, Daisy. "On Top of the Mountain." *Publishers Weekly* (June 10, 2002).

"Meet the Author: Jan Karon." BookPage. *http://www.bookpage.com/9904bp/jan_karon.html* (viewed March 31, 2003).

Mitford Books Web site. *http://www.mitfordbooks.com/books.asp* (viewed March 31, 2003)

Peacock, Scot, ed. Jan Karon entry, *Contemporary Authors*. Vol. 204. Detroit: Gale Research, 2003.

Penguin Readers Guide to The Mitford Years Series. New York: Penguin Putnam, 2001.

Ten Eishof, Phyllis. "Why Jan Karon Left Mitford." *Christian Reader* (May/June 2001).

Winner, Lauren F. "New Song, Familiar Tune: Jan Karon's latest Mitford installment changes locales to talk about living where you're at." *Christianity Today* (July 12, 1999).

Faye Kellerman

◆ Mystery

St. Louis, Missouri
1952

◆ *Peter Decker/Rina Lazarus Series*

About the Author and the Author's Writing

The relationship between Los Angeles homicide detective Peter Decker and his wife, Rina Lazarus, gives their long-running and popular crime series by Faye Kellerman a distinct spin. It's no surprise Kellerman makes crime solving a family affair. After all, she and her husband, Jonathan, are a crime-solving duo in real life, both being mystery writers. Each produces a new novel a year, his published in winter, hers in summer.

Faye Marder was born in 1952 in St. Louis, Missouri, the daughter of a retailer. She received a bachelor of arts degree in 1974 from the University of California in Los Angeles and a doctorate in divinity studies degree from the same institution four years later. She married Jonathan Kellerman in 1972, and they have four children. Jonathan is a psychologist as well as novelist; since 1974, Faye has been an independent investor and real estate manager in Los Angeles.

Faye Kellerman began writing after the birth of her first child. Her husband was her inspiration. None of those early romances saw print, but in 1986 her first mystery, *The Ritual Bath*, did. It was the first book to feature the Decker/Lazarus duo; *Stalker*, in 2000, featured another family member, eldest daughter Cindy Decker, now an LAPD officer, who reappeared in *Street Dreams*.

To keep her books fresh, Faye Kellerman wrote *Stalker* in Cindy Decker's voice. The author said on the HarperCollins Web site that this allowed her to take a younger perspective: "I could be more brash, more bold, more careless and she could get herself into tight situations . . . things her father wouldn't do because he's too experienced and he's a different character altogether. He's more reserved, more thoughtful, he thinks more."

Kellerman has said she believes it is the realistic depiction of her main characters, and their relationship, that makes them so popular. Decker has married into an Orthodox Jewish family. "Religion is a major factor in my life," Kellerman told interviewer Jill Zaklow.

"I consider myself a modern Orthodox Jewish woman with attachments to my synagogue, my children's religious school and the community at large."

Aside from the Jewish subtext, Kellerman is known for the high level of violence in her books. She notes much of it is after-the-fact, crime-scene detail vital to the realistic depiction of a crime investigation.

"Crime novels speak to the most basic human drives and instincts," Kellerman said in speaking with Bookreporter.com. "There is nothing as compelling as murder. It addresses the darkest recesses of human nature much in the same way that religion does. I like to contrast the two, the sacred and the profane."

Kellerman lists among her favorite authors Joyce Carol Oates, James M. Cain, Ross MacDonald, Elmore Leonard, Chaim Potok, Joseph Wambaugh, Sue Grafton, the Brontes, and, of course, Jonathan Kellerman.

Critic Gilliam Rodgerson described Kellerman as "a powerful, inventive writer whose plots and characters hold the readers' attention from beginning to end. She truly understands modern America and the prejudices and pressures that lurk behind its facade of flag-waving family values. All of her novels reflect her keen intelligence and her special ability to advance her stories principally in dialogue perfectly tailored to her characters."

Kellerman has her stories well plotted and outlined before she begins a book, though there is leeway to allow for creativity along the way from crime to solution. Rina Lazarus is partly based on the author, partly different. "To write a really interesting character, you have to step outside your personal confines, otherwise there's no objectivity," she told Ben P. Indick. "Rina's feelings and her love of Judaism are probably reflected from my own love. Peter Decker only partially reflects my husband, Jonathan."

"It's very important in crime fiction to flesh out characters, at the same time cutting out extraneous things and keeping the plot moving," Kellerman told Susan Salter Reynolds of *Publishers Weekly*. "I take about 60% to 70% of [her agent's] advice. But I myself am a merciless editor. Every 50 to 100 pages or so I'll give the manuscript to Jonathan, who will tell me which scenes drag and where I make illogical leaps that don't work."

Kellerman has written two stand-alone books, *Moon Music*, a contemporary thriller, and *The Quality of Mercy*, a historical set in Elizabethan England. In the last, the main female character disguises herself as a man, meets up with William Shakespeare, and falls in love with him. If that sounds something like the plot of the movie *Shakespeare in Love*, well, Kellerman in 1999 sued the Oscar-winning screenwriters of that film claiming plagiarism.

Works by the Author

Fiction

The Quality of Mercy (1992)
Moon Music (1998)

Peter Decker/Rina Lazarus Series

The Ritual Bath (1986)
Sacred and Profane (1987)
Milk and Honey (1990)

Day of Atonement (1992)
False Prophet (1992)
Grievous Sin (1993)
Sanctuary (1994)
Justice (1995)
Prayers for the Dead (1996)
Serpent's Tooth (1997)
Jupiter's Bones (1999)
Stalker (2000)
The Forgotten (2001)
Stone Kiss (2002)
Street Dreams (2003)
Therapy (2004)

Written with Jonathan Kellerman

Double Homicide (2004)

Anthologies

Sisters in Crime, edited by Marilyn Wallace (1989)
Sisters in Crime 3, edited by Marilyn Wallace (1990)
A Woman's Eye (1991)
Women of Mystery (1992)
Deadly Allies II (1994)
A Modern Treasury of Great Detective and Murder Mysteries (1994)
Hard-Boiled (1995)
Murder for Love (1996)
The Night Awakens (1998)
Mothers & Daughters: Celebrating the Gift of Love With 12 New Stories, edited by
    Jill M. Morgan (1998)
Diagnosis Dead (1999)
Mystery Midrash (1999)
Fathers & Daughters: Celebrating the Gift of Love With 12 New Stories, edited by Jill
    Morgan (2000)
World's Finest Mystery and Crime Stories, edited by Edward Gorman (2000)

For Further Information

Carter, Dale. Jonathan Kellerman entry, *St. James Guide to Crime & Mystery Writers*.
    4th edition, edited by Jay P. Pederson. Detroit: St. James Press, 1996.

Dunn, Adam. "There are ways of doing it." PW Talks with Faye Kellerman biography.
    Meet the Writers. *http://www.barnesandnoble.com/writers/writerdetails.asp?
    userid-0H4KV3ZHMT&cid=881727#bio* (viewed May 24, 2003).

Faye Kellerman interview. HarperCollins. *http://www.harpercollins.com/hc/authors/ stalker.asp* (viewed May 24, 2003).

Flamm, Matthew. "Between the Lines." *Entertainment Weekly* (April 9, 1999).

Indick, Ben P. "PW talks with Faye Kellerman." *Publishers Weekly* (July 1, 2002).

Jones, Daniel, and John D. Jorgenson, eds. Faye Kellerman entry, *Contemporary Authors New Revision Series*. Vol. 60. Detroit: Gale Research, 1998.

Kornbluth, Jesse, and Jennifer Levitsky. Faye Kellerman interview. Bookreporter. *http://www.bookreporter.com/authors/au-kellerman-faye-asp* (viewed May 24, 2003).

Mudge, Alden. "Partners in crime: The Kellermans share a knack for suspense." BookPage (December 2000). *http://www.bookpage.com/0012bp/jonathan_fye _kellerman.html* (viewed March 31, 2003).

Reynolds, Susan Salter. "Faye Kellerman: murder on her mind." *Publishers Weekly* (August 18, 1997).

Rodgerson, Gillian, and Don Sandstrom. Faye Kellerman entry, *St. James Guide to Crime & Mystery Writers*. 4th edition, edited by Jay P. Pederson. Detroit: St. James Press, 1996.

Zaklow, Jill. Faye Kellerman interview. Bookreporter. *http://www.bookreporter.com/ authors/au-kellerman-faye-asp* (viewed May 24, 2003).

Elmer Kelton

◆ Westerns ◆ Historical

Andrews, Texas
1926

◆ *The Day the Cowboys Quit*

Credit: Jim Bean.

About the Author and the Author's Writing

Voted all-time best western author by the Western Writers of America, Elmer Kelton remarked before the Texas Folklore Society, "As a fiction writer I have always tried to use fiction to illuminate history, to illuminate truth, at least as I see the history and truth. A fiction writer can fire a reader's interest enough to make him want to dig into the true story and make him search out the real history to find out for himself what happened."

Kelton was born in 1926 at the Scharbauer Cattle Company's horse camp at Five Wells Ranch in Andrews County, Texas, the son of a cowboy and a teacher. He grew up on the McElroy Ranch near Crane, Texas, where his father worked as foreman. Kelton learned about roping and herding cattle, but he always dreamed of becoming a writer.

After serving in Austria during World War II, he married Anna Lipp in 1947. The next year, he completed requirements for a bachelor of arts degree in journalism from the University of Texas. A Methodist in religion, an independent in politics, he became an agricultural journalist for the *San Angelo Standard-Times* (starting in 1948), *Sheep and Goat Ranchers* magazine (editor, beginning in 1963), and *Livestock Weekly* (associate editor, 1968 until he retired in 1990).

At the same time, he wrote fiction part-time. His first short story was "There's Always Another Chance" for *Ranch Romances* in 1948. Then in 1955, his first full-length book, *Hot Iron*, appeared. It was followed by, on average, a book a year ever since.

His novels have garnered four Western Heritage Awards from the National Cowboy Hall of Fame and seven Western Writers of America Spur awards, including the 2002 Spur Award for best western novel, *The Way of the Coyote*.

As a reporter, Kelton visited ranches and watched the livestock business firsthand. He collected stories and learned how cowboys worked, spoke, and acted. He saw how close to nature ranch people are, how connected to the soil. Although his regular job consumed a lot of his time, Kelton said, it provided job security. He didn't *have* to write novels, and consequently he could write the novels he wanted to.

To get a handle on westerns when he started out, he read the works of Luke Short and Ernest Haycox. He was already familiar with Zane Grey, from reading that author's works in his youth, but he looked more for stylistic hints in Will James, S. Omar Barker, W. C. Tuttle, Wayne D. Overholser, and others.

"The conflict quite often in Kelton's Westerns is not supplied by the formulary hero vs. villain convention," observed Deane Mansfield-Kelley in *Encyclopedia of Frontier and Western Fiction*, "but rather by confrontations between opposing beliefs or viewpoints."

"The strength of his fiction lies in the historical background, the folklore, and the development of his characters," added Dorys C. Grover in *Twentieth-Century Western Writers*. "He is especially good with dialogue and he certainly knows Texas history."

Indeed, Kelton has made Texas history his hallmark. The author told *Twentieth-Century Western Writers*, "I have chosen various periods of change or of stress in which an old order is being pushed aside by the new, and through the fictional characters try to give the reader some understanding of the human reason for and effects of these changes."

Kelton is seen as a driving force in a new style of western writers who shun stereotypes and explore new aspects of the genre. He has written about everything from buffalo hunting to the aftermath of the Civil War as it related to African Americans to the birth of the Texas Rangers. His Buckalew quartet followed one family through Texas history; his Sons of Texas trilogy, written under the penname Tom Early, looks at the Lewis family's role in Lone Star State history; and his Texas Rangers series explores the early days of that legendary law enforcement agency.

As he progressed as a writer, Kelton has observed, he has placed more emphasis on character and less on action. His plots have become more intricate and history has come to play a greater role.

His *The Day the Cowboys Quit* is based on a real 1883 incident, a cowboy strike on the Canadian River. *The Time It Never Rained* follows stubborn Charlie Flagg who is determined to wait out a seven-year drought in West Texas in the 1950s. Wes Hendrix is a cattle rancher who refuses to sell out in another modern-day novel, *The Man Who Rode Midnight*. Kelton creates strong and value-driven characters, women as well as men, yet they are individuals who are vulnerable or flawed in some way. Hewey Calloway in *The Good Old Boys*, for example, was put together from several cowboys he knew as a youth. (That book was made into a TNT television movie in 1995 with Tommy Lee Jones.)

Kelton recognizes westerns are a shrinking market, but asserts they are no less valid. "I've heard many people say that 'Star Wars' was the best Western they'd ever seen," Kelton said in an interview with Liz Cordingley. "Of course there's the pioneering aspects of science fiction and space as a new frontier, but detailed scientific language leaves the West behind. Part of the Western's charm is in its nostalgia for simpler times."

Kelton has been a member of Western Writers of America since 1955. He has served on its board and as its president. His papers through 1985 are archived at Texas Tech University Southwest Collection/Special Collections Library.

Kelton's westerns are also great literature. "A good novel of the West is just as valid as a novel set anywhere as long as it is honest and reflects reality," Kelton told Dale L. Walker in a *Louis L'Amour Western Magazine* interview. "My real subject is the human condition, and this is universal."

Works by the Author

Fiction

Hot Iron (1955)
Buffalo Wagons (1956)
Barbed Wire (1957)
Shadow of a Star (1959)
The Texas Rifles (1960)
Donovan (1961)
Bitter Trail (1962)
Horsehead Crossing (1963)
Llano River (1966)
Captain's Rangers (1968)
Hanging Judge (1969)
The Day the Cowboys Quit (1971)
Wagontongue (1972)
The Time It Never Rained (1973)
Manhunters (1974)
The Good Old Boys (1978)
Barbed Wire (1979)
The Wolf and the Buffalo (1980)
Stand Proud (1984)
Dark Thicket (1985)
There's Always Another Chance (1986)
The Man Who Rode Midnight (1987)
Honor at Daybreak (1991)
Slaughter (1992)
The Far Canyon (1994)
The Pumpkin Rollers (1996)
Cloudy in the West (1997)
Traildust (1997)
The Smiling Country (1998)
A Thousand Miles of Mustangin' (1998)
Dark Thicket (1999)
Legend (1999)

Buckalew Series

Massacre at Goliad (1965)
After the Bugles (1967)
Bowie's Mine (1971)
Long Way to Texas (1976), written as Lee McElroy

Texas Heritage Series

Christmas on the Ranch (2003)

Texas Ranger Series

The Buckskin Line (1999)
Badger Boy (2001)
The Way of the Coyote (2001)
Ranger's Trail (2002)
Lone Star Rising: The Texas Ranger Trilogy (2003), omnibus
Texas Vendetta (2003)
Jericho Road (2004)

Written as Alex Hawk

Shotgun Settlement (1969)

Written as Lee McElroy

Joe Pepper (1975)
Eyes of the Hawk (1981)

Written as Tom Early

Sons of Texas Series

The Raiders (1989)
Sons of Texas (1989)
The Rebels (1990)

Collections

The Big Brand (1986)
There's Always Another Chance and Other Stories (1986)
Wagontongue (1996)

Anthologies

Trails of the Iron Horse (1975)
Water Trails West (1978)
Western Hall of Fame Anthology, edited by Dale L. Walker (1997)
A Century of Great Western Stories, edited by John Jakes (2000)

Nonfiction

Looking Back West (1972)
Frank C. McCarthy: The Old West (1981)
Permian, A Continuing Saga (1986)

Living and Writing in West Texas (1988)
The Art of Frank McCarthy (1992)
The Art of Howard Terpning (1992)
The Art of James Bama (1993)
Elmer Kelton Country (1993)
The Indian in Frontier News (1993)
My Kind of Heroes (1995)
Judge Roy Bean Country (1996)
My Kind of Heroes (2004), essays

Contributor

Ranching Traditions, by Kathleen Jo Ryan (1989)
Cowboys Who Rode Proudly (1992)
This Place of Memory: A Texas Perspective, edited by Joyce Gibson Roach (1992)
Texas (1995)

Editor

Yesteryear in Ozona and Crockett County, by VI. Pierce (1980)

Television Movies Based on the Author's Works

The Good Old Boys (1995)

For Further Information

Alter, Judy. Elmer Kelton and West Texas: A Literary Relationship. Denton: University of North Texas Press, 1989.

"Books by Elmer Kelton." *http://www.kelton.org/notables/books.html* (viewed April 5, 2003).

Clayton, Lawrence. "Elmer Kelton Responds to the Movie Version of The Good Old Boys." *Roundup Magazine* (July–August 1995).

Clayton, Lawrence. *Elmer Kelton*. Boise, ID: Boise State University Press, 1986.

Cordingley, Liz. "Interview: Elmer Kelton." Citysearch. *http://austin.citysearch.com/feature/19335/* (viewed May 9, 2003).

"Elmer Kelton *The Time It Never Rained* Curriculum Guide." *//www.cyberways waterways/com/en/curricula/langarts/kelton_resources.jhtml* (viewed May 9, 2003).

Elmer Kelton Web site. *http://www.elmerkelton.net/* (viewed April 6, 2003).

Graebner, Janet E. "New Frontiers for Westerns." *Bloomsbury Review* (September/October 1998).

Grover, Dorys C. "Elmer Kelton and the Popular Western Novel." *Southwest Heritage* 8 (summer 1978).

Grover, Dorys C. Elmer Kelton entry, *Twentieth-Century Western Writers*. 2nd edition, edited by Geoff Sadler. Chicago: St. James Press, 1991.

"Inventory for the Elmer Kelton Papers, 1948–1985." Texas Tech University. *http://www.lib.utexas.edu/taro/ttusw/00041/tsw-00041.html* (viewed April 6, 2003).

Lee, Billy C. "Elmer Kelton: A PQ Interview." *Paperback Quarterly* 1 (summer 1978).

"Legislature honors San Angelo author." Austin *Reporter-News* (May 29, 1977).

Mansfield-Kelley, Deane, with Vicki Piekarski. Elmer Kelton entry, *Encyclopedia of Frontier and Western Fiction*, edited by John Tuska and Piekarski. New York: McGraw-Hill, 1983.

Peacock, Scot, ed. Elmer Kelton entry, *Contemporary Authors New Revision Series*. Vol. 85. Detroit: Gale Research, 2000.

"Story of Elmer Kelton." *http://www.kelton.org/notables/elmer.html* (viewed April 5, 2003).

"Texas Institute of Letters gives cash awards to top state writers." *Dallas Morning News* (March 22, 1987).

Walker, Dale L. "A Conversation with Elmer Kelton." *Louis L'Amour Western Magazine* (July 1994).

Stephen King

◆ Horror ◆ Fantasy

Portland, Maine
1947

◆ *Carrie*

About the Author and the Author's Writing

Stephen King nearly died when, taking his daily four-mile walk along a narrow highway in June 1999, he was struck to the ground by a wayward motorist driving a Dodge minivan. Bones askew, a lung collapsed, King was hospitalized, uncertain if he would walk again. Within five weeks, he was writing again—so much is the craft part of his being—finishing *On Writing*, a combination how-to and memoir.

"If there is an opposite of writer's block, King has it," marveled Stephen J. Dubner in the *New York Times Magazine*, who noted that by the time he was a second-year college student the author had finished five novels.

King these days writes in the comfort of an office in his Bangor, Maine, mansion, a giant step up from the mobile home where he wrote the novel *Carrie* in 1970. *Carrie*, a more ambitious piece than the short stories he was turning out for men's magazines such as *Cavalier*, was King's first novel to become a hit.

With an enormous output, King thrives on innovation: He's tried pseudonyms (Richard Bachman); he's tried serial novels (*The Green Mile*) and illustrated novels (*Creepshow*) and electronic stories (*Riding the Bullet*). His popularity is so high that a writer for the *New York Times* wondered in print if any publisher could afford him, when in 1997 he went looking for a new print deal.

After the car accident, King dove into writing the novel *Dreamcatcher*. He had to work propped up on pillows, writing in longhand because of his pain, and it was enormously cathartic. "A lot of [the book] was about going through a really painful experience and coming out changed, like something inside me had taken possession and changed me forever," he told Joseph P. Kahn of the *Boston Sunday Globe*. (*From a Buick Eight*, which involves a nasty auto accident, was written before King's injury but held back until after *Dreamcatcher*'s release.)

In 2003, however, he said he was inclined to slow the pace, promising only to complete the last three chapters of the Dark Tower opus, which would answer some questions about a few earlier, nonseries novels. The Dark Tower has particular meaning for the author, as the initial episode, *The Gunslinger*, was the first novel he wrote. Once the epic is complete, 4,000 pages in seven volumes, it will be, he believes, the "longest popular novel of all time."

America's preeminent horror and suspense writer was born in 1947 in Portland, Maine, the son of a merchant seaman who abandoned the family when King was two. King's mother struggled to keep the family together. King has said that as a youngster he felt overweight and uncoordinated. He dreamt of his inadequacies, had an active imagination, and at times became preoccupied with death. For example, he kept a scrapbook of the 1950s mass murderer Charlie Starkweather. He also went to horror and science fiction movies and watched television. And then he took a part-time sports writing job with the Lisbon *Enterprise*. "This editor was the man who taught me everything I know about writing in ten minutes. His name was John Gould," King said in *The Writer* for June 1975.

In 1970, King received a bachelor of science degree from the University of Maine at Orono. A year later he married Tabitha Jane Spruce, a poet and novelist. They have three children. Before he made his name as a writer, King worked variously as a janitor, laundryman, and knitting mill hand. He taught English in Hampden, Maine, from 1971 to 1973 and in 1978–1979 was writer-in-residence at University of Maine at Orono.

Rising above the modest-paying short story market, King submitted *Carrie* to the publisher Doubleday. It was accepted with a $2,500 advance.

Carrie "lives out a nightmare that all teen-agers go through," the author told Lois Lowry for *Down East*. "Not being accepted by peers. And all high school kids are full of suppressed violence. Remember how you used to go home and throw your books across a room if you'd flunked a quiz? Carrie lets people relive that violent urge of adolescence."

King's second book, *Salem's Lot*, owes something to the movie *Invasion of the Body Snatchers*. The writer told Stefan Kanfer, only half seriously, "I've had about three original ideas in my life. The rest of them were bounces. I sense the limitation of where my talents lie."

King turned out more prose than his publisher wanted to bring out in a year's time. Thus, his novel *Rage* was issued under the name Richard Bachman—the "Richard" swiped from a Richard Stark novel that was on his desk at the time, the "Bachman" from a record on the player by Bachman-Turner Overdrive. There were two more Bachman books before readers recognized his style.

In 1978, King's *The Stand* appeared. The story starts with a rampant plague wiping out much of civilization. It was difficult to write, King said, and was shortened by the publisher. A full version appeared years later, at the author's insistence, when he could comfortably command it. In 1980, King became the first author to have three books simultaneously on the *New York Times* best-seller list: *Firestarter, The Dead Zone*, and *The Shining*.

When director Brian DePalma's film version of *Carrie* came out in 1976, it was one of the top money-earners of the year. There followed more than two dozen motion picture versions of King stories. King has since become the writer most frequently adapted to film and television.

Horror stories strike at the human subconscious and act as a curative, according to Dean R. Koontz, another popular suspense writer. "And if the lead characters of such stories have honor and courage—and are portrayed with depth—the tales may also serve as examples of how one can face death, loss, loneliness, and other real-life tragedies with dignity. In other words, suspense fiction can provide both thrills and subtle—heed that word 'subtle'—moral lessons."

King's works have been subjected to censorship over the years. Some people, for example, wanted *The Shining* or *Cujo* removed from library shelves. Profanity in *Christine*, according to Herbert N. Foerstel, prompted parents in a Michigan community to ask that the book be removed from a high school curriculum. But censorship has not hurt his sales.

"Stephen King is the most remarkable publishing phenomenon in modern literature," summed up S. T. Joshi. He is a "writer who has purportedly 'humanized' the weird tale by enmeshing it in the everyday lives of ordinary people."

King makes it all look easy. In *Nightmares and Dreamscapes*, he commented, "After twenty years of writing popular fiction and being dismissed by the more intellectual critics as a hack (the intellectual's definition of a hack seems to be 'an artist whose work is appreciated by too many people') I will gladly testify that craft is terribly important, that the often tiresome process of draft, redraft, and then draft again is necessary to produce good work, and that hard work is the only acceptable practice for those of us who have some talent but little or no genius."

He explained in *On Writing* that "once I start work on a project, I don't stop and I don't slow down unless I absolutely have to." He writes every day, and when he's not writing, the characters may be dancing around in his head.

King's most recent project at this writing is for *Kingdom Hospital*, a television miniseries based on a European program created by Danish filmmaker Lars von Trier. King took the concept of a medical facility from hell and, recovering from his 1999 auto accident, cathartically wrote the scripts from his hospital bed. He wrote a second season's worth of scripts in late 2003, while recovering from pneumonia. One wonders, would he even want a third season?

What's the reward of all this hard work, aside from financial gain? "All writers basically want one thing," the author told Dana Kennedy for *Entertainment Weekly*. "They're dyin' for as many people as possible to read their stories."

Oh, well, and maybe a National Book Award might be nice. Which is just what he received in 2003.

Works by the Author

Fiction

Carrie (1974)
Salem's Lot (1975)
The Shining (1977)
The Stand (1978; full length restored 1990)
Dead Zone (1979)
Firestarter (1980)
Cujo (1981)
The Mist (1981)
The Plant (1982/1983/1985/2000)
Christine (1983)
Pet Sematary (1983)
It (1986)
Eyes of the Dragon (1987)

Misery (1987)
The Tommyknockers (1987)
My Pretty Pony (1988)
The Dark Half (1989)
Needful Things: The Last Castle Rock Story (1991)
Dolores Claiborne (1992)
Gerald's Game (1992)
Insomnia (1994)
The Shawshank Redemption: The Shooting Script, with Frank Darabont (1994)
Rose Madder (1995)
Desperation (1996)
Rage (1997)
Bag of Bones (1998)
Blood and Smoke (1999)
The Girl Who Loved Tom Gordon (1999)
Storm of the Century (1999)
Secret Windows (2000)
Dreamcatcher (2001)
From a Buick Eight (2002)

The Dark Tower Series

The Gunslinger (1982)
The Drawing of the Three (1987)
The Waste Lands (1992)
Wizard and Glass (1997)
Wolves of the Calla (2003)
The Dark Tower (2004)
Song of Susannah (2004)

Green Mile Serial

The Bad Death of Eduard Delacroix (1996)
Coffey on the Mile (1996)
Coffey's Hands (1996)
The Mouse on the Mile (1996)
Night Journey (1996)
Two Dead Girls (1996)
The Green Mile (1997) collected

Talisman Series, written with Peter Straub

The Talisman (1984)
Black House (2001)

Collections

Night Shift (1978)
Creepshow (1982)
Different Seasons (1982), four novellas.
Selected Works (1983)
Skeleton Crew (1985)
Maximum Overdrive (1986)
Four Past Midnight (1990)
Night Shift: Excursions into Horror (1991)
Gray Matter and Other Stories (1993)
Nightmares & Dreamscapes (1993)
Hearts in Atlantis (1994)
Six Stories (1997)
Stephen King Omnibus (1999)
Everything's Eventual: Fourteen Dark Tales (2002)
The Man in the Black Suit: Four Dark Tales (2002)

Chapbooks

The Breathing Method (1984)
Dolan's Cadillac (1989), later included in *Nightmares & Dreamscapes*.
My Pretty Pony (1989), non-horror short story, limited edition.
The Langoliers (1990)
The Library Policeman (1991)
Secret Window, Secret Garden (1991)
The Body (1994)
The Shawshank Redemption (1995)
Apt Pupil (1998)
Stephen King's F-13 (1999)
Riding the Bullet (2000), electronic book
LT's Theory of Pets (2001)

Anthologies

Modern Masters of Horror (1976)
Shadows (1978)
Tales of Unknown Horror (1978)
The Year's Finest Fantasy (1978)
Best Detective Stories of the Year—1979, edited by Edward D. Hoch (1979)
More Tales of Unknown Horror (1979)
The Year's Best Horror Stories VII (1979)
The 21st Pan Book of Horror Stories (1980)
Dark Forces (1980)
New Tales of the Cthulhu Mythos (1980)

Fantasy Annual III (1981)
Fantasy Annual IV (1981)
The Giant Book of Horror Stories (1981)
Horrors (1981)
Shadows 4 (1981)
New Terrors 2 (1981)
International Treasury of Mystery and Suspense, edited by Marie R. Reno (1983)
The Science Fiction Weight-Loss Book (1983)
I Shudder at Your Touch (1984)
Realms of Darkness (1985)
A Treasury of American Horror Stories (1985)
Legends (1986)
The Puffin Book of Horror Stories (1986)
Blood Thirst: 100 years of Vampire Fiction (1987)
The Dark Descent: The Colour of Evil (1987)
Masques 2 (1987)
Mystery Scene Reader edited by Ed Gorman (1987)
New Adventures of Sherlock Holmes, edited by Martin H. Greenberg and Carol-Lynn
    Rossel Waugh (1987)
Dark Visions (1988)
Horror Stories (1988)
The Mammoth Book of Short Horror Novels (1988)
Prime Evil (1988)
Book of the Dead (1989)
Dark Voices: The Best from the Pan Book of Horror Stories (1990)
The Best of the Best (1994)
Young Blood (1994)
The Vampire Omnibus (1995)
The Year's Best Fantasy and Horror Eighth Annual Collection (1995)
American Gothic Tales (1996)
Twists of the Tale (1996)
The Year's Best Fantasy and Horror Ninth Annual Collection (1996)
Dancing with the Dark (1997)
Robert Bloch's Psychos, edited by Robert Bloch (1997)
Eternal Lovecraft: The Persistence of H.P. Lovecraft in Popular Culture (1998)
The Playboy Book of Science Fiction (1998)
999 (1999)
A Haunting Collection (1999)
Legends: Short Novels by the Masters of Modern Fantasy. Vol. 1, edited by Robert
    Silverberg (1999)
Tales of the Cthulhu Mythos (1999)
Technohorror: Tales of Terror, Suspense and Intrigue (1999)
Vintage Science Fiction (1999)
The Year's Best Fantasy and Horror Twelfth Annual Collection (1999)

Necon 20th Anniversary Program (2000)
Best American Mystery Stories of the Century, edited by Otto Penzler and Tony Hillerman (2001)
Century of Great Suspense Stories, edited by Jeffrey Deaver (2001)
McSweeney's Mammoth Treasury of Thrilling Tales, edited by Michael Chabon (2003)
Thrilling Tales, edited by Michael Chabon (2003)
Best American Mystery Stories, edited by Nelson DeMille (2004)
McSweeney's Enchanted Chamber of Astonishing Stories, edited by Michael Chabon (2004)
Transgressions, edited by Ed McBain (forthcoming)

Books for Children

The Girl Who Loved Tom Gordon: A Pop-Up Book (2004)

Illustrated Stories

Creepshow (1982)
Cycle of the Werewolf (1984)

Nonfiction

Danse Macabre (1981)
Nightmares in the Sky: Gargoyles and Grotesques, with f-stop Fitzgerald (1988)
Stephen King Live (1999)
On Writing: A Memoir of the Craft (2000)
Secret Windows (2000)
Faithful: Two Diehard Boston Red Sox Fans Chronicle The 2004 Season, with Stewart O'Nan (2004)

Written as by Richard Bachman

Rage (1977)
The Long Walk (1979)
Roadwork (1981)
The Running Man (1982)
Thinner (1984)
The Bachman Books (1985)
The Regulators (1996)

Motion Pictures and Television Movies and Series Based on the Author's Works

Carrie (1976)
Salem's Lot (1979)

The Shining (1980)

Knightriders (1981)

Creepshow (1982)

Christine (1983)

Cujo (1983)

The Dead Zone (1983)

Disciples of the Crow (1983)

Firestarter (1984)

Stephen King's Children of the Corn (1984), based on a short story from *Night Shift*

Cat's Eye (1985), film scripted by King and based the new story "The General" and "Quitters, Inc." and "The Ledge" from *Night Shift*

Silver Bullet (1985)

Stephen King's Night Shift Collection (1985), includes "The Boogeyman" and "The Woman in the Room" from *Night Shift*

Stephen King's Silver Bullet (1985), from the novelette *Cycle of the Werewolf*

Tales from the Darkside (1985), television episode "Word Processor of the Gods," from the story in *Skeleton Crew*

Maximum Overdrive (1986), film written and directed by King

Stand By Me (1986), film based on "The Body" from *Different Seasons*

The Twilight Zone (1986), television episode "Gramma," based on the King story from *Skeleton Crew*

Creepshow II (1987)

A Return to Salem's Lot (1987)

The Running Man (1987)

Tales from the Darkside (1987), television episode "Sorry, Right Number," from a King teleplay

Pet Sematary (1989)

Stephen King's World of Horror (1989)

Graveyard Shift (1990), based on the short story from *Night Shift*

It (1990), television miniseries

Misery (1990)

Tales from the Darkside (1990)

Stephen King's Golden Years (1991), television miniseries

Stephen King's Sometimes They Come Back (1991), based on a short story.

The Lawnmower Man (1992), based on a short story

Pet Sematary II (1992)

Sleepwalkers (1992)

Stephen King's Sleepwalkers (1992), from a King script

Children of the Corn II—The Final Sacrifice (1993)

The Dark Half (1993)

Needful Things (1993)

The Tommyknockers (1993), television movie

Sometimes They Come Back (1994)

The Shawshank Redemption (1994), based on the story "Rita Hayworth and the Shawshank Redemption" from *Different Seasons*

The Stand (1994), television miniseries

Children of the Corn 3 (1995)

Dolores Claiborne (1995)

The Langoliers (1995), television movie

Mangler (1995), based on the story from *Night Shift*

Stephen King's The Langoliers (1995), television miniseries

Children of the Corn 4 (1996)

Sometimes They Come Back Again (1996)

Thinner (1996)

The Night Flier (1997)

Quicksilver Highway (1997)

The Shining (1997) television movie

Trucks (1997)

Apt Pupil (1998)

Children of the Corn 5 (1998)

Children of the Corn 666 (1999)

The Green Mile (1999)

The Rage: Carrie 2 (1999)

Sometimes They Come Back for More (1999)

Storm of the Century (1999), King wrote screenplay for television movie

Children of the Corn 7 (2001)

Hearts in Atlantis (2001)

Paranoid (2001)

The Dead Zone, (2002) television series

Firestarter 2: The Next Chapter (2002)

The Mangler 2 (2002)

Rose Red (2002), television movie

Dreamcatcher (2003)

Salem's Lot (2003), television movie

Stephen King's The Night Flyer (2003)

Secret Window (2004)

Stephen King's Kingdom Hospital (2004), television series

Bag of Bones, announced movie

Carrie, announced television series

Firestarter, announced television series

The Girl Who Loved Tom Gordon, announced movie

The Mist, announced movie

For Further Information

Beahm, George, ed. *The Stephen King Companion*. Kansas City: Andrews & McMeel, 1989.

Beahm, George, ed. *The Stephen King Story—A Literary Profile*. Kansas City: Andrews & McMeel, 1991.

Bloom, Harold. "Dumbing down American readers." *Boston Globe* (September 24, 2003).

Carvajal, Doreen. "Who Can Afford Him? Stephen King Goes in Search of a New Publisher." *New York Times* (October 27, 1997).

Collings, Michael R. *Stephen King as Richard Bachman*. San Bernadino, CA: Borgo Press, 1985.

Collings, Michael R. *The Annotated Guide to Stephen King: A Primary & Secondary Bibliography of the Works of America's Premier Horror Writer*. San Bernadino, CA: Borgo Press, 1986.

Collings, Michael R. *The Films of Stephen King*. San Bernadino, CA: Borgo Press, 1986.

Collings, Michael R. *Horror Plum'd: An International Stephen King Bibliography and Guide 1960–2000*. Hiram, GA: Overlook Connection Press, 2003.

Collings, Michael R. *The Many Facets of Stephen King*. San Bernadino, CA: Borgo Press, 1985.

Collings, Michael R. *The Work of Stephen King: An Annotated Bibliography and Guide*. San Bernadino, CA: Borgo Press, 1994.

Collings, Michael R., and David Engebretson. *The Shorter Works of Stephen King*. San Bernadino, CA: Borgo Press, 1985.

Doherty, Brian, ed. *American Horror Fiction: From Brockden Brown to Stephen King*. New York: St. Martin's Press, 1990.

Dubner, Stephen J. "What is Stephen King Trying To Prove?" *New York Times Magazine* (August 13, 2000).

Foerstel, Herbert N. *Banned in the USA: A Reference Guide to Book Censorship in Schools and Public Libraries*. Westport, CT: Greenwood Press, 1994.

Furth, Robin. Stephen King's *The Dark Tower: A Concordance*. New York: Scribner, 2003.

Goldstein, Bill. "War Would Upend Plans Of Publishers and Retailers; Canceled Promotions Could Cut Into Sales." *New York Times* (March 10, 2003).

Grant, Charles L. "Stephen King: 'I Like to Go for the Jugular.'" *Rod Serling's The Twilight Zone Magazine* (April 1981).

Herron, Don, ed. *Reign of Fear: The Fiction and the Films of Stephen King*. Novato, CA: Underwood-Miller, 1992.

Hoppenstand, Gary, and Ray B. Browne, eds. *The Gothic World of Stephen King: Landscape of Nightmare*. Bowling Green, OH: Bowling Green University Press, 1987.

Immell, Myra, ed. *The Young Adult Reader's Advisory: The Best in Literature and Language Arts, Mathematics and Computer Science*. New Providence, NJ: R. R. Bowker, 1989.

Jensen, Jeff. "Kingdom Hospital." *Entertainment Weekly* (January 23/30, 2004).

Joshi, S.T. "The King's New Clothes." *Million* (January–February 1993).

Kahn, Joseph P. "Into the Woods with Stephen King." *Boston Sunday Globe* (March 16, 2003).

Kanfer, Stefan. "King of Horror." *Time* (October 6, 1986).

Kennedy, Dana. "Going for Cheap Thrillers: Stephen King's Paperback Series, 'The Green Mile,' Takes It One Month at a Time." *Entertainment Weekly* (February 23, 1996).

King, Stephen. "'Ever Et Raw Meat?' and Other Weird Questions." *New York Times Book Review* (December 6, 1987).

King, Stephen, introduction. *Nightmares & Dreamscapes*. New York: Viking, 1993.

King, Stephen. *The Writer* (June 1975).

King, Tyson. *The Unseen King*. West Linn, OR: Starmont House, 1989.

Kirkpatrick, David D. "A Literary Award For Stephen King." *New York Times* (September 15, 2003).

Koontz, Dean R. "Keeping the Reader on the Edge of His Seat." In *How to Write Tales of Horror, Fantasy & Science Fiction*, edited by J. N. Williamson. Cincinnati: Writer's Digest Books, 1987.

Lloyd, Ann. *The Films of Stephen King*. New York: St. Martin's, 1994.

Lowry, Lois. "King of the Occult." *Down East* (1978).

Magistrale, Anthony. *Landscape of Fear: Stephen King's American Gothic*. Bowling Green, OH: Bowling Green University Press, 1988.

Magistrale, Anthony. *Moral Voyages of Stephen King*. San Bernadino, CA: Borgo Press, 1989.

Magistrale, Anthony. *Stephen King: The Second Decade: Danse Macabre to the Dark Half*. New York: Macmillan, 1992.

Magistrale, Anthony, ed. *Casebook on 'The Stand.'* San Bernadino, CA: Borgo Press, 1992.

Magistrale, Anthony, ed. *The Dark Descent: Essays Defining Stephen King's Horrorscape*. Westport, CT: Greenwood, 1992.

O'Hehir, Andrew. "The Quest for the North Central Positronics." *New York Times Book Review* (January 4, 2004).

Reino, Joseph. *A to Z: A Dictionary of People, Places and Things in the Works of the King of Horror*. Ann Arbor, MI: Popular Culture, 1994.

Reino, Joseph. *The First Decade, Carrie to Pet Sematary*. New York: Macmillan, 1988.

Saidman, Anne. *Stephen King: Master of Horror*. Minneapolis, MN: Lerner, 1992.

Schweitzer, Darrell, ed. *Discovering Stephen King*. San Bernadino, CA: Borgo Press, 1985.

Shindler, Dorman T. "Gleaning Tower." *Pages* (November/December 2003).

Spignesi, Stephen J. *The Complete Stephen King Encyclopedia: The Definitive Guide to the Works of America's Master of Horror*. Chicago: Contemporary Books, 1993.

"Stephen King and Jerry Williamson awarded the Bram Stoker award for Lifetime Achievement." Stephen King newsletter. *http://www.stephenkingnews.com* (viewed April 14, 2003).

Stephen King News. *http://www.stephenkingnews.com/tvseries/html* (viewed March 16, 2003).

"Stephen King's Haunted Hospital." *Time* (September 8, 2003).

Stephen King Web site. *http://www.stephenking.com* (viewed May 11, 2003).

Terrell, Caroll F. *Stephen King: Man and Artist*. Cincinnati: North Lights, 1991.

Tomashoff, Craig. "Medical Nightmare." *TV Guide* (February 26–March 5, 2004).

Underwood, Tim, and Chuck Miller, eds. *Feast of Fear: Conversations with Stephen King*. New York: McGraw-Hill, 1989.

Underwood, Tim, and Chuck Miller, eds. *Fear Itself The Horror Fiction of Stephen King*. San Francisco: Underwood-Miller, 1982.

Underwood, Tim, and Chuck Miller, eds. *Kingdom of Fear: The World of Stephen King*. New York: New American Library, 1987.

Van Hise, James. *More Stephen King and Clive Barker: The Illustrated Guide to the Masters of the Macabre*. Las Vegas: Movie Publications Services, 1992.

Van Hise, James. *Stephen King and Clive Barker, Illustrated Guide*. Las Vegas: Movie Publications Services, 1990.

Winter, Douglas E. *Stephen King: The Art of Darkness*. New York: New American Library, 1986.

Sandra Kitt

Credit: John Pinderhughes.

New York, New York
1947

◆ *The Color of Love*

About the Author and the Author's Writing

Sandra Kitt didn't sell her first book the conventional way. A professional artist and librarian, she wrote in her spare moments, ending up with two romance manuscripts. At first she didn't consider trying to have them published. Then, reading in the newspaper one day that a major publisher, Harlequin, had opened a New York office, she phoned an editor there, arranged an appointment, showed her work—and went home with a contract. Within a month, she sold two other manuscripts and her second career was off and running.

Kitt was born in Harlem in 1947. She graduated from the Music & Art High School in New York and earned an associate's degree from Bronx Community College of the City University of New York, a bachelor of arts degree from City College of the City University of New York in 1969, and a master's degree in fine arts from the same institution in 1975. She attended the School of Visual Arts, the New School for Social Research, and the University of Guadalajara. When she was twenty-one, she hitchhiked across Canada, and she has since traveled to China, Japan, and the former Soviet Union. Divorced, she lives in New York.

Kitt worked as an art assistant for Philip Gips Studios, a teacher in the Cloisters Workshop Program, a staff member of the Children's Art Center, a teacher at Printmaking Workshop, and a librarian for the city of New York before joining the American Museum of Natural History in New York in 1992 as manager of library services at the Richard S. Perkin Library, Hayden Planetarium. She has taught a creative writing course at County College of Morris in New Jersey. At the same time, she has been a freelance graphic artist (she did illustrations for two of Isaac Asimov's books and one of her own, *Love Everlasting*), a greeting card designer (for UNICEF), and a printmaker. And she has been a writer of romance and suspense novels.

Considering her workload, Kitt fortunately is a fast worker, generally completing a manuscript in less than six months. "I have to be disciplined," she said in an African American Literature Book Club (AALBC) interview, explaining she has had to prepare better outlines as her contractual obligations have grown. "Each book gets more detailed. Now I write a synopsis that acts as a guidepost or map to guide me."

She didn't set out to write romances. Rather, Kitt said in a Wonderful World of Color interview, she wanted to write stories about relationships—between men and women, between parents and children, between siblings. "Yes, I wanted to have a love relationship in my books, but I never considered them strictly romances. I guess the early influences were 'gothic' writers like Mary Stewart and Victoria Holt even though their stories were suspenseful. There was more than just romance going on in their books." The author also admires the writing of Janet Dailey for her realistic, ordinary characters; Kathleen Eagle; Tess Gerritson; Chassie West; and Elizabeth Berg.

Although Kitt has become popular for her works depicting African Americans, her very first book was about Caucasians. She has explored a variety of themes: *She's the One* is about a woman whose friend who has become the guardian of her biracial daughter and, at the same time, is falling in love with a man from a lower economic class. *The Color of Love* looks at interracial relationships, *Between Friends* at a character's dealing with being the child of a mixed marriage. In *Close Encounters*, an innocent black woman is wounded by a white undercover cop.

The author often writes about relationships between African Americans and those of other races. She explains that she really is simply writing about people who have different skin colors and are accepting of change. With the cultural mix of New York City—Asians, Middle Easterners, Hispanics, mixed-race, to name a few—it is obvious the nation's complexion is rapidly changing.

"I guess to some extent I'm a selfish writer, in that I want to write what I want to write. . . . What motivates me is always trying to understand the complex nature of what brings people together, to either love or hate each other," the author said in an All About Romance interview. "I do believe in a 'positive' and upbeat ending."

Kitt generally starts formulating a novel with the characters' personalities, adding physical details, establishing conflicts, and building the plot later. She is very visually descriptive. She carefully paces her books; there are no scenes of intimacy in the first half, as people just getting to know each other usually hold off on sex, she observes. Her characters, she asserts, are not perfect; they have the same flaws as most everyone has.

Kitt hopes her reputation will spur other black writers. "I've always considered myself a writer who's Black, rather than a Black writer, because I always wanted to make sure I had the options of writing anything and being seen capable of doing more than just another 'Black' work."

She's not likely to run out of ideas soon. "For many years I've had an idea I've wanted to write about an African American woman and an American Indian man," she said in a New People interview. "I happen to believe that the spirituality between the two groups are very similar, and I think there is much that we share. I'm also particularly interested because of my own American Indian background from both my mother and father's family."

With black fiction just coming into its own, Kitt has enormous opportunity ahead.

Works by the Author

Fiction

All Good Things (1984)
Love Everlasting (1993)

Serenade (1994)
The Color of Love (1995)
Sincerely (1995)
Significant Others (1996)
Suddenly (1996)
Between Friends (1998)
Family Affairs (1999)
Close Encounters (2000)
She's the One (2001)
First Touch (2004)
Southern Comfort (2004)

Harlequin American Romance Series

48. *Rites of Spring* (1984)
86. *Adam and Eva* (1984)
97. *Perfect Combination* (1985)
112. *Only with the Heart* (1985)
148. *With Open Arms* (1987)
280. *An Innocent Man* (1989)
327. *The Way Home* (1990)
399. *Someone's Baby* (1991)

Anthologies

Friends, Families and Lovers (1993)
Baby Beat (1996)
For the Love of Chocolate (1996)
Merry Christmas, Baby (1996)
Sisters (1996)
Girlfriends (1999)
Valentine Wishes (2001)

Nonfiction

Illustrator

Asimov's Guide to Halley's Comet by Isaac Asimov (1985)
Beginnings: The Story of Origin . . . by Isaac Asimov (1986)

For Further Information

"Interview with Author Sandra Kitt." Wonderful World of Color Page. *http://www
.geocities.com/bellesandbeaux/Kitt.html* (viewed May 24, 2003).

"Interview with Sandra Kitt." Your Interracial e-Mag. *http:newpeople/.weblogger
.com/feature* (viewed May 24, 2003).

Mendoza, Sylvia. "Sandra Kitt; Bringing 'The Color of Love' to Romance Novels." *http://www.sylvia-mendoza.com/SDWMSep97.htm* (viewed May 24, 2003).

Peacock, Scot, ed. Sandra Kitt entry, *Contemporary Authors New Revision Series*. Vol. 91. Detroit: Gale Research, 2000.

Sandra Kitt interview. African American Literature Book Club. *http://www.aalbc.com/authors/sandrakitt.htm* (viewed May 24, 2003).

Sandra Kitt interview. *http://www.writersandpoets.com/newsletter/sandra_kitt_interview.htm* (viewed May 24, 2003).

"Sandra Kitt: A Matter of Hope." All About Romance (September 11, 2000). *http://www.likesbooks.com/sandrakitt.html* (viewed May 24, 2003).

Sandra Kitt Web site. *http://www.sandrakitt.com* (viewed May 24, 2003).

Dean Koontz

◆ Suspense ◆ Fantasy ◆ Horror

Everett, Pennsylvania
1945

◆ *Dark Rivers of the Heart*

About the Author and the Author's Writing

Best-selling authors generally hem and haw about how they get ideas for their books. Dean Koontz did not mind explaining the genesis of one of his suspense novels, *False Memory*. He came across an article about a rare psychological disorder called autophobia, literally the fear of one's self. He knew immediately it would make a great hinge for a book. But of course there was more to it, as he explained on his Web page: "Because complex themes underlie a good novel, a story has to have a structure that grows from those themes and supports them. For this reason, I needed to know why my lead character would develop autophobia and how she would free herself from it before I could decide to write her story."

He mulled the idea for about a year, came up with a solution and began writing. At first, he told his wife, Gerda, he was afraid he did not have enough material to sustain a 320-page novel. She ignored him. He kept writing. Pretty soon, he was going so strong, he began to fret the book would be too long. Again, his wife paid no heed. When he was done, he had a 627-page thriller, one he said was perhaps the most enjoyable to write of all his work. And Koontz has a lot of work to his credit, having been a full-time writer since 1969.

Dean Ray Koontz was born in 1945 in Everett, Pennsylvania. His family was poor, his father an abusive alcoholic. Koontz nevertheless is relentlessly upbeat in person and his novels frequently carry themes of transcendence, hope, and redemption.

The author paid his own way through college. *The Atlantic Monthly* published a story he wrote for college English class, "Kittens." He received a bachelor of arts degree from Shippensburg State College in 1966 and that same year married his high school girlfriend, Gerda Ann Cerra. He worked briefly in the Appalachian Poverty Title III Program and as a high school English teacher before turning to writing. Often categorized a horror writer, he is more accurately a writer of suspense, and has given romances, supernatural stories, and science fiction a shot as well.

A workaholic, he turned out book after book under several names and in several genres ("Brian Coffey" wrote fast-paced novels, "Leigh Nichols" was known for intrigue, "Deanna Dwyer" swooned through gothics). Fairly early on he became dissatisfied working within a single genre, and blended elements of fantasy or horror into a suspense novel.

"I knew that I wanted to bring various genres together and knit them up into a mainstream novel, so some of my decisions were conscious and calculated," he said in an interview with Stanley Waiter. "But creativity is as much an unconscious process, and many of the techniques and approaches I came up with were not obvious to me until I had been using them a while. You can't coldly calculate and plan a new style. All you can do is determine what you hope to achieve, then create the mental environment that will let art happen on deeper levels of consciousness."

He labored with little recognition until finally *Midnight* stormed onto the bestseller lists in 1989 and *The Key to Midnight* followed the next year. Lest his Leigh Nichols penname for *Key* become more popular than his own name, he eventually abandoned all aliases. Many of his early works have come back into print, though, being a perfectionist, he has refused to reissue some and has rewritten others. When he set out to rewrite *Shattered*, it turned into a longer, new work, *Winter Moon*.

"Whether exploring the boundaries of identity (*Mr. Murder*), the vagaries of intelligence (*Watchers*) or the limits of re-engineering human response (*Strangers*), Koontz challenges his readers to reflect on their own experience, their relationship to the world, and their responsibility to 'make' their own lives," assert Nick Gillespi and Lisa Snell.

"The imagination comes from a lifetime of pumping bizarre fiction into myself as a reader," the author said in a Doorly.com interview. "And part of it is my skewed view of the world. If you keep your eyes open to the real world around us, there is nothing more bizarre than what happens around us on the street. Ninety percent of my books are just about that."

His favorite (and most influential) writer is John D. McDonald, though James M. Cain, Ray Bradbury, and Charles Dickens had some sway. These days he reads Stephen King and Ed McBain, among others.

The Southern California resident put in sixty- and seventy-hour work weeks when writing *False Memory*. *Intensity* took six months, *Dark Rivers of the Heart* nearly twelve.

The Book of Counted Sorrows was a non-existent book, an in-joke from which Koontz frequently quoted in his novels—until fan demand ensured issuance of an actual *Book of Counted Sorrows* in 2001. Most of his books are standalones, but he wrote *Seize the Night* as a sequel to the Christopher Snow–Sasha Goodall story *Fear Nothing*, and has promised a third.

"I think the world is a magical place," Koontz said in a *Pages* interview. "When I look at the world, I see a planet where a single butterfly flapping its wings can have a subtle impact around the globe. Many times, it's been molecular biology and quantum mechanics that have most directly bolstered my faith."

"Increasingly, his fictions confront the issues of individual responsibility in a world moving beyond the limits of reason and rationality," observed Michael R. Collings in *St. James Guide to Crime & Mystery Writers*. "His characters are increasingly isolated— 'outsiders' in the classical sense—burdened with their own intricate psychological problems. All must confront complex difficulties, with levels of mysteries to be solved, of dangers to be faced. . . ."

There are big doses of humor in many of Koontz's books, and *The Face*, in the view of Scott Brown, is pure self-parody: "The villain, for example, is one Vladimir 'Corky' Laputa, a bloodthirsty English professor-cum-anarchist who dabbles in every dastardly deed, from murder to graffiti to nontraditional approaches to literature. Corky plans to assault the Bel-Air manse of vapid superstar Channing 'The Face' Manheim. . . ."

The life of an author? Koontz wouldn't have any other. "Writing a novel is like making love," he wrote in *Mystery Scene*, "but it's also like having a tooth pulled. Pleasure and pain. Sometimes it's like making love while having a tooth pulled."

Works by the Author

Fiction

Star Quest (1968)
The Fall of the Dream Machine (1969)
Fear That Man (1969)
Anti-Man (1970)
Beastchild (1970)
Dark of the Woods (1970)
The Dark Symphony (1970)
Hell's Gate (1970)
The Crimson Witch (1971)
A Darkness in My Soul (1972)
The Flesh in the Furnace (1972)
Starblood (1972)
Time Thieves (1972)
Warlock (1972)
Demon Seed (1973)
Hanging On (1973)
The Haunted Earth (1973)
A Werewolf Among Us (1973)
After the Last Race (1974)
Nightmare Journey (1975)
Night Chills (1976)
Time Thieves (1977)
The Vision (1977)
Whispers (1980)
Darkness Comes (1983), published in United Kingdom as *Darkfall*
Phantoms (1983)
Twilight Eyes (1985)
Voice of the Night (1985)
Strangers (1986)
Watchers (1987)
Lightning (1988)
Oddkins (1988)

The Shadow Sea (1988)
The Bad Place (1989)
Midnight (1989)
Relampagos (1989)
The Key to Midnight (1990)
Cold Fire (1991)
Hideaway (1991)
Three Complete Novels (1991), includes *Lightning, The Face of Fear,* and *The Vision*
Dragon Tears (1992)
Mr. Murder (1993)
Trapped (1993), with Ed Gorman
Winter Moon (1993)
Dark Rivers of the Heart (1994)
Three Complete Novels (1994), includes *Strangers, The Voice of the Night,* and *The Mask Intensity* (1995)
Koontz I: The House of Thunder, Cold Fire, Dragon Tears (1996)
Koontz II: Voice of the Night, Darkfall, Midnight (1996)
Koontz III: The Bad Place, Mr. Murder, Cold Fire (1996)
Santa's Twin (1996)
Tick-Tock (1996)
Demon Seed/Cold Fire/Dragon Tears/The House of Thunder/Lightning/Mr. Murder/ The Servants of Twilight: Mixed (1997)
Sole Survivor (1997)
Key to Midnight, Shattered, and House of Thunder (1998)
False Memory (1999)
Storm Front (1999)
From the Corner of His Eye (2000)
The Book of Counted Sorrows (2001)
One Door Away from Heaven (2001)
Three Complete Novels: Cold Fire, Hideaway, Key to Midnight (2001)
By the Light of the Moon (2002)
The Face (2003)
Odd Thomas (2003)
The Taking (2004)

Moonlight Bay Series

Fear Nothing (1998)
Seize the Night (1999)

Collections

Strange Highways (1991)
The Paper Doorway: Funny Verse and Nothing Worse (2001)

Anthologies

Future City, edited by Roger Elwood (1973)
Criminal Justice Through Science Fiction, edited by Joseph D. Olander (1977)
Mystery Scene Reader, edited by Ed Gorman (1987)
Night Visions 4 (1987)
Under the Gun, edited by Ed Gorman (1990)

Written as Aaron Wolfe

Invasion (1975)

Written as Anthony North

Strike Deep (1974)

Written as Brian Coffey

Blood Risk (1973)
Surrounded (1974)
The Wall of Masks (1975)
The Face of Fear (1977)
The Voice of the Night (1980)

Written as David Axton

Prisoner of Ice (1976), retitled *Icebound* as by Dean R. Koontz (1995)
Stolen Thunder (1993)
Dragon Jet (1994)

Written as Deanna Dwyer

The Demon Child (1971)
Legacy of Terror (1971)
Children of the Storm (1972)
The Dark of Summer (1972)
Dance With the Devil (1973)

Written as John Hill

The Long Sleep (1975)

Written as K. R. Dwyer

Chase (1972)
Shattered (1973), rewritten as *Winter Moon* as by Dean Koontz (1994)
Dragonfly (1975)
Face of Fear (1978)

Written as Leigh Nichols

The Key to Midnight (1979)
The Eyes of Darkness (1981)
The House of Thunder (1982)
The Servants of Twilight (1984)
Twilight (1984), also published as *The Servants of Twilight* (1990)
The Door to December (1987)
Shadow Fires (1987)

Written as Owen West

The Funhouse (1980)
The Mask (1981)

Written as Richard Paige

New American (1985)

Nonfiction

The Pig Society, with Gerda Koontz (1970)
The Underground Lifestyles Handbook, with Gerda Koontz (1970)
Writing Popular Fiction (1972)
CIA Flaps and Seals Manual (1975)
How to Write Best Selling Fiction (1981)

Anthologies

Final Stage (1974)
The Architecture of Fear (1987)
Night Visions Hardshell (1987)
Between Time and Terror (1990)
Cyber-Killers (1991)
Predators (1993)
The Ultimate Witch (1993)

Motion Pictures and Television Movies Based on the Author's Works

The Face of Fear (1990)
Hideaway (1995)
Intensity (1997), television miniseries
Sole Survivor (1997), television miniseries
Cold Fire (1998), based on Koontz script
Phantoms (1998)
Mr. Murder (1999), television miniseries

For Further Information

Brown, Scott. "Oddest Proposal." *Entertainment Weekly* (May 30, 2003).

Chapman, Jeff, and Pamela S. Dean, eds. Dean R. Koontz entry, *Contemporary Authors New Revision Series*. Vol. 52. Detroit: Gale Research, 1996.

Christopher Snow Web page. *http://www.randomhouse.com/features/koontz/christopher snow/world.html* (viewed May 30, 2003).

Collings, Michael R. Dean R. Koontz entry, *St. James Guide to Mystery & Crime Writers*. 4th edition. Detroit: St. James Press, 1996.

Dean Koontz interview. Barnes & Noble. *http://www.bookbrowse.com/index/ cfm?page =author&authorID=260&view=interview* (viewed May 27, 2003).

Dean Koontz long fiction. *http://web.tiscali.it/no-redirect-tiscali/luigiurato/longfiction/ .long.htm* (viewed May 27, 2003).

Dean Koontz pseudonyms. *http://web.tiscali.iot/no-redirect-tiscali/luigiurato/pseudo/ pseudo1.htm* (viewed May 27, 2003).

Dean Koontz Web page. *http://www.randomhouse.com/features/koontz/index2.html* (viewed May 27, 2003).

Dean Koontz non-fiction. *http://web.tiscali.it/no-redirect-tiscali/luigiurato/nonfiction/ nonfiction.htm* (viewed May 27, 2003).

Gillespie, Nick, and Lisa Snell. "Contemplating Evil: Novelist Dean Koontz on Freud, Fraud and the Great Society. Reasononline. *http://web.tiscali.it/no-redirect-tiscali/ luigiurato/interv/cont_evil.htm* (viewed May 27, 2003).

Greenberg, Martin H., Ed Gorman, and Bill Munser, eds. The *Dean Koontz Companion*. New York: Berkley, 1994.

Halem, Dann. "Night Light: Dean Koontz finds brightness in life's dark mysteries." *Pages* (January/February 2003).

Hatchigan, Jessica. "Born to Write." *The Writer* (December 2003).

Koontz, Dean. "Koontz on Koontz." *Mystery Scene*, no. 59 (1997).

Kotker, Joan G. Dean Koontz bibliography. *http:www.bcc.ctc.edu'lmc/reserve/kotler/ koonbib.htm* (viewed May 27, 2003).

Lybarger, Dan. "Unread Books and the Ancient Enemy: An Interview with Dean Koontz." *Pitch Weekly* (January 28–February 4, 1999).

Munster, Bill. *Sudden Fear: The Horror and Dark Suspense Fiction of Dean R. Koontz*. San Bernardino, CA: Borgo, 1990.

Ramsland, Katherine Marie. *Dean Koontz: A Writer's Biography*. New York: Harper-Prism, 1998.

Springen, Karen. "The Cheery Titan of Terror." *Newsweek* (February 11, 1991).

Taylor, Marlene, and Sean Doorly. Dean Koontz interview. Doorly.com. *http://www.doorly.com/writing/DeanKoontz/htm* (viewed May 27, 2003).

Wiater, Stanley. "Dark Dreamer: Dean R. Koontz." *http://web.tiscali/it/no-redirect-tiscali/luigiurato/interv/deramers.htm* (viewed May 27, 2003).

Wiater, Stanley. "Dean R. Koontz in the Fictional Melting Pot." *Writer's Digest* (November 1989).

Jayne Ann Krentz

◆ Romance ◆ Historical ◆ Science fiction

San Diego, California
1948

◆ *Eclipse Bay*

About the Author and the Author's Writing

The women share an office, sit at the same desk, compose their stories on the same Dell laptop computer. Jayne Ann Krentz is there, writing her contemporary suspense novels, alternating with Amanda Quick, who is finishing off her latest historical romance. Jayne Castle doesn't come as often to do her stories with a futuristic bent, though she might show up any day. And Jayne Taylor, Jayne Bentley, Amanda Glass, and Stephanie James are just looking on, all apparently retired from romance writing.

The writers all get on well, as they should, since they are all one and the same person.

Jayne Ann Krentz immediately squashed one theory about the frequent use of pseudonyms in the romance genre. It is not because the writers are ashamed to have books come out under their real names, and hide under aliases. Romance novels, she explained in an essay in *Romance Reader's Handbook*, are novels of strong emotions, and the authors put a lot of their own emotions into them. "A romance novel is an extraordinarily personal thing to the author—very much an extension of herself—very much her baby," Krentz said. "A great deal of creative energy, time, effort, sweat, blood, and tears are invested in it. You don't send it out into the world if you are ashamed of it. . . ."

Rather, she went on, pseudonyms are used when the publisher insists, in order to tie the author to a specific line of books; to alleviate reader confusion when an author works in more than one style or sub-genre; to allow an author to make a fresh start if he or she has become mired in midlist doldrums; to give a veteran author an opportunity to try to recreate his or her own success a second time.

The second reason applies to Krentz herself. She suffered six years worth of rejection slips before seeing her first book come into print, and she has gone on to turn out at least two or three books a year since. These days she uses her birth name, her married name and a made-up name—Amanda Quick, chosen because there were barely any authors in the "Q" section of her bookstore.

The author, who has had more than thirty-two consecutive *New York Times* bestsellers, was born Jayne Castle in San Diego, California, in 1948. As a young girl her favorite books included Walter Farley's *The Black Stallion*, Nancy Drew mystery novels, and science fiction by Robert Heinlein. Any wonder what became her three main genres when she entered the writing profession? "I now write romantic-suspense, often with a psychic twist and a dog," she joked to interviewer Claire E. White.

She received her bachelor of arts degree in history from the University of California, Santa Cruz, and her master's in library science from San Jose State University in 1971. She and her husband, Frank Krentz, a fellow vegetarian, live in Seattle, Washington.

Krentz worked in academic and corporate libraries, including Duke University's library, for several years. She wanted to become a writer, and she wrote, and wrote some more, until she found a publisher. One thing she did—and she urges aspiring writers to do the same—was maintain faith in her own literary voice and refuse to compromise.

Admitting that writing is a compulsion, she is at the keyboard almost daily at 7:00 in the morning, working on books such as her recent *Light in Shadow.* That book is about Zoe Luce, a Whispering Springs, Arizona, interior designer with psychic abilities who has been committed by her in-laws to an institution. The man she hires to help her escape and solve the puzzle of one of her client's dark secrets is investigator Ethan Traux, a man with his own problems, namely three failed marriages.

Jumping back to the Regency era, Amanda Quick's recent *Don't Look Back* again features a pair of witty private lovers/detectives, Lavinia Lake and Tobias March, who probe crime among both the very well-to-do and the seedier elements of London.

The Lake-March books have a lively style, in the view of reviewer Kristin Ramsdell in describing *Late for the Wedding*, "proving that with well-matched, engaging protagonists and careful attention to sexual tension and romantic plot line, romances can, indeed, successfully maintain a series featuring one couple."

Jumping ahead to the future, the next Jayne Castle title will see the return of Fuzz, "the dynamic dust-bunny."

Many of Krentz's books require research, something Krentz is comfortable with, given her librarian background. Her engineer-husband helps with technical matters. She usually drafts a two-page outline, but from experience knows she will likely abandon parts of it once she's engaged in the story. "Things happen in the writing process that change the story," she said in a Washington Post Viewpoint online chat. "The finished book never looks much like the original outline. But I think the uncertainty is part of the lure for me as a writer."

A plotline is usually triggered by "a sense of the conflict that will push my characters apart even as it pulls them together," she said on her Web site in answer to a question from a reader.

She often keeps characters or setting for a second book, because they have become so comfortable and easy to write about.

"I love writing stories that have a psychic twist," she told interviewer Bonnie Rock for Writerspace. "Most people have had some experience at some point in their lives that they believe was an episode of psychic awareness . . . I think the psychic thing adds another dimension to my plots without taking them beyond the bounds of probability."

Krentz also finds it natural to mix romance and mystery. "I have always loved that blend," she said in an iVillage conversation. "The romance raises the stakes in the mystery, and the mystery adds an edge to the romance."

The author writes a little of herself into her heroines, though, as she told a reader on her Web site, "By their very nature, heroes and heroines in popular fiction are larger-than-life . . . they aren't supposed to be just like you and me. That's what makes it fun to read about their adventures." One of the characters in her *Dawn in Eclipse Bay* she based on her husband, something she did without telling him.

Krentz's books are known for their sparkling dialogue. "I think people kind of miss the moves from the '40s and '50s," she told *Tacoma News Tribune* reporter Betsy Model. "I think they miss some of the verbal repartee that movies were famous for then. I also think that there's a real desire to see some old-fashioned ethics and style. . . ."

Most of the books by this Romance Writers of America RITA Lifetime Achievement Award-winning author remain in print or are periodically rereleased. Exceptions include titles she wrote for a now-defunct publisher, McFadden, to which she has rights but for the moment has no interest in reissuing.

Krentz has little patience with literary critics who dismiss romances. She responds that genre writing comes from the heroic tradition of storytelling. "They feature the ancient heroic virtues: honor, courage, determination and the healing power of love," she told White. "Most modern literary critics are stuck in a time warp that dates back to the middle of the twentieth century when the only fiction that was considered *good* fiction was that which was heavily in-fluenced by existentialism, various social agendas and psychological theory."

As far as the author is concerned, romances have more than proven themselves. In a speech at Bowling Green State University in 2000, Krentz declared the romance novel has climbed out of its literary ghetto. Over the previous two decades, she said, "I have watched my genre take its rightful place alongside the other genres of popular fiction such as mystery and suspense, thrillers, science fiction, etc. The answer to the question, 'Are We There Yet?' for romance is *yes*. It has, as they say in the marketing business, been mainstreamed."

Works by the Author

Fiction

Twist of Fate (1986)
The Coral Kiss (1987)
Midnight Jewels (1987)
The Golden Chance (1990)
Sweet Fortune (1991)
Family Man (1992)
Perfect Partners (1992)
Hidden Talents (1993)
Wildest Hearts (1993)
A Grand Passion (1994)
Trust Me (1995)
Absolutely, Positively (1996)
Deep Waters (1997)
Flash (1998)
Sharp Edges (1998)
Eye of the Beholder (1999)
Soft Focus (2000)
Lost and Found (2001)
Smoke in Mirrors (2002)

Worth the Risk (2002)
Deep Waters (2003)
Dangerous Affair (2004)
Truth or Dare (2004)

Eclipse Bay Series

Eclipse Bay (2000)
Dawn in Eclipse Bay (2001)
A Summer in Eclipse Bay (2002)

Harlequin Intrigue Series

10. *Legacy* (1985)
17. *The Waiting Game* (1985)

Harlequin Temptation Series

11. *Uneasy Alliance* (1984)
21. *Call It Destiny* (1984)
34. *Ghost of a Chance* (1984)
45. *Man With a Past* (1985)
74. *Witchcraft* (1985)
91. *True Colors* (1986)
109. *The Ties That Bind* (1986)
146. *The Family Way* (1987)
157. *The Main Attraction* (1987)
168. *Chance of a Lifetime* (1987)
177. *Test of Time* (1987)
191. *Full Bloom* (1988)
219. *Joy* (1988)
229. *Dreams - Part One* (1988)
230. *Dreams - Part Two* (1988)
241. *A Woman's Touch* (1989)
270. *Lady's Choice* (1989)
341. *Too Wild to Wed?* (1991)
265. *The Wedding Night* (1991)
377. *The Private Eye* (1992)

Ladies and Legends Trilogy, Harlequin Temptation Series

287. *The Pirate* (1990)
293. *The Adventurer* (1990)
302. *The Cowboy* (1990)

Lost Colony Books

Crystal Flame (1986)
Sweet Starfire (1986)
Shield's Lady (1996), written as Amanda Glass, later issued as by Jayne Ann Krentz

Verity/Jonas Books

Gift of Gold (1988)
Gift of Fire (1989)

Written as Jayne Bentley

Maiden of the Morning (1979)
A Moment Past Midnight (1979)
Turning Towards Home (1979)
Hired Husband (1981)
Sabrina's Scheme (1981)
Shield's Lady (1989)

Written as Jayne Castle

Double Dealing (1984)
Trading Secrets (1985)
Harmony (2002)
After Glow (2004)

Candlelight Ecstasy Romance Series

2. *Gentle Pirate* (1980)
17. *Wagered Weekend* (1981)
23. *Right of Possession* (1981)
26. *Bargain with the Devil* (1981)
45. *Relentless Adversary* (1982)
36. *A Man's Protection* (1982)
55. *Affair of Risk* (1982)
58. *A Negotiated Surrender* (1982)
79. *Power Play* (1982)
91. *Spellbound* (1982)
130. *Conflict of Interest* (1983)

Guenevere Jones Series

The Chilling Deception (1986)
The Desperate Game (1986)
The Fatal Fortune (1986)
The Sinister Touch (1986)

McFadden Series

132. *Vintage for Surrender* (1979)
157. *Queen of Hearts* (1980)

Psynergy Inc. Series

Amaryllis (1996)
Zinnia (1997)
Orchid (1998)
Charmed (1999), short story
After Dark (2000)

Written as Amanda Quick

Seduction (1990)
Surrender (1990)
Rendezvous (1991)
Scandal (1991)
Ravished (1992)
Reckless (1992)
Dangerous (1993)
Deception (1993)
Desire (1993)
Mistress (1994)
Mystique (1995)
Mischief (1996)
Affair (1997)
Wicked Widow (2000)
Late for the Wedding (2003)

Whispering Springs Series

Light in Shadow (2003)

Lavinia Lake/Tobias March Books

Slightly Shady (2001)
Don't Look Back (2002)
Late for the Wedding (2003)

With This Ring Books

With This Ring (1998)
I Thee Wed (1999)

Written as Jayne Taylor

Whirlwind Courtship (1980), later issued as by Jayne Ann Krentz (1991)

Written as Stephanie James

Men Made in America Series

44. *To Tame the Hunger* (1995)

Silhouette Desire Series

1. *Corporate Affair* (1982)
11. *Velvet Touch* (1982)
19. *Lover in Pursuit* (1982)
25. *Renaissance Man* (1982)
31. *A Reckless Passion* (1982)
37. *The Price of Surrender* (1983)
49. *Affair of Honor* (1983)
55. *Gamemaster* (1983)
85. *The Silver Snare* (1983)
97. *Battle Prize* (1983)
103. *Body Guard* (1983)
115. *Gambler's Woman* (1984)
127. *Fabulous Beast* (1984)
145. *Night of the Magician* (1984)
163. *Nightwalker* (1984)
211. *Wizard* (1985)
235. *Golden Goddess* (1985)
253. *Cautious Lover* (1986)
277. *Green Fire* (1986)
307. *Second Wife* (1986)
342. *The Challoner Bride* (1987)
Saxon's Lady (1987), promotional

Colter Books, Silhouette Desire Series

127. *Fabulous Beast* (1984)
187. *The Devil to Pay* (1985)

Silhouette Intimate Moments Series

9. *Serpent in Paradise* (1983)
21. *Raven's Prey* (1983)

Silhouette Romance Series

89. *A Passionate Business* (1981)

Silhouette Special Edition Series

15. *The Dangerous Magic* (1982)
35. *Stormy Challenge* (1982)

Anthologies

Dreamscape (1993)
Everlasting Love (1995)
Stranded (1995), Stephanie James story
Heart's Desire (1998)
Dangerous Desire (1999)
Legacies of Love (1999)
A Shared Dream (2001)
Stolen Memories (2001)
Take 5 II (2001)
Family Passions (2002)
Bedazzled (2002)
Witchcraft (2003)

Editor

Dangerous Men and Adventurous Women: Romance Writers on the Appeal of Romance (1992)

Television Movie Based on the Author's Works

The Waiting Game (2000)

For Further Information

"Amanda Quick, A Writer for Any Era." Washington Post Viewpoint (November 30, 2000). *http://www.washingtonpost.com/wp-srv/liveonline/advertisers/quick.html* (viewed May 1, 2003).

"Jayne Ann Krentz (Amanda Quick, Jayne Castle)." Happily Ever After. *http://www .teresciaharvey.com/hea/authors/krentz.html* (viewed April 20, 2003).

Jayne Ann Krentz bibliography. Mystical Unicorn. *http://www.myunicorn.com/bibl2/ bibl0278.html* (viewed April 29, 2003).

Jayne Ann Krentz Web site. *http://www.krentz-quick.com/* (viewed April 29, 2003).

"Jayne Ann Krentz: Fiction Is My First Love." iVillage. *http://www.ivillage.com/ books/intervu/romance/articles/0,11872,240796_219221,00.html* (viewed April 29, 2003).

Jones, Daniel, and John D. Jorgenson, eds. *Contemporary Authors New Revision Series.* Vol. 63. Detroit: Gale Press, 1998.

Krentz, Jayne Ann. "A.K.A. Jayne Ann Krentz." *Romance Reader's Handbook,* Kathryn Falk, Melinda Helfer, Kathe Robin, compilers. Brooklyn Heights, NY: Romantic Times Books, 1989.

Krentz, Jayne Ann. "Are We There Yet? Mainstreaming the Romance." Keynote speech, Bowling Green State University Conference on Romance (August 2000). *http://www.krentz-quick/bgspeech.html* (viewed May 1, 2003).

Model, Betsy. "Jayne First in her class." *Tacoma News Tribune* (February 29, 2000).

Moore, Arlene. Jayne Ann Krentz entry, *Twentieth-Century Romance and Historical Writers.* 2nd edition, edited by Lesley Henderson. Chicago: St. James Press, 1990.

Ramsdell, Kristin. *Late for the Wedding* review. *Library Journal* (May 15, 2003).

Rock, Bonnie. Jayne Ann Krentz interview. Writerspace. *http://www.writerspace.com/interviews/krentz1202.html* (viewed April 29, 2003).

White, Claire E. "A Conversation With Jayne Ann Krentz." Writers Write (January–December 2003). *http://www.writerswrite.com/journal/dec02.krentz.htm* (viewed April 29, 2003).

Louis L'Amour

◆ Westerns ◆ Historical ◆ Adventure

Jamestown, North Dakota
1908–1988

◆ *Sackett Series*

Courtesy of Bantam Books.
Credit: © John Hamilton/Globe
Photos.

About the Author and the Author's Writing

A Congressional Gold Medal, a Presidential Medal of Freedom—Louis L'Amour received the honors, in 1983 and 1984, respectively, solidifying his reputation as America's premiere frontier storyteller.

The Louis L'Amour Companion biographer Robert E. Weinberg said, "Louis L'Amour led a life more incredible than most of the characters in his novels. A high-school dropout, he sailed around the world before his eighteenth birthday. . . . His books sold in the millions of copies, and by the time he died at age eighty, L'Amour was by far the best-selling Western novelist of all time."

All 122 L'Amour books so far are still in print. They have sold more than 275 million copies.

The irresistible lure of L'Amour's writing, in the view of *New York Times* writer Bruce Weber, is the story. "He wrote with a fearless omniscience, entering the minds of cowboys and Indians, sheriffs and cattle rustlers, women, children and even animals."

"I am writing about men and women who were settling a new country," L'Amour explained in *Education of a Wandering Man*, "finding their way through a maze of difficulties and learning to survive despite them."

Louis Dearborn LaMoore was born in Jamestown, North Dakota, in 1908. His father had emigrated from Canada. One of three boys, Louis learned from his farm machinery salesman-livestock inspector-veterinarian father a love for horses and athletics, and from his housewife mother a love for books and stories. The family had a library of at least 500 books and the nearby Alfred Dickey Free Library provided more.

"I left school at 15, and never did go back," the author told columnist Pete Hamill. "So I educated myself. Just by reading everything. I always had books in my pockets." He read world histories and the biography of Socrates; he read minerology and geology; he read aviation history.

During hard times in the 1920s, when the family was living in the Southwest, L'Amour (he changed the spelling back to the traditional) left home and began a period of what he called yondering. He skinned cattle in Texas, roamed the Far East, boxed, loaded freight, baled hay, toiled in a hardrock mine, handled elephants for a circus, picked fruit, prospected for gold, and, during World War II, he was a tank destroyer officer in the U.S. Army, rising to the rank of first lieutenant. L'Amour married Katherine Elizabeth Adams in 1956 and they had two children.

"Louis started writing poetry and two-line fillers and jokes for farm magazines—anything he could get published," Mrs. L'Amour said. "*Yondering* has some of his best early stories." He wrote for *New Mexico Quarterly Review* and other publications for which payment was in copies. But to make ends meet, he shifted to the pulp magazine market.

After the war, L'Amour settled in Los Angeles and wrote adventures, sports, and private eye stories, which he sold at a rapid pace. "The pulps ate up his material," Mrs. L'Amour said. "One year he wrote sixty stories." One editor phoned to ask if he had any westerns. He didn't, but he said yes. And he started to write westerns.

L'Amour became fond of frontier stories but also wrote contemporary thrillers such as *Last of the Breed*, his best-selling title, and stories with exotic settings such as those included in *Night Over the Solomons*. There's been a *Louis L'Amour Western Magazine* and a Louis L'Amour Book Club.

L'Amour listened to what people asked for in bookstores, and learned early on how important it was to keep one's name before the public. He also learned to start a novel's action on the first page. When the pulp market waned, he wrote books for paperback houses. He could have found hardcover publishers, Mrs. L'Amour said, but those companies wanted to hold onto a large portion of the film and paperback rights. L'Amour wisely resisted. He wrote four adventures of Hopalong Cassidy when the iconic hero's originator, Clarence E. Mulford, declined to produce new adventures to take advantage of the character's radio and television popularity. L'Amour wrote Hoppy in the same rough-hewn vein as Mulford, but the publisher insisted they be edited to make the character more like the then-blossoming television hero. As he was paid strictly by the job, $900 a book, L'Amour had little recourse. They came out under a house name, Tex Burns.

He also wrote two books as Jim Mayo. Then a book that had come out under his own name, *Hondo*, was made into a hit movie starring John Wayne. It was the first of more than thirty of his novels and stories to be made into films or television movies, and dozens more have been dramatized on audio. From then on, he didn't use a penname again.

L'Amour worked steadily at his craft. He left the paperback publisher Fawcett, which only wanted one book a year, for Bantam Books, which would print three. L'Amour stuck with Bantam, which now has begun republication of seven volumes of early L'Amour stories collected for the first time in hardcover.

L'Amour looked upon his work with some modesty. "If I have written good stories, much is due to those with whom I worked or saw around town, and who contributed their bits of western lore or their memories of the old days and the people who lived them," he said in *The Sackett Companion*. Among his acquaintances were Elfago Baca and Bill Tighman, legendary lawmen. He also knew a seventy-nine-year-old wrangler who had been raised by Apaches and had ridden with Geronimo.

Historic detail was a hallmark of the author's work. He developed characters in three ongoing series, the longest the Sackett saga. L'Amour stressed authenticity, noting how hoked up Hollywood plots were. Yes, there were gunfighters, he said in *Writer's Digest*. "He was a natural part of the times, but there were very few men who really wanted to be known as gunfighters. They got their reputation largely by accident. They were cowboys who simply had a natural skill with guns. By the time they'd won two or three fights they had the reputation as gunfighters whether they wanted it or not. And frankly, most of them didn't want it."

L'Amour's readership never diminished, even as the western genre faded behind him. "There's always been something romantic about any horseman," he commented to *Los Angles Times* reporter John Riley. "He's the knight in armor, the Cossack, the Bedouin. The man who could move on horseback . . . captured the people's attention."

On another occasion, speaking with Donald Dale Jackson, L'Amour observed, "Writing is sharing. I'm working for the reader."

L'Amour amassed a library of more than 10,000 volumes of western material. He cherished the idea of establishing a Library of Americana in the Four Corners region (he had a ranch in later years in Durango, Colorado). He also endorsed an effort to develop an authentic western town of the late nineteenth century, something of a Cowboy Williamsburg, to be called Shalako. Neither came about before his death, though Mrs. L'Amour has continued to support the establishment of the Mesa Verde National Park Cultural Center.

In his later years, L'Amour refused to write on a computer, after his son Beau told him it might take six weeks to become comfortable with the electronics. Six weeks would be a book lost, he reasoned, so he stuck with his typewriter. Even though it might take only six weeks to physically put the words of a new book on paper, L'Amour once said it actually took a lifetime to write a book; that is how long he had gathered experiences and material and capability. He might scribble a few notes, but otherwise he never outlined his tales before writing.

"I just tried to write the best I could about things I knew," he told Jean Henry-Mead shortly before his death.

"Louis had enormous energy," said Mrs. L'Amour, "and his energy just flowed out of his fingers into the typewriter. That energy is what captures people's imagination—it makes him hard to put down."

Works by the Author

Fiction

Westward the Tide (1950)
Hondo (1953)
Crossfire Trail (1954)
Heller With a Gun (1954)
Kilkenny (1954)
Guns of the Timberlands (1955)
To Tame a Land (1955)
The Burning Hills (1956)
Silver Canyon (1956)
Last Stand at Papago Wells (1957)
Sitka (1957)
The Tall Stranger (1957)
Radigan (1958)
The First Fast Draw (1959)
Taggart (1959)

Flint (1960)
High Lonesome (1962)
Killoe (1962)
Shalako (1962)
Catlow (1963)
Dark Canyon (1963)
Fallon (1963)
How the West Was Won (1963), based on James R. Webb's screenplay
Hanging Woman Creek (1964)
The High Graders (1965)
The Key-Lock Man (1965)
Kiowa Trail (1965)
The Broken Gun (1966)
Kid Rodelo (1966)
Kilrone (1966)
Matagordo (1967)
Chancy (1968)
Down the Long Hills (1968)
Conagher (1969)
The Empty Land (1969)
The Man Called Noon (1970)
Reilly's Luck (1970)
Brionne (1971)
Tucker (1971)
Under the Sweetwater Rim (1971)
Callaghen (1972)
The Man from Skibbereen (1973)
The Quick and the Dead (1973)
The Californios (1974)
The Rider of Lost Creek (1976)
Where the Long Grass Blows (1976)
Bendigo Shafter (1978)
The Mountain Valley War (1978)
The Iron Marshall (1979)
The Proving Trail (1979)
Lonely in the Mountains (1980)
Comstock Lode (1981)
The Cherokee Trail (1982)
The Shadow Riders (1982)
The Tall Stranger (1982)
The Lonesome Gods (1983)
Son of a Wanted Man (1984)
The Walking Drum (1984)
Passin' Through (1985)

Last of the Breed (1986)
A Trail to the West (1986)
West of the Pilot Range (1986)
The Haunted Mesa (1987)
Merrano of the Dry Country (1990)
Smoke from this Mountain (1990)

Bowdrie Series

Bowdrie (1983)
Bowdrie's Law (1984)

Chantry Series

North to the Rails (1971)
The Ferguson Rifle (1973)
Borden Chantry (1977)
Fair Blows the Wind (1978)

Sackett Series

The Daybreakers (1960)
Sackett (1961)
Lando (1962)
Mojave Crossing (1964)
The Sackett Brand (1965)
Mustang Man (1966)
The Sky-Liners (1967)
The Lonely Men (1969)
Galloway (1970)
Ride the Dark Trail (1972)
Treasure Mountain (1972)
Sackett's Land (1974)
To the Far Blue Mountains (1976)
Sackett's Gold (1977)
Lonely on the Mountain (1980)
The Warrior's Path (1980)
Ride the River (1983)
Jubal Sackett (1985)

Talon Series

Rivers West (1974)
The Man from the Broken Hills (1975)
Milo Talon (1981)

Short Story Collections

War Party (1975)
The Strong Shall Live (1980)
Yondering (1980/1989)
Buckskin Run (1981)
The Hills of Homicide (1983)
Law of the Desert Born (1983)
The Trail to Crazy Man (1984)
Dutchman's Flat (1986)
Night Over the Solomons (1986)
The Rider of the Ruby Hills (1986)
Riding for the Brand (1986)
West from Singapore (1987)
Lonigan (1988)
Long Ride Home (1989)
The Outlaws of Mesquite (1991)
Valley of the Sun: Frontier Stories (1995)
West of Dodge (1996)
End of the Drive (1997)
Monument Rock (1998)
Beyond the Great Snow Mountains (1999)
Off the Mangrove Coast (2000)
May There Be a Road (2001)
With These Hands (2002)
Collected Short Stories of Louis L'Amour: the Frontier Stories, volume 1 (2003)
From the Listening Hills (2003)
Collected Short Stories of Louis L'Amour: the Frontier Stories, volume 2 (2004)

Written as Jim Mayo, reissued as by Louis L'Amour

Showdown at Yellow Butte (1954)
Utah Blaine (1954)

Written as Tex Burns, reissued as by Louis L'Amour

Hopalong Cassidy Series

The Riders of the High Rock (1951)
The Rustlers of West Fork (1951)
The Trail to Seven Pines (1951)
Trouble Shooter (1952)

Anthologies

Western Hall of Fame Anthology, edited by Dale L. Walker (1997)
A Century of Great Western Stories, edited by John Jakes (2000)

The Golden West, edited by Jon Tuska (2002)
Stagecoach, edited by Ed Gorman and Martin H. Greenberg (2003)
The Untamed West, edited by Jon Tuska (2004)

Poetry

Smoke from This Altar (1939)

Nonfiction

Louis L'Amour's Frontier (1984)
The Sackett Companion: A Personal Guide to the Sackett Novels (1988)
Education of a Wandering Man (1989)
A Trail of Memories: The Quotations of Louis L'Amour, edited by Angelique L'Amour (1988)

Motion Pictures and Television Movies Based on the Author's Works

East of Sumatra (1953), based on L'Amour screenplay written with Frank J. Gill Jr. and Jack Natteford
Hondo (1953)
Four Guns to the Border (1954), based on L'Amour screenplay written with George Van Marter and Franklin Coen, also known as *The Shadow Valley*
Stranger on Horseback (1955), based on L'Amour screenplay written with Herb Meadow and Don Martin
Treasure of the Ruby Hills, with Tom Hubbard and Fred Eggers (1955)
Blackjack Ketchum, Desperado (1956), based on *Kilkenny*
The Burning Hills (1956)
The Tall Stranger (1957), based on *Showdown Trail*; also known as *The Rifle* and *Walk Tall*
Utah Blaine (1957)
Apache Territory (1958), based on *Last Stand at Papago Wells*
Guns of the Timberland (1959), also titled *Stampede*
Heller in Pink Tights (1960), based on *Heller With a Gun*
Taggart (1965)
Kid Rodelo (1966), based on L'Amour screenplay written with Jack Natteford
Hondo and the Apaches (1967), based on "The Gift of Cochise"
Shalako (1968)
Catlow (1971)
Cancel My Reservation (1972), based on *The Broken Gun*
The Man Called Noon (1972)
The Sacketts (1979)
The Shadow Riders (1982)
The Cherokee Trail (1986)

Down the Long Hills (1987)
The Quick and the Dead (1987)
Conagher (1991)
Shaughnessy (1996), based on *The Iron Marshal*
Crossfire Trail (2001)
Diamond of Jeru (2001)

For Further Information

Ellison, Harlan. "Lunch With Louis 'n' Me: A Few Casuals by Way of Reminiscence." *http://www.louislamourbooks.com/aboutlouis/louis_n_me.htm* (viewed May 20, 2003).

"Famed Author Louis L'Amour Still Inspiring Preservation of a Bygone Era." PR Newswire (September 13, 2002).

Gale, Robert L. Louis L'Amour entry, *Twentieth-Century Western Writers*. 2nd edition. Chicago: St. James Press, 1991.

Gonzalez, Arturo F. Jr. "Louis L'Amour: Writing High in the Bestseller Saddle." *Writer's Digest* (December 1980).

Hamill, Pete. "The Fastest Typewriter West of the Pecos, Pardner." New York *Daily News* (January 31, 1979).

Henry-Mead, John. *Maverick Writers*. Evansville, WY: Medallion Press, 1989.

Jackson, Donald Dale. "World's fastest literary gun: Louis L'Amour." *Smithsonian Magazine* (1987). *http://www.louislamourbooks.com/aboutlouis/smithsonian.htm* (viewed May 20, 2003).

L'Amour, Katherine. Telephone conversation with the author. March 6, 2004.

Louis L'Amour bibliography. Mystical Unicorn. *http://www.myunicorn.com/bibl4/bibl0457.html* (viewed May 20, 2003).

Louis L'Amour bibliography. *http://www.hycyber.com/WEST/lamour_louis.html* (viewed May 22, 2003).

Louis L'Amour bibliography. *http://www.veinotte.com/lamour/sackets.htm* (viewed May 20, 2003).

Louis L'Amour Web site. *http://www.louislamour.com* (viewed April 5, 2003) and Web page *http://www.louislamourbooks.com/* (viewed May 20, 2003).

Riley, John. "The West Lives On in Louis L'Amour." *Los Angeles Times* (October 19, 1975).

Trisky, Susan M., ed. Louis L'Amour entry, *Contemporary Authors New Revision Series*. Vol. 40. Detroit: Gale Research, 1993.

Tuska, Jon, and Vicki Pierkarski. *Encyclopedia of Frontier & Western Fiction*. New York: McGraw-Hill, 1983.

Unofficial Tribute to Louis L'Amour. *http://louis-lamour-fan.com/* (viewed May 20, 2003).

Valby, Karen. "Tome Raiders: Reports of their demise are greatly exaggerated: How dead authors are 'writing' new books." *Entertainment Weekly* (May 4, 2001).

Weber, Bruce. "The Proust of the Prairie Gallops On: A Decade After His Death, Louis L'Amour Remains a Publisher's Dream." *New York Times* (June 10, 1998).

Weinberg, Robert. *The Louis L'Amour Companion*. Kansas City: Andrews and McMeel, 1992.

John le Carré

Poole, Dorsetshire, England
1931

◆   *The Spy Who Came In From the Cold*

About the Author and the Author's Writing

David John Moore Cornwell led a life of deceit as tense and, at times, nearly as dangerous as that of the fictional spies he wrote of under a penname.

Born in Poole, Dorsetshire, England, in 1931, he attended the University of Berne, 1948–1949, to study French and German, then joined the British Army Intelligence Corps in 1949. He completed his studies at Lincoln College, Oxford, from which he received a first-class honors degree in modern languages in 1956. He has three children by his first marriage to Alison Sharp in 1954, one by his second to Valerie Eustace in 1971.

The author taught junior high school in England for two years, then became a tutor at Eton College, Buckinhamshire, England, where he worked from 1956 to 1958. Over the years, according to his publisher, he also sold bath towels, washed elephants, and wiped out a flock of Welsh sheep when he failed to follow the instructions of his gunnery officer. He became second secretary in the British Foreign Office in Bonn, West Germany, and was political consul in Hamburg, from 1960 to 1964. It was in this period he began writing, adopting the pseudonym John le Carré to mask his identity.

Le Carré dismisses his undercover service: "In the old days it was convenient to bill me as a spy turned writer. I was nothing of the kind. I am a writer who, when I was very young, spent a few ineffectual but extremely formative years in British Intelligence." He recruited Soviet agents from a group of refugees living in Austria. "The relationship between agent and agent-runner was sacrosanct," he told reporter Tim Sullivan. "You promised that you would never reveal what he did."

Le Carré knew firsthand of deceit from his childhood as the son of a confidence man and convicted felon. Today he has the bearing of a British aristocrat, but as a youth, in a home from which his mother had fled by the time he was three, the author and his younger brother attended private British schools and had to pretend they were of the upper crust. In reality, he wouldn't know what danger his father might bring home any night, or, for that matter, when his father might next go to jail. He grew up much as a spy, in an entire world that was the enemy, risking discovery at any turn.

Is it any wonder the author has such a masterful hold on the morally vague world of Cold War espionage such as emerges in *The Spy Who Came In from the Cold*? The main character, Alec Leamas, is fifty, tired of the spy game, and anxious to step out of it. But first, he must complete one more assignment.

Reviewer Anthony Boucher appreciated the intricacies of the main character, who must live a life of deception: "He must protect himself not only from without but from within, and against the most natural of impulses: though he earn a fortune, his role may forbid him the purchase of a razor; though he may be erudite, it can befall him to mumble nothing but banalities; though he be an affectionate husband and father, he must under all circumstances withhold himself from those in whom he should naturally confide."

Le Carré's theme continues through his oeuvre. The character Oliver Single in *Single and Single* eludes his corrupt father to become a magician. Le Carré identifies with this character because, when he was growing up, he was often the entertainer to the rest of the family. The cathartic, autobiographical *A Perfect Spy* is about a British spy about to become a traitor, a con man much like his father. The character of Rick Pym is something of an exception; the author told reporter Mary Ann Gwinn, "There is no such thing as a fictional character literally drawn from life—you can draw an inflection or a mannerism (from an actual person), but finally you have to fill that person with the possibility of your own character."

The book bears a lighter tone than the rest of le Carré's works, something he attributes to his maturity: Given the world situation, at his age, one either laughs or commits suicide. (It should be noted that le Carré isn't unrelievedly serious, despite his mien; Jeeves-Bertie Wooster creator P. G. Wodehouse is at the top of his list of favorite authors.)

Le Carré, who lives above a cliff on the Cornish coast, does considerable background research for his books, often going to actual locations, and fills his head with the main character's thoughts and motivations.

"I write in longhand," he told interviewer Chris Nashawaty in *Entertainment Weekly*. "And I always write first thing in the morning. If it's really going, I'll start at 4 or 5 o'clock and that will go through until lunchtime. And if it's gone well, I'll have a couple glasses of wine with lunch as a reward."

The end of the Cold War wasn't the end of his career, by any means. Le Carré simply shifted to mobsters, gun runners, and deceitful Western governments. In *The Tailor of Panama*, as another example, he reworks the duality of his life with a more comic edge. The book is about ex-con Harry Pendel who, blackmailed into becoming an informant but lacking any crucial information to pass on, invents a plot about Asians who want to stir up a revolution and grab the Panama Canal. In *Absolute Friends*, the author circled around to espionage again and a very current topic: the war in Iraq. (He takes a position strongly opposed to America's strong-armed handling of international politics.)

George Smiley, the glum-but-solid British spy, has figured in many of Le Carré's books beginning with the first, *Call for the Dead*, and perhaps reaching his pinnacle in the trilogy in which he faces the Communist master spy Karla. That sequence took inspiration from the case of the treacherous British spy, Kim Philby, the author has said.

For *The Honourable Schoolboy*, Le Carré already had the characters, the reliable George Smiley and Jerry Westerby, previously introduced but now in a major role. He explained the genesis of the book to Michael Barber of the *New York Times*: "I set off for the Far East with those two people and a rough idea of the evanescence of the Western presence in

Southeast Asia; beyond that, I felt, I had no preconceptions. I found myself referring to Jerry and George as 'my secret sharers.' So it was an act of complicity, I suppose, between myself and the characters, that we finally drew the story out of their motivations."

In a Salon interview with Andrew Ross, Le Carré drew the distinction that his books are credible, but not authentic. In the real world of spies, he pointed out, there is seldom resolution, characters are not always caught in the dilemma of wrong or right, and their motives may not always be dangerous.

"So I use the furniture of espionage to amuse the reader," le Carré said, "to make the reader listen to me, because most people like to read about intrigue and spies. I hope to provide a metaphor for the average reader's daily life. Most of us live in a slightly conspiratorial relationship with our employer and perhaps with our marriage. I think what gives my works whatever universality they have is that they use the metaphysical secret world to describe some realities of the overt world."

Reviewer Bill Ott noted a change in the author's work with *The Constant Gardener*, citing a "profound cynicism" with a hero who feels betrayed by his own country. George Smiley, at least, always felt his government, whatever its shortcoming, was better than anyone else's.

Le Carré, after all, has established himself with readers. If any further testimonial to the accuracy of his work is needed, the CIA has reportedly adopted some of his jargon, including "mole," "lamplighter," and "scalp-hunter," into its own universe.

Works by the Author

Fiction

A Small Town in Germany (1968)
The Naïve and Sentimental Lover (1971)
The Little Drummer Girl (1983)
A Perfect Spy (1986)
The Russia House (1989)
The Night Manager (1993)
Our Game (1995)
The Tailor of Panama (1996)
Single and Single (1999)
The Constant Gardener (2001)
Absolute Friends (2004)

Smiley Series

Call for the Dead (1961), retitled *The Deadly Affair* (1966)
A Murder of Quality (1962)
The Spy Who Came In From the Cold (1963)
The Incongruous Spy (1964), includes first two books
The Looking Glass War (1965)
Tinker, Tailor, Soldier, Spy (1974)
The Honourable Schoolboy (1977)
Smiley's People (1980)

The Quest for Karla (1982), omnibus; includes *Tinker, Tailor, Soldier, Spy, The Hon-
  ourable Schoolboy*, and *Smiley's People*
The Secret Pilgrim (1990)
John le Carré: Three Complete Novels (1995), includes *Tinker, Tailor, Soldier, Spy,
  Honourable Schoolboy*, and *Smiley's People*

Teleplays

Dare I Weep, Dare I Mourn (1966)
Smiley's People, with John Hopkins (1982)

Nonfiction

The Clandestine Muse (1986)
Vanishing England, with Gareth H. Davies (1987)

Motion Pictures and Television Movies Based on the Author's Works

The Spy Who Came in from the Cold (1965)
The Deadly Affair (1967), based on *Call for the Dead*
The Looking Glass War (1970)
Tinker, Tailor, Soldier, Spy (1980)
The Little Drummer Girl (1984)
The Russia House (1990)
A Perfect Spy (1999)

For Further Information

Barber, Michael. "John le Carré: An Interrogation." *New York Times* (September 25, 1977).

Boucher, Anthony. "Temptations of a Man Isolated in Deceit." *New York Times* (January 12, 1964).

Freeman, Alan. *Absolute Friends* review. *Sunday Republican*, Waterbury, CT (January 18, 2004).

Gwinn, Mary Ann. "Author John le Carré digs deep in his own past for the themes of his work." *Seattle Times* (March 25, 1999).

Harris, Mark. *Absolute Friends* review. *Entertainment Weekly* (January 16, 2004).

Homberger, Eric. *John le Carré*. New York: Ungar, 1985.

John le Carré Web site. *http://www.johnlecarre.com/* (viewed May 30, 2003).

Jones, Daniel, and John J. Jorgenson, eds. David Cornwell entry, *Contemporary Authors New Revision Series*. Vol. 59. Detroit: Gale Research, 1998.

Le Carré Breaks his Silence. Random House. *http://www.randomhouse.com/features/ lecarre/author/html* (viewed May 30, 2003).

Le Carré, John. "The United States of America has gone mad." Times Online (January 15, 2003). *http:www.timesonline.co/uk/article/0,1072-543296,00.html* (viewed May 30, 2003).

Lelyveld, Joseph. "Le Carré's Toughest Case." *New York Times Magazine* (March 16, 1986).

Monaghan, David. *Smiley's Circus; A Guide to the Secret World of John le Carré.* London: Orbis, 1986.

Monaghan, David. *The Novels of John le Carré.* Oxford: Blackwell, 1985.

Nashawaty, Chris. "The Spy Who Came In From the Cold War." *Entertainment Weekly* (January 16, 2004).

Ott, Bill. *Constant Gardener* review. *American Libraries* (February 2002).

Ross, Andrew. "John le Carré on deception, storytelling and American hubris." Salon .com. *http://www.salon.com/weekly/lecarre961021.html* (viewed May 30, 2003).

Snyder, John. John le Carré entry, *St. James Guide to Crime & Mystery Writers.* 4th edition, edited by Jay P. Pederson. Detroit: St. James Press, 1996.

Sullivan, Tim. "John le Carré still holding back some secrets." Associated Press (November 22, 1996). *http://cgi.canoe.ca/JamBooksFeatures/lecarre_john.html* (viewed May 30, 2003).

Wolfe, Peter. *Corridors of Deceit: The World of John le Carré.* Bowling Green, OH: Bowling Green University Popular Press, 1987.

Ursula K. Le Guin

♦ Science fiction ♦ Fantasy

| Berkeley, California |
| 1929 |

♦ *Earthsea Series*

Credit: © Marian Wood Kolisch.

About the Author and the Author's Writing

A prolific crafter of fantasy, science fiction, and realistic fiction, a poet as well as a prose writer, a storyteller for children as well as adults, Ursula K. Le Guin has won Hugo, Nebula, Pushcart, PEN, Pilgrim, and National Book awards; she is one of the most widely read and respected authors in her field.

Ursula Kroeber was born in Berkeley, California, in 1929, the daughter of anthropologist Alfred Kroeber and writer Theodora Kroeber (*Ishi in Two Worlds*). She had a happy childhood in a family that included three brothers and a great-aunt. They spent summers at an old ranch in the Napa Valley, and Ursula attended public school. Because of her father's college professorship, there were frequent visitors to the home and lots of talking and exchanging of ideas. During World War II, with her brothers in the service, she was on her own a lot and wandered the outdoors. "I think I started making my soul then," she said on her Web site.

Ursula attended Radcliffe College, where she earned a bachelor of arts degree in French and Italian literature in 1951. Then, she went on to Columbia University for her master's degree the next year. She was a member of Phi Beta Kappa at Radcliffe and a Columbia University Fellow at Columbia. In 1953 she became a Fulbright Fellow. She has also received honorary degrees from nine institutions including Lewis & Clark College and Portland State University. She has been an instructor in French at two colleges and a lecturer or writer in residence at sixteen colleges, conferences, or workshops. Her manuscripts are held by the University of Oregon Library in Eugene.

She married Charles A. Le Guin, a historian, in 1953 in Paris. Raising three children, they have lived in Portland, Oregon, since 1958. With her husband's blessing and support, she began writing. *Rocannon's World* came out in 1966. There followed in a rush of creative energy seven science fiction and three fantasy novels, nine poems, and sixteen essays over the next six years.

Le Guin said in a discussion with Jonathan White that she gravitated to science fiction and fantasy because that's where the prose she wanted to write most comfortably fit in. "Both realism and science fiction deal with stories that might be true. Fantasy, on the other hand, tells a story that couldn't possibly be true. With fantasy, we simply agree to lift the ban on the imagination and follow the story, no matter how implausible it may be."

Why is she drawn to imaginative fiction? Because the future is one big void. "The emptiness of the future is why it is so useful to SF," she said in *The Writer* in 2003. "Fitting an invented country into 19th- [and] 20th-century Europe—well, Europe is full. So is history."

In her early work, Le Guin followed convention with mostly male characters. Her science fiction book *The Left Hand of Darkness* began her exploration of gender issues. *The Dispossessed* and *Always Coming Home* look at utopias, while *Searoad* explores contemporary small-town Oregon. Her Catwings books about flying cats who have found a new home in the country found a large audience among younger readers.

The Hainish, or Ekumen books, starting with *Rocannon's World*, are set in universes spawned by inhabitants of the planet Hain. "Each work employs the alien as the embodiment of alienation presenting to the hero the challenge of transcending fear itself, thoroughly embracing the unknown Communication, whether through telepathic 'mindspeech' or by means of the amazing ansible [a spontaneous communication] is significant, often the symbolic crux of each climax," according to Rosemary Herbert.

There are all sorts of elements in Le Guin's stories, from Norse mythology to Taoist philosophy, the latter particularly evident in her best-known fantasies, the Earthsea novels. At the beginning of the series, the main character, Ged, is studying at a school for wizards on the island of Roke. "As a self-proclaimed Taoist," notes Jan M. Griffin, "Le Guin manufactures a world based on two of the main principles of Taoism: 1) the theory of inactivity in which one acts only when absolutely necessary, and 2) the relativity of opposites which is the belief that opposites are interdependent, and their interdependence results in the equilibrium."

How does this translate into prose? Lin Carter had high praise for the author's description of Ged's descent into Hell in the third Earthsea book, *The Farthest Shore*: "The entire sequence of events as young Ged and his squire traverse the underworld to its utmost depths is a harrowing masterpiece of emotional intensity, held under tight control and told in terms of quiet understatement."

Le Guin has revisited her series years later, revisioning some of what had happened in Earthsea and further exploring elements of Ekumen.

"What is remarkable in Le Guin's work is the subtlety with which she spins her tales and draws us into their moral universe—for she is a writer very much concerned with morals, though these stories could hardly be regarded as polemic," observed Elizabeth Hand in the *Washington Post*.

Le Guin sees far beyond entertainment value in her imaginative fiction: "It widens the soul," she told interviewer Faith Justice. Indeed it does.

Works by the Author

Fiction

The Lathe of Heaven (1971)
The Word for World Is Forest (1972)

From Elfland to Poughkeepsie (1973)
Very Far Away from Anywhere Else (1976), also titled *A Very Long Way from Anywhere Else* (1976)
The Eye of the Heron (1978)
Malafrena (1979)
The Beginning Place (1980), also titled *Threshold*
Gwilans Harp (1981)
In the Red Zone (1983)
Always Coming Home (1985)
A Visit from Dr. Katz (1988)
Fire and Stone (1989)
The Ones Who Walk Away from Omelas (1991)
Searoad: Chronicles of Klatsand (1991)
Fish Soup (1992)
A Ride on the Red Mare's Back (1992)
Blue Moon over Thurman Street (1993)
A Fisherman of the Inland Sea (1994)
Four Ways to Forgiveness (1995)
The Shobies' Story (1998)
The Telling (2000)
Tom Mouse (2002)
Changing Planes (2003)

Earthsea Series

A Wizard of Earthsea (1968)
The Tombs of Atuan (1971)
The Farthest Shore (1972)
Tehanu (1990)
The Earthsea Quartet (1993)
Earthsea Revisioned (1993)
The Other Wind (2001)
Tales from Earthsea (2001)

Hainish or Ekumen Series

Planet of Exile (1966)
Rocannon's World (1966)
City of Illusions (1967)
The Left Hand of Darkness (1969)
The Dispossessed: An Ambiguous Utopia (1974)
Worlds of Exile and Illusion (1998), includes first three books; also called *Three Hainish Novels*
The Telling (2000)

Prose Chapbooks

A Winter Solstice Ritual for the Pacific Northwest, with Vonda N. McIntyre (1991)
The Art of Bunditsu (1993)
Findings (1992)

Collections

The Wind's Twelve Quarters (1975)
The Wind's Twelve Quarters Volume One (1975)
The Wind's Twelve Quarters Volume Two (1975)
Orsinian Tales (1976)
Earthsea Trilogy (1977)
Ursula K. Le Guin: Five Complete Novels (1979)
Edges (1980)
The Compass Rose (1982)
Buffalo Gals and Other Animal Presences (1987)
Science Fiction Stories (1994)
Searoad: Chronicles of Klatsand (1995)
Unlocking the Air: And Other Stories (1996)
The Birthday of the World: And Other Stories (2002)
Changing Planes (2003)

Translations

Lao Tzu: Tao Te Ching: A Book About the Way and the Power of the Way (1997)
The Twins, The Dream / Las Gemelas, El Sueno, with Diana Bellessi (1998)
Kalpa Imperial: The Greatest Empire That Never Was, by Angélica Gorodischer (2003)

Editor

Nebula Award Stories 11 (1977)
Edges, with Virginia Kidd (1980)
Interfaces, with Virginia Kidd (1980)
The Norton Book of Science Fiction, with Brian Attebery (1993)
Selected Stories of H. G. Wells (2004)

Anthologies

Great Science Fiction of the 20th Century (1968)
Nebula Award Stories 5 (1969)
The Year's Best Science Fiction 3 (1969)
Again Dangerous Visions Book 1 (1972)
The Best Science Fiction of the Year (1972)
The Golden Road (1973)
The Best Science Fiction of the Year 3 (1974)

Fellowship of the Stars (1974)
Modern Science Fiction (1974)
Women of Wonder (1974)
Nebula Award Stories 10 (1975)
Universe 5 (1975)
The Best of New Dimensions (1979)
The Black Magic Omnibus Volume 1 (1976)
Black Water (1976)
Nebula Award Stories 11 (1976)
New Dimensions 9 (1979)
A Century of Fantasy 1980–1989 (1980)
Timegates (1981)
Future Primitive: The New Ecotopias (1982)
Killing Me Softly (1982)
Unicorns! (1982)
The Mammoth Book of Fantasy All-Time Greats (1983), also titled *The Fantasy Hall of Fame* (1984)
The Best from Universe (1984)
Top Fantasy (1984)
Top Science Fiction (1984)
Visions of Wonder (1985)
Afterlives (1986)
Legends (1986)
A Magic-Lover's Treasury of the Fantastic (1986)
New Legends (1988)
Women Who Run with the Werewolves: Tales of Blood, Lust, and Metamorphosis (1988)
The Year's Best Fantasy First Annual Collection (1988)
Amazing Stories: The Anthology (1991)
Full Spectrum 3 (1991)
The Night Fantastic (1991)
Nebula Awards 26 (1992)
The Oxford Book of Science Fiction Stories (1992)
Xanadu (1992)
The Norton Book of Science Fiction (1993)
Omni Best Science Fiction Three (1993)
Xanadu 2 (1993)
The Ascent of Wonder (1994)
The Best from Fantasy And Science Fiction: The 50th Anniversary Anthology (1994)
Blue Motel: Narrow Houses Vol. 3 (1994)
Explorers: SF Adventures to Far Horizons (1994)
Horses! (1994)
New Eves: Science Fiction About the Extraordinary Women of Today and Tomorrow (1994)

The Year's Best Fantasy and Horror Seventh Annual Collection (1994)
The Good Old Stuff (1995)
The Penguin Book of Modern Fantasy by Women (1995)
Tales in Space (1995)
The Year's Best Science Fiction Twelfth Annual Collection (1995)
American Gothic Tales (1996)
Modern Classics of Fantasy (1996)
Nebula Awards 30 (1996)
The Wizards of Odd: Comic Tales of Fantasy (1996)
The Year's Best Fantasy and Horror Ninth Annual Collection (1996)
Year's Best Science Fiction (1996)
The Year's Best Science Fiction Thirteenth Annual Collection (1996)
Dragons: The Greatest Stories (1997)
Dying for It (1997)
More Amazing Stories (1997)
Nebula Awards 31 (1997)
The Best of Crank! (1998)
The Fantasy Hall of Fame (1998)
Mistresses of the Dark: 25 Macabre Tales by Master Storytellers (1998)
The Playboy Book of Science Fiction (1998)
The Unexplained: Stories of the Paranormal (1998)
Far Horizons (1999)
The Year's Best Science Fiction Sixteenth Annual Collection (1999)
Legends: Short Novels by the Masters of Modern Fantasy, volume 1, edited by Robert
    Silverberg (1999)
Isaac Asimov's Utopias (2000)
The Year's Best Fantasy And Horror Thirteenth Annual Collection (2000)

Poetry

Wild Angels (1975)
Hard Words: And Other Poems (1981)
Wild Oats and Fireweed: New Poems (1987)
Blue Moon Over Thurman Street, with Roger Dorband (1993)
Going Out With Peacocks: And Other Poems (1994)
Sixty Odd: New Poems (1999)

Poetry Chapbooks

Walking in Cornwall (1976)
Tillai and Tylissos, with Theodora Kroeber (1979)
In the Red Zone, with Henk Pander (1983)
The Visionary: The Life Story of Flicker of the Serpentine of Telina-Na (1984)
No Boats (1992)

Books for Children

Leese Webster (1979)
A Visit from Dr. Katz (1988)
Fire and Stone (1989)
Fish Soup (1992)
A Ride on the Red Mare's Back (1992)
Tom Mouse (2002)

Adventures in Kroy Series

The Adventures of Cobbler's Rune (1982)
Solomon Leviathan's Nine-Hundred and Thirty-First Trip Around the World (1983)

Catwings Series

Catwings (1988)
Catwings Return (1989)
Jane On Her Own (1992)
Wonderful Alexander and the Catwings (1994)
Tales of the Catwings (1996)

Nonfiction

Dreams Must Explain Themselves (1975)
The Language of the Night: Essays on Fantasy and Science Fiction (1979), revised (1989)
Steering the Craft: Exercises and Discussions on Story Writing for the Lone Navigator or the Mutinous Crew (1984)
Dancing at the Edge of the World: Thoughts on Words, Women, Places (1989)
The Way of the Water's Going: Images of the Northern California Coastal Range (1989)

Television Movies Based on the Author's Works

The Lathe of Heaven (1979/2000)
Legend of Earthsea (2004)

For Further Information

Bloom, Harold. *Ursula K. Le Guin.* Oakland, CA: Potlatch 4, 2000.

Bratman, David S. *Ursula K. Le Guin: A Primary Bibliography.* Broomall, PA: Chelsea House, 1995.

Bucknall, Barbara J. *Ursula K. Le Guin.* New York: Ungar, 1981.

Carter, Lin. *Imaginary Worlds.* New York: Ballantine, 1973.

Changing Planes review. *Publishers Weekly* (April 14, 2003).

Cummins, Elizabeth. *Understanding Ursula K. Le Guin*. Columbia: University of Southern California Press, 1990.

Drumming, Neil. "Sunken Treasure." *Entertainment Weekly* (December 17, 2004).

Gevers, Nick. "Driven by a Different Chauffeur: An Interview With Ursula K. Le Guin."

Griffin, Jan M. "Ursula Le Guin's Magical World of Earthsea." *ALAN Review* (spring 1996).

Hand, Elizabeth. "Science and Fantasy." *Washington Post* (October 29, 1995).

Herbert, Rosemary. Ursula K. Le Guin entry, *Twentieth-Century Science-Fiction Writers*. 3rd edition, edited by Noelle Watson and Paul E. Schellinger. Chicago: St. James Press, 1991.

Justice, Faith. "Steering Her Craft: An Interview with Ursula LeGuin." *http://www.writing-world.com/sf/leguin/shtml* (viewed June 10, 2004).

Kersten, Denise. "Now boarding at Gate 13: Ursula Le Guin's flights of plane fantasy." *USA Today* (July 31, 2003).

Kolish, Marian. "An Interview with Ursula K. Le Guin." *http://www.sfsite.com/03a/ul123.htm* (viewed May 30, 2003).

Le Guin, Ursula K. "Exercises & Discussion on Story Writing for the Lone Navigator or the Mutinous Crew." Ursula K. Le Guin Web site. *http://www.ursulakleguin.com/AlternateTitles.html* (viewed May 30, 2003).

Le Guin, Ursula K. "Some Genres I Write In." Ursula K. Le Guin Web site. *http://www.ursulakleguin.com/AlternateTitles.html* (viewed May 30, 2003).

"Miscellany." *The Writer* (August 2003).

Peacock, Scot, ed. Ursula K. Le Guin entry, *Contemporary Authors New Revision Series*. Vol. 74. Detroit: Gale Research, 1999.

Reid, Suzanne Elizabeth. *Ursula K. Le Guin*. Boston: Twayne, 1997.

SF site (November/December 2001). *http://www.sfsite.com/03a/ul123.htm* (viewed May 30, 2003).

Ursula K. Le Guin Web site. *http://www.ursulakleguin.com* (viewed May 30, 2003).

White, Donna R. *Dancing With Dragons: Ursula K. Le Guin and the Critics*. Rochester, NY: Camden House, 1999.

White, Jonathan. "Coming Back from the Silence: An Interview with Ursula K. Le Guin." *http://www.geocities.com/Area51/2593/fuliv.htm* (viewed May 30, 2003).

Elmore Leonard

◆ Mystery ◆ Western

New Orleans, Louisiana
1925

◆ *Get Shorty*

Courtesy of HarperCollins. Credit:
Linda Solomon.

About the Author and the Author's Writing

Elmore Leonard is known for his gritty realism, skewed characters, and crackling dialogue. *New York Times Book Review* critic Charles Taylor remarked on the author's style: "There are plenty of literary luminaries who could learn a lot from the discipline and craft of writers pigeonholed—or dismissed—as genre writers. My Christmas wish this year was that when Cormac McCarthy, Michael Ondaatje and Toni Morrison, to name but three, looked under their trees, they found that some kind soul had been thoughtful enough to send them a copy of Elmore Leonard's latest."

Born in New Orleans in 1925, Elmore John Leonard Jr. had lived in Dallas, Oklahoma City, Memphis, and Detroit by the time he was ten; his father was a location scout for General Motors. Leonard attended Catholic elementary school and the Jesuit-run University of Detroit High School—an experience he years later credited with giving him the ability to "think clearly." His nickname "Dutch" comes from his love of baseball; Emil "Dutch" Leonard was a knuckleball pitcher for the Washington Senators in those days.

Leonard signed on with the Navy Seabees in 1944 and was stationed near New Guinea, in the Admiralty Islands. After World War II, he attended the University of Detroit, where he studied English and philosophy and developed an interest in writing.

Married three times, the author has five children. He lives in Bloomfield Hills, Michigan.

Joining Campbell-Ewald, an advertising agency that included Chevrolet among its clients, Leonard wrote advertising copy from 1950 to 1961. His first published story was "Trail of the Apache" for *Argosy* magazine in 1951. He continued to write western fiction—largely because he liked oater movies, and he knew there was a market—early mornings, before leaving for his day job. He wrote stories for magazines including *Zane Grey's Western, Dime Western*, and *The Saturday Evening Post*, and he produced five novels for book publishers. Two stories, "3:30 to Yuma" and "The Tall T," were made into motion pictures.

How did someone living in Detroit capture the flavor of the wild West? "The first thing I did, once I decided to set my stories in the Southwest, was subscribe to *Arizona Highways*. And once I had a stack of the magazines, I was all set. When I needed a description of the terrain, including the growth, trees, cactus, the kind of rocks, I'd go through the magazines until I found a photo that was suitable," he told interviewer Dale L. Walker. "In my case this was better than being there, for the caption would describe trees and brush that I would never be able to identify." Other references provided information on six-shooters and Apaches and the like.

Leonard worked as a freelance copywriter and scripted industrial and educational films for two years, then operated his own advertising agency, 1963–1966.

After his novel *Hombre* was sold for a film in 1966, Leonard, cognizant the saturated western field was on the wane, shifted to crime fiction with *The Big Bounce*. He also adapted his own *The Moonshine War* for film—and for a while made more money writing scripts than books. In the early 1970s, he returned to crime stories, most of them with a Detroit setting, among them *Swag* and *Unknown Man No. 89*. In 1985 his best-selling novel *Glitz* caught the attention of *Newsweek* magazine, which put Leonard on the cover.

Did any single author influence his work? Leonard said in a discussion with Joel M. Lyczak for *The Armchair Detective*, "I was not greatly influenced by any popular Western writers. My inspiration came from Ernest Hemingway, his lean style. I saw *For Whom the Bell Tolls* as a Western, studied closely how he wrote action sequences as well as dialogue."

Leonard said he prefers writing novels to screenplays. The former affords him the isolation to maintain his writing voice. The latter is a group endeavor, often several writers tinkering with dialogue and plot. His works have continued to sell to motion picture producers, however. Recent films *Get Shorty* and *Jackie Brown*, in the author's view, captured his "sound" well. The character of a woman U.S. marshal, Karen Sisco, from the film *Jackie Brown*, which was based on the book *Rum Punch*, appeared in a television series in 2003.

Leonard's characters are not drawn in black-and-white. His heroes have rough edges, his villains have good qualities. "If I do a good-guy cop," the author explained to Tom Nolan for *Mary Higgins Clark Mystery*, "he's not going to be all good; he's going to cut corners if he sees the opportunity. Then there's the good guy with a past, maybe a criminal past. I like that kind of guy because you're not sure which way he's going to go. He can always revert—pull something he's learned before. Chili Palmer's [from *Get Shorty and Be Cool*] probably the best example of that."

"My purpose is to entertain and please myself," Leonard said on his Web site. "I feel that if I am entertained, then there will be enough other readers who will be entertained too."

He stressed, in a piece for the *New York Times* about writing, that he strives to "remain invisible when I'm writing a book," to show, not tell, the story. He employs a researcher and does his own leg work, interviewing cops on the beat and bail bondsmen and convicts on death row.

It takes Leonard about six months to complete a book. He writes every day, in longhand (he began writing with a 29-cent Scripto then switched to a 98-cent pen, he has said), later typing his draft on an IBM electric typewriter; he does not use a word processor. He also does not outline. "I learn where the plot is going at the same time as my lead character," he told Anthony Wilson-Smith of *Maclean's*.

"A *New Yorker* editor used to ask me for stories," Leonard told *Newsweek's* Malcolm Jones, "and I'd say, 'I don't write your kind of stories.' My stories have endings."

Calling Leonard one of today's most innovative writers, Jeff Zaleski in *Publishers Weekly* noted other characteristics of the author's works: "His power arises from his unique style—instantly recognizable, working through narratives set along the margins of society, featuring characters charged with life . . . the stories told in dreamy prose, always flowing from a particular character's point of view . . . and distinguished by dialogue as pitch perfect as any in fiction."

And he has succeeded. In the view of critic George Grella: "His thugs and pimps, convicts and con men, stockbrokers and coke dealers, his ex-Marines, retired cops, and reformed rummies act and, especially, speak as we know (or think we know) they should."

Leonard, with his quirky characters and snappy dialogue, has established a brand for himself that is often imitated but never equaled.

Works by the Author

Fiction

The Bounty Hunters (1953)
The Law at Randado (1954)
Escape from Five Shadows (1956)
Last Stand at Saber River (1959)
Hombre (1961)
The Big Bounce (1969)
The Moonshine War (1969)
Valdez Is Coming (1970)
Forty Lashes Less One (1972)
Fifty-Two Pickup (1974)
Mr. Majestyk (1974)
Swag (1976)
The Hunted (1977)
Unknown Man No. 89 (1977), sequel to *Swag*
The Switch (1978)
Gunsights (1979)
City Primeval (1980)
Gold Coast (1980)
Split Images (1981)
Cat Chaser (1982)
LaBrava (1983)
Stick (1983)
Dutch Treat (1985), omnibus
Double Dutch Treat (1985), omnibus
Glitz (1985)
Bandits (1987)
Touch (1987)
Freaky Deaky (1988)
Killshot (1989)
Get Shorty (1990)

Maximum Bob (1991)
Rum Punch (1992)
Pronto (1993)
Riding the Rap (1995), sequel to *Pronto*
Out of Sight (1996)
Cuba Libre (1998)
Be Cool (1999), sequel to *Get Shorty* (1990)
Pagan Babies (2000)
Fire in the Hole (2001)
Tishomingo Blues (2002)
Mr. Paradise (2003)
A Coyote's in the House (2004)

Collections

Tonto Woman: And Other Western Stories (1998)
When the Women Come out to Dance: And Other Stories (2002)

Anthologies

Roundup: A Treasury of Great Stories by the Western Writers of America (1982)
Arbor House Treasury of Great Western Stories, edited by Bill Pronzini and Martin
    H. Greenberg (1985)
New Black Mask 2, edited by Matthew J. Bruccoli and Richard Layman (1985)
Western Hall of Fame Anthology, edited by Dale L. Walker (1997)
Best American Mystery Stories 2003, edited by Michael Connelly (2003)
McSweeney's Mammoth Treasury of Thrilling Tales, edited by Michael Chabon
    (2003)
Thrilling Tales edited by Michael Chabon (2003)

Contributor

Naked Came the Manatee (1996)

Screenplays

Jesus Saves (1970)
The Moonshine War (1970)
American Flag (1973)
Joe Kidd (1973)
Mr. Majestyk (1974)
High Noon, Part II: The Return of Will Kane (1980)
The Rosary Murders (1982)
Stick (1983)

Motion Pictures, Television Movies, and Television Series Based on the Author's Works

Moment of Vengeance (1956), television
The Tall T (1957)
3:10 to Yuma (1967)
Hombre (1967)
The Big Bounce (1969)
The Moonshine War (1970)
Valdez Is Coming (1971)
Joe Kidd (1972)
Mr. Majestyk (1974)
High Noon, Part II (1980), television
Stick (1985)
Fifty-Two Pick-Up (1986)
Desperado (1987), television
The Rosary Murders (1987)
Glitz (1988), television
Cat Chaser (1989)
Border Shootout (1990), television
Split Images (1992)
Get Shorty (1995)
Elmore Leonard's Gold Coast (1997), television
Jackie Brown (1997), based on *Rum Punch*
Last Stand at Saber River (1997), television
Pronto (1997), television
Touch (1997)
Out of Sight (1998)
Maximum Bob (1998), television series
Karen Sisco (2003–2004), television series based on *Jackie Brown*
Be Cool (2004)
The Big Bounce (2004)

For Further Information

Bianco, Robert. " 'Karen Sisco' should be a sure-fire hit." *USA Today* (October 1, 2003).

Dirda, Michael. Mr. Paradise review. *Washington Post Book World* (January 18, 2004).

Elmore Leonard Web site. *http://www.elmoreleonard.com/home.htm* (viewed June 13, 2003).

Fister, Barbara. "A Full-Time Researcher Helps the Renowned Mystery Writer Keep It Real." *American Libraries* (April 2001).

Grella, George. Elmore Leonard entry, *St. James Guide to Crime & Mystery Writers.* 4th edition, edited by Jay P. Pederson. Detroit: St. James Press, 1996.

Jones, Malcolm. Elmore Leonard interview. *Newsweek* (December 23, 2002).

Leonard, Elmore. "Writers on Writing: Easy on the Adverbs, Exclamation Points and Especially Hooptedoodle." *New York Times* (July 16, 2001).

Lyczak, Joel M. "An Interview With Elmore Leonard." *The Armchair Detective* (summer 1983).

Nolan, Tom. "Elmore Leonard: Regular Guys—and Gals—With a Twist." *Mary Higgins Clark Mystery* (summer–fall 1997).

Peacock, Scot, ed. Elmore Leonard entry, *Contemporary Authors New Revision Series.* Vol. 76. Detroit: Gale Research, 1999.

Sheppard, R. Z. "Neither Tarnished nor Afraid: Hard-boiled fiction continues to influence and entertain." *Time* (June 16, 1986).

Taylor, Charles. "I Can Hear Their Voices." *New York Times Book Review* (December 29, 2002).

Walker, Dale L. "A Conversation with Elmore Leonard." *Louis L'Amour Western Magazine* (May 1994).

Wilson-Smith, Anthony. "The master of crime; Elmore Leonard's 35th novel shows him at the top of his form." *Maclean's* (March 29, 1999).

Zaleski, Jeff. "Dutch in Detroit." *Publishers Weekly* (January 21, 2002).

Robert Ludlum

◆ Suspense ◆ Adventure

New York, New York
1927–2001

◆ *The Bourne Identity*

About the Author and the Author's Writing

"Robert Ludlum [became] an eagerly collected author because of sheer immense popularity," noted Otto Penzler. "His type of action-espionage thriller has influenced so many subsequent writers that the term 'Ludlum-esque' has become an accepted shorthand definition of the sort of novel that he single-handedly made so incredibly popular."

If Ludlum's stories have the sharpness of a dramatic script, and his characters speak with the crispness of actors, it's because the author's first career was as a stage performer and television actor.

Robert Ludlum was born in 1927 in New York City, the son of a businessman and his wife. He grew up in Short Hills, New Jersey. His career choice was evidenced early on; at age sixteen he landed a part in the Broadway show *Junior Miss*. It went on the road, to venues in such places as Detroit. While in that Michigan city, he crossed the border into Canada and tried to enlist in the Canadian Air Force only to be rejected for his youth. He returned home and, when he was old enough, joined the U.S. Marine Corps, seeing action in the South Pacific. He graduated with a bachelor of arts degree from Wesleyan University in 1951. While there he met Mary Ruducha, who became his wife. They had three children.

For eight years, from 1952 to 1959, both Ludlums acted in summer stock and on and off Broadway. Robert Ludlum appeared in some 200 television drama episodes, including *Studio One* and *Kraft Television Theater*. Ludlum also established and produced plays at North Jersey Playhouse in Fort Lee, New Jersey, from 1957 to 1969, then for the next decade produced shows in New York City (including *The Owl and the Pussycat*) and at Playhouse-on-the-Mall in Paramus, New Jersey.

The spark to his writing career was unusual; one day he saw two photographs in a magazine, one a postwar scene in Germany, depicting a man pushing a wheelbarrow that brimmed with paper money—barely enough to buy a loaf of bread. The other was of soldiers wearing new, pressed uniforms. He immediately wondered: If bread cost so much, how did the government get the money to buy clothing for its soldiers? This created the premise for a book, and he began to write *The Scarlatti Inheritance*. It is about a group of European financiers who after World War I put up the cash for Adolf Hitler's charge into the Third Reich. It climbed onto the best-seller list, as did each of the nearly dozen books that followed.

Ludlum theorized it was his storytelling ability that set him apart from other contemporary writers. AshGroveAudioBook.com quoted him from a 1986 interview: "When I came along writing novels in 1971, so much of the previous generation of novelists was very self-indulgent. It was always me, me, me. . . . The craft of storytelling was kind of gone out the window for the sake of the writer himself. And I think I came along at a time when people were sick and tired of that. They wanted stories again. And I'm basically a storyteller."

Ludlum's hallmark is the arena of mega-power, elected or appointed, deserved or stolen. His twisting, turning tales delve into governmental secrets, huge conspiracies, and vile corruption, all well-paced. Yet from such a dark morass rises the Ludlum hero, an idealist, a democrat, an individualist, tolerant yet strong and loyal.

"Ludlum chooses somewhat ordinary men as his heroes to fight against these evils [cabals and enemy governments] . . . ," explains Karen Hinckley in *St. James Guide to Crime & Mystery Writers*. "Although he may be promised help and protection by those he is working for, inevitably he finds himself alone with only his wits to save him."

Never a typist, much less a computer user, Ludlum wrote his manuscripts by hand on a yellow pad. A book typically took three months to research, and as long as fifteen months to write.

As have several fantasy writers, and fellow suspense writer Tom Clancy, Ludlum conceived the idea of a series of books. His series featured an elite, top-secret team of troubleshooters headed by Colonel Jonathan Smith whose mission was to fight crime and corruption at the highest levels. The actual novels have been written by others, including Gayle Lynds, who observed on Mystery Ink, "As a writer of fiction, Robert Ludlum opened many doors for all of us not only politically but literarily. He brought passion, an informed sense of history, and a deep concern for the future to all his works. He was also unafraid to create strong female characters."

When the best-selling author died in 2001, with only one book in a seven-book, eight-figure contract completed with publisher St. Martin's Press, there was never any doubt one nearly completed manuscript, *The Sigma Protocol*, would be finished by editor Keith Kahla. Kahla went on to finish another, three-quarters complete Ludlum manuscript, *The Janson Directive*. There remain two or three more partial books that will likely appear to meet reader demand.

Works by the Author

Fiction

The Scarlatti Inheritance (1971)
The Osterman Weekend (1972)
The Matlock Paper (1973)
The Rhinemann Exchange (1974)
The Gemini Contenders (1976)
The Chancellor Manuscript (1977)
The Holcroft Covenant (1978)

The Parsifal Mosaic (1982)
The Aquitaine Progression (1984)
The Icarus Agenda (1988)
The Road to Omaha (1992)
The Scorpio Illusion (1993)
The Apocalypse Watch (1995)
The Prometheus Deception (2001)
The Sigma Protocol, completed by Keith Kahla (2001)
The Janson Directive, completed by Keith Kahla (2002)
The Tristan Betrayal, completed by Keith Kahla (2003)
The Lazarus Vendetta, completed by Keith Kahla (2004)

Brandon Scofield Novels

The Matarese Circle (1979)
The Matarese Countdown (1995)

Jason Bourne Trilogy

The Bourne Identity (1980)
The Bourne Supremacy (1986)
The Bourne Ultimatum (1990)

Covert-One Series, created by Robert Ludlum

The Hades Factor, by Gayle Lynds (2000)
The Cassandra Compact, by Jonathan Smith (2001)
The Paris Option, by Gayle Lynds (2002)
The Altman Code, by Gayle Lynds (2003)

Written as Michael Shephard

The Road to Gandolfo (1975)

Sherlock Holmes Series

Sherlock Holmes and the Case of Dr. Freud (1985)

Written as Jonathan Ryder

Trevayne (1973), reissued as by Robert Ludlum (1989)
The Cry of the Halidon (1974)

Motion Pictures Based on the Author's Works

The Osterman Weekend (1983)
The Holcroft Covenant (1985)

The Bourne Identity (1988, television; 2002, film)
The Bourne Supremacy (2004)

For Further Information

Greenberg, Martin H., ed. *The Robert Ludlum Companion*. New York: Bantam, 1993.

Hinckley, Karen. Robert Ludlum entry, *St. James Guide to Crime & Mystery Writers*. 4th edition, edited by Jay P. Pederson. Detroit: St. James Press, 1996.

Jones, Donald, and John D. Jorgenson, eds. Robert Ludlum entry, *Contemporary Authors New Revision Series*. Vol. 68. Detroit: Gale Research, 1998.

Lynds, Gayle. "How I Came to Collaborate with Bob Ludlum." *Mystery Scene*, no. 68 (2000).

Lynds, Gayle. "Remembering Robert Ludlum (1927–2001)." Mystery Ink. *http://www.mysteryinkonline.com/ludlumrip.htm* (viewed June 10, 2003).

MacDonald, Gina. *Robert Ludlum: A Critical Companion*. Westport, CT: Greenwood Press, 1997.

Maryles, Daisy. "Ludlum's legacy." *Publishers Weekly* (October 28, 2002).

Penzler, Otto. "Collecting Mystery Fiction: Robert Ludlum." *The Armchair Detective* (fall 1989).

Robert Ludlum bibliography. AuthorsOnTheWeb.com. *http://www.authorsontheweb.com/features/lists/li-ludlum.robert.asp* (viewed June 10, 2003).

Robert Ludlum bibliography. Mystical Unicorn. *http://www.myunicorn.com/bibl5/bibl0505.html* (viewed June 10, 2003).

Robert Ludlum biography. Barnes & Noble. *http://www.barnesandnoble.com/writers/writerdetails.asp?userid=2UHJZHFY29&cid=91353#bio* (viewed June 10, 2003).

Robert Ludlum entry, *Newsmakers*. Vol. 1. Detroit: Gale Group, 2002.

Robert Ludlum interview. Bookreporter.com. *http://www.bookreporter.com/features/020614-ludlum.asp* (viewed June 10, 2003).

Robert Ludlum obituary. AshGroveAudioBook.com. *http//www.ashgroveaudiobook.com/grove/info_authors_ludlum.html* (viewed June 10, 2003).

Robert Ludlum Web site. *http://www.ludlumbooks.com/* (viewed June 10, 2003).

Valby, Karen. "Tome Raiders: Reports of their demise are greatly exaggerated: How dead authors are 'writing' new books." *Entertainment Weekly* (May 4, 2001).

Ed McBain

♦ Mystery ♦ Science fiction

New York, New York
1926

♦ *87th Precinct Series*

Credit: Dragica Hunter.

About the Author and the Author's Writing

Ed McBain began writing police procedural novels in the era of Jack Webb's *Dragnet* and has continued strong through the times of Stephen Boccho's *NYPD Blue*, his prose always seeming as gritty and relevant as those popular television programs. His solid cast of 87th Precinct cops has suffered many loves and losses, bullet wounds, and comic mishaps. The author's pristine, sardonic, deceptively plain prose has proven a winner in more than fifty novels and still counting—a bookshelf that secured for him the Mystery Writers of America Grand Master Award in 1986 and the British Crime Writers Association lifetime achievement Cartier Diamond Dagger award in 1999.

Salvatore Albert Lombino was born in 1926 in Manhattan and grew up in East Harlem and North Bronx. He wanted to be a cartoonist, so he studied art at the Cooper Union. He left to join the U.S. Navy, serving aboard a ship in the Pacific, but just missing World War II action. While in the service, he began submitting short stories to periodicals. Returning home, he studied at Hunter College and graduated Phi Beta Kappa in 1950. He has married three times, has been twice divorced, and has four children. He and his wife, Dragica Dimitrijevic, live in Connecticut.

Out of college, Lombino played jazz piano and sold lobsters to support himself. He continued to sell stories to pulp fiction magazines and digests such as *Manhunt*, and placed two science fiction novels.

Writing recently for the *New York Times*, the author likened the rapid production of short stories to "reaching into a box of chocolates and being surprised by either the soft center or the caramel or the nuts. There were plenty of nuts in crime fiction, but you never knew what kind of story would come out of the machine until it started taking shape on the page."

The author's writing method has not changed all that much over the years; he told Court TV he generally begins with a title, "one that has a lot of resonance, and usually I start with a dead body, or someone about to become a dead body, and I don't know any more than the police know at the beginning of the book, with rare exceptions."

When he took a job as a literary agent, he helped his own career as well as those of other writers. He wrote a novel of his experiences teaching at a vocational school. *The Blackboard Jungle* drew instant attention. (By this time he had already legally changed his name to Evan Hunter, a name he said he "invented out of whole cloth.") The author wrote the screenplay to the classic Alfred Hitchcock picture *The Birds*, among other films. But it is his next byline that has become the most enduring: Ed McBain, which he affixed to a trio of crime novels he contracted to write for Pocket Books, a publisher concerned at the time that its hottest mystery writer, Erle Stanley Gardner, was on the wane.

McBain did a lot of research for those first books, and his accuracy and feeling of authenticity became hallmarks for the 87th Precinct series. McBain has never shunned violence in his books—after all, that's what real-life police see all the time; riding with police, "there'd be a guy lying in the gutter with his brains all over the sidewalk. There'd be a police photographer snapping pictures, people crying or shouting in the background, blood splattered all over the brick wall. . . . As a writer, I felt you couldn't pull punches in this area. If you wanted your books to be authentic, then it was essential to tell the truth," he said in an interview with Barry Forshaw. (McBain said he stopped riding the beat with cops one night in Houston when there was a shootout with a convenience store robber—and McBain was the only one there without a firearm.)

The books are set in Isola, which feels like New York, but with its boroughs skewed to the point where even the author, writing in Mysterious Press's newsletter *Mysterious News*, admitted "the invented city of Isola has evolved over the years from novel to novel, and even I don't know where it's going next." He began inventing the city when he realized he couldn't keep up with all of New York's changes—buildings would be replaced, the police would alter their policies. So he devised Isola.

"To say that McBain invented the police procedural is only technically inaccurate," John C. Carr stated in *The Craft of Crime*. "There were others before him (after all, Sherlock himself is a sort of honorary copper), but the modern police procedural began with McBain, and its present practitioners can now be found not only in the United States and Great Britain but also in France, Scandinavia, Japan, and, of course, South Africa." Carr credits McBain's longevity to one simple thing: his style.

"I respect the craftsmanship and the commitment which has gone into these books . . . ," novelist Stephen King wrote in a *Mystery Scene* tribute issue to McBain, "There is also McBain's wonderful lack of pretension and artifice. . . . he has never used his novels either as a soapbox (as does the endlessly annoying Tom Clancy) or as a psychiatrist's couch (pick your own favorite 'literary writer')."

Critic James McClure marvels, in *Murder Ink*, that McBain dove into writing procedurals without imposing his own sensibility. McBain "accepts things as they are: if the field that engrosses him is knee-high in clichés, so be it. In he goes, as eager and uncompromising as a child, to grasp the thistle that grows between the rows."

Steve Carella is the main character in the books, though he very nearly was killed off in the third in the series (and suffered another close brush in *The Big Bad City*). But McBain often gives the stage over to others of the squad room, including Fat Ollie Weeks, who in the 2003 entry has at last completed the manuscript for his sure-to-be-a-best-seller crime novel.

Reviewer Ted Fitzgerald pointed out in *The Drood Review* the characters Carella, Meyer, Bert Kling, Artie Brown, Eileen Burke, Hal Willis, Captain Peter Byrnes, and others have found affectionate readers: "Shifting his focus among the different detectives from book to book, McBain imbues them with personalities, tragedies, experiences that instill an intimacy with the reader and provide an underlying consistency of character that has allowed them to function successfully across four decades in an irrevocably changed society."

McBain is amused that other writers have copied his format, sometimes a little too religiously. Noting the twenty-four hours before a crime and the twenty-four hours after are critical to cops in reconstructing the victim's actions, and in pursuing the assailant, he told *Armchair Detective's* Charles L. P. Silet, "I labeled this the '24/24' and a guy in one of his books went into this whole business about the 24 hours preceding and the 24 hours after and he said, 'In police jargon, this is known as the 24/24.' Well, I *invented* that! It doesn't *exist* in police work! So I found that very funny." He was less amused by similarities between the television program *Hill Street Blues* and the 87th. The 87th appeared in thirteen episodes of its own American television program in the early 1960s, and also became a popular show on Japanese television.

McBain has sometimes been disparaging of cozies and other mysteries featuring amateur detectives. "I felt that the only people who should be investigating crime were cops," he told Bookreporter.com, "not private eyes, not amateur sleuths. I further felt that a repertory company, so to speak, would give me wider range in what I hoped would be a long-lived series."

The author's novel *Money, Money, Money* was prescient, its subject counterfeiters and terrorists. He was on a promotional tour in September 2001 when he heard of the airplane attacks on New York and Washington, D.C. "I thought, my God, it's really happening, this is what my book is about . . . ," he related to interviewer Mike Stotter. "It was a kind of eerie feeling for me because much of the research on terrorism was done on the Internet. I thought, Jesus, if I can get information on terrorism off the Internet why can't the people who are meant to be protecting us do the same? It wasn't classified material, you know?"

McBain wrote a second series featuring lawyer Matthew Hope, but ended it after thirteen books, he said, because a lawyer is not naturally a crime solver. The last book in that series, *The Last Best Hope*, includes a visit by Carella to help Hope track a missing man.

Does McBain enjoy writing? He said in a Mystery One Bookstore online chat, "No time clock to punch. Lots of interesting people in the room every time I sit down at the computer. And an enduring joy in my work."

Works by the Author

Fiction

Written as Curt Cannon

Deadlier Than the Mail (1953)
Good Deal (1953)
Dead Men Don't Dream (1958)
The Death of Me (1958)
Die Hard (1958)
I'm Cannon—for Hire (1958)
Now Die in It (1958)

Written as Ed McBain

The Big Fix (1952)
Cut Me In (1954)
Runaway Black (1954)
The Spiked Heel (1957)
The April Robin Murders, with Craig Rice (1958)
Even the Wicked (1958)
The Sentries (1965)
Where There Is Smoke (1975)
Guns (1976)
Walk Proud (1979)
Another Part of the City (1986)
Downtown (1989)
Jeopardy (2004)

87th Precinct Series

Cop Hater (1956)
The Mugger (1956)
The Pusher (1956)
The Con Man (1957)
Killer's Choice (1957)
Killer's Payoff (1958)
Killer's Wedge (1958)
Lady Killer (1958)
King's Ransom (1959)
'Til Death (1959)
The Empty Hours (1960)
Give the Boys a Great Big Hand (1960)
The Heckler (1960)
Lady, Lady, I Did It (1960)
See Them Die (1960)
Lets Hear It for the Deaf Man (1961)
Like Love (1962)
Ax (1963)
Ten Plus One (1963)
Doll (1965)
He Who Hesitates (1965)
Eighty Million Eyes (1966)
Fuzz (1968)
Shotgun (1968)
Jigsaw (1970)
Hail, Hail, the Gangs All Here (1971)
Sadie, When She Died (1972)
Hail to the Chief (1973)

Bread (1974)
Blood Relatives (1975)
So Long As You Both Shall Live (1976)
Long Time No See (1977)
Calypso (1979)
Ghosts (1980)
Heat (1981)
Ice (1983)
Lightning (1984)
Eight Black Horses (1985)
Poison (1987)
Tricks (1987)
McBain's Ladies: The Women of the 87th (1988), collection
Lullaby (1989)
McBain's Ladies Too (1989), collection
Vespers (1989)
Widows (1991)
Kiss (1992)
Mischief (1993)
And All Through the House (1994)
Romance (1995)
Nocturne (1997)
The Big Bad City (1998)
The Last Dance (1999)
Money, Money, Money (2001)
Fat Ollie's Book (2003)
The Frumious Bandersnatch (2004)
Hark (2004)

Matthew Hope Series

Goldilocks (1977)
Jack And the Beanstalk (1981)
Rumplestiltskin (1981)
Beauty And the Beast (1982)
Mary, Mary (1982)
Snow White And Rose Red (1985)
Cinderella (1986)
Puss in Boots (1987)
The House That Jack Built (1988)
Three Blind Mice (1990)
There Was a Little Girl (1994)
Gladly the Cross-eyed Bear (1995)
The Last Best Hope (1997)

Collections

The Jungle Kids (1956)
The McBain Brief (1957)
I Like 'em Tough (1958)
The Last Spin (1960)
Happy New Year, Herbie (1963)
The Beheaded (1971)
Seven (1972)
Hot Cars (1982)
Running from Legs and Other Stories (2000)

Editor

Crime Squad (1968)
Downpour (1968)
Homicide Department (1968)
Ticket to Death (1969)
The Best American Mystery Stories 1999 (1999)
Transgressions (forthcoming)

Anthologies

Three Times Three Mystery Omnibus, edited by Howard Haycraft (1964)
Best Detective Stories of the Year—1974, edited by Allen J. Hubin (1974)
Masterpieces of Mystery: Amateurs & Professionals, edited by Ellery Queen (1978)
Tales of Unknown Horror (1978)
Alfred Hitchcock: The Best of Mystery (1980)
Arbor House Treasury of Mystery and Suspense, edited by Bill Pronzini (1981)
The Giant Book of Horror Stories (1981)
Great Tales of Mystery and Suspense (1981)
Top Crime, edited by Josh Pachter (1983)
Baker's Dozen: 13 Short Mystery Novels, edited by Bill Pronzini (1984)
Great Detectives, edited by David Willis McCullough (1984)
Academy Mystery Novellas 2: Police Procedurals, edited by Martin H. Greenberg (1985)
Detecives A to Z, edited by Frand D. McSherry Jr. (1985)
Ethnic Detectives, edited by Bill Pronzini (1985)
Great Tales of Mystery and Suspense, edited by Bill Pronzini (1985)
101 Mystery Stories, edited by Bill Pronzini (1986)
Great Modern Police Stories, edited by Bill Pronzini (1986)
New Black Mask 7, edited by Matthew J. Bruccoli and Richard Layman (1986)
Prime Suspects, edited by Bill Pronzini (1987)
Suspicious Characters, edited by Bill Pronzini (1987)
Uncollected Crimes, edited by Bill Pronzini (1987)

Criminal Elements, edited by Bill Pronzini (1988)
Mammoth Book of Private Eye Stories, edited by Bill Pronzini (1988)
Deadly Doings, edited by Martin H. Greenberg (1989)
Felonious Assaults, edited by Bill Pronzini (1989)
Great American Mystery Stories of the Twentieth Century (1989)
Sport of Crime, edited by Carol-Lynn Rossel Waugh (1989)
Six of the Best Short Novels by Masters of Mystery, edited by Ellery Queen (1989)
The Best of the Best (1994)
Knights of Madness: Further Comic Tales of Fantasy (1998)
Vintage Science Fiction (1999)
World's Finest Mystery and Crime Stories, edited by Edward Gorman (2000)
Mysterious Press Anniversary Anthology: Celebrating 25 Years (2001)
World's Finest Mystery and Crime Stories: Third Annual Collection, edited by Ed Gorman (2002)
Dangerous Women, edited by Otto Penzler (2004)

Written as Evan Hunter

Don't Crowd Me (1952)
The Evil Sleep (1952)
The Blackboard Jungle (1953)
Second Ending (1956)
Strangers When We Meet (1958)
A Matter of Conviction (1959)
Buddwing (1961)
Mothers And Daughters (1961)
The Paper Dragon (1966)
A Horses Head (1967)
Last Summer (1968)
Sons (1969)
Nobody Knew They Were There (1971)
Every Little Crook And Nanny (1972)
Come Winter (1973)
Streets of Gold (1974)
The Chisholms (1976)
Love Dad (1981)
Far from the Sea (1982)
Lizzie (1984)
Criminal Conversation (1994)
Privileged Conversation (1996)
Candyland (2000)

Books for Children

Find the Featured Serpent (1952)
Danger: Dinosaurs! (1953)

The Remarkable Harry (1959)
The Wonderful Button (1961)
Me And Mr. Stenner (1976)

Collections

The Last Spin (1960)
Happy New Year, Herbie (1963)
The Easter Man (1972)
Barking at Butterflies and Other Stories (2000)

Anthologies

Best Detective Stories of the Year 1955 (1955)
Homicide Department, edited by Ed McBain (1968)
Manhattan Mysteries, edited by Bill Pronzini (1987)
Second Black Lizard Anthology of Crime, edited by Ed Gorman (1988)
Best American Mystery Stories 2000, edited by Donald E. Westlake (2000)
Best American Mystery Stories of the Century, edited by Otto Penzler and Tony
    Hillerman (2000)
World's Finest Mystery and Crime Stories, edited by Edward Gorman (2000)

Stage Plays

The Easter Man (1964)
The Conjuror (1969)
Stalemate (1975)

Screenplays

Strangers When We Meet (1960), based on his own novel
The Birds (1963), based on a Daphne du Maurier short story
Fuzz (1972), based on his own novel
Walk Proud (1979), based on his own novel
The Chisholms (1979–1980)
The Legend of Walks Far Woman (1980)
Dream West (1986)

Nonfiction

Me and Hitch, written as Ezra Hannon (1997)
Doors, written as Hunt Collins (1975)
Tomorrow's World (1956)
Tomorrow and Tomorrow (1957)
Sucker (1958)

Written as Richard Marsten

Rocket to Luna (1952)
Murder in the Navy (1955)
Vanishing Ladies (1957)
Big Man (1959)

Motion Pictures and Television Films Based on the Author's Works

The Blackboard Jungle (1955)
Cop Hater (1958)
The Muggers (1958)
The Pusher (1960)
The Young Savages (1961), based on *A Matter of Conviction*
87th Precinct (1961–1962), NBC television series
High and Low (1963), based on *King's Ransom*
Mr. Buddwing (1967), based on *Buddwing*
Last Summer (1969)
Le Cri du cormoran le soir au-dessus des jonques (1971), based on *A Horse's Head*
Sans Mobile apparent (1971), based on *Ten Plus One*
Every Little Crook and Nanny (1972)
Wagamachi (1992–1998), Japanese television series based on 87th Precinct novels

For Further Information

Block, Lawrence. "Evan Hunter was my Hero." *Mystery Scene*, no. 70 (2001).

Campbell, Colin. "Evan Hunter Is a Serious Novelist, But Ed McBain Sells a Lot More Books." *People* (December 19, 1977).

Carr, John C. *The Craft of Crime: Conversations with Crime Writers*. Boston: Houghton Mifflin, 1983.

Dove, George N. Ed McBain entry, *St. James Guide to Crime & Mystery Writers*. 4th edition, edited by Jay P. Pederson. Detroit: St. James Press, 1996.

Ed McBain entry, *Authors and Artists for Young Adults*. Vol. 39. Detroit: Gale Group, 2001.

Ed McBain interview. Bookreporter.com. *http://www.bookreporter.com/authors/au-mcbain-ed.asp* (viewed June 27, 2003).

Ed McBain Web site. *http://www.edmcbain.com* (viewed June 27, 2003).

Ed McBain/Evan Hunter interview. Mystery One Bookstore. *http://www.mysteryone.com/EdMcBainInterview.htm* (viewed June 27, 2003).

"Evan Hunter/Ed McBain: The author discusses his 87th Precinct novels . . . and more." Court TV (May 29, 2001). *http://www.courttv.com/talk/chat_transcripts/ 2001/0529hunter.html* (viewed June 27, 2003).

Fitzgerald, Ted. "Steve Carella's turning forty." *Drood Review* (January/February 1999).

Forshaw, Barry. "Interviews: Ed McBain." Crime Time. *http://www.crimetime.co.uk/ interviews/edmcbain.html* (viewed June 27, 2003).

Gorman, Ed. "Evan Hunter/Ed McBain." *Mystery Scene*, no. 70 (2001).

Hamill, Pete. "The Poet of Pulp." *Mystery Scene*, no. 70 (2001).

Healy, Jeremiah. "Evan Hunter as Ed McBain." *Mystery Scene*, no. 70 (2001).

Hunter, Evan. E-mail to the author (January 15, 2004).

Jakes, John. "My Pal Evan." *Mystery Scene*, no. 70 (2001).

Jones, Daniel, and John D. Jorgenson, eds. Evan Hunter entry, *Contemporary Authors New Revision Series*. Vol. 62. Detroit: Gale Research, 1998.

Kaminsky, Stuart M. "On Evan Hunter and Ed McBain." *Mystery Scene*, no. 70 (2001).

King, Stephen. "On Ed McBain." *Mystery Scene*, no. 70 (2001).

Leitch, Thomas. "The Importance of Ed McBain." *Mystery Scene*, no. 70 (2001).

McBain, Ed. "Creating the 87th." *Mystery Scene*, no. 70 (2001).

McBain, Ed. "Ed McBain in Another Part of the City." *Mysterious News* (April 1986).

McBain, Ed. "She Was Blond. She Was in Trouble. And She Paid 3 Cents a Word." *New York Times* (March 29, 1999).

McClure, James. "Carella of the 87th." *Murder Ink: The Mystery Reader's Companion*, edited by Dilys Winn. New York: Workman Publishing, 1977.

Silet, Charles L. P. "The 87th Precinct And Beyond: Interview With Ed McBain." *Armchair Detective* (fall 1994).

Silet, Charles L. P. "Writing for Hitch: An Interview with Ed McBain." Mysterynet .com. *http://www.mysterynet.com/hitchcock/mcbain.shmtl* (viewed June 27, 2003).

Stasio, Marilyn. "Crime" (*Frumious Bandersnatch* review). *New York Times Book Review* (December 28, 2003).

Stotter, Mike. "Ed McBain." Magazine for Crime & Mystery. *http://www.shotsmag .co.uk/mcbain.htm* (viewed June 27, 2003).

"Wanted Evan Hunter aka Ed McBain." Ed McBain Web site. *http://www.edmcbain.com/eljefe/bio.asp* (viewed June 27, 2003).

"Wassup, McBain? Ed serves up sardonic thriller about rap diva's kidnapping." New York *Daily News* (January 11, 2004).

Westlake, Donald E. "Uprising." *Mystery Scene*, no. 70 (2001).

Anne McCaffrey

◆ Fantasy ◆ Science fiction

Cambridge, Massachusetts
1926

◆ *Pern Series*

Courtesy of Virginia Kidd
Agency. Credit: Christine Coneri.

About the Author and the Author's Writing

When she first began writing science fiction, Anne McCaffrey ran into an attitude: The science fiction genre was seen as one for males. But many women watched the *Star Trek* television series and they sought books of similar themes. McCaffrey was there and waiting.

"I never had trouble with editors and publishers," she said in an ssfworld.com interview. "I had trouble getting male readers to believe I was serious, and a good enough writer to interest them."

McCaffrey considers herself first and foremost a storyteller. She expanded in *Literature for Today's Young Adults*, "[I] unconsciously reflect in my stories the pressures, the problems, and the ambiance which beset me and our world while I am writing a story." *The Ship Who Sang* is one of the author's favorite books, as it afforded her an opportunity to deal in print with the premature death of her father in 1963.

McCaffrey was born in Cambridge, Massachusetts, in 1926, the daughter of a city administrator and U.S. Army colonel and of a real estate agent. She attended high schools in Staunton, Virginia, and Montclair, New Jersey. In 1947, she earned a bachelor of arts degree cum laude in Slavonic languages and literature from Radcliffe College. She did graduate study in meteorology at the University of City of Dublin. She studied voice for nine years and appeared in a summer music circus in New Jersey, sparking an interest in the stage direction of opera. Divorced from H. Wright Johnson, she has three children.

McCaffery's first book, *Restoree*, takes a jab at the portrayal of women in science fiction. Her "concern with women's roles and struggles in Pern's society is most vividly realized in *Dragonsong* (1976) and *Dragon Singer* (1977), which center on Mennolly, a young woman whose ambition to be a harper runs counter to Pern's social norm for women," said Linda Mainero in *American Women Writers*. "Mennolly achieves her goals through perseverance, courage and quick wit."

McCaffrey is best known for her fantasy novels featuring the dragonriders of Pern. The small planet Pern had an erratic neighboring red star that spun off spore life "which proliferated at an incredible rate on the Red Star's wild surface, spun off into space and bridged the gap to Pern. The spores fell as thin threads on the temperate, hospitable planet, and devoured anything organic in their way, seeking to establish burrows in Pern's warm earth from which to set out more voracious Threads," the author explained in *Dragonsong*.

The Thread took a toll on crops and vegetation, and on people. To fight them, inhabitants bred a specialized dragon, which moved by teleportation and which, after consuming phosphine-bearing rock, emitted a flaming gas that destroyed the Threads in air. There developed six Weyrs, each with its own dragons and fighters, for the protection of Pern. The rest of the population lived in cavernous Holds, and tithed to support the Weyrs. As time stretched between arrivals of Thread, Pern inhabitants forgot their danger, until eventually, there was only a single Weyr left on the plant. When the red star once again spun close enough to send its Thread to Pern, dragon riders F'lar and his half brother F'nor retrieved the last golden egg of a dying queen dragon and began to rally their scant and long-forgotten resources.

The idea for the books, McCaffrey said, came from the simple question posed one day as she sat in her living room in Long Island: What if dragons were the good guys? She shaped her thoughts into a short story, "Weyr Search," and was pleased with it. "Rather wonderful to have an intelligent partner that loves you unconditionally," she said on her Web site of the dragonriders. "Who wouldn't like a forty-foot telepathic dragon as their best friend?" She sold the story to John Campbell for *Analog*, then expanded it to the first Pern novel.

When McCaffrey was a girl, her mother read her the Rudyard Kipling Mowgli stories. "When I was about ten, my mother also suggested I read A. Merritt's *The Ship of Ishtar*, then a serial in *Argosy* magazine," she said in *Books I Read When I Was Young*. "I devoured any of Mr. Merritt's books I could find. You might say that between Kipling and Merritt the groundwork was laid for my fascination with science fiction and science fantasy. When she was fourteen, she discovered Austin Tappan Wright's *Islandia*, and it greatly influenced her later writing.

Before her success as a short story crafter and novelist, McCaffrey worked as a writer and layout designer for Liberty Music Shops in New York City, a copywriter, and a secretary for Helena Rubinstein. She sold her first story, barely 1,000 words, to Sam Moskowitz for *Science Fiction Plus* in 1952. "My mother was thrilled and my father said, 'Hmph!' That's all, but I wasn't unencouraged. I had got my hundred dollars for a short story that I had written, and I would continue to try and write and get more money," she told interviewer Anne Gay.

McCaffrey kept at her writing, but didn't sell another story for five years. That was "Lady in the Tower," appearing in *Magazine of Fantasy and Science Fiction* in 1959. The story and a sequel, "A Meeting of Minds," involved parapsychology and romance.

McCaffrey is adept at shorter fiction forms, according to Mary Turzillo Brizzi in *Twentieth-Century Science Fiction Writers*. "In all, her style has a neo-classic flavor in wit, sarcasm, and clarity. She is at her strongest depicting love and bonding, between lovers, family members, humans and animals, humans and aliens. Her flight imagery—dragons, Pegasus, spaceship—is compelling. With these, her characterization and world-building make her a significant science-fiction writer."

"I've accomplished a few firsts in my life," the author said in an AOL Book Report interview. "I was the first in my field, a bona fide science-fiction writer, to get on the *New York Times* bestseller list." She acknowledges women science fiction writers have made some gains since she first published *Restoree*, noting three-fifths the membership of Science Fiction Writers of America is female.

In recent years the author has teamed with other writers—Mercedes Lackey, Elizabeth Ann Scarborough, Jody Lynn Nye, Margaret Ball, S. M. Stirling, and her son Todd—to give her a break and to give greater exposure to those midlist writers.

McCaffrey now lives in Ireland in a home she calls Dragonhold-Underhill. She maintains a private livery stable, though she does not ride in competition. "Ireland is a relaxed country," McCaffrey told interviewer Jessica Palmer. "It's a peaceful place and quiet. I'm allowed my own space. If a fan wants to come visit me, he's got to travel thousands of miles to do it."

Works by the Author

Fiction

Restoree (1967)
The Mark of Merlin (1971)
The Ring of Fear (1971)
The Kilternan Legacy (1975)
The Coelura (1983)
Stitch in Snow (1984)
The Girl Who Heard Dragons (1985)
Habit is an Old Horse (1986)
To Ride Pegasus (1986)
The Year of the Lucy (1986)
The Lady: A Tale of Ireland (1987), retitled *The Carradyne Touch* (1988)
Three Gothic Novels—Omnibus: Ring of Fear, Mark of Merlin, The Kilternan Legacy (1990)
Generation Warriors, with Elizabeth Moon (1991)
Three Women (1992)
Treaty Planet, with Jody Lynn Nye (1994)
An Exchange of Gifts (1995)
Black Horses for the King (1996)
No One Noticed the Cat (1996)
If Wishes Were Horses (1998)
Nimisha's Ship (1998)
On Dragonwings (2003)

Acorna Series

Acorna: The Unicorn Girl, with Margaret Ball (1997)
Acorna's Quest, with Margaret Ball (1998)
Acorna's People, with Elizabeth Ann Scarborough (1999)
Acorna's World, with Elizabeth Ann Scarborough (2000)

Acorna's Search, with Elizabeth Ann Scarborough (2001)
Acorna's Rebels, with Elizabeth Ann Scarborough (2003)
Acorna's Triumph, with Elizabeth Ann Scarborough (2004)
First Warning: Acorna's Children, with Elizabeth Ann Scarborough (2005)

Catteni Series

Freedom's Landing (1995)
Freedom's Choice (1997)
Freedom's Challenge (1998)
Freedom's Ransom (2002)

Crystal Singer Series

Crystal Singer (1981)
Killashandra (1985)
Crystal Line (1992)
Crystal Singer Trilogy (1996), omnibus

Dinosaur Planet Series

Dinosaur Planet (1978)
Dinosaur Planet Survivors (1984)
The Ireta Adventure (1985), includes the first two books; also titled *The Mystery of Ireta*
Dinosaur Planet Omnibus (2001)

Doona Series

Decision at Doona (1969)
Crisis on Doona, with Jody Lynn Nye (1992)
Treaty at Doona, with Jody Lynn Nye (1994)

Dragonriders of Pern Series

Dragonflight (1968)
Dragonquest:(1971)
The White Dragon (1978)
The Dragonriders of Pern (1988), includes first three books
Dragoneye (1996)
Dragon's Kin, with Todd McCaffrey (2004)

Harper Hall of Pern Series

Dragonsong (1976)
Dragonsinger (1977)

Dragondrums (1978)
The Harper Hall of Pern (1979), includes first three books
Harper Hall Trilogy (1983), includes first three books
Dragonharper—Crossroads Adventure in the World of Anne McCaffrey's Pern, by Jody Lynn Nye (1987)
Dragonfire—Crossroads Adventure in the World of Anne McCaffrey's Pern, by Jody Lynn Nye (1988)

Pegasus Series

To Ride Pegasus (1973)
Pegasus in Flight (1990)
Pegasus in Space (2000)

Petaybee Series, with Elizabeth Scarborough

Power Lines (1994)
Powers That Be (1994)
Power Play (1995)
The Petaybee Trilogy (2002), omnibus

Planet Pirates Series

The Death of Sleep, with Jody Lynn Nye (1990)
Sassinak, with Elizabeth Moon (1990)
Generation Warriors, with Elizabeth Moon (1991)
The Planet Pirates, with Elizabeth Moon and Jody Lynn Nye (1993)

Renegades of Pern Series

The Dragonlover's Guide to Pern, with Jody Lynn Nye (1989)
Get Off the Unicorn (1977), short stories
Moreta: Dragonlady of Pern (1983)
Nerilka's Story (1986)
Dragonsdawn (1988)
The People of Pern, with Robin Wood (1988)
The Renegades of Pern (1989)
All the Weyrs of Pern (1991)
Rescue Run (1991)
The Chronicles of Pern: First Fall (1993), short stories
Dragonflight Graphic Novel (1993)
The Dolphin's Bell (1994)
The Dolphins of Pern (1994)
Red Star Rising: Second Chronicles of Pern (1996)

The Masterharper of Pern (1997)
The Skies of Pern (2001)
Dragon's Kin, with Todd McCaffrey (2004)

The Ship Who Sang Series

The Ship Who Sang (1969)
PartnerShip, with Margaret Ball (1992)
The Ship Who Searched, with Mercedes Lackey (1992)
The City Who Fought, with S. M. Stirling (1993)
The Ship Who Won, with Jody Lynn Nye (1994)
The Ship Errant, with Jody Lynn Nye (1996)
The Ship Avenged, with S. M. Stirling (1997)
The Ship Who Saved the Worlds, with Jody Lynn Nye (2003)
The City and the Ship, with S. M. Stirling (2004)

The Tower and Hive Series

The Rowan (1990)
Damia (1991)
Damia's Children (1993)
Lyon's Pride (1994)
The Tower and the Hive (1999)

Collections

A Time When: Being a Tale of Young Lord Jaxom, His White Dragon, Ruth, and Various Fire-Lizards (1975)
The Worlds of Anne McCaffrey (1981)
Habit Is an Old Horse (1984)
The Girl Who Heard Dragons (1994)
A Gift of Dragons (2002)

Chapbooks

Duty Calls (1988)

Editor

Alchemy and Academe (1970)
Cooking Out of This World (1973)
Serve It Forth: Cooking with Anne McCaffrey, with John Betancourt (1996)
Space Opera, with Elizabeth Scarborough (1996)

Anthologies

The Hugo Winners 1968–1970 (1962)
Nebula Award Stories 3 (1967)
Nebula Award Stories 4 (1968)
Crime Prevention in the 30th Century (1969)
The Disappearing Future (1970)
Infinity One (1970)
The Many Worlds of Science Fiction (1971)
Demon Kind (1973)
Future Quest (1973)
Omega (1973)
Science Fiction Tales (1973)
Ten Tomorrows (1973)
Continuum (1974)
Women of Wonder (1974)
Future Love (1977)
Cassandra Rising (1978)
The Great Science Fiction Series (1980)
Visitors' Book (1980)
The Best of Randall Garrett (1982)
David Copperfield's Beyond Imagination (1982)
Top Fantasy (1984)
Top Science Fiction (1984)
Visions of Wonder (1985)
Legends (1986)
Time Wars (1986)
Animal Brigade 3000 (1987)
New Destinies 3 (1989)
Confederacy of the Dead (1990)
The Ascent of Wonder (1994)
A Dragon-Lover's Treasury of the Fantastic, edited by Margaret Weis (1994)
New Eves: Science Fiction About the Extraordinary Women of Today and Tomorrow (1994)
Great Writers and Kids Write Spooky Stories (1995)
The Penguin Book of Modern Fantasy by Women (1995)
The Ultimate Alien (1995)
Don't Forget Your Spacesuit, Dear (1996)
Space Opera (1996)
Dancing with the Dark (1997)
Dragons: The Greatest Stories (1997)
Far Horizons (1999)
Fathers & Daughters: Celebrating the Gift of Love With 12 New Stories, edited by Jill Morgan (2000)

Legends: Short Novels by the Masters of Modern Fantasy, volume 1, edited by Robert
   Silverberg (1999)
Legends II, edited by Robert Silverberg (2003)

Television Series Based on the Author's Work

Pern (announced)

For Further Information

Anne McCaffrey interview. AOL Book Report (April 6, 1997). *http://www
   .randomhouse.com/delrey/pern/amcc/TBRtranscript.html* (viewed June 2, 2003).

Anne McCaffrey interview. sffworld.com. *http://www.sffworld.com/authors/m/
   mccaffrey_anne/interviews/200005.html* (viewed June 2, 2003).

Anne McCaffrey Web site. *http://www.annemccafrey.org/* (viewed June 2, 2003).

Arbur, Rosemarie. *Leigh Brackett, Marion Zimmer Bradley and Anne McCaffrey:
   Primary and Secondary Bibliography*. New York: G. K. Hall, 1982.

Benson, Gordon, and Phil Stephensen-Payne. *Anne McCaffrey*. San Bernardino, CA:
   Borgo Press, 1990.

Brizzi, Mary T. *Anne McCaffrey: A Reader's Guide*. Westfinn, OR: Starmont, 1986.

Brizzi, Mary Turzillo. "Anne McCaffrey." In *Twentieth-Century Science-Fiction
   Writers*. 3rd edition, edited by Noelle Watson and Paul E. Schellinger. Chicago:
   St. James Press, 1991.

Cassada, Jackie. *Acorna's Rebels* review. *Library Journal* (February 15, 2003).

Chapman, Jeff, and John D. Jorgenson, eds. Anne McCaffrey entry, *Contemporary
   Authors New Revision Series*. Vol. 55. Detroit: Gale Research, 1997.

Cullinan, Bernice, and M. Jerry Weiss, eds. *Books I Read When I Was Young: The Favorite Books of Famous People*. New York: Avon, 1980.

Donelson, Kenneth L., and Alleen Pace Nilsen. *Literature For Today's Young Adults*.
   Glenview, IL. Scott, Foresman, 1980.

Gay, Anne. "Flights of Fancy." Tiscali Entertainment. *http://www.tiscali.co.uk/
   entertainment/scifi/interviews/anne_mccaffrey.html* (viewed June 2, 2003).

Hargreaves, Mathew D. *Anne Inez McCaffrey, Forty Years of Publishing, An International Bibliography*. Seattle, WA: Hargreaves, 1992.

Mainero, Lina, ed. *American Women Writers from Colonial Times to the Present:
   A Critical Reference Guide*, vol. 3. New York: Ungar, 1981.

McCaffrey, Anne. "Building a World: Notes on the Invention of Pern." Random House. *http://www.randomhouse.com/delrey/pern/amcc/article.html* (viewed June 2, 2003).

Palmer, Jessica. "Dragons and Beyond." *Million* (May–June 1991).

Roberts, Robin. *Anne McCaffrey: A Critical Companion*. Westport, CT: Greenwood Press, 1996.

World of Pern Web page. Random House. *http://www.randomhouse.com/delrey/pern/amcc/bio.html* (viewed June 2, 2003).

Colleen McCullough

◆   Historical

Wellington, Australia
1937

◆   *The Thorn Birds*

About the Author and the Author's Writing

Colleen McCullough lives on Norfolk Island in the South Pacific, where half of the population of 1,700 is descended from H.M.S. *Bounty* mutineers and the Tahitian women they married. It is about 900 miles from her native Australia, and the remote island has provided refuge in the years following publication of her novel *The Thorn Birds*.

McCullough was born in Wellington, New South Wales, in 1937, to an Irish father and New Zealander mother. She grew up largely in Sydney, though the family for a time lived in the arid Outback. McCullough was a voracious reader as a girl, and she did well in her studies, hoping she might become a doctor. She attended Holy Cross College and the University of Sydney, where she learned she had a soap-caused allergy that would make it impossible to ever scrub for surgery. So she taught school, supervised a library, and drove a bus in the Outback. She worked as a journalist then became a researcher in neurophysiology in Sydney. In 1967, she moved to Connecticut to do the same work for the Yale University School of Internal Medicine.

McCullough began writing while living in New England, though she eventually discarded those manuscripts. She methodically crafted a novel in the teary vein of Erich Segal's *Love Story*, circulated it to publishers, received only rejections, then engaged the services of agent Frieda Fishbein, who quickly peddled the book *Tim* to Harper & Row. The story of a romance between an older woman and a developmentally disabled young man was released in 1974 and was eventually made into a motion picture.

After earning $50,000 from that book, McCullough decided to write a multigenerational work three times as long, in hopes of making three times the money. *The Thorn Birds*, published in 1977, begins by chronicling the lives, loves, and losses of Meggie Cleary, who with her family relocates to remote Australia when her father becomes manager of the sheep station Drogheda. She develops a crush on a handsome priest, Father Ralph, who has been banished by church hierarchy.

The book sold spectacularly worldwide, and made the headlines when paperback rights sold for $1.9 million, a record at the time. It was transformed into a ten-hour miniseries for American television, though the result repulsed the author, as did a subsequent *The Thorn Birds: The Missing Years* in 1996. The sudden fame prompted the author's removal into island isolation, where she continued to write. In 1984 she married Ric Robinson, a housepainter.

McCullough has written a cookbook, a fairy tale, a whodunit, and a biography of Victoria Cross recipient Sir Roden Cutler. She wrote a novel titled *An Indecent Obsession*, she said in an online chat, "because I was interested in exploring a situation wherein one woman was in control of a group of men." The South Pacific romance, set near the end of World War II, is about Australian nurse Sister Honour Langtry's romantic involvement with two of her male patients, the guilt-ridden Neil and the angry Michael.

"Colleen McCullough has created fully drawn and believable characters, and she keeps her plot moving along nicely," said William A. Nolen in *Washington Post Book World*, in his review of the book.

The most ambitious of McCullough's recent endeavors is a series of novels set in ancient Rome, something she dreamed of doing for three decades. She hired researcher Sheelah Hidden and outlined her project. Her longtime publisher backed away, so the author signed on with a new publisher, Morrow. The first book in the sequence, *The First Man in Rome*, came out in 1990.

"Exhaustively researched for historical accuracy and humanized through a plethora of small, telling details that bring Roman politics and society vividly to life, this is a complex story that requires respectful attention," Sybil Steinberg wrote in *Publishers Weekly*.

In 2001, McCullough diverged to retell the story of Helen and Paris in *The Song of Troy*, a book that *Publishers Weekly* found "a laudable interpretation of the epic, rendered with both sweep and intimacy."

The author concluded her Rome sequence with *The October Horse* in 2002. Another *Publishers Weekly* reviewer noted that "the skillfulness of McCullough's portrait of Octavian will make readers wish more novels were in the offing. Introduced as a guarded, talented youth, he is transformed by Caesar's assassination into a merciless, retributive man—or perhaps he simply shows his true colors."

In 2003, *The Touch*, another late-19th-century Australian saga, centered on Alexander Kinross; his child bride Elizabeth, who hates him; and Ruby, the madam who loves him.

McCullough has a mystery novel in the works, but finds her ability to write curtailed by progressive hemorrhagic macular degeneration, which has already taken the sight in one eye.

"So much of me is tied up in writing and reading. It's my life. It's what I love most to do," she told an AFP reporter in June 2004.

Works by the Author

Fiction

Tim (1974)
The Thorn Birds (1977)
An Indecent Obsession (1981)
A Creed for the Third Millennium (1985)
The Ladies of Missalonghi (1987)

Three Complete Novels (1999), includes *Tim, An Indecent Obsession*, and *The Ladies of Missalonghi*
Morgan's Run (2000)
The Song of Troy (1998)
The Touch (2003)

Masters of Rome Series

The First Man in Rome (1990)
The Grass Crown (1991)
Fortune's Favorites (1993)
Caesar's Women (1996)
Caesar; Let the Dice Fly (1997)
The October Horse (2002)

Nonfiction

An Australian Cookbook (1982)
Roden Cutler, V.C. (1998)

Motion Pictures or Television Miniseries Based on the Author's Work

Tim (1981)
The Thorn Birds (1983)
An Indecent Obsession (1985)
The Thorn Birds: The Missing Years (1996)

For Further Information

Chang, Suna. "She plays on words: 'Thorn Birds' author Colleen McCullough." *Entertainment Weekly* (February 16, 1996).

Colleen McCullough chat. Nineman.com. *http://aca.ninemsn.com/au/stories/114.asp* (viewed July 7, 2003).

Colleen McCullough entry, *Authors and Artists for Young Adults*. Vol. 36. Detroit: Gale Group, 2000.

Colleen McCullough entry, *Contemporary Authors Online*. Detroit: Gale, 2002.

Dam, Julie K.L., and John Hannah. "Thorny Bird: Australian author Colleen McCullough lives large, says what she thinks and doesn't sweat the consequences." *People Weekly* (November 27, 2000).

DeMarr, Mary Jean. *Colleen McCullough: A Critical Companion*. Westport, CT: Greenwood Publishing, 1996.

Lipton, Michael A. "The Curse of Colleen." *People Weekly* (January 29, 1996).

Nolen, William A. An Indecent Obsession review. *Washington Post Book World* (October 11, 1981).

October Horse review. *Publishers Weekly* (November 4, 2002).

Patteson, Jean. *Touch* review, *Sunday Republican*. Waterbury, CT (January 18, 2004).

Song of Troy review. *Publishers Weekly* (July 16, 2001).

Steinberg, Sybil. "Colleen McCullough: the indefatigable Australian author has embarked on a five-volume series set in ancient Rome." *Publishers Weekly* (September 14, 1990).

"Thorn Birds Author Colleen McCullough Going Blind." Vision Connection. *http://www.visionconnection.org/Content/News/Community/TheThornBirdsAuthor ColleenMcCulloughGoingBlind.htm?cookie%5Ftest=1* (viewed June 10, 2004).

Terry McMillan

◆　Women's fiction

Port Huron, Michigan
1951

◆　*Waiting to Exhale*

About the Author and the Author's Writing

Terry McMillan made believers out of publishers who doubted there was an audience for a fresh, vibrant black voice in literature. Her third novel, *Waiting to Exhale*, was months on the *New York Times* best-seller list, and when it was made into a motion picture, it was a major event.

Terry McMillan was born in 1951 in Port Huron, Michigan, the oldest of five children. Her parents divorced when she was thirteen and her father, a sanitation worker and an abusive alcoholic, died three years later. McMillan attended public schools, but it was only when she took a job shelving books at a local library that she encountered the magic of literature—she was in awe of women writers such as the Bronte sisters and Louisa May Alcott, and of black writers including James Baldwin and Langston Hughes. Reading Ring Lardner, she came to realize the humor to be found in tragedy.

In 1979, McMillan received a bachelor of arts degree in journalism from the University of California at Berkeley. During her college years, her first short story, "The End," was published. Moving to New York, she studied film at Columbia University and earned her master of fine arts degree. She worked as a word processor and took a workshop at the Harlem Writers Guild. In the early 1980s, she had a child and struggled with alcohol and drug abuse.

McMillan worked hard to promote her first novel, *Mama*, published in 1987. "[C]ritics praised McMillan for her realistic detail and powerful characterization of her heroine, Mildred Peacock," noted Voices from the Gaps. "They loved Mildred's energy and zest for life."

Added *Contemporary Novelists*, "*Mama* is at once a response to the myth of the black welfare queen that gained significant cultural currency in the 1980s, and the earlier image of a castrating black woman popularized by the now infamous Moynihan Report. The character of Mildred provides a counter-image to these stereotypes: she is complex, dignified, and committed to raising her children to be capable, responsible adults."

Two years later, McMillan followed the novel of a strong woman struggling to keep her family together with *Disappearing Acts*. Her son's father took exception to the way he was portrayed in the book and sued McMillan for slander. His suit was dismissed in court. Nevertheless, McMillan has frequently been criticized for her negative depictions of black men.

"I do extensive profiles of my characters before I write the stories," the author told *Essence* in 2001. "I ask my characters questions: Do you lie? Do you have a secret? If so, what is it? Do you pay your bills on time? If you could change something about yourself, what would it be, and why?"

Of decisions made by men and women, McMillan said in a Bookbrowse.com interview, "[H]ow many of us are actually 'smart' when it comes to relationships? We do what we want to and suffer the consequences later."

Critic Andrew B. Presler noted the author's close examination of cultural expectations and relationships, which cross professional, gender, and family lines: "*Mama* depicts an acceptance by an intellectual daughter of her flawed mother. *Disappearing Acts* follows a love affair between a professional, responsible woman and an uneducated tradesman. *Waiting to Exhale* builds an ambitious collage of images from all three types of relationships."

McMillan was an instructor at the University of Wyoming in Laramie from 1987 to 1990, then became a professor at the University of Arizona in Tucson for two years. In 1988, she held a National Endowment for the Arts fellowship. She edited an anthology of black fiction, *Breaking Ice*, in 1990, the same year she was a judge for the National Book Award for fiction. She now lives in Danville, California.

Waiting to Exhale energized the black reading community, not only establishing McMillan's career, but, it was widely believed, also opening doors for other ethnic writers. McMillan disputes this latter categorization as simply good marketing; there were many active ethnic writers before she came on the scene, she asserts.

The story of four middle-class, smart, hip women, *Waiting to Exhale* "told the world that not all black people live in ghettos," said BBC World Service. "Displaying a level of determination and ambition, McMillan's characters could have been created in the author's own image. . . . Depicting sexy, black determined women is unsurprisingly McMillan's forte as she openly admits that she enjoys writing about her own 'evolution.'"

The author intended to follow *Exhale* with *A Day Late and a Dollar Short*, a depiction of a loving mother. But in 1993 her own mother, to whom she felt extremely close, died following an asthma attack. On top of this, one of McMillan's best friends, novelist Doris Jean Austin, died of cancer the following year. Devastated, the grieving McMillan traveled to Jamaica to find healing.

She next completed the largely autobiographical *How Stella got Her Groove Back*, in which the main character is a professional woman in her forties, raising a son as a single parent, who travels to Jamaica and meets and falls in love with a younger man—just as McMillan did, marrying a twenty-four-year-old hotel management student named Jonathan Plummer. This novel was longer in gestation than McMillan was accustomed to, the writing disrupted by personal issues.

"I am a fast writer," she said on her PenguinPutnam Web page. "My drafts usually come quickly, in a rush. *Mama* took about a month; *Disappearing Acts*, two weeks; *Exhale*, a few months. These are just rough drafts, the versions you don't dare show a soul. The rewriting and revisions took close to a year. *A Day Late* took its own title quite seriously, but the story was important to me and I had to dredge up all the courage I had to finish it."

A Day Late and a Dollar Short, which came out in 2001, examines the dynamics of family life through all generations—children are still children to their parents even as the children age through the years. "I've come to realize that people don't tell everything," the author told interviewer Esther Iverem. "As much as you love your siblings, there are things you just don't share. You think, this is my sister or brother, they tell me everything, and then you realize they don't tell you everything. And maybe they shouldn't. Maybe some things shouldn't be shared."

"McMillan writes intimately, sometimes mockingly, about a middleclass black experience in which white America is largely irrelevant," summarizes *Newsweek's* John Leland. "Her best work captures the foibles and rhythms around her in lusty vernacular."

In an article in *The Writer* McMillan stated why she loves her craft: "I write because the world is an imperfect place, and we behave in an imperfect manner. I want to understand why it's so hard to be good, honest, loving, caring, thoughtful and generous. Writing is about the only way (besides praying) that allows me to be compassionate toward folks who, in real life, I'm probably not that sympathetic toward. I want to understand myself and others better, so what better way than to pretend to be them?"

Works by the Author

Fiction

Mama (1987)
Disappearing Acts (1989)
Waiting to Exhale (1992)
How Stella got Her Groove Back (1996)
A Day Late and a Dollar Short (2001)

Screenplays

Waiting to Exhale, with Ronald Bass (1996)

Editor

Breaking Ice: An Anthology of Contemporary African-American Fiction (1990)

Nonfiction

Five for Five: The Films of Spike Lee, with others (1991)

Motion Pictures Based on the Author's Works

Waiting to Exhale (1996)
How Stella Got Her Grove Back (1998)
Disappearing Acts (2000)

For Further Information

Bass, Patrik Henry. "Terry McMillan's Triumphant Return." *Essence* (January 2001).

"Interview with Terry McMillan." Bookbrowse.com. *http://www.bookbrowse.com/index.cfm?page=author&authorID=542&view=interview* (viewed June 27, 2003).

Iverem, Esther. "Interview with Terry McMillan." Seeingblack.com (September 26, 2002). *http://www.seeingblack.com/x092602/mcmillan.shtml* (viewed June 27, 2003).

Jones, Daniel, and John D. Jorgenson, eds. Terry McMillan entry, *Contemporary Authors New Revision Series*. Vol. 60. Detroit: Gale Research, 1998.

Leland, John. "How Terry got her groove." *Newsweek* (April 29, 1996).

"McMillan Finally Exhales." *Time* (September 21, 1996).

Patrick, Diane. *Terry McMillan: The Unauthorized Biography*. New York: St. Martin's Press, 1999.

Presler, Andrew B. Terry McMillan entry, *American Ethnic Writers*. Vol. 2. Edited by David Peck. Pasadena, CA: Salem Press, 2000.

Richards, Paulette. *Terry McMillan: A Critical Companion*. Westport, CT: Greenwood Press, 1999.

" 'Stella' in South Africa: Still looking for her groove, best-selling author Terry McMillan reveals new details of art-imitating-life love affair." *Ebony* (December 1996).

Terry McMillan entry, *Contemporary Novelists*. 7th edition. Detroit: St. James Press, 2001.

Terry McMillan interview. BookPage. *http://www.bookpage.com/0102bp/terry_mcmillan.html* (viewed March 31, 2003).

Terry McMillan Web page. Penguin Putnam. *http://www.penguinputnam.com* (viewed June 27, 2003).

"Terry McMillan." *The Writer* (August 2001).

Terry McMillan biography. Voices from the Gaps. *http://www.voices.cla.umn.edu/authors/MCMILLANtery.html* (viewed June 27, 2003).

Wilkerson, Isabel. "On top of the world." *Essence* (June 1996).

Larry McMurtry

◆ Western   ◆ Mainstream

Wichita Falls, Texas
1936

◆ *Lonesome Dove*

About the Author and the Author's Writing

Texas Monthly declared Larry McMurtry's Pulitzer Prize-winning, 830-page epic *Lonesome Dove* the Texas novel of the century. It could as easily be the American western novel of the century, so powerful and influential was its story of Texas Rangers Woodrow F. Call and Jake Spoon and a 2,500-mile trail drive to Montana in quest of bad men, Indians, and redemption.

McMurtry wrote his landmark novel despite an earlier disdain for his home state. Early in his career, he once called the Lone Star State "a country literate America hopes to hear no more about."

"I'm a critic of the myth of the cowboy," he told writer Mervyn Rothstein for the *New York Times*. "I don't feel that it's a myth that pertains, and since it's a part of my heritage I feel it's a legitimate task to criticize it." He elaborated that most notorious gunslingers actually led mundane, boring lives, and that the rural way was not all it has been made out to be. His novel *Anything for Billy* is largely about the dime novelist, Ben Sippy, who contributes to the romanticization of the west.

Larry Jeff McMurtry was born in Wichita Falls, Texas, in 1936. His father and eight uncles were cowboys and ranchers. He received a bachelor of arts degree from North Texas State College in 1958 and a master's from Rice University in Houston in 1960. He also studied at Stanford University in 1960. He has one son from his marriage to Josephine Ballard in 1959; they divorced in 1966.

McMurtry was an instructor at Texas Christian University in Fort Worth from 1961 to 1962 and a lecturer in English and creative writing at Rice from 1963 to 1969 (and also managed a book store and scouted collectible books for dealers). In 1970, he was a visiting professor at George Mason College, and the year after that, at American University. A resident of Archer City, Texas, he resides in the house that previously belonged to his grandparents.

The author's first three novels had a contemporary setting, often a barely disguised version of his home town. He abandoned seriousness for lightness in works such as *All My Friends Are Going to Be Strangers*; and he moved his locales out of Texas for books such as *Cadillac Jack*. *Lonesome Dove* appeared in the Old West time period. Suggests Bookreporter.com, "No other author has so thoroughly and delightfully debunked the ill-advised romanticism of the American West. McMurtry's immense talent punctures the cowboy mythology with such finesse that the reader never feels the prick; we just joyfully go along for the ride of a lifetime." But not all readers appreciated the fact that *Lonesome Dove* was debunking the Texas mythos.

"He is often concerned with displaced characters searching for something to provide their lives with stability and purpose," observed Mark Busby, "especially since the elements that provided direction in the past have disappeared. . . . Although their lives are ultimately fraught with difficulty, pain, and uncertainty, McMurtry demonstrates how these characters take pleasure in moments of creativity, love, or humor."

After *Lonesome Dove*, McMurtry wrote sequels to earlier novels, experimented with memoir, honed his essays, and produced a handful of non-Texan westerns. McMurtry is a fast writer, producing ten or so pages a day on his manual typewriter, then editing at the rate of twenty pages a day.

Films and television miniseries made from his works have won praise—*Hud*, *The Last Picture Show*, *Terms of Endearment*, and *Lonesome Dove*.

In 1991, the author underwent quadruple bypass surgery, then suffered severe depression. "I faded out of my life," he told Barnes & Noble. "Suddenly I found myself becoming an outline, and then what was within that outline vanished."

He recuperated at the home of friend Diana Ossana, who stayed with him during several years of depression and recovery, helping him complete *Streets of Laredo* in 1993 and collaborating on screenplays such as *Pretty Boy Floyd*. They also wrote *Zeke and Ned* together.

"His characters are rich and emotionally accessible," observed Ossana in *Entertainment Weekly*. "He likes to take them through their lives from beginning to end."

Streets of Laredo garnered nearly as strong, favorable reviews as its predecessor, though a darker work. Call, now nearly seventy years old and retired as a ranger, takes on the private assignment to hunt down a train robber for a railroad. It proves a bloody undertaking.

"This is a story about divided loyalties, and about the trouble visited upon those with one foot planted in civilization and the other in the wilderness," said *Newsweek's* Malcolm Jones in 1993. Two more volumes have appeared to complete the sequence. "The myth is intact, if a tad tattered by McMurtry's darkly comedic touch and sly debunking of chivalric conventions," suggests reviewer Bill Bell. "But at its core are McMurtry's respect and gift for exaggerated and fanciful pageantry and heroic form."

McMurtry in the early 1970s bought downtown real estate in his old hometown Archer City and opened an antiquarian and secondhand book store. According to *Texas Monthly* writer Kathryn Jones, "Some still haven't forgotten or forgiven the gloomy portrayal of their town in the book and the movie *The Last Picture Show*, McMurtry's semiautobiographical story about small-town love and loss that was filmed here. Or they grumble that the downtown stores are full of old books instead of things they really need and that Archer City is turning into a tourist town—'McMurtryville.'"

The author struggled to explain to *Smithsonian* magazine his affinity for books: "Even dedicated readers don't always understand," he said. "It seems to be a pure affinity, like some people have for horses. Or fine china."

By 1997, McMurtry told *Texas Monthly* he was about ready to hang up his writing spurs. He was involved in his several Booked Up stores—he still relishes the hunt for good books in unlikely places—and his screenwriting had ebbed. He was writing quite a few essays and nonfiction. Of course he eventually changed his mind, turning in recent years to writing by himself, producing among other books the Berrybender quartet depicting the exploits of an odd English family in the rugged west.

Noted writer Don Graham, "McMurtry has been the reigning King of Texas Literature for more than four decades. That is a long time to dominate a literary scene, but McMurtry has done it by dint of brilliance, talent, hard work, and rock-solid discipline."

Works by the Author

Fiction

Horseman, Pass By (1961), retitled *Hud* (1961)
Leaving Cheyenne (1963)
Moving On (1970)
All My Friends Are Going to Be Strangers (1972)
Terms of Endearment (1975)
Somebody's Darling (1978)
Cadillac Jack (1982)
The Desert Rose (1983)
Anything for Billy (1988)
Some Can Whistle (1989), sequel to *All My Friends Are Going to Be Strangers*
Buffalo Girls (1990)
The Evening Star (1992), sequel to *Terms of Endearment*
Pretty Boy Floyd, with Diana Ossana (1994)
Three Best-selling Novels (1994), includes *Lonesome Dove*, *Leaving Cheyenne*, and
    The Last Picture Show
The Late Child (1995)
Zeke and Ned, with Diana Ossana (1997)
Boone's Lick (2000)
Loop Group (2004)

Berrybender Narratives

Sin Killer (2002)
By Sorrow's River (2003)
The Wandering Hill (2003)
Folly and Glory (2004)

Lonesome Dove Series

Lonesome Dove (1985)
Streets of Laredo (1993)

Dead Man's Walk (1995)
Comanche Moon (1997)

Last Picture Show Trilogy

The Last Picture Show (1966)
Texasville (1987)
Duane's Depressed (1999)

Screenplays

The Last Picture Show, with Peter Bogdanovich (1971)
Montana (1990)
Falling from Grace (1992)
Memphis, with Cybill Sheperd (1992)
Streets of Laredo, with Diana Ossana (1995)
Dead Man's Walk, with Diana Ossana (1996)
Johnson County War, with Diana Ossana (2002), based on a novel by Frederic Manfred

Nonfiction

In a Narrow Grave: Essays on Texas (1968)
It's Always We Rambled: An Essay on Rodeo (1974)
Film Flam: Essays on Hollywood (1987)
Crazy Horse (1999)
Walter Benjamin at the Dairy Queen (1999)
Roads: Driving America's Great Highways (2000)
Paradise (2001)
Sacagawea's Nickname: Essays on the American West (2001)

Contributor

Texas in Transition (1986)
Rodeo: No Guts, No Glory (1994)

Motion Pictures and Television Movies Based on the Author's Works

Hud (1962), based on *Horseman, Pass By*
The Last Picture Show (1971)
Lovin Molly (1974), based on *Leaving Cheyenne*
Terms of Endearment (1983)
Lonesome Dove (1989)
Return to Lonesome Dove (1993)

Lonesome Dove: The Series (1994–1996), syndicated television series
Larry McMurtry's Streets of Laredo (1995)
Dead Man's Walk (1996)

For Further Information

Bell, Bill. "Grand Old Man of Western Lit." *Dallas News* (November 9, 1997).

Busby, Mark. Larry McMurtry entry, *Twentieth-Century Western Writers*. 2nd edition, edited by Geoff Sadler. Chicago: St. James Press, 1991.

Busby, Mark. *Larry McMurtry and the West: An Ambivalent Relationship*. Denton: University of North Texas Press, 1995.

Dingus, Anne. "Book of the Century." *Texas Monthly* (December 1999).

Estleman, Loren D. "Lonesome Dove: Star Robert Duval Says: It's Going to Be Like a Western Godfather." *TV Guide* (February 9, 1989).

Graham, Don. "Not moving on: despite his past statements to the contrary, Larry McMurtry is still writing fiction. And I for one am glad." *Texas Monthly* (May 2003).

Horowitz, Mark. "Larry McMurtry's Dream Job." *New York Times* (December 7, 1997).

Jones, Daniel, and John D. Jorgenson, eds. Larry McMurtry entry, *Contemporary Authors New Revision Series*. Vol. 64. Detroit: Gale Research, 1998.

Jones, Kathryn. "I've written enough fiction." *Texas Monthly* (December 1997).

Jones, Malcolm. "The Ghost Writer at Home on the Range." *Newsweek* (August 2, 1993).

Jones, Malcolm. "The Poet Lariat." *Newsweek* (January 11, 1999).

Jones, Roger Walton. *Larry McMurtry and the Victorian Novel*. Texas University Press, 1994.

Landless, Thomas. *Larry McMurtry*. Austin, TX: Steck Vaughn, 1969.

Larry McMurtry biography. Barnes & Noble. *http://www.barnesandnoble.com/writers/writerdetails.asp?userid=2UHJZHFY29&cid=701973#bio* (viewed June 24, 2003).

Larry McMurtry biography. Bookreporter.com. *http://www.bookreporter.com/authors/au-mcmurtry-larry.asp* (viewed June 24, 2003).

Larry McMurtry entry, *Contemporary Southern Writers*. Detroit: St. James Press, 1999.

Lich, Lera Patrick Tyler. *Larry McMurtry's Texas: Evolution of the Myth*. Austin, TX: Eakin Press, 1987.

Neinstin, Raymond L. *The Ghost Country: A Study of the Novels of Larry McMurtry*. Berkeley, CA: Creative Arts Book, 1976.

Peavy, Charles D. *Larry McMurtry*. Boston: Twayne, 1977.

Reynolds, Clay, ed. *Taking Stock: A Larry McMurtry Casebook*. Dallas, TX: Southern Methodist University Press, 1989.

Rothstein, Mervyn. "A Texan Who Likes to Deflate The Legends of the Golden West." *New York Times* (November 1, 1988).

Schmidt, Dorey, ed. *Larry McMurtry: Unredeemed Dreams*. Mexico City, Mexico: School of Humanities, Pan American University, 1978.

Thompson, Anne. "Cowboy Junkies." *Entertainment Weekly* (May 10, 1996).

Tucker, Ken. "Best of the West." *Entertainment Weekly* (May 10, 1996).

Watson, Bruce. "Racing to Round Up Readers." *Smithsonian* (March 1999).

Weinman, Irving. "McMurtry's still tall in the saddle." *Boston Globe* (August 3, 1993).

Wylie, Andrew. *By Sorrow's River* review. *Publishers Weekly* (August 25, 2003).

James A. Michener

◆ Historical

New York or Pennsylvania
1907(?)–1997

◆ *Centennial*

About the Author and the Author's Writing

James A. Michener has practically created a fiction genre of his own: the robust, roaming, historical family sagas that take on not just generations or decades, but entire nations.

James Albert Michener was born either in New York or Pennsylvania—he never really knew—probably in 1907. He was raised by Quakers Albert and Mabel Michener in Doylestown, Pennsylvania, under impoverished circumstances. Biographer John Hayes says Mabel Michener was his unwed birth mother who told everyone she had adopted the orphan boy. Michener took his uncertain parentage philosophically and got on with his life. Lynn Rossellini writing in *U.S. News & World Report* in 1991 suggested, "If he couldn't figure out his own identity, perhaps it would be possible to figure out his place in the world by analyzing and locating what he saw around him. 'He will go out of this world not knowing who he was,' says [Michener's editorial assistant John] Kings. 'So he wants to leave something behind.' "

At Doylestown High School, Michener excelled in basketball. As a teenager, he began the travels that he would enjoy all his life: He hitchhiked across the country. "Those were years of wonder and enchantment," he wrote in *The World Is My Home*, ". . . some of the best years I would know. I kept meeting American citizens of all levels who took me into their cars, their confidence and often their homes."

In 1929, he graduated summa cum laude from Swarthmore College (which he attended on a scholarship) with an A.B. degree (his triple major was English, history, and philosophy); then earned an A.M. degree from Colorado State College of Education (now University of Northern Colorado) in 1936. He did research at the University of Pennsylvania, the University of Virginia, Ohio State University, Harvard University, St. Andrews University, and University of Siena. Three times wed and twice divorced, he survived his third wife, Mari Yoriko Sabusawa, who died in 1994.

Michener tried his hand at various careers. He wrote a sports column at age fifteen; he acted with a traveling show; and he became a teacher at Hill School in Pennsylvania in 1932. He later became an associate professor at Colorado State University, 1936 to 1941, before joining the publisher Macmillan in New York City as an associate editor of textbooks. He served in the U.S. Naval Reserve from 1942 to 1945, achieving the rank of lieutenant commander and serving as naval historian in the South Pacific. This latter task fed his natural curiosity; he observed with great interest the interactions—the clashes—of different cultures. A near accident while landing at an airfield in French New Caledonia prompted Michener to make bold plans for his life. While still in the service, he began developing ideas for books, and after briefly returning to Macmillan following the war, he became a full-time freelance writer.

Michener's first fiction was *Tales of the South Pacific*, which grew out of his experiences during World War II, and it won him the Pulitzer Prize. The linking stories follow a romance between a young soldier, Joe Cable, and islander Liat, set against a backdrop of the Allied invasion. It was adapted to the stage as the Rogers and Hammerstein musical *South Pacific*.

After that book was published, the author still had plenty to say about the South Pacific, and he put it into travel sketches and other works of nonfiction. When Macmillan rejected his *The Fires of Spring*, he found a willing Random House, where Bennett Cerf became his publisher and Albert Erskine his editor.

Michener's travels influenced much of his writing. While staying in Honolulu in 1956, he started writing the novel that grew into the million-word *Hawaii*. The saga follows the many people who came to settle on the islands. Later, his travels to Israel inspired *The Source*; a journey to Poland inspired on eponymous novel, and so on.

Michener's curiosity served him well and came despite his schooling. "I was the child solely of an English-type education," he said in an Academy of Achievement interview. "Never had any American History or Canadian or anything like that. It was always English. That's what counted in those days. And I went out to Colorado, and I suddenly saw there was an Hispanic component, a French component in the old days. And above all, a liberal free-swinging component."

Although many suspect Michener employed researchers to provide the vast material that went into each of his novels, he said, in fact, he had the help of only secretaries and occasionally graduate student assistants and otherwise did the work himself. "His editorial assistant, John Kings, has been with him since 1972," explained Jim Shahin in the *Saturday Evening Post* in 1990. "Kings, who often travels with Michener, reads and comments on the manuscripts before publication. . . . 'What I need is very simple,' Michener says. 'A good library and access to an airport.' "

Of course, Michener's work is far more than a stringing together of facts. "A lot of my writing comes from the heart, not just from research," Michener told the *Saturday Evening Post* in 1985. "I tell young people that that is the best way to write. I don't advise anybody to work the way I do. My method works for me, but there's a better way to write, and that is to write out of one's self."

Author Nelson DeMille, quoted in a Michener obituary in *People Weekly*, observed, "He's the grand old man of historical fiction. Those big hardcovers used to be in everybody's houses. He was a man of the old school who didn't play with the facts. He got them across in such a way that you actually learned something."

Though cautious with spending, as a result of his impoverished upbringing, Michener was a generous philanthropist, making major donations (some $117 million worth, all told) to the University of Texas at Austin for a creative writing program, for example, establishing the James A. Michener Art Museum in Bucks County, Pennsylvania; and awarding $10,000 annually in the Journey Prize for Canadian short stories.

Besides creating his own television series in 1959, *Adventures in Paradise*, Michener served as board member, chairman, or consultant to a wide range of organizations from President John F. Kennedy's Food for Peace Program to the U.S. State Department Advisory Committee on the Arts to the U.S. Postal Service Advisory Committee. He received more than twenty honorary degrees as well as the Navy Gold Cross, the Franklin and the Einstein awards, and the Medal of Freedom.

The author's manuscripts are held by the Library of Congress in Washington, D.C. The James A. Michener Special Collection at the University of Northern Colorado holds the author's *Centennial* research notebook.

Though he came to know considerable fame, Michener accepted it with great humility. In 1997, he told Kira Albin, "[Famous] is a word I never use myself, about myself."

Works by the Author

Fiction

The Fires of Spring (1949)
The Bridges at Toko-Ri (1953)
Sayonara (1954)
The Bridge at Andau (1957)
Hawaii (1959)
Caravans (1963)
The Source (1965)
Texas (1965)
The Drifters (1971)
Centennial (1974)
Chesapeake (1978), retitled *The Watermen* (1979)
The Covenant (1980)
Space (1982)
Poland (1984)
Legacy (1987)
Alaska (1988)
Caribbean (1989)
Journey (1989)
The Eagle and the Raven (1990)
The Novel (1991)
Mexico (1992)
Recessional (1994)
Miracle in Seville (1995)

Short Stories

Tales of the South Pacific (1947)
Return to Paradise (1951)
Creatures of the Kingdom: Stories of Animals and Nature (1993)

Poetry

A Century of Sonnets (1997)

Nonfiction

The Unit in the Social Studies, with Harold M. Long (1940)
The Voice of Asia (1951), retitled *Voices of Asia* (1952)
The Floating World (1954)
Rascals in Paradise, with A. Grove Day (1957)
Selected Writings (1957)
Japanese Prints from the Early Masters to the Modern (1959)
Report of the County Chairman (1961)
The Modern Japanese Print: An Introduction (1962)
Iberia: Spanish Travels and Reflections (1968)
The Subject is Israel: A Conversation Between James A. Michener and Dore Shary (1968)
Presidential Lottery: The Reckless Gamble in Our Electoral System (1969)
Facing East: A Study of the Art of Jack Levine (1970)
The Quality of Life (1970)
Kent State: What Happened and Why (1971)
A Michener Miscellany 1950–1970, edited by Ben Hibbs (1973)
About "Centennial": Some Notes on the Novel (1974)
Sports in America (1976), retitled *Michener on Sports* (1976)
Collectors, Forgers—and a Writer: A Memoir (1983)
Testimony (1983)
Six Days in Havana, with John Kings (1989)
Pilgrimage; A Memoir of Poland and Rome (1990)
James A. Michener's Writer's Handbook: Explorations in Writing and Publishing (1992)
My Lost Mexico (1992)
The World Is My Home: A Memoir (1992)

Editor

The Future of the Social Studies: Proposals for an Experimental Social-Studies Curriculum (1939)
The Hokusai Sketch Books: Selections from the Manga (1958)
Firstfruits: A Harvest of 25 years of Israeli Writing (1973)

Anthology

The Writing Life: Writers on How They Think and Work, edited by Marie Arana (2003)

Stage Plays, Motion Pictures, or Television Programs Based on Author's Works

South Pacific (1949), play
Return to Paradise (1953), film
The Bridges at Toko-Ri (1954), film
Men of the Fighting Lady (1954), film
Sayonara (1957), film
Until They Sail (1957), film
South Pacific (1958), film
Hawaii (1966), film
Centennial (1978–1979), TV miniseries
Space (1985), TV miniseries

For Further Information

Albin, Kira. "James Michener: An Epic Life" (1997). *http://www.grandtimes.com/michener.html* (viewed June 30, 2003).

Becker, G. I. *James A. Michener*. New York: Ungar, 1983.

Day, A. Grove. *James A. Michener*. New York: Twayne, 1964 and 1977.

Dybwad, G. L., and Joy V. Bliss. *James A. Michener: The Beginning Teacher and His Textbooks*. Albuquerque, NM: The Book Stops Here, 1995.

Gander, John. "James Michener: Not Just a Famous Author, But My Friend!" Sagazines .com. *http://www.sagazine.com.archive_event.htm* (viewed June 30, 2003).

Harwell, Jenny Andrews. "At Home with James A. Michener." *Saturday Evening Post* (September 1985).

Hayes, J. P. *James A. Michener: A Biography*. Indianapolis: Bobbs-Merrill, 1984.

James A. Michener Art Museum Web site. *http://www.michenerartmuseum/org/about/* (viewed June 30, 2003).

James A. Michener entry, *Contemporary Popular Authors*. Detroit: St. James Press, 1997.

James A. Michener obituary. *Maclean's* (October 27, 1997).

James A. Michener obituary. *People Weekly* (November 3, 1997).

James A. Michener obituary. *U.S. News & World Report* (October 27, 1997).

"James A. Michener: Pulitzer Prize-Winning Novelist." Interview, Academy of Achievement (January 10, 1991). *http://www.achievement.org/autodoc/page/mic0int-1* (viewed June 30, 2003).

James A. Michener Special Collection. University of Northern Colorado. *http://library.unco.edu/jam/centennial/* (viewed June 30, 2003).

Jones, Daniel, and John D. Jorgenson, eds. James A. Michener entry, *Contemporary Authors New Revision Series*. Vol. 68. Detroit: Gale Research, 1998.

Magnuson, James. "James Michener." *Texas Monthly* (December 1997).

"Novelist James Michener dies." CNN.com (October 17, 1997). *http://www.cnn.com/US/9710/16/michener.obit/* (viewed June 30, 2003).

Rossellini, Lynn. "The man who loves facts." *U.S. News & World Report* (June 17, 1991).

Severson, Marilyn S. *James A. Michener: A Critical Companion*. Westport, CT: Greenwood Press, 1996.

Shalin, Jim. "The continuing sagas of James A. Michener." *Saturday Evening Post* (March 1990).

Walter Mosley

◆ Mystery ◆ Science fiction

Los Angeles, California
1952

◆ *Easy Rawlings Series*

About the Author and the Author's Writing

Walter Mosley learned a lot about the craft of prose writing while enrolled in a poetry program at City College. "[S]tudying poetry taught me the major things I needed to know about fiction," he said in a Bookpage interview with Alden Mudge. "I already had a narrative voice, and I already loved characters and character development. But the other stuff I had to think about was condensation, the music in language, how simile works, how metaphor works, how to make a sentence say one thing and mean other things also."

Walter Ellis Mosley was born in 1952 in Los Angeles, California. He was an only child of a black man from Louisiana and a Jewish woman—thus he felt the influence of two cultures when growing up, southern black and Eastern European. His father served in the military during World War II—an experience that brought him to realize, when German soldiers were shooting at him, that no matter his skin color, he was an American. The author went through a similar epiphany following the September 11 terrorist attacks—when the airplanes smashed into the World Trade Center, they were attacking all of America, no matter about skin color.

"My father always taught by telling stories about his experiences," Mosley relates in the memoir *What Next*. "He told me what it meant to be a man and to be a Black man. He taught me about love and responsibility, about beauty, and how to make gumbo. My father's instructions have sustained me in the complex life we live here in America. Some of his lessons I'm still working out over forty years later."

After graduating from Hamilton High School in 1970, Mosley attended Goddard College in Vermont. He received a political science degree from Johnson State College in 1977. He attended the University of Massachusetts at Amherst and City College of the City University of New York. In 1987, he married dancer and choreographer Joy Kellman, but they later divorced. He now lives in Greenwich Village in New York City.

Mosley worked as a potter, caterer, and computer programmer before becoming a writer. (Mosley briefly considered becoming a nurse, but did not because he does not like to see blood.) He wrote a coming-of-age story of a black man and, as he has said, since it was before Terry McMillan had achieved popularity, it found no publisher. McMillan opened doors for black authors, as did Mosley, in turn, when President Bill Clinton said Easy Rawlins was one of his favorite fictional characters.

Mosley has been president of Mystery Writers of America, a member of PEN American Center's executive board, and a member of the National Book Awards board of directors. He won a Grammy award in 2002 for best liner notes for a boxed set of Richard Pryor recordings.

Best known are his Ezekiel "Easy" Rawlins noir crime novels—the first one, *Devil in a Blue Dress*, won the Private Eye Writers of America Shamus Award in 1990 for best first P. I. novel. The Easy Rawlins stories are set in post-WWII Los Angeles, where a just-discharged soldier ends up a detective. Time moves ahead a few years with each new novel; Rawlins acquires real estate and a new job, finds a mate and family, befriends an ex-gangster named Mouse Alexander. The series will take Rawlins through the 1960s, according to the author.

"[T]he books are really about Black life in Los Angeles," the author said in an *Armchair Detective* interview. "[T]here are all these important events since WWII, contemporary, historical events which Black people have been edited out of. I'm talking about, for instance, in *A Red Death* the juxtaposition of the lives of Black people and the lives of those people who were destroyed by McCarthy. So there's all this important history."

Although Chester Himes paved the way for black writers, Mosley read the Himes books only after he began writing his own. Among Mosley's favorite novels are *One Hundred Years of Solitude*, *The Adventures of Huckleberry Finn*, and *Their Eyes Were Watching God*.

Black men read his books, the author has said, "because I won't embarrass them," and black women read him because he addresses important issues such as racism, sexism, and discrimination.

"All his works share an abiding interest in the moral dimensions of everyday life," observed reviewer Ben Greenman.

In his books, Mosley develops a complex relationship between Rawlins and his son Juice. "What I write about are black, male heroes," the author said in an interview on his Web page at twbookmark. "A big part of being a hero in a community is raising children from one way or another. I don't have any kids. But, I know this role from my own father. I wanted to write it specifically, which this book *Bad Boy Brawly Brown* does, and it talks about black men and their sons and their friends' sons."

How do the stories come together? The author does not outline before he starts writing. "I never have the plot worked out when I start writing," he said in a NYTimes.com chat. "My ideal situation is to have a first sentence that captures the voice of my story—with that I don't need anything else." He continues to edit and polish his manuscript until he reaches the point where he no longer knows how to fix things.

Mosley has also launched two other series characters, ex-con Socrates Fortlow and bookseller Paris Minton. In reviewing the second book in the series, *Fear Itself*, Jeanne Russell of the *Montreal Gazette* remarked on the author's ability to investigate the darker side of racism: "The contrast evoked by two close male friends helps underscore and explain the tension of being black in 1950s Los Angeles."

Mosley has also written a science fiction novel, *Blue Light*, and brought out a collection of imaginative stories, *Futureland*. "The best thing that science fiction can do," he said in an online SciFi.com chat, "is to break you out of ruts in the way you see the world and to shatter one's illusions about progress. It should not make people feel cozy but it should make people question their good fortune about being born at any one moment in time."

Mosley has taken the hard-boiled private detectives of Dashiell Hammett and Raymond Chandler into new and interesting directions, weaving in social commentary.

"For blacks who emigrated to the west and north," the author said in a BookPage discussion with Robert Fleming, "there was a deep concern for one another. There was a strong bond among blacks during the days of Jim Crow. They realized there was no chance of help coming from outside the community. They knew they were only a hair's breadth from misfortune happening to any one of them if they didn't help each other. I'm very interested in this quality."

Are there other genres Mosley still wants to explore? "I might, one day, write a western," he told *Black Issues Book Review*. "But I'm not dying to do it. I have pretty much done most things I've wanted to."

Works by the Author

Fiction

RL's Dream (1995)
Blue Light (1998)
The Greatest (2000)
Whispers in the Dark (2000)
The Man in My Basement (2004)

Easy Rawlins Series

Devil in a Blue Dress (1990)
A Red Death (1991)
White Butterfly (1992)
Black Betty (1994)
A Little Yellow Dog (1995)
Gone Fishin' (1996)
Bad Boy Brawly Brown (2002)
Little Scarlet (2004)

Paris Minton and Fearless Jones Series

Fearless Jones (2001)
Fear Itself (2003)

Socrates Fortlow Series

Always Outnumbered, Always Outgunned (1997)
Walkin' the Dog (1999)

Collections

Futureland: Nine Stories of an Imminent World (2001)
Six Easy Pieces (2003)

Editor

Black Genius (1999)
The Best American Short Stories 2003 (2003)

Introduction

The Man Who Cried I Am, by John A. Williams (1985)

Anthologies

Constable New Crimes 2 (1993)
The New Mystery (1993)
The Plot Thickens (1997)
Best American Mystery Stories 1998, edited by Sue Grafton (1998)
Best American Mystery Stories 2003, edited by Michael Connelly (2003)
Dangerous Women, edited by Otto Penzlor (2004)

Nonfiction

Working on the Chain Gang: Shaking Off the Dead Hand of History (1999)
What Next: A Memoir Toward World Peace (2003)

Motion Pictures Based on the Author's Works

Devil in a Blue Dress (1994)

For Further Information

Benson, Christopher. "What's behind the boon in Black mystery writers?" *Ebony* (September 2003).

Chapin, Jeff, and John D. Jorgenson, eds. Walter Mosley entry, *Contemporary Authors New Revision Series*. Vol. 57. Detroit: Gale Research, 1997.

"Easy Rawlins." Thrilling Detective. *http://www.thrillingdetective.com/rawleasy.html* (viewed May 24, 2003).

Fleming, Robert. "Interview with Walter Mosley." BookPage.com. *http://www.bookpage.com/9607bp/mystery/littleyellowdog.html* (viewed May 24, 2003).

Greenman, Ben. "What Lies Beneath: Subterranean homestead blues in Walter Mosley's new novel." *New Yorker* (January 19, 2004).

"How My Father Shaped My Life." *Ebony* (June 2003).

"In His Own Words." twbookmark.com. *http://www.twbookmark.com/features/ waltermoslye/article.html* (viewed May 24, 2003).

Lindsay, Tony. "BIBR talks with Walter Mosley." *Black Issues Book Review* (July–August 2002).

Mosley, Walter. "Writers on Writing: For Authors, Fragile Ideas Need Loving Every Day." *New York Times* (July 3, 2000).

Mudge, Alden. "New crime fiction with a twist from noir master Walter Mosley." BookPage.com. *http://www.bookpage.com/0106bp/walter_mosley.html* (viewed May 24, 2003).

Petersen, James R. "Easy Does it." *Playboy* (August 2002).

Russell, Jeanne. "Hot Reads: Paris Minton and Fearless set out on a wacky tale." *Montreal Gazette* (August 30, 2003).

Silet, Charles L. P. "The Other Side of Those Mean Streets." *Armchair Detective* (fall 1993).

"10 Questions for . . . Walter Mosley." NYTimes.com (April 14, 2003). *http://www .nytimes.com/2003/04/14/readersopinions/15MOS1.html* (viewed April 20, 2003).

Villinger, Binti L. Six Easy Pieces review. *Black Issues Book Review* (January–February 2003).

Walter Mosely Web page. W. W. Norton. *http://www.wwnorton.com/catalog.featured/ mosley/welcome.htm* (viewed May 24, 2003).

Walter Mosley interview. SciFi.com. *http://www.scifi.com/transcripts/2001/mosley_chat .html* (viewed May 24, 2003).

Walter Mosley Web page. *http://www.twbookmark.com/features/waltermosley/ bookhsl.html* (viewed May 24, 2003).

Weeks, Linton. "Of Life and Depth: For Mystery Writer Walter Mosley, Easy Rawlins Is Just the Beginning of the Intrigue." *Washington Post* (August 5, 2002).

Williams, Juan. "Walter Mosely: 'What Next.'" National Public Radio (March 17, 2003). *http://www.npr.org/display_pages.features/feature_1192760.html* (viewed May 24, 2003).

Gloria Naylor

♦ Women's fiction

New York, New York
1950

♦ *The Women of Brewster Place*

Credit: Sigrid Estrada.

About the Author and the Author's Writing

Author Gloria Naylor won the American Book Award immediately out of the gate, with her 1982 novel *The Women of Brewster Place*. The novel follows seven diverse African American women, women with common fears, weaknesses, and strengths, as they go through love, grief, sex, and birth. "Her women feel deeply, and she unflinchingly transcribes their emotions. . . . Vibrating and undisguised emotion, *The Women of Brewster Place* springs from the same roots that produced the blues. Like them, her book sings of sorrows proudly borne by black women in America," remarked reviewer Diedre Donohue.

Noting Naylor's novels center on enclosed black communities with characters coming to grips with themselves and their environments, Christine H. King further observed, "Naylor's powerful settings combine elements of the ordinary with the otherworldly, allowing for magical events and mythic resolutions."

The author was born in 1950 in New York City, the daughter of a master framer/transit worker and a telephone operator. Her parents had been sharecroppers in Mississippi who relocated to the North. She credits her mother with opening her eyes to the wonderful world of books. Her mother gave her a blank diary when she was twelve, and that's where she wrote down those emotional things she had a hard time articulating otherwise.

After graduating from high school in 1968, Naylor was baptized a Jehovah's Witness, becoming a minister in the faith. Still living at home, she worked as a switchboard operator for six years before venturing to North Carolina and Florida as a full-time worker for her religion. In 1975, she left the Jehovah's Witnesses, suffered a nervous breakdown, recovered, and began taking nursing courses at Medgar Evers College. After discovering the work of feminist advocates and seeing the emergence of black literature from the hands of Toni Morrison and Zora Neale Hurston, among others, she transferred to Brooklyn College of CUNY to study English, earning her degree in 1981. She married in 1980 but divorced the next year. During this time, with encouragement from an editor at *Essence* magazine, she wrote *The Women of Brewster Place*, which was published in 1982.

"The novel began with my using, in an odd way, the sort of confessional writing that I began with in my diary," the author said in a National Book Foundation interview. Feeling anxious over a relationship, "I just felt I was going to die. So I said to myself, what could make another woman hurt the way I'm hurting? That's when I invented 'Luciella' Louise Turner. It wasn't my situation, but I imagined a woman who loses her husband, loses her unborn child and loses her toddler."

From there, Naylor conceived the other six women in the book, variations on the experiences of black women in this country. As she comes from a large, extended, and close family, she naturally explored family issues.

"Naylor's success," suggests *Contemporary Novelists*, "lies, in part, in the intensity of her presentation of such social issues as poverty, racism, discrimination against homosexuals, the unequal treatment of women, the value of a sense of community among blacks, and the failure of some upper middle-class educated blacks to address racial problems and social injustice."

In 1983, Naylor received a master of arts degree in Afro-American studies from Yale University; the novel *Linden Hills* was her master's thesis. She was writer-in-residence at Cummington Community of the Arts and a visiting lecturer at George Washington University that year. Naylor was a National Endowment for the Arts fellow in 1985 and scholar-in-residence at the University of Pennsylvania the year after. She was a visiting lecturer at Princeton University (1986) and Boston University (1987) and senior fellow in the Society for Humanities at Cornell University in 1988. She received a Guggenheim fellowship also in 1988.

Her next books, *Mama Day* and *Bailey's Café*, completed an interrelated sequence, the accomplishment of which, the author said in *The Writer*, gave her great satisfaction. "When I finished the last of that quartet, it was an exciting, exciting moment for me, to realize that I had set that goal and achieved it. You know, a whole lot can happen in 10 years of an adult life, and I had written through all of that."

Today Naylor has her own film production company, One Way Productions, which promotes a positive African American image. She nevertheless continues to explore her themes and write powerful fiction. *The Men of Brewster Place* (1998) responds to queries from readers about where the men were. "Like many in this country I was profoundly moved by the Million Man March and the images of all those black men calling themselves to task, promising to return home and be better citizens by concentrating on being better fathers and brothers," the author said on her Penguin Putnam's Web page. "It has taken me these many years to decide finally that I wanted to give the men who had appeared briefly in *The Women* a voice of their own."

Works by the Author

Fiction

The Women of Brewster Place: A Novel in Seven Stories (1982)
Linden Hills (1985)
Mama Day (1988)
Bailey's Café (1992)
The Men of Brewster Place (1998)

Stage Plays
Bailey's Café (1992)

Editor
Children of the Night: The Best Short Stories by Black Writers, 1967 to the Present (1995)

Nonfiction
Centennial (1986)
Revolution of the Heart: A New Strategy for Creating Wealth, with Bill Shore (1996)

Anthologies
The Writing Life: Writers on How They Think and Work, edited by Marie Arana (2003)

Motion Pictures Based on the Author's Works
The Women of Brewster Place (1989)

For Further Information

Awkward, Michael. *Inspiring Influences: Tradition, Revision, and Afro-American Women's Novels*. New York: Columbia University Press, 1991.

"Conversation with Gloria Naylor." *Essence* (June 1998).

Denison, D. C. "Interview with Gloria Naylor." *The Writer* (December 1994).

Donahue, Diedre. *The Women of Brewster Place* review. *Washington Post* (October 21, 1983).

Felton, Sharon, and Michelle Loris, eds. *Naylor: The Critical Response to Gloria Naylor*. Westport, CT: Greenwood Press, 1997.

Fowler, Virginia. *Gloria Naylor: In Search of Sanctuary*. New York: Twayne, 1996.

Gloria Naylor biography. Voices from the Gaps: Women Writers of Color. *http://voices.cla.umn.edu/authors/NAYLORgloria.html* (viewed May 27, 2003).

Gloria Naylor entry, *Contemporary Novelists*. 7th edition. Detroit: St. James Press, 2001.

Gloria Naylor interview. National Book Foundation. *http://www.nationalbook.org/authorguide_gnaylor.html* (viewed May 27, 2003).

Hall, Chekita T. *Gloria Naylor's Feminist Blues Aesthetic*. New York: Garland, 1998.

Harris, Trudier. *The Power of the Porch: The Storyteller's Craft in Zora Neale Hurston, Gloria Naylor, and Randall Kenan*. Athens: University of Georgia Press, 1996.

Kelley, Margot Anne, ed. *Gloria Naylor's Early Novels*. Gainesville: University Press of Florida, 1999.

Peacock, Scot, ed. Gloria Naylor entry, *Contemporary Authors New Revision Series*. Vol. 74. Detroit: Gale Research, 1999.

King, Christine H. Gloria Naylor entry, *American Ethnic Writers*. Vol. 2, edited by David Peck. Pasadena, CA: Salem Press, 2000.

Montgomery, Maxine Laura. *Conversations with Gloria Naylor*. Jackson: University Press of Mississippi, 2004.

Unofficial Gloria Naylor Homepage. *http://www.lythastudios.com/gnaylor/chron.html* (viewed May 27, 2003).

Whitt, Margaret Earley. *Understanding Gloria Naylor*. Columbia: University of South Carolina Press, 1999.

Women of Brewster Place Reading Guide. Penguin Putnam. *http://www.penguinputnam .com/static/rguides/us/women_of_brewster_place.html* (viewed May 27, 2003).

Patrick O'Brian

♦   Historical

Buckinghamshire, England
1914–2000

♦ *Aubrey-Maturin Series*

Courtesy of W. W. Norton &
Company. Credit: Rex Features.

About the Author and the Author's Writing

For years Patrick O'Brian quietly translated the works of writers such as Simone de Beauvoir and Henri Charriere into carefully phrased English. At the same time he wrote his own fiction, and over three decades—Richard Snow in the *New York Times Book Review* in 1991 called him "the best author you have never heard of "—he saw his solidly researched and lovingly rendered sea tales of the Napoleonic era emerge to find an enthusiastic audience.

His sea adventures, noted *Entertainment Weekly* in 2001, "are most truly about the two friends living them. Blustery, confident naval officer Jack Aubrey and the reflective, opium-addicted surgeon/spy Stephen Maturin were best mates through 20 novels."

Indeed, said O'Brian biographer Dean King in *Entertainment Weekly* in 2000, "He blew the genre away. His books were probably the most profound literature on friendship of this half century."

They are not necessarily easy reading. "The books have a music of their own," explained Richard Lacayo in *Time*, "though occasionally compressed into passages that are a trial by vocabulary for shore-hugging readers ('and then these fluttock-plates at the rim here hold the dead-eyes for the topmast shrouds')." But the books have drawn a navy of readers into history and onto the sea.

"Under the O'Brian spell you move into an unfamiliar but entirely convincing world. Quite likely you start with no special interest in the British navy in the age of sail. But who could have predicted the appeal of Tolkien's fantasies?" asked Brian Duffy in *U.S. News & World Report*.

The author was born near Galway, Ireland, in 1914, to a Roman Catholic family. Raised by a governess, he became fluent in Gaelic, Latin, and other languages. Whoa! That's the invented story. King revealed in 1998 that O'Brian was really born Richard Patrick Russ. He was Protestant, one of nine children, and the son of a physician of German extraction and his English wife, both living near London. His mother died when he was four, and he was educated at a Devon boarding school. He took the name Patrick O'Brian in 1945 and gradually submerged his old identity for a new one.

"He was not the first, and he will not be the last person to invent himself as someone entirely new," observed Patrick West in *New Statesman*. The change of nationality? "Irishness has always been an attractive nationality for the English. To them, it conjures up notions of romance, spirituality, rugged masculinity—qualities more alluring than a stuffy, prosaic Englishness."

Belying the camaraderie of his characters Maturin and Aubrey, O'Brian had failed relationships with his father and his son. He also abandoned his first wife and children, and the marriage ended in divorce. Adding to this turmoil, a daughter died of spina bifida, a congenital defect in the spinal column.

He had published a successful first novel at age fifteen. He took refuge in a small village called Collioure in southern France, "because it was cheap, at least in the early days when he was poor," observed an obituary writer for the *Economist*. "Several pre-Aubrey novels sank without trace, and Mr. O'Brian and his [second] wife Mary [Tolstoy] lived on his earnings as a translator; he may not have known much Irish, but he had far more useful French."

O'Brian infrequently submitted to public conversation. As he told Francis X. Clines of the *New York Times* in 1993, "I very much dislike being interviewed by the kind of journalist who tries to dig into your private life."

Some O'Brian fans no doubt cut their teeth on C. S. Forester's heroic Horatio Hornblower series. But O'Brian was particularly skilled at introducing and explaining period details—from orlops to pintles to marline spikes—and at dialogue. "To listen in on such accomplished people," marveled Edward T. Wheeler in *Commonweal*, "gimballing over the ocean on impossible missions, making erudite remarks on sea birds, on navigation, or on the intricacies of foreign policy, is to experience the 'felt life.' I supposed only some of us can translate all the Latin or understand the technicalities of sailing trim, but we are content to read ourselves into the company of these people."

"It's impossible for writers of historical fiction to completely expunge modern sensibilities from their work," observed Brian Bethune in *Maclean's*, "but O'Brian came closer than anyone else."

O'Brian was intrigued with the limited sphere of a shipboard adventure. He said in a BookPage interview, "[T]he people in it are cut off from outer influences—they react with other members of the crew, no one else; and this, clearly, heightens the reaction."

The author might not have made as dramatic a crossing of the ocean had not a W. W. Norton executive editor, Starling Lawrence, read the British paperback edition of *The Reverse of the Medal* while returning to the United States in 1990 and immediately recognized their appeal. Norton negotiated rights to the backlist and to new books in the Aubrey series. "I've never received so much mail as we've had on O'Brian," the editor told *Publishers Weekly* in 1992.

From 1992 to 1996, Norton issued *The Patrick O'Brian Newsletter* to further unify the author's audience. In the first issue, O'Brian explained he decided to write of the sea after completing a particularly difficult manuscript. He decided he wanted to do something for fun and chose an actual historical event as it relieved him of the task of having to make up characters and situations. He wrote about Anson's voyage around the world in 1740. The book did only modestly well, but an American publisher a few years later expressed an interest, so O'Brian went to sea again, this time using a setting of the Napoleonic Wars.

"In my subsequent naval tales I have rarely had everything, character, plot and ending, handed to me on a salver," he said, "but I have often found a comfortable kernel of fact for my fiction; for example I borrowed Cochrane's taking of the immensely superior Cacafuego in *Master and Commander*, Linois's unsuccessful action against the Indiamen in *HMS Surprise*, and Captain Riou's collision with an iceberg in *Desolation Island*."

The author admitted in *Patrick O'Brian: Critical Essays and a Bibliography*, that he became locked in time: "Obviously, I have lived very much out of the world; I know little of present-day Dublin or London or Paris, even less of post-modernity, post-structuralism, hard rock or rap, and I cannot write with much conviction about the contemporary scene."

O'Brian listed Jane Austen as one of his favorite writers, and indeed many compared his descriptions of Nelson's navy to Austen's richly depicted small towns in the country. O'Brian was sometimes compared with Forester, but as Al Navis countered, "The Aubrey/Maturin books bear as little resemblance to the Hornblower tales as the series' main characters do to one another. Aubrey is the antithesis of Hornblower. Where Hornblower is short and slight, Aubrey is six feet tall and well over 200 pounds. Where Hornblower is introspective, vulnerable and hesitant, Aubrey is masterful and self-confident. Hornblower's marriage was a disaster; Aubrey is happily married. Hornblower is tone deaf, while Aubrey has a passionate flair for the violin."

At his death, O'Brian had completed, in his usual longhand fashion, three chapters of his next novel, of which the estate was in no hurry to publish. Even if it is never finished, O'Brian's legacy appears ready to endure. For one reason, said biographer King on HeartOfOak.com, because his best works are "set 200 years before they were written, the novels have been tempered against anachronism." In other words, O'Brian never let setting overwhelm character; his books may be set in the past, but their sensibilities are very much in the present.

Works by the Author

Fiction

Caesar (1930)
Hussein (1938)
Testimonies (1952), in England as *Three Bear Witness* (1952)
The Catalans (1953), in England as *The Frozen Flame* (1953)
The Road to Samarcand (1954)
The Golden Ocean (1956), revised (1970)
The Unknown Shore (1959)
Richard Temple (1962)

Aubrey-Maturin Series

Master and Commander (1969)
Post Captain (1972)
H.M.S. Surprise (1973)
The Mauritius Command (1977)
Desolation Island (1978)

The Fortune of War (1979)
The Surgeon's Mate (1980)
The Ionian Mission (1981)
Treason's Harbour (1983)
The Far Side of the World (1984)
The Reverse of the Medal (1986)
The Letter of Marque (1988)
The Thirteen-Gun Salute (1989)
The Nutmeg Consolation (1991)
The Truelove (1992), in England as *Clarissa Oakes* (1992)
The Wine-Dark Sea (1993)
The Commodore (1995)
The Yellow Admiral (1996)
The Hundred Days (1998)
Blue at the Mizzen (1999)
Boxed Set of all 21 books (2004)
No. 21: The Unfinished Twenty-First Novel in the Aubrey/Maturin Series (2004)

Collections

The Walker and Other Stories (1955), in England as *Lying in the Sun and Other Stories* (1956)
The China Wine and Other Stories (1974)
The Last Pool and Other Stories (1980)
The Rendezvous and Other Stories (1995)

Editor

A Book of Voyages (1947)
Men-of-War (1974)
Picasso: A Biography (1976), in England as *Pablo Ruiz Picasso: A Biography* (1976)
Joseph Banks: A Life (1987)

Translator

The Daily Life of the Aztecs on the Eve of the Spanish Conquest, by Jacques Soustelle (1961)
Daily Life in the Time of Jesus (1962), in England as *Daily Life in Palestine at the Time of Christ* (1962)
St. Bartholomew's Night: The Massacre of Saint Bartholomew, by Philippe Erlanger (1962)
The Wreathed Head, by Christine de Rivoyre (1962)
A History of the U.S.A.: From Wilson to Kennedy, by Andre Maurois (1964); also titled *From the New Freedom to the New Frontier: A History of the United States from 1912 to the Present* (1964)

A History of the USSR: From Lenin to Kruschev, by Francoise Mallet-Joris (1964)

When the Earth Trembles, by Haroun Tazieff (1964)

Munich: Peace in Our Time, by Henri Nogueras (1965); in England as *Munich or, The Phoney Peace* (1965)

The Delights of Growing Old, by Maurice Goudeket (1966)

The Uncompromising Heart: A Life of Marie Mancini, Louis XIV's First Love, by Simone de Beauvoir (1966)

The Italian Campaign, by Michel Mohrt (1967)

Memoirs, by Clara Malraux (1967)

The Quicksand War: Prelude to Vietnam, by Lucien Bodard (1967)

The Horsemen, by Joseph Kessel (1968)

Les Belles Images, by Simone de Beauvoir (1968)

The Japanese Challenge, by Robert Guillian (1970)

A Life's Full Summer, by Andre Martinerie (1970)

Papillon, by Henri Charriere (1970)

The Coming of Age, by Simone de Beauvoir (1972); in England as *Old Age* (1972)

The Assassination of Heydrich: 27 May 1942, by Miroslav Ivanov (1973)

Further Adventures of Papillon, by Henri Charriere (1973)

All Said and Done, by Simone de Beauvoir (1974)

The Paths of the Sea, by Pierre Schoendoerffer (1977)

Obsession: An American Love Story, by Yves Berger (1978)

When Things of the Spirit Come First: Five Early Tales, by Simone de Beauvoir (1982)

Adieux: A Farewell to Sartre, by Simone de Beauvoir (1984)

De Gaulle, by Jean Lacouture (1990); in England as *De Gaulle: The Rebel, 1890–1944* (1990)

Motion Pictures Based on the Author's Works

Master and Commander (2003)

For Further Information

"Ahoy! Patrick O'Brian sails again." *Commoneal* (November 8, 1996).

"An Interview with Dean King, Author of Patrick O'Brian: A Life Revealed." *http://www.heartofoak.com/interview2.htm* (viewed May 24, 2003).

"Anchors Aweigh!" *Time* (November 30, 1998).

Bethune, Brian. "Men of the Deep." *Maclean's* (November 24, 2003).

Clines, Francis X. "In the Glare of the Short-Toed Eagle, Or What You Read is All You'll Get." *New York Times* (November 14, 1993).

Cunningham, Arthur. *Patrick O'Brian: Critical Essays and a Bibliography*. New York: Norton, 1994.

Duffy, Brian, and Bruce B. Auster. "A Master of Tales of the Sea." *U.S. News & World Report* (January 17, 2000).

Flynn, Gillian. "Larger Than Life." *Entertainment Weekly* (January 5, 2001).

Goldberg, Carole. "Writer Lied About Past, Deserted His Wife, Son, Dying Daughter." *Hartford Courant* (November 14, 2003).

Grossman, Anne Chotzinoff, and Lisa Grossman. *Lobscouse and Spotted Dog: Which Is a Gastronomic Companion to the Aubrey/Maturin Novels of Patrick O'Brian.* New York: Norton, 1997.

"His Ship Sails On: Author Patrick O'Brian's tales were top-deck adventures." *Entertainment Weekly* (January 21, 2000).

King, Dean. *Patrick O'Brian: A Life Revealed.* New York: Henry Holt, 2000.

King, Dean, with John B. Hattendorf. *A Sea of Words: A Lexicon and Companion for Patrick O'Brian's Seafaring Tales.* New York: Owl Books, 1995.

King, Dean, with John B. Hattendorf. *Harbors and High Seas: An Atlas and Geographical Guide to the Aubrey-Maturin Novels of Patrick O'Brian.* New York: Henry Holt, 1996.

King, Dean, with John B. Hattendorf and J. Worth Estes. *A Sea of Words: A Lexicon and Companion for Patrick O'Brian's Seafaring Tales.* New York: Henry Holt, 1997.

Lacayo, Richard. "At the Heart of the Ocean." *Time* (November 10, 2003).

Lavery, Brian. *Jack Aubrey Commands: An Historical Companion to the Naval World of Patrick O'Brian.* Annapolis, MD: Naval Institute Press, 2003.

McGregor, Tom. *The Making of Master and Commander: The Far Side of the World.* New York: W. W. Norton, 2003.

"Meet the Author: Patrick O'Brian." BookPage. *http://www.bookpage.com/9911bp/patrick_obrian.html* (viewed May 24, 2003).

Navis, Al. "Collecting Patrick O'Brian: The Four-Decade Overnight Sensation." *Firsts* (September 1995).

O'Neill, Richard. *Patrick O'Brian's Navy: The Illustrated Companion to Jack Aubrey's World.* Running Press, 2003.

"Patrick O'Brien." *The Economist* (January 15, 2000).

Peacock, Scot, ed. Patrick O'Brien entry, *Contemporary Authors New Revision Series.* Vol. 74. Detroit: Gale Research, 1999.

Simson, Maria. "Patrick O'Brian: full speed ahead at Norton." *Publishers Weekly* (October 26, 1992).

Snow, Richard. "An Author I'd Walk the Plank For." *New York Times* (November 7, 1991).

Taylor, Robert. "A Rousing Addition to O'Brian's Sea Saga." *Boston Globe* (November 10, 1993).

Tyrangiel, Josh. "The Bold Man and the Sea." *Time* (November 10, 2003).

World of Patrick O'Brian Web page, including newsletter. W. W. Norton. *http://www .wwnorton.com/pob* (viewed May 24, 2003).

West, Patrick. "The secret lives of our Walter Mitties." *New Statesman* (October 30, 2000).

Janette Oke

◆ Historical ◆ Romance ◆ Christian

Champion, Alberta, Canada
1935

◆ *Seasons of the Heart Series*

Credit: Photo Visions by Colin.

About the Author and the Author's Writing

"I see my writing as an opportunity to share my faith," said Janette Oke, a pioneer in inspirational romantic and historical fiction.

"We live in a hurting, confused world that is searching for answers and purpose," she continued on her Web site. "Many are also searching for love. Not frothy romance, though they may feel that is the answer to their inner need, but love, constant and committed, is what they really seek."

The writer was born Janette Steeves in Champion, Alberta, in 1935, the daughter of American citizens, a farmer and his wife. Her ancestors had come from Germany to Nova Scotia in 1766, a decade after the Acadians were banished by the British. They survived thanks to help from a French man named Belliveau.

In 1957, she graduated from Mountain View Bible College in Didsbury, Alberta, and married Edward L. Oke, a professor. They raised four children. The Okes pastored at churches in Indiana and Alberta. Oke also worked as a bank teller, proofreader, bookkeeper, and mail clerk. She was treasurer for Mountain View Bible College and a loan officer and teller at Royal Bank of Canada, both in Alberta. Her husband died in 1984, after serving as president of Mountain View Bible College.

After thinking long and hard about it, Oke wrote a draft of a novel in summer 1977. The first publisher she sent it to returned the manuscript. It sat on a shelf; she tried another publisher. The third publisher, Bethany Fellowship, agreed to publish *Love Comes Softy* in 1979. She quickly wrote a sequel, and her career was underway.

When she began writing, she was drawn to the history of her country, Canada.

"My interest in writing the type of material that I have comes from a personal interest in that era of our history, and a feeling that little had been written with a Christian slant on the time period. I also have the feeling that society is searching for a deeper, more committed type of lasting love. Letters from readers have confirmed this," she told *Contemporary Authors*.

Oke said she believes strongly in family values and opposes the depiction of sex in romantic novels. She hopes to impart a sense of moral values, particularly to her younger readers.

"Even as a child Janette had enjoyed putting words together," said Laurel Oke Logan in a biography of her mother, "but she had always promised herself that she would not attempt to write for publication until she received special training. Occasionally she chaffed against her self-imposed restriction. . . . There had just never been the time nor the money for it."

Oke has said that her characters are composites of real people, but not based specifically on anyone she knows. She led something of a rugged life in her early years in Alberta and has accumulated research material since to give her books a feeling of authenticity. Oke has written many of her books in seclusion at a condominium in the Canadian mountains, producing an initial draft in as few as seven days. She aims her stories at young women.

When Calls the Heart, the first book in the author's Canadian West series, is about pretty, cultured, and educated Elizabeth Thatcher. Raised in the eastern part of Canada, she's not prepared for a teaching position on the frontier. But she meets her task with love and humor, and determination. She meets Wynn, a mounted policeman who is determined never to marry. Can Elizabeth change his mind?

Oke's fans weren't satisfied four books told the whole story, and repeated requests prompted the author to write two more books, this time centering on two children of the original characters. In the same fashion, the Prairie Legacy series carries on with four books featuring grandchildren of Marty and Clark Davis of the Love Comes Softly series.

Heart of the Wilderness, one of the Women of the West books, tells the story of trapper George McMannus, who travels night and day from his wilderness cabin when he learns that his daughter and son-in-law have died in a river accident. His only granddaughter, Kendra Marty, is not quite four years old and he must provide for her. But is his backwoods life proper for the little girl?

The 1992 recipient of the President's Award from the Evangelical Christian Publishers Association for her significant contribution to Christian fiction, Oke has also written poetry, devotionals, and children's books. A half dozen of her Women of the West books were repackaged specifically for teen readers. She has collaborated in recent years with her daughter and with writer T. Davis Bunnon on the Song of Acadia books. These novels follow the friendship of two young women, Louise Belleveau and Catherine Price, one French, one English, in the turbulent 1750s in what was then called Acadia, present-day Canada.

Oke is pleased with the strong following for her books. She commented on her Web site, "My hope is that my books, which I do not regard as 'romance novels' but as slices of life, will show readers that a personal faith in God and the fellowship of family and selected friends will bring harmony and inner peace to their lives."

Works by the Author

Fiction

The Red Geranium (1995)
Nana's Gift (1996)
The Matchmakers (1997)

Canadian West Series

When Calls the Heart (1983)
When Comes the Spring (1985)
When Breaks the Dawn (1986)
When Hope Springs New (1986)
Beyond the Gathering Storm (2000)
When Tomorrow Comes (2001)

Love Comes Softly Series

Love Comes Softly (1979)
Love's Enduring Promise (1980)
Love's Long Journey (1982)
Love's Abiding Joy (1983)
Love's Unending Legacy (1984)
Love's Unfolding Dream (1987)
Love Takes Wing (1988)
Love Finds a Home (1989)

Prairie Legacy Series

The Tender Years (1998)
A Quiet Strength (1999)
A Searching Heart (1999)
Like Gold Refined (2000)

Seasons of the Heart Series

Once Upon a Summer (1981)
The Winds of Autumn (1987)
Winter is Not Forever (1988)
Spring's Gentle Promise (1989)

Women of the West Series

The Calling of Emily Evans (1990)
Julia's Last Hope (1990)
Roses for Mama (1991)
A Woman Named Damaris (1991)
The Measure of a Heart (1992)
They Called Her Mrs. Doc (1992)
A Bride for Donnigan (1993)
Heart of the Wilderness (1993)
Too Long a Stranger (1994)
The Bluebird and The Sparrow (1995)

A Gown of Spanish Lace (1995)
Drums of Change (1996)

Written with T. Davis Bunn

Return to Harmony (1996)
Another Homecoming (1997)
Tomorrow's Dream (1998)

Song of Acadia Series

The Meeting Place (1999)
The Sacred Shore (2000)
The Birthright (2001)
The Beloved Land (2002)
The Distant Beacon (2002)

Written with Laurel Oke Logan

Dana's Valley (2001)

Collections

Hey, Teacher (1981)
Quiet Places, Warm Thoughts (1983)
Too Long a Stranger (1994)

Books for Children

Spunky's Diary (1982)
New Kid in Town (1983)
The Prodigal Cat (1984)
Duck Tails (1985)
The Impatient Turtle (1986)
A Cote of Many Colors (1987)
Prairie Dog Town (1988)
Maury Had a Little Lamb (1989)
Trouble in a Fur Coat (1990)
This Little Pig (1991)
Pordy's Prickly Problem (1993)
Who's New at the Zoo? (2001)

Poetry

Janette Oke: My Favorite Verse (1987)

Devotional Books

The Father Who Calls (1988)
The Father of Love (1989)
Father of My Heart (1990)
Janette Oke's Reflections on the Christmas Story (1994)

For Further Information

Cash, Amy. "Janette Oke." *http://falcon.jmu.edu/~ramseyil/oke.htm* (viewed May 15, 2003).

Janette Oke interview. Christian Books. *http://www.christianbook.com/Christian/Books/cms_sp/49580906?sp=1001&file=DPEP/Interview/oke_interview.htm&event-SP1001* (viewed May 15, 2003).

Janette Oke Web site. *http://www.janetteoke.com/* (viewed May 15, 2003).

Jones, Daniel, and John D. Jorgenson, eds. Janette Oke entry, *Contemporary Authors New Revision Series*. Vol. 58. Detroit: Gale Research, 1997.

Logan, Laurel Oke. *Janette Oke: A Heart for the Prairie: The untold story of one of the most beloved novelist of our time*. Minneapolis: Bethany House, 1993.

Diana Palmer

◆ Romance ◆ Historical

Cuthbert, Georgia
1946

◆ *Long Tall Texan Series*

Credit: Maureen Stead.

About the Author and the Author's Writing

Paperback romance writer Diana Palmer starting churning out several romances a year beginning in 1979, but it was not until 2002 that she saw her first novel published as a hardcover. She certainly paid her dues.

Susan Spaeth was born in Cuthbert, Georgia, in 1946, but grew up with grandparents in Calhoun County while her parents completed their college educations. Her father became a college professor, her mother a nurse and journalist. She married James Edward Kyle, a computer consultant, in 1972, and they have one son.

Through the 1970s, the author worked as a newspaper reporter for the *Gainesville Times*, *TriCounty Advertiser*, and *Atlanta Constitution*. She was also active on the board of her local American Cancer Society chapter. When her husband returned to college to earn a diploma in computer programming in 1995, the author enrolled at Piedmont College to complete requirements for a major in history and a double minor in archaeology and Spanish. She continued to work toward her master's in history at California State University, specializing in Native American studies.

Given her string of love stories, it may come as a surprise to learn that the author's first published novel was science fiction. That and several of her earliest books were published under her real name before she took pennames so she would not compete with herself as she contracted with various publishers. The author was also known as Diana Blayne and Katy Currie—and of course Diana Palmer, the name that established her reputation. She wrote mainstream romances for MIRA Books, contemporary series romances for Silhouette, and historical romances for Fawcett Books—ultimately garnering *Romantic Times Magazine's* Lifetime Achievement Award.

Palmer's Long Tall Texan series has stayed in print for more than fifteen years. She also has a handful of other series, or books written years apart but linked by common characters. Several of her early books have been reissued.

The Savage Heart, typical of the author's books, is set in 1891 in Montana and follows the years-long relationship of Matt Davis, actually a Sioux named Raven Following, with Tess Meredith, who nurses him back to health following a massacre. *The Texas Ranger* is about Josette Langley, branded a vicious tease for apparently falsely accusing a boy of rape. The policeman who investigated the case, Marc Brannon, continues to encounter Josette, and they of course fall in love, despite great obstacles. Cord Romero and Maggie Barton are featured in *Desperado*. Cord is a ranch owner; Maggie is an office worker. They suffer a love-hate you romance, but manage to work out their differences.

Lawless finds Texas Ranger Judd Dunn secretly wed to a sixteen-year-old, Chrissy Gaines, as a way of helping her escape an abusive father. Judd figures to back out of the marriage when Chrissy turns twenty-one; Chrissy, however, is very much in love with Judd and has to deal with a rival when an actress comes to their ranch to make a movie. A *Publishers Weekly* reviewer criticized the book for unbelievable characters, but suggested that "readers looking for steamy, undemanding escapism will find this fits the bill."

The author said in *Twentieth-Century Romance and Historical Writers* she relies on her journalism background to glean telling details in researching her books. "My books are hallmarked by their regional settings, old-fashioned morality and virtues, spirited heroines, and rugged, uncompromising heroes," she said.

Barbara E. Kemp, in *Twentieth-Century Romance and Historical Writers*, noted Palmer's ability to create initially unappealing heroes and transform them through love into decent, believable men.

Characters are obviously vital in Palmer's books, but setting also plays an important role. As she avidly read Zane Grey novels as a youth, Palmer loves writing about the state of Texas. But, she cautions would-be writers on the Harlequin Web site, "Your own uniqueness is the thing that will help you sell your work. Never try to write like anyone else."

Works by the Author

Fiction

Lacy (1991), sequel to *The Cowboy and the Lady*
Amelia (1993)
Nora (1993)
Noelle (1993)
Trilby (1993)
Magnolia (1996/1997)
The Savage Heart (1997)
Midnight Rider (1998)
Once in Paris (1998)
3-in-1 Montana Mavericks (1999), includes *Rogue Stallion*
Paper Rose (1999)
Lord of the Desert (2000)
The Texas Ranger (2001), sequel to *Lord of the Desert*
Desperado (2002)
Lawless (2003)
Renegade (2004)

Long Tall Texans Series

Calhoun (1988), Silhouette Romance 580
Justin (1988), Silhouette Romance 592
Sutton's Way (1989), Silhouette Romance 670
Tyler (1989), Silhouette Romance 604
Connal (1990), Silhouette Romance 741
Ethan (1990), Silhouette Romance 694
Evan (1991), Silhouette Romance 819
Harden (1991), Silhouette Romance 783
Donavan (1992), Silhouette Romance 843
Emmet (1992), Silhouette Romance 910
Long, Tall Texans I (1994), includes *Calhoun/Justin/Tyler*
Regan's Pride (1994), Silhouette Romance 1000
Abduction and Seduction (1995), includes novella
Long, Tall Texans II (1995), includes *Sutton's Way, Ethan,* and *Connal*; reprinted as
     Texans at Heart (2003)
That Burke Man (1995), Silhouette Desire 913
Coltrain's Proposal (1996), Silhouette Romance #1103
Husbands on Horseback (1996), includes novella
Lone Star Christmas (1997), includes story
A Long Tall Texan Summer (1997), collection
Long, Tall Texans III (1997), includes *Harden, Evan,* and *Donovan*
Beloved (1999), Silhouette Desire 1189
Callaghan's Bride (1999), Silhouette Romance 1355
Long, Tall Texans IV (1999), includes *Emmett, Regan,* and *Burke*
Love with a Long, Tall Texan (1999), collection
Weddings in White (1999), includes *The Princess Bride/Callaghan's Bride/Unlikely
     Lover*
Matt Caldwell: Texas Tycoon (2000), Silhouette Special Edition 1297
Long, Tall Texan Weddings (2001), includes *Coltrain's Proposal, Beloved,* and *Paper
     Husband*
Lionhearted (2002), Silhouette Romance 1631; sequel to *A Man of Means*
A Man of Means (2002), Silhouette Desire 1429
Evan (2004)

MacFadden Romances

127. *Now and Forever* (1979)
139. *Storm Over the Lake* (1979)
150. *To Have and To Hold* (1979)
179. *Sweet Enemy* (1980)
218. *Love on Trial* (1980)
223. *Dream's End* (1980)
250. *Bound By A Promise* (1980)

256. *To Love and To Cherish* (1980)
268. *If Winter Comes* (1981)
278. *At Winter's End* (1981)

Montana Mavericks Series

Rogue Stallion (1994)
Montana Mavericks Weddings (1998), novellas

Most Wanted Series

The Case of the Confirmed Bachelor (1992), Silhouette Desire 715
The Case of the Mesmerizing Boss (1992), Silhouette Desire 702
The Case of the Missing Secretary (1992), Silhouette Desire 733
Most Wanted (2000), includes first three books

Silhouette Desire Series

12. *The Cowboy and the Lady* (1982)
26. *September Morning* (1982), sequel to *Here Come the Grooms*
50. *Friends and Lovers* (1983), sequel to *Rage of Passion*
80. *Fire and Ice* (1983)
102. *Snow Kisses* (1983)
110. *Diamond Girl* (1984)
157. *The Rawhide Man* (1984)
175. *Lady Love* (1984)
193. *Cattleman's Choice* (1985)
252. *Love By Proxy* (1985), Men Made in America
271. *Eye of the Tiger* (1986)
289. Loveplay (1986)
306. *Rawhide and Lace* (1986), sequel to *Unlikely Lover*
325. *Rage of Passion* (1987)
349. *Fit for a King* (1987), sequel to *Reluctant Father*
391. *Betrayed by Love* (1987)
469. *Reluctant Father* (1989)
492. *Hoodwinked* (1989)
528. *His Girl Friday* (1989)
606. *Hunter* (1990), sequel to *His Girl Friday*
618. *Nelson's Brand* (1991)
643. *The Best Is Yet to Come* (1991)
799. *Night of Love* (1993)
829. *Secret Agent Man* (1994), sequel to *King's Ransom*
1000. *Man of Ice* (1996)
1099. *The Patient Nurse* (1997)
The Wedding in White (2000), online promo

Silhouette Romances Series

254. *Darling Enemy* (1983)
301. *Roomful of Roses* (1984)
314. *Heart of Ice* (1984)
328. *Passion Flower* (1984)
406. *After the Music* (1986)
436. *Champagne Girl* (1986)
472. *Unlikely Lover* (1986)
532. *Woman Hater* (1988)
971. *King's Ransom* (1993), sequel to *Night of Love*
1210. *Mystery Man* (1997)
1282. *The Princess Bride* (1998)
1718. *Cattleman's Romance* (2004)

Silhouette Special Edition Series

33. *Heather's Song* (1982), sequel to *Passion Flower*
239. *The Australian* (1985)
991. *Maggie's Dad* (1995)
1417. *The Last Mercenary* (2001)

Soldier of Fortune Series

Soldier of Fortune (1985), Silhouette Romance 340
The Tender Stranger (1985), Silhouette Desire 230
Enamored (1988), Silhouette Desire 420
Mercenary's Woman (2000), Silhouette Romance 1444
Soldiers of Fortune (2000), includes *Soldier of Fortune*, *The Tender Stranger*, and *Enamored*
The Winter Soldier (2001), Silhouette Desire 1351

Collections and Anthologies

Silhouette Christmas Stories (1987)
Duets 1 (1990), includes *Sweet Enemy* and *Love on Trial*
Duets 2 (1990), includes *Storm Over the Lake* and *To Love and To Cherish*
Duets 3 (1990), includes *If Winter Comes* and *Now and Forever*
Duets 4 (1990), includes *After the Music* and *Dream's End*
Duets 5 (1990), includes *Bound By a Promise* and *Passion Flower*
Duets 6 (1990), includes *To Have and To Hold* and *The Cowboy and the Lady*
Silhouette Summer Sizzlers (1990)
Silhouette To Mother With Love (1993)
Love's Legacy (1996)
Lone Star Christmas, with Joan Johnston (1997)

With a Southern Touch (2002), includes sequel to *The Texas Ranger*
Blessings in Disguise (2003), includes novella
A Hero's Kiss (2003)

Written as Diana Blayne

Denim and Lace (1990)

Candlelight Ecstasy Series

94. *A Waiting Game* (1982)
113. *A Loving Arrangement* (1983)
138. *White Sand Wild Sea* (1983)
184. *Dark Surrender* (1983)

Candlelight Ecstasy Supreme Series

49. *Color Love Blue* (1984)
110. *Tangled Destinies* (1986)

Written as Katy Currie

Silhouette Inspirational Series

5. *Blind Promises* (1984), Love Inspired

Written as Susan Kyle

The Morcai Battalion (1980)
Diamond Spur (1988), rewritten (2002)
Fire Brand (1989)
Night Fever (1990)
True Colors (1991)
Escapade (1992)
After Midnight (1993)
All That Glitters (1995)

For Further Information

"An Interview with Diana Palmer." Harlequin Books. *http:www/eharlequin.com/cms.authors/authorDetail.jhtml;jsessionid=SXSKVKPORQH4HLAUEAKSAOQ?authorID=155&type=interview* (viewed May 29, 2003).

Desperado review. All About Romance. *http://www.likesbooks.com/jane105.html* (viewed May 29, 2003).

Diana Palmer Web site. *http://www.dianapalmer.com* (viewed May 28, 2003).

Kemp, Barbara E. Diana Palmer entry, *Twentieth-Century Romance and Historical Writers.* 2nd edition, edited by Lesley Henderson. Chicago: St. James Press, 1990.

Lawless review. *Publishers Weekly* (June 16, 2003).

Olendorf, Donna, ed. Susan Kyle entry, *Contemporary Authors*. Vol. 141. Detroit: Gale Research, 1994.

The Savage Heart review. All About Romance. *http://www.likesbooks.com/anne13 .html* (viewed May 29, 2003).

The Texas Ranger review. All About Romance. *http://www.likesbooks.com/jeny97.html* (viewed May 29, 2003).

Sara Paretsky

◆   Mystery

Ames, Iowa
1947

◆   *V. I. Warshawski Series*

Courtesy of Dominick
Abel Literary Agency, Inc.
Credit: Steven E. Gross.

About the Author and the Author's Writing

Along with Marcia Muller, P. D. James, and Sue Grafton, Sara Paretsky is a mother of the modern female private eye novel. Perhaps more than the others, Paretsky has probed society's darker underbelly, garnering awards including the Silver Dagger from the British Crime Writers Association (for *Blood Shot* in 1988) and the Marlowe Award from the German Crime Writers Association (for *Guardian Angel* in 1993).

The author was born in Ames, Iowa, in 1947, the daughter of a scientist and a librarian. Her first prose was a short story published in *American Girl* magazine when she was eleven. She received a bachelor of arts degree in political science from the University of Kansas in 1967.

She moved to Chicago and completed studies toward her MBA and Ph.D. in history degrees, which she received in 1977 from the University of Chicago. She held a variety of jobs while at the university, including bottle washer and conference manager. She went on to spend a decade as a marketing manager with CNA Insurance in Chicago—and later put her background in the financial world to good use in her novels.

Maintaining her interest in writing, Paretsky in the mid-1970s decided to work on a mystery novel. She had read Rex Stout mysteries as a teen, Raymond Chandler when in her twenties. She felt women were not particularly well treated in the private detective genre. A simple feminine version of Philip Marlowe would not work, she decided; her character had to experience sexism and social pressures.

Paretsky formed a strong female detective "who could be a whole person, which meant that she could be a sexual person without being evil. That she could be an effective problem solver, as women are in reality, but not very often in fiction or on the screen," the author told Linda Richards for *January* magazine.

Paretsky admits to having the same sharp tongue as her heroine V. I. Warshawski, the same part-Polish background, the same love for the Chicago Cubs, and the same fondness for golden retrievers. They differ in other ways, however. For one thing, Paretsky is married, since 1976, to Courtney Wright, a physics professor who has three sons by a previous marriage; V. I. has had a number of lovers and has abandoned them. For another thing, V. I. packs a gun, Paretsky wouldn't keep one in the house. And there is one more difference—V. I. grew up in the shadow of South Chicago's steel mills, Paretsky in Kansas, where she attended a country school and played third base for the ball team.

"Almost everything she wears is in my wardrobe," the mystery writer told *The Writer's* Elfrieda Abbe. "I have those Bruno Magli pumps. But she wears colors I can't wear because she's dark and I'm very fair. I keep wanting to deduct my clothes as research, but the accountant won't let me."

Paretsky wrote three books in the evenings while still working full time, tutoring, and singing in a choir. It was easiest to utilize her own working background in insurance to devise a plot about workers' compensation fraud—learning about some of the common and not-so-common scams from older workers in her office.

Paretsky said library sales helped launch her career. "My first book, *Indemnity Only*, sold 4,500 copies; 2,500 of those were to libraries. The sales were enough for my publisher to request a second book," she explained in *New Statesman*.

Not a fast writer, the author joked in an Amazon.co.uk interview—"self-doubt makes me write a sentence then go to bed for six weeks while I think about it." Paretsky has produced a dozen novels in twenty years. She is not fond of research, but does as much as it takes to make her story convincing.

"The novels . . . are dense with the atmosphere of Chicago, a single woman's life amidst friends and family, the professional relationship of a detective with the police and other connections, and the difficulty of affecting more than a minute aspect of contemporary social injustice," Katherine Gregory Klein wrote in *St. James Crime & Mystery Writers*. "Amidst a raft of new detective novelists focusing on women as private investigators, Sara Paretsky makes a unique and lasting contribution."

V. I. ages gradually in the course of the books, and readers have reacted in different ways, the author has said. Women Paretsky's age—in their mid-fifties—want the heroine to get older, but younger women and men readers seem to wish she would stay young.

Paretsky says she made her decision "because although she [V. I.] is a fictional character," the crime writer said on her Web site, "she is grounded in historical events: she came of age during the civil rights movement and the anti-war movement. . . . [H]er cases are all based on real events."

In *Killing Orders*, V. I.'s Aunt Rosa is suspected of placing counterfeit securities in the safe of St. Albert's Roman Catholic Church. *Tunnel Vision* is set against a background of Chicago's homeless. But *Total Recall*, coincidentally released barely a week before the Twin Towers and Pentagon terrorist attacks, finds V. I.'s journalist boyfriend Morrell going to Afghanistan to investigate the Taliban. That came closer to anticipating the news than the author ever expected.

What drives Warshawski? According to Kathleen Gregory Klein in *The Woman Detective*, "V. I. has become a private investigator not only to be her own boss but also—'a la Doña Quixote perhaps'—to redress the imbalances between guilty and innocent she'd seen in the public defenders office. . . . As a detective, she contrasts herself unfavorably with [Dorothy L. Sayers'] Lord Peter Wimsey, who would have charmed rather than bullied; favorably with [Mickey Spillane's] Mike Hammer, who could barely think."

Paretsky's only non-V. I. novel so far is *Ghost Country*. Writing in the *New York Times* the author said, "I don't sit down to write books of social or political commentary. Both as a reader and a writer, I'm pulled by stories, not by ideas; I see the world in the stories of the people around me. It's just that the stories that speak most to me are those of people . . . who can't speak for themselves, who feel powerless and voiceless in the larger world."

In 1986, the author helped start and served as a president of Sisters in Crime, an international organization of women mystery writers—now 3,200 strong, with forty-six local chapters—who, feeling overshadowed by men, worked to obtain more reviews of their works and otherwise promote themselves.

Paretsky told *Armchair Detective* interviewer Catherine M. Nelson that reader reaction to her novels is gratifying. Women particularly have told her "that reading about my character has given them courage to face difficult situations in their lives. And the thought that I've done something that has helped people in such an intimate way really moves me more than I can say. It's probably my strongest impetus to keep writing about V. I."

Works by the Author

Fiction

Ghost Country (1998)

V. I. Warshawski Series

Indemnity Only (1982)
Deadlock (1984)
Killing Orders (1985)
Bitter Medicine (1987), in England as *Toxic Shock* (1988)
Blood Shot (1988)
Burn Marks (1990)
Guardian Angel (1992)
Tunnel Vision (1994)
Hard Time (1999)
Total Recall (2001)
Blacklist (2003)
Fire Sale (2005)

Collections

Windy City Blues (1995), in England as *V. I. for Short* (1995)
V. I. x 2 (2002), chapbook

Editor

Beastly Tales: The Mystery Writers of America Anthology (1989)
A Woman's Eye: Original Crime Stories by Women (1991)
Women on the Case (1996) in the United Kingdom as *Woman's Other Eye* (1996)

Anthologies

The Eyes Have It (1984)
The Eyes Have It, volume 2 (1986)
Mean Streets edited by Robet J. Randisi (1986)
Murder and Mystery in Chicago, edited by Carol-Lynn Rossel Waugh (1987)
New Black Mask volume 8, edited by Matthew J. Bruccoli and Richard Lamnay (1987)
Suspicious Characters, edited by Bill Pronzini (1987)
Lady on the Case, edited by Marcia Muller (1988)
Raymond Chalndler's Philip Marlow, edited by Byron Preiss (1988)
City Sleuths and Tough Guys, edited by David Willis McCullough (1989)
Homicidal Acts, edited by Bill Pronzini (1989)
Ms. Murder, edited by Marie Smith (1989)
New Crimes, edited by Maxim Jakubowski (1989)
Reader, I Murdered Him, edited by Alison Hennegan (1989)
Sisters in Crime, edited by Marilyn Wallace (1989)
Year's Best Mystery and Suspense Stories, edited by Edward D. Hoch (1989)
Sisters in Crime 3, edited by Marilyn Wallace (1990)
Third WomanSleuth Anthology (1990)
Under the Gun, edited by Ed Gorman (1990)
1st Culprit (1993)
2nd Culprit (1994)
Reader, I Murdered Him Too (1995)
A Taste of Life and Other Stories (1995)
Best American Mystery Stories of the Century, edited by Otto Penzler and Tony Hillerman (2000)
Century of Great Suspense Stories, edited by Jeffrey Deaver (2001)
Most Wanted, edited by Robert J. Randisi (2002)
Oxford Book of Detective Stories, edited by Patricia Craig (2002)
World's Finest Mystery and Crime Stories: Third Annual Collection, edited by Ed Gorman (2002)

Motion Pictures Based on the Author's Works

V. I. Warshawski (1991)

For Further Information

Abbe, Elfrieda. "Risky business: Sara Paretsky pushes the boundaries of her detective series." *The Writer* (October 2003).

Klein, Kathleen Gregory. Sara Paretsky entry, *St. James Guide to Crime & Mystery Writers.* 4th edition, edited by Jay P. Pederson. Detroit: St. James Press, 1996.

Klein, Kathleen Gregory. *The Woman Detective; Gender & Genre*. Urbana: University of Illinois Press, 1988.

Nelson, Catherine M. "Trouble is Her Business." *Armchair Detective* (summer 1991).

Paretsky, Sara. "The new censorship." *New Statesman* (June 2, 2003).

Paretsky, Sara. "Writers on Writing: A Storyteller Stands Where Justice Confronts Basic Needs." *New York Times* (September 25, 2000).

Peacock, Scot, ed. Sara Paretsky entry, *Contemporary Authors New Revision Series*. Vol. 95. Detroit: Gale Research, 2001.

Richards, Linda. Sara Paretsky interview. *January Magazine. http://www.january magazine.com/profiles/paretsky.html* (viewed April 28, 2003).

Sara Paretsky interview. Amazon.com. *http://www.amazon.co.uk/exec/obidos/tg/feature/-/66967/ref=ed_art_83926_txt_1/026-9976128-8595614* (viewed May 20, 2003).

Sara Paretsky Web site. *http://www.saraparetsky.com/* (viewed May 20, 2003).

Swanson, Jean, and Dean James. *By a Woman's Hand: A Guide to Mystery Fiction by Women*. 2nd edition. New York: Berkley, 1996.

Robert B. Parker

Springfield, Massachusetts
1932

◆ *Spenser Series*

Courtesy of Helen Brann Agency.
Credit: John Earle.

About the Author and the Author's Writing

Writing book after book featuring the same hero can be tricky. You have to be careful how you introduce the character each time: give just enough information to make things clear to the new reader, but not so much as to bore an old one. With a series, the reader knows from the start the hero will survive whatever ordeal he or she faces, so again the author has to carefully portray the character as just vulnerable enough to make things interesting.

Spenser creator Robert B. Parker said in *The Writer* in 1981 that there are opportunities as wells challenges in having a series characcater. "If you create a character in one book that you like (Hawk, for instance, in *Promised Land*), you can use him again. And if you didn't get him right the first time, you have another chance, and another. Moreover, you have the chance to develop your hero over a sequence of books and during a span of real time. Thus Spenser, who first appeared when I was 41, can grow, as I have."

Robert Brown Parker was born in Springfield, Massachusetts, in 1932, the son of a telephone company executive and his wife. He grew up reading pulp fiction magazines and detective stories. He earned a bachelor of arts degree from Colby College in 1954 and his master's degree in English and his doctoral degree in literature from Boston University in 1957 and 1970, respectively. He married Joan Hall in 1956, and they have two sons.

Parker served in the U.S. Army in Korea from 1954 to 1956. After working as a management trainee, technical and advertising writer, advertising partner, film consultant, and lecturer in English, he became an instructor in English at Massachusetts State College at Lowell in 1964. He lectured at Suffolk University from 1965 to 1966, taught at Massachusetts State College at Bridgewater from 1966 to 1968, and worked his way up to professor of English at Northeastern University, leaving in 1979 for a full-time career writing mystery novels. This was all part of a plan; Parker said in one interview that he sought his doctorate specifically so he could enjoy the short work week of university professorships, allowing him to devote the rest of his time to writing fiction.

Having written his dissertation, titled "The Violent Hero, Wilderness Heritage and Urban Reality: A Study of the Private Eye in the Novels of Dashiell Hammett, Raymond Chandler, and Ross Macdonald," and teaching a course called "The Novel of Violence" at Northeastern, he was comfortably prepared to create his own variant on the American private eye, Spenser, which he did with *The Godwulf Manuscript* in 1974.

"When it came time to write the book, that's what I knew how to do. I always wanted to write, and when I got to the point where I had an opportunity to do so . . . ," he said in an interview with Amanda Smith, "I sat down and began to write it. I didn't decide, I think I'll choose this genre rather than that one. I started typing, and that's what came out. And I stay with it cause I like it and because I know how."

In the years since, with a deceptively plain but powerful style, with a barb-tongued, literate hero who spends nearly as much time in the kitchen preparing meals and schmoozing with his longtime companion Susan Silverman as he does quizzing sources and grappling with thugs, Parker has risen to the top of the private detective genre.

"Parker's influence on the detective novel is, arguably, nearly as great as Poe's or Conan Doyle's," according to *Publishers Weekly's* Jeff Zaleski. "Through his primary hero, Spenser . . . , Parker has modernized the American private eye novel beyond its pulp roots, bringing to it psychological realism and sociopolitical awareness."

"Spenser's first four novels were an explosive opening salvo that has still to be matched," said an enthused a writer on the Thrilling Detective Web site. "Here was a P.I. who wasn't a California-bound loser and loner, who actually enjoyed his life, and was capable, it seemed, of having an actual relationship with a woman who wasn't a ditzy housewife or some psycho-killer nympho. He's as cold and ruthless as Hammer, but as chivalric as Marlowe, and as plain spoken as The Continental Op."

The hero owes a lot to the creator, as Parker explained in an interview with Tom Auer: "Spenser is entirely made up of stuff which comes out of my interior, and therefore, it is reasonable to see that he probably reflects what's going on in my life. I mean, writers write out of what they've got, and what they've got is whatever's going on. So I'm not consciously trying to update him."

Parker's Spenser has appeared in a regular television series, *Spenser for Hire*, and in A&E made-for-TV movies, the latter based on Parker scripts derived from the novels. Parker developed another fiction series about private eye Sunny Randall at the request of actress Helen Hunt and with an eye toward a motion picture series.

Joan Parker, with whom the author has cowritten two nonfiction books, is an important resource for this series. "I have to rely quite heavily on Joan to write Sunny Randall," Parker told the *Boston Globe's* Robin Dougherty. "She'll say, 'It's not called rouge anymore' or explain how to put on pantyhose. I don't think I could have undertaken [Sunny] without Joan."

The author has a third ongoing series featuring police chief Jesse Stone. The third-person point of view in these books, in the view of *Boston Globe* reviewer Richard Dyer, gives Parker "options he doesn't have in the Spenser novels. He introduces the serial killers as early as page one [in *Stone Cold*], and we follow their plans as they tilt against Jesse." (Stone also shows up briefly in a Spenser novel, *Back Story*.)

Parker also completed a Raymond Chandler manuscript featuring Philip Marlowe, and wrote a new novel in the series. A recent novel, *Double Play*, features the black baseball player Jackie Robinson.

Parker excels in the long form, and long resisted writing short stories until lured into it by *Playboy*. "They offered good pay, an autographed picture of Hefner, that type of thing,"

Parker said in an April 2000 interview with Bookreporter. "So I wrote a short story, featuring Spenser, titled 'Surrogate.' And *Playboy* rejected it!" The story was eventually published elsewhere, but only rarely—such as "The Kitchen Caper" for the *Boston Globe Magazine* in 2003—has he tried short fiction again.

The author has a regular writing routine, five days a week, beginning in late morning and ending when he has produced five manuscript pages. After lunch, he works on screenplays or other projects. After that he works out.

What does Parker have to say about the craft of writing? "Writing is not an unintellectual activity," he told *Boston Globe* writer John Koch, "but in some ways it's like playing the piano—which I can't do, but I know some good piano players who can play the piano and talk to you at the same time."

And about Spenser's popularity? "I guess it has something to do with a story about someone who doesn't fail," he told *PW's* Zelseki. "And they're about love, they're about courage, they're about honor. And I guess they're well told. . . . I have always thought that writing should be about the most meaning with the fewest words."

Works by the Author

Fiction

Wilderness (1979)
Love and Glory (1983)
All Our Yesterdays (1994)
Gunman's Rhapsody (2001)
Double Play (2004)

Jesse Stone Series

Night Passage (1997)
Trouble in Paradise (1998)
Death in Paradise (2001)
Stone Cold (2003)

Philip Marlowe Series

Poodle Springs, with Raymond Chandler (1989)
Perchance to Dream (1990), sequel to *The Big Sleep* by Raymond Chandler

Spenser Series

The Godwulf Manuscript (1973)
God Save the Child (1974)
Mortal Stakes (1975)
Promised Land (1976)
The Judas Goat (1978)
Looking for Rachel Wallace (1980)
Early Autumn (1981)

A Savage Place (1981)
Ceremony (1982)
The Widening Gyre (1983)
Valediction (1984)
A Catskill Eagle (1985)
Taming a Sea Horse (1986)
Pale King and Princes (1987)
Crimson Joy (1988)
The Early Spenser: Three Complete Novels (1989), includes *The Godwulf Manuscript. God Save the Child*, and *Mortal Stakes*
Playmates (1989)
Stardust (1990)
Pastime (1991)
Double Deuce (1992)
Paper Doll (1993)
Walking Shadow (1994)
Thin Air (1995)
Chance (1996)
Small Vices (1997)
Sudden Mischief (1998)
Hush Money (1999)
Hugger Mugger (2000)
Potshot (2001)
Widow's Walk (2002)
Back Story (2003)
Bad Business (2004)

Sunny Randall Novels

Family Honor (1999)
Perish Twice (2000)
Shrink Rap (2002)

Anthologies

New Black Mask, edited by Matthew J. Bruccoli and Richmard Layman (1985)
New Crimes 3 (1993)
Murderer's Row (2001)
Best American Mystery Stories 2002, edited by James Elroy (2002)

Teleplays

B. L. Stryker: Blues for Buder (1989)
B. L. Stryker: High Rise (1990)
Spenser: Ceremony (1993)

Spenser: Pale King and Princes (1993)
Spenser: The Judas Goat (1994)
Spenser: A Savage Place (1995)
Small Vices (1999)
Thin Air (2000)
Walking Shadow (2001)
Monte Walsh (2003)

Television Movies or Series Based on the Author's Works

The Promised Land (1985)
Spenser for Hire (1985–1988), series
Spenser (1993–) made-for-television movies A&E

Nonfiction

The Personal Response to Literature (1970), contributor
Order and Diversity: The Craft of Prose, with Peter L. Sandberg (1973)
Sports Illustrated Weight Training: The Athlete's Free-Weight Guide, with John R. Marsh (1974)
Three Weeks in Spring, with Joan Parker (1978)
The Private Eye in Hammett and Chandler (1984)
Parker on Writing (1985)
A Year at the Races, with Joan Parker (1990)
Spenser's Boston (1994)
Boston: History in the Making (1999)

For Further Information

Auer, Tom, with James Anderson. "Robert B. Parker: The Man Who Would Be Philip Marlowe." *Bloomsbury Review* (June 1991).

Bullets and Beer: The Spenser Home Page. *http://www.mindspring.com/~boba4/* (viewed May 30, 2003).

Charm, Robert E. "Spenser For Sale." *New England Business* (May 19, 1986).

Donnelly, Barry. "A Catcher in the Rye." *The Armchair Detective* (winter 1990).

Dougherty, Robin. "For Spenser Fans, a 30th Installment." *Boston Sunday Globe* (March 9, 2003).

Dyer, Richard. "Parker's Second Sleuth Is First-Rate." *Boston Globe* (October 7, 2003).

Fretts, Bruce. "Mass. Murder." *Entertainment Weekly* (March 31, 2000).

Hoffman, Carl. "Spenser: The Illusion of Knighthood." *The Armchair Detective* (spring 1983).

"Interview with Robert B. Parker." Mystery One Bookstore. *http://www.mysteryone.com/RobertParkerInterview.htm* (viewed May 30, 2003).

Jones, Malcolm. "Helen Hunt's Mystery Date." *Newsweek* (October 4, 1999).

Koch, John. "Perpetually Robert Parker." *Boston Globe* (May 29, 1992).

Marling, William. "Robert B. Parker." Hard-Boiled Fiction. *http://www.cwru.edu/artsci/engl/marling/hardboiled/Parker.HTM* (viewed May 30, 2003).

McGee, Celia. "He's the Old Ball Parker." New York *Daily News* (May 31, 2004).

Parker, Robert B. "Creating a Series Character." *The Writer* (January 1981).

Peacock, Scot, ed. Robert B. Parker entry, *Contemporary Authors New Revision Series.* Vol. 89. Detroit: Gale Research, 2000.

Ponder, Anne. "A Dialogue with Robert B. Parker." *The Armchair Detective* (fall 1984)

Robert B. Parker biography. Authors and Creators. *http://www.thrillingdetective.com/trivia/parker.html* (viewed May 30, 2003).

Robert B. Parker biography and interviews (April 4 and October 6, 2000). Bookreporter. *http://www.bookreporter.com/authors/au-parker-robert.asp* (viewed May 30, 2003).

Smith, Amanda. "Robert Parker: The private eye as pensive wise-guy." *Boston Phoenix* (September 29, 1981).

Spensarium, Unofficial Robert B. Parker fan site. *http://www.spensarium.com/* (viewed May 30, 2003).

"Spenser Turns 25." Amazon.com. *http://www.amazon.com/exec/obidos/ts/feature/4841/102256298-9751302* (viewed March 31, 2003).

Stasio, Marilyn. "A Landmark for Spenser." *New York Times* (March 9, 2003).

Zaleski, Jeff. "PW Talks with Robert B. Parker." *Publishers Weekly* (October 8, 2001).

James Patterson

♦ Suspense-thriller ♦ Mystery

Newburgh, New York
1947

♦ *Four Blind Mice*

Credit: Sue Solie Patterson.

About the Author and the Author's Writing

Thirty-one publishers said no to James B. Patterson's first manuscript. But when a thirty-second brought it into print, *The Thomas Berryman Number* won the Mystery Writers of America Edgar Award for best first novel.

Patterson was born in Newburgh, New York, in 1947. When attending a Catholic high school there, he said he hated to read (and still doesn't bide *Silas Marner*). The family moved to Massachusetts after his senior year. With few friends, working at a mental hospital to pay his way through college, something clicked. He rediscovered books. "I'd hang out in the library," he said in *TV Guide*. "I became a serious reader. And I was scribbling on the side."

An English major, the author graduated summa cum laude from Manhattan College in 1969 and earned a master's degree summa cum laude at Vanderbilt University the next year. He became a copywriter for J. Walter Thompson advertising agency, working on Toys 'R' Us, Ford Motor Company, and other campaigns. He rose to chief executive officer in 1988, chairman in 1990. He continued writing, and his *Along Came a Spider*, about a deranged math teacher who kidnapped two students, ratcheted him into the upper bracket of popular writers. In 1996, he retired from advertising to devote his full energy to fiction writing.

Having read *Ulysses* and recognizing he could not match it, Patterson found himself drawn to more escapist fare such as *The Exorcist* and *Day of the Jackal*. He decided that's what he wanted to write: books that would make air flights shorter.

Spider was the first of Patterson's Alex Cross series, about a detective psychologist working in the Washington, D.C., area. Those kidnapped children are not just any high school students; they are the daughter of a Hollywood actress and the son of the Treasury secretary. Cross, tall and athletic (Morgan Freeman played him on screen), lost his wife to a drive-by killer. The murder was never solved. Now a widower with three children, Cross, who calls himself Dragonslayer, relentlessly pursues psychopaths and high-profile killers. Patterson said he made Cross an African American because of a family he had known and respected when growing up in Newburgh in the 1950s.

The author switched genders for a second series featuring the members of the Women's Murder Club—four females who are disgusted with the way men handle things and work together to show the guys up. They are homicide detective Lindsay Boxer, reporter Cindy Thomas, medical examiner Claire Washburn, and lawyer Jill Bernhardt. (One of them dies in the third book in the series.)

Patterson finds the feminine voice comes to him comfortably. "I grew up in a house full of women—grandmother, mother, three sisters, two female cats," he explained to interviewer Steven Womack. "I cooked for my grandmother's restaurant. I've always been most comfortable talking to women. My best friends generally tended to be women. I liked the way they talk, the fact that a lot of subjects weave in and out of conversations. Sometimes men are a little bit more of a straight line."

Patterson, who lives with his wife, Susan Solie, and son in Florida, has accelerated his book production in recent years, working on some books with coauthors. (At least one reviewer, for *Publishers Weekly*, found *The Lake House* perhaps too hastily written: "Exclamation points do not engender deep emotions with readers!")

Besides thrillers and crime-mystery novels, Patterson has written a romance, *Suzanne's Diary for Nicholas*; a legal thriller, *The Beach House*; a novel with spiritual overtones, *Cradle and All*; and a medieval romantic adventure, *The Jester*.

In discussing his writing, Patterson has said he never bases his characters on real people. But his personal experience may figure in a story; when he was in his early thirties, he lost a close woman friend to cancer. It was several years before he loosened up enough to establish a new, close relationship with someone. Thus, *Suzanne's Diary* for Nicholas is about love lost, love regained. It was his best-selling book.

The author outlines his books to save time, but he omits specifics that emerge in the course of writing. He says he's never quite sure how things will turn out until he gets there. He generally starts writing (with pencil and pad) at 6:00 or 6:30 in the morning and quits at about 4:00 p.m., seven days a week. Patterson may have more than one book in the works at a time, and he employs professional researchers to dig up some information for his books. He claims he pursues those topics that intrigue him the most, keeping a folder with notes on ideas, and referring to it frequently to see what might work next.

The idea for *The Jester* evolved that way. "I've had that story in my head for a dozen years," he told Edward Morris. "Most history has been written from the point of view of nobles or the people they've commissioned. the notion of a common person—particularly a common person with a sense of humor—was a story that really appealed to me. What we have here is a hero who's part Braveheart and part Jerry Seinfeld and Sherlock Holmes. That's kind of a fun combination."

Patterson trademarks are his short, rapid-paced chapters and his character-driven plots. "I think it's an easier way of reading," he said in a Lycos conversation. Each chapter is built around a dramatic moment that propels the story, "and turns on the movie projector in our heads. That's what I'm trying to do with the short chapters."

Each book, Patterson said in an iVillage interview, is an attempt "to create the perfect amusement park ride: lots of twists and turns, swoops and heights on the ride."

Works by the Author

Fiction

The Thomas Berryman Number (1976)
The Season of the Machete (1977)
The Jericho Commandment (1979), retitled *See How They Run* (1997)
Virgin (1980), rewritten as *Cradle and All* (2000)
Black Market (1986), retitled *Black Friday* (1989)
The Midnight Club (1989)
The Thirteen (1995)
Hide and Seek (1996)
Miracle on the 17th Green, with Peter de Jonge (1996)
Suzanne's Diary for Nicholas (2001)
The Beach House, with Peter de Jonge (2002)
The Jester, with Andrew Gross (2003)
Sam's Letters to Jennifer (2004)

Alex Cross Series

Along Came a Spider (1993)
Kiss the Girls (1995)
Jack and Jill (1996)
Cat and Mouse (1997)
Pop! Goes the Weasel (1999)
Roses Are Red (2000)
Violets Are Blue (2001)
Four Blind Mice (2002)
The Big Bad Wolf (2003)
London Bridges (2004)

Winged Children Series

When the Wind Blows (1998)
The Lake House (2003)

Women's Murder Club Series

1st to Die (2001)
2nd Chance, with Andrew Gross (2002)
3rd Degree (2004)

Books for Children

Santakid (2004)

Nonfiction

The Day America Told the Truth: What People Really Believe About Everything That Matters, with Peter Kim (1991)
The Second American Revolution, with Peter Kim (1994)

Motion Pictures Based on the Author's Works

Child of Darkness, Child of Light (1991), based on *Virgin*
Kiss the Girls (1997)
Miracle on the 17th Green (1999)
Along Came a Spider (2001)
1st to Die (2003)
2nd Chance (announced)

For Further Information

Ashley, Mike, ed. James Patterson entry, *The Mammoth Encyclopedia of Modern Crime Fiction*. New York: Carroll & Graf, 2002.

Brookman, Rob. "Have You Read a Patterson Lately?" *Book* (March–April 2003).

James Patterson biography. Bookbrowse. *http://www.bookbrowse.com/index/cfm?page=author&authorID-289* (viewed April 11, 2003).

James Patterson interview. Bookreporter. *http://www.bookreporter.com/reviews/0316969680.asp* (viewed April 11, 2003).

James Patterson interview. Written Voices. *http://www.writtenvoices.com/authorfeature.asp?namelast-patterson* (viewed April 11, 2003).

James Patterson interview. Lycos (March 20, 2003). *http://clubs.lycos.com/live/Events/Transcripts/james_patterson.asp* (viewed May 17, 2003).

James Patterson Web page. *http://www.twbookmark.com/features/jamespatterson/press.html* (viewed May 17, 2003).

"James Patterson: I Never Stop Writing." iVillage. *http://www.ivillage.com/books/intervu/myst/articles/0,11872,240795_219210,00.html* (viewed April 11, 2003).

Jones, Daniel, and John D. Jorgenson, eds. James Patterson entry, *Contemporary Authors New Revision Series*. Vol. 72. Detroit: Gale Research, 1999.

Kotler, Joan G. *James Patterson: A Critical Reader*. Westport, CT: Greenwood, 2004.

Lake House review. *Publishers Weekly* (May 19, 2003).

Morris, Edward. "A jester on crusade: James Patterson plumbs medieval history for his newest hero." *BookPage* (March 2003).

Murphy, Mary. "Along came a writer." *TV Guide* (February 22, 2003).

Womack, Steve. "Stretching the Boundaries of the Thriller." BookPage. *http://www .bookpage.com/0006bp/james_patterson.html* (viewed April 11, 2003).

Sharon Kay Penman

◆ Historical ◆ Mystery

New York, New York
1944

◆ *Here Be Dragons*

About the Author and the Author's Writing

Considering her experience with her first manuscript, one wonders why Sharon Kay Penman didn't become a writer of horror, rather than historical, novels. While working a regular job, she wrote a 500-page draft about the life of Richard III, which she left one day under the seat in her car. It was stolen from a busy parking lot in 1972, and never recovered. The experience brought on a prolonged writer's block and it was not until 1978 and a new career that she was able to rewrite the book. It became her first published work, *The Sunne in Splendor*, in 1982. The novel was sufficiently successful that it enabled her to become a full-time writer.

"Penman creates memorable characters from several social strata," observed *Contemporary Authors*, "and strives to show how 'history,' as chronicled—the foreign alliances, the intrigues at court—affected ordinary lives."

All of her books have been well received by critics, but it was Penman's first Medieval mystery, *The Queen's Man*, that became a finalist for an Edgar Award for Best First Mystery from Mystery Writers of America.

The author was born in New York City's Greenwich Village and grew up in Atlantic City, New Jersey, before it became a gambling mecca. She created her own newspaper when a child, and she and her brother often engaged in imaginative play, making up their own worlds. She attended Penn State University and Louisiana State University, and received a bachelor of arts degree in history from University of Texas in 1969. She accepted her law degree from Rutgers University in 1974.

Penman taught in a parochial school in Hawaii before becoming a tax and corporate lawyer for four years. As she began writing more historical novels, she made herself a fixture at libraries, accumulated shelves of reference materials of her own, and as often as possible visited England and Wales. Discovery of a revisionist history of Richard III while she was a college student triggered Penman's fascination with the time period; the book, though finding Richard guilty of killing the Little Princes in the Tower, absolved him of other crimes for which he has been blamed by historians, and by Shakespeare.

"I wanted to find out more about him," Penman told interviewer Wendy Zollo, "and soon discovered—to my amazement and indignation—that this was the classic case of history being rewritten by the victor."

Penman followed her Richard III novel with *Here Be Dragons*, the first of a Welsh trilogy, telling the story of Llewelyn the Great and Joanna, the illegitimate daughter of King John. With little information available on Joanna, the author had to be very creative. The fact that Llewelyn forgave Joanna for a very public indiscretion, to her thinking, suggested they were very much in love. Penman has said she found it both gratifying and challenging to be able to work with a lesser-known, yet vital, historical figure.

"Writers have more in common with alchemists than many people realize," the author said in a Chelsea Forum Web page, "as we both struggle to transform dross into gold. I write the most remarkable novels in my head but they seem to suffer a mysterious sea change by the time they reach the page, even when I am quite satisfied with the results."

She further explained she has a full image of the chapter in mind before she begins. Things may change as she composes that chapter; for example, Davydd ap Gruffydd, a secondary character in *Falls the Shadow* and *The Reckoning*, of his own volition emerged as a more dynamic and interesting figure as she wrote. This in fact, she admitted, is much of the charm of being a writer—discovering what's inside yourself, waiting to emerge.

Penman's Medieval mysteries center on Justin de Quincy, a young squire in Winchester in the 1190s who becomes an accidental detective. His investigations at times involve royalty and often reveal the frailties of the upper crust.

Penman has written two books about Henry II and Eleanor of Aquitaine, whom the author has described as intrigued and at the same time dysfunctional. She sees parallels with our own times.

"The medieval times definitely echo our times: The church-versus-state clashes, the greatest friend becoming the greatest foe, the question of nationality," she said in an interview with Jessica Turner. "We're still asking, 'What part does religion play in daily life?' And still trying to decipher those boundaries."

"By using a changing viewpoint [in *Time and Chance*], Penman shows us life through the eyes of Henry, Eleanor, Thomas Becket, and a purely fictional character, Ranulf, who was also featured in *When Christ and His Saints Slept*," observed reviewer Tamara Mazzei, "and who gives a certain measure of continuity to the story."

In addition to attracting an adult audience, Penman's books have become popular with young adult readers as well.

The author explained her feeling of obligation about accuracy in an interview in *Artists & Authors for Young Adults*: "I try to be honest with my readers; if I have to take any liberties with known facts, I make sure to mention it in my Author's Note. Obviously, a novel is by its very nature a work of the imagination, but I believe a historical novel requires a sound factual foundation if the structure is to survive."

Works by the Author

Fiction

The Sunne in Splendor (1982)
When Christ and His Saints Slept (1995)
Time and Chance (2002), sequel to *When Christ and His Saints Slept*

Justin de Quincy Medieval Mystery Series

The Queen's Man (1996)
Cruel as the Grave (1998)
Dragon Lair (2003)

Welsh Series

Here Be Dragons (1985)
Falls the Shadow (1988)
The Reckoning (1991)

For Further Information

Mazzei, Tamara. Time and Chance review. *http://www.triviumpublishing/com/articles/timeandchance.html* (viewed June 30, 2003).

Peacock, Scot, ed. Sharon Kay Penman entry, *Contemporary Authors*. Vol. 200. Detroit: Gale Research, 2002.

Sharon Kay Penman biography. Chelsea Forum. *http://ww.chelseaforum.com/speakers/Penman.htm* (viewed June 30, 2003).

Sharon Kay Penman entry, *Authors and Artists for Young Adults*. Vol. 43. Detroit: Gale Group, 2002.

Sharon Kay Penman Web site. *http://www.sharonkaypemna.com/* (viewed June 30, 2003).

Turner, Jessica. "A stolen manuscript almost waylaid Sharon Kay Penman's career." City Beat Time Bandits. *http://www.citybeat.com/2002-0307.books.shtml* (viewed June 30, 2003).

Vasudevan, Aruna, ed. Sharon Kay Penman entry, *Twentieth-Century Romance and Historical Writers*. 3rd edition. Detroit: St. James Press, 1994.

Zollo, Wendy. Sharon Kay Penman interview. Trivium Publishing. *http://www.triviumpublishing.com.articles/penman/html* (viewed June 30, 2003).

Anne Perry

◆ Mystery ◆ Fantasy

London, England
1938

◆ *Charlotte and Thomas Pitt Series*

Courtesy of Anne Perry.

About the Author and the Author's Writing

Anne Perry spends most of her days immersed in the Victorian age, though she's quite pleased to return to modern plumbing and health care by evening. She considers herself as much a historian as a writer. "The differences between their time and ours is a challenge which is fun to explore," she said in *Contemporary Novelists*, "and the exercise of transporting a drama from the present into another age brings into sharp relief what is transient and what is permanent, part of the core of human nature."

The author was born Juliet Marion Hulme in Blackheath, London, where she also spent her early years. Her father was an astronomer, mathematician, and nuclear physicist. Frequent family relocations in wartime and her poor health interrupted her education in private schools. But at her parents' urging, she read a lot, her favorites the works of authors such as Lewis Carroll and Charles Kingsley early on.

Later in life, Juliet held clerical and retail jobs. She worked as an airline stewardess from 1962 to 1964 then for two years was an assistant buyer for Newcastle Upon Tyne from 1964 to 1966. Residing in California from 1967 to 1972, she was a limousine dispatcher and insurance underwriter for Muldoon and Adams. (She has also lived in the Bahamas and Toronto briefly.)

But all she really ever wanted to do was write. That is something she began seriously when in her twenties, though another twenty years went by before one of her manuscripts was accepted by a publisher. The book was *The Cater Street Hangman* and it was published in 1979. This first effort was set in Victorian London after her stepfather made a remark that Jack the Ripper was probably a member of Parliament. She explored what happens to people who are interrogated by police.

Only years later did readers learn that the author described this topic from a very personal viewpoint. As a teen in 1954, she was convicted and sent to jail for her role in the beating death of her best friend Pauline Parker's mother in a New Zealand park. At the time of the murder, the author was ill and taking medication that was later banned because it altered the user's perspectives and judgment.

"Everybody who wants to look into the subject, which is hopefully not everybody, knows I was on medication," Perry told reporter Shelly Decker in 1998, "knows that I was under extreme pressure, knows that I believed the other girl would take her own life if I didn't join her. I felt that would be my fault. That's really all there is to say." She was freed when she was twenty-one. (The episode was depicted in the 1995 motion picture *Heavenly Creatures*.)

Today, Perry offers teenage criminals the message that a mistake doesn't have to be end of everything, that they should not give up on becoming comfortable or successful in life.

A further effect of her experience shows in Perry's depictions of relationships and motives. "I figure that to make a good mystery," she said to reporter Wilder Penfield III, "the motive must be understandable and powerful—passionate, and intense, and real, at least to the person concerned. . . . Fear makes people behave very, very differently from the way they normally do. How people behave under pressure is what the story's always about, I think."

A convert to Mormonism and never married, Perry lived with her father's support until her writing career kicked in. She generally writes six days a week, in longhand, from her home in the Scottish Highlands.

The Cater Street Hangman introduced Inspector Thomas Pitt and his upper-class wife, Charlotte, who, though Perry didn't anticipate they would at first, became series characters. Perry said she was drawn to the time period by the dramatic class differences, wealth living so close to squalor, high manners coexisting with crude rowdyism. "[T]he intelligent and socially conscious Charlotte aids her educated and sensitive husband in all his cases. Using her own family connections as an entrée to the homes of the wealthy and powerful, Charlotte, often assisted by her sister Emily (who married as far up the social scale as Charlotte married down), pokes her nose into the secrets of the Victorian upper crust," explained Jean Swanson and Dean James in *By a Woman's Hand*.

"This framework provides Perry with a realistic means of presenting a broader range of locations and characters than she could with a single detective," commented Helga Borck in *St. James Guide to Crime & Mystery Writers*.

Perry writes books about another policeman, William Monk, and Crimean war nurse Hester Latterley. The second series, set in the 1850s and 1860s, the author has said, provided opportunity to explore an even darker character. Because Monk is amnesiac, he has no recollection of some acts in his life.

Hester has something of a sharp tongue. "It's much more fun to have a character who's tart," the author told Bethanne Kelly Patrick. "Laughing is good for you and just because I'm writing mysteries doesn't mean there can't be humor." By the latest title in the series, Hester and her close friend have married, and William has become a private investigator, for a time anyway.

The author found a strong readership outside her native England, where publishers were slow to bring out her books. She has also written fantasy novels, including *Tathea*, about a quest for truth, and *The One Thing More*, which takes place during the reign of Louis XVI. A third mystery series, beginning with *No Graves as Yet*, is set in Cambridge in 1914, on the eve of World War I. That time period interests her, as her grandfather was a Presbyterian during the conflict.

"I just wanted to try something different," she told *Publishers Weekly* in 2003. "I like to write stories in which there is a real moral conflict: what is right and what is wrong, or what is wrong and what is even more wrong."

Perry thrives on the writing life, committed to turning out two books and perhaps a few short stories each year. Her short story "Heroes" won a Mystery Writers of America Edgar Award in 2000.

"Almost everything about [writing] is enjoyable for me," she told *January Magazine's* Linda Richards. "About the only thing I don't like is when the editor calls you from two books back and you've forgotten what it's about. And she says, 'On page 372 about half way down, did you mean this or did you mean that?' And you can't remember the story."

Works by the Author

Fiction

Riders Ready! (1985)
Shadow Mountain (1999)
Talthea (1999)
The One Thing More (2000)
A Dish Taken Cold (2001)
A Christmas Journey (2003)
Come Armageddon (2003), sequel to *Talthea*

Charlotte and Thomas Pitt Series

The Cater Street Hangman (1979)
Callander Square (1980)
Paragon Walk (1981)
Resurrection Row (1982)
Rutland Place (1983)
Bluegate Fields (1984)
Death in the Devil's Acre (1985)
Cardington Crescent (1987)
Silence in Hanover Close (1988)
Bethlehem Road (1990)
Highgate Rise (1991)
Belgrave Square (1992)
Farriers' Lane (1993)
The Hyde Park Headsman (1994)
Traitors Gate (1995)
Pentecost Alley (1996)
Ashworth Hall (1997)
Brunswick Gardens (1998)
Bedford Square (2000)
Half Moon Street (2000)
The Whitechapel Conspiracy (2001)
Southampton Row (2002)
A Christmas Journey (2003)

Seven Dials (2003)
The Shifting Tide (2004)

Monk and Hester Series

The Face of a Stranger (1990)
A Dangerous Morning (1991)
Defend and Betray (1992)
A Sudden, Fearful Death (1993)
The Sins of the Wolf (1994)
Cain His Brother (1995)
Weighed in the Balance (1996)
The Silent Cry (1997)
A Breach of Promise (1998)
The Twisted Root (1999)
Slaves and Obsession (2000)
A Funeral in Blue (2001)
Death of a Stranger (2002)
The Shifting Tide (2004)

Peavley Family Series

No Graves as Yet (2003)
Shoulder the Sky (2004)

Editor

A Century of British Mystery and Suspense (2000)
Death by Horroscope, with Martin H. Greenberg (2001)
Death by Dickens (2004)

Anthologies

Canine Crimes (1993)
Holmes for the Holidays (1996)
Murder for Love (1996)
Crime Through Time (1997)
Crime Through Time II (1997)
Murder They Wrote II (1998)
Women of Mystery (1998)
First Lady Murders (1999)
Holmes for the Holidays II (1999)
Midnight Louie's Pet Detectives (2000)
Unholy Orders (2000)

World's Finest Mystery and Crime Stories, edited by Edward Gorman (2000)
Malice Domestic 10 (2001)
Murder and Obsession (2001)
World's Finest Mystery and Crime Stories: Fourth Annual Collection, edited by Ed Gorman and Martin H. Greenberg (2003)
Dangerous Women, edited by Otto Penzler (2004)
The Mighty Johns and Other Stories, edited by Otto Penzler (2004)
Powers of Detection, edited by Dana Stabenow (2004)

Television Movies Based on the Author's Works

The Cater Street Hangman (1998)

For Further Information

Anne Perry biography. Crime Time. *http://www.crimetime.co/uk/profiles/anneperry.html* (viewed March 31, 2003).

Anne Perry entry, *Contemporary Novelists*. 7th edition. Detroit: St. James Press, 2001.

Anne Perry Web site. *http://www.anneperry.net/news/htm* (viewed March 31, 2003).

Bliss, Laurel. *No Graves Yet* review. *Library Journal* (August 2003).

Borck, Helga. Ann Perry entry, *St. James Guide to Crime & Mystery Writers*. 4th edition, edited by Jay P. Pederson. Detroit: St. James Press, 1996.

Come Armageddon review. *Publishers Weekly* (August 18, 2003).

Decker, Shelly. "Anne Perry would rather not talk about her murderous past." *Express* (October 26, 1998).

Lipez, Richard. *No Graves As Yet* review. W*ashington Post Book World* (September 28, 2003).

Menconi, Ralph. "Murder on the eve of war." *Publishers Weekly* (June 30, 2003).

Nolan, Tom. "Anne Perry: Double Detecting in Victorian England." *Mary Higgins Clark Mystery* (spring 1997).

Patrick, Bethanna Kelly. "In the Trenches." *Pages* (January/February 2003).

Peacock, Scot, ed. Anne Perry entry, *Contemporary Authors New Revision Series*. Vol. 84. Detroit: Gale Research, 2000.

Penfield, Wilder III. "Heavenly Creature-Turned-Hit Novelist Anne Perry Survives Exposure." *Toronto Sun* (February 5, 1995).

Perry, Anne. "Breach of Promise." *Mystery Scene*, no. 62 (1999).

Richards, Linda. Anne Perry interview. *January Magazine. http://www.january magazine.com/profiles/perry.html* (viewed May 23, 2003).

Swanson, Jean, and Dean James. *By a Woman's Hand: A Guide to Mystery Fiction by Women.* New York: Berkley, 1996.

Elizabeth Peters

◆ Mystery ◆ Romantic suspense

Canton, Illinois
1927

◆ *Amelia Peabody Series*

Credit: © 1997 Osmund Geier.

About the Author and the Author's Writing

Detectives often have to really dig into the past for clues, but archaeologist-heroine Amelia Peabody really digs into the *far* past in Elizabeth Peters popular mystery series.

The author was born Barbara G. Mertz in Canton, Illinois, in 1927. She evidenced a way with words while in high school, when a sonnet she wrote on assignment was so good, her teacher wondered if it hadn't been plagiarized. She passed by traditional teen reading such as Nancy Drew and instead devoured classic mystery writers Agatha Christie and Dorothy L. Sayers, Ellery Queen, and Raymond Chandler. Her father influenced her to explore the weird tales of H. P. Lovecraft and the adventures of H. Rider Haggard and John Buchan.

When a great-aunt took Barbara to the Oriental Institute Museum, the young girl fell in love with anything and everything Egyptian. In postsecondary studies, she received her Ph.D. from the University of Chicago in 1947, a master's degree three years later and a Ph.D. in Egyptology from the university's Oriental Institute two years after that. She married Richard R. Mertz in 1950 and started a family.

Feminist Betty Friedan sparked a change in the author's life. "It wasn't until *The Feminine Mystique*," she told *Time* magazine, "that I began to get those 'clicks' that she talks about, and they came like a machine gun." Her marriage ended soon after.

Gender issues, which limited field research to women at the time (unless they were with their husbands), dissuaded her from entering academia, though she has written three nonfiction books about Egypt's history and politics under her real name, Barbara Mertz. When she began writing fiction, she turned out dozens of romantic suspense novels under the penname Barbara Michaels.

On the Unofficial Barbara Michaels Web page, Monica Sheridan praises the books as not only "being skillfully crafted and carefully researched, [but also] they are fun to read. . . . And even more important are the interesting, intelligent characters who often congregate in the kitchen to argue, to eat, and to talk."

The Master of Blacktower, a gothic published in 1967, began a stream of books so steady her publisher eventually requested she use a second name for some lighter, more contemporary works. She chose a literary alias based on the names of her children, Elizabeth and Peter, under which she eventually wrote her first Peabody puzzle. (At the time, she had no anticipation it would become a series.)

As her career progressed, Peters "soon invested her work with a healthy sense of humor and some rather innovative notions about the abilities of women and their relationships with men—ideas that were quite radical for the mystery and romantic suspense fiction of the time," observed Dean James in *Mystery Scene*, no. 53.

The first change came with *Witch* in 1973. Explains Dean James in *Mystery Scene*, no. 71, "Ellen March [the heroine] is a divorcee in her late 30s. Heroines of romantic suspense novels were usually in their early 20s and virgins, for crying out loud! Michaels helped break the mold with this and other books."

Peters remains proud of that book to this day; "I think having a woman who is a strong character and able to stand on her own feet appealed to a lot of women," she told T. Liam McDonald.

The next change in the author's work, the addition of humor, began with *The Camelot Caper*, her second book under the Peters name. "What is better than laughing aloud at a clever line, a wicked comment, or the perfect deflating of the overly inflated?" asked Susan Dunlap in *Mystery Scene*, no. 71, a Peters tribute issue. "The better the humor, the more we delight in it. Unfortunately, the better it is, the smoother it flows, the easier it seems as if it must be to write."

If readers noticed, they enjoyed it. And if they noticed that series characters art historian Vicky Bliss and librarian Jacqueline Kirby had freer ideas and more gumption than some heroines, they enjoyed that too.

Background became an important element in the stories by the time the Peabody series took hold. The fifteenth in the series, *Children of the Storm*, continues the adventures of Victorian amateur investigator Peabody and her husband, Radcliffe Emerson, son Ramses, and ward Nefret to uncover a new tomb or treasure.

The author works hard to portray the period accurately (these were days before the advent of scientific archaeology, thus her heroine is legitimately Indiana Jones-ish), as well as the setting. She has gone to all the exotic places her series character has. "I try to get to Egypt at least once a year for three or four weeks," Peters told Lee Smith. "I like to hang around and talk about the latest theories."

She also works hard on building her characters. Peters' heroines' personalities generally, she has said, are modeled somewhat on herself. Or, she has become more like Amelia Peabody as she's gotten older, becoming more firm in making decisions, less tolerant of bad manners. In an iVillager interview, the author further explained, "Emerson was inspired by William Flinders Petrie, who was one of the first people with a scholarship. I wanted Emerson to be better than Petrie. Amelia was inspired by many people; her name is inspired by Amelia B. Edwards, but she bears no resemblance to her. There are many people like her who are exploring in the world; she is an archetype."

"Once Amelia and Emerson stormed onto the stage," Peters said in an article for *The Armchair Detective*, "all resemblance between them and other characters living or dead ceased to exist. They became themselves. I know them so well now that I don't have to invent their conversations or actions or opinions; I simply put them into a particular situation and describe their reactions."

As the series has progressed, Peabody's son Ramses has grown up and taken a greater role, particularly in his relationship with Nefret. The author enjoys the added dimension of contrasting their issues with the older generation's.

The hardest work for each book is in the research and preparation, the author told Debbie Stier for *Mystery Scene*, no. 71. "The actual writing process takes less time than the preliminaries, working out the plot in my head and doing the research, which can take months. When I actually sit down to write I stick to it for as many hours a day as my creaking body can stand."

The books are thoroughly grounded, but not overwhelming so, assured Edward Marston: "The archeological detail was fascinating but never overwhelming. Some writers feel the need to show their readers just how much research they've done. 'I've suffered,' they say, 'and so will you.' Not Elizabeth Peters. She never poses or patronizes."

Aaron Elkins, a mystery novelist with his own archaeologist hero, tells the story of how he challenged Peters on a particular point while once touring the ancient site of Memphis with her and his wife, Charlotte. He later looked it up, found he was wrong, and, in the course of phoning to apologize, realized the entry in the reference book he was reading had been written by "BGM." Barbara G. Mertz. "I was flabbergasted. I don't mean about the extent of her scholarship, but about her restraint. Can you imagine? Arguing—at tedious length—with a rank amateur like me about something in which she was a certified, respected expert, and never once saying, maybe not in so many words: 'Will you shut up already, you presumptuous twerp? I wrote the Memphis article in the *Encyclopedia Britannica!*'"

As much as she enjoys Egyptology, Peters said she knows that if she had actually lived in that time, she would have been a slave girl, not a queen. She'll stay in the present, thank you, and continue writing books.

Works by the Author

Fiction

The Jackal's Head (1968)
The Camelot Caper (1969)
The Dead Sea Cipher (1970)
The Night of Four Hundred Rabbits (1971)
The Legend in Green Velvet (1976)
Devil May Care (1977)
Summer of the Dragon (1979)
The Love Talker (1980)
The Copenhagen Connection (1982)

Amelia Peabody Series

Crocodile on the Sandbank (1975)
Curse of the Pharaohs (1984)
The Mummy Case (1985)
Lion in the Valley (1986)
Deeds of the Disturber (1988)
The Last Camel Died at Noon (1991)

The Snake, The Crocodile and The Dog (1992)
The Hippopotamus Pool (1996)
Seeing a Large Cat (1997)
The Ape Who Guards the Balance (1998)
The Falcon at the Portal (1999)
He Shall Thunder in the Sky (2000)
Lord of the Silent (2001)
The Golden One (2002)
Children of the Storm (2003)
Guardian of the Horizon (2004)
The Serpeant on the Crown (2004)

Jacqueline Kirby Series

The Seventh Sinner (1972)
Murders of Richard III (1974)
Die for Love (1984)
Naked Once More (1989)

Vicky Bliss Series

Borrower of the Night (1973)
Street of the Five Moons (1978)
Silhouette in Scarlet (1983)
Trojan Gold (1987)
Night Train to Memphis (1994)

Anthologies

The Mummy's Tomb (1989)
Sisters in Crime edited by Marilyn Wallace (1989)
The Mammoth Book of Historical Whodunits (1993), retitled *Historical Whodunits*
Women on the Edge (1994)

Written as by Barbara Michaels

The Master of Blacktower (1967)
Sons of the Wolf (1967), retitled *Mystery on the Moors* (1968)
Prince of Darkness (1969)
Dark on the Other Side (1970)
The Crying Child (1971)
Greygallows (1972)
Witch (1973)
House of Many Shadows (1974)
The Sea King's Daughter (1975)
Patriot's Dream (1976)

Wings of the Falcon (1977)
Wait for What Will Come (1978)
The Walker in Shadows (1979)
The Wizard's Daughter (1980)
Someone in the House (1981)
Black Rainbow (1982)
Here I Stay (1983)
The Grey Beginning (1984)
Be Buried in the Rain (1985)
Search the Shadows (1987)
Smoke and Mirrors (1989)
Into the Darkness (1990)
Vanish with the Rose (1992)
House of Stone (1993)
The Dancing Floor (1997)
Other Worlds (1998)

Georgetown House Series

Ammie, Come Home (1968)
Shattered Silk (1986)
Stitches in Time (1995)

Nonfiction

Amelia Peabody's Egypt, with Kristen Whitbread (2003)

Written as by Barbara Mertz

Two Thousand Years in Rome, with Richard Mertz (1968)
Red Land, Black Land (1978)
Temples, Tombs and Hieroglyphs (1978)

Anthologies

The Writing Life: Writers on How they Think and Work, edited by Marie Arana (2003)

Television Motion Pictures Based on the Author's Works

Ammie Come Home (1969)

For Further Information

Dunlap. "Barbara Mertz." *Mystery Scene*, no. 71 (2001).

Elizabeth Peters biography. *http://www.angelfire.com/ut/westbound341/peters.html* (Viewed May 24, 2003).

Elizabeth Peters biography. Fantastic Fiction. *http://www.fantasticfiction.co/uk/ authors/Barbara_Michaels.htm* (viewed May 24, 2003).

"Elizabeth Peters: I've Been in Love With Egypt Since I Was 13." iVillagers. *http:// www.ivillage.com/books/intervu/myst/articles/0,11872,240795_81682,00.html* (viewed May 24, 2003).

Elkins, Aaron. "A Thousand Miles up the Nile with Amelia Peabody." *Mystery Scene*, no. 71 (2001).

Grape, Jan, Dean James, and Ellen Nehr, eds. *Deadly Women*. New York: Carroll & Graf, 1998.

James, Dean. "Elizabeth Peters." *Mystery Scene*, no. 53 (1996).

James, Dean. "The 'Gothic' World of Barbara Michaels." *Mystery Scene*, no. 71 (2001).

Maron, Margaret. "Peters and Peabody." *Mystery Scene*, no. 71 (2001).

McDonald, T. Liam. "Will the Real Author Please Stand Up?" *The Armchair Detective* (spring 1993).

Nicholas, Victoria, and Susan Thompson. *Silk Stalkings: When Women Write of Murder*. Berkeley, CA: Black Lizard, 1988.

Peacock, Scot, ed. Barbara Mertz entry, *Contemporary Authors New Revision Series*. Vol. 82. Detroit: Gale Research, 2000.

Peters, Elizabeth. "Amelia Meets Her Maker." *The Armchair Detective* (summer 1992).

Sachs, Andrea. "Mystery Tours: Barbara Mertz (a.k.a. Elizabeth Peters) takes her readers on suspenseful trips through Egypt." *Time* (June 2, 2003).

Sitier, Debbie. "A Conversation with Elizabeth Peters." *Mystery Scene*, no. 71 (2001).

Smith, Lee. "The Jewel of the Nile." *Book* (March/April 2003).

Unofficial Elizabeth Peters/Barbara Michaels/Barbara Mertz Page. *http://www.autopen .com/elizabeth.peters.shmtl* (viewed May 24, 2003).

Susan Elizabeth Phillips

◆ Romance ◆ Women's ◆ Historical

Cincinnati, Ohio

◆ *First Lady*

About the Author and the Author's Writing

Susan Elizabeth Phillips comes up with plot ideas by contemplating what-ifs. What if a woman with no interest in football suddenly inherits a national team (*It Had to Be You*)? What if a good ol' boy Texan becomes a golf pro (*Fancy Pants*)? What if an American president dies, his successor is a bachelor, and the First Lady is asked to carry on her role as the country's chief hostess (*First Lady*)?

"I love so many of the traditional elements of romance, but maybe my favorite is the marriage of convenience," the author said on her Web site. "It's an extremely difficult plot device to bring off in contemporary romance, but I had to try (*Kiss an Angel*)."

The author was born Susan Elizabeth Titus in Cincinnati, Ohio, the daughter of a corporate recruiter and a teacher. She received a bachelor of fine arts degree in theater from Ohio University. She married William C. Phillips in 1971, they have two sons, and the family lives in Chicago. Phillips has taught high school speech, drama, and English.

The author's first romance novel was published in 1983. She wrote it with a friend, initially as a lark, but finished it when an editor from Dell agreed to publish it. She followed the book with two historicals, then four big women's fiction volumes. She bought back the rights to one novel, *Risen Glory*, a bodice-ripper, and rewrote and released it under a new title, *Just Imagine*.

Phillips' Chicago Stars series took the author's writing in a new direction and caught on in great part because of their comedic elements. Is she a football fan? "The Bears suck," she said in a BookPage interview. "I think I watched part of the Super Bowl last year. I can't stand watching baseball because the players spit. Watching golf is less interesting than watching grass grow. Favorite players? You've got to be kidding. I'm just not much of a fan."

In a Romance Review interview the author said, "I start with a premise and go from there—no outline. It's an insane way to work, but I seem to be stuck with it." It can take

Phillips anywhere from eleven to fourteen months to write a novel, which is an improvement over her first efforts, which were two years in gestation.

"The familiar tricks of the trade are refreshingly revamped in this lively contemporary romance set in Tuscany," *Publishers Weekly* said of *Breathing Room*. In this book, Isabel Favor, a self-help guru, finds herself in the unlikely position of having to negotiate a summer rental with Lorenzo "Ren" Gage, a playboy movie star with whom she had an unfortunate one-night stand the evening before. Although their gradual falling in love follows convention, the evolution of their personalities makes the book sparkle. And the appearance in an otherwise light romance of Gage's pregnant ex-wife and kids sends the plot into a spin.

On occasion, Phillips has spotted a secondary character with an obvious story to tell; thus Bobby Tom Denton got his own book in *Heaven, Texas*; and Gabe and Ethan Bonner showed up in *Dream a Little Dream*, brothers of a quarterback in the Chicago Stars series.

There are humorous elements in all of Phillips' books, including the historicals, and this may account for her large young adult following. "I'm not a particularly funny person in person," she said in an All About Romance interview. "I can't tell jokes, but it just seems like it happened when I started to write. It wasn't anything that was planned. I'm a very intuitive writer; I just sort of let the characters talk to me and they start saying funny things. So I wrote them down!"

Phillips' achievements have not gone without notice. The author holds the Romantic Times Lifetime Achievement Award, and in 2001, she was inducted into the Romance Writers of America Hall of Fame.

Works by the Author

Fiction

Risen Glory (1984), revised as *Just Imagine* (2001)
Glitter Baby (1987)
Fancy Pants (1989)
Hot Shot (1991)
Honey Moon (1993)
Kiss an Angel (1996)
Dream a Little Dream (1998), spin-off from *Nobody's Baby But Mine*
Lady Be Good (1999), spin-off from *Fancy Pants*
First Lady (2000)
Breathing Room (2002)
Ain't She Sweet (2003)

Chicago Stars Series

It Had to Be You (1994)
Heaven, Texas (1995)
Nobody's Baby But Mine (1997)
This Heart of Mine (2001)

Written as Justine Cole

The Copeland Bride (1983)

For Further Information

Breathing Room review. *Publishers Weekly* (June 3, 2002).

Huseby, Sandy. "A touchdown from the queen of romantic comedy." BookPage (February 2001). *http://www.bookpage.com/0102bp/susan_elizabeth_phillips.html* (viewed May 31, 2003).

"Interview with Susan Elizabeth Phillips." A Romance Review. *http://www.aromance review.com/artmonth/susanelizabethphillips.phtml* (viewed July 2, 2003).

Maryles, Daisy, and Dick Donahue. "It's Not Who You Think." *Publishers Weekly* (February 21, 2000).

Olendorf, Donna, ed. Susan Elizabeth Phillips entry, *Contemporary Authors*. Vol. 142. Detroit: Gale Research, 1994.

"Some Time with Susan Elizabeth Phillips." All About Romance (1997). *http://www .likesbooks.com/int3.html* (viewed July 2, 2003).

Susan Elizabeth Phillips Web site. *http://www.susanephillips.com/* (viewed July 2, 2003).

Terry Pratchett

◆ Fantasy ◆ Humor

Beaconsfield, England
1948

◆ *Discworld*

Courtesy of HarperCollins.

About the Author and the Author's Writing

Is there room for humor in fantasy? Terry Pratchett's twenty-eight volumes and counting in his Discworld series certainly says there is. Should his opinion count? Of course. After all, he *was* named an Officer of the British Empire in 1998 for "services to literature."

Pratchett was born in Beaconsfield, England, in 1948, the son of an engineer and a secretary. Drawn at an early age to writing, he published his first story when he was thirteen and made his first commercial sale at seventeen. He graduated from Wycombe Technical High School in Buckinghamshire. Today, the author and his wife, Lyn, have one child and live in Wiltshire, about a dozen miles from Stonehenge.

Pratchett worked as a journalist in Buckinghamshire, Bristol, and in Bath, England, from 1965 to 1980, during which time his humorous fantasy novel *The Carpet People* came out. His first Discworld novel, *The Color of Magic*, was published during the seven years he was a press officer for Central Electricity Board's Western Region.

Pratchett ventured briefly into science fiction with *The Dark Side of the Sun* and *Strata*, which makes a nod to the works of writer Larry Niven. Of the latter title, critic Don D'Ammassa said, "[T]he best part of the novel is the richly creative background of aliens, religious and philosophical speculations, and exotic settings. Pratchett's light-hearted approach succeeds in making what would otherwise be a standard adventure story into a witty exercise of the imagination."

Pratchett sometimes writes books for younger readers, but his main thrust has been Discoworld and its universe, which is held up by four elephants who are standing on the back of a giant turtle as it swims forever through space. The author's light approach to fantasy incorporates frequent barbs aimed at J.R.R. Tolkien or other fantasy writers, and satirical takes on New Age practices, religion, and politics. For example, a dying wizard in *Equal Rites* passes on his powers and legacy to a baby, who happens to be female. As years pass, the girl becomes a female wizard who has to deal with the ire of a profession dominated by prejudiced males. *The Fifth Elephant* finds a group of neo-Nazi werewolves trying to destabilize Uperwald, a mineral-rich country, control of which is sought by the citizens of Ankh-Morpork. In *Hogfather*, the title figure, something of a Santa Claus who makes his rounds in a sleigh pulled by four huge pigs, is kidnapped.

Discworld is a world filled with trolls and witches, gnomes and wizards. But all is not cute and cuddly. Later Discworld books have an element of violence. Pratchett explained its necessity in an ssfworld.com interview about *Night Watch*: "[Y]ou can't build a plot out of jokes. You need tragic relief. And you need to let people know that when a lot of frightened people are running around with edged weaponry, there are deaths. Stupid deaths, usually. I'm not writing 'The A-Team'—if there's a fight going on, people *will* get hurt. Not letting this happen would be a betrayal."

"Discworld is a place where any story can be told, and its geography is fluid" explains *St. James Guide to Fantasy Writers*. "Events are governed by a steely common-sense which may only be overruled by the important need to insert another joke or demented footnote. When the chief city Ankj-Morpork goes up in flames, there is good reason: a tourist has introduced the delighted underworld to the concept of fire insurance."

Running characters include Death, whose speech is RENDERED IN BIG LETTERS; Captain Samuel Vimes, whose City Watch force includes a werewolf and troll; Rincewind, an inept wizard; the Luggage, a magical suitcase; the Igors; Granny Weatherwax, and the Auditors.

Pratchett likes to take a logical twist on characters. Angua, for example, the she-werewolf, is a vegetarian in human form, but must consume blood the one week a month she is lycanthropic.

"Angua is screwed up. Granny Weatherwax is screwed up. They are not at ease with themselves, and that makes them fun for the author," Pratchett said in Writers Write. "That makes their heads very interesting places for the author to be."

Pratchett pictures his Discworld stories as a continguous piece, much in the way English humorist P. G. Wodehouse's Bertie Wooster and Jeeves and other stories took place in the same realm.

"Taken together, these novels create an imaginative zone that is rich and strange," suggests a critic in *Contemporary Novelists*, "offering the reader both the pleasures of discovery, as new aspects are revealed, and of recognition, as familiar figures recur."

Pratchett's two latest Discworld books, *The Wee Free Men* (for young adult readers) and *Monstrous Regiment*, focus on female characters. In the former, Tiffany Aching, a witch in training, is "funny, sassy and spirited," according to a *Publishers Weekly* reviewer, as she seeks out her kidnapped brother armed with only a frying pan and aided by the impish Nac Mac Feegle. In the latter, innkeeper's daughter Polly Perks disguises herself as a man in search of her brother.

Pratchett sets about writing a novel with a general idea in mind. "I start with a handful of semi-formed ideas and play around with them until they seem to make some sense," he said in an interview for Discworldshop.com. "Actually typing is important to me—it kind of tricks my brain into gear. I've got a packrat mind, like most writers, and once I start thinking hard about a new project all kinds of odd facts and recollections shuffle forward to get a place on the bus." The author also admits the beginning of a book is more pleasurable than wrapping up the ending, typing up loose ends, and editing.

In a *January Magazine* interview, Pratchett said he feels he's grown as a writer. "Humor comes out of a deep soil," he said. "Humor puts down roots. Now wit: you can grow wit in a windowbox. And what Discworld now has is more humor, less wit. . . . I would not have the readership I have if I'd written effectively in terms of style, the same book 28 times."

Works by the Author

Fiction

The Carpet People (1971)
The Dark Side of the Sun (1976)
Strata (1981)
The Unadulterated Cat, with Gray Joliffe (1989)
Good Omens, with Neil Gaiman (1990)

Discworld Series

The Colour of Magic (1983)
The Light Fantastic (1986)
Equal Rites (1987)
Mort (1987)
Sorcery (1988)
Wyrd Sisters (1988)
Guards! Guards! (1989)
Pyramids (1989)
Eric (1990)
Moving Pictures (1990)
Reaper Man (1991)
Witches Abroad (1991)
Small Gods (1992)
Lords and Ladies (1992)
Men at Arms (1993)
Interesting Times (1994)
Soul Music (1994)
Maskerade (1995)
Feet of Clay (1996)
Hogfather (1996)
Jingo (1997)
Carpe Jugulum (1998)
The Last Continent (1998)
The Fifth Elephant (1999)
The Truth (2000)
The Last Hero, with Paul Kidby (2001)
Thief of Time (2001)
Night Watch (2002)
Monstrous Regiment (2003)
Going Postal (2004)

Discworld Young Adult Series

Amazing Maurice and His Educated Rodents (2001)
The Wee Free Men (2003)
A Hat Full of Sky (2004), sequel to *The Wee Free Men*

Books of the Nomes, Young Adult Series

Truckers (1988)
Diggers (1990)
Wings (1990)
The Bromeliad Trilogy (2003), omnibus

Johnny Maxwell Series

Only You Can Save Mankind (1992)
Johnny and the Dead (1993)
Johnny and the Bomb (1996)
The Johnny Maxwell Trilogy (1999), omnibus

Collections

The Bromeliad (1998)
Death Trilogy (1998)
The City Watch (1999)
The Color of Magic/The Light Fantastic (1999)
Rincewind the Wizzard (1999)
Gods Trilogy (2000)

Anthologies

Legends (1986)
The Flying Sorcerers (1987)
Gaslight and Ghosts (1988)
Hidden Turnings (1989)
Digital Dreams (1990)
Cyber-Killers (1991)
Shivers for Christmas (1995)
The Wizards of Odd: Comic Tales of Fantasy (1996)
Knights of Madness: Further Comic Tales of Fantasy (1998)
The Mammoth Book of Comic Fantasy (1998)
Legends: Short Novels by the Masters of Modern Fantasy. Volume 1, edited by
    Robert Silverberg (1999)
Vintage Science Fiction (1999)

Nonfiction

The Science of Discworld, with Jack Cohen and Ian Stewart (1992)
Streets of Ankh Morpork (1993)
The Discworld Companion, with Stephen Briggs (1994)
The Pratchett Portfolio (1996)
A Tourist Guide to Lancre, with Stephen Briggs and Paul Kidby (1998)
Death's Domain: A Discworld Mapp, with Paul Kidby (1999)
Discworld Assassins' Guild Yearbook and Diary 2000 (1999)
Nanny Ogg's Cookbook, with Stephen Briggs and Tina Hannan (1999)
The Discworld Fools' Guild Yearbook and Diary 2001 (2000)
The Discworld Mapp, with Stephen Briggs (2000)
Discworld Also (2001)
The Discworld Fools' Guild Yearbook and Diary 2002 (2001)
The New Discworld Companion (2002)
The Science of Discworld II: The Globe (2002)
Nanny Ogg's Cookbook, with Stephen Briggs and Paul Kidby (2003)
The Second Discworld Portfolio (2003)

For Further Information

"Conversation with Terry Pratchett." Writers Write. *http://www.writerswrite.com/ journal/apr00/pratchett.htm* (viewed July 2, 2003).

D'Ammassa, Don. Terry Pratchett entry, *Twentieth-Century Science-Fiction Writers*. 3rd edition, edited by Noelle Watson and Paul E. Schellinger. Chicago: St. James Press, 1991.

Fifth Elephant review. *Publishers Weekly* (March 6, 2000).

Hogfather review. *Publishers Weekly* (October 26, 1998).

Howard, Jennifer. *Monstrous Regiment* review. *Washington Post Book World* (September 28, 2003).

Monstrous Regiment review. *Publishers Weekly* (September 8, 2003).

Peacock, Scot, ed. Terry Pratchett entry, *Contemporary Authors New Revision Series*. Vol. 87. Detroit: Gale Research, 2000.

Richards, Linda. Terry Pratchett interview, *January Magazine* (August 2002). *http://www.januarymagazine/com/profiles/tpratchett2002.html* (viewed July 2, 2003).

Terry Pratchett entry, *Contemporary Novelists*, 7th edition. Detroit: St. James Press, 2001.

Terry Pratchett entry, *St. James Guide to Fantasy Writers*, 1st edition. Detroit: St. James, 1996.

Terry Pratchett interview.sffworld.com. *http://www.sffworld.com/authors/p/pratchett_terry/interviews/200212.html* (viewed July 2, 2003).

Terry Pratchett Web site. *http://www.terrypratchettbooks./com* (viewed July 2, 2003).

"*Wee Free Men*: An Interview with Terry Pratchett." Discworldshop.com. *http://www.discworldshop.com/interview01.html* (viewed July 2, 2003).

Wee Free Men review. *Publishers Weekly* (May 12, 2003).

Mary Jo Putney

♦ Romance ♦ Historical

Upstate New York

♦ *Dearly Beloved*

Credit: Franco.

About the Author and the Author's Writing

Dominic Renbourne reluctantly agrees to his twin brother Kyle's plea to switch places, and Dominic ends up wooing an orphaned heiress with an eccentric reputation. Little does he anticipate he will fall in love with the woman, Lady Meriel Grahame. The time period: just after the Regency era. The novel: *The Wild Child*. The author: Mary Jo Putney, who enjoys a reputation as a solid stylist, sharp portrayer of character, and deft plotter. She is also known for taking on topics not expected in historical romances, such as alcoholism and domestic abuse.

Putney was born in upstate New York and earned bachelor of arts degrees in English and in industrial design from Syracuse University. She worked as an industrial and graphic designer in California and England before becoming a writer full-time. She now lives in Baltimore, Maryland.

Putney claims on her Web site that she was born with a reading addiction and has yet to overcome it. Her outlet is to write. "I'd always enjoyed romantic elements in stories, and I fell in love with the novels of Georgette Heyer when I was in college. A few months before I bought my first computer, I discovered the Heyer-ish Walker Regency romances in the library, so that's what came to mind once I figured out how to use my word processing program."

Putney wrote a historical novel, sold it based on a partial manuscript, and has gone on to publish more than twenty-five books since her first book, *The Diabolical Baron*, appeared in 1987.

Putney described what she believes is the lure of the Regency in an All About Romance Internet interview. "It was the dawn of the modern age," she said, "where revolutions and industrial change were creating the society we recognize now. The old regime was dead, and the people of that time period speak in voices we can recognize. They are accessible. It was also an age of wonderful writers, of Jane Austen and the Romantic poets."

"Putney knows how to create characters attractive enough to enchant readers without being too good to be true," said *Publishers Weekly* in a review of the author's *The Bartered Bride*.

The Regency period is familiar enough, yet sufficiently remote to be appealing. It was the time of the Napoleonic wars, which allows for certain plot intrigues.

The author often brings in social themes. "I'm intrigued by stories of redemption, about people who heal and learn to make themselves stronger and happier . . . ," she said in a Romance Catalogue interview. "I want my work to be accurate as well as hopeful. As to alcoholism in particular, well, I knew an alcoholic. Doesn't everybody?"

With recent books, Putney has begun to alternate modern with historical fiction. "My natural 'voice' is historical, and I love the fantasy and the over-the-top qualities of historical romance," she said on her Web site. "But I started to fear that I might burn out on historicals, and the Muse began sending me ideas that would only work as contemporaries."

The award-winning author works in short as well as long forms, frequently contributing short stories or novellas to anthologies. Putney is a relatively quick writer, a novel taking generally six to seven months, not including time for research and revision.

"I'm very linear," she said in a Crescent Blues interview. "I start at the beginning and inch my way through to the end. If I don't know what happens next, I tread water and edit until I figure out how to proceed. I can't even imagine writing in pieces and stringing them together; to me, the writing process is organic, with each section growing out of what happened previously."

Her approach to writing may be linear, but the author readily admits a little craziness can't hurt when thinking up plot spins.

Works by the Author

Fiction

Lady of Fortune (1988)
Carousel of Hearts (1989)
The Controversial Countess (1989)
The Rogue and the Runaway (1990)
Uncommon Vows (1991)
The Would Be Widow (1992), rewritten as *The Bargain* (1999)
The Diabolical Baron (1994)
Dearly Beloved (1997)
The Wild Child (1999), sequel to *Uncommon Vows*

Bride Trilogy

The Wild Child (1999)
The China Bride (2000)
The Bartered Bride (2002)

Circle of Friends Series

The Burning Point (2000)
The Spiral Path (2002)
A Twist of Fate (2003)
A Kiss of Fate (2004)

Davenport Series

The Diabolical Baron (1987)
The Rake and the Reformer (1991)
The Rake (1998)
Christmas Revels (2002)

Fallen Angel Series

Petals in the Storm (1993)
Thunder and Roses (1993)
Dancing on the Wind (1994)
Angel Rogue (1995)
River of Fire (1996)
Shattered Rainbows (1996)
One Perfect Rose (1997)

The Silk Trilogy

Silk and Shadows (1991)
Silk and Secrets (1992)
Veils of Silk (1992)

Anthologies

A Regency Christmas III (1991)
A Regency Christmas IV (1992)
A Victorian Christmas: Five Stories (1992)
Rakes and Rogues (1993)
A Regency Christmas II: Five Stories (1993)
Promised Bride (1994)
Dashing and Dangerous (1995)
A Stockingful of Joy (1997)
Faery Magic (1998)
In Our Dreams (1998)
Captured Hearts (1999)
Bride by Arrangement (2000)
A Constellation of Cats (2001)

For Further Information

"All About Romance: Mary Jo Putney on the Regency." LikesBooks. *http://www.likesbooks.com/quickie5.html* (viewed May 4, 2003).

Bartered Bride review. *Publishers Weekly* (May 6, 2002).

Krozser, Kassia. "Identity and Transformation: Mary Jo Putney on Mad Heroines and Other Favorite Themes" (1998). *http//www.booksquare.com/subversion/parlor .int006.cfm* (viewed May 4, 2003).

Mary Jo Putney interview. All About Romance (August 6, 1998). *http://www.likesbooks/ com/wb6.html* (viewed May 4, 2003).

Mary Jo Putney interview. Crescent Blues. *http://www.crescentblues.com/4_4issue/ int_mary_jo_putney.shtml* (viewed May 4, 2003).

Mary Jo Putney interview. Romance Catalogue (July 18, 2001). *http://romance.narod .ru/putney/inter_e.htm* (viewed May 4, 2003).

Mary Jo Putney Web site. *http://www.maryjoputney.com/* (viewed May 4, 2003).

Peacock, Scot, ed. Mary Jo Putney entry, *Contemporary Authors*. Vol. 164. Detroit: Gale Research, 1998.

Russotto, Tammy. Mary Jo Putney interview (May 2000). *http://members.aol.com/ ladycheyenne1441.putney/* (viewed May 4, 2003).

Twist of Fate review. *Publishers Weekly* (June 30, 2003).

Francis Ray

◆ Romance ◆ Suspense ◆ Historical

Texas
1944

◆ *The Turning Point*

Credit: William H. Ray.

About the Author and the Author's Writing

Francis Ray's novels have consistently drawn praise. Eric Jerome Dickey, for instance, said the author "creates characters and stories that we all love to read about. Her stories are written from the heart."

Ray was born in Texas in 1944 and still lives in the Lone Star State with her husband and daughter. She is a graduate of Texas Woman's University and works as a school nurse practitioner with the Dallas Independent School District.

She wrote and sold sixteen confession stories to publications such as *Black Romance* magazine. After reading and enjoying Kathleen Woodiwiss's *Shanna*, she decided to write a novel. "The book captivated me," she told a Wonderful Women and Men of Color interviewer. "I didn't know such wonderful love stories existed. The next day I went out and bought every book I could find by her. By the third book I knew I wanted to create similar stories of monogamous relationships with strong, sensitive and dependable men and the equally strong, caring and independent women they loved."

Once she found a publisher for her first manuscript, she continued to represent herself through nine more books and four novellas for collections. Her first imprint, Odyssey, a pioneer in bringing out romances specifically for the black market, went out of business after her first book, and she had to move on to other book publishers. Her decision in 1999 to move into mainstream fiction prompted her to engage an agent.

Some of Ray's plots come from actual experiences, such as *The Turning Point*, which grew from her macular surgery and slower-than-anticipated recovery. She created the character of ace neurosurgeon Adam Wakefield, who fears he is going blind. Lilly Crawford, another featured character, is dealing with her own issue of suddenly being penniless.

Once she has her characters in mind, the author said, she generally writes a several-pages description, and then comes up with a what-if.

"Since I try to start each book with conflict," she told Alvin Romer, "I have to know why my characters act or don't react, what makes them who they are. I pay particular attention to their childhood. I strongly believe that this is where we are shaped."

Break Every Rule centers on Dominique Falcon, who is separated from her abusive millionaire husband and has sworn off men and romance. Moving to Dallas to start a photography business, she doesn't know how to react to the magnetic neighbor, trucking company owner Trent Masters.

Ray found an unusual plot twist for *I Know Who Holds Tomorrow*. After the loss of her child, television talk show host Madison Reed finds herself withdrawn from her TV correspondent husband Wes Reed. Wes and a woman companion die in a car accident, Wes revealing in his last breath he has been unfaithful to Madison and has a nine-month-old daughter. Overwhelmed, Madison struggles with Wes's last request—to raise the other woman's child.

Ray has written several interrelated books featuring strong Taggart, Grayson, and Falcon men, who are African American and part Native American.

Until There Was You adds a suspense element; private investigator Luke Grayson, seeking relaxation in his mountain cabin, instead finds himself held at gun point by child psychologist Catherine Stewart, who has a frightful secret.

Ray's novels sometimes require research, such as *Until There Was You*, for which Ray had to learn more about the Santa Fe Highway Patrol, and *The Turning Point*, for which she consulted a head trauma specialist and others. Even though she has a full-time job, she generally can complete a novel in four months, a novella for an anthology in three weeks.

Ray's novel *Incognito* was optioned and made into the first made-for-television movie for Black Entertainment Network.

The author said she believes the publishing industry has come to recognize a market for her type of book. "I feel my greatest accomplishment has been creating stories that touch people's lives and impact them in a positive way," she said in a Romance in Color interview. "African-Americans do have love and romance in their lives, and we do live happily ever after."

Works by the Author

Fiction

Fallen Angel (1992)
The Bargain (1995)
Undeniable (1995)
Incognito (1997)
Silken Betrayal (1997)
The Turning Point (2001)
I Know Who Holds Tomorrow (2002)
Someone Knocking at My Door (2003)
Like the First Time (2004)
Troubles Don't Always Last (2004)

Taggart/Falcon/Grayson Series

Forever Yours (1994)
Only Hers (1996)
Break Every Rule (1998)
Heart of the Falcon (1998)
Until There Was You (1999)
Falcon Saga (2004), omnibus

Anthologies and Collections

Spirit of the Season (1994)
Winter Nights (1998)
Rosie's Curl and Weave (1999)
Della's House of Style (2000)
Welcome to Leo's (2000)
Going to the Chapel (2001)
Gettin' Merry (2002)
Living Large (2003)
First Touch, with Sandra Kitt and Eboni Snoe (2004)
Let's Get It On (2004)

Television Movies Based on the Author's Work

Incognito

For Further Information

"Author of the Month—Francis Ray." Romance in Color. *http://www.romanceincolor.com/authormthray.htm* (viewed June 5, 2003).

Francis Ray interview. Wonderful Women and Men of Color Page. *http://www.geocities.com/ bellesandbeaux/Ray.html* (viewed June 2, 2003).

Francis Ray Web site. *http://www.francisray.com/bio/htm* (viewed June 2, 2003).

I Know Who Holds Tomorrow review. *Publishers Weekly* (April 29, 2002).

I Know Who Holds Tomorrow. Reading Group Guides. *http://www.readinggroupguides.com/ guide3/i_know_who_holds_tomorrow.asp* (viewed June 5, 2003).

Osborne, Gwendolyn. *Break Every Rule* review. The Romance Reader. *http://www.theromancreader.com/ray-break.html* (viewed June 5, 2003).

Peacock, Scot, ed., Francis Ray entry, *Contemporary Authors*. Vol. 180. Detroit: Gale Research, 2000.

Ramsdell, Kristen. *Until There Was You* review. *Library Journal* (August 1999).

Romer, Alvin. Francis Ray interview. *http://myshelf.com/haveyouheard/01/ray.htm* (viewed June 2, 2003).

Winter Nights review. *Publishers Weekly* (October 26, 1998).

Ruth Rendell

London, England
1930

♦ *Chief Inspector Wexford Series*

Courtesy of Crown Publishing
Group.

About the Author and the Author's Writing

Ruth Rendell is three writers in one. She is the author of the Chief Inspector Reginald Wexford police procedural novels; she is the author of stand-alone crime suspense novels; and she is Barbara Vine, author of longer, darker tales often of multigenerational suspense. Oh, and since 1997 she has been a working Labour Peer, Baroness Rendell of Babergh.

Ruth Barbara Grasemann was born in 1930 in London, the only child of an English father (Arthur Grasemann) and a Swedish mother (Ebba Kruse). She grew up in South Woodford, Essex, where her parents worked as school teachers. Referring to her father in a BBC interview, the author said, "I loved him very much. I learned discipline from my father, if a thing's worth doing it's worth doing well." In fact, her character Wexford's dry wit, literate tastes, and liberalness reflect her dad.

Ruth read Anthony Trollope and Thomas Hardy, Dorothy Sayers and Agatha Christie, among others; years later she read Somerset Maugham and Elmore Leonard. After finishing school, she became a reporter for *The Chigwell Times*. There she met her future husband, Donald Rendell, a writer for London's *Daily Mail*. The author quit journalism after four years, frustrated with the profession and needing to care for a newborn son. She began crafting fiction for amusement.

"I wrote lots of novels and never tried to get any of them published," she told *People Weekly*. When she did submit a manuscript, the publisher asked if she had anything else. She did, and it became her first sale, the first Wexford.

It took nearly fifteen years of writing before Rendell caught on, winning the Mystery Writers of America Edgar Allan Poe Award two times (her pseudonym Barbara Vine—her own middle name plus her great-grandmother's maiden name—also won one) and the Arts Council National Book Award.

"If you always write detective stories, you're stuck in quite a tight scheme," the author said in a JamBook interview. "That's why I write the other books, so that I'm not stuck with a detective story format for the rest of my life. Some people like that. It suits them, but it wouldn't suit me. I want to do more than that."

Rendell writes the Wexford stories to satisfy public demand. The sharp-tongued hero is very intelligent, and very empathetic. "One cannot be sure *exactly* which way the Inspector will react," suggests critic Jane S. Bakerman. "He is equally capable of shrugging off or lashing out at an opponent, of intimidating or encouraging a subject, of telling off or sustaining a subordinate. One knows his repertoire of responses, but Wexford's choice of response remains tantalizingly uncertain."

Rendell crafts stories of character, rather than of detectives solving puzzles. The Wexfords are her most conventional, "their quality and individuality resists easy pigeon-holing," according to *Contemporary Novelists*. "Like all her writing they are notable for superb plotlines, excellent atmosphere and memorable characters, not least Wexford and his 'Watson' figure Inspector Mike Burden. The pair are marvelous foils for each other, the large, sometimes irascible Wexford whose painstaking deductions are allied to intuitive hunches striking sparks from his decent but stiff, by-the-book subordinate."

Rendell is known for her characterizations. "I like writing dialogue . . . ," she told Susan L. Clark for *The Armchair Detective* in 1989, "and I love using my ears. . . . I take a lot of time. I rewrite and rewrite. Well, now I use a word processor. I do that on a screen, which is lovely for me, because I used to write things sometimes five or six times, sometimes as many as ten times. And that simply becomes very tedious when you're doing it by hand or on a typewriter."

Rendell often delves into psychology in her works of fiction. "I do write about obsession," the author allowed in a *Publishers Weekly* interview, "but I don't think I have an obsession for writing. I like to watch obsession in other people, watch the way it makes them behave."

No manner what means she uses to write her mysteries, Rendell has proven a reliable, dedicated, and enduring wordsmith.

Works by the Author

Fiction

To Fear a Painted Devil (1965)
Vanity Dies Hard (1965)
The Secret House of Death (1968)
One Across, Two Down (1971)
The Face of Trespass (1974)
A Demon in My View (1976)
A Judgment in Stone (1977)
Make Death Love Me (1979)
The Lake of Darkness (1980)
Talking to Strange Men (1980)
Master of the Moor (1982)
The Killing Doll (1984)

The Tree of Hands (1984)
Live Flesh (1986)
Heartstones (1987)
The Bridesmaid (1989)
Going Wrong (1990)
Ruth Rendell Omnibus (1992)
The Crocodile Bird (1993)
Ruth Rendell Omnibus Vol. 2 (1993)
Omnibus Fiction: Ruth Rendell (1994)
The Second Ruth Rendell Omnibus (1994)
The Keys to the Street (1996)
Thornapple (1998)
Adam and Eve and Pinch Me (2001)
The Rottweiler (2003)

Chief Inspector Wexford Series

From Doon with Death (1964)
A New Lease of Death (1967)
Sins of the Fathers (1967)
Wolf to the Slaughter (1967)
The Best Man to Die (1969)
A Guilty Thing Surprised (1970)
No More Dying Then (1971)
Murder Being Once Done (1972)
Some Lie and Some Die (1973)
Shake Hands Forever (1975)
A Sleeping Life (1978)
Put On by Cunning (1981)
The Speaker of Mandarin (1983)
An Unkindness of Ravens (1985)
Wexford: An Omnibus (1987)
The Second Wexford Omnibus (1988)
The Veiled One (1988)
The Third Wexford Omnibus (1989)
The Fourth Wexford Omnibus (1990)
Ruth Rendell Mysteries: Three Inspector Wexford Mysteries as Seen on Television (1990)
Kissing the Gunner's Daughter (1992)
Simisola (1994)
Road Rage (1997)
Harm Done (1998)
A Sight for Sore Eyes (1998)

The Babes in the Wood (2002)
Sixth Wexford Omnibus (2002), in United States as *Three Cases for Chief Inspector Wexford* (2002)

Collections

The Fallen Curtain and Other Stories (1976), in the United States as *The Fallen Curtain: Eleven Mystery Stories by an Edgar Award-Winning Writer* (1976)
The New Girlfriend and Other Stories (1978)
Means of Evil and Other Stories (1979), in United States as *Five Mystery Stories by an Edgar Award-Winning Writer* (1980)
The Copper Peacock and Other Stories (1980)
The Fever Tree and Other Stories (1982), in the United States as *The Fever Tree and Other Stories of Suspense* (1982)
Collected Short Stories (1987) in United States as *Collected Stories* (1988)
Collected Stories (1988)
Blood Lines: Long and Short Stories (1996)
A Dark Blue Perfume and Other Stories (1996)
A Needle for the Devil and Other Stories (1996)
The New Girl Friend and Other Stories of Suspense (2000)
Piranha to Scurfy and Other Stories (2000)
Thornapple (2000)

Edited by Ruth Rendell

A Warning to the Curious: The Ghost Stories of M. R. James (1986)
Undermining the Central Line, with Colin Ward (1989)
The Reason Why: An Anthology of the Murderous Mind (1995)

Anthologies

Ellery Queen's Murdercade, edited by Ellery Queen (1975)
Winter's Crimes 7 (1975)
Ellery Queen's Crime Wave, edited by Ellery Queen (1976)
Fallen Curtain (1976)
Best Detective Stories of the Year—1977, edited by Edward D. Hoch (1977)
Ellery Queen's Searches and Seizures, edited by Ellery Queen (1977)
Ellery Queen's A Multitude of Sins, edited by Ellery Queen (1978)
Best Detective Stories of the Year—1979, edited by Edward D. Hoch (1979)
Ellery Queen's Scenes of the Crime, edited by Ellery Queen (1979)
Masterpieces of Mystery: The Seventies, edited by Ellery Queen (1979)
Best Detective Stories of the Year, edited by Edward D. Hoch (1980)
Ellery Queen: The Best of Suspense (1980)
Ellery Queen's Circumstantial Evidence, edited by Ellery Queen (1980)

John Creasey's Crime Collection 1980, edited by Herbert Harris (1980)
Who Done It?, edited by Alice Laurence and Isaac Asimov (1980)
Year's Best Mystery and Suspense Stories, edited by Edward D. Hoch (1980)
Best Detective Stories of the Year—1981, edited by Edward D. Hoch (1981)
Ellery Queen's Crime Cruise Round the World, edited by Ellery Queen (1981)
Haunted Houses: The Greatest Stories (1983)
Year's Best Mystery and Suspense Stories, edited by Edward D. Hoch (1983)
Best of Ellery Queen, volume 2 (1984)
Great Detectives, edited by David Willis McCullough (1984)
I Shudder at Your Touch (1984)
Murder on the Menu, edited by Carol-Lynn Rossel Waugh (1984)
Penguin Classic Crime Omnibus, edited by Julian Symons (1984)
Year's Best Mystery and Suspense Stories, edited by Edward D. Hoch (1984)
Ellery Queen's More Lost Ladies and Men, edited by Eleanor Sullivan (1985)
Year's Best Mystery and Suspense Stories, edited by Edward D. Hoch (1985)
Best of Winter Crimes, volume 2, edited byGeorge Hardinge (1986)
Ellery Queen's Blighted Dwellings, edited by Eleanor Sullivan (1986)
Mammoth Book of Modern Crime Stories, edited by George Hardinge (1986)
Academy Mystery Novellas 5: Women Write Murder, edited by Martin H. Greenberg
    (1987)
Ellery Queen Masters of Mystery (1987)
John Creasey's Crime Collection 1987, edited by Herbert Harris (1987)
Ladykillers (1987)
The Mammoth Book of Haunted House Stories (1987)
Prime Suspects, edited by Bill Pronzini (1987)
Ellery Queen's Crimes and Punishments, edited by Eleanor Sullivan (1988)
English Country House Murders, edited by Thomas F. Godfrey (1988)
Haunted Women (1988)
John Creasey's Crime Collection 1989, edited by Herbert Harris (1989)
Ms. Murder, edited by Marie Smith (1989)
Scare Care (1989)
New Edgar Winners (1990)
More Ms. Murder (1991)
Mystery Cats (1991)
The Picador Book of the New Gothic (1991)
Scarlet Letters (1991)
1st Culprit (1992)
Murder on the Menu (1992)
Murder Takes a Holiday (1992)
Women of Mystery (1992)
More Murder Most Cozy (1993)
Murder British Style (1993)
3rd Culprit (1994)

Little Deaths (1994)
Murder by the Glass (1994)
Murder for Father (1994)
Murder for Mother (1994)
Tales of Obsession (1994)
Tales from the Rogues Gallery (1994)
Women of Mystery II (1994)
Garden of Deadly Delights (1996)
Lethal Kisses (1996)
London After Midnight (1996)
Murder at Teatime (1996)
Murder Most British (1996)
Murder on the Railways (1996)
Win, Lose or Die (1996)
Women on the Case (1996)
Love Kills (1997)
Simply the Best Mysteries (1997)
Whydunit? Perfectly Criminal 2 (1997)
Crime After Crime (1998)
Crossing the Border; Tales of Erotic Ambiguity (1998)
The Cutting Edge (1998)
The Mammoth Book of Twentieth-Century Ghost Stories (1998)
Mistresses of the Dark: 25 Macabre Tales by Master Storytellers (1998)
Past Crimes: Perfectly Criminal III (1998)
Women of Mystery III (1998)
Missing Persons (1999)
Creme de la Crime (2000)
Murder Most Delectable (2000)
World's Finest Mystery and Crime Stories, edited by Ed Gorman (2000)
Blood Threats & Fears (2001)
Century of Great Suspense Stories, edited by Jeffrey Deaver (2001)
Feline Felonies (2001)
World's Finest Mystery and Crime Stories: Third Annual Collection, edited by Ed
    Gorman (2002)

Written as Barbara Vine

A Dark Adapted Eye (1986)
A Fatal Inversion (1987)
The House of Stairs (1988)
*Yes, Prime Minister: The Diaries of the Right Honorable James Hacker, Jonathan
    Lynn, Anthony Jay, and Antony Jay* (1988)
The Barbara Vine Novels (1990), omnibus

Gallowglass (1990)
King Solomon's Carpet (1991)
Asta's Book (1993)
No Night Is Too Long (1994)
The Brimstone Wedding (1996)
The Chimney Sweeper's Boy (1998)
The Blood Doctor (2002)

Nonfiction

Ruth Rendell's Suffolk (1992)

Motion Pictures Based on the Author's Works

The Housekeeper (1987), based on *A Judgment in Stone*
Several episodes of *Masters of Mystery* series on Arts & Entertainment Network

For Further Information

Anable, Stephen. "PW Talks with Ruth Rendell." *Publishers Weekly* (January 28, 2002).

Bakerman, Jane S. "Great Expectations Generously Fulfilled: The Work of Ruth Rendell/Barbara Vine." *The Armchair Detective* (summer 1993).

Bakerman, Jane S. Ruth Rendell entry, *St. James Guide to Crime & Mystery Writers*. 4th edition, edited by Jay P. Pederson. Detroit: St. James Press, 1996.

Clark, Susan L. "A Fearful Symmetry." *The Armchair Detective* (summer 1989).

Neill, Michael. "To make the skin crawl." *People Weekly* (December 18, 1995).

Peacock, Scot, ed. Ruth Rendell entry, *Contemporary Authors New Revision Series*. Vol. 74. Detroit: Gale Research, 1999.

"Rendell keys in on state of Britain in recent novels." JamBooks (November 19, 1996). *http://www.canoe.ca/JamBooksFeatures/rendell_ruth./html* (viewed July 1, 2003).

Rowland, Susan. *From Agatha Christie to Ruth Rendell*. New York: St. Martin's Press, 2000.

"Ruth Rendell, Baroness Rendell of Babergh." Books by Author, BBC. *http://www.bbc .co/uk/arts/books/authorrendell/* (viewed July 1, 2003).

Ruth Rendell biography. Bastulli Mystery Library. *http://www.bastuli/.com/Rendell/ RENDELL./htm* (viewed July 1, 2003).

Ruth Rendell books. Malicebooks.com. *http://www.malicebooks.com/web_pages/ britauth/rendell.htm* (viewed July 1, 2003).

Ruth Rendell books. *http://www.twbooks/co/uk/authors/rendell/html* (viewed July 1, 2003).

Ruth Rendell entry, *Contemporary Novelists*. 7th edition. Detroit; St. James Press, 2001.

Anne Rice

Courtesy of Knopf Publicity.
Credit: Joyce Ravid.

♦ Horror ♦ Fantasy

New Orleans, Louisiana
1941

♦ *Interview With the Vampire*

About the Author and the Author's Writing

There's a mystique about writer Anne Rice, whose fascination with vampires is exceptional. She sees them as the quintessential outsiders. "They never leave me alone," she told interviewer Linda Richards for *January Magazine*. "They're like a world of people that I've created. I'm no longer writing just books about Lestat, I'm writing novels that thrill me because of their metaphysical content, their horror content, their philosophical content, their sexual content and the vampires are my main characters. They're my people, they're my gang."

The author was born in 1941 in New Orleans, Louisiana, and was named Howard Allen O'Brien by a rather Bohemian mother and a father who had always smarted from being teased about his name—which was Howard Allen O'Brien—as a child. She gave her name as "Anne" the first day of parochial school and her mother allowed it to stick.

When Anne was fourteen, her mother died and her postal worker father remarried. Two years later the family relocated to Richardson, Texas. Anne did not want to move, and she felt out of place in Texas. "That sense of alienation intensified over the years as I moved to California to work my way through college and then stayed on," she said in *Time* magazine. "At first I loved the freedom and radical spirit of the place. But as the years passed, I became bitter about not going home. I really didn't fit in with my liberal friends. In California, people's lifestyles are acquired—their taste, their decor, their behavior—but in New Orleans, where people stay with their families, they inherit their lifestyles. All those years I was writing about New Orleans and obsessively longing for it, but I couldn't get there for more than a few days a year." (By 1989, Rice was able to move to New Orleans to a home in the Garden District.)

While attending Richardson High School, the author met her future husband, Stan Rice. They married in 1961 and had two children. Her husband, who attended college the same years she did, became a college professor.

Rice attended Texas Woman's University, 1959 to 1960, then received her bachelor's degree in political science and creative writing from San Francisco State College (later renamed San Francisco State University) in 1964. While in college, she published her first short story, "October 4, 1948," in a student journal. She did graduate work at the University of California at Berkeley from 1969 to 1970, but left to complete her master's in creative writing at San Francisco State in 1972. She held jobs ranging from waitress and cook to theater usher and insurance claims adjuster before becoming a writer.

After the Rices' first child died of leukemia in 1972, they went through a period of mourning, from which Anne emerged in 1973 to write *Interview With the Vampire* in a five-week rush. Initially rejected by publishers, the author met an agent while attending a writer's conference, and that agent, Phyllis Seidel, sold the book to Knopf.

Interview with the Vampire centers on Louis, a young vampire in New Orleans infected by an older and more cynical French vampire, Lestat. Louis relates his experiences to a journalist, expressing his anguish at having the blood lust, because in his heart, he is repulsed at taking a human life. "While other vampires in literature, including Lestat, the Brat Prince, have embraced their evil and murderous natures without conscience," observes critic Kathleen Rout, "Anne Rice was the first to show the moral ambivalence a fledgling vampire might feel."

Rice outspokenly opposed the casting of Tom Cruise to play Lestat in the 1994 film version of *Interview with the Vampire*, though she later admitted he played the role admirably. She would have preferred to see Leonardo DiCaprio in the part. A decade later, Elton John and his songwriting partner Bernie Taupin were reportedly at work on a musical version of the novel, which would head for Broadway perhaps in 2005.

Rice did not set out to write multiple volumes about vampires. But as she said in a BookEnds interview, "[W]hen I slip into the character of Armand, or Louis, or Lestat, or any of these immortals, I find myself in possession of a crystal clear lens through which to see my own time, and any lessons I have learned."

Despite its imaginative world, Rice does considerable research. Digging up background for *The Vampire Armand*, for example, prompted her to seek out information about the Monastery of the Caves in Kiev and about Russia and Ukraine.

The author puts in twelve-hour days at her writing, working in an office filled with reference books and handwritten notes. She refuses to go outside and eats while at her desk. She works frantically to complete a manuscript in a short time, while the material is vibrant in her mind. She outlined her first books heavily, but more recently has simply begun sitting at a computer keyboard with characters in mind, perhaps an ending conceived, but the rest just waiting to emerge. *Cry to Heaven*, *Violin*, *Memnoch the Devil*, and *Tale of the Body Thief* were well worked out ahead of time; *Interview With the Vampire*, *Taltos*, and most of *The Vampire Armand* were written spontaneously.

Rice has recently alternated her longer vampire novels with shorter books (she calls them novelettes) featuring characters such as Pandora and Vittorio who were peripheral to earlier works.

Even as her vampire tales grew in popularity, the author explored the world of erotica in novels written as Anne Rampling and A. N. Roquelaure. The books in the Beauty trilogy, written under the latter name are graphic fantasies meant to be not lurid but authentic and playful, Rice said. The Columbus, Ohio, library removed the books from its shelves after one patron complained, despite wide circulation. Rice decried the library's decision, and noted its lack of a definition of "pornography."

"Censorship is foolish," she said on her Veinotte.com Web page. "I grew up under censorship where you couldn't get James Joyce's *Ulysses*. People will not be hurt with what we read; we can't make that decision for others."

In the meantime, Rice continues to write, and readers continue to read her books. What drives Anne Rice to write? "A deep desire to be read," she told *Success* in 2000, "a need for self-expansion, to make a mark."

Works by the Author

Fiction

The Feast of Saints (1979)
Cry to Heaven (1982)
The Mummy: or Ramses the Damned (1989)
Servant of the Bones (1996)
Violin (1997)

Lives of the Mayfair Witches Series

The Witching Hour (1990)
Lasher (1993)
Taltos (1994)
The Mayfair Witches Collection (2000)

New Tales of the Vampires Series

Pandora (1998)
Vittorio the Vampire (1999)

Vampire Chronicles Series

Interview With the Vampire (1976)
The Vampire Lestat (1985)
The Queen of the Damned (1988)
The Complete Vampire Chronicles (1989), omnibus
The Tale of the Body Thief (1992)
The Vampire Chronicles Collection (1992), includes four previous books
Memnoch the Devil (1995)
The Vampire Armand (1998)
Merrick (2000)
Blood and Gold (2001)
Blackwood Farm (2002)
Blood Canticle (2003)

Written as Anne Rampling

Exit to Eden (1985)
Belinda (1986)

Written as A. N. Roquelaure
Sleeping Beauty Series

The Claiming of Sleeping Beauty (1983)
Beauty's Punishment (1984)
Beauty's Release (1985)
The Sleeping Beauty Novels (1991)

Collections

The Anne Rice Reader (1996)

Anthologies

Vampires, Wine and Roses (1983)
The Ultimate Zombie (1985)
Blood Thirst: 100 Years of Vampire Fiction (1987)
Into the Mummy's Tomb (1989)
The Picador Book of New Gothic (1991)
The Vampire Omnibus (1995)
American Gothic Tales (1996)
The Vampire Hunters' Casebook (1996)
Night Shade: Gothic Tales by Women (1999)

Stage Plays

The Vampire Lestat (announced 2005)

Motion Pictures Based on the Author's Works

Exit to Eden (1994)
Interview with the Vampire (1994), screenplay

For Further Information

Anne Rice interview. BookEnds. *http://w62.173.95.217/bookends/chat/rice.asp?TAG= &CID=* (viewed April 5, 2003).

Anne Rice entry, *St. James Guide to Horror, Ghost & Gothic Writers*. Detroit: St. James Press, 1998.

Anne Rice Web page. Random House. *http://www.randomhouse.com/features/ annerice/author.html* (viewed July 1, 2003).

Anne Rice Web page. *http://www.veinotte.com/anne/bio/htm* (viewed July 1, 2003).

Behm, George, ed. *The Unauthorised Anne Rice Companion*. Andrews and McMeel, 1996.

Blood Canticle review. *Library Journal* (September 1, 2003).

Dickinson, Joy. *Haunted City: An Unauthorized Guide to the Magical, Magnificent New Orleans of Anne Rice*. Secaucus, NJ: Carol Publishing Group, 1993.

"Fangs for the Memories." *Publishers Weekly* (October 30, 2000).

"Heading Home." *Time* (October 22, 2001).

Hofler, Robert. "Warner's vamping." *Variety* (May 12, 2003).

Hoppenstand, Gary, and Ray B. Browne, eds. *The Gothic World of Anne Rice*. Green, OH: Bowling Green Popular Press, 1996.

"In the Blood." *People Weekly* (October 23, 2000).

Marcus, Jana. *In the Shadow of the Vampire: Reflections from the World of Anne Rice*. New York: Thunder's Mouth Press, 1997.

"New and Nightmarish." *U.S. News & World Report* (November 3, 1997).

Peacock, Scot, ed. Anne Rice entry, *Contemporary Authors New Revision Series*. Vol. 74. Detroit: Gale Research, 1999.

Ramsland, Katherine M. *Prism of the Night: A Biography of Anne Rice*. New York: Dutton, 1991.

Richards, Linda. "Anne Rice: Literary Diva of the Dark." *January Magazine. http://www.januarymagazine.com/rice.html* (viewed July 1, 2003).

Riley, Michael. *Conversations with Anne Rice*. New York: Ballantine, 1996.

Roberts, Bette B. *Anne Rice*. New York: Twayne, 1994.

Route, Kathleen. "Who Do You Love? Anne Rice's Vampires and Their Moral Transition." *Journal of Popular Culture* (winter 2003).

Simeon, Furman. "Anne Rice." *Success* (October 2000).

Smith, Jennifer. *Anne Rice: A Critical Companion*. Westport, CT: Greenwood Press, 1996.

"String duet." *People Weekly* (March 9, 1998).

Nora Roberts

◆ Romance ◆ Women's fiction ◆ Fantasy ◆ Mystery

Washington, D.C.
1950

◆ *MacGregor Series*

About the Author and the Author's Writing

There are popular authors, and then there's Nora Roberts. In spring 2003, *Publishers Weekly* reported that her books sold on average of eighteen a minute every minute for the past twenty-one years!

Eleanor Marie Robertson was born in Washington, D.C., in 1950. Her father was a movie projectionist who later started a lighting company. In 1968, Eleanor married high school sweetheart Ronald Aufdem-Brinke, and they had two children before they divorced in 1985. She did not attend college. When she was wed a second time in 1983, to Bruce Wilder, the media could not resist commenting, as it was to a man who works as a carpenter and whom she first met when he came to build her a bookcase. "I am living proof," she responded to *People Weekly* in 1999, "that what I write about can happen in real life."

The author worked for Wheeler & Korpjeck in Silver Springs, Maryland, as a legal secretary from 1968 to 1970, and then was a clerk and a secretary for the Hecht Co., 1970–1972, and R&R Lighting, 1972–1975. She has been a full-time writer since 1979, producing an enormous number of romance books for paperback publishers and, with *Honest Illusions*, breaking into hardcover (though continuing to write paperback originals). She's produced some 150 titles, with no sign of letting up.

How did she go from clerical worker and homemaker to writer? Roberts says it was during the February blizzard of 1979 when she was home in rural Maryland with two young sons. "Every morning when school was canceled, I wept," she told *People Weekly* in 1996. "We couldn't even get out to buy Oreos. I decided I would write a story—I had made them up in my head since childhood—just to give myself an outlet until the snow melted." She wrote a Harlequin-esque romance set in Spain. It never found a market, nor did the next five manuscripts she crafted. But the one after that did when the then-new publishing house Silhouette brought out *Irish Thoroughbred* in 1981.

Roberts writes at a frantic pace. In 1998, she had eleven books on the *New York Times* best-seller list—four of them hit number one.

Although she does some research for settings, usually on the Internet (she intensely dislikes flying), her novels tend to be character-, rather than story-driven. She writes of emotions, successes, and losses. Several of her series revolve around families, albeit sometimes unusual families, such as the Donovan Legacy trilogy about three cousins who have unusual powers or the Royal Family of Cordina series, which is set in an imaginary Mediterranean country.

The MacGregor series includes historicals (*Rebellion* and *In From the Cold*) as well as contemporary (*The MacGregor Brides* among others). The series was unintentional; Roberts only planned the first book, *Playing the Odds*. But she fell in love with the brothers of the main character, Serena, so that led to at least three additional books to explore their lives and loves. A popular figure from the series is Daniel McGregor, matchmaking patriarch of the Scottish clan. "Daniel just came almost fully developed into my head," the author said in an All About Romance interview. "He's a very powerful man. There's a bit of my father in him, but for the most part he's just Daniel. When a writer is lucky enough to have a character like Daniel insisting on being part of her work, she listens."

Roberts seldom writes issues-oriented books. "I write strictly for entertainment, romances with a lot of suspense. If issues are a part of the story, that's a plus. But I don't seek to raise issues or write about them," she said in an interview with Susan Farrington.

The author is an unflagging cheerleader for the romance genre. She has pushed the genre, introducing multiple viewpoints—including male narrators—and exploring the supernatural. She has introduced premarital sex and humor as well as suspense.

She also enjoys ventures into fantasy, as in the Hornblower books, which are set three centuries in the future. Her very popular pseudonymous series featuring New York City police detective Eve Dallas—written under the J. D. Robb byline (the initials taken from her sons' first names)—are set in the 2050s and blend crime with science fiction, along with some pretty lively romance. One reason she created the series was simply her fast pace of writing; her publishers could not keep up with the backlog. So Berkley brought out the Robb books, initially making no reference to the author's real identity.

"I wanted to try something a little different," the author said in a Paranormal Romance Reviews interview. "I love writing romance and suspense but also wanted a twist. The near future setting provided this and allowed me to more or less create a world. What would it be like in 2058? I could decide."

For fans of the two authors, *Remember When* is "cowritten" by Roberts and Robb and combines contemporary romance with futuristic suspense. While Laine Tavish in the present grapples with the sudden reappearance and death of her fugitive father, Detective Eve Dallas in the future sorts out issues surrounding Laine's secret fortune.

The author shrugs off questions about her output. "I just have a steady pace," Roberts told *Publishers Weekly* in 1988, "it's like having green eyes." She generally takes two days off between books. She writes six to eight hours a day. If she runs into a plot block, she simply forces her way through.

The year 1997 was not a pleasant one for the author; a reader tipped her off there were passages in two novels by fellow romance writer Janet Dailey that appeared to have been lifted from Roberts books. Dailey later admitted borrowing plot ideas as well as entire passages from ten Roberts novels. Feeling somehow violated, Roberts decided to sue, but reached an agreement with Dailey out of court. She donated the settlement to Literacy Volunteers of America, the Authors Guild Foundation, and the Authors League Fund.

Roberts works methodically and tirelessly. She generally writes a fast and slim first draft to be sure of the story. She then goes back over the manuscript, fleshing out the story and characters. A final pass is for language.

These days the author generally writes two hardcover romantic suspenses a year as Roberts, two romantic mystery paperbacks as Robb, and a trilogy book or two.

One wonders when she has time to read—avocations include gardening, and she works out every day—but she reads many sister romance writers, as well as mystery writers John Sanford and Lawrence Block, women's fiction author Elizabeth Berg; fantasy author Terry Pratchett; and historical romance writer Mary Stewart. "When I read for pleasure, give me a story," she said in a *Book* magazine interview.

Roberts enjoys writing. "I really love the entire process of writing," she said on Subversion Parlor. "The crafting of the story, the building of characters, the surprises when I'm doing both and each goes its own way. I love the fiddling and polishing to make it the best story I can at that time. And I'm madly in love with the basic writer perks. No makeup, no pantyhose, no commuting in traffic."

"I don't count on inspiration," said the recipient of Romance Writers of America's Lifetime Achievement Award in an iVillager interview. "I think it's overrated. Wait for it and you can be waiting a *long* time. I believe in storytelling, in being driven to tell the story, and in the joy of it. I really love the process of writing, and so far, I don't have a problem with coming up with ideas. I think ideas are just part of the process."

What's the secret of her success? Her answer, according to *The Writer* in 2003: "My people win. That's what people buy me for. They're not buying me to write King Lear."

Works by the Author

Fiction

Promise Me Tomorrow (1984)
Hot Ice (1987)
Sacred Sins (1987)
Brazen Virtue (1988), sequel to *Sacred Sins*
Sweet Revenge (1989)
Public Secrets (1990)
Genuine Lies (1991)
Carnal Innocence (1992)
Divine Evil (1992)
Honest Illusions (1992)
Private Scandals (1993)
Hidden Riches (1994)
True Betrayals (1995)
Montana Sky (1996)
Sanctuary (1997)
Home Port (1998)
The Reef (1998)
River's End (1999)
Carolina Moon (2000)

Midnight Bayou (2001)
The Villa (2001)
Three Fates (2002)
Birthright (2003)
Boon O'Hurley (2004)
Jake's Ladder (2004)
Northern Lights (2004)

Calhoun Women Series

Courting Catherine (1991), Silhouette Romance 801
For the Love of Lilah (1991), Silhouette Special Edition 685
A Man for Amanda (1991), Silhouette Desire 649
Suzanna's Surrender (1991), Silhouette Intimate Moment 397
Catherine, Amanda, Lilah, Suzanne—The Calhoun Women (1996)
Megan's Mate (1996), Silhouette Intimate Moment 745
Catherine, and Amanda—The Calhoun Women (1998)
Lilah and Suzanna—The Calhoun Women (1998)

Concannon Sisters Series

Born in Fire (1994)
Born in Ice (1995)
Born in Shame (1996)

Gallagher's Pub Series

Jewels of the Sun (1999)
Heart of the Sea (2000)
Tears of the Moon (2000)

Harlequin Intrigue Series

Night Moves (1985)

In the Garden Trilogy

Blue Dahlia (2004)
Black Rose (2005)
Red Lily (2005)

Irish Thoroughbred Series

Irish Thoroughbred (1981), Silhouette Romance 81
Irish Rose (1988), Silhouette Intimate Moments 232

Irish Heart (2000)
Irish Rebel (2000), Silhouette Special Edition 1328

Jack's Story Series

Best Laid Plans (1989), Silhouette Special Edition 511
Lawless (1989), Harlequin H 21
Loving Jack (1989), Silhouette Special Edition 499

Key Trilogy

Key of Knowledge (2003)
Key of Light (2003)
Key of Valor (2003)

Language of Love Series

1. *Irish Thoroughbred* (1992)
2. *The Law Is a Lady* (1992)
3. *Irish Rose* (1992)
4. *Storm Warning* (1992)
5. *First Impressions* (1992)
6. *Reflections* (1992)
7. *Night Moves* (1992)
8. *Dance of Dreams* (1992)
9. *Opposites Attract* (1992)
10. *Island of Flowers* (1992)
11. *Search for Love* (1992)
12. *Playing the Odds* (1992)
13. *Tempting Fate* (1992)
14. *From This Day* (1992)
15. *All the Possibilities* (1992)
16. *The Heart's Victory* (1992)
17. *One Man's Art* (1992)
18. *Rules of the Game* (1992)
19. *For Now, Forever* (1992)
20. *Her Mother's Keeper* (1992)
21. *Partners* (1992)
22. *Sullivan's Woman* (1992)
23. *Summer Desserts* (1992)
24. *This Magic Moment* (1992)
25. *Lessons Learned* (1993)
26. *The Right Path* (1993)
27. *The Art of Deception* (1993)
28. *Untamed* (1993)

29. *Dual Image* (1993)
30. *Second Nature* (1993)
31. *One Summer* (1993)
32. *Gabriel's Angel* (1993)
33. *The Name of the Game* (1993)
34. *A Will and a Way* (1993)
35. *Affaire Royale* (1993)
36. *Less of a Stranger* (1993)
37. *Command Performance* (1993)
38. *Blithe Images* (1993)
39. *The Playboy Prince* (1993)
40. *Treasures Lost, Treasures Found* (1993)
41. *Risky Business* (1993)
42. *Loving Jack* (1993)
43. *Temptation* (1993)
44. *Best Laid Plans* (1993)
45. *Mind Over Matter* (1993)
46. *The Welcoming* (1993)
47. *Boundary Lines* (1994)
48. *Local Hero* (1994)
Mysterious (2003), reprints *This Magic Moment*, *Search for Love*, and *The Right Path*
Suspicious (2003), reprints *Partners*, *The Art of Deception*, and *Night Moves*

MacGregor Series

All the Possibilities (1985), Silhouette Special Edition 247
One Man's Art (1985), Silhouette Special Edition 259
Playing the Odds (1985), Silhouette Special Edition 225
Tempting Fate (1985), Silhouette Special Edition 235
For Now, Forever (1987), Silhouette Special Edition 361
Rebellion (1988), Harlequin H 4
Harlequin Christmas Stories (1990), short story
The MacGregor Brides (1997)
The MacGregor Grooms (1998)
The MacGregors—Serena and Caine (1998)
The Winning Hand (1998), Silhouette Special Edition 1202
The MacGregors—Alan and Grant (1999)
The MacGregors—Daniela and Ian (1999)
The Perfect Neighbor (1999), Silhouette Special Edition 1232

MacKade Brothers Series

The Pride of Jared MacKade (1995), Silhouette Special Edition 1000
The Return of Rafe MacKade (1995), Silhouette Intimate Moments 31
The Fall of Shane MacKade (1996), Silhouette Intimate Moments 1022

The Heart of Devin MacKade (1996), Silhouette Intimate Moments 697
The MacKade Brothers: Devin and Shane (2004), omnibus
The MacKade Brothers: Rafe and Jared (2004), omnibus

Chesapeake Bay/Quinn Brothers Series

Rising Tides (1998)
Sea Swept (1998)
Inner Harbor (1999)
Chesapeake Blue (2004)

Silhouette Intimate Moments Series

2. *Once More With Feeling* (1983)
12. *Tonight and Always* (1983)
25. *This Magic Moment* (1983)
33. *Endings and Beginnings* (1984)
49. *A Matter of Choice* (1984)
70. *Rules of the Game* (1984)
85. *The Right Path* (1985)
94. *Partners* (1985)
114. *Boundary Lines* (1985)
123. *Dual Image* (1985)
131. *The Art of Deception* (1986)
150. *Treasures Lost, Treasures Found* (1986)
160. *Risky Business* (1986)
185. *Mind Over Matter* (1987)
264. *The Name of the Game* (1988)
300. *Gabriel's Angel* (1989)
433. *Unfinished Business* (1992)

Silhouette Intimate Moments: Hornblower Brothers Series

313. *Time Was* (1989)
317. *Times Change* (1990)
Time and Again (2001)

Silhouette Intimate Moments: Night Tales Series

365. *Night Shift* (1991)
373. *Night Shadow* (1991)
529. *Night Shade* (1993)
595. *Night Smoke* (1994)
1027. *Night Shield* (2000)
Night Tales (2000)

Silhouette Intimate Moments: Royal Family of Cordina Series

142. *Affaire Royale* (1986)
198. *Command Performance* (1987)
212. *The Playboy Prince* (1987)
The Cordina Royal Family (1999)
1448. *Cordina's Crown Jewel* (2002)
Cordina's Royal Family (2002)

Silhouette Intimate Moments: The Stars of Mithra Series

811. *Hidden Star* (1997)
823. *Captive Star* (1997)
835. *Secret Star* (1998)

Silhouette Romance

127. *Blithe Images* (1982)
143. *Song of the West* (1982)
163. *Search for Love* (1982)
180. *Island of Flowers* (1982)
199. *From This Day* (1983)
215. *Her Mother's Keeper* (1983)
252. *Untamed* (1983)
274. *Storm Warning* (1984)
280. *Sullivan's Woman* (1984)
299. *Less of a Stranger* (1984)
529. *Temptation* (1987)

Silhouette Special Edition

59. *The Heart's Victory* (1982)
175. *The Law Is a Lady* (1984)
162. *First Impressions* (1984)
199. *Opposites Attract* (1984)
345. *A Will and a Way* (1986)
427. *Local Hero* (1988)
553. *The Welcoming* (1989)

Silhouette Special Edition: Banion Series

100. *Reflections* (1983)
116. *Dance of Dreams* (1983)
1279. *Considering Kate* (2001)

Silhouette Special Edition: Celebrity Magazine Series

288. *Second Nature* (1986)
306. *One Summer* (1986)
Summer Pleasures (2002)

Silhouette Special Edition: Chief Series

271. *Summer Desserts* (1985)
318. *Lessons Learned* (1986)

Silhouette Special Edition: Donovan Legacy Series

768. *Captivated* (1992)
774. *Entranced* (1992)
780. *Charmed* (1992)
961. *Enchanted* (1999)
The Donovan Legacy (1999)

Silhouette Special Edition: O'Hurley Triplets Series

451. *The Last Honest Woman* (1988)
463. *Dance to the Piper* (1988)
475. *Skin Deep* (1988)
625. *Without a Trace* (1990)
Born O'Hurley (2002)

Silhouette Special Edition: Those Wild Ukrainians Series

583. *Taming Natasha* (1990)
709. *Luring a Lady* (1991)
810. *Falling for Rachel* (1993)
872. *Convincing Alex* (1994)
1088. *Waiting for Nick* (1996)
Natasha and Rachel—The Stanislaski Sisters (1997)
Mikhail and Alex—The Stanislaski Brothers (2000)
1379. *Considering Kate* (2001)

Templeton Dream Trilogy

Daring to Dream (1996)
Finding the Dream (1997)
Holding the Dream (1997)

Three Sisters Island Series

Dance Upon the Air (2001)
Heaven and Earth (2001)
Face the Fire (2002)

Anthologies

Silhouette Christmas Stories (1986)
Silhouette Summer Sizzlers (1989)
Birds, Bees and Babies (1994)
Jingle Bells, Wedding Bells (1994)
From the Heart (1996)
Once Upon a Castle (1998)
Once Upon a Star (1999)
Once Upon a Dream (2000)
Once Upon a Rose (2001)
A Little Magic (2002)

Written As Jill March

Melodies of Love (1982)

Written As J. D. Robb

Eve Dallas Mysteries

Glory in Death (1995)
Naked in Death (1995)
Immortal in Death (1996)
Rapture in Death (1996)
Ceremony in Death (1997)
Vengeance in Death (1997)
Holiday in Death (1998)
Conspiracy in Death (1999)
Loyalty in Death (1999)
Witness in Death (2000)
Betrayal in Death (2001)
Seduction in Death (2001)
Reunion in Death (2002)
Imitation in Death (2003)
Remember When, with Nora Roberts (2003)
Visions of Death (2004)

For Further Information

Birthright review. *Publishers Weekly* (April 14, 2003).

Donahue, Dick. "Roberts rules redux." *Publishers Weekly* (September 8, 2003).

Elley, Karen Trotter. "Nora Roberts deals with destiny in Three Fates." BookPage. *http://www.bookpage.com/0204bp/nora_roberts.html* (viewed June 17, 2003).

Farrington, Susan. "An Interview with Nora Roberts." *Sanford Herald* (April 24, 2003).

Foege, Alec. "Close to Home: Romance writer Nora Roberts found her own true love with the man who came to build her a bookcase." *People Weekly* (April 12, 1999).

Imitation in Death review. *Publishers Weekly* (August 25, 2003).

J. D. Robb interview. Paranormal Romance Reviews. *http://pnr.thebestreviews.com/author2* (viewed June 17, 2003).

Kloberdanz, Kristin. "Thought you could dismiss it? Think again: Meet Nora Roberts, the queen of the genre, who reigns over a changed landscape." *Book* (March/April 2002).

Little, Denise, and Lara Hayden. *The Official Nora Roberts Companion*. New York: Berkley, 2003.

Maryles, Daisy. "Breaking Her Record." *Publishers Weekly* (July 16, 2001).

Maryles, Daisy. "Roberts Rules." *Publishers Weekly* (November 1, 1999).

Maryles, Daisy, and Dick Donahue. "A Jewel of an Author." *Publishers Weekly* (December 6, 1999).

Maryles, Daisy, and Dick Donahue. "Nora's #1 'Birthright.' " *Publishers Weekly* (April 14, 2003).

McMurran, Kristin. "Page Churner." *People Weekly* (July 1, 1996).

Mowery, Linda, and Laurie Likes Books. "Nora Roberts on her MacGregor Series, All About Romance (September 22, 1997). *http://www.likesbooks.com/roberts/html* (viewed June 17, 2003).

Nora Roberts entry, *St. James Encyclopedia of Popular Culture*. Detroit: St. James Press, 2000.

Nora Roberts entry, *Twentieth-Century Romance & Historical Writers*. 3rd edition. Chicago: St. James Press, 1994.

"Nora Roberts: I'm Not Planning to Retire." iVillager. *http://www.ivillage.com/books/intervu/romance/articles/0,11872,192493_82603,00.html* (viewed June 17, 2003).

Nora Roberts interview. *http://www.die-buecherecke.de/roberts2.HTM* (viewed June 17, 2003).

Patrick, Diane. "Daily, Roberts settle." *Publishers Weekly* (May 4, 1998).

Quinn, Judy. "Nora Roberts: a celebration of emotion." *Publishers Weekly* (February 23, 1998).

Remember When review. *Library Journal* (September 1, 2003).

"Resolved." *People Weekly* (May 4, 1998).

Rist, Curtis. "Bodice rip-off." *People Weekly* (August 18, 1997).

"Roberts will sue Dailey after all." *Publishers Weekly* (September 8, 1997).

Tichemer, Louise. "Drive, Discipline, and Desire." *Writer's Digest* (February 1997).

Wachsmith, Maudeen. "No Makeup, No Commuting: Nora Roberts on Reading, Writing, and Relaxing." Subversion Parlor. *http://www.booksquare.com/subversion/parlor/int002.cfm* (viewed June 17, 2003).

"What makes readers love Nora Roberts' romances?" *The Writer* (September 2003).

Peter Robinson

♦ Mystery

Castleford, Yorkshire, England
1950

♦ *Inspector Banks Series*

Courtesy of Peter Robinson.

About the Author and the Author's Writing

> Marshall had gone missing in 1965, and Banks had in the years since lived
> with guilt. A few months before, a man had made a sexual approach, which
> Banks fended off but never reported out of embarrassment. He'd always fig-
> ured that predator had come back for Graham.
>
> *—Close to Home*

Today's police procedural mystery is as apt to find the protagonist grappling with personal or relationship issues as with a kidnapping or murder; witness Peter Robinson's richly textured, deeply plotted and entertaining series featuring the Yorkshire detective chief inspector. In the novel *Close to Home*, Alan Banks has to not only work closely with an ex-girlfriend, Detective Inspector Annie Cabbot, but also must cultivate a new one, Detective Inspector Michelle Hart, as he confronts a suppressed fear he once did something terribly wrong.

Robinson was born in Castleford, Yorkshire, England, in 1950, the son of a photographer and a homemaker. Growing up in England, his first attempts at writing were retellings of Robin Hood and other stories, complete with his own illustrations, in a notebook. After he earned a bachelor of arts degree, with honors, from University of Leeds in 1974, he was drawn to Canada by the prospect of a course in creative writing at the University of Windsor in Ontario. "I think the main thing I learned from Joyce Carol Oates [his instructor there] was to take myself seriously as a writer, to believe in myself," he said in a HarperCollins interview.

In 1983, after traveling back and forth between England and Canada, he completed requirements for a doctoral degree at York University in Ontario.

Robinson wrote poetry and stories, but he was not drawn to mystery fiction until he visited his father one rainy summer and devoured his father's copies of Raymond Chandler and Georges Simenon books. Something clicked.

"Crime fiction was immediately attractive because of its formal and structured nature," he said in an interview on the HarperCollins Web site, "though I have tried to move away from some of the stricter requirements since then—that's probably what keeps me there, the feeling that you can push at the boundaries, go further with each book."

He took direction from writers such as Ruth Rendell, "who were able to take a part of England and create a detective through whose eyes they could examine the area as much as investigating crimes," he told J. Kinsston Pierce for *January Magazine*. By then firmly settled in Canada, where he found employment opportunity as a teacher, he decided to create, largely through nostalgia, a Yorkshire town (Eastvale, modeled largely on Richmond).

Opera-loving Banks has freshly arrived in the Dales in the first book, *Gallows View*, but he finds the countryside far from tranquil as he has to immediately deal with a Peeping Tom, a burglar, and a murderer. Banks is entirely imaginary, though his name, the author has said, was cribbed from an old school friend. Even though he may have similarities to Simenon's Jules Inspector Maigret or Rendell's Chief Inspector Reginald Wexford, Robinson said he has made him more modern, more musical, more political, more proletarian, more rebellious.

Robinson knew from the start he wanted his main character to react to his new setting. As the series has gone on, Banks has become more introspective, his marriage has broken up, he has begun to cherish life more. Robinson told Pierce, "He's thinking more about his youth and his childhood. I think it's opened him up an awful lot to the readers."

> The Chameleon, a serial killer who has abducted five young women in Yorkshire, has a grim surprise in store for Police Constables Janet Taylor and Dennis Morrisey when they are called to a reported domestic disturbance. Acting Detective Superintendent Banks soon has the brutal Terence Payne in custody—but that's only the beginning of the horror.
>
> *—Aftermath*

Aftermath was universally praised by reviewers: "Seemlessly plotted" (*Fort Lauderdale Sun-Sentinel*); "A winner" (*Houston Chronicle*), "Highly textured" (*Tampa Tribune*); "[A]n excellent crime novel" (*Milwaukee Journal-Sentinel*). Still, Kathy Phillips suggested in *Drood Review of Mystery*, Robinson took a risk by reversing the usual plot progression. The killer is caught right off, and the book follows the police as they reconstruct the crimes.

"I'm far more interested in what combination of circumstances caused a person to commit a crime," Robinson told *Publishers Weekly's* Tim Peters. "I find the term 'police procedural' sort of boring actually. My novels are often less about Banks as detective than they are about Banks and what happens to the people around him, in his work and his life. But I hope to get the procedural part accurate, too!"

A full-time writer since 1987, Robinson has also taught community college writing and literature classes for twenty years. He is married to Sheila Halladay, a lawyer. Hobbies include music, reading, travel, walking, and visiting pubs.

Among Robinson's awards are a Mystery Writers of Canada Arthur Ellis Award in 1990 and 1991 for *The Hanging Valley* and *Past Reason Hated*, respectively, and a French Grand Prix de Littérateur Policiére in 2000 for *In a Dry Season*. He has also received the British Crime Writers Association Dagger in the Library award.

"Robinson quietly pushes the boundaries of crime fiction while shrugging off the genre wars," observed Brian Bethune in *Maclean's*.

The author has avoided writing a novel with an American protagonist, as he believes it would require a voice foreign to him. His one story set in the United States, *No Cure for Love*, has a British woman as the main character.

Robinson does not outline his books, he said on his HarperCollins Web page: "The plot develops organically as I write . . . I tend to go back more often and add layers and new details as I go, so that I end up with a draft far closer to the final one than I used to."

Nor does the author try to replicate true-life conversation. "I just look at dialogue as an extension of narrative," he said in *The Writer*. "I try to keep in mind that when two people are talking, each wants something from the other or is trying to get something across. I think if you keep that in mind, it helps you to focus the dialogue."

He elaborated in a Mystery One conversation, "I let the characters and events take me places, and sometimes those places turn out to be dead ends. It's not a method I'd recommend. I always tell my students to know how their story ends before they begin writing it, but don't practice that technique myself."

Banks only gradually gets a handle on his relationships—with his ex-wife, with his son, with his former girlfriend, with his superiors on the police force. Chief Constable Jeremiah "Jimmy" Riddle is particularly prickly—so much so, he contemplates a shift to the National Crime Squad. Then . . .

> Riddle calls Banks to his house. It's certainly not a social visit. Riddle's sixteen-year-old daughter Emily has run away. Nude pictures of her show up on a pornographic Web site. To investigate, Banks must go where he doesn't wish to go—into Riddle's private life.
>
> —*Cold is the Grave*

Works by the Author

Fiction

Caedmon's Song (1990)
No Cure for Love (1995)

Inspector Banks Series

Gallows View (1987)
A Dedicated Man (1988)
The Hanging Valley (1989)
A Necessary End (1989)
Past Reason Hated (1991)
Wednesday's Child (1992)
Final Account (1994), in England as *Dry Bones That Dream*
No Cure for Love (1995)
Innocent Graves (1996)
Blood at the Root (1997), in England as *Dead Right*
Cold is the Grave (2000)
Aftermath (2001)
Close to Home (2002)
Playing With Fire (2004)
Strange Affair (2005)

Collections

Not Safe After Dark (1998)
In a Dry Season (1999)

Anthologies

Cold Blood II, edited by Peter Sellers (1989)
Best American Mystery Stories 1997, edited by Robert B. Parker (1997)
Best American Mystery Stories 1999, edited by Ed McBain (1999)

Poetry

With Equal Eye (1979)
Nosferatu (1981)

For Further Information

Aldrich, Chris. Peter Robinson interview. *Mystery News* (February/March 2003).

Ashley, Mike. Peter Robinson entry, *Mammoth Encyclopedia of Modern Crime Fiction*. New York: Carroll & Graf, 2002.

Bethune, Brian. "Working-Class Boys Made Good." *Maclean's* (February 23, 2004).

Cold Is the Grave description. Mystery Net.com. *http://www.mysterynet.com/robinson/* (viewed April 21, 2003).

"Cold Is the Grave: Peter Robinson." USAToday.com. *http://www.usa.today.com/community/chatp/1116robinson.htm* (viewed April 21, 2003).

Colley, Kimberly. *Closer to Home* review. *RT Bookclub* (February 2003).

"Conversation with Peter Robinson." Mostly Fiction. *http://www.mostlyfiction.com/authorqa/robinson.htm* (viewed April 20, 2003).

In a Dry Season description. *http://www.inspectorbanks.com/dry.html* (viewed April 21,2003).

In a Dry Season description. *http://www.twbooks.co.uk/authors/probinsn.html#Cold%20is%20the%20Grave* (viewed April 21,2003).

Jones, Daniel, and John D. Jorgenson, eds. Peter Robinson entry, *Contemporary Authors New Revision Series*. Vol. 67. Detroit: Gale Research, 1998.

Peter Robinson interview. HarperCollins. *http://www.harpercollins.com/hc/features/mystery/0380978083fea.asp* (viewed April 21, 2003).

Peter Robinson interview. Mystery One Bookstore. *http://www.mysteryone.com/PeterRobinsonInterview.htm* (viewed April 20, 2003).

Peters, Tim. "Inspector Banks Goes home (PW Talks with Peter Robinson)." *Publishers Weekly* (December 9, 2002).

Phillips, Kathy. "Banks comes full circle." *Drood Review of Mystery* (September/October 2001).

Pierce, J. Kingston. "There's Nothing Dry About Peter Robinson." *January Magazine* (July 1999).

Robinson, Peter. "How I Write." *The Writer* (September 2003).

John Saul

Pasadena, California
1942

◆ *Suffer the Children*

Credit: Mike Sack.

About the Author and the Author's Writing

John Saul suffers frequent comparison to Stephen King. Both write novels of horror and psychological suspense. Saul published his Blackstone Chronicles serially—an innovation Stephen King had done a year before him. But when King moved on to e-books, Saul went in a different direction and adapted a story into a computer game, *Blackstone Chronicles: An Adventure in Terror*. Saul had embraced the electronic world in 1978, when word processing computers cost about $15,000, and he played Zork for years. He could barely wait for the technology to enable him to bring his own story to CD-ROM.

"The game is its own story," the author told Randy Sluganski, explaining why the game's premise will not be turned into a book, "and that story only works for me as a CD-ROM based game. It's structured for media. The puzzle aspect of it, the fact that you can explore from different sequences and in any direction . . ."

John Woodruff Saul III was born in 1942 in Pasadena, California. He attended Antioch College, Montana State University, and San Francisco State College. He traveled the country for several years and held a variety of jobs including working for a drug and alcohol program, technical writing, office typist temping for Western Girls, and assistant managing an auto rental agency. He was director of Tellurian Communities from 1976 to 1978 and was a director of Seattle (Washington) Theater Arts for the next two years. He has been a full-time writer since. He has homes in Seattle and Maui, Hawaii.

Saul considers himself a writer of psychological thrillers. "Basically, I see myself as an entertainer," he told interviewer Al Giovetti. "Providing people a fun read is what I enjoy doing. Ever since I was a small child I always knew I would be writing to entertain. This has been my motivation."

Saul's success was not immediate. He wrote spicy novels (a couple of which were published under pseudonyms), humorous crime novels, and a novel about the citizen's band radio craze, but none sold.

His literary agent suggested he try writing a long summer horror novel. As Saul told *The Advocate* in a 2001 interview, he and his life partner, Michael Sack, mulled the idea as they drove home that day in 1976. "Suddenly Michael said, 'What if there were two little girls and everyone thought one of them was crazy, but it was actually the other one who's crazy?' I said, 'I like that idea, because that means we can have one little girl killing all of their friends but everyone thinks it's her sister.' And that became *Suffer the Children*."

That working partnership between Saul and Sack has continued through more than two dozen books. They come up with a plot together, Sack outlines the plot and key developments, and Saul writes the book. Although contracts with publishers are in both their names, Saul, it is agreed, does all the publicity. Sack is a trained psychotherapist who has run the Wisconsin state drug and alcohol rehabilitation program.

Saul frequently uses young protagonists because, as he told *Charlotte Austin Review*, "Teenagers and children are not yet responsible for their actions and serve as excellent protagonists and antagonists for this genre."

Saul does not write gay fiction, but some of the themes he explores such as teased and rejected children and people haunted by their repressed sexuality, ring true with gay readers. The only openly homosexual characters thus far, however, have been a lesbian veterinarian in *Guardian* and a gay couple, Kevin and Mark in *Midnight Voices*. Saul said this doesn't mean there aren't other gays in the books, he just doesn't say so, anymore than he specifies the race of his characters.

In an interview with *January Magazine*, the author remarked he does as little research as he can get away with. "They pay me to tell lies," he said. "That's the great thing about fiction; you make it up as you go along. That's one of the reasons I always make up the towns too. If you use a real place—for instance, I did set a book in Seattle, and I did set a book on Maui—and suddenly you've got to have it right, or people go crazy."

Works by the Author

Fiction

Suffer the Children (1977)
Punish the Sinners (1978)
Cry for the Strangers (1979)
Comes the Blind Fury (1980)
When the Wind Blows (1981)
The God Project (1982)
All Fall Down (1983)
Nathaniel (1984)
Brainchild (1985)
Hellfire (1986)
The Unwanted (1987)
Fear Factor (1988)
The Unloved (1988)
Creature (1989)
Second Child (1990)
Sleepwalk (1990)
Darkness (1991)

Shadows (1992)
Guardian (1993)
The Homing (1994)
Black Lightning (1995), omnibus
Three Terrifying Best-selling Novels (1996), omnibus
John Saul 3 Novels (1997), omnibus
The Presence (1997)
The Right Hand of Evil (1999)
Nightshade (2000)
The Manhattan Hunt Club (2001)
Midnight Voices (2002)
Black Creek Crossing (2004)

Blackstone Chronicles

An Eye for an Eye: The Doll (1996)
Ashes to Ashes: The Dragon's Flame (1997)
Asylum (1997)
The Blackstone Chronicles (1997), includes all the books
In the Shadow of Evil: The Handkerchief (1997)
Day of Reckoning: The Stereoscope (1997)
Twist of Fate; The Locket (1997)

For Further Information

Bail, Paul. *John Saul: A Critical Companion*. Westport, CT: Greenwood Press, 1996.

Giovetti, Al. "John Saul and his game The Blackstone Chronicles." The Computer Show. *http://www.thecomputershow.com/computershow/interviews/johnsaul blackstonechron.htm* (viewed June 17, 2003).

John Saul entry, *St. James Guide to Horror, Ghost & Gothic Writers*. Detroit: St. James Press, 1998.

Peacock, Scot, ed. John Saul entry, *Contemporary Authors New Revision Series*. Vol. 81. Detroit: Gale Research, 1999.

Richards, Lidna. John Saul interview. *January Magazine. http://www.januarymagazine .com/profiles/saul.html* (viewed June 17, 2003).

Sluganski, Randy. John Saul interview, Just Adventure (November 7, 1998). *http:// www.justadventure.com/Interviews/John_Saul_Interview.shtm* (viewed June 17, 2003).

Steele, Bruce C. "Fear and loving in the best-seller rack." *The Advocate* (August 28, 2001).

Steele, Bruce C. "John and Mike and Kevin and Mark." The Advocate (July 9, 2002). *http://www.advocate.com/html/stories/868/868_saul.asp* (viewed June 17, 2003).

Tomasso, Phillip III. "Interview with best-selling author John Saul." *Charlotte Austin Review.* *http://collection.nlc-bnc.ca/100/202/300/charlotte/2000/10-15/pages/ interviews/authors/johnsaul.htm* (viewed June 17, 2003).

Winter, Stanley. *Dark Dreamers: Conversations with the Masters of Horror.* New York: Avon, 1981.

Anne Rivers Siddons

◆ Women's fiction

Fairburn, Georgia
1936

◆ *Peachtree Road*

About the Author and the Author's Writing

Anne Rivers Siddons came to realize very quickly the power of the written word. She attended Auburn University during the racially turbulent 1950s when protesters boycotted buses in Montgomery, Alabama, and attempted to desegregate Alabama University. In a column generally devoted to more mundane subjects, she wrote a piece that embraced integration. When she refused to withdraw it, the university's administration inserted a disclaimer saying it did not agree with her view. The column drew national attention. When she attempted a second piece on the same subject, she was dismissed from her position.

"At Auburn, and before that when I wrote local columns for the Fairburn paper, writing came so naturally that I didn't value it," she said on her HarperCollins Web page. "I never even thought that it might be a livelihood, or a source of great satisfaction. Southern girls, remember, were taught to look for security."

Sybil Anne Rivers (she doesn't use the first name) was born in 1936, the only child of a lawyer and his wife, the seventh generation of her family to live in the community. She was an A student, a cheerleader, homecoming queen, and centennial queen of Fairburn, the small railroad town just south of Atlanta where she grew up. She received a B.A.A. degree from Auburn in 1958 and then attended Atlanta School of Art.

In 1959, the author worked for Retail Credit, then for Citizens & Southern National Bank from 1961 to 1963, in the company's advertising department. She started out doing layout and design, but frequently rewrote copy as well. After stints at Burke-Dowling Adams, 1967–1969, and Burton Campbell Advertising, 1969–1974, she became a full-time journalist. She became a senior editor for the new *Atlanta* magazine and came to know many leaders of the civil rights movement of the time.

The author's magazine experiences provided the background for her novel *Downtown*, in which the main character, Smoky O'Donnell, is a writer for a trendy Atlanta magazine in the 1960s who observes an exciting time in civil rights activism but is disappointed at so little result.

In 1966 the author married Heyward L. Siddons; he had four sons by a previous marriage.

After an editor at Doubleday read one of her pieces, he offered Siddons a two-book contract, which resulted in a collection of essays, *John Chancellor Makes Me Cry*, and her first novel, *Heartbreak Hotel*, about her college years. When that editor, Larry Ashmead, moved on to Simon & Schuster, and then to Harper & Row, Siddons followed. She wrote a haunted house story, *The House Next Door*, which Stephen King proclaimed "the new American Gothic."

She continued to write novels, and *Peachtree Road* in 1988 boosted her onto the bestseller lists. Later, as she struggled to overcome severe depression, she went through a three-year period without writing.

Siddons lived and wrote for many years in Brookhaven, Atlanta, and had a summer place in Brooklin, Maine. She wrote in a cottage, a home office at the rear of the property. She and her husband read and edited each day's output over cocktails in the evening.

"Anne is simply one of the best writers writing about the South today," observed author Pat Conroy, quoted on the Barnes & Noble Meet the Writers Web page. "*Gone with the Wind* comparisons drive Anne crazy, but the truth is, she is covering the territory Margaret Mitchell would have covered if she'd lived. The difference is that Anne is a much better writer." And less a romantic, the author herself adds.

Siddons' novel *Up Island* is about Molly Redwine's discovery that her Coca-Cola executive husband is having an affair. She does not know what to do when he suddenly leaves her for another woman, her mother dies suddenly, and her children scatter. After spending the summer with a friend on Martha's Vineyard, she takes a modest job and housing arrangement in order to stay on in the off season. She befriends a cancer patient living next door, comforts her grieving father, and slowly comes to grip with reality: She has abandoned her old, Atlanta way of life and must find new strength.

The author now lives in Charlotte, South Carolina, and that city shows up in her novel *Low Country*, which carries the theme of coastal development versus preservation of natural assets. The heroine of *Low Country*, Caroline Venable, inherited a pristine island from her grandfather. There's a small cottage on it, otherwise inhabitants are largely wildlife. Caroline's husband, Clay, is rich from his resort developments. But facing sudden bankruptcy, he sees selling the island as his only salvation. Caroline obviously faces the greatest decision of her life. The plot grew from Siddons' own experience writing promotional material for an island resort on Hilton Head, South Carolina.

Islands apparently mean a lot to the author—she used islands in two novels, where they play a symbolic role as well as a physical one. "I think it's the idea that they're totally apart from the world," the author explained in an interview with Alice Cary for BookPage. "An island has some sort of magnetic pull. It makes all these promises that it will keep you safe and nurture you. Of course this is not true, but I still never sleep as soundly as I do on an island or on our little peninsula in Maine."

Works by the Author

Fiction

Heartbreak Hotel (1976)
The House Next Door (1978)
Fox's Earth (1980)
Homeplace (1987)

Peachtree Road (1988)
King's Oak (1990)
Outer Banks (1991)
Colony (1992)
Hill Towns (1993)
Downtown (1994)
Fault Lines (1995)
Up Island (1997)
Low Country (1998)
Nora, Nora (2000)
Islands (2003)

Nonfiction

John Chancellor Makes Me Cry (1975)
Go Straight on Peachtree (1976)

Motion Picture Based on the Author's Works

Heart of Dixie (1989), based on *Heartbreak Hotel*

For Further Information

Anne Rivers Siddons biography. Barnes & Noble. *http://www.barnesandnoble.com/ writers/writerdetails.asp?cid=883628* (viewed April 11, 2003).

Ann Rivers Siddons biography. Bookreporter. *http://www.bookreporter.com/authors/ au-siddons-anne-river.asp* (viewed April 11, 2003).

Anne Rivers Siddons entry, *St. James Guide to Horror, Ghost & Gothic Writers*. Detroit: St. James Press, 1998.

Anne Rivers Siddons Fan Web page. *http://www.geocities.com/Athens/Delphi/8435/* (viewed April 11, 2003).

Anne Rivers Siddons Web page. HarperCollins. *http://www.harpercollins.com/cata-log/author_xml.asp?authorID-9057* (viewed April 11, 2003).

Cary, Alice. "Anne Rivers Siddons preserves natural treasures in *Low Country*." BookPage (July 1998). *http://www.bookpage.com/9807bp/anne_rivers_siddons .html* (viewed April 11, 2003).

King, Stephen. *Danse Macabre*. New York: Everest House, 1981.

Nora, Nora review. iVillager. *http://www.ivillage.com/books/recread/review/articles/ 0,,220641_218754,00.html* (viewed June 13, 2003).

Peacock, Scot, ed. Anne Rivers Siddons entry, *Contemporary Authors New Revision Series*. Vol. 81. Detroit: Gale Research, 1999.

Up Island review. Reading Group Guide. *http://www.readinggroupguides.com/guides/up_island.asp* (viewed June 13, 2003).

Danielle Steel

◆ Romance ◆ Women's fiction

New York City
1947

◆ *Once in a Lifetime*

About the Author and the Author's Writing

Romantic tales of the rich and famous, strong women making major decisions, life's crises crunching on the unsuspecting—these are author Danielle Steel's hallmarks in a career that has produced more than sixty novels. By the time you read this, the statistic will change. But Steel has had one or another book on the *New York Times* best-seller list for more than 390 consecutive weeks!

Steel's heroines are from the luxury class, but they nevertheless suffer some romantic or other tragedy. "These heroines, brimming with brains and talent, must overcome many obstacles to find happiness and fulfillment," explains Patricia Altner in *Twentieth-Century Romance and Historical Writers*. "Some find a way to accomplish this through love. . . . There is an element of soap-opera inherent in all of Steel's tales, but her characters, despite some physical and social similarities, are distinctive and appealing. Her ear for dialogue is excellent."

The author has an easy, inviting style. Her locales are exotic, her characters attractive, her plots tangled. "Steel has the ability to give such formula writing enough strength to not collapse into an exhausted state of cliché," commended reviewer Petty Hill in 1988.

Danielle Fernande Schuelein-Steel was born in New York, in 1947. Educated in France, she came to enjoy French literature and writers such as Colette. She attended Parsons School of Design in 1963 and New York University, 1963 to 1967. As a teen, she wrote poetry, and she completed her first manuscript for a novel when she was nineteen. She is a Christian Scientist. Her fourth husband is John Traina, a businessman, and she has two children from earlier marriages, two stepchildren, and five children from her present marriage.

Steel's career in the public relations field began with Supergirls Ltd. in New York as vice president of public relations, 1968 to 1971, followed by two years as a copywriter for Grey Advertising in San Francisco. She also held other advertising writing and public relations positions before becoming a full-time novelist.

There were many rejections before her first book found a welcoming publisher. One of her early novels, *Once in a Lifetime*, tells the story of a popular novelist Daphne Fields who fiercely guards her privacy. She has secrets from a tragic fire years before. Strong-willed, she nevertheless finally admits she can't face the future alone.

Ideas for her books, Steel has said aren't easily explained. They often take root over long periods of time. She does not use experiences from her own life, and seldom bases characters on real people.

Steel has written books with serious themes such as child abuse, abduction, and infertility; she explores family issues and tragedy. A couple's teenaged daughter in *Accident* has suffered brain injury, for example.

The author has also written illustrated storybooks for young readers—she's certainly had plenty of experience, rearing nine children—dealing with such issues as a new sibling or the loss of a grandparent.

More than twenty of Steel's books have been adapted to television, among them *Jewels*, a four-hour miniseries that garnered two Golden Globe nominations.

She has seemingly done everything an author could do, but she has never written a sequel to one of her books. She does considerable research for many of her novels, sometimes over several years and while she has other writing going on. Once she starts a book—using her 1946 Olympia manual typewriter—she stays with it upwards of twenty hours a day.

Steel has been national chairman for the American Library Association and a spokeswoman for the National Committee for the Prevention of Child Abuse and the American Humane Association.

Steel's nonfiction work, *His Bright Light*, is a poignant portrait of her son Nick Traina's life and his death at nineteen to drug overdose after losing a long battle with manic depression.

"*His Bright Light* will make a difference for countless others who are seeing the early signs of mental illness," said Laurie Flynn, executive director of National Alliance for the Mentally Ill, in a letter found on the Random House Danielle Steel Web site.

The book was written, Steel said in a NAMI interview, to honor her son and "to share with people the challenges we faced, so that they feel less alone and less isolated with their pain, in similar situations. It wrote it to give people hope and strength as they follow a similar path to ours." Issues of mental health so concerned the writer she testified in 2000 before a congressional hearing on funding for suicide prevention.

That same year, in an unusual celebration of the publication of the author's fiftieth novel, *Journey*, her publisher Delacorte Press printed and distributed free through booksellers one million copies of a commemorative edition of Steel's three most popular paperback novels, *Family Album*, *Kaleidoscope*, and *Fine Things*.

Works by the Author

Fiction

Going Home, (1973)
Passion's Promise (1977)
Now and Forever (1978)
The Promise (1978), based on screenplay by Garry Michael White
The Ring (1980)
Season of Passion (1980)

Summer's End (1980)
Loving (1981)
To Love Again (1981)
Palomino (1981)
Remembrance (1981)
Crossings (1982)
Once in a Lifetime (1982)
Changes (1983)
A Perfect Stranger (1983)
Thurston House (1983)
Full Circle (1984)
Family Album (1985)
Secrets (1985)
Wanderlust (1986)
Fine Things (1987)
Kaleidoscope (1987)
Zoya (1988)
Daddy (1989)
Star (1989)
Message from Nam (1990)
Heartbeat (1991)
No Greater Love (1991)
Jewels (1992)
Mixed Blessings (1992)
Vanished (1993)
Accident (1994)
The Gift (1994), *El Regalo* (1994), Spanish edition with Maria Jose Rodellar
Wings (1994)
Five Days in Paris (1995)
Lightning (1995)
Malice (1996)
Silent Honor (1996)
The Ghost (1997)
The Ranch (1997)
Special Delivery (1997)
The Klone and I (1998)
The Long Road Home (1998)
Mirror Image (1998)
Bittersweet (1999)
Granny Dan (1999)
Irresistible Forces (1999)
The House on Hope Street (2000)
Journey (2000)
The Wedding (2000)

The Kiss (2001)
Leap of Faith (2001)
Lone Eagle (2001)
Answered Prayers (2002)
The Cottage (2002)
Sunset in St. Tropez (2002)
Dating Game (2003)
Johnny Angel (2003)
Safe Harbour (2003)
Echoes (2004)
Miracle (2004)
Ransom (2004)
Second Chance (2004)

Books for Young Adults

Amando (1985)

Martha Series

Martha's Best Friend (1989)
Martha's New Daddy (1989)
Martha's New School (1989)
Martha's New Puppy (1990)
Martha and Hilary and the Stranger (1991)

Max Series

Max and the Baby-Sitter (1989)
Max's Daddy Goes to the Hospital (1989)
Max's New Baby (1989)
Max Runs Away (1990)
Max and Grandma and Grandpa Winky (1991)

Freddie Series

Freddie and the Doctor (1992)
Freddie's Accident (1992)
Freddie's First Night Away (1992)
Freddie's Trip (1992)

Poetry

Love: Poems (1984)

Nonfiction

Having a Baby (1984), coauthor
His Bright Light (1998)

Television Movies Based on the Author's Works

Now and Forever (1983)
Crossings (1986)
Fine Things (1990)
Kaleidoscope (1990)
Changes (1991)
Daddy (1991)
Palomino (1991)
Jewels (1992)
Secrets (1992)
Heartbeat (1993)
Message from Nam (1993)
Star (1993)
Family Album (1994)
Once in a Lifetime (1994)
A Perfect Stranger (1994)
Mixed Blessings (1995)
Vanished (1995)
Zoya (1995)
Full Circle (1996)
No Greater Love (1996)
Remembrance (1996)
The Ring (1996)

For Further Information

Altner, Patricia. Danielle Steel entry, *Twentieth-Century Romance and Historical Writers*. 2nd edition, edited by Lesley Henderson. Chicago: St. James Press, 1990.

Bane, Vickie L., with Lorenzo Benet. *The Lives of Danielle Steel: The Unauthorized biography of America's #1 Best-Selling Author*. New York: St. Martin's, 1994.

Danielle Steel biography. Meet the Writers, Barnes & Noble. *http://www.barnes andnoble.com/writers/writerdetails.asp?userid=0H4KV3ZHMT&cid=748011# bio* (viewed May 9, 2003).

"Danielle Steel, Bipolar Disorder, and Suicide." YourCongress.com. *http://www .yourcongress.com/ ViewArticle.asp?article_id=79* (viewed April 10, 2003).

"Danielle Steel's Million Paperback March." *Publishers Weekly* (November 20, 2000).

Danielle Steel Web page. *http://www.randomhouse.com/features/steel/profile.html* (viewed April 10, 2003).

Hill, Peggy. *Zoya* review, *Toronto Globe & Mail* (July 9, 1988).

Jones, Daniel, and John D. Jorgenson, eds. Danielle Steel entry, *Contemporary Authors New Revision Series*. Vol. 65. Detroit: Gale Research, 1998.

"NAMI's Interviews With Danielle Steel & Kay Jamison Provide Advance Glimpse of Tuesday Hearing." National Alliance for the Mentally Ill. *http://www.nami/org/pressroom/000204.html* (viewed May 9, 2003).

Peter Straub

◆ Horror   ◆ Suspense   ◆ Fantasy

Milwaukee, Wisconsin
1943

◆ *Ghost Story*

Credit: Jerry Bauer.

About the Author and the Author's Writing

Peter Straub became hooked on frightful stories as a young teen when he read the Modern Library *Great Tales of Terror and the Supernatural*, with its tales by Machen, James, Lovecraft, and others.

In a *Locus* interview, Straub said he does not read much horror these days, but he is enamored of its concept: "The idea of a nasty, subversive genre, the purpose of which is to up-end conventional ideas of good taste, and to speak truths otherwise ignored or suppressed. I think that's really worthy. I'd like to see a little more of it. Good works of horror are immensely impressive."

The author was born in 1943 in Milwaukee, Wisconsin, about ten miles from where years later notorious cannibalistic serial killer Jeffrey Dahmer would lure his victims. As a kid, Straub devoured comic books, everything from Nancy and Sluggo and Donald Duck to Batman and Captain Marvel.

By the time he reached school, Straub disdained the usual Dick and Jane readers in favor of what he could find at the library or the Stratemeyer syndicate series books, such as the Hardy Boys, sold at Woolworth's. By sixth grade, he was a fan of A. E. Van Vogt, Robert Heinlein, and a host of science fiction and fantasy authors. When he reached high school, he embraced Thomas Wolfe and Jack Kerouac.

Straub early accepted the belief one could not trust the world; he was severely injured when struck by an automobile. A stutter limited his social activity so he took refuge in reading. "And his storytelling," according to the author's net-site.com Web site, "for in spite of everything he was still a sociable child with a lot of friends, took a turn toward the dark and the garish, toward the ghoulish and the violent. He found his first 'effect' when he discovered that he could make this kind of thing funny."

Straub attended private Milwaukee Country Day School on a scholarship. With a bachelor of arts degree in English from the University of Wisconsin, Madison, he obtained his master's degree from Columbia University in 1966. He married Susan Bitker, a counselor, in 1966; they have two children.

For three years, Straub taught English at his former high school in Wisconsin, and then in 1969, he relocated to Ireland where he began work toward a doctoral degree at University College, Dublin. He composed poetry, two volumes of which were published in 1972, but he became disenchanted. He wrote a novel, *Marriages*, an exercise in poetic prose that received favorable reviews but only modest sales.

His next novel, *Under Venus*, was more conventional, but found no publisher. At the urging of his agent, Straub wrote *Julia*, his first gothic novel, inspired by his renewed reading of Robert Block, Richard Matheson, and Peter Blatty. It is about a woman living in England who is haunted by the specter of a murdered child.

"Horror was not about the invention of clever puzzles," Straub explained in a Dark Echo interview in 1997. "It dealt with profound emotions and real mysteries. . . . Horror could touch people, change them, make them think. While it was certainly entertaining, there was much more to it than mere weightless entertainment."

In 1979, *Ghost Story* became a best-seller—it is about a woman's spirit extracting revenge on those responsible for her death in a New England town. "When I was writing *Ghost Story*," Straub said in an interview with Michael McCarty, "I was very aware that I was at another level from the work I had done before that. I knew something was going to happen, I knew my life was going to change in some way."

Since then the author has topped the charts with novels such as *Shadowland*. His Blue Rose trilogy is suspense without supernatural elements. One of the volumes, *Koko*, brought Straub the 1989 World Fantasy Award. He has also won the British Fantasy and the Bram Stoker awards. Straub has pushed himself as a writer, not only venturing into various genres, but honing his craft, striving to accomplish something new each time out.

In 1984, he collaborated with Stephen King on *The Talisman*. They began the book together at Straub's home in Westport, Connecticut, and then sent material back and forth by modem. "We decided to do it as a kind of lark . . . ," Straub said in an Omnimag online discussion in 1997. "It was perfectly dandy most of the time, and King was a hero. I don't think either one of us would ever do it again. Too many compromises. But I have to say that writing that last 100 pages at his house in Maine was one of the richest experiences of my life." Of course, they did work together again, for a sequel, *Black House*, among other things an homage to Charles Dickens' *Bleak House*, just as *The Talisman* paid its respects to Mark Twain's *The Adventures of Tom Sawyer*.

Straub said he generally works without detailed outline. But he and King worked out a 75-page outline for *The Talisman*, an overly ambitious work they eventually had to trim back.

Momentarily knocked back by the emotional blow of the attacks on the World Trade Center in 2001, Straub recovered slowly, writing an introduction to a Lawrence Block collection and guest-editing an issue of the literary journal *Conjunctions*, in which he invited contributions from writers known for erasing genre boundaries.

The author's recent *Lost Boy Lost Girl* marked the reappearance of familiar Blue Rose characters: novelist Tim Underhill and private detective Tom Pasmore. About this book, a reviewer at *Publishers Weekly* said, "With great compassion and in prose as supple as mink, Straub has created an exciting, fearful, wondrous tale about people who matter, in one of his finest books to date."

Works by the Author

Fiction

Marriages (1973)
Julia (1975), in England as *Full Circle* (1977)
If You Could See Me Now (1977)
Ghost Story (1979)
Shadowland (1980)
Floating Dragon (1983)
The Talisman, with Stephen King (1984)
Wild Animals: Three Novels (1984), includes *Julia, If You Could See Me Now* and
        Under Venus
Blue Rose (1985)
Under Venus (1985)
The Hellfire Club (1996)
Mr. X (1999)
Black House, with Stephen King (2001), sequel to *The Talisman*
In the Night Room (2004)

Blue Rose Series

Koko (1988)
Mystery (1991)
The Throat (1993)
Lost Boy, Lost Girl (2003)

Short Stories and Novellas

The General's Wife (1982)
Houses Without Doors (1991)
Mrs. God (1991)
Magic Terror (1997)

Editor

Peter Straub's Ghosts (1995)

Anthologies

Cutting Edge (1978)
The Armless Maiden and Other Tales for Childhood's Survivors (1985)
Prime Evil (1988)
Best New Horror 2 (1991)
The Picador Book of the New Gothic (1991)
The Year's Best Fantasy and Horror Fourth Annual Collection (1991)

Shadows of Fear: Foundations of Fear 1 (1992)
Best New Horror 4 (1993)
The Year's Best Fantasy and Horror Sixth Annual Collection (1993)
Borderlands 4 (1994)
The Giant Book of Terror (1994)
Dark Terrors (1995)
Great Writers and Kids Write Spooky Stories (1995)
American Gothic Tales (1996)
Dark Terrors 2 (1996)
The Mammoth Book of Best New Horror 10 (1999)
The Year's Best Fantasy and Horror Twelfth Annual Collection (1999)
Dark Terrors 5 (2000)
The Mammoth Book of Best New Horror 11 (2000)
Mothers & Sons edited by Jill Morgan (2001)
The Museum of Horrors edited by Dennis Etchinson (2003)

Poetry

Ishmael (1972)
Open Air (1972)
Leeson Park and Belsize Square: Poems 1970–1975 (1983)

Motion Pictures and Television Movies Based on the Author's Work

Ghost Story (1981)
The Haunting of Julia (1981), as *Full Circle* in England

For Further Information

Baker, John F. "Straub's next thriller for random." *Publishers Weekly* (August 11, 2003).

Givens, Ron. "Slow and spooky does it." *Daily News*, New York (October 26, 2003).

Jones, Daniel, and John D. Jorgenson, eds. Peter Straub entry, *Contemporary Authors New Revision Series*. Vol. 63. Detroit: Gale Research, 1998.

Lost Boy Lost Girl review. *Publishers Weekly* (September 15, 2003).

McCarty, Michael. "Man of Mystery Peter Straub reaches into his pocket and pulls out a novel." SciFi.com. *http://www.scifi.comsfw/issue264/interview.html* (viewed June 17, 2003).

Peter Straub biography. *http://www.alat.books.peter-straub* (viewed April 10, 2003).

Peter Straub interview. DarkEcho. *http://www.darkecho.com/darkecho/archives/straub.html* (viewed April 10, 2003).

Peter Straub interview. OmniVisions. *http://www.omnimag.com/archives/chats/ov060597.html* (viewed April 10, 2003).

Peter Straub interview. Ténèbres Magazine (2000). *http://members.tripod.com/~charnelhouse/straubinterview2.html* (viewed June 17, 2003).

Peter Straub Web page. *http://www.net-site.com/straub/bio/htm* (viewed April 10, 2003).

"Peter Straub: Seeing Double." *Locus Magazine* (December 1998).

Petrella, Alba. "Interview with Peter Straub." I.H. magazine. *http://www.ihmagazine.it/articoli/en24.html* (viewed June 17, 2003).

Winter, Douglas E. "House of Horrors." *Washington Post Book World* (December 21, 2003).

Bodie Thoene

Bakersfield, California
1951

Brock Thoene

♦ Christian ♦ Historical ♦ Western

Bakersfield, California
1952

♦ *Zion Series*

About the Authors and the Authors' Writings

A knowledge of the history of Jerusalem and other ancient lands at the time of Jesus can give modern-day Christians a firmer grasp of the meaning of the Bible. So believe authors Brock and Bodie Thoene, who give as an example the custom in Christ's day of honoring those who have done well. Athletes received laurel leaf crowns, civic leaders oak leaf crowns. The Roman army awarded the corona obsidianalis to heroic soldiers who saved their number from sure ruin; it was made of weeds that grew on the particular battlefield where the honor was earned.

"Now if you recall in Genesis, the ground after the fall of Man was cursed to bring forth only thorns and thistles," the Thoenes wrote in an article for the *Page Turner's Journal.* "So when the soldiers put a crown of thorns on Jesus's head, they were really giving him a corona obsidianalis, and it fit: Jesus was giving his life to redeem the whole earth from the curse . . . from certain destruction." The soldiers were mocking Christ with their crown, but it obviously was appropriate.

Born a year apart, Bodie (named Roberta, nicknamed "Birdie," which evolved into "Bodie") in 1951 and William Brock Thoene in 1952, the multiple Evangelical Christian Publishers Association Gold Medallion Award-winning writers grew up in the same Bakersfield, California, community, though their romance came in their high school years. Bodie was known as class clown in school; Brock was known for his intelligence. She studied journalism and political science in college; he took courses in history and education. They were involved in Campus Crusade and other lay ministries, and they married in 1971, when both were college sophomores. They now reside in Lake Tahoe, Nevada, though they spend a great deal of time in London, England, which is closer to their research.

Bodie was the first to gravitate to writing; at age fourteen she received fifty cents a column inch for articles she wrote for a weekly newspaper. She later followed the Vietnam War protest movement in the Bay area for *U.S. News & World Report*. She began writing fiction when the couple relocated to Waco, Texas, where Brock could attend Baylor University. As the first of their three children was born, Bodie took the tales she heard from old Texas cowboys and crafted them into prose. In the meantime, Brock finished his undergraduate degree and went on to earn a master's degree in education from California State University.

Soon after publication of Bodie's novel *The Fall Guy*, the Thoenes went to work for actor John Wayne's Batjac Productions and ABC Television as screenwriters and researchers. Bodie also wrote for *American West, The Saturday Evening Post*, and *Smithsonian* magazine. Keenly interested in the history of Israel—her father is Jewish, her mother of Irish ancestry—Bodie received encouragement from actor Wayne to write what became the first of the Zion Chronicles. "That's one you ought to do," Wayne told her. "It's the story of the Jewish Alamo!"

The first book the Thoenes wrote together was *Gates of Zion*, which was originally intended to be a screenplay. Brock Thoene explained to interviewer Etta Wilson the word Zion carries both biblical and prophetic aspects of Israel. "No other state has gone out of existence and come back centuries later. The Pope has called the establishment of Israel the most significant event of the 20th century."

The Thoenes have made frequent trips to Israel to do research, to speak with scholars and others there, and to soak in the atmosphere. They use some Hebrew and Arabic words in their dialogue in an effort to re-create an authentic sound of the time.

Their fascination with Israel has, if anything, amplified in recent years with new Zion and other series. *Jerusalem Vigil*, the first of the Zion Legacy series, is set in a very narrow time slot: the first weeks after May 14, 1948, when the modern state of Israel was created.

The Thoenes see great prophetic importance to Christians in the reestablishment of Israel. They are trying to counter misinformation that appears elsewhere. "It is phenomenally important to us today, to our faith and our beliefs, that God keeps his promises," Bodie Thoene said in speaking with Christianbook.com. "And yet, all of that is being downplayed as if Israel was always the big, bad dog on the block. It's an enormous distortion. The place is a postage stamp surrounded by millions and millions of hostile people."

Brock, of German-Swiss lineage, grew up in a Christian home. He wrote a few books on his own, including *The Legend of Storey County*, which depicts a hundred-year-old Jim Canfield who escaped slavery, fought in the Civil War, and had adventures in the rugged West. Although it is unstated, reviewers suggested the character is surely Jim from Mark Twain's *The Adventures of Huckleberry Finn*.

The two also wrote Christian westerns in the Saga of the Sierras. The authors are equally comfortable in the present; *The Twilight of Courage*, for instance, is set in Europe at the dawning of World War II.

The Thoenes often divide their chores when writing together. Brock is the main researcher, Bodie the crafter of story and dialogue. Characters are often composites of actual people. For the Zion books, the history provides the firm outline for the story. Bodie suffered dyslexia from an early age, and while her parents and a young teacher helped her overcome many of its limitations, she still finds reading difficult. She writes chapters each day, and the next morning Brock reads them back to her and they edit them together.

"I'm convinced that being read to aloud like that has a lot to do with Bodie's writing because she has such a sharp ear for cadences and speech patterns," Brock Thoene told writer Robin Jones Gunn. "It's different from someone whose own reading experience is all in the eye. You don't reproduce dialogue and dialect the same as when it's introduced through the ear."

The Zion Chronicles and Zion Covenant books at first bore only Bodie's name, even though they both produced them. They switched publishers for that reason and now both names appear on the books. How do they produce two or more books a year? Their answer is simple: They're professionals.

Works by Bodie Thoene and Brock Thoene

Fiction

The Twilight of Courage (1994)
Shiloh Autumn (1996)

A. D. Chronicles Series

First Light (2003)
Second Touch (2004)
Third Watch (2004)

Galway Chronicles Series

Only the River Runs Free (1997)
Of Men and of Angels (1998)
Ashes of Remembrance (1999)
All Rivers to the Sea (2000)

Saga of the Sierras Series

The Man from Shadow Ridge (1990)
Riders of the Silver Rim (1990)
Gold Rush Prodigal (1991)
Sequoia Scout (1991)
Cannons of the Comstock (1992)
The Year of the Grizzly (1992)
Shooting Star (1993)
Flames of the Barbary Coast (1994)
A New Frontier (1998), omnibus
A Land Without Laws (2000), omnibus

Wayward Wind Series

Winds of Promise (1997)
To Gather the Wind (1998)
Winds of the Cumberland (1999)

Zion Chronicles Series

The Gates of Zion (1986)
A Daughter of Zion (1987)
The Return to Zion (1996)
The Key to Zion (1998)
A Light in Zion (1998)

Zion Covenant Series

Danzig Passage (2000)
Jerusalem Interlude (2000)
Munich Signature (2000)
Prague Counterpoint (2000)
Vienna Prelude (2000)
Warsaw Requiem (2000)

Zion Legacy Series

Jerusalem Vigil (2000)
Thunder from Jerusalem (2000)
Jerusalem's Crown (2001)
Jerusalem's Heart (2001)
The Jerusalem Scrolls (2001)
Jerusalem's Hope (2002)
Stones of Jerusalem (2002)
First Light (2003)

Nonfiction

Writer to Writer (1990)

Works by Bodie Thoene

Shiloh Legacy Series

My Father's House (1993)
A Thousand Shall Fall (1994)
Say to This Mountain (1995)

Nonfiction

The Fall Guy: 30 Years as the Duke's Double, by "Bad Chuck" Roberson with Bodie
Thoene (1980)
A Thousand Shall Fall (1993)

Works by Brock Thoene

Fiction

The Legend of Storey County (1995)
Delta Passage (1997)
Hope Valley War (1997)
The Listening Hills (1997)
To Gather the Wind (1998)

Nonfiction

Protecting Your Income and Your Family's Future (1989), as William Brock
Thoene

For Further Information

Alger, Emily S. "Flying High: An interview with Bodie and Brock Thoene, Suite101
.com (July 3, 2000). *http://www.suite101.com/article/cfm/6104/42995* (viewed
May 18, 2003).

Bodie and Brock Thoene Web site. *http://www.thoenebooks.com/* (viewed May 18,
2003).

Bodie Thoene interview. Christianbook.com. *http://www.christianbook.com/
Christian/books/cms_content/106988044?page=6450&sp=1001* (viewed May
18, 2003).

"Brock and Bodie Thoene." Tracy's Book Nook. *http://www.tracysbooknook.com/
authors/brockbodiethoene.html* (viewed May 18, 2003).

First Light review. *Publishers Weekly* (July 7, 2003).

Gunn, Robin Jones. Bodie and Brock Thoene profile. *Ink* (October 1994).

Peacock, Scot, ed. Brock Thoene entry, *Contemporary Authors*. Vol. 167. Detroit:
Gale Research, 1999.

Thoene, Brock and Brodie. "Not One Careless Word." Page Turner's Journal

(December 6, 2002). *http://www.movingfiction.net/pt_archive/issue13/issue13 .html* (viewed May 18, 2003).

Wilson, Etta. "Birth of a nation: Thoenes focus on Israel's first days." BookPage. *http://www.bookpage.com/0003bp./bodie_brock_thoene.html* (viewed May 18, 2003).

J.R.R. Tolkien

◆ Fantasy

Bloemfontein, South Africa
1892–1973

◆ *Lord of the Rings*

About the Author and the Author's Writing

J.R.R. Tolkien has had a profound impact on literature, to such an extent, he should have been named author of the century, in the view of *Maclean's* writer Brian Bethune. "Tolkien essentially invented the modern fantasy epic, which has become such a huge branch of publishing that no book since can match [Lord of the Rings'] influence among fiction writers."

Tolkien wrote of medieval quests and battles. "But," explained Alison Lurie, "the message of *The Hobbit* (1937) was new. It presented a world in which the forces of evil might at times overcome the forces of good, and the true hero was no longer strong, handsome, aristocratic, and victorious in combat."

Noting Tolkien's attention to detail, including the use of long appendices, writer Lin Carter said, "No author in the history of fantasy has created so convincingly detailed and overwhelmingly realistic an imaginary world, and few have ever created so colorful a story."

"With appeal for all ages, the stories are filled with myth and legend; interesting characters with remarkable names; humor; warmth; and daring." added Susan Roman.

James Cawthorn and Michael Moorcock included Tolkien's *The Lord of the Rings* among their 100 best fantasy books, remarking on its impact: "There are no irresistible warriors, male or female, in Tolkien's saga. Its strength lies in its embracing sweep, a combination of the panoramic view with a wealth of homely detail. Power, wisdom and authority rest largely in the hands of the older generations, and in Middle-Earth 'older' can be old indeed, for the Elves are virtually immortal."

John Ronald Reuel Tolkien (1892–1973) was born in Bloemfontein, South Africa, the son of a bank manager. At age three, his mother brought Tolkien and his brother back to England for health reasons. His father, who stayed on in South Africa, died of rheumatic fever a short time later.

That change in country had an impact on the writer, who in a BBC *Radio 4* interview in 1971 told how such a thing "bites into your memory and imagination. . . . If your first Christmas tree is a wilting eucalyptus and if you're normally troubled by heat and sand . . . then, to have just at the age when imagination is opening out, suddenly find yourself in a quiet Warwickshire village, I think it engenders a particular love of what you might call central Midlands English countryside."

The family didn't have much, but Tolkien's mother managed to introduce her son to Andrew Lang's fairy books and George MacDonald's Curdie stories. His mother died in 1904, after the family had moved into the village of Birmingham, and the boys were entrusted to a Catholic priest. Religion would become a dominant force in Tolkien's creative output.

Tolkien began to study the classics at Exeter College in Oxford, but switched to English and literature. He wrote poetry and continued an interest in language, even making up his own, supposedly spoken by elves.

During the First World War, Tolkien served as a signal officer. The loss of two close friends inspired him to start writing *The Silmarillion*, an epic work that wasn't published until much later. He married Edith Mary Bratt, a pianist, in 1916. (She died in 1971.) After the war, he began to teach and, at age thirty-three, he became one of Oxford's youngest professors. Instead of trying to find a publisher for *Silmarillion*, he wrote bedtime stories for his four children, all born by 1929.

One of Tolkien's children's stories was *Mr. Bliss*, published years after his success with the Rings trilogy. In 1930, he began writing *The Hobbit*, completing it seven years later. Pressed to pen a sequel, he came up with The Lord of the Rings. Fellow writer C. S. Lewis, a colleague at Oxford, encouraged Tolkien. Completed in 1949, the trilogy didn't come out in print until five years later. It was enormously popular.

The books audience was initially seen as a young one. "All historians of children's literature . . . agree in placing that book among the very highest achievements of children's authors during the 20th century," noted Humphrey Carpenter and Mari Prichard in *The Oxford Companion to Children's Literature*. "Tolkien himself came to believe that no author could write especially 'for' children—the first edition of *The Hobbit* contains a number of patronizing 'asides' to the child-audience, but many of these were removed later, when its author's views on the subject changed."

Tolkien held up publication of Lord of the Rings. He hoped to have the even longer (but still not completed) *Silmarillion* come out at the same time. In 1954, *The Fellowship of the Ring* and *The Two Towers* were finally published; *The Return of the King* came out the next year. By 1965, international copyright on the books lapsed. An American paperback publisher, Ace, brought the trilogy out in softcover, but without paying royalties. Tolkien revised the work slightly for a new, "authorized" edition from his own publisher. The notoriety of the royalties dispute brought wide attention to the book, which was at the time very popular with college students. Ace later paid royalties to Tolkien and withdrew its edition. By the end of 1968, about three million copies of the *Lord of the Rings* had sold worldwide. Tolkien's son Christopher completed *The Silmarillion* after Tolkien's death, and it was published in 1977.

Tolkien wrote many nonfiction works on topics of English literature, among them *A Middle English Vocabulary* (1922), *Beowulf: The Monsters and the Critics* (1937), and *Chaucer as a Philologist* (1943).

Tolkien's popularity has hardly waned over the years, and the release of film versions of his tales reawakened interest in the early 2000s; the trilogy held places six, ten, and fifteen in the ranking of all-time United States box office champions in mid-2004.

A new biography came out in 2001: Michael Coren's *J.R.R. Tolkien: The Man Who Created The Lord of the Rings*. Scholarly discussion continues unabated: *Christian Century* recently mulled Christian faith and hope as found in the trilogy and *Gay & Lesbian Review* pondered homoeroticism in the Lord of the Rings, to give two examples.

The author has been much imitated but never equaled, in the estimate of Ralph Wood, author of *The Gospel According to Tolkien*. Why? "The answer I give," Wood told *Pages*, "is that no one has taken the trouble to learn what Tolkien knew: a raft of ancient languages, the myth lore of the Greco-Roman world and the Northern European world. That's what gives his work its inexhaustible richness."

Works by the Author

Fiction

Farmer Giles of Ham (1949 and revisions 1950, 1975, 1978)
The Adventures of Tom Bombadil and Other Verses from the Red Book (1962)
Tree and Leaf (1964)
The Tolkien Reader (1966), includes *The Homecoming of Beorhtnoth, Tree and Leaf, Farmer Giles of Ham*, and *The Adventures of Tom Bombadil*
The Road Goes Ever On: A Song Cycle (1967)
Smith of Wootton Major (1967)
The Father Christmas Letters, edited by Baillie Tolkien (1976)
Pictures by J.R.R. Tolkien (1979)
Poems and Stories (1980)
Unfinished Tales of Numenor and Middle-Earth, edited by Christopher Tolkien (1980)
Mr. Bliss (1982)
Finn and Hengest: The Fragment and the Episode (1982)

Middle Earth Series

The Hobbit; or, There and Back Again (1937 and revisions 1951, 1966, 1978)
The Fellowship of the Ring (1954)
The Two Towers (1954)
The Return of the King (1955)
The Silmarillion edited by Christopher Tolkien (1977)
Bilbo's Last Song (1990), verse extracted from *The Hobbit*

History of Middle Earth Series, edited by Christopher Tolkien

The Book of Lost Tales, Part 1 (1983)
The Book of Lost Tales, Part 2 (1984)
The Lays of Beleriand (1985)
The Shaping of Middle-Earth: The Quenta, the Ambarkanta, and the Annals (1986)
The Lost Road and Other Writings: Language and Legend before The Lord of the Rings (1987)

The Return of the Shadow: The History of The Lord of the Rings, Part 1 (1988)
The Treason of Isengard: The History of The Lord of the Rings, Part 2 (1989)
The War of the Ring: The History of The Lord of the Rings, Part 3 (1990)
Sauron Defeated: The History of The Lord of the Rings, Part 4 (1992)
Morgoth's Ring: The Later Silmarillion, Part 1 (1993)

Editor

A Spring Harvest by Geoffrey Bache Smith, with C. L. Wiseman (1918)
Sir Gawain and the Green Knight, with Eric V. Gordon (1925)
Songs for the Philologists, with Eric V. Gordon et al. (1936)
Beowulf: The Monsters and the Critics (1937)

Translator

Sir Gawain and the Green Knight, Pearl, Sir Orfeo, edited by Christopher Tolkien (1975)
The Old English Exodus, edited by Joan Turvile-Petre (1981)

Contributor

Oxford Poetry, edited by G.D.H. Cole and T. W. Earp (1915)
A Northern Venture: Verses by Members of the Leeds University English School Association (1923)
Realities: An Anthology of Verse, edited by G. S. Tancred (1927)
Report on the Excavation of the Prehistoric, Roman, and Post-Roman Sites in Lydney Park (1932)
Essays Presented to Charles Williams (1947)
Angles and Britons: O'Donnell Lectures (1963)
Winter's Tales for Children 1, edited by Cazroline Hillier (1965)
The Image of Man in C.S. Lewis, edited by William Luther White (1969)
The Hamish Hamilton Book of Dragons, edited by Robert Lancelyn Green (1970)
A Tolkien Compass, edited by Jared Lobdell (1975)
J.R.R. Tolkien: Scholar and Storyteller, edited by Mary Salu and Robert T. Farrell (1979)

Nonfiction

A Middle English Vocabulary (1922)
Chaucer as a Philologist (1943)
The Monsters and the Critics and Other Essays, edited by Christopher Tolkien (1984)

Motion Pictures Based on the Author's Work

The Hobbit (1977)
The Lord of the Rings (1978)

The Fellowship of the Ring (2001)
The Two Towers (2002)
Return of the King (2003)

For Further Information

Anderson, Douglas A. *The Annotated Hobbit*. Boston: Houghton Mifflin, 1988.

Bertenstam, Åke. A Chronological Bibliography of the Writings of J.R.R. Tolkien. *http://www.forodrim.org/arda/tbchron.html* (viewed April 5, 2003).

Bethune, Brian. "The Lord of the Bookshelves." *Maclean's* (December 23, 2002).

Birzer, Bradley. *J.R.R. Tolkien's Sanctifying Myth: Understanding Middle-Earth*. Wilmington, DE: ISI Books, 2002.

Carpenter, Humphrey. "Our Brief Encounter." *Sunday Times Magazine* (November 25, 2001).

Carpenter, Humphrey. *Tolkien: A Biography*. Boston: Houghton Mifflin, 1978.

Carter, Lin. *Imaginary Worlds: The Art of Fantasy*. New York: Ballantine, 1973.

Carter, Lin. *Tolkien: A Look Behind The Lord of the Rings*. Boston: Houghton Mifflin, 1969.

Cathorn, James, and Michael Moorcock. *Fantasy The 100 Best Books*. New York: Carroll & Graf, 1988.

Day, David. *A Tolkien Bestiary*. New York: Ballantine, 1979.

Duriez, Colin. *Tolkien and the Lord of the Rings: A Guide to Middle-Earth*. Mahwah, NJ: Hidden Spring, 2001.

Fonstad, Karen Wynn. *The Atlas of Middle-Earth*. Boston: Houghton Mifflin, 1981.

Foster, Robert A. *A Guide to Middle-Earth*. Manchester, MD: Mirage Press, 1971. (Revised as *The Complete Guide to Middle-Earth*. Del Rey, 1981.)

Gerrolt, Dennis. "An Interview with J.R.R. Tolkien." BBC Radio 4 program Now Read On . . . (January 1971). *http://www.geocities.com/Area51/Shire/5014/interview.html* (viewed April 6, 2003).

Giles, Jeff. "Secrets of 'The King.'" *Newsweek* (December 1, 2003).

Harvey, Greg. *The Origins of Tolkien's Middle-Earth for Dummies*. San Francisco: For Dummies, 2003.

Johnson, Judith A. *J.R.R. Tolkien: Six Decades of Criticism*. Westport, CT: Greenwood Press, 1986.

J.R.R. Tolkien issue. *Christian History*, no. 78 (summer 2003).

Johnson, Judith A. *J.R.R. Tolkien: Six Decades of Criticism*. Westport, CT: Greenwood Press, 1986.

Kaufman, Roger. "Lord of the Rings taps a gay archetype." *The Gay & Lesbian Review Worldwide* (July–August 2003).

Kramer, Kathryn. "Writers on Writing: Middle earth Enchants A Returning Pilgrim." *New York Times* (December 30, 2002).

Lesniak, James G., ed. J.R.R. Tolkien entry, *Contemporary Authors New Revision Series*. Vol. 36. Detroit: Gale Research, 1992.

Lurie, Alison. *Don't Tell the Grown-Ups: Why Kids Love the Books They Do*. New York: Avon, 1990.

Noel, Ruth S. *The Languages of Tolkien's Middle-Earth*. Boston: Houghton Mifflin, 1980.

Roman, Susan. *Sequences: Annotated Guide to Children's Fiction in Series*. Chicago: American Library Association, 1985.

Shippey, T.A. *The Road to Middle-Earth*. Boston: Houghton Mifflin, 1983.

Stimpson, Catherine R. *J.R.R. Tolkien*. New York: Columbia University Press, 1969.

Tolkien, J.R.R. *Letters of J.R.R. Tolkien*. Selected by Humphrey Carpenter and Christopher Tolkien. Boston: Houghton Mifflin, 1988.

Tolkien, John, and Priscilla Tolkien. *The Tolkien Family Album*. Boston: Houghton Mifflin, 1994.

West, Richard C. *Tolkien Criticism: An Annotated Checklist*. Kent, OH: Kent State University Press, 1970 (revised 1981).

Wood, Ralph. "Frodo's faith." *Christian Century* (September 6, 2003).

Wood, Ralph. *The Gospel According to Tolkien*. Westminster: John Knox Press, 2003.

Scott Turow

◆ Mystery ◆ Suspense

Chicago, Illinois
1949

◆ *Presumed Innocent*

Credit: David Joel Photography.

About the Author and the Author's Writing

Scott Turow has quite a deep pocket of personal experience to dip into for his stories of criminal mischief and legal suspense. *Personal Injuries*, as an example, follows an ambulance-chasing lawyer named Robbie Feaver who goes undercover to help break open corruption among judges.

Turow witnessed many of the events in the book in his role as an assistant United States attorney in Chicago. "There was one large undercover project, called Operation Greylord, that was aimed at the judiciary in Illinois," he told James Buckley Jr. "I was assigned to run a decoy, above-ground, highly visible investigation of judicial corruption in one court, while the undercover operation was going on in the criminal court. Then I was assigned to try to flip a criminal lawyer whom we had a case on." Turow had to work with limited knowledge of all that was going on around him.

The author's ability to create complex characters and intricate plots grows from Turow's own undercover dealings with witnesses and criminals; their relationships with their handlers are at times dicey, morally and personally. One has to be their friends, to be persuasive and supportive, in spite of being truly repulsed by things they have done. And that emerges as a common Turow theme: duality. Robbie Feaver may be a pushy, dubious lawyer, but he also has his assets.

Turow was born in Chicago in 1949, the son of a physician and a writer. At New Trier High School in the suburb of Winnetka, Turow edited the school paper—despite having nearly flunked English. In 1971, he married Annette Weisberg, an artist; they have three children. He is of the Jewish faith and is an avid Chicago Cubs fan.

Turow's parents hoped he would follow his father into a career in medicine. But Turow wanted to become a writer. He received a bachelor of arts degree in 1960 from Amherst College and accepted a Mirrielees Fellowship to the Stanford University Creative Writing Center,

1970–1972. For the next three years, he taught creative writing at Stanford as part of the endowed E. J. Jones Lecturer program. He received a master's degree from Stanford in 1974 and a law degree from Harvard University in 1978. He clerked in the Suffolk County District Attorney's Office in Boston, and then became assistant United States attorney in the United States Court of Appeals, Seventh District, in Chicago, from 1978 to 1986. Among his high-profile cases was the prosecution with others of Illinois Attorney General William J. Scott on tax fraud charges. He also served as president of Authors Guild 1997–1998. Since 1986, he has been with the law firm Sonnenschein, Carlin, Nath & Rosenthal.

Turow's first published book was a work of nonfiction, *One L*, describing his first year as a law student at Harvard. It was a decade before he realized a longtime dream of publishing a novel, *Presumed Innocent*. That first novel (not counting a few manuscripts still in the drawer) drew considerable attention both because it was put to bid among publishers and because he accepted, not the highest bid, but the one from a publishing house, Straus & Giroux, whose reputation the author felt gave his book literary credence. (It was also the only firm, years before, that had sent him an encouraging rejection for an earlier fictional effort called "The Way Things Are.")

In the book, set in fictional Kindle County—obviously modeled on Cook County in Illinois—Rusty Sabich, chief deputy prosecuting attorney, is implicated in the murder of an attractive, sharp, corruptible coworker. "Despite its familiar plot idea—circumstantial evidence incriminating the 'innocent' man—in Turow's first novel, *Presumed Innocent*, perceptions shift rapidly with each new piece of information," relates *St. James Guide to Crime & Mystery Writers*. "The result is . . . a psychological study of a morose man seeking an ephemeral, beguiling illusion in a world of corruption, betrayal, and inescapable pain."

"I am defined by the legal universe," Turow told interviewer David Zivan. "I refuse to change its rules, so I have got to try to make people understand the way lawyers think about certain things."

Today Turow writes while continuing his law practice. He works in the area of white-collar criminal litigation, and does a lot of pro bono work. Opposed to the death penalty, he was appointed to an Illinois board in 2000 to review the state's capital punishment laws. The experience became the grist for a nonfiction book, *Ultimate Punishment: A Lawyer's Reflections on Dealing With the Death Penalty*, in 2003. "This measured weighing of the facts will be most valuable to those who, like Turow, are on the fence—they will find an invaluable, objective look at both sides of this critical but highly charged debate," suggested *Publishers Weekly*.

The author said on his Web site that the writers who have most influenced him are Saul Bellow and Charles Dickens; in an interview with *Book* magazine he singled out Leo Tolstoy and James Joyce.

Turow does not write a novel from beginning to end. Rather, he writes in blocks of text, scenes that, thanks to the flexibility of the word processor, he can rearrange as needed. "I used to read about [Isaac] Nabokov who would write paragraphs out on index cards all over his books, and I thought, 'How can the guy do that? You've got to have it all in order in your head.' But I'll be damned. That's now the way I write," he said on his Web site. He doesn't put together an outline until he's in his second or third draft. This fractured writing method worked well on his daily commutes to and from work in the Windy City.

Turow often finds himself deeply entwined in his characters, such as black defense lawyer Hobie Tuttle in *The Laws of Our Fathers*. The character became one of his favorites. "He was originally just part of the mechanics of the novel," he said to Alden Mudge, "but he took over. I love his character. Hobie Tuttle is one clever dude."

From Erle Stanley Gardner's Perry Mason to television's *Law & Order*, the courtroom has had a broad audience. For Turow the prosecutor, the mystery novel brings something real life cannot: Truth about the guilt or innocence of a defendant. In the books, the reader learns all. In real life, the jury can only make an educated guess.

Works by the Author

Fiction

Presumed Innocent (1987)
The Burden of Proof (1990)
Pleading Guilty (1993)
The Laws of Our Fathers (1996)
Personal Injuries (1999)
Reversible Errors (2002)

Anthologies

Best American Short Stories (1971)
Best American Short Stories (1972)
Guilty As Charged (2004)

Nonfiction

One L: An Inside Account of Life in the First Year at Harvard Law School (1977)
Ultimate Punishment: A Lawyer's Reflections on Dealing With the Death Penalty (2003)

Anthologies

The Writing Life: Writers on How they Think and Work, edited by Marie Arana (2003)

Motion Pictures and Television Movies Based on the Author's Works

Presumed Innocent (1990)
Scott Turow's Reversible Errors (2004)

For Further Information

"Author of the Month: Scott Turow." Authors on the Web. *http://www.authorsontheweb .com/features/authormonth/0211turow/turow-scott.asp#facts* (viewed May 26, 2003).

Buckley, James Jr. "Going undercover in life and law: A talk with Scott Turow." Book-Page. *http://www.bookpage.com/9910bp/scott_turow.html* (viewed April 5, 2003).

Flynn, Gillian. *Ultimate Punishment* review. *Entertainment Weekly* (September 26, 2003).

Jones, Daniel, and John D. Jorgenson, eds. Scott Turow entry, *Contemporary Authors New Revision Series*. Vol. 65. Detroit: Gale Research, 1998.

Mudge, Alden. "When characters slip from the confines of plot: A Talk with Scott Turow." BookPage. *http://www.bookpage.com/9610bp0.mystery/thelawsofour fathers.html* (viewed April 5, 2003).

Scott Turow entry, *St. James Guide to Crime & Mystery Writers*. 4th edition. Chicago: St. James Press, 1996.

Scott Turow Web site. *http://www.scottturow.com/* (viewed April 5, 2003).

Turow Scott. "Odyssey That Started With Ulysses." *New York Times* (November 22, 1999).

Ultimate Punishment review. *Publishers Weekly* (August 25, 2003).

Zivan, David. "The Double Life of Scott Turow." Book (September/October 1999).

Stuart Woods

◆ Mystery ◆ Suspense

Manchester, Georgia
1938

◆ *Stone Barrington Series*

Courtesy of Penguin Group, Inc.
Credit: Harry Benson.

About the Author and the Author's Writing

Stuart Woods's mystery series heroes have a common thread in solid police training: Holly Barker, chief in Orchid Beach, Florida, was once a military police commander; Stone Barrington was a police officer wounded in the line of duty, now pursuing a second career as a lawyer. All of the books are briskly paced, and many flirt with the world of glitz and glitter.

Woods was born Stuart Lee in 1938 in Manchester, Georgia. He legally adopted his stepfather's surname in 1955. His mother taught him to read at an early age and he devoured Mark Twain and Charles Dickens, as well as a slew of horse and dog stories. His father was an ex-convict who had left the family within two years of the author's birth.

Woods received a bachelor of arts degree in sociology from the University of Georgia in 1959. He was a member of the Air National Guard from 1960 to 1968 and served a year in Germany on active duty. Married for a time, Woods now lives the life of a bachelor at homes in Florida, Maine, and New York City.

From 1960 to 1969 Woods worked as an advertising copywriter and creative director in New York City (his employers included such firms as Young & Rubicam and J. Walter Thompson). The author also spent three years as a consultant to advertising agencies in London, then moved to south County Galway in Ireland to become a consultant to Irish agencies in Dublin and to begin work on his first novel. He has been a freelance writer since 1973.

Woods was momentarily sidetracked from his writing by an interest in sailing, sparked when a friend asked him to help shuttle a yacht up the Irish coast. A bequest from his grandfather in 1976 enabled him to commission a craft and take part in the 1976 Observer Single-handed Transatlantic Race. He completed his lap from Plymouth, England, to Newport, Rhode Island, in forty-five days, solo. He settled in Georgia and wrote a nonfiction account of his race experience, *Blue Water, Green Skipper*, as well as the first of several travel guides, *A Romantic's Guide to the Country Inns of Britain and Ireland*. He continued competitive sailing and was among survivors of the storm-struck Fastnet race in 1979. Woods is also a licensed airplane pilot.

The American publisher of his travel book also accepted Woods's first novel, based on sample chapters. *Chiefs* came out in 1980 and won a Mystery Writers of America Edgar Allan Poe Award. It was turned into a six-hour television miniseries.

Woods in an interview for *Mystery Scene* said the idea for the book came from his youthful discovery of a shoe box in his grandmother's house. Among the memorabilia and photographs inside was a policeman's badge with the legend "Chief of Police Manchester." It had been partially shot away by buckshot. An aunt revealed the badge had been his maternal grandfather's, who had been killed in the line of duty. "That story, combined with others from my hometown and family history, was the basis for the novel, which I began to write some 25 years later," he said.

Where does the author come up with his ideas? He gave this answer on his Web site: "I have a fevered imagination and a rich fantasy life, which helps with the sex scenes. I've never really had any trouble coming up with ideas; they just grow, like weeds. Writers are always astonished to be asked this question: the answer seems so obvious."

Woods, who worked in Jimmy Carter's 1976 campaign and on Ted Kennedy's 1980 effort, allows some of his personal political views to enter his books, such as *Grass Roots* and *The Run*, in which he is critical of the Republican efforts to impeach President Bill Clinton. The books feature as the main character William Henry Lee IV, a former senator from Georgia who by *Capital Crimes* has risen to become president of the United States.

Meanwhile, Woods's longest-appearing series hero, Stone Barrington, in his latest outing encounters for the second time the beautiful British Intelligence agent called simply "Carpenter," who soon involves him in a world of international intrigue against a band of female assassins.

Woods initially resisted book series, but he came to admit he finds it easier not to have to develop characters from scratch for each new novel. He has said he works hard to not write the same book over and over, but to bring fresh characterizations and ideas to his work. He writes several introductory chapters and an outline, for his editors' acceptance, and once he gets the green light, he said on his Web site, he chucks out the outline and just jumps in to see where the story will take him. He averages two books a year.

The author tries to write a chapter at a sitting—five to ten pages. "I do try to make each chapter a small story in itself," he told interviewer Claire E. White, "with a beginning, a middle and an end, and I try to end each one in such a way as to lead naturally into the next one. It seems to work."

Works by the Author

Fiction

Deep Lie (1986)
Under the Lake (1987)
White Cargo (1988)
Palindrome (1991)
Santa Fe Rules (1992)
L.A. Times (1993)
Dead Eyes (1994)
Heat (1994)

Choke (1995)
Imperfect Strangers (1995)

Holly Barker Series

Orchid Beach (1998)
Orchid Blues (2001)
Blood Orchid (2002)

Stone Barrington Series

New York Dead (1991)
Dirt (1996)
Dead in the Water (1997)
Swimming to Catalina (1998)
Worst Fears Realized (1999)
L.A. Dead (2000)
Cold Paradise (2001)
Dirty Work (2001)
The Short Forever (2002)
Reckless Abandon (2004)

Rick Barron Series

The Prince of Beverly Hills (2004)

Will Lee Series

Chiefs (1980)
Run Before the Wind (1983)
Grass Roots (1989)
The Run (2000)
Capital Crimes (2003)

Nonfiction

Blue Water, Green Skipper (1977)
A Romantic's Guide to the Country Inns of Britain and Ireland (1979)
A Romantic's Guide to London (1980)
A Romantic's Guide to Paris (1981)
A Romantic's Guide to the Country Inns of France (1981)

Television Miniseries Based on the Author's Works

Chiefs (1981)
Grass Roots (1989)

For Further Information

"A Few Minutes With . . . Stuart Woods." *Mystery Scene*, no. 68 (2000).

Capital Crimes review. *Publishers Weekly* (August 18, 2003).

Dirty Work review. *Publishers Weekly* (March 17, 2003).

Jones, Daniel, and John D. Jorgenson, eds. Stuart Woods entry, *Contemporary Authors New Revision Series*. Vol. 72. Detroit: Gale Research, 1999.

Stuart Woods biography. Bookbrowse. *http://www.bookbrowse.com/index.cfm?page=author&authorID=391* (viewed April 5, 2003).

Stuart Woods Web site. *http://www.stuartwoods.com/* (viewed April 5, 2003).

Swanson, Jean and Dean James eds. Stuart Woods entry, *Killer Books: A Reader's Guide to Exploring the Popular World of Mystery and Suspense*. New York: Berkley Prime Crime, 1998.

White, Claire E. "A Conversation with Stuart Woods." Writers Write. *http://www.writerswrite.com/journal/jul98/woods.htm* (viewed April 5, 2003).

Author/Title Index

Genre Index

About the Author

BERNARD A. DREW is a freelance writer/editor and book author of numerous articles and books, including *100 Most Popular Young Adult Authors* and *100 More Popular Young Adult Authors,* both published with Libraries Unlimited.